King and Congress

King and Congress

THE TRANSFER
OF POLITICAL LEGITIMACY,

1774–1776

JERRILYN GREENE MARSTON

PRINCETON UNIVERSITY PRESS
PRINCETON, NEW JERSEY

Library of Congress Cataloging in Publication Data will be
found on the last printed page of this book

ISBN 0-691-04745-6

Publication of this book has been aided by a grant from the
Whitney Darrow Fund of Princeton University Press

This book has been composed in Linotron Palatino

Clothbound editions of Princeton University Press books
are printed on acid-free paper, and binding materials are chosen for strength and
durability. Paperbacks, although satisfactory
for personal collections, are not usually suitable for library rebinding

Printed in the United States of America by Princeton University Press,
Princeton, New Jersey

Designed by Joanna V. Hill

For R.C.M.

Elizabeth's spirits soon rising to playfulness again, she wanted Mr. Darcy to account for his having ever fallen in love with her. "How could you begin?" said she. "I can comprehend your going on charmingly, when you had once made a beginning; but what could set you off in the first place?"

"I cannot fix on the hour, or the spot, or the look, or the words, which laid the foundation. It is too long ago. I was in the middle before I knew that I had begun."

—Jane Austin, *Pride and Prejudice*

Contents

Acknowledgments

This book has been a long time in coming, and along the way I have incurred many debts to many people, to all of whom I am most grateful. In addition, there are a few people I would like to thank particularly and individually.

My debt to John Murrin is, quite simply, enormous. He gave generously of his time and energy at each stage in bringing this project to fruition. His extensive and thoughtful critique of my dissertation served as a blueprint for the extensive revisions that followed, he served as a continual source of intellectual and personal encouragement through the years since, and his faith in both me and my work never wavered. My thanks as well to Stanley Katz, colleague and friend, for introducing me to my present field of legal history and for his unstinting support both in the publication of this book and in general. Both of these scholars represent to me all that is finest in our profession—incisive intellects, wide-ranging imaginations, and generous hearts.

I owe much to my colleagues and teachers. This book began as a dissertation at Boston University many years ago. I would like to thank my dissertation advisor, Richard Bushman, for his advice and support during the preparation of the original dissertation. During the formative stage of this manuscript, he gave me freedom to develop the ideas; encouragement to carry them through and intellectual direction to shape them.

The major revisions in the work were done during the period I spent as a postdoctoral fellow at what was then Bicentennial College of the University of Pennsylvania, forerunner to the present Center for Early American History. During that period, the manuscript benefited greatly from extensive discussions with my colleagues there, Stephanie Wolf and Richard A. Ryerson. My thanks to them both for their helpful critiques of early chapters of this book, and for introducing me to a wide range of source materials in early American history that have both enriched my understanding of the field and, I hope, enhanced this work. My thanks also to Michael Zuckerman, whose informal "colonial group" provided an ideal forum in which to share ideas and exchange information. I also appreciate a similar opportunity provided to me by Gordon Schocket in the political theory seminar at Columbia University. The book was much improved, at the final revision stage, because of the detailed and perceptive comments of Eugene Sheridan, who read the manuscript for Princeton University Press. The care and insight of his critique made the task of revision both rewarding and efficient. My thanks also to my second reader whose constructive comments I found most helpful.

Historians can never fully repay the debts they incur to research librarians, whose knowledge of their collections and generous help make our work efficient, accurate, and pleasurable. I thank the scholars at all the institutions to which I traveled in the course of researching this manuscript. I owe particular thanks to Caroline Sung, of the Manuscript Room of the Library of Congress, where I "lived" for several months, and also to Peter Parker of the Historical Society of Pennsylvania, where my "residence" was also extensive. I owe a particular debt to Dr. Paul Smith, the editor of the *Letters of Delegates to Congress, 1774–1776*, and to his able staff, for allowing me free access to the files of the project, which was at that time in its earliest stages. This generosity saved me much time and effort and gave me an early indication of the wealth of material that was available on the subject. The current published version of the *Letters*, an enormous scholarly undertaking, fully vindicates the care and enthusiasm that I saw in the projects' cramped offices at the Library of Congress during those early days. My thanks also to the staff of Van Pelt Library of the University of Pennsylvania, where much of the work on this book was done.

In addition, I wish to acknowledge my debt to a gentleman and scholar who had no direct contact with the work but whose influence upon me, and thus indirectly upon my work, is great. My thanks to the Honorable Edmund B. Spaeth, Jr., former President Judge of the Superior Court of Pennsylvania, from whom I learned that honor and integrity are neither irrelevant nor anachronistic, and that a short, clear sentence is usually a better sentence.

I wish also to thank two able typists and silent editors whose fine work made mine so much easier. Mary McCutcheon typed both the dissertation and the first revised version of the manuscript, in pre-word-processing days, with accuracy and perseverance. Paul Hiles did an outstanding job on the final version of the manuscript and introduced me to the author's nirvana of word processing, in which all revisions are possible and footnote numbers always come out right. His great good humor and patience are much appreciated.

Most of all, my thanks to my family. My mother and father instilled in me a love of scholarship and an appreciation for quality. My children, Heather and Hilary, have lived with this manuscript all their lives. Their direct contribution to it was minimal, although I thank them for never once getting peanut butter on the manuscript. Nevertheless, the life that went on irrespective of this work was immeasurably enriched by them both. I thank them for becoming the kind of people I am proud to know. They are both the best.

Finally, to the dedicatee. He neither typed the manuscript, edited it, nor critiqued it. Nevertheless, he alone is aware of all the reasons why this manuscript would never have been written or published without him. I thank him profoundly for each and every one of them.

Philadelphia
1986

King and Congress

Introduction

You may exert Power over, but you can never govern, an unwilling people.

       —Thomas Pownall, April 12, 1769

Force is always on the side of the governed, the governors have nothing to support them but OPINION.

       —Virginia Gazette, June 22, 1775

Thomas Pownall was one of the ablest of the royal governors appointed by the king to govern his fractious colony of Massachusetts Bay, and he expended considerable effort in analyzing the basis of British imperial authority over its American colonies.[1] Yet his observation regarding the ultimately consensual nature of British rule was neither unique nor unusual, as the maxim laid down by an anonymous colonial essayist in 1775 emphasizes. In fact, both Pownall and the essayist were remarking upon a basic precondition of all political life. Barring the extremes of anarchy and totalitarianism, government cannot exist unless the ruled voluntarily submit to the rules of their society and to the authority of their rulers. For the ruled to do this, they must believe implicitly that their rulers have the right to ask that they obey, that is, that they believe that their government possesses "political legitimacy."

The concept of legitimacy is basic to that of government.[2] As one scholar has remarked, "the desire for legitimacy is so deeply rooted in human communities that it is hard to discover any sort of historical government that did not either enjoy widespread authentic recognition of its existence or try to win such recognition."[3] Yet, because the phenomenon is so widespread, the concept is also diffuse and thus renders precise discussion difficult, for, as another student has observed, "in some time and place, almost every conceivable political arrangement—feudalism, monarchy, oligarchy, hereditary aristocracy, plutocracy, representative government, direct democracy—has acquired so much legitimacy that men have volunteered their lives in its defense."[4]

Political legitimacy, as the term is used here, refers to the belief of the governed that their government rightfully exercises authority over them. It is, as Friedrich notes, the belief of the ruled in the "just title of the rulers to rule." Thus for Friedrich, the basic question of legitimacy "is a factual one, whether a given rulership is believed to be based on good title by most men subject to it or not." Therefore, while legitimacy exists in the minds of the ruled, rulers are not passive spectators, for, as Dahl explains, "leaders in a political system try to ensure that whenever governmental means are used to deal with conflict, the decisions arrived at are widely accepted not solely from fear of violence, punishment, or coercion, but also from a belief that it is morally right and proper to do so."[5]

The bases upon which the ruled have endowed their rulers with legitimacy have been as varied as man's capacity for political imagination. Thus, the legitimacy of the Egyptian Pharaohs stemmed from their divine descent, and that of early western kings from religious consecration, custom and tradition, and magic.[6] In all modern constitutional systems, however, one essential basis for political legitimacy has been the consent of the governed both to a given system of rule and to a given ruler. Thus, for most modern regimes, "popular consent, although not the whole essence of legitimate government, is one of its most important criteria." But consent is not the only—or, indeed, an exclusive—basis for legitimacy. A powerful factor reinforcing the legitimacy of existing regimes is that of custom and tradition. As Edmund Burke observed in 1782, there is "a presumption in favor of any settled scheme of government against any untried scheme" because "a nation has long existed and flourished under it." Thus, writes one scholar, "the sanction of tradition plays its part in almost every kind of legitimacy."[7] Moreover, just as a regime's legitimacy may be bolstered by the past, so may it be strengthened by the present. Thus, a regime's continued ability to perform its functions in a way acceptable to the ruled renders more powerful the latter's belief in the legitimacy of the regime. This "pragmatic" basis of legitimacy, as Friedrich terms it, is rooted in a government's ability to protect its citizens from enemies within and without and to assure that they inhabit an orderly and prosperous society.[8]

Once a regime has acquired legitimacy, the ruled rarely have occasion to articulate their belief in the just title of their rulers. Because of this, some scholars have characterized the obedience of the ruled to legitimate authority as habitual and unreflective. Thus, as Schochet notes, "obeying one's government is generally not a thought-out action, but rather it is a learned and habituated response." The habitual quality of legitimacy ought not be confused with irrationality, however. As Friedrich explains, the authority possessed by a legitimate ruler is "rooted in the capacity for reasoned elaboration." That is, based upon the community of values and beliefs that he shares with the ruled, the legitimate ruler is always capable of giving a reasoned elaboration of why he requires obedience, and that elaboration is one that the ruled will accept as true. Because of this, Friedrich insists, the obedience that the ruled render to legitimate authority is rational, but because it is based upon shared assumptions and reasoning, there is no need for the rationale to be articulated.[9]

Based upon these criteria, British imperial rule over the colonies in 1774 was legitimate. The colonists rarely articulated the grounds upon which they acquiesced in British rule, but when they did—in periods of transition, for example, or during periods of political crisis—they did so very clearly.[10] To the eve of independence, the colonists elaborately expressed their satisfaction with the British constitution established by the Glorious Revolution of 1688. Within the system established by that constitution, the authority exercised by the king was legitimate, for it was based upon colonial consent, upon custom and tradition, and upon the performance by the king of essential imperial functions. While the colonists expressed their discontent, quite vociferously, with the politics and the corruption of certain British ministers, which they believed threatened to undermine the constitution, they rarely questioned the legitimacy of the system itself or of the imperial authority exercised under the constitution by George III.[11]

Political legitimacy is no fragile flower. Once a regime has acquired legitimacy, as had that of Great Britain, nothing is more difficult than to convince its subjects that the regime to which they have habitually subordinated themselves no longer deserves their allegiance. It is perhaps for this reason that revolutions are always more intelligible to historians than to contemporary participants. Yet it is clear that by 1776 neither the king nor the officials acting under his authority were able, absent coercion, to command the acquiescence of Americans; the bases of American belief in the propriety of British authority had crumbled; the British imperial government had lost political legitimacy.[12] Simultaneously, however, Americans had begun to acquiesce in the authority of a new continental institution that did not exist prior to 1774. By 1776, the Continental Congress had acquired most of the attributes of a legitimate continental government. The present study attempts to explain the process by which this came about.

I begin by examining the bases of legitimate British authority in the colonies. The primary source of imperial authority was the king, and the institutions, governments, and officials invested with his authority. George III's just title to rule his American subjects was based, in a post-Lockean world, upon their consent to the specific terms of a political agreement, or contract. By the terms of this contract, Americans looked to the king for the performance of certain basic governmental functions that both symbolized and epitomized the imperial link. The king was the source of security, of unity, and of the legitimate authority possessed by subordinate institutions and officials. The consent of Americans to this system of rule was buttressed by tradition and custom. From 1774 on, however, the king was directly implicated in the British response to the American resistance movement, and that response, Americans believed, attacked the very bases upon which their consent to British authority rested. As Americans viewed it, the king's course of action in the period after 1774 destroyed the legitimacy of the British imperial government.

Simultaneously, however, Americans began to believe that a new continental institution, the Continental Congress, was imbued with the characteristics of legitimate government. From 1774, the Congress's authority was based on consent, although its mandate was not to govern but rather to coordinate a united continental resistance. With the coming of the war, the potential that the Congress had for becoming a true legitimate government was realized. As one scholar has noted, the circumstances under which a new institution will acquire legitimacy occur "only as the new government begins governing."[13] As the continental delegates began to accept and perform the executive and administrative functions of the vacating royal government, and thus to conform to their constituents' expectations regarding the nature of imperial authority, the Congress began to assume the attributes of a legitimate continental government.

Having thus baldly stated the thesis that the following chapters endeavor to support, it is appropriate to explain the limitations of the study and thus to warn the reader of what he or she will not find in the following pages. The time frame I have chosen, 1774 through 1776, is not, of course, the only one that could have been chosen. It is, however, explained by the purposes of the study. The period of the American Revolution, if inclusive of the total process of American disillusionment with British authority, obviously must be measured in decades. Some historians have argued that American alienation from British institutions began almost as soon as transplanted Englishmen began to breathe the freer air of the New World.[14] A narrower, and frequently used, period is that between 1763 and 1776, when British efforts at imperial reorganization clashed with American aspirations for greater autonomy. Recognizing the many justifications for such a time frame, I argue here that it is not the only one possible, because, despite rancor and dissension since 1763, the fact remains that the vast majority of Americans in 1774 believed that their continuation within the British empire was not only possible but necessary and, for some, desirable. Additionally, 1774 is an excellent starting point, for our purposes, because a vital shift in the colonists' constitutional position took place in that year. Before 1774, American expressions of discontent with British policies had focused upon the British Parliament. But by 1774 such a point of bitterness had been reached that most Americans refused absolutely to admit the legitimacy of any parliamentary authority over the colonies. This meant, however, given the continued desire to remain within the empire, that the king remained the sole legitimate imperial authority recognized by the colonists. Similarly, 1776 is a reasonable place to end the study, for with independence the Rubicon had been crossed. Americans might be dissatisfied with their new continental and provincial governments, and they might—and, indeed, did—change their form, but they could not reestablish the legitimacy of British imperial government. Humpty Dumpty had taken too great a fall.[15]

Within this time frame, the study is further limited. I have not attempted to present any detailed account of the institutions of British imperial government. This has, of course, been done with great care and precision by the great historians of the imperial school, and any similar description here would simply reiterate that work.[16] Thus, while I will assert that the king was responsible for protecting the empire, I will not describe how this function was carried out by the Secretary of War or the Commanders-in-Chief, or how the Treasury financed the imperial wars.[17] Similarly, while I note that the boundary disputes were resolved by means of the king's authority, I do not describe the process by which the Privy Council actually heard and decided these disputes. Such limitations are justified, I believe, by the focus of the study on political expectations. Thus, the expectation that a particular institution will perform certain functions, and its ability to satisfy such expectations, may be an essential component of political legitimacy; the process by which the institution performs those responsibilities, however, will vary over time for reasons unrelated to the questions addressed here. In what follows, the emphasis is on the existence of these functions and the process by which the Congress assumed them. The way in which they were performed, either by king or Congress, is alluded to only where necessary to clarify these themes.

This focus also explains a second limitation of the study. Because I concentrate upon the expectations and beliefs of the governed, there is little said about the delegates' *own* view of their role. I do not contend, therefore, that the delegates thought of themselves as primarily an executive body, and, indeed, there is surprisingly little evidence about their institutional self-conception.[18] It appears that the delegates conceived of themselves in 1774, as a convention modeled upon the great "conventions" of English history, that of the barons at Runnymede and the Convention of 1689.[19] After 1774 the evidence demonstrates a frantic attempt to keep up with mounting executive and administrative responsibilities, which left little time for self-contemplation. Nevertheless, during the only debates that necessarily concerned this issue—those in the summer of 1776 over confederation—the delegates displayed intense confusion over their role as a national legislature, which contrasted sharply with their confidence in their role as a national executive.[20]

Finally, the pages that follow give an extended account of the manner in which Congress assumed and began to perform various royal functions. Again, the viewpoint adopted, that of constituent expectations, may give an unwarranted impression that I believe that the Congress was "successful" in performing its functions as a "plural executive." Even if I believed that such a relative concept provided a useful analytical tool, and I do not, it quickly became obvious that the Congress was *not* a successful plural executive.[21] In fact, the very idea that essential executive functions could be durably performed by a numerous body is almost a contradiction in terms, and this contradiction became increasingly clear in the years immediately following independence.[22]

What I do contend, however, is that American expectations regarding the proper functions of a legitimate central government were formed under the British monarchy. When necessity forced Americans to look elsewhere for the performance of these important functions, they did not fragment the king's imperial role among the newly sovereign states but rather transferred it almost intact to the successor to the king's imperial authority, the Continental Congress. I have implied in this study, therefore, that the American adoption of republican institutions and values in 1776, so evident in the early state constitutions, nevertheless took on a peculiar cast on the continental level, because classical republican doctrine pointed out a different path for Americans to follow as they created new continental institutions. That path led to a diminished executive role, and yet Americans chose an enhanced one. It led to an elevated conception of the legislature, yet Americans created a continental legislature that was relatively weak. It led to values of equality and virtue, yet continental institutions like the army would be based upon hierarchy and authority. The colonists' actions become more intelligible, I believe, when one recognizes that their vision of the legitimate authority of a continental government was based, not upon a republican model of the future, but upon an idealized British monarchical model from the past. As a future delegate contended in 1774, Americans would not create a new continental political structure but rather would adopt the British constitution "purged of its impurities," and thus would "build an empire upon the ruins of Great Britain."[23]

PART I

King

CHAPTER 1

The King's Authority

I went a few days ago . . . to visit the House of Lords. . . . I felt as if I walked on sacred ground. I gazed for some time at the Throne with emotions that I cannot describe. I asked our guide if it was common for strangers to set down upon it. He told me no, but upon my importuning him a good deal I prevailed upon him to allow me the liberty. . . . When I first got into it, I was seized with a kind of horror which for some time interrupted my ordinary train of thinking. . . . I endeavored to arrange my thoughts into some order, but such a crowd of ideas poured in upon my mind that I can scarcely recollect one of them.

—Benjamin Rush, October 22, 1768

Thus did Benjamin Rush, committed republican of the 1770s, take his seat in 1768 upon his monarch's throne. Rush's feelings were not unique; many of his fellow colonists were similarly reverent when confronted with the aura of royalty. "There is something that Strikes an awe," noted one young American, "when you enter the Royal presence."[1] The vast majority of colonists, who never crossed the Atlantic, demonstrated their sense of identification with their king in a more mundane manner through the familiar rituals that occurred regularly throughout the year. Royal birthdays were joyous holidays, royal marriages and births were celebrated with familial enthusiasm, and royal deaths were mourned, both officially and personally. A New England farmer, therefore, saw no incongruity in recording the death of a king in his journal along with other matters of importance to him:

> Oct. 9. 1760. Bo't my Cart Wheels of Mr. Gove for 30 £.
> Oct. 17. 1760. I Enter'd the 43rd year of my Age. this year I tan 39 Hides & 114 Calfskins.
> Oct. 25. 1760. King George the 2nd Died.

Even the son of that steadfast pair of revolutionaries, John and Abigail Adams, when asked what gift he wished his father to bring him upon returning from the Continental Congress, chose "the History of king and Queen."[2]

As the crisis with Great Britain grew graver in the mid-1770s, radical American Whigs expressed disgust and impatience with their fellow colonists' reluctance to throw off old habits of obedience to and affection for the monarch.[3] They incessantly warned their compatriots not to allow their political judgment to be affected by the glittering facade of the monarchy. Thus "A.Z." begged his readers no longer to be "wretchedly imposed upon by Shew and Parade." Americans should be "very cautious" about allowing the pomp of monarchy to work their "Mind[s] into a Rapture," lest they become "enamoured with we know not what, or who." American radicals constantly assured one another that they were immune to the "golden mists" that surrounded the monarch. An agent of the Boston committee of correspondence, Josiah Quincy, Jr., when recording his private impressions of the king's ceremonial opening of Parliament in 1774, made it a point to note virtuously, "I was not awe-struck with the pomps." Even as late as 1776, Charles Thomson, dubbed the "Sam Adams of Philadelphia," worried that his countrymen's minds were still "too much depraved with monarchical principles."[4]

Patriot fears of a resurgence of "monarchical principles" did not end with independence but rather deepened to become a major political theme during the early years of the American republic.[5] Leading American statesmen publicly and privately expressed apprehension that their experiment in republicanism would end in a return to some form of monarchy. In 1787 Hugh Williamson of North Carolina thought "it was pretty certain . . . that we should at some time or other have a King." Alexander Hamilton's conclusions were well known to his contemporaries, and even George Washington seemed to share the assumption. He believed, Thomas Jefferson later recalled, that the noble American experiment "must at length end in something like a British constitution." The aged Benjamin Franklin perhaps best summarized the hopes of a few and the fears of many that "the government of these states may in future times end in a monarchy." On the basis of a lifetime's political observation and participation, Franklin wearily concluded that "there is a natural inclination in mankind to kingly government."[6]

Such expressions raise interesting questions about the supposed ease with which Americans abandoned monarchical government after

1776.[7] Important recent studies have explained the smooth transfer from monarchy to republic in terms of long-term developments that, prior to the Revolution, had sharply differentiated American attitudes and political institutions from those of Great Britain. Scholars have shown how Americans gradually developed greater autonomy and individuality, and among some classes became desirous of social change, characteristics that made them poor members of the rigidly hierarchical and stratified British social system.[8] Similarly, semirepublican political institutions had emerged at both the local and provincial levels, and they progressively assumed greater autonomy and power at the expense of British imperial institutions.[9] These developments caused British influence and institutions to wither away, such scholars imply, rendering the American embrace of republican governments after 1776 simply a confirmation of developments that had long since transformed colonial politics and society.[10]

Such interpretations have greatly advanced our understanding of the speed and totality with which Americans at every political level—local, provincial, and continental—embraced new republican political institutions after 1776. The sincerity of the conversion to republicanism cannot be questioned. Despite often-expressed fears of a resurgence of "monarchical principles," the few Americans who seriously advocated an American king received scant consideration.[11] In the light of such evidence, confirmed by decades of virulent attacks on monarchs and monarchy, it would be wrong to suggest that Americans after 1776 were somehow latent monarchists. Yet despite the overwhelming American commitment to a republican experiment after 1776, even the most confirmed republicans worried that Americans, if sufficiently unwary or unvirtuous, might yet return to some form of monarchical government.[12]

What, then, was the attraction of monarchy that caused such apprehensions among even committed republicans? To answer this, one must examine the political perceptions of Americans, and those of the English political authorities upon whom they depended, about the role of the monarch in a rational system of government. Such a study reveals that while few preferred a monarchical form of government in theory, many considered it to be the most workable system in practice, because it was best suited to the fallible and imperfect nature of man. In short, political thinkers on both sides of the Atlantic accepted, with varying degrees of enthusiasm, the fact that the king, the embodiment of the principle of authority in government, fulfilled certain essential political roles that could not as certainly or durably be filled by existing republican alternatives.

Americans drew their ideas of the proper role of the monarch from a great variety of works of political theory. They were, in fact, voracious consumers of such works, stocking their libraries with the ancients and moderns—Renaissance Italians, French philosophers, and, more important, English Whigs.[13] Within the Whig political spectrum, however, there were important differences of emphasis.[14] At one end stood the "real" or "radical" Whigs, men like Algernon Sydney, John Trenchard, and Robert Viscount Molesworth whose decisive influence upon the colonists has been well established. These were men who had either themselves witnessed or participated in the great events of 1688 or who were close to the generation that had. Their characteristic ideological stance was suspicion of unlimited political power, the symbol of which was James II, and their characteristic political demand was for sure and certain boundaries to such power.[15]

As the eighteenth century progressed and the threat of Stuart despotism diminished, other political theorists emerged. These men were Whigs too, for they were the inheritors and beneficiaries of the Revolution Settlement of 1689. They were not radicals, however, for they did not wish to change or alter the political settlement arrived at in 1689, but rather sought to preserve and support it. They are therefore here termed "establishment Whigs."[16] While these men shared certain basic political perceptions with their radical colleagues, they nevertheless emphasized themes that the radicals only implied. In order to implement their goal of preserving the fruits of liberty that their Whig forbears had won in 1689, they emphasized the need to maintain a continual balance in political life between the forces of "authority" and those of "liberty," between executive and legislature, between the fallible ruler and the equally imperfect ruled. To maintain this vital balance, they were more likely than the radicals to acknowledge that the king, the embodiment of the principle of authority in government, filled certain necessary political roles in a rational system of government.

The King's Limitations

It was to the radical Whigs that Americans owed their fervent belief that all legitimate political power must have definite limits. This radical Whig conviction stemmed from a basic political belief, shared by all Whigs, in the absolute duality of political life. Throughout history, English Whigs believed, political life had been a tense struggle between the forces of liberty and those of authority, and they used certain code words to express this concept. Authority, usually termed "power," was associated with rulers, the executive, or simply the king. "Liberty," on the other hand, was usually coupled with "the people," or, in institutional terms, their representatives in the House of Commons. Since authority could not be eliminated from any government that retained the name, and since liberty could not be lost in any government that remained free, Whigs acknowledged that an uneasy opposition of the two principles was a basic precondition of all political life. As "Cato" (that is, John Trenchard and Thomas Gordon) explained the dilemma, "whereas Power can . . . subsist where Liberty is not, Liberty cannot subsist without Power," which meant that liberty had "as it were, the Enemy always at her Gates."[17]

Whigs in particular believed the situation to be dangerous, because they viewed mankind with a skeptic's eyes. "In truth," wrote "Cato," "there are so many Passions and . . . so much Selfishness belonging to human Nature, that we can scarce be too much upon our Guard against each other." James Burgh, a direct midcentury heir of the radical Whig tradition, reiterated the conviction that man, "whom we dignify with the honourable title of Rational," is in truth an imperfect being primarily influenced "by supposed interest, by passion, by sensual appetite, by caprice, by any thing, by nothing."[18] To trust such an imperfect being with unlimited power, Whigs believed, was to court disaster. Because they so feared unbounded political authority, and because they could see no way to eliminate the need for such authority, radical Whigs concerned themselves with setting sure limits on the exercise of power.[19]

In order to limit the considerable power vested in the executive by the eighteenth-century constitution, Whigs relied on a basic tenet of contemporary political theory, the governmental contract. The idea of a contract between subject and prince is as old as the principle of monarchy itself.[20] Many Whigs, however, believed that their notion of such a contract had come from John Locke. This may well not be true, for Locke's "contract" had been primarily concerned with an original agreement between all members of society to form a political entity; he left implicit the original and subsequent agreements between rulers and ruled that specified the reciprocal obligations of both. Locke's eighteenth-century followers, however, were primarily interested in the latter contract, between rulers and ruled, which appealed to Whigs as an ideal theoretical construct with which to limit executive authority.[21]

The terms of the contract, as Whigs conceived them, were so simple and clear that they could be understood by the meanest member of society: The subject swore allegiance to the prince, in return for which the prince was obligated to protect the subject's person, property, and rights. The idea of an uncomplicated, mutually binding contract was so essential to Whig theory that the terms of the contract became an eighteenth-century political cliché reiterated by Whigs on both sides of the Atlantic. Thus "Cato" laid down as a political maxim "that Protection and Allegiance are reciprocal." "A true Whig is of the Opinion," Molesworth asserted, "that the *Executive* Power has as just a Title to the Allegiance and Obedience of the Subject . . . as the Subject has to *Protection*." By midcentury, Blackstone had incorporated the concept into his lectures and ultimately into his *Commentaries*, giving semilegal status to the idea that "allegiance is the tie, or *ligamen*, which binds the subject to the King, in return for that protection which the King affords the subject."[22]

In America, colonists of every political persuasion echoed their English mentors in referring to the terms of the governmental contract. "Are not Protection and Allegiance reciprocal?" queried John Adams in 1765. "In every government," Joseph Galloway answered some ten years later, "protection and allegiance . . . are reciprocal duties" that are "so inseparably united that one cannot exist without the other." From their pulpits, ministers drummed the political catechism into their parishioners' heads. "The duties of Rulers and Subjects are reciprocal, and mutually imply each other," declared one cleric in a typical election sermon. "The duty of rulers and subjects is mutual," exhorted another, so that "rulers ought to love their people and to seek their welfare; and the people on their part, ought to be subject to the higher powers." With this long tradition, it is not surprising that after 1765 the idea that the ruler and the ruled were bound by mutual obligations became a standard theme in colonial resistance literature. Thus James Wilson insisted that "liberty is, by the Constitution, of equal Stability, of equal Antiquity, and of equal Authority with Prerogative." This meant, he scribbled in the margin of a speech delivered in January 1775, that "the Compact between the King and People is mutual, and both are equally bound."[23]

The vital corollary to this theory of a contract between rulers and ruled was that if either side failed to perform its contractual duties, the contract was dissolved. If the ruler was the miscreant, the people were under no further obligations of allegiance and could legitimately resist any unjust exercise of executive authority. The right of the people to resist the illegal encroachments of the executive was thus integral to Whig political theory, and it constituted the ultimate check upon unbounded executive power. David Hume announced it to be a *"general principle"* that "in the case of enormous tyranny and oppression 'tis lawful to take arms against supreme power" because, as government is "a mere human invention for mutual advantage and security, it no longer imposes any obligation . . . when once it ceases to have that tendency." The Americans' claim that their resistance was legitimate was buttressed, therefore, by the most influential political authorities. "They know little of the English Constitution," James Wilson declared, "who are ignorant" of "the Lawfulness of Resistance on the part of the governed against illegal Exertions of Power on the Part of those who govern."[24]

This theory provided an effective check on the discretionary powers of the king. Any king who abused his authority by turning from protector to tyrant effectively broke the governmental contract. The king's tyranny therefore constituted a de facto abdication of his throne. After he broke the contract, the tyrant-king was to be considered a usurper to the legal title of ruler against whom resistance was not only justified but demanded. The king of England's "very attempt" to tyrannize his people, one American explained, "at once destroys his right to [reign] over them."[25]

Although some believed that the governmental contract was simply a useful abstraction that helped explain the limits of executive power, most Whigs conceived of it as a real agreement, with a fixed term that had been publicly sworn to by both parties. Following Locke, Whigs certainly believed that at some point in the distant past the terms of the governmental contract had been agreed upon when man first entered civil society. But additionally, and more relevant to their present situation, English and American Whigs insisted that both the right of resistance and the exact limits of executive authority had been settled "to a plain certainty," as Blackstone put it, by the Glorious Revolution. By virtue of the precedent of 1688, he laid down as "the law of redress against public oppression" that if "any future prince should endeavour to subvert the constitution by breaking the original contract between king and people," his actions would legally "amount to an abdication, and the throne would be thereby vacant."[26] It was particularly incumbent upon George III to heed the lessons of 1688, Americans were quick to point out, for as the scion of the House of Brunswick, he owed his throne to the Glorious Revolution. The king had an undoubted right to the British throne, a typical American asserted, but "his right thereto" was founded "on the people's right to resist, and set aside evil and wicked rulers."[27]

Furthermore, Whigs asserted, both rulers and ruled publicly swore to this contract at the king's coronation, with all the pomp and solemnity the occasion required. Every king was required to swear a coronation oath, the terms of which had been significantly revised in 1689.[28] Only after the new king had sworn to the oath did his subjects swear allegiance to him. Thus "the terms of the original contract between king and people," Blackstone affirmed, were "couched in the coronation oath," which must be sworn to by every ruler "who shall succeed to the imperial crown of these realms."[29]

The King's Powers

The consistent Whig emphasis upon restraining executive authority came not from a desire to eliminate the executive but from a clear recognition that discretionary authority, however dangerous to liberty, was essential to the orderly conduct of political life. The executive, quite simply, had legitimate and important functions that could neither be dispensed with nor easily performed by an alternative authority. As Richard Price observed, "Wisdom, union, dispatch, secrecy, and vigour" are as essential to a well-ordered government as liberty, and these tasks must of necessity be entrusted to "a Supreme executive Magistrate at the head of all."[30]

While radical Whigs admitted the necessity of an executive, they tended to assume that political authority, being of an expansive and encroaching nature, needed few advocates. The establishment Whigs, ever conscious of the need to preserve the precious balance between liberty and authority, were quicker to defend authority and explain its advantages when they sensed that the balance had tipped too far on the side of liberty. Although "liberty is the perfection of human society," Hume wrote, still he wished his readers to remember that "authority must be acknowledged essential to its very existence."[31]

In their concern for maintaining a proper balance between the basic political forces, the establishment Whigs were more likely than the radicals to point out that restraints against excesses of liberty were as necessary as those against excesses of authority. They shared the common Whig view that man is an irrational creature whose natural inclination when entrusted with power is to dominate and to tyrannize. But whereas the radical Whigs were concerned chiefly with the behavior of rulers, the establishment theorists counseled vigilance also against the excesses of the people. This was especially true in "free" states, where the people possessed considerable political power and thus, like rulers in a similar situation, were liable to abuse that power.[32] As Ferguson explained, "it is under a just restraint only that every person is safe" for "if any one were unrestrained, and might do what he pleased, to the same extent also every one else must be exposed to suffer what ever the free men of this description were inclined to inflict." This, he noted, would be worse than the "usurpation of the most outrageous tyrant." The necessity of some restraint on popular excesses was assumed, although not emphasized, by radical Whigs as well. "Liberty does not exclude restraint," James Burgh wrote, "it only excludes unreasonable restraint."[33]

Only the executive, most theorists agreed, could exercise the necessary restraint upon which orderly government depended. Thus, in a section of the *Commentaries* in which Blackstone explained the theoretical basis of the king's role in the eighteenth-century constitution, he observed that "civil liberty, rightly understood, consists in protecting the rights of individuals by the united force of society." This could not be done without entrusting to "some sovereign power" (in the British case, the king) the power to enforce the law by restraining the subject, for "obedience is an empty name, if every individual has a right to decide how far he himself shall obey."[34]

A powerful executive was not only necessary in a negative sense, as a counterweight to popular excesses, but also because the executive in a positive sense performed certain functions and filled certain roles that were essential to the contemporary concept of government. Authority, a modern scholar has noted, is necessary in all political systems "in order for functional processes, each of which regards some aspect of the common good, to be directed toward the whole of the

common good."[35] In the eighteenth-century British system, this positive role of authority included several preeminent royal functions: The
king was responsible for the maintenance of order and stability in
society; he preserved unity among his subjects and dominions; he
protected his people from domestic and foreign enemies; and he
provided—through commissions, charters, and various other legal
agencies—the legitimate authority by which government proceeded.

The Whig conviction that a powerful executive is necessary to a
well-ordered society stemmed from the belief that society naturally
and inevitably assumes a hierarchical order. Liberty, explained Ferguson, must not be confused with "equality of station or fortune." "It
is impossible to restrain the influence of superior ability," he explained, "of property, of education, or the habits of station. It is impossible to prevent these from becoming in some degree hereditary;
and of consequence it is impossible, without violating the principles of
human nature, to prevent some permanent distinction of ranks."[36]

Far from denouncing the natural social hierarchy, establishment
theorists insisted that it provides important political benefits by maintaining order and stability. "It is impossible that government can be
maintained without a due subordination of rank," wrote Blackstone,
"that the people may know and distinguish such as are set over them,
in order to yield them their due respect and obedience." It is in the in-
equalities of rank and station, Ferguson reiterated, that one would
find the "germ of subordination . . . so necessary to the safety of individuals and the peace of mankind."[37]

Americans, too, recognized the necessity in any well-ordered state
of a due subordination of ruled to rulers. Few election sermons were
complete without exhortations that the "Strength & Glory of a People"
consisted of their "due Obedience to all proper Authority." The lack
of such submission, one cleric warned characteristically, would destroy the "Mechanic Order of all society," for where men are "uneasy
in their proper station and troublesome to their Superiors," the state is
filled "with Disorder & Confusion."[38] Up to the final break with England, few overt condemnations of the hierarchical order of society appeared. While there was much criticism of the king's ministers, for example, and increasing dissatisfaction with the king himself, until the
appearance of Paine's *Common Sense* there was little uneasiness expressed about the relationship between subject and king. Americans
constantly asserted that they did not resent their inferior status vis-à-

vis the king but were merely contending for an equality of subjecthood with their fellow Britons.[39]

Thus, when the revolutionary crisis threatened to overthrow the existing "mechanic Order" of society, it is not surprising that some colonists continued to use the long-familiar rhetoric that called for due subordination to those in authority, be those rulers old or new. "When all are Masters," a "New-York Freeholder" feared, "there can be no Security, consequently no true Liberty." The continuance of stability in the midst of revolution depended upon "order and just subordination," a Philadelphia cleric warned. In all political situations, but especially during revolutionary turmoil, every man was "bound to keep the place and duty assigned him." "In every government," the youthful Alexander Hamilton summarized, "there must be a supreme absolute authority lodged somewhere . . . to which all the members of that society are subject." Otherwise, he declared, "there could be no supremacy, or subordination, that is, no government at all."[40]

An essential advantage of a limited monarchy, Whigs believed, lay in the king's social and political primacy. He capped both the political and social hierarchies, all ranks descending in gradation from him. The king's uniquely superior position in a political culture that was convinced that hierarchy was the natural order of society gave him the right to exercise the restraining influence on popular excess upon which stability and order depended. "The prince or leader exclaims against every disorder, which disturbs his society," explained Hume, and because of his primacy he is "readily followed" by those in inferior ranks, whose own stations in the hierarchy ultimately depend upon the king.[41]

To bolster the king's ability to preserve order, Whigs supported a variety of legal conventions along with the traditional pomp and grandeur of the monarchy, all of which enabled the king to maintain his elevated political and social position. These conventions became political clichés, whose functions were understood by all participants in the eighteenth-century political process. The most important of these was probably the assumption that the king was politically perfect, i.e., that he could do no wrong. Political wrongs, this convention held, could only be attributed to evil ministers and advisers, not to the king himself. Blackstone clearly explained the political function of this convention. It meant that "whatever is exceptionable in the conduct of public affairs, is not to be imputed to the king," for to hold the monarch personally responsible for his actions would "totally destroy" the king's superior status, which is "necessary for the balance of power in our free and active . . . constitution."[42] This was a convention to which Americans adhered ever more tenaciously as the quarrel between the colonies and Britain escalated, leaving the king as the last remaining bond of empire. "If the ——— is served by a set of Rascals," one American wrote, "yet spare the beloved Name, and let the Odium be cast on them who deserve it." George III, a pamphleteer assured his readers, was "a Prince, whose goodness of soul, and unsuspecting heart" had "unfortunately . . . betrayed him into the ensnaring measures of designing men."[43]

Some Americans continued to follow the conventional rules of political discourse even after the outbreak of war, which led to considerable confusion and absurdity. Thus a minister admonished a Pennsylvania militia unit about to set out for Massachusetts in 1775 to "continue to revere royalty, and observe your allegiance to the King," for "your drawing the sword must not be against the person of his Majesty; but the mal-administration of his government, by designing, mischief-making ministers."[44]

Of less obvious political use, but of powerful psychological significance, was the image of the king as the "royal father" of the national and the imperial community. Even the sober Blackstone justified the considerable prerogative powers that remained to the king by recurring to the evocative filial metaphor. The king, he wrote, is the *"pater familias* of the nation," to "whom it pertains by his regal office to protect the community."[45] Colonial Americans frequently referred to the king in this traditional filial manner. They had been more "habituated," as a minister wrote, to consider him "under the amiable and endearing character of a father, than the more awful one of a sovereign." Even to cynical Benjamin Franklin, the king was "truly the common father of his people."[46] As the conflict between Britain and America deepened, the colonists continued to evoke the image of the royal father, references that assumed increasingly emotional overtones as the quarrel grew more bitter. As one of the strongest of the early revolutionary pamphlets pleaded, "Where can an affectionate, but *afflicted* people go, but to the bosom of their affectionate *Sovereign*? . . . Where can children who are in danger of being disinherited . . . flee to, but to the breast of their royal *Father*, their friend, their guardian."[47]

The literature is thus replete with examples of the regular colonial use of the familial metaphor, with the king cast as paterfamilias, to characterize the imperial bond, though assessing the effect of the use of such evocative symbolism is difficult. It is important, however, that we not dismiss the usage as empty rhetoric.[48] One imaginative study has, in fact, found in the ubiquitous familial metaphor a psychological explanation of both the tenacity with which Americans bound themselves to the father-king even to the final months of the imperial crisis and the bitterness and righteous indignation with which they reproached him for what they considered to be his ultimate paternal betrayal.[49]

The king's symbolic role was bolstered by the grand and glorious face that the eighteenth-century monarchy presented to the nation. The British monarch has always been surrounded by grandeur and magnificence, which on one level satisfies a universal affection for pomp and parade. It was just such affection, in fact, that caused radicals to warn one another not to be blinded by the "golden mists" of monarchy. The mass of subjects, moreover, saw their king, if they saw him at all, at the great state occasions: coronations, holidays, and openings of Parliament. At these times the king appeared in the full magnificence of his office, dressed in gold, ermine, and velvet, carrying the jeweled symbols of royalty, and riding in a golden coach.[50]

Americans, who rarely viewed such ceremonies personally, appeared to take great delight in the ample colonial newspaper coverage of these occasions, which attempted to convey a vicarious sense of the royal magnificence. Thus, for example, the numerous newspaper accounts of the king's official review of his fleet at Portsmouth in 1773 emphasized the glory and pageantry of the occasion, the magnificent appearance of the royal party, the silken banners and golden ropes, the "saluting with guns, acclamations, and other demonstrations of joy," and the illumination of houses all along the royal route. The account in Rind's *Virginia Gazette* assured its readers that "no words can describe the grandeur of the scene," everything "conspired to heighten its splendor."[51]

The political significance of such pomp and ceremony was not lost on contemporary observers. The sovereign, noted Ferguson, "owes a great part of his authority to the sounding titles and the dazzling equipage which he exhibits in public." It was proper that this should be so, he explained, for it was necessary to ascribe to the king whatever "impose[s] upon the imagination of men," so that "so armed, the sovereign may be able to repress every disorder." Once again, however, it was Blackstone who most clearly understood the importance of bolstering the king's authority by grandeur and political convention. This is essential to the maintenance of political order, he wrote, because "the mass of mankind" would "be apt to grow insolent and refractory, if taught to consider their prince as a man of no greater perfection than themselves." Thus, law and custom ascribe to him grandeur and political attributes "of a great and transcendent nature; by which the people are led to consider him in the light of a superior being, and to pay him that awful respect, which may enable him with greater ease to carry on the business of government."[52]

Whigs acquiesced in the king's supremacy not only because they believed his elevated status maintained order but because his position aided his performance of a second preeminent function of the executive. The king, who was theoretically above selfish interest and political party, was uniquely qualified to represent all his people and his dominions. While members of Parliament still came to Westminster in the mid-eighteenth century to champion their borough, their county, or their patron, the king alone, as a Pennsylvanian noted in 1775, was the sovereign "representative of our whole state."[53] Because the king virtually embodied the national interest, it was his responsibility to harmonize the differences that threatened to divide his people and dominions, to unite disparate elements within his realms, and to direct the efforts of all toward the common good.[54] "As the King is the centre of union," "America Solon" summarized in 1772, ". . . the various parts of the great body politic will be united in him; he will be the spring and soul of the union, to guide and regulate the grand political machine."[55]

In the eighteenth century, the expansion of the empire both magnified the problems of unity and increased the emphasis on the king's role as imperial unifier. "Great empires," Ferguson reminded his readers, were prey to "disunion and dismemberment of provinces." Such tendencies could only be curbed, he believed, by the unifying authority of a powerful king. Americans, conscious of their tendency to quarrel among themselves as well as with the mother country, placed particular emphasis upon the king's unifying authority. For Benjamin Franklin, therefore, the greatest importance of "the King's Supreme Authority over all the Colonies" lay in his role as "a dernier Resort, for settling all their Disputes, a Means of preserving Peace among them with each other, and a Center in which their Common Force might be united." "To the king," James Wilson stated flatly, "is intrusted the direction and management of the great machine of government." He is therefore "fittest to adjust the different wheels, and to regulate their motions in such a manner as to cooperate in the same general designs." The most comprehensive claims for the king as imperial unifier were made, however, by Alexander Hamilton. In the "person and prerogative of the King," he declared, the "connecting, pervading principle" of the British empire is to be found. He it is "that conjoins all these individual societies into one great body politic." He it is that preserves "their mutual connexion and dependence" and he it is that makes them "all co-operate to one common end[,] the general good." It was left to the king, therefore, to "guide the vast and complicated machine of government, to the reciprocal advantage of all his dominions." "The authority of his Majesty over the whole," Hamilton concluded, "will, like a central force, attract them all to the same point."[56]

The king's theoretical responsibility to unify the empire entailed certain specific powers and duties that were of great significance to Americans. As the representative of the entire national community, it was the king's responsibility to present a unified national position in all negotiations with foreign powers. Americans agreed that it must "for ever . . . remain to the Magistrate an EXCLUSIVE RIGHT, of declaring Peace and War, and indeed of transacting most of the publick Business, which relates to their Neighbours." "Connexions, alliances and treaties," a colonist conceded, ". . . are royal prerogatives . . . vest in the King, without murmur of complaint."[57]

The king was also responsible for preserving the internal unity of the empire; he was the "sovereign umpire" who resolved all intra-imperial disputes for the common good. It was "properly his business," asserted Richard Wells, "to confine" each colony "within our proper spheres." In short, observed "A Philadelphian," Britain's kings had always served as "the Umpires of our Disputes, and the Center of our Union."[58] Americans expressed few doubts regarding the legitimacy of this royal function, and right up to the eve of the final separation they continued to bring boundary and jurisdictional disputes to London for final resolution by "the king-in-council." Alternative solutions, in the form of bilateral negotiations or third-party arbitration had often been tried but had seldom been successful. As the imperial crisis deepened, Tories played effectively upon colonial fears that should the king's unifying authority be removed, the colonies would sink into internal dissension and ultimately civil war.[59]

The supreme function with which Whigs charged their king—indeed, the function upon which the governmental contract depended—was that of protection. Men entered political society, explained "Cato," to obtain "mutual Protection and Assistance," and it had been "to make such Protection practicable" that "Magistracy was formed, with Power to defend the Innocent from Violence, and to punish those that offered it." Only to further "this good End" by defending "every Man and his Property from foreign and domestick Injuries" had the magistrate been "instructed with conducting and applying the united Force of the Community." "To wield the national force" for protection against internal and external enemies, Ferguson reiterated simply, "is the office of the executive power."[60]

The principle that the king owed his subjects protection was an ancient one that was adopted by eighteenth-century theorists precisely because it was so compatible with their conception of a contract between ruler and ruled. The statement, "protection and allegiance are reciprocal" encapsulated, in a simplified form, the mutual obligations of king and subject, and thus it became a Whig political cliché that appeared with regularity in almost every form of political literature.[61] Protection, as conceived of by these theorists, was a concrete function of the executive that conveyed specific benefits to the subject. It referred primarily to the king as the military leader of the empire and to his responsibility to provide his subjects with security against foreign enemies and internal disorders. "The king is considered," Blackstone reminded his readers, ". . . as the generalissimo, or the first in military command, within the kingdom," and he was responsible in this capacity for directing "the united strength of the community" to protect "the weakness of individuals." As "the supreme protector of the empire," Hamilton explained, the king is vested with the power of making war and peace. "He it is that has defended us from our enemies," Hamilton emphasized, "and to him alone, we are obliged to render allegiance and submission."[62]

To enhance the image of the king as protector, sovereigns were invested both metaphorically and actually with all the accoutrements of military glory. George II, Jonathan Mayhew claimed, "was a prince of an heroic and martial spirit." His minor victory at Dettingen in 1743, during which battle he had personally led his troops, was hailed out of all proportion to its military importance because it added luster to the king's image as protector. Public accounts emphasized the military competence of George III, a most unlikely martial leader, precisely because such competence was considered to be integral to his kingship. For this reason, the king's commanders traditionally affected to act upon the personal orders of their sovereign. Thus, General James Wolfe, upon arriving in America in 1759, immediately issued a proclamation that established an intimate connection between his mission and his monarch's desires. "The King, my Master," Wolfe wrote, being "highly offended" by "the insolent treatment that has been offered his Subjects in North America" has "resolved to check" the "arrogant and hostile proceeding[s]" of France. In "obedience to his Majesty's commands," therefore, Wolfe would lead "a well appointed Sea and Land force . . . into the heart of Canada."[63] Such personal identification of the sovereign with his troops added to American bitterness toward the king after Lexington and Concord.[64]

In less troubled times, however, British protection seemed to afford Americans considerable security, and they frequently and extravagantly expressed their gratitude to the monarch who protected them. Significantly, American gratitude often was not expressed to the British nation but rather to the protector-king. Thus, after the fall of Quebec in 1759, a New England cleric announced that Americans were indebted "not only for their present Security and Happiness, but perhaps, for their very Being, to the paternal Care of the Monarch." Similarly, Thomas Foxcroft declared in 1760 that "Above all, we owe our humble *Thanks* to his MAJESTY and with loyal Hearts full of joyous Gratitude, we bless the *King*, for his Paternal Goodness in sending such effectual Aids to his American Subjects, . . . when we so needed the Royal Protection."[65]

Not only in wartime did Americans receive the concrete benefits of royal protection. In peacetime as well, American traders sailed the waters of the globe under the protection of His Majesty's navy. "I shall not forget that we are Colonies," James Duane declared in 1774, and "that we are indebted" to Great Britain for "the Blessings of Protection" of our trade. In 1776 many Americans feared independence simply because the removal of the protection afforded by the British navy would render the trade of the colonies, as one patriot noted, "a prey to some of the maritime Princes." As Samuel Seabury observed, Tories delighted in playing upon general fears that the colonies could "have no trade but under the protection of Great-Britain."[66]

In addition to the individual tasks of kingship, the king filled an essential political role that was the basis of his specific powers and duties. Although all Whigs believed that original political power resided always in the body of the people (who conveyed it to both the king and their representatives), after the people delegated their authority to the king at the inception of a reign, he continued in possession of residual political authority in the state until he died or was deposed. Thus, for the duration of his reign, actions taken under the aegis of the king's authority were legal; those taken in the absence of such sanction were not.[67]

The royal authority to legitimate political actions and officers referred in practice to the host of discretionary, or prerogative, powers still exercised by the king after 1688. Whigs, consistently suspicious of unlimited power, attempted to devise firm boundaries to the exercise of the royal prerogative. They had difficulty in doing so, however, for if some discretionary political powers were deemed necessary (and most agreed that they were), then those who were entrusted with the exercise of such powers must be allowed to exercise discretion. As Blackstone put it, "in the exertion of lawful prerogative the king is and ought to be absolute." Yet the idea of unlimited power was too fearful a concept for most eighteenth-century theorists. As Hume carefully stipulated, "a legal authority, though great, has always some bounds." The king's prerogative was no exception, and thus his discretionary powers, according to Blackstone, were limited "by bounds so certain and notorious that it is impossible he should ever exceed them."[68] The solution to the seeming contradiction of "unlimited power" limited by "certain and notorious" bounds lay in the definition of the "just" or "lawful" prerogative. As one midcentury theorist defined "this Power . . . called PREROGATIVE of Magistracy," it was "no more than a Power to DO GOOD WITHOUT LAW." In this way, an American cleric noted, kings were "ministers of GOD for good." Thus, "Cato" explained, the British constitution had once again contrived a happy medium; the prince was lawfully empowered with "all the Means of doing good, and none of doing ill."[69]

With the very definition of the king's prerogative precluding the abuse of such discretionary power, Whigs could defend the considerable prerogative powers that the eighteenth-century constitution confided in the king. The theoretical justification for these powers lay in the king's role as the reservoir of all legitimate power in the state.[70] Although all political power ultimately resided in the people, once it had been granted to the king at his coronation he was empowered to delegate this legitimate authority to subordinate jurisdictions and officers. Since the king was "the Head & Fountain of Civil Power," an American observed, so the "subordinate Authority" of all civil magistrates was a stream "issuing there from." As the dispenser of legitimate authority, the king appointed all subordinate officers of government, civil and military. He was, as Blackstone noted, "the fountain of honour, of office, and of privilege." As the embodiment of legitimate authority, he was the ultimate source of all justice in the realm; he was "the reservoir," Blackstone explained in the ubiquitous watery metaphor, "from whence right and equity are conducted . . . to every individual."[71]

In this capacity, moreover, the king alone could delegate governing authority to subordinate jurisdictions. Thus charters—whether for borough, university, or colony—had to be *royal* charters if they were to convey governmental powers.[72] The king's prerogative power to legitimate all subordinate governments was further enhanced in the case of the American colonies by his legal ownership of all the lands within his realms. As Arthur Lee reminded Samuel Adams, "all territory taken possession of . . . by the King's subjects, vest absolutely in him." Most of the colonies were legally, therefore, creations of the king's prerogative powers to grant land and issue charters.[73]

Far from protesting this legal position, in the political battles of the 1760s and 1770s the colonists began to emphasize their dependence upon the king's prerogative, in part to counteract claims of parliamentary sovereignty and in part because there was, as yet, no legal alternative. "The main body of the American colonies are constitutional whigs," observed "Obadiah," and "as such, they approve of the King's constitutional prerogative in all its branches, and are ready to defend it with their lives and fortunes."[74] Though many Americans mistrusted and even despised George III by 1774, it is also true that few saw an easy or tranquil way of replacing his political authority.

A brief and by no means exhaustive survey of the king's role on the eve of the Revolution reveals that the power of the eighteenth-century executive remained ample and that his functions continued to be important. This was perhaps even more true in the imperial than in the domestic context, because, as noted, the nature of the imperial relationship depended on the sovereign's prerogative powers to settle

lands, issue charters, and protect his subjects, and also because the
dramatic expansion of parliamentary power after 1689 was a major
source of colonial discontent. So large was the king's role that radical
Whigs constantly warned their readers to guard against executive encroachments. Yet they never favored abolishing the king's prerogative
powers, nor did they argue for contracting his constitutional role.
They did not do so because they could not, as yet, discern a practical
alternative to the existing British system.

All Whigs were, of course, familiar with the examples of both the ancient and modern republics and frequently alluded to the fact that in
such systems the functions of authority were exercised by various institutions under direct popular control.[75] As advocates of liberty,
therefore, most Whigs conceded the theoretical advantages of republics. Even Hume believed that of all systems of government, "the Republican Form . . . is by far the best." But changing governments inevitably brought turmoil and dislocation; it was a course to be
advocated only in the most extreme circumstances. Furthermore,
Whigs realized that in practice the forces of liberty and those of authority must always be opposed, whether the forces of authority derived their power from the people or by heredity. The question concerning British theorists therefore was not, as Hume noted,
"concerning any fine imaginary republic, of which a man may form a
plan in his closet," but in preserving the balanced stability of the present British constitution. As "Cato" admitted, "Liberty may be better
preserved by a well poised Monarchy, than by any popular Government that I know now in the World."[76]

The key to making the British constitution live up to such expectations lay in maintaining the proper balance between liberty and authority. While Whigs worried most that the balance would be tipped
toward authority, they were also concerned that too great a curtail-
ment of the executive might end in the "worst Effect, Licentiousness."
As Hume warned, "if we have reason to be more jealous of monarchy,
because the danger is more imminent from that quarter, we have also
reason to be more jealous of popular government because that danger
is more terrible." For thoughtful men the lesson was clear: Authority
without liberty was tyranny, but liberty without authority was anarchy. This was a lesson that Americans learned well. Thus, after the
Stamp Act riots of 1765 in Boston, a young Josiah Quincy, Jr., wrote
revealingly in his journal: "Who, that marks the riotous tumult, con-

fusion, and uproar of a democratic, the slavery and distress of a despotic, state,—the infinite miseries attendant of both,—but would fly for refuge from the mad rage of the one, and oppressive power of the other, to that best asylum, that glorious medium, the British Constitution?"[77]

The problem of maintaining the proper balance between liberty and authority, however, did not become acute in the colonies until the struggle to maintain American liberty threatened to eliminate all vestiges of authoritative government.[78] For Elbridge Gerry, a Massachusetts radical of longstanding, the need to temper "undue" liberty was apparent as early as 1775. Since the people had been harangued so incessantly about their power "from the frequent delineations of their rights," he worried that "they now feel rather too much their own importance, & it requires great skill in gradually checking them to such a subordination as is necessary to good Government." A New England cleric warned in a similar vein of the chaos that must ensue when men "under the notion of a zeal for liberty, run into most excessive licentiousness . . . pulling down and destroying houses, abusing persons, endangering men's lives, destroying their property." By 1776 even John Adams, who had been first to call for the erection of new, popular provincial governments, expressed apprehension that in those new governments "the People will have unbounded Power." For he had read widely enough in the standard works of political theory to realize that "the People are extreamly addicted to Corruption and Venality, as well as the Great."[79]

These conceptions suggest a major reason why many Americans hung back from the final renunciation of George III long after he had lost all title to their allegiance. They were loathe to destroy the precious constitutional balance by removing the symbol of political authority, the king. So some Americans continued to invoke the king's name in courthouse and legislature, to petition him for redress, and to put the best face upon his actions long after all affection for and trust in George III was gone, because right up to the brink of independence their understanding of the nature of imperial politics left them little alternative. In answer to a question that troubled many of his countrymen, a Virginian thus gave a blunt and revealing answer. He realized that many of his fellow Americans were asking themselves how they could "again be reconciled to a King who has violated the rights of the subject, and broke through the barriers of the constitution?" But he considered it imperative that they attempt such a reconciliation. Although he also "detest[ed] the principles of George III" and would "at all times oppose his unjust encroachments," yet, he wrote, "I mean to preserve the constitution by retaining the King."[80]

Such absurdities, however, could not continue forever. Americans could not indefinitely, wrote one disgusted patriot, "swear Allegiance to the power that is Cutting our throats."[81] By 1776 the king had, by his own actions, destroyed the very foundations upon which a Whig king held his throne, and thus he forced the colonists to search for political alternatives. Some Americans, of course, embraced the opportunity that George III's tyranny provided to create new republican institutions based entirely upon popular authority. They welcomed the challenge of building, in a young and virtuous society, something entirely new in political history—a durable, extensive, and stable popular government. These were the hopeful men who plunged into the creative process of political experimentation that characterized many of the new American states in the years after independence.[82] They believed that in 1776 an American revolution had truly begun, because they were among the first to define "revolution" in its modern sense, as a movement forward into a different and better future.[83]

But for other Americans, "revolution" remained what it always had been—a return to a happier past, to an Eden that had existed prior to 1763, prior to 1603, or prior to 1066.[84] For them, resistance to the authority of George III was justified by the same sources that warned them against political experimentation. They looked at the various provincial governments after 1774 not as challenges but as failures, as improvised structures of committees and congresses superimposed upon the vestiges of royal government that were incapable of carrying out the tasks of authoritative government. These Americans, who also felt the need to oppose tyranny but who worried about the consequent vacuum of authority, turned initially to the Continental Congress, the only American institution that seemed capable, in the troubled years after 1774, of carrying the burden of authority.

CHAPTER 2

The Abdication of George III

You surprise me with your Account of the Prayers in publick for
an Abdicated King, a Pretender to the Crown.
                    —*John Adams, October 8, 1776*

In May 1776, Gouverneur Morris rose to speak in the New York Provincial Congress. He was annoyed by his colleagues' hesitation over taking decisive steps toward declaring independence and organizing a new provincial government, and he chided them for seeking to defer such action until the arrival of royal peace commissioners who, rumor had it, were on their way to America.[1] "Will you trust these commissioners?" he asked. "No, they come from the King. We have no business with the King." "We did not quarrel with the King," Morris continued, but George III had made the final break inevitable by officiously thrusting himself into the middle of the dispute. "Trust crocodiles, trust the hungry wolf in your flock, or a rattlesnake in your bosom," Morris warned, and "you may yet be something wise. But trust the King, . . . it is madness in the extreme!"[2]

The anger at George III and the extreme distrust of his intentions expressed by Morris in 1776 was the culmination of a long series of events that effectively quenched the huge reservoir of respect, affection, and veneration that the colonists long had shown toward their sovereign.[3] So strong had the attachment been, wrote Oliver Wolcott on the eve of independence, "that the Abilities of a Child might have governed" the colonists.[4] George III possessed abilities considerably greater than those of a child, and his intentions, invariably, were to govern his overseas dominions with justice and with the strictest adherence to the principles of the English constitution.[5] But the king's iron determination to do his duty, combined with his understanding of the eighteenth-century constitution, led him to undertake a series of actions from 1774 to 1776 that directly affected the colonists' conception of the grounds upon which he held his throne. The king's behavior during this critical period led Americans, fully cognizant of Whig theories of kingship, to the conclusion that George III had irrevocably broken the governmental contract that bound king and colonist together and that he had thereby abdicated his American thrones.

The king's direct entrance into the American controversy could not have come at a worse stage of the continuing crisis between Britain and America. By 1774, American Whigs had completely disavowed the authority of Parliament and had flung themselves into the arms of the royal prerogative to an extent that horrified their English compatriots. In appealing directly to the king himself, they let themselves in for a final, and perhaps inevitable, disillusionment with British authority. From 1774 through 1776 the king repeatedly and publicly scorned American overtures and seized every opportunity to demonstrate his approval of a harsh American policy. By 1776, over a year's experience of dependence upon George III had convinced even those colonists who had previously wavered that the king had, by his own actions, renounced his just title to rule his American subjects.

Dependence upon the King

The colonists' relations with the king had undergone a series of changes since George III had ascended the throne in 1760 to extravagant expressions of joy.[6] American Whigs felt themselves a part of the English opposition movement that had battled with the king through the 1760s over his policies, his advisers, and, climactically, over the improbable Whig hero John Wilkes. American enthusiasm for Wilkes matched and occasionally surpassed that of the English radicals. American faith in their sovereign was correspondingly undermined by the king's contemptuous treatment of Wilkes and the petitions of his supporters. By 1770 the exaggerated American hope that George III would be a true "Patriot King" had effectively been dashed. Some colonists drew the conclusion that the king's tyranny at home had completely destroyed his right to rule in America.[7]

Although by the early 1770s some Americans felt released from their bonds of allegiance, and a great many more had begun to distrust the king's intentions, most colonists would still have to travel a considerable political distance before they would approve the antimonarchical sentiments expressed in *Common Sense* and in the Declaration of Independence.[8] The journey was made more difficult in 1774, at the outset

of the final stage of the controversy, by the realities of the colonial constitutional position.

By 1774 American political theorists were faced with an apparently
insoluble constitutional dilemma. The colonists were utterly sincere in
their desire to remain within the British empire; despite British suspicions, independence was still the goal of only a few. Yet Americans
were determined to deny the authority of the British Parliament over
them, for by 1774 they had come to believe that the corrupt Parliament
was the source of all their grievances. The logic of this position forced
them to emphasize to a greater degree than they ever had before their
utter dependence upon the king and his prerogative.[9] Benjamin
Franklin was an early exponent of this new American position. "From
a long and thorough consideration of the subject," Franklin informed
his son in 1773, he was "of opinion, that the parliament has no right to
make any law whatever, binding on the colonies," and furthermore,
that only "the king, and not the king, lords, and commons collectively, is their sovereign; and that the king with their respective parlia-
ments, is their only legislator."[10]

Other Americans expanded upon Franklin's theme, which became
central to the arguments of some persuasive pamphlets in 1774 and
early 1775. Franklin's fellow Pennsylvanian, James Wilson, argued in
an essay that appeared in England and the colonies in mid-1774 that
the phrase the "dependence of the colonies on Great Britain" meant
"the obedience and loyalty, which the colonists owe to the *kings* of
Great Britain." "Those who launched into the unknown deep, in quest
of new countries," he observed, ". . . took possession of the country
in the *king's* name: . . . they established governments under the sanction of *his* prerogative, or by virtue of *his* charters." This was the dependence, Wilson insisted, that the colonists had always acknowledged and would continue to acknowledge, for it was "a dependence
founded upon the principles of reason, of liberty, and of law." Americans were the subjects of a still-powerful king, he concluded, and this
relationship was the basis of the connection between the colonies and
Britain.[11]

In his answer to Tory pamphleteer Samuel Seabury, Alexander
Hamilton presented perhaps the most complete expression in pamphlet form of this inflation of the king's imperial role. Americans could
not be considered independent of Britain, he wrote, even though they
completely denied parliamentary authority, for they bore the strictest

and most faithful allegiance to the king. "He is King of America,"
Hamilton noted, "by virtue of a compact between us and the Kings of
Great-Britain." From this compact, he continued, arose the mutual obligations of king and subject, the one to protect, the other to swear allegiance. The source of American allegiance, therefore, was "that protection which we have hitherto enjoyed from the Kings of Great
Britain," for the king was "the supreme protector of the Empire." "He
it is that has defended us from our enemies," noted Hamilton, "and to
him alone, we are obliged to render allegiance and submission."[12]

This theme was popular throughout the colonies in late 1774 and
early 1775. "The British Parliament is nothing but your elder sister,"
"Hampden" assured the Virginia burgesses. "Affection is due to her;
but obedience is a tribute due only to a King."[13] A New England minister echoed that allegiance was not due "to the power of Parliament"
but was only "due to the King." In short, an "Anxious By Stander"
announced, "I declare my allegiance to George the Third. I won him
for my Sovereign, and I will admit of no intermediate parliamentary
power, between an American legislation and his Royal Throne."[14]

The specter of American Whigs heedlessly throwing themselves
upon the king's pleasure was one that amused American Tories and
British ministers but that alarmed the friends of America in England.
In a speech to the House of Commons, Lord North even claimed that
since the "administration contended for the right of parliament, while
the Americans talked of their belonging to the crown," that "their language therefore was that of Toryism." Not only British ministers noted
the strange turn of the American position in 1774. English radicals[15]
were aghast at the apparent American willingness to "throw themselves into the arms of prerogative, and [put] all their confidence in the
. . . pleasure of the crown." "Who could believe," one troubled writer
asked, "that patriotism could even speak a language like this?"[16]

One may question the strength of the American commitment to the
constitutional position sketched out in 1774 by the colonial pamphlet-
eers and argue that the colonists were merely casting about in desperation for a way to reconcile two apparently contradictory impulses—a
desire to remain within the empire and a determination to deny parliamentary authority. The inflation of the king's imperial role, one might
observe, was simply a hasty colonial solution to the dilemma, quickly
seized upon and just as quickly abandoned. There is no evidence to
suggest, however, that the colonial theorists were insincere in their ar-

guments. Nor is there any reason to suppose that they did not speak for a great many moderate Americans who continued until 1776 to act upon the very assumptions expressed by the theorists by actively seeking a reconciliation that would have permitted them to remain under the king's, although not Parliament's, authority. Furthermore, the imperial connection that the colonial theorists envisioned in 1774 was not inherently absurd, but rather may well have been an imaginative, if premature, solution to the problem of imperial federation. A relationship very similar to that outlined by Wilson and Hamilton successfully enabled first Canada and subsequently other dominions to remain within the British empire.[17]

Yet in the particular situation of 1774 the exaggeration of the king's role had a corollary that, given George III's determination to play the role assigned to him by the Revolution Settlement of 1689, boded ill for the future stability of the first British empire. Precisely because the king was the last constitutional link with the empire that the colonists still considered to be legitimate, George III was destined to become, as Gerald Stourzh has noted, "the final scapegoat."[18]

Assent to Unjust Laws

George III opened Parliament on January 13, 1774, with a speech concerned mainly with European affairs. Relations between England and her colonies continued to be quiescent, and the most alarming news the king reported was the failure of peace negotiations between Turkey and Russia.[19] On January 27 the calm ended when news of the Boston Tea Party reached London. The Tea Party, which Britons viewed as a mob attack upon private property, raised a storm of outrage throughout the nation. Nowhere did the tempest rage more furiously than in the king's chambers, where the monarch and his ministers agreed that they must pursue a firm policy toward the colonies. A week after the news arrived, Lord Dartmouth, Secretary of State for the Colonies, informed a general on service in America that it was "the king's firm Resolution;—upon the unanimous Advice of His Confidential Servants, to pursue such Measures as shall be effectual for securing the Dependence of the Colonies upon this Kingdom."[20] George III's attitude toward the Americans remained virtually unchanged until the end of the war, and at critical times it proved decisive in stiffening the resolve of wavering ministers. His conviction that until the colonies submitted to the authority of Parliament there could be no reconciliation, and that only coercion could induce such a submission, proved especially disastrous in the critical years from 1774 through 1776, when moderates on both sides of the Atlantic still believed that a reconciliation on terms other than submission was possible and were working desperately to bring it about.

The king's views should have come as no surprise to Americans. English radical diatribes against the sovereign, which far surpassed any American efforts in invective, were widely reprinted in colonial newspapers. Thus the colonists were aware of the malevolent disposition attributed to the king by his discontented subjects at home.[21] They received similar indications from the private correspondence of Americans living in London, like William and Arthur Lee, Benjamin Franklin, and Ralph Izard. The ministry's harsh measures, Franklin hinted to his son in 1773, had been "very much the King's own." By November 1774 Izard had concluded that "the King's determined inflexibility cuts off all hope" of reconciliation.[22]

Yet, on the eve of revolution most Americans continued to suppress the suspicion, fed by the English papers and private letters, that the king himself was behind the measures directed against them. The constitutional position of many colonists, and the personal preferences and habits of others, led them to continue to profess loyalty to the king.[23] Had the colonists been apprised of the facts about the king's role in the ministry's coercive policy, they would have been hard pressed to maintain this position for as long as they did. The opposition Whigs were more correct than they knew concerning the king's attitude toward the Americans, and this became increasingly difficult to hide after 1774 as Americans began to appeal their case directly to George III.

The king's course of action during the crises of 1774 resulted from the combination of his personality and his perception of his political role. George III was a man of many admirable qualities. Among the most attractive features of his personality were courage, faith in God, devotion to duty, and an unwillingness to let obstacles deter him from performing his duty once he had determined where his duty lay. It is, however, but a short step from these qualities to others—obstinacy, inflexibility, stubbornness—that were also attributed to the king.[24]

George III's conception of where his duty lay was formed in the early years of his reign, when he had learned about the proper role of a Hanoverian king. The House of Brunswick had been called to the throne by Parliament, and as its scion he realized that the great mistake of the Stuarts had been to attempt to enlarge their prerogative powers by curtailing those of Parliament. His duty, he knew, lay in *upholding* the rights of Parliament, an institution whose power had increased and would continue to do so throughout his reign. At issue in 1774 was not his own power but rather the power of Parliament to legislate for the colonies. On such a fundamental issue he could accept no compromise, even had his personality permitted such flexibility. His duty was absolutely clear, as his biographer puts it: "He would be the defender of the constitution; the protector of the 'rights of Parliament.' " As the king wrote in September 1775, he was "fighting the Battle of the legislature, [and] therefore [had] a right to expect almost unanimous support."[25]

The king's conviction that he must not yield when such a fundamental issue was at stake was strengthened by his experiences during the early years of his reign, when ministerial instability had induced him to consent to the repeal of the Stamp Act. Instead of reconciling Americans to the principle of parliamentary sovereignty—insisted on in the Declaratory Act—repeal had only engendered stiffened resistance and increased recalcitrance. The lesson of 1765 was clear, and the king recurred to it often: There could be no true reconciliation until the colonists acknowledged the sovereignty of Parliament, and as weakness only encouraged resistance, only a steady policy of firmness could ever induce them to do so.[26]

Although he took pains to inform himself about the facts of the American situation from those who might have been expected to know, there is no evidence that he was influenced by—or, indeed, even heard—facts that conflicted with these convictions. Thus, after an interview with Thomas Hutchinson in 1774, the king informed Lord North that the former Massachusetts governor had convinced him that the Bostonians would submit to the Port Bill. Hutchinson, however, recalled his advice to his sovereign in entirely different terms. He had informed the king, he recorded soon after the interview, that the Port Bill would bring "the greatest distress upon the town, and many of the tradesmen" and suggested that, unless amended, it would injure Britain's best friends without distressing her enemies.[27]

Through the final crisis years, the king's unswerving commitment to a firm policy shows not only in all his public pronouncements but in his private correspondence as well. In May 1774, when the Coercive Acts were before Parliament, the king remarked that "perseverance and . . . firmness seem the only means of either with credit or Success terminating public affairs." In September of the same year he again pronounced his credo. "The dye is cast," he wrote, "the Colonies must either submit or triumph." While he did "not wish to come to severer measures," he added, "we must not retreat." In March 1775 he continued to insist, as he did until the end of the war, that the more he revolved in his mind the proper line of conduct toward the Americans, the more he was convinced that "rectitude, candour, and becoming firmness, if properly attended to[,] must with time be crowned with success."[28]

After the arrival of the news of the Boston Tea Party, the king's determination to punish the Bostonians echoed the enraged sentiment not only in government circles but in the nation at large. "There never has been a time when the nation in general has been so united against the Colonies," Thomas Hutchinson reported soon after his arrival in England. This unity had determined the ministry "not to recede."[29]

This determination found expression in March, 1774 when a unanimous cabinet presented a harsh plan for subordinating Massachusetts to Parliament. The plan had been developed during feverish interviews and consultations in February.[30] On March 7, 1774, the king formally announced to Parliament the news of the "outrageous proceedings at . . . Boston." One week later, Lord North introduced the punitive Boston Port Bill. The rationale for this bill, which was to cause an unprecedented uproar in the colonies, was almost self-evident to the ministers who proposed it. Thus Lord Dartmouth, the supposed moderate in the ministry, informed Hutchinson that since Boston had abused its status as a commercial center, the best means of punishment would be to suspend "all the privileges at present enjoyed" by the town "as a Seat of Government and a place of Trade."[31] The full plan became apparent by the end of March, when the government introduced the Massachusetts Government Bill and the Administration of Justice Bill, both of which passed with large majorities. In April the government introduced the Quebec Bill, which the colonists classed with the previous measures, although it had not been intended by the ministry to be part of the coercive package against Massachusetts. By the time Parliament was dissolved on June 22, the king had assented to all the bills. The "great Majority" by which these measures had been approved, he observed in early May, had given him "infinite satisfaction."[32]

When news of the Coercive Acts reached America, a wave of resentment against their authors swept through the continent.[33] While most of the anger was directed against the ministry, the first fruits of the new dependence upon the king began to ripen as Americans looked more closely at the sovereign's role in the business. "What reflections or feelings of humanity," Josiah Quincy, Jr., asked bitterly, passed through the mind of "that generous prince stiled THE FATHER OF ALL HIS PEOPLE" as he united with his ministry in passing "this terrible act" and thereby "solemnly consign[ed] thousands—if not millions—to ruin, misery and desperation?"[34]

As one by one the rest of the Coercive Acts arrived from across the Atlantic in the summer of 1774, Americans expressed increasing anger at the king. The Quebec Act was particularly disturbing, the colonists charged, for by consenting to the establishment of Roman Catholicism in that province, the king had breached his coronation oath, in which he had sworn to uphold the Protestant religion. "I must not say that our King *hath* committed wilful and corrupt *Perjury* by forswearing his oath," noted a "Scotchman," "I will not say that he hath thereby been guilty of High Treason against the Majesty of the People; neither do I assert that the People are now *absolved from their Allegiance*." But, he added, *"nobody can be hanged for thinking."* "Phocian" summarized the effect of the Coercive Acts on American sentiments toward the king. "To YOU we look for protection," he reminded the king, and therefore colonial grievances must be traced "up to the throne," for Americans realized that the hated acts could not have become laws to "affect and oppress" them "without *your* approbation."[35]

The colonists responded to the Coercive Acts by calling a continental congress to establish a concerted opposition to the new British measures. The king and his ministers had expected that their firm policy would convince the Bostonians to retreat.[36] Instead, the entire continent had taken up Boston's cause. Not only did the Congress issue a ringing declaration of colonial rights, but the delegates went even further. To bring about changes in British policy, they adopted a Continental Association, which pledged the colonies to a total, continent-wide commercial boycott of Great Britain. This Association, the king believed, would result in the utter destruction of imperial commerce.[37]

Although the harsh measures of 1774 had not secured the desired end of colonial submission, neither the king nor his ministers seriously considered the alternative policy of seeking an accommodation on terms the Americans were likely to accept. As the Americans had not retreated, so the British leadership resolved to make their stand upon the rights of Parliament as upheld in the Coercive Acts. Thus when General Thomas Gage (the new governor of Massachusetts) suggested repealing the acts as a first step toward reconciliation, the king firmly rejected the idea. The colonists, he believed, were "ripe for mischief" and repeal would only demonstrate irresolution on the part of the mother country and encourage colonial recalcitrance. The government had determined, Hutchinson reported in early November, "that it was too far gone. There was no possibility of receding."[38]

The harsh ministerial response to the First Continental Congress was due in part to the unfortunate sequence in which reports of its actions arrived in London, for the news could not possibly have come in a worse way for those on both sides who were working and praying for an accommodation. There were many such men in London, and they, above all, awaited the outcome of the Congress with interest and anxiety. Thus Lord Dartmouth confided to Hutchinson on August 31 that "he supposed nothing was to be done until the result of the Congress was known."[39] Not until late October did the first news arrive in London about the delegates' activities in Philadelphia, and the reports horrified English moderates. The American delegates, from whose reputed good sense and prudence the British moderates had expected much, had approved the inflammatory resolves of Suffolk County, Massachusetts.[40]

It was unfortunate that this action—by far the most radical step taken by the delegates—should have been the first news of congressional activity to reach London. That it did so was a byproduct of the delegates' agreement to preserve an appearance of unanimity by conducting their deliberations in secret. They had breached their self-imposed obligation of secrecy in the case of the Suffolk Resolves in order to forestall an immediate outbreak of war near Boston.[41] But whatever the domestic reasons for their action, one result was that it provided Englishmen with their first impression of the Continental Congress. As General Frederick Haldimand acidly noted, by the delegates' approval of the Resolves, "The Spirit of the Congress may easily be guessed."[42]

The news could not have failed to harden the position of the king and his ministers, who at this point reflected the aroused opinion in the country. Even the colonists' best friends within the government, like Dartmouth and John Pownall, seemed thunderstruck by the news. Dartmouth concluded unhappily that the Americans had in effect declared war upon the mother country.[43]

The king's reaction to the report can perhaps best be described as relief. At least in his mind, there could be no further doubt by what name to characterize American actions. The Suffolk Resolves had proved Massachusetts to be "in a State of Rebellion." The other colonies' support for the rebellious province had shown them also to have "thrown off the mask" of prudence. The actions, he wrote, had dictated "the proper plan to be followed"; henceforth "blows" would decide the future status of the rebellious colonies.[44]

This was the state of opinion regarding America when the ministry, convinced that it now faced a long colonial struggle, abruptly dissolved Parliament and called for new elections. No further news of the Congress arrived until the elections were over, the result of which was victory for the ministry and for the king, who had taken a great interest in the campaign.[45] But it would have made little difference in the outcome even if further news of the Congress had arrived prior to the elections, for Englishmen would have learned, as they did on November 10, that the Congress had voted to ban all British imports. Upon reading the full text of the Continental Association, which this early action foreshadowed, even Dartmouth concluded that "every one who had signed" it "was guilty of Treason" and that the only possible British response to "such an insult" must be to pursue "the most vigorous measures" in order to punish the colonists.[46]

The carefully written declaration of rights upon which the delegates had lavished so much time and thought and that had conceded to the British Parliament the power (if not the right) to regulate colonial trade, did not arrive in Britain until mid-December, after the new Parliament had met and had recessed for the long holiday season. Not until the very end of December, when almost no one of importance was still in London, did the British see John Dickinson's elegant and correct petition to the king. Out of respect for the monarch, the delegates had declined to publish the text until the petition had been formally presented to His Majesty's representative, which was done, finally, on December 21, 1774.[47]

The petition made little difference, however, for minds had been made up almost two months previously when news of the Suffolk Resolves had arrived. On November 30 the king had opened his new Parliament with a belligerent speech that publicly announced the conclusions that he and his ministers had reached upon first hearing the news of the Congress. He announced that, "unhappily," despite the Coercive Acts, the "daring spirit of resistance and disobedience to the law" still prevailed in Massachusetts. The administration had not yet decided what specific measures to take in response, but the general direction was clear. Coercive policy must be pursued without let or deviation. Of the king's personal acquiescence in this policy there can be no doubt. "The King's Speech as it appears in print is strong," Hutchinson related to a friend in Massachusetts. "If you had heard him deliver it you would have thought it much stronger."[48] The printed text, however, was bad enough, and the colonists received the news of the ministry's overwhelming election victory and the king's speech with sadness and shock. "The die is cast," wrote Abigail Adams, unknowingly echoing her sovereign. "Yesterday brought us such a Speach from the Throne as will stain with everlasting infamy the reign of G[e]orge the 3."[49]

The policy implications of the king's speech were not worked out until the government reassembled in London in January 1775. In part this was due to the seemingly inviolable English holiday hiatus. It was also due, however, to policy disagreements as to the best way of dealing with the situation created by the First Congress. It was all very well to announce one's support for a firm policy, but it was a different matter entirely to agree upon the specific actions that such firmness ought consist of, especially since there was as yet no fighting and thus (some argued) no overt rebellion. For example, although Dartmouth agreed that coercion was necessary, he wished to see it accompanied by some conciliatory action, such as the dispatch of peace commissioners to America. The more bellicose ministers, like Suffolk, argued strenuously against making any concessions until the colonists had submitted. These disagreements rendered the king, who was "more his own Min[ister] than any of his Predecessors," more influential than he might otherwise have been, and he was firmly and perhaps decisively on the side of those who favored coercion alone. These divisions within the cabinet produced a delay in adopting a plan of response to the First Congress. "I am told there are many Cooks," Hutchinson reported to a correspondent during this period, "which makes me fear what the Broth will be."[50]

The broth, which was eventually served up to the House of Commons in January and February 1775, was undiluted coercion soup. By January 12, very early in their discussions, the government had formally dismissed the only plan of accommodation that had any chance of success by deciding that the congressional petition to the king did not supply a basis for negotiation.[51] Having summarily dismissed the American peace initiative, the ministry embarked upon a two-part policy. First, largely to satisfy Dartmouth, North decided to offer his own reconciliation plan in the Commons. The North plan—which was far from conciliatory as far as the colonists were concerned—allowed the American legislatures rather than Parliament the right to apportion and collect such taxes as Parliament saw fit to levy. North's plan was not considered a serious effort, even by knowledgeable Englishmen. The plan, noted Hutchinson, "seems rather calculated to Stop the mouths of people here than to serve any valuable purpose with the people in America."[52]

The second line of policy, to which the major portion of the ministers' time and effort were devoted, was that of coercion. To deal with the congressional trade embargo, trade was to be stopped, first with the New England colonies, and then any other provinces that adhered to the Association. This method of dealing with colonial economic coercion had been discussed as soon as rumors of a possible renewed commercial boycott had reached London. North had noted in September 1774 that if the colonies "refused to trade with Great Britain, G[reat] B[ritain] would take care they should trade no where else." Despite pleas by merchants and resident Americans that such a policy would harm only Britain's best friends in the colonies, the simplicity of the measure (so like the Boston Port Bill) appealed to a majority of the cabinet, and they refused to give it up.[53] Dealing with a rebellion that was not yet a rebellion proved somewhat more difficult. Unwilling to initiate the military action which they increasingly believed was inevitable, the ministers decided to strengthen British land and sea forces in America and to order them to stand ready to meet any new colonial encroachments with force.[54]

The ministry's dual policy was pursued simultaneously through the late winter of 1775. On January 21 the Privy Council agreed to present North's conciliation plan to the Commons and also voted to send General Gage the substantial reinforcements he had requested. On February 10 the bill to restrain the trade of the New England colonies was introduced, and it was followed shortly by similar bills for the southern colonies. To emphasize that the ministers planned to depend on coercion rather than conciliation, Dartmouth fully explained the administration's position in secret instructions written to Gage on January 27, 1775. Whereas the governor had hitherto been cautioned "to act upon the Defensive," he was thenceforth to "take a more active & determined part" by using the substantial military manpower that the government was dispatching. American conduct had proved that the colonists were in "actual Revolt," Dartmouth observed. Under such circumstances, "the King's Dignity & the Honour and Safety of the Empire" required that "Force should be repelled by Force." The ministry's plans to send more troops to America were made public in the king's "Message for an Augmentation of the Forces" of February 10, 1775.[55]

Dartmouth's letter to Gage provides a key to British policy in the late winter and early spring of 1775. In effect, the ministers appear to have united in favor of the position that the king had announced several months previously. All were now agreed that the measures of the First Congress amounted to rebellion and that rebellion could be dealt with only by force. As Hutchinson noted, many prominent men felt that "a restr[aint] upon trade is no punishment for Rebellion." Thus, while the British, like the Americans, had no desire to fire the first shot, nevertheless the correspondence indicates a clear wish that the first shot be fired, so that the cabinet could get on with the concrete tasks of waging war and leave behind the complexities of colonial politics and graded responses. By early March, therefore, many of the men in power "wish[ed] to hear of an Engagement." Even Dartmouth, who was "very apprehensive that the New England people will resist the King's troops" did "not know but some action between them will be best." By March 1775, therefore, even the most conciliatory of the king's ministers had concluded with their master that henceforth "Blows must decide between Britain and the colonies."[56]

The king's determination to treat American resistance as rebellion and his expectation that the dispute would soon degenerate into armed conflict was abundantly clear to the Americans, even without having access to the sovereign's private papers. Every one of the king's public announcements (all of which were widely reported in the colonial press) breathed the same spirit as his private correspondence. "It is a lamentable circumstance," wrote Jefferson, "that the only mediatory power acknowledged by both parties, . . . should pursue the incendiary purpose of still blowing up the flames as we find him constantly doing in every speech and public declaration."[57]

Even before the events of April 1775, the Americans were therefore well aware of the king's personal approval of the harsh coercive measures undertaken by the ministry. The faith of many colonists in the king's disposition to abide by his contractual duties was accordingly shaken. Nevertheless, although much colonial affection for the king had been dissipated by early 1775, many colonists continued to express a desire to remain his subjects. Perhaps Samuel Stillman, pastor of the First Baptist Church in Boston, best summed up American attitudes toward George III on the eve of Lexington and Concord. "In this Province all is quiet," he wrote. "Rebellion, shocking Word, undeserved Charge, they never tho't of. They revere the House of Hanover: but submit to the present Measures they will not." "We wish not for Independence," he emphasized, "nor are we disaffected to his Majesty: but we have too great a Sense of the Privileges of Englishmen . . . to consent to be Slaves."[58]

"Blows Must Decide"

In early 1775 moderates on both sides of the Atlantic tried desperately to find a peaceful solution to the escalating conflict between Britain and America. As yet, the dispute had been carried on by the peaceful methods of petitions, pamphlets, and commercial warfare. But by late 1774, even moderates suspected that the situation could not long continue. By October 1774 a New York doctor feared that it was already "almost too late to enter into a calm discussion of constitutional rights" for "men's hands are already laid to the hilts of their swords, & a few riotous Townsmen, or irritated Soldiers may light up a flame, not to be extinguished but by the blood of thousands." By mid-February 1775 an observer in London had concluded that "we seem to be upon the rough edge of battle."[59]

These expectations were soon realized. The opening of hostilities in April 1775 brought with it all the animosity common to civil conflict. After Lexington each side spread atrocity stories about the conduct of the other. Britons shocked each other with tales of bloodthirsty Yankees scalping helpless redcoats, while Americans spread their own stories of the "black catalogue" of British deeds. At the end of June,

John Winthrop acknowledged that "both parties . . . have gone too far to think of retreating," and "War now rages . . . in all its fury."[60] The commencement of hostilities also inflamed American passions against the king, whose troops and ships were wreaking destruction and shedding American blood. A New England farmer, upon receiving the news of his son's death from smallpox in the army in Canada, bitterly wrote in his diary that the boy had come to his end "in the prime of life by means of that wicked Tyranical Brute (Nea worse than Brute) of Great Britain."[61]

But the inflamed passions did not result from the simple fact of war itself, for colonists who wished to do so could have continued to view the king's troops as agents of the ministry, not of the king.[62] Rather, it was the manner in which the war was conducted, according to policies openly advocated and even initiated by the king, that made continued allegiance to George III a patent impossibility for most Americans.

Problems in America were far from most Englishmen's minds during the spring of 1775. As Parliament wound up its business, in fact, one ministry official called upon Hutchinson and seemed "to be without apprehensions of much further difficulty with America." The calm was in some degree due to the old problem of communications. When Parliament rose on May 26, the latest news from the colonies dated from the end of March.[63]

The next day, however, startling reports arrived aboard an express vessel that the Massachusetts Provincial Congress had dispatched in ballast on April 29. The dispatches related that there had been engagements between British and provincial troops at Lexington and Concord. Although the British had behaved barbarously, the reports said, the provincials had been completely victorious. By May 28 the news was all over London and beyond.[64] But, considering the source of the report, the ministers refused to believe it; instead, they waited impatiently for the official packet boat that would bring Gage's version of the encounter. Their wait stretched out to a seemingly interminable two weeks, during which time the version of the Provincial Congress spread through Britain. When Gage's dispatches finally arrived on June 10, they differed only in detail and emphasis from those of the Provincial Congress.[65]

The news of the ignominious British retreat from Concord shocked the British public. "I have not courage to write about America," the historian Edward Gibbon declared. "We talk familiarly of Civil War[,]

Dissolutions of Parliament, Impeachments and Lord Chatham." Many who "were strong for the measures of Parliament are much discouraged," he noted. Suffolk, who favored a coercive policy, was disgusted by the effect of the news upon his ministry colleagues. "This American Business," he observed, "makes Lambs of us All."[66] In fact, the ministry was in disarray and uncertain as to the best way to proceed. In the cabinet meeting called to respond to Gage's dispatches, Dartmouth continued to press for milder measures, North inclined toward some middle course, as ever, and others, like Suffolk and Sandwich, favored more vigorous measures. In this feverish atmosphere of advice and counteradvice, the king's influence on the ultimate direction of policy vastly increased, and his policy remained one of "firmness." "I am certain," he wrote to North during this period, that "any other conduct but compelling obedience" by the Americans "would be ruinous and culpable," and "therefore no consideration could bring me to swerve from the present path which I think Myself in Duty bound to follow."[67]

The king's firmness was needed in the months ahead, as news arrived in late July of the first major battle of the war, Bunker Hill. Prior to Bunker Hill, the ministry had treated the American conflict purely as a police action, a civil war that, for all its fierceness, still pitted brother against brother. The early military policy of the government had therefore been to reinforce the British troops in the colonies with regiments from home, as seen in the king's February 10 "Message for an Augmentation of the Forces." But Bunker Hill proved this policy to be completely insufficient. Now the king's ministers were faced with a critical choice. Either they must retreat or they must proceed to prosecute the war vigorously. The king, supported by the cabinet's "hawks," ruled out retreat. "I am clear as to one point," George III wrote on July 26, "that we must persist and not be dismayed by any difficulties." Thus the government turned to the fatal alternative of fighting the Americans as they would have fought a European enemy. "The War is now grown to such a height," North wrote to the king in late July, "that it must be treated as a foreign war, & that every expedient which would be used in the latter case should be applied in the former." After long conversations with Dartmouth, Hutchinson reported to his son that the government had decided that "the same force will be employed" in America "as if the inhabitants were French or Spanish enemies."[68]

The basic decision to fight the American conflict as a foreign land war entailed certain strategic policies that were followed until the end of the war. These policies immeasurably increased American consciousness of George III's enmity. Great Britain was not a militaristic country; her land wars in continental Europe had consistently been fought with a majority of foreign troops. Even the army of the great duke of Marlborough had consisted largely of Dutch and Germans. The ministry's decision meant that America, like France before her, would soon do battle with British-paid mercenaries culled from all over Europe. "Scotch highlanders, Irish papists, Hanoverians, Canadians, Indians," Gibbon noted, would all be employed.[69] It is important to note that the military strategy adopted by the king and his ministers in mid-1775 was not the only course available to them. Responsible officers in America, aware of the difficulties of fighting a land war with limited men and supplies in hostile territory, called instead for a total naval blockade of American ports. The main work, as one such officer put it, "must be done by our fleet," and the role of the land troops should be only to assist the primary naval effort.[70] Moreover, the ministry was well aware of the probable American reaction to the use of foreign troops. Early in 1775, when the outbreak of war in the colonies seemed imminent, the cabinet recalled the Swiss-born general Frederick Haldimand, then second-in-command of British forces in North America. Given "the Prejudices & Opinion of Mankind," Dartmouth had written delicately to Haldimand, it would "create great difficulties" if the command should possibly devolve upon Haldimand, for then Britain would be in the position of fighting "her own Sons & Subjects" with a foreign-born general.[71] Yet, in the summer of 1775 the cabinet took the irrevocable decision to send not one, but some 20,000 foreign troops to America, a decision that the king supported and undertook to carry out.

The possibility of using foreign troops had been discussed by the king and his ministers toward the end of 1774, but the project was not taken up in earnest until after Bunker Hill. At the end of July one minister wrote wearily that "my Head is full of Troops and Treatys." Since the treaties involved in the engagement of foreign troops were with individual foreign sovereigns, the conduct of the negotiations came under the king's prerogative power to conduct the nation's foreign affairs. George III entered into the project with energy and a characteristic devotion to detail. In the European situation of the mid-

1770s, there appeared to be two plausible sources of the required troops. First, there were the petty states of Germany, to whom the British had traditionally resorted. But the cabinet also appealed to a previously untapped source of cheap manpower—Russia.[72]

Given the availability of German troops, it is a measure of both the government's desperation and the scale of planned operations in America that the ministry first applied to Catherine of Russia. Having recently concluded an expensive war with Turkey, Catherine was left with a huge war debt and a still-mobilized army. What better and cheaper source of large numbers of troops for America, the king and his servants reasoned, than the Russian steppes? The cabinet entered into the Russian negotiations with enthusiasm, and Guy Carleton, the governor of Canada, was told to expect 20,000 Russian troops by the following spring. The idea that these troops would introduce a ferocious brand of Eastern warfare to America seems not to have troubled the British leaders. Suffolk even callously remarked that the Russians would make "charming Visitors at New-Yorke, and civilize that part of America wonderfully." Despite such sanguine hopes, the attempt to recruit the Russians came to nothing. Catherine had merely been toying with the British and flatly turned down the king's personal request. "Could not his majesty," Catherine suggested practically, "make use of Hanoverians?"[73]

His majesty planned to do precisely that. At the same time that the unsuccessful negotiations for the Russian troops were being pursued, the king had determined to secure men from Britain's traditional German recruiting grounds. The easiest sovereign with whom to negotiate was, of course, the elector of Hanover, George III himself. He swiftly gave orders that his electoral troops were to be taken into British pay and deployed at Gibraltar and at Port Mahon on Minorca to free the garrisons there for service in America.[74] The various sovereigns of Brunswick, Hesse-Cassel, and Waldeck proved only marginally more difficult to deal with. The troops hired from these princes were expensive; the miserly Prince William IV of Hesse acquired his legendary fortune largely from such British payments. But by the end of March 1776 Parliament had approved treaties ratifying the administration's agreements to hire some 20,000 German troops. The parliamentary opposition, aware that the news of foreign troops would be bitterly received in America, unsuccessfully attempted to defeat the treaties. David Hartley predicted that sending foreigners against the

Americans would mean that "the possibility of reconciliation is totally cut off."[75]

The English radicals had gauged American sentiment accurately. In colonial eyes, the king's role in procuring foreign mercenaries undermined his legal title to his American thrones. The contract between subject and prince was based almost exclusively on the reciprocal obligations of protection and allegiance. By early 1776 it was apparent not only that the king had failed to fulfill his obligations as protector but also that he was personally levying war upon his colonial subjects.[76]

Reports of the king's efforts had begun to filter through to America by the fall of 1775, and George III's part in the negotiations with the various sovereigns had been so obvious that Americans could not ignore his instrumental role in procuring the foreign troops.[77] "I have great reason to think we shall have a severe trial this summer," observed Josiah Bartlett, "with Britons, Hessians, Hanoverians, Indians, negroes and every other butcher the gracious King of Britain can hire against us." In short, noted another New Englander, the hiring of the mercenaries proved that "the ——— of England delights in blood, yea, thirsteth for the blood of America."[78] Americans of every political persuasion denounced the king for procuring the foreign troops. The news of the mercenaries confirmed radicals in their belief that the king had broken the governmental contract and had rendered both independence and foreign alliances inevitable. As Elbridge Gerry queried, "If they are sending to Hanover for troops . . . is it not time for us to think of alliances?" A Virginian pointed to the expected Russians and Hanoverians and concluded that Great Britain "deserved" to have Americans "declare [them]selves independent of her."[79]

The news wrought perhaps the greatest change of sentiment among those American moderates who in early 1776 still clung to the hope of reconciliation. "God forbid," one such Pennsylvanian wrote, that the colonists should ever "be driven to the Necessity" of declaring independence. But, he reported, most people he knew believed that although the continental delegates had been "hitherto averse to that Measure," they would "embrace it as indispensably necessary, when ever the Government shall actually determine to employ foreign Troops to reduce us."[80]

Many colonists believed that the ministry's search for troops did not end with efforts to engage Russians and Germans. They suspected the

British also of attempting to call into their service Indians and black slaves. "From newspapers & private Letters we are assured that next Summer will be a bloody one," William Hooper wrote to Samuel Johnston. "The Sovereign has declared (we hear) that he will pawn the Jewels of his Crown or humble America. Indians, Negroes, Russians, Hanoverians & Hessians are talked of as the Instruments to accomplish this blessed purpose."[81] In fact, the use of slaves and Indians was not official government policy. As Lord North explained, "there never was any idea of employing the negroes or the Indians, until the Americans had first applied to them." North's statement was accurate; the British did not use their Indian allies for offensive action until the colonists had begun to do so, and the use of slaves was not official government policy but rather a desperate expedient resorted to by the troop-starved royal governor of Virginia, Lord Dunmore.[82] Nevertheless, the colonists believed the use of Indians and slaves to be official government policy, and they increasingly laid the responsibility for such barbarity at the door of the sovereign himself. "We are told from the throne," an American wrote, that the king had "acted with a spirit of moderation and forbearance, anxious to prevent the effusion of the blood of [his] subjects." "Let the wanton butchery" of the royal troops, "the destruction of thousands of innocent and helpless women on our frontiers" by "tribes of savages," not to mention the "horrid massacre" by black slaves, be a measure of "the truth of this *royal declaration*."[83]

Americans had a better basis for perceiving that the British were deliberately prosecuting the war in a barbarous manner when they looked to British naval policy. As part of the British military buildup in late 1774, Vice Admiral Samuel Graves, commander of the North American fleet, was sent the reinforcements he had requested. In late December 1774, His Majesty's ships *Asia, Boyne*, and *Scarborough* arrived in Boston harbor with a full complement of ten companies of marines.[84] The navy's mission in these early months was, however, vague and ill-defined, in part due to Graves's deficiencies as a commander. His ships began to patrol the New England waters aimlessly, seeking supplies for the land forces and opportunities to bolster British authority in the coastal towns.[85] Thus, for example, Captain Wallace of H.M.S. *Rose* cruised Narragansett Bay, seizing ships and supplies and returning the occasional fire from coastal towns. By August 1775 he had grown bolder, bombarding Bristol, Rhode Island, when the town refused to comply with his supply requisitions. On their part, the colonists took every opportunity to harass isolated navy patrol ships, capturing several of them and taking the crews prisoner. Thus, on August 8, 1775, townsmen on shore fired on H.M.S. *Falcon*, which was seeking supplies off Cape Anne Harbour (Gloucester, Massachusetts). *Falcon* returned the fire and tried unsuccessfully to burn the town before being driven off. Patriots in Portsmouth, New Hampshire, similarly fired on one of the small boats detached from H.M.S. *Scarborough*, also on a supply mission.[86]

Graves, having received Admiralty authorization to take offensive action, resolved to repay the insults to his ships. He dispatched Captain Henry Mowatt with a flotilla of five ships and 100 marines on a mission to "chastize" the coastal towns. Mowatt, who had himself been held prisoner in Falmouth (now Portland, Maine) was ordered "to proceed along the Coast, and lay waste, burn and destroy such Seaport towns as are accessible to his Majesty's ships," and he was also to take advantage of "favorable Circumstances, to fall upon and destroy . . . other Towns or places."[87]

Mowatt anchored in Casco Bay, off Falmouth, late on October 16, 1775. He immediately called for an assembly of the townspeople. Mowatt's messenger began by recounting the "many premeditated Attacks on the legal Prerogatives of the best of Sovereigns, . . . the repeated Instances you have experienced in Britain's long forbearance of the Rod of Correction; and the Merciful and Paternal extension of her Hands to embrace you, again and again." These had all "been regarded as vain and nugatory. And in place of a dutiful and grateful return to your King and Parent State, you have been guilty of the most unpardonable Rebellion." The townspeople were therefore given two hours, later extended to the following morning, to remove the "human species" from the town.[88] The next day, Mowatt bombarded the town from 9:30 AM to sunset. An eyewitness recorded that "about three quarters of the town was consumed and between two and three hundred families who twenty-four hours before enjoyed in tranquility their commodious habitation were now in many instances destitute of a hut for themselves and families; and as a tedious winter was approaching, they had before them a most gloomy and distressing prospect."[89]

The official British policy of deliberately attacking civilians and indiscriminately destroying civilian property shocked and horrified

Americans, most of whom lived on or near the seacoast. "We have just heard that the pirates . . . have destroyed two-thirds of Falmouth burnt down, and have orders to destroy every port from Boston to Pemmaquid," James Warren informed John Adams. "This is savage and barbarous in the highest stage. What can we wait for now?" As with other British war policies, the colonists were more inclined to lay the blame for the coastal raids at the door of the sovereign in whose name the destruction was carried out. Benjamin Franklin wrote, "We have just receiv'd Alarm of the burning of Falmouth Casco Bay; and are assur'd that Orders are come over to burn, ravish and destroy the Sea Coast; such is the Government of the best of Princes!"[90]

The cruel nature of war itself, and the animosities generated by the particular policies chosen by the British government to carry on the American war, snapped the remaining bonds of affection that had united the colonists to their king. Perhaps even more important at this late stage in the crisis were the ideological implications of the king's actions. Americans quickly drew a connection between the king's withdrawal of protection and their own obligations of allegiance. To "Johannes in Eremo" the conclusion was clear. The king's attempts to carry out the parliamentary program "by force of arms" had "totally dissolved allegiance to the King of England as our King," for Americans had sworn allegiance to him "as *King*, not as *Tyrant*—as *Protector*, not as a *Destroyer*." The failure of the king to fulfill his constitutional duty of protection was cited by almost every colonial legislature as the justification for organizing governments independent of his authority. As Oliver Wolcott succinctly summarized the changed attitude toward the king that the war had brought, "to swear allegiance" to "an Authority which had not only cast us out of its Protection but for so long a Time has been carrying on the Most cruel War against us," was ". . . not only Absurd but impious."[91]

Abdication of the American Thrones

Despite hostilities, the final break between Britain and America was not declared in 1775. Though the majority of Americans had become convinced of the king's enmity, still they remained reluctant (as the radicals in Congress found to their dismay) to take the positive step of declaring their independence of him. Even this final hesitation was soon removed by their sovereign, however. Determined to remove all ambiguity regarding the legal position of the colonists, he formally cast the colonists out of his protection by declaring them to be rebels, and he specified the practical consequence of this legal status by declaring their persons and property found on the high seas to be forfeit.

He did this because the military policy the British administration decided upon after Bunker Hill could only be justified if the colonists were placed in the category of a foreign foe or a rebellious subject people. The former denomination was clearly inappropriate, for it would have meant British recognition of the independence of the colonies. But the latter category was not precisely correct either, for the Americans had not, by the summer of 1775, explicitly been declared to be in rebellion. This was an oversight that the king was determined to correct, for a public declaration of rebellion would have the added advantage of rendering legally treasonable the verbal support and concrete aid that the English opposition was giving to the colonists. By the end of July, therefore, the king and the Bedford faction pushed through a decision to make an immediate proclamation of rebellion.[92] Lord North, aware that such a step would end any possibility of success for the contemplated Howe peace mission, attempted to forestall the implementation of the decision. But the king refused to countenance any delay. With his approval, two of the more belligerent officials, Suffolk and William Eden, produced a draft proclamation of rebellion. By August 18, a bare three weeks after the arrival of the news of Bunker Hill, the king was pushing a reluctant North to accept the Suffolk-Eden draft. "There has been much delay in framing a Proclamation declaring the conduct of the Americans Rebellious," he wrote. "From the time it was first suggested," the king emphasized, he had seen it as "most necessary," first because it put the English opposition "on their guard," and second, and perhaps more important, because "it shews the determination of prosecuting with vigour every measure that may tend to force those deluded People to Submission."[93] Unable to oppose both his sovereign and a powerful faction within the administration, North agreed to the harshly worded proclamation "For Suppressing Rebellion and Sedition." It was accordingly issued in the king's name on August 23, 1775.[94]

At the same time that the ministry was considering the proclamation, another sequence of events relating to America was proceeding in London. On July 8, with much reluctance, Congress had agreed to issue one last petition to the British king. The moderates, led by John

Dickinson and perhaps influenced by the great difficulties they had encountered in procuring a petition, could not believe a peace initiative offered in the midst of war would suffer the ignominious fate of former petitions. They pinned considerable hopes on this Olive Branch Petition, the more so because it was to be carried to the king by the respected former governor of Pennsylvania, Richard Penn.[95] Penn arrived in Bristol on August 13, 1775. Aware of the urgent nature of his business, he hurried to London, hoping to present the plea of Congress to the king immediately. But he got no higher in the English bureaucracy than Dartmouth, to whom he informally showed the petition on August 21. The king refused to see him or to receive the petition until he had issued the proclamation of rebellion that rendered Penn's mission nugatory.[96]

George III had no intention of regarding the Olive Branch Petition any differently than he had previous congressional efforts. On August 18 he informed North that a discussion with Haldimand had strengthened his conviction that nothing but force could bring the colonists to reason. The general, the king recorded, "ownes that till they have suffered for their Conduct . . . it would be dangerous to give ear to any propositions they might transmit." These sentiments coincided with the king's own, and he hastened to make public his attitude toward the American peace initiative. On September 1 he finally condescended to receive the petition, but he signified his attitude toward it quite clearly (as he had previously done with a City of London petition) by refusing to receive it formally while seated on his throne and by refusing to answer it. Penn was instructed simply to hand the petition to Dartmouth for eventual submission to the king.[97]

Though the August 23 proclamation and the reception of the Olive Branch Petition were two separate events, news of them arrived in America simultaneously in early November. "We find by a Vessel from Cork," a Massachusetts man bitterly observed, "a Proclamation from that stupid ——— Wretch of a K——g declaring us all Rebels." "The die is cast," a Rhode Islander concluded, "the union of the Colonies with Britain is at an end," for the proclamation had proved the king to be "unalterably determined to be absolute Master of *America*." In view of the king's proclamation, James Warren wrote to John Adams, "I think your Congress can be no longer in any doubts and hesitancy about taking capital and effectual strokes" toward independence. "We shall certainly expect it."[98]

Nowhere was the uproar caused by the proclamation of rebellion and the failure of the Olive Branch Petition greater than in the State House in Philadelphia. It is no coincidence that the delegates took several important steps toward independence in early November 1775.[99] Yet, preparing for independence is not the same as declaring it, and it is clear that Congress was not ready to pass a resolution for independence in November 1775. Events transpiring in London, however, helped to remove any final hesitation. The ministry's basic decision to depend upon coercion involved a host of corollary decisions. By the fall of 1775, more legislation was thought necessary to carry out the war policy. This was foreshadowed in the king's Opening Address to Parliament on October 26, 1775. He reported that since the previous spring, "the rebellious war now levied is become more general, and is manifestly carried on for the purpose of establishing an independent empire." The government had resolved, therefore, "to put a Speedy end to these disorders by the most decisive exertions."[100]

On November 20, 1775, Lord North introduced the American Prohibitory Bill in the House of Commons. Its terms were relatively simple and drastic. As the rebellion had now spread from Massachusetts through all the colonies, all the colonies must be punished; therefore, all American trade with all other countries was prohibited. To enforce this draconian measure, the navy was given the major role: all American ships, cargoes, and seamen were subject to being declared prizes and prisoners of war, and the Courts of Admiralty were forbidden to declare them otherwise. This meant that should a British naval vessel capture an American vessel, regardless of the political sympathies of the owners, the ship and cargo were to be sold and the proceeds distributed among the crew of the capturing ship. The American crews were subject to imprisonment or impressed service in the Royal Navy. Because this measure, when combined with military victories ashore, was expected to reduce the colonies within a short period of time, the bill also made provision for the appointment of royal commissioners empowered to accept the submission of individual colonies or parts of colonies and to pardon individuals. Finally, because the bill was intended to embody in legislation the wholly military policy of the government, it also included provisions for repealing several of the Coercive Acts of 1774, which had embodied policies that were inappropriate to a wartime situation.[101] As Lord North explained the bill's rationale, previous policy had adopted "civil coercions against civil crimes; but we being now at war, the provisions were incapable, and other provisions were necessary: those provisions he now proposed were such as would be made use of in case of war with any country in the world." The parliamentary opposition protested that the ministry policy amounted to what might be termed a self-fulfilling prophecy, that is, by declaring Americans rebels and outlaws and legalizing piracy against their civilian vessels, the government had in effect declared the colonies beyond the royal protection and therefore independent. The opposition protests were futile. The bill passed with large majorities on December 20 as the members prepared to leave for their holidays, and the royal assent came two days later.[102]

The English opposition had, if anything, underestimated the effect of the Prohibitory Act on the colonies.[103] News of Lord North's proposal arrived in late February 1776, a month after the publication of Thomas Paine's *Common Sense*. Despite the fact that the Prohibitory Act was much more a product of the cabinet than such measures as the recruitment of foreign troops, Americans were no longer disposed to make fine distinctions between ministry, parliament, and king. John Adams, whose decision for independence had long since been made, saw in the act all the justification any waverer would need:

> I know not whether you have seen the Act of Parliament call'd the restraining Act, or prohibitory Act, or piratical Act, or plundering Act, or Act of Independency, for by all these Titles is it called. I think the most apposite is the Act of Independency, for King, Lords and Commons have united in Sundering this Country and that I think forever. It is a compleat Dismemberment of the British Empire. It throws thirteen Colonies out of the Royal Protection, levels all Distinctions and makes us independent in Spight of all our supplications and Entreaties.[104]

Perhaps more interesting was the response of Robert Alexander, a Maryland conservative who, at the final moment, would be incapable of severing the tie. While Adams had identified the act as emanating from Parliament, Alexander did not:

> I shall make no Comments on this Act, it is only a further Step in that System of Tyranny, hitherto persued by that ——— who under the Influence of a Scotch Junto now disgraces the British Throne. What Measures Congress may persue in Consequence of this Act, I know not; with me every Idea of Reconciliation is pre-

cluded by the Conduct of G. Britain, & the only Alternative, absolute Slavery, or Independancy. The latter I have often repudiated both in publick & private, but am now almost convinced
the Measure is right & can be justified by Necessity.[105]

For years, many Americans had repressed fears and doubts about
their king. Initially, they had done so because of sincere affection for
the young sovereign; subsequently, their reasons probably involved
constitutional prudence. But the long period during which Americans
had expressed real or ritual devotion to George III tended to turn such
attitudes into habits, and habits are not easy to break.[106] They continued to protest their loyalty to the king through the years of imperial
crisis that began in the early 1760s. This tendency was intensified in
1775 when Americans reached the final and perhaps inevitable end of
the constitutional road that had led them to deny, bit by bit, the authority of British institutions—first that of a corrupt ministry, then of
Parliament, until only the authority of the king was left. In 1774 many
moderates took the political position that their ties to the king, and
those alone, were sufficient to bind them to the empire. The ominous
corollary of this position, however, was that their continuation in the
empire depended upon the king's ability and desire personally to redress their grievances by overriding both his Parliament and his ministers.

George III had neither the desire nor, indeed, the power to do so. In
private and in public, he never wavered either in his commitment to a
coercive policy or in his conviction that there was no alternative to
American submission to parliamentary authority. The implications of
the sovereign's attitude were devastating for Americans steeped in
Whig theories of kingship. What the king regarded as a rigid adherence to duty, the colonists could only interpret as total destruction of
the grounds upon which he rightfully held his throne. George III had
assented to unjust laws, he had withdrawn protection, he had proclaimed them all rebels (thereby formally casting them beyond his protection), and he had sealed their fate by declaring them outlaws and
making their property subject to legalized plunder. Like all the previous English kings whose tyranny had cost them their thrones,
George III also had abdicated his American thrones.[107]

No wonder, then, that in January 1776 colonists of all political per-
suasions seized upon Thomas Paine's *Common Sense* with excitement

and enthusiasm. Conclusions about George III that bitter experience had forced upon them but that habits of loyalty rendered them unable to express were clearly and forcefully stated in Paine's spirited prose. Like the boy in the fairy tale who could not see the emperor's new clothes and declared that his emperor was in fact naked, Paine looked at his lawful king and pronounced him in fact a tyrant. In doing so, he brought conclusions about George III from the deepest recesses of the colonists' minds to the tips of their tongues. "It matters very little now what the king of England either says or does," Paine wrote. "He hath wickedly broken through every moral and human obligation, trampled nature and conscience beneath his feet, and by a steady and constitutional spirit of insolence and cruelty procured for himself a universal hatred."[108] It was in fertile intellectual soil, enriched by a year's experience of pleading with a king turned tyrant, that Paine sowed his general condemnation of monarchy and his particular indictment of George III.

Although most Americans believed that the king had forced them into independence and were relieved by Paine's justification of their declaring themselves to be a separate people, many acquiesced in the Declaration of Independence with a profound sense of sorrow. "I wish things may answer our Expectations after we are Independant," wrote a doubtful John Penn on June 28, 1776, but he added, "I fear most people are too sanguine." Having lived all their lives in a world in which cherished political goals of order, stability, unity, and protection had ultimately been guaranteed by a king, they could take little pleasure in the fact that one particular king had, as they saw it, wantonly removed himself from the position of supreme authority. His actions had forced the Americans into a position where, Edward Rutledge wrote, they "must bid adieu . . . to Ease and Happiness." He had launched them "into an unknown Ocean." What for some, like John Adams, was an occasion for perpetual joy and celebration, was for others a sad necessity. Thus, Henry Laurens of South Carolina refused the appellation "rebel." "Driven away by my King," he declared, "I am at worst a Refugée.[109]

PART II

Congress

CHAPTER 3

The First Congress Assumes Authority

Mr. Deane says . . . that the resolutions of the Congress shall be the laws of the Medes and Persians; that the Congress is the grandest and most important assembly ever held in America, and that the all *of America is intrusted to it and depends upon it.*

—John Adams, August 15, 1774

On a sultry Monday afternoon, August 29, 1774, four dusty-looking gentlemen mounted their horses at the Red Lion Tavern in Bristol, Pennsylvania and nudged them onto the Philadelphia road.[1] This would be the last leg of an exhausting but exhilarating trip that brought them some 500 miles overland and an immeasurable distance in political sophistication. They had left New England almost three weeks before, most of them for the first time, to represent Massachusetts Bay at the Congress that was scheduled to assemble shortly in Philadelphia. The delegation, consisting of Robert Treat Paine, Thomas Cushing, and the "brace of Adamses," Samuel and John, had been chosen in a stormy June 17 session of the Massachusetts House of Representatives. As an emissary of the new royal governor had pounded on the locked chamber door, proclaiming that the session was dissolved and the proceedings inside were therefore illegal, the legislators had issued a call for a general congress, named a site—Philadelphia—and set a date—September 1, 1774.[2]

The instructions that the Massachusetts House gave its delegates charged them with difficult tasks. They, and such colleagues as might join them in Philadelphia, were to deliberate "upon wise and proper Measures" to recover and establish the "just rights and liberties of the colonies." Unstated but strongly implied in these instructions was the fear that the fate of Boston hung upon the proceedings of the continental assembly.[3]

The meeting to which the delegates journeyed would, over the course of the next year, evolve into the institution that served as the central government for a new American state through eight years of war and five years of uneasy peace. But in 1774 the delegates had no conception that their assembly would become a government. They had come to Philadelphia not to replace the British imperial government but to reform it. Had the delegates themselves been asked to state the precedents for their meeting, they might well have cited not governmental institutions but the English conventions of 1215 and 1689, which, like the Congress, had met to correct abuses in government so that order and legitimate authority might be restored.

Yet, for men with such vague precedents, the delegates acted with a remarkable degree of unity and speed. There was almost no division among them over their basic goals. Almost all agreed, for example, that they must make a strong and immediate demonstration of support for Boston, whose imminent danger had precipitated their meeting. To relieve the town, the delegates knew they would also have to devise a plan that would pressure the British government to repeal at least the Coercive Acts of 1774 and possibly to redress all the grievances that had disturbed imperial harmony since 1763. Finally, the delegates themselves intended to issue a definite statement of the rights that the colonists possessed as British subjects and as men. Relatively little disagreement surfaced during the two months of their deliberations over these goals.

The basic unity of the delegates in 1774 was not based upon their personalities or their abilities, although both were formidable. Their consensus mirrored and echoed a remarkable cohesion of political opinion that became apparent during the summer of 1774. The news of the Boston Port Bill had mobilized Americans at the local and provincial level throughout the colonies. As the summer wore on, they assembled in scores of local meetings to state their conception of the nature of the crisis and their recommendations for its solution. The local resolves varied little from colony to colony, and this fundamental agreement was transferred to the delegates to the Congress, almost all of whom owed their presence in Philadelphia to their participation in and basic approval of the expressions of popular opinion. They could proceed to speedy action in Philadelphia because they came to the Congress with a true mandate, in the modern sense of the word, for a specific course of action.

But the mandate was a limited one. The local resolutions dealt particularly with the immediate crisis of 1774, so the delegates were directed to respond specifically to British aggression against Boston. The unity they demonstrated was thus limited to issues related to the immediate crisis, and in the actions they took to respond to the crisis they relied upon the great outpouring of popular opinion throughout the summer that had concerned precisely these issues. By responding to this popular opinion, however, the delegates gained enormous political authority for a new and untried institution. This authority persisted long after events had gone beyond the crisis issues upon which it was based and long after the Congress had evolved into a far different institution than it had been in 1774.

The popular sentiment that formed the basis for the unity at the First Congress was suitable to guide a convention that would meet for one heroic session, fulfill popular demand, and then dissolve. But if the Congress were to continue as an institution beyond the crisis of 1774—if it were to become a government—the delegates' tasks could never again be as clearly defined or as closely monitored by their constituents as they were in 1774. For clues to the direction in which the Congress would move as a government, rather than as a convention, one must go beyond the issues upon which there was a consensus and examine those few instances in which the delegates' actions were relatively unconstrained by popular demands.

The Summer of 1774

On May 10, 1774, news of the Port Bill reached Boston. Most of the city's inhabitants had been expecting some British response to the Tea Party of the previous December, but virtually no one was prepared for the swiftness or the severity of the government's action. Even Samuel Adams, who had perhaps the darkest view of ministerial intentions, had believed that the most likely policy of the administration would be to send additional troops.[4] Instead, the ministry had not only sent troops but had ordered them to enforce the provisions of the Port Bill. If the harbor were closed on June 1 as scheduled, Bostonians of all classes would be effectively deprived of their major source of food and income.

The radical leadership of the Boston committee of correspondence responded quickly to the crisis. They had two immediate concerns. First, they realized that the town could not by itself resist British aggression effectively; a united colonial response was absolutely essential. Moreover, the reaction had to be not only united but timely. The port would be closed in less than a month, so the disastrous effects of the trade stoppage would be felt by the city's inhabitants almost immediately. How long the Bostonians could survive the closure of the harbor without either capitulating and paying for the tea or erupting in violence was a question the committeemen felt ill-prepared to answer. All they knew for certain was that it would be exceedingly difficult, as Samuel Adams observed, "to restrain the Resentment of some within the proper Bounds, and to keep others who are more irresolute from sinking."[5]

To secure the sufficient and timely response that Boston's desperate situation required, the committeemen dashed off letters to their sister committees in the other colonies. By May 14 the committee express rider, Paul Revere, was headed south to deliver Boston's plea. The attack on the town, they wrote, was "doubtless designed for every other Colony, who will not surrender their sacred Rights & Liberties into the Hands of an Infamous Ministry." In these circumstances, they asked patriots farther south to determine "whether *you* consider Boston as now suffering in the Common Cause, & sensibly feel and resent the Injury and Affront offerd to her?"[6]

The news of the Boston Port Bill caused an unprecedented upsurge of political activity all over the continent. While such activity might have been expected in previously politicized areas like New England, which had local institutions suitable for the expression of popular sentiment, a similar outpouring of opinion emerged from the middle and southern colonies as well. Citizens met in local assemblies throughout the colonies almost as soon as the Boston committee's pleas reached their provinces, and each meeting formally declared not only the participants' sense of outrage but also their conception of the proper colonial response. As news of the full scope of the ministerial program arrived through the spring and summer—of the Administration of Justice, the Massachusetts Government, and Quebec acts—the meetings grew in number and the resulting resolutions became more urgent.[7]

These local and provincial proceedings, taken collectively, constitute an extraordinary cross section of colonial opinion toward the crisis of 1774. The local meetings represented the basis of the political authority of most delegates to the Congress, for they were, in large measure, selected by provincial conventions composed of delegates chosen by these local meetings.[8] Out of prudence and by conviction, the delegates echoed the opinions expressed in the local resolutions and were faithful in carrying out the program that the resolutions mandated. To understand the actions taken by the delegates upon their arrival in Philadelphia, therefore, it is important to examine the political climate that conditioned their behavior. The local and provincial resolutions agreed upon during the summer of 1774 provide useful evidence regarding this political climate.

Of the 108 resolutions examined for this study, 98 began with some general statement of political attitude. Thus, for example, 63 percent of these resolutions began with a ritual statement of loyalty to George III. The most overwhelming issues in 1774, however, were obviously those concerning the immediate crisis. While 64 percent of the sample condemned the Revenue Acts of the 1760s, 92 percent specifically condemned the Boston Port Act, or, as the summer progressed, the Coercive Acts in general.

Furthermore, such condemnations were usually accompanied by a forceful declaration that Boston's trials were the concern of the entire continent. Such convictions frustrated Tory attempts throughout the summer to isolate the Bostonians and to build upon old stereotypes of Boston's supposed extremism. Thus, for example, one Pennsylvania conservative[9] observed in June 1774 that Boston's "patriots will find themselves deceived in the general support of the other Provinces." In Pennsylvania, he asserted, "they will find none."[10] Such sentiments were little more than wishful thinking. Of the twelve Pennsylvania resolutions examined, nine declared that Boston suffered in the common cause, and seven of the nine proceeded to raise a subscription for the beleaguered town. Further, the Pennsylvanians' expressions of support were typical. Eight of the ten resolutions in the sample that expressed no other political attitude specifically declared their support for Boston. Of the 108 resolutions in the sample, 76 percent declared that Boston suffered in the "common cause" and 44 percent proceeded to raise money to aid the town's inhabitants. The reaction to the Boston Tea Party, the act that had initiated the crisis, demonstrates the strength of the support for Boston. Tories had condemned the destruction of the tea as an outrageous assault upon private property, and some conservatives had echoed this view. Yet in the resolutions examined here, no one called on the Bostonians to comply with British demands that they pay for the tea. Only two of the resolutions indicated that the participants would welcome such a gesture, and these two called for the money to be raised by continental subscription.[11] The resolutions indicate the enormous compassion felt for the Bostonians, the submergence of former enmity, if any, and the urgent desire to bring the suffering inhabitants some relief. In the face of this outpouring of sympathy, it would have been inconceivable for the Continental Congress not to make some substantial gesture of solidarity with the Bostonians.

While 98 of the resolutions in the sample expressed sentiments from which one can extrapolate more general political attitudes, all of the 108, even those of only a few lines, stated the goal they hoped resistance would achieve. Stated on the most general level, all the resolutions asked either for a redress of grievances, called specifically for repeal of the Coercive Acts, or used a catch phrase to indicate similar sentiments, such as praying for the establishment of colonial rights on a permanent foundation. More important, the resolutions reflect remarkably little division over the choice of the instrument by which these general goals were to be achieved. Seventy-two of the resolutions specifically called for an intercolonial conference, and an additional twenty-one implied a similar desire for united action.[12] Ninety-three of the 108 resolutions (86 percent of those studied) expressed the opinion that only united colonial action could bring about the desired alterations in British policy. The call for a congress was accompanied by an enormous and spontaneous grant of political authority. With virtually no knowledge of whom the delegates were to be or what measures they would adopt, 48 percent of those calling for a congress agreed in advance to consider themselves bound by any decisions such a congress might make. As the inhabitants of Lancaster, Pennsylvania, pledged on July 9, 1774, "We will sincerely and heartily agree to and abide by the measures which will be adopted by the Members of the General Congress of the Colonies."[13]

While localities delegated enormous political authority to the congress, the grant was not, in general, discretionary. The delegates were given authority to do *something*. In some cases, the constraints were not stated in very strong language; such resolutions ask only that the congress not break up without devising some plan of resistance. The inhabitants of Westchester, New York, were among the most eloquent of those who left the delegates free to choose for themselves the most effective plan of action. Since "to obtain a redress of our grievances it has been thought most advisable in the Colonies to appoint a general

Congress," they resolved, "we will take shelter under the wisdom of those gentlemen who may be chosen to represent us, and cheerfully acquiesce in any measures they may judge shall be proper on this very alarming and critical occasion."[14]

Most of the resolutions, however, contain more specific demands for congressional action. There were several calls, for example, that the congress adopt a declaration of American rights and grievances. When these instructions are added to the numerous general demands for the "restoration of colonial rights on a permanent foundation," the delegates might well have concluded that their constituents hoped they would devise a unified statement of colonial rights. Similarly, there was some desire expressed for a petition to the king. While only three localities expressed any interest in such a petition, four provincial meetings noted that they would favor such a measure.[15]

By far the most compelling demand made by those areas calling for a congress, however, was that the delegates adopt a continental plan of commercial opposition. The proposed commercial plans varied in detail, with local meetings calling for variously timed trade boycotts of Britain, Ireland, and the West and East Indies. The common theme of all these plans, however, was that the only effective strategy of resistance would be a united plan of commercial opposition. Sixty-six percent of the resolutions that called for a congress also demanded the adoption of some kind of nonimportation plan. Because of the difficulties that would be caused by an immediate ban on the exportation of tobacco, the staple crop of Virginia and Maryland, there was less support in these colonies for nonexportation than for nonimportation. Yet, despite such difficulties, 50 percent of the meetings in question announced themselves in favor of nonexportation as well.[16] The strength of opinion favoring a commercial boycott was such that twenty-two of the sixty-one resolutions favoring a boycott took steps to begin executing local trade embargoes prior to the meeting of the congress. While most of these agreements were made contingent upon such alterations as the general congress might adopt, it is clear that a significant minority of Americans were prepared to undertake a commercial boycott irrespective of continental action. Thirty-nine of the resolutions supporting a boycott, however, indicated the participants' willingness to wait until the congress adopted a unified continental plan.[17]

The local resolutions made the popular sentiments abundantly clear to the delegates to the First Congress. The same popular opinion that had called the Congress into being had strongly indicated the actions that the colonists wanted the delegates to take. First, the delegates should make some strong gesture of support for Boston. Next, the participants generally seemed to favor some kind of declaration of American rights and had indicated, on the provincial level at least, a degree of support for a petition to the king. Finally, and most important, they demanded that their delegates devise a plan of action to obtain redress of the numerous American grievances. Though a minority of the localities left the delegates the discretionary power to decide for themselves what that plan might consist of, a sizeable, perhaps a compelling, majority demanded a commercial plan of opposition.

The significance of the 1774 resolutions goes beyond the specific opinions expressed. The political mobilization that their very creation symbolized, for example, was not an ephemeral phenomenon. It was clear that the participants in the meetings would not leave the political arena as swiftly as they had entered it. The purpose of many of the meetings was to select delegates to provincial conventions, and, not surprisingly, 88 percent of the resolutions in the sample did so. Perhaps even more important in the long run was the appointment of local committees in previously quiescent areas of the southern and middle colonies. While many towns in New England had formed resistance committees during the crises of the early 1770s, for example, a similar process had not occurred farther south, except in the few large cities that had participated in the Townshend Acts boycott.[18] The crisis of 1774 began to change this. Of the ninety-six local resolutions examined, fifty-eight included the appointment of a new local committee. Clearly, the participants did not expect the struggle to be resolved by mere statements of political opinion, the designation of delegates to provincial conventions, or, indeed, the meeting of the congress. Those who felt the need to express their opinions on the crisis issues also contemplated the necessity for continuing the resistance activity at the local level.

The question of who participated in this process is a vital one, but one that is impossible to answer. No attendance lists of the meetings were compiled; the only names that appear on the records are those of the moderator, the higher officials, and the appointees to the new committee, if one was chosen. There is some evidence, however, that the resolutions express the opinions of a wider spectrum, if not a larger number, of people than would have ordinarily been included in the political process. While 25 percent of the resolutions note that only freeholders attended the meeting, 74 percent record that the gatherings included both freeholders and "other Inhabitants." Some expansion of the political process was probably involved, although the exact dimensions of the expansion are unclear.[19]

Many of the delegates to the First Congress had been active participants in the local or provincial proceedings, whose very raison d'être was to select and instruct delegates to provincial conventions that would in turn select and instruct delegates to the Congress.[20] In only two colonies, Connecticut and Rhode Island, were the delegates selected and instructed entirely by regularly constituted institutions.[21] In most others they were chosen by these provincial conventions. While the conventions were variously facilitated and approved by established institutions and provincial leaders,[22] it is nevertheless clear that the continental delegates owed their political authority directly to the extralegal meetings engendered by the crisis of 1774. These meetings, as an examination of the resolutions they produced has shown, demonstrated a remarkable convergence of opinion throughout the colonies on the specific issues raised by the crisis. The delegates thus were in closer touch with local opinion than they would ever be again, and in most cases they were in personal agreement with the sentiments their constituents had expressed. They came to Philadelphia, therefore, with a specific agenda and with the political authority to carry it out.

The Congress Meets

On August 29 the Massachusetts delegates reached Frankford, a suburb of Philadelphia. At every step of their journey from Boston they had been greeted and feted by leading local figures. They were therefore pleased, but no longer surprised, to see yet another welcoming committee coming by carriage from the city. Carried off by this party of fellow delegates to the elegant new City Tavern at Second and Chestnut streets, the New Englanders again responded graciously to the toasts in their honor.[23] In truth, however, the elaborate courtesies that had been showered upon them since they had left Boston had begun to wear thin. Through the summer and into the fall, in newspapers, public meetings, and private correspondence, colonists had charged their delegates with nothing less than the salvation of America. They were to be given, a New Jersey committee wrote, "a power equal to any wherewith human nature alone was ever invested." To them, the Jerseymen observed, "the whole Interest of this free and august Continent are to be delegated." "Never in this country," observed a New Yorker, "has more depended upon one assembly of men, than depends upon this."[24] The delegates were thus burdened with the enormous confidence that Americans had placed in "the assembled gods" in Philadelphia; they felt weighed down with inflated expectations, but they were ready to begin.[25]

The anxiety of the delegates to begin substantive work was reflected in the speed with which they disposed of complex organizational and procedural matters. Soon after they assembled at the City Tavern early on Monday, September 5, they marched two blocks to inspect the new hall of the Carpenters' Company, offered to them by the city as a meeting place. The delegates quickly agreed that the site was adequate, and, ignoring an offer by the Speaker of the Pennsylvania Assembly, Joseph Galloway, that they use the new Pennsylvania State House about two blocks away, they immediately voted to accept the offer of Carpenters' Hall. Similar organizational motions followed, all offered by Thomas Lynch, a veteran of the Stamp Act Congress and of South Carolina resistance politics. Lynch first proposed that Charles Thomson of Philadelphia, who was Galloway's "Sworn opposite" and thus not a member of the Pennsylvania delegation, be appointed Secretary of the Congress. The appointment was debated briefly and accepted, apparently unanimously. Lynch then nominated Peyton Randolph, Speaker of the Virginia House of Burgesses, to preside at the Congress. This motion was also approved without dissent.[26] One potentially divisive procedural issue did arise near the end of the day on September 5. As James Duane of New York later framed the issue, the question was "whether the Congress should Vote by Colonies & what weight each Colony should have in the determination."[27] The delegates reserved the issue for full debate and decision the next day.

Patrick Henry of Virginia opened the debate as soon as Congress met at ten o'clock the following morning. In a long and fiery speech, he staked out the position of the larger colonies. As they had more at risk, Henry declared, their votes ought to be given greater weight than those of the smaller colonies. Each colony, he reasoned, must be given "a Just weight in [the congressional] deliberations in proportion to its opulence & number of Inhabitants its Exports & Imports." The issue must be instantly resolved, Henry reasoned, for the crisis had dissolved all former government and had thrown the colonies into "a State of Nature"; it was up to the delegates, therefore, to design a new voting procedure to govern the future congresses that might, and probably would, be necessary. Samuel Ward of Rhode Island answered with what would come to be the classic "small state" reply. The Rhode Islanders were prepared, "if necessary to make a Sacrifice of our All & that the weakest Colony by such a Sacrifice would suffer as much as the greatest." In answer to this, Patrick Henry's fellow Virginian, Benjamin Harrison, "insisted Strongly on the Injustice that Virginia should have no greater Weight in the determination than one of the smallest Colonies."[28]

The remarkable unity the delegates had heretofore displayed over preliminary procedural matters thus threatened to shatter over this issue, which was, indeed, destined to become a perennial sore point in future debates over a continental form of government. Yet at the First Congress the delegates pulled back; as Duane recorded, the debate "took a different Turn." Several delegates noted practically that they could not possibly resolve the complicated issue of an equitable basis for proportional voting without having much more elaborate statistical data on the relative wealth and population of the colonies. In its absence, as Christopher Gadsden observed, "I cant see any Way of voting but by Colonies."[29] Other delegates, however, saw more basic reasons for avoiding the issue. Contrary to Henry's view, John Jay did not believe that all government had yet been dissolved, and he did not, accordingly, believe that the delegates had been charged with the responsibility of devising a permanent structure of continental government; he could not "suppose, that We came to frame an American Constitution." John Rutledge similarly reminded his colleagues that they had "no legal Authority," and the adherence of their constituents to their measures would not depend upon voting procedure but upon "the reasonableness, the apparent Utility, and Necessity" of the substantive measures they devised to deal with the crisis of 1774. As the Virginian Richard Bland observed, "the Question is whether the Rights and Liberties shall be contended for, or given up to arbitrary Power." The delegates thereupon voted "that the Sense of the Congress shall be taken by Voting in Colonies each to have one Vote."[30]

While the debate over the basis for representation certainly occasioned greater debate and revealed greater potential division among the delegates than any other preliminary issue, nevertheless it too was resolved, if not without acrimony, at least with dispatch.

By September 7 the delegates were thus ready to proceed to substantive business. Two committees were created, the first to examine the British commercial system so that the colonists could identify particularly oppressive trade regulations. A second and more important committee was directed "to State the rights of the Colonies in general, the several instances in which these rights are violated or infringed, and the means most proper to be pursued for obtaining a restoration of them." With the appointment the following day of the membership of both the trade committee and what became known as the Grand Committee, the outline of activity in the First Congress was drawn. Thus, by the afternoon of September 7, two days after the delegates had marched in a body to Carpenters' Hall, the Grand Committee had begun to deliberate.[31]

Historians have long searched for an explanation of the delegates' ability to organize and define their duties so rapidly. A prevalent answer has been that of a conspiracy, that is, that congressional radicals led by the Adamses had concerted their actions beforehand and rammed their decisions through an unsuspecting Congress before sufficient opportunity for debate had emerged.[32] It has recently been demonstrated that such an interpretation is almost entirely dependent upon the recollections of one man, Joseph Galloway, who was the great loser in all the early proceedings.[33] Galloway was particularly incensed by the decisions to reject his offer of the State House and to elect his enemy, Charles Thomson, as Secretary. These matters, he observed ominously, "were privately settled by an Interest made out of Doors," a reference that has usually been interpreted to mean by Samuel Adams and company.[34] Galloway's recollections have heavily influenced subsequent accounts of the First Congress. He depicts an assembly divided from the beginning by factional strife, out of which the Massachusetts radicals, through cunning and a talent for conspiracy, emerged triumphant.[35] But such an interpretation obscures the most important features of the Congress, and thus it will be useful to examine the reliability of Galloway's evidence.

Although certain of the early congressional decisions were undoubtedly prearranged, as Galloway suspected, his explanation of this fact—that the Massachusetts radicals had conspired to realize their secret plans—is neither sufficient nor entirely plausible. In the first place, the "conspiracy" that supposedly brought about the early procedural agreements was hardly an exclusive one. Indeed, everyone appears to have been included, except for Galloway and his close allies. It is true, of course, that the Massachusetts delegates had been in constant contact, during the journey and after their arrival in Philadelphia, with all those from whom they might learn about the abilities and politics of the unknown men who were soon to be their associates. Their discussions included men of every political persuasion from nearly every colony. But the Massachusetts men were not alone in such hectic activity. Evidence from sources other than John Adams's diary, while fragmentary, indicates that members of all the delegations were feverishly seeking out their future colleagues and engaging them in "frequent Conversations." Only Galloway, it seems, despite attempts to "find out the Temper of the Delegates," had difficulty finding opportunities of "sounding them."[36]

The role played by the Massachusetts radicals may have been considerably more passive. On August 29 several Philadelphia radicals who had welcomed them at Frankford had reiterated warnings that the New Englanders had been receiving since they had left Boston. They strongly advised the Adamses to keep themselves in the background and to assume a modest demeanor that would help alleviate suspicions of New England fanaticism.[37] They appear to have taken such advice seriously. It is probably for this reason, for example, that all the procedural resolutions of September 5 had been introduced, undoubtedly by prearrangement, by a southerner (Lynch), while the Massachusetts delegates acquiesced in the behavior pressed upon them by their allies and sat quietly in their seats.[38]

There is some indication, moreover, that the passivity of the New Englanders was more than a tactical pose. Certain important early congressional decisions appear to have been taken without consulting the Bostonians. The choice of a congressional meeting place, for example, which Galloway appeared to lay at the Adamses' door, seems to have been made prior to September 5 by a coalition of radical and moderate Pennsylvanians headed by John Dickinson. On August 30, the day after John Adams arrived in Philadelphia and before much opportunity for political maneuvering had presented itself, he paid a visit to "the Carpenters Hall[,] where," he wrote flatly, "the Congress is to Sit."[39]

Perhaps the most telling argument against the conspiracy theory, however, is also the most obvious one. Whatever machinations had preceded the early decisions, there was ample opportunity to oppose them in the congressional debates. Yet no debate on any of the early procedural decisions, other than that on the basis for representation, was recorded. Whatever qualms individual delegates may have had were clearly subordinated to the greater goal of unity.[40] Where tactical decisions did affect the proceedings, as in the attempt to keep the Massachusetts delegates in the background, they were pressed upon the New Englanders by fellow delegates anxious to prevent the surfacing of old animosities that might mar the prevailing spirit of unity and consensus. Whatever would come later, the decisions of early September do not provide evidence of early factionalism among the delegates but rather illuminate their fundamental agreement as to the tasks they faced and the means by which they might be accomplished.

If the remarkable consensus that marked the early days of Congress ought not to be attributed to a conspiracy, neither can it be explained by precedent, for the delegates had few precedents to guide them. The periodic crises of the past decade had impressed upon resistance leaders the importance of coordinating resistance efforts among the several colonies.[41] This conclusion led to early calls by radicals for an intercolonial conference that would formulate a united plan of resistance.[42] Once before, Americans had met in a similar conference. The Stamp Act Congress of 1765, however, provides an interesting contrast with, rather than a precedent for, the 1774 congress.

The delegates to the 1765 congress had not been appointed in response to a popular call for an intercolonial conference; neither the need for a conference nor reports of the proceedings very often appeared in the public print or private letters. The Stamp Act Congress was called into being by a circular letter of the Massachusetts Assembly to which the assemblies of eight other colonies responded by appointing delegates. The Stamp Act delegates, therefore, were largely the legitimate representatives of the colonial assemblies. They believed they were acting for the entirely constitutional purpose of petitioning the king and remonstrating with Parliament. When this self-image was shattered by Lieutenant Governor Cadwallader Colden of New York, who informed one surprised delegation that he considered the Congress to be not only unprecedented but unconstitutional, the delegates were distressed. If their meeting was not a legal assembly, they had no alternative model for what it should be.[43]

Not surprisingly, given the weakness and disunity of the 1765 congress, the 1774 delegates dismissed it as a precedent for their own proceedings. Thomas McKean and Caesar Rodney of Delaware, two of the nine delegates who were present at both congresses, regaled their 1774 colleagues with little anecdotes of the "pretended Scruples and Timidities" of delegates at the previous congress. Patrick Henry was even clearer. Perhaps remembering Virginia's absence in 1765, he asserted on the opening day of debate that the 1774 assembly "was the first general Congress which had ever happened—that no former Congress could be a Precedent."[44]

More important as a precedent for the Continental Congress, although more remote in time, were the extralegal conventions that had met in England in 1215, 1660, and 1688. The raisons d'être of these conventions were the failures of successive English governments to rule adequately or justly. Their purpose had been to remedy the errors or excesses into which the government had fallen and thereby to allow legitimate government to resume its functions. They were by design temporary gatherings whose success would be measured by the disappearance of the causes that had brought them into being. Americans were quick to draw parallels between the 1774 Congress and the great conventions, comparisons that added prestige as well as precedent to the colonial assembly. "It cannot be supposed," wrote a Pennsylvanian, "that any English subject" would "condemn the three noblest Assemblies which dignify the pages of [English] history." "The Barons who obtained Magna Carta from King John, the Assembly which restored Charles the Second and monarchy," and the Convention of 1689 "were all Congresses," he claimed, "formed on the same principles and the same necessities as the late American Congress." The delegates to the Congress, "A Jersey Farmer" concluded, were "undoubtedly the Barons of North-America."[45]

Although the convention precedent was not necessarily a dominant influence on the delegates, they referred to their body as "the Convention" before formally voting to call themselves "the Congress." Perhaps more important, they realized that the nature of their authority was much more analogous to that of a convention than to that of a legislature. When Edward Rutledge of South Carolina carefully explained the scope and nature of congressional authority on the opening day of business, he noted that "We have no coercive or legislative Authority."[46] Although the great English conventions provided a general model that helped the delegates define the scope of their authority and the nature of their task, they cannot provide a sufficient explanation for the substantial consensus that continued throughout the congressional session.

Yet that consensus, first displayed in the early procedural votes, carried through to most of the major substantive issues that the delegates were to face in the next two months. In that relatively short period of time they accomplished all their major goals. They voted strong, although limited, support for Boston; they delineated the extent of colonial rights; they listed those British acts they considered to be infringements of their rights; and most important, they adopted a comprehensive commercial boycott of Great Britain, Ireland, and the West Indies. On these matters one must remember that the delegates did not arrive in Philadelphia either uninstructed or unconstrained. Their constituents had, in the same process by which they selected the delegates, also instructed them as to all these matters and delegated to them specific political authority to carry those instructions into execution. The delegates themselves, as participants in that process, were therefore close to the political temper of their constituents. If they appeared to agree on most matters and displayed a sense of urgency that enabled them to subordinate their differences on others, it was because they accurately reflected the unity of their constituents throughout the continent regarding the specific issues raised by the crisis of 1774.[47]

In the process of fulfilling the inflated expectations of their constituents regarding those issues, the delegates also did more. They seized the transitory political authority that had been delegated to them to deal with the crisis and transferred it to a new political body, the Continental Congress. The seizure and institutionalization of political authority in 1774 marked the beginning of the process that would transform the transitory convention of 1774 into a permanent continental government.

The Congress Acts

On Tuesday, September 6, as soon as the delegates had settled most of the initial organizational and procedural problems, dispatches from Israel Putnam, a former British officer who now resided in Connecticut, arrived from New England. They contained distressing news. General Gage, he related, had attempted to seize by force the military supplies that the colonists had stockpiled in Charlestown. The countrymen had opposed him, and shots had been fired. As Putnam wrote his report to the Congress, armed men marched toward Boston from all over New England. In retaliation against the citizens who had fired upon his troops, Putnam wrote, Gage had ordered the warships in the harbor to begin shelling the town of Boston.[48] The citizens of Philadelphia were shocked. Muffled bells tolled throughout the city, Silas Deane recorded, and "all Faces gather paleness, but they all gather indignation, & every Tongue pronouncs Revenge." The delegates inside Carpenters' Hall shared the emotions of the townspeople. The anxiety was particularly acute for the New Englanders, who sat helplessly in Philadelphia, uncertain as to the fate of their families and friends.[49] Not until Thursday, September 8, did the delegates get accurate news from the north. Gage was indeed fortifying Boston Neck—an alarming enough prospect—but his troops had not been attacked, nor had the British ships fired on the town. "To Our Joy," Deane reported, "*Putnam's* blundering Story is contradicted, and that every thing as yet wears the most favorable aspect which Zeal & Unanimity can promise Us."[50] The delegates' relief was enormous; they could, for the present at least, proceed with the deliberate course of action that they had plotted two days previously.

While the immediate threat was over, the situation in Massachusetts remained critical. At any moment, and over any trivial incident, war might break out. The prospect of impending bloodshed hung over the delegates through the entire length of the session. Boston's urgent problems repeatedly intruded upon the proceedings and elicited an immediate congressional response. Through all their deliberations, the delegates half feared, half expected, to receive news that war had begun.[51]

After the initial crisis had passed, the delegates settled into the routine that would occupy them through September. The Congress as a whole body adjourned from day to day, while the individual members worked in the Grand Committee and its subcommittees, struggling with the matters assigned to them. Before the committeemen could determine which colonial rights had been infringed and propose methods of obtaining redress, they realized that they must agree upon a precise definition of those rights. Through early September the delegates attempted unsuccessfully to resolve this troublesome issue. It was in the midst of the continuing, often deadlocked, debate over colonial rights that the problem of Boston again came to the fore and brought the delegates back from the abstract realm of political theory to the urgent and perhaps comforting concreteness of Boston's immediate plight.

On Friday, September 16, the express rider of the Boston committee arrived in Philadelphia. He carried with him the Bostonians' response to Gage's new fortifications, which took the form of a series of resolves that had been adopted by the Suffolk County Convention on September 9.[52] Revere hurried to deliver the Suffolk Resolves to the waiting Massachusetts delegates. It is highly likely that he also delivered the committee's request that the delegates secure explicit congressional approval of the Bostonians' course of action. The next morning, the Massachusetts delegates laid the dispatch before a specially convened session of the full Congress. By that afternoon the delegates had voted unanimously to approve the Suffolk Resolves and ordered that their vote be made public.[53]

The Suffolk Resolves, largely written by Joseph Warren, presaged the end of effective royal government in Massachusetts. Although several of the nineteen resolves were similar to those adopted in other Massachusetts meetings—the acknowledgment of allegiance to George III, for example, and the agreement to commence commercial nonintercourse—others were considerably more drastic. The meeting recommended, for example, that all local taxes collected be withheld from the provincial government and that the newly appointed royal councilors resign their seats. The delegates also advised the various towns to begin to arm and drill their local militia companies under captains of their own choosing. As to their policy regarding hostilities, the Bostonians were equally blunt: They were "determined to act merely upon the defensive, so long as such conduct may be vindicated by reason and the principles of self-preservation, but no longer."[54]

Tories and English officials interpreted the endorsement of the Suffolk Resolves as a sign that the Congress had been captured by the New England radicals and would thenceforth do their bidding. The unanimous congressional approval of the inflammatory principles of Suffolk County proved, Tories claimed, that the delegates had thrown off their spurious mask of prudence to reveal that they were in reality as reckless as the Bostonians themselves.[55] Certainly such assessments are accurate if one looks at the immediate effect of the endorsement of the Resolves, for this early action was the first act of the Congress to be made public. Radicals like John Adams rejoiced: "This was one of the happiest Days of my Life," he wrote with uncharacteristic exuberance. "This Day convinced me that America will support Massachusetts or perish with her."[56]

Yet one ought not look to the substantive provisions of the Resolves for clues to the delegates' future policies toward support for Boston or toward military preparedness. The speed with which the delegates acted precluded any careful study of those provisions, and in fact, the delegates adopted the Resolves for reasons independent of the substantive positions the Bostonians had taken. This is clear from the manner in which they acted on this issue, which differs significantly from their practice in considering other important issues. In contrast to the careful study they devoted to the subject of the proposed declaration of rights, for example, no committee was appointed to study and report on the Resolves, and there is no evidence of extensive debate in the full Congress. If, therefore, the delegates regarded their vote as a firm policy commitment to the positions the Bostonians had taken, they were uncharacteristically lax in the amount of debate and analysis that preceded that commitment. If, on the other hand, they regarded their action as a limited response to an immediate problem, the reasons for the swiftness of their action and its limited significance become clearer.

Given the sentiments expressed during the summer of 1774 and the horrified reaction of the delegates to the initial news of the bombardment of Boston, it was predictable that they would make some expression of support for the town whose trials had, after all, occasioned their meeting. The action of the Boston committee apparently provided an opportunity to make that gesture of support (as the committee had hoped and expected it would). It is clear that the committee had hoped to spur the delegates by specifically requesting that the Congress approve the Suffolk Resolves. As George Read, a delegate from Delaware, wrote on September 18, his planned departure from Philadelphia had been delayed because the arrival of the Resolves had forced an immediate vote of "approbation of the conduct of the people of Boston." They had acted so "suddenly," he explained, "in consequence of an application from Boston to the Congress for their advice upon the late measures of General Gage, in fortifying the neck of land that leads into Boston."[57] In approving the Suffolk Resolves, then, the delegates did not necessarily view themselves as committed to the specific course of action the Bostonians had undertaken. Rather, their response to the request of the Boston committee was probably intended primarily as a statement of support for the town and disapproval of Gage's conduct. The decision to publicize the vote constituted an unmistakable warning to the governor that Boston did not stand alone, a warning calculated to deter Gage from undertaking a military solution to his problems.[58]

Approval of the Suffolk Resolves marked the limit to which the delegates were prepared to go in supporting their northern brethren. In the face of Gage's apparently imminent attack, they were willing to endorse defense preparations by the Bostonians. They were not ready, however, to approve any civil or military action by the town's leaders that looked toward a general preparation for war or that indicated a belief that war was inevitable. John Adams himself recognized this: "The Congress will support Boston and the Massachusetts or Perish with them," he assured his brother-in-law Richard Cranch, "but they earnestly wish that Blood may be spared if possible, and all Ruptures with the Troops avoided."[59] The limited extent of congressional support for Massachusetts soon became evident in the debate over an unlikely vehicle for military discussion, the petition to the king.

Even before the Congress met, some radicals had come to believe that war could not be avoided and that military preparations must be made. "A capital branch of the business of congress," Joseph Hawley had avowed on the eve of the Massachusetts delegates' departure, ought to be the settlement of a "certain clear plan, for a constant, adequate and lasting supply of arms and military stores." Christopher Leffingwell had similarly asserted that the Congress must recommend "to have eighty or a hundred thousand men . . . under regular Discipline," a proposal that Israel Putnam had been avidly circulating in various newspapers.[60] Several of the Massachusetts delegates themselves shared such sentiments. John Adams, for one, particularly felt the need for strong measures. "What avails, Prudence, Wisdom, Policy, Fortitude, Integrity," he asked, "without Power, without Legions?" When Demosthenes had gone through Greece to unite opposition to Philip of Macedon, Adams observed, "he did not go to propose a Non-Importation or Non-Consumption Agreement!!!"[61] So when the Adamses arrived in Philadelphia they did not have to look far for allies on the subject of military preparedness. Particular support came from Virginians Patrick Henry and Richard Henry Lee. In early October the radicals attempted to win congressional approval for military preparations. They focused their efforts in the committee appointed on October 1 to draw up a petition to the king. The delegates usually attempted to preserve an ideological balance in all their actions by appointing relatively conservative committees to implement relatively radical policies and vice versa. Accordingly, the petition committee was dominated by radicals.[62]

Lee, as a member of the committee, hoped to shape the petition to radical purposes. On the day the committee was appointed, he attempted to procure a resolution instructing it to include in their final document a clause recommending the arming and equipping of the colony militias.[63] Debate on Lee's controversial proposal was deferred until October 3. When discussions resumed after the weekend, Patrick Henry took the floor to issue a ringing statement of support for the proposal. "A preparation for Warr is Necessary to obtain peace," he declared. "We ought to ask Ourselves," he reminded his colleagues, what they would do "should the planns of Non-im[portatio]n & Nonexp[ortatio]n fail of success." "In that Case," Henry observed, "Arms are Necessary, & if then, it is Necessary Now." "Arms are a Resource to which We shall be forced, . . ." he concluded, "& why . . . are We to hesitate providing them Now whilst in Our power."[64]

The radical position was quickly and passionately denounced. John Rutledge, also a member of the petition committee, pronounced his colleague's proposal "out of the Line" of the Congress's business and noted that it constituted a declaration of war. If the delegates intended such an action, he observed, "no other Measure ought to be taken up" and they should "speak out at Once." Benjamin Harrison of Virginia mildly restated the point. Arming the militia, he noted, would "tend, only to irritate, whereas Our Business is to reconcile." Edmund Pendleton then rose to offer an alternative to the gauntlet Lee wanted to throw down before George III. He proposed that his countryman's resolution be amended, and after further debate an amended instruction was in fact passed. The committee was instructed to do little more than reiterate Whig clichés in favor of a militia and promise that the colonial militia would vigorously support the king's cause in the event of war. Lee was so disgusted with the toned-down resolution that he refused to support it, and he bitterly endorsed his own proposal, "A motion made in Congress by R. H. Lee to apprize the public of danger, and of the necessity of putting the colonies in a state of defence," even though, he said, "a majority had not the spirit to adopt it."[65]

Despite this rebuff, on October 21 Lee managed to place before his colleagues a strongly worded draft petition.[66] His continuing efforts to use the petition to make a firm statement of the colonial position, however, were as unavailing as his attempt to make it the vehicle for military preparedness. His draft was ordered to be recommitted and the newly elected Pennsylvania delegate, John Dickinson, whose great reputation as a writer had preceded him to Congress, was added to the petition committee. It was Dickinson who wrote the elegantly worded petition to the king that the delegates adopted on October 24. Lee's original draft, Dickinson later remembered, had been discarded because it had been "written in language of asperity very little according with the conciliatory disposition of Congress."[67] Dickinson's assessment of the temper of the delegates, a disposition that they displayed on every occasion in which they were not constrained by superheated public opinion, was an accurate one. Most delegates steadfastly refused to contemplate civil or military preparations for a rupture that they earnestly believed they might still prevent. As the Massachusetts radicals came to understand the basically moderate aims of their colleagues, their disillusionment with the Congress grew.

The delegates' eagerness to avoid military measures, a disposition that was to fade so rapidly in the following winter that its determining influence at the First Congress is scarcely credible, shaped early congressional policy toward Massachusetts, the most likely site for a war to begin. From personal conviction and in response to public opinion, the delegates had been anxious to express their support for Boston from the day the Congress opened, and this wish had been satisfied by the approval of the Suffolk Resolves. Once common cause had been made with Boston, however, they could determine the limits of continental support for Massachusetts. They demonstrated on this, as on the few other occasions when their policy was discretionary, that their ruling principles were caution and prudence. Tangible continental support for Massachusetts, the delegates quickly made clear, would be limited by their determination to avoid hostilities. The Bostonians were informed that they could expect no continental assistance for any offensive military action, nor would they countenance the civil counterpart of such action, the organization of a new provincial government.

The wariness with which the delegates approached the explosive situation in Massachusetts demonstrates their own temperate inclinations and their determination to satisfy, but in no case to go beyond, the expectations of their constituents. None of the local or provincial proceedings mention or even hint at the necessity to prepare for war. The delegates' decision to avoid any possibility of war, therefore, was stiffened by the lack of overt popular support for policies that might lead to bloodshed. What the Massachusetts radicals began to scorn as congressional timidity was in fact the delegates' reluctance to commit themselves to policies that they personally did not favor and that might not command popular support.

By the end of September, private conversations in and outside of Congress had convinced Samuel and John Adams that the congressional support for Boston that had been voted on September 17 had been hedged with conditions. They hastened to warn their compatriots not to be carried away by the approval of the Suffolk Resolves. In sharp contrast to his earlier euphoria, John Adams cautioned a friend in Massachusetts that "the Delegates here are not Sufficiently acquainted with our Pr[ovince] and with the Circumstances you are in, to form a Judgment [of] what Course it is proper for you to take. . . . They Shudder at the Prospect of Blood."[68]

The reason for the gloom soon became apparent. Hoping to translate the congressional approval of the Suffolk Resolves into more definite support, the Boston committee again dispatched Revere to Philadelphia with an extremely alarming account of events in Boston. Gage was continuing to fortify all the entrances to and high points in the town, the committeemen wrote, with the intention of making Boston into "a garrisoned town." They reported that government was suspended and intimated that anarchy threatened, and in this distressing situation they again requested "the advice of the Congress."[69] What the committeemen ardently desired from the Congress, and hoped to prompt by this letter, was some indication that the Bostonians would have continental support if they launched a preemptive attack on Gage's troops. Furthermore, they wanted an assurance that should war commence, the province would not be left without government. Specifically, they wanted a congressional resolution granting them the authority to organize a virtually independent government in Massachusetts by resuming the old charter of 1629.[70] There had been some calls to take up the old charter even prior to the crisis of 1774. In the fall of 1774, with effective government in the province suspended by the citizens' refusal to submit to the Coercive Acts, sentiment for resuming the old charter grew, and it was especially strong in the fiery western counties of the province.[71]

But from extensive conversations with their colleagues, both Adamses concluded that the Congress would never approve the creation of an independent provincial government in Massachusetts. Their apprehension was fully justified. Revere reached Philadelphia with the Boston committee's letter on Thursday, October 6. Debate on the proper congressional response occupied the delegates through the weekend and into the following week. The basic outlines of that response, however, were clear by Monday, October 10. The delegates flatly refused to countenance the resumption of the old charter. They advised the inhabitants of Massachusetts simply to "submit to a suspension of the administration of Justice, . . . under the rules of their present charter, and the laws of the colony founded thereon." His colleagues, John Adams fumed when he realized their intention, desired the Bostonians to "Stand Stock Still, and live without Government, or Law. . . . We hear, perpetually, the most figurative Panegyricks upon our Wisdom Fortitude and Temperance," he added, and "the most fervent Exhortations to perseverance, But nothing more is done."[72]

The delegates were equally adamant in their refusal to countenance offensive military action by the Bostonians. On October 7, John Adams warned a friend about his colleagues' attitude toward the issue. "If it is the secret Hope of any, as I suspect it is, that the Congress will advise to offensive Measures," he cautioned, "they will be mistaken." The majority of the delegates, he noted, would not vote "to raise Men or Money, or Arms or Ammunition. Their Opinions are fixed against Hostilities and Ruptures." The next day, the delegates proceeded to bear out Adams's predictions, resolving to support military action by the New Englanders only if Gage went beyond his current preparations and actually attacked the citizens. Significantly, they refused to construe Gage's preparations as the necessary attack.[73]

When debate on policy toward Massachusetts resumed after the weekend, the delegates continued to demonstrate their prudence. In their letter the members of the Boston committee had requested advice on whether the Bostonians ought to respond to Gage's acts by evacuating the city. The delegates read into this request, probably accurately, a design by the Bostonians to besiege the governor within the town. This they refused to approve, and they voted down a Richard

Henry Lee motion to advise such an evacuation. On October 11 the delegates put the finishing touches on their policy toward the British troops who had come with General Gage. They categorically denied that their approval of the Suffolk Resolves had countenanced an attack upon the governor. On the contrary, they admonished the Boston men to "peaceably and firmly persevere in the line [in which] they are now conducting themselves, on the defensive."[74] While Massachusetts radicals chafed under the congressional advice, moderates in that province were cheered by what they regarded as the calming influence of the continental delegates. Revere's return with the continental resolves had made at least one such moderate, John Andrews, "a little easier in regard to matters," for he now had some basis to hope that the continental advice "will have some influence upon the councils" of the provincial firebrands and would "check their impetuous zeal."[75]

The delegates' refusal to approve offensive action, either civil or military, was a setback for Massachusetts radicals. The limits of congressional support for Massachusetts had been made clear. Thus, when Samuel Adams, for his own purposes, attempted upon his return to Massachusetts to misrepresent congressional sentiment and intimated that he had received assurances of support for an attack on Gage's troops, Thomas Cushing retorted, "That is a lie Mr. Adams, and I know it and you know that I know it."[76]

The caution that the delegates displayed in responding to Massachusetts also characterized their response to most other discretionary issues that they faced, including the Galloway Plan of Union. The plan, introduced by Joseph Galloway on September 28, was a bold one that would have made substantial constitutional changes in the British imperial system. It called for an American parliament that would have controlled domestic and trade affairs of the colonies under the executive leadership of a British-appointed governor general.[77] Prior to the meeting of Congress, there had been few calls for such extensive imperial reorganization. Such discussion as there had been had centered in Philadelphia among merchants who may well have been in contact with Galloway and to whom he may have confided his intention to propose a plan of union at the coming Congress.[78] Support for such a plan was not widespread, however, and the surprising thing about the Galloway plan was not its defeat—which has been interpreted as a radical triumph[79]—but rather that it was almost successful. The considerable support for the plan that emerged in the Congress is all the more bewildering when one considers Galloway's rapidly diminishing influence in Congress and in his power base, the Pennsylvania Assembly.

From the beginning of congressional deliberations, Galloway had sensed that he and his handpicked Pennsylvania delegates were not participating in important decisions. Galloway's sense of isolation, confessed to William Franklin during the opening days of the Congress, became increasingly obvious as the session continued. The only committee assignment his fellow delegates bestowed on him during the entire session was an appointment on October 21 to the committee "to revise the minutes of the Congress."[80] Even more damaging, in the long run, was the erosion of Galloway's political strength within the Pennsylvania Assembly. Never a personable figure, his political ability alone had kept him in a leadership position. By 1774 his stubborn opposition to majority opinion, and even to the opinion of his old mentor, Benjamin Franklin, had brought both his ability and his sincerity into question. In the early October elections to the Pennsylvania Assembly, which took place while the Congress was in session, two of Galloway's enemies, Thomson and Dickinson, won seats. Almost as soon as the new Assembly met, Dickinson was added to Pennsylvania's congressional delegation. Galloway's leadership was repudiated in more direct ways as well. The new legislature elected Edward Biddle as Speaker, displacing Galloway from the position he had held almost continuously for the past eight years.[81]

From a weak position within Congress and a crumbling political base without, therefore, Galloway introduced his Plan of Union. It was an indication of the delegates' great desire for some plan of reconciliation that they seriously debated a scheme that had so little popular support and that was sponsored, moreover, by a soon-to-be-repudiated political leader. The considerable interest that the plan did generate was due more to the peculiar situation in the Congress in late September, however, than to the merits of the plan itself. By the end of that month, the delegates were in the midst of seemingly endless wrangles in the Grand Committee and its subcommittee over the question of parliamentary authority over colonial trade. The issue had brought deliberations on the declaration of rights virtually to a standstill, and Galloway introduced his plan as a possible solution. Since all agreed that to avoid chaos the power to regulate trade must reside in some supracolonial entity, Galloway suggested that his proposed

American legislature, rather than Parliament, might best do the job.[82]

But the plan, although a tempting resolution of the intractable trade problem, was simply too far removed from immediate, crisis-related issues, and its author was too suspect, for it to succeed. The radicals attacked the plan, somewhat disingenuously, by playing upon the moderates' fears that the delegates lacked the authority to approve the far-reaching constitutional changes that Galloway proposed. By the end of the day's debate, the plan was tabled by a vote of six to five. After the adoption of the declaration of rights in late October settled the issue of colonial trade, the plan was expunged from the official journal.[83]

The Galloway plan, which has loomed so large in subsequent accounts of the Congress, was of relatively minor importance to contemporaries. A far more important task, they believed, lay in devising a definitive statement of colonial rights and grievances.[84] The delegates may well have been more anxious to obtain a declaration of rights than their constituents had been. Few specific demands for such a document had been expressed during the summer, either at the local or the provincial level. There were many vague calls, however, for the delegates to "establish American rights upon a permanent foundation," and the delegates may well have considered such expressions a sufficient authorization for their attempts to compile a colonial bill of rights.[85] But nowhere was the need for such a document absolutely pressed upon them; in no case was the desire for such a declaration as compelling, for example, as the demands for a plan to relieve Boston. The declaration of rights, then, was another of those issues upon which the 1774 delegates might exercise their discretion.

Despite the lack of specific authorization and the complexity of the undertaking, however, the delegates—"these great Witts, these subtle Criticks, these refined Genius's, these learned Lawyers," as a disgruntled John Adams described his colleagues—were exceedingly "fond of shewing their Parts and Powers." A project that would precisely define the bases and extent of colonial rights had attractions for men of this disposition, and they were determined to undertake it.[86] One of the tasks confided to the Grand Committee on the opening day of business was therefore to "State the rights of the Colonies in general." On September 9 the Grand Committee began its work on the subject by appointing a subcommittee to draft a statement of colonial rights.[87]

As John Adams later recalled in his autobiography, the major debates over the statement, both in the Grand Committee and in its sub-committee, involved two questions. First, Adams remembered, the delegates had wrangled over the proper foundation for American rights. Should colonial rights be sanctioned by the law of nature, or should they be based upon "the British Constitution and our American Charters of Grants" alone? Adams recalled that this issue had decisively separated radicals from conservatives. He himself, he wrote, had argued very strenuously to uphold the radical position, which favored the law of nature. He depicted himself as a prescient figure, eloquently conjuring up the events of 1776 from the situation in 1774. Adams informed his colleagues, he recalled, that the law of nature was "a Resource to which We might be driven, by Parliament much sooner than We were aware." In all this, he noted, he was vigorously opposed by conservatives determined not to go beyond the comforting confines of the British constitution.[88]

Adams's account is a skewed one, however, which conflicts with several contemporary pieces of evidence, his own diary among them. In fact, there appears to have been little controversy over the proper foundation for American rights, and such debate as did occur does not demonstrate a clear radical-conservative split. Thus, as Adams recorded in his diary, the delegates agreed rather quickly upon the proper basis of colonial rights. The issue arose in the Grand Committee on September 8 and was debated and settled on the following day, even before the rights subcommittee was appointed. The compromise solution that the Grand Committee reached was neither particularly surprising, particularly inventive, nor particularly significant ideologically. The committee simply listed all the possible bases for colonial rights. The members agreed, Samuel Ward recorded, "to found our Rights upon the Laws of Nature, the Principles of the English Constitution, & Charters & Compacts."[89]

This compromise solution appealed to radicals and conservatives alike and did not seem to divide the delegates along any clearly discernible ideological lines. Although Adams recalled, for example, that the radicals had argued strongly against the inclusion of the British constitution as a basis for colonial rights, it was one of his closest allies, Richard Henry Lee, who opened the September 8 debate by declaring that colonial rights must be based upon "Nature, on the british Constitution, on Charters, and on immemorial Usage." One might even argue that, far from dividing conservatives from radicals, the issue was one upon which they could find common ground. Thus John Jay, who is generally placed in the conservative camp, rose to support Lee's formulation, arguing that "it is necessary to recur to the Law of Nature and the british Constitution," because "the Constitution of G[reat] B[ritain] will not apply to some of the Charter Rights."[90]

Adams was accurate, however, in his recollection that much controversy developed over a substantive issue. The delegates argued at great length over the right of Parliament to regulate colonial trade. This was a question upon which they had no clear guidance, either from instructions or constituents, and was one, moreover, upon which many had strong personal opinions. Thus, Christopher Gadsden announced that he was violently opposed to "allowing to Parliament any Power of regulating Trade, or allowing that they have any Thing to do with Us."[91] But opinions on the other side of the question were held with equal vehemence. Many delegates thought that the protection of the Royal Navy was essential to American trade. If Americans claimed such protection, they reasoned, they must submit to the regulatory power of Parliament. "I am one of those who hold the Position," Samuel Chase declared, "that Parliament has a Right to make Laws for us in some Cases, to regulate the Trade—and in all Cases where the good of the whole Empire requires it."[92]

Because of these strong convictions, and because there was no compelling popular sentiment on either side of the question, compromise did not come easily. The differing views were first thrashed out in the rights subcommittee that had been appointed on September 9. The subcommittee debated the problem through the weekend and on into the following week. After a week of fruitless wrangling, John Rutledge finally suggested to John Adams that he draft a compromise resolution. Rutledge thought the conservatives would accept a clause that allowed Parliament the power to regulate colonial trade by reason of colonial acquiescence in its necessity, rather than by right, and that concurrently denied Parliament any authority over taxation. Adams complied and the subcommittee unanimously accepted the compromise, although no one was completely satisfied with it. The compromise was reported back to the Grand Committee on September 14. In the full committee, as in the subcommittee, the compromise aroused little enthusiasm. The issue was debated for two full days before the need to act on the Suffolk Resolves interrupted the debate. On September 22 the Grand Committee laid the compromise report before the

full Congress, where on September 24 the delegates resolved to postpone consideration of the troublesome issue in order to make some
progress on the Association.[93]

The delegates resumed consideration of the issue on October 12. According to Adams, when the delegates debated the Grand Committee's report, they found they were almost evenly divided: five colonies
favored accepting parliamentary authority to regulate colonial trade,
five were against, and the delegations of two—Massachusetts and
Rhode Island—were split among themselves. After an acrimonious
debate, which continued through the next day, the full Congress accepted the compromise that the rights subcommittee had worked out
a month previously. The final statement of rights and grievances,
probably drafted by John Dickinson, allowed Parliament the authority
to regulate colonial trade but based it upon colonial acquiescence and
"the necessity of the case." The Congress agreed to concede to Parliament the power but not the right.[94]

When Adams recalled the compromise, he emphasized the general
dissatisfaction with the measure and the halfhearted spirit in which it
had been adopted. "The general Sense of the Members," he recalled,
"was that the Article demanded as little as could be demanded, and
conceeded as much as could be conceeded with Safety." But his opinion may have been colored by the fact that if any group lost by the compromise, it was the radicals. As he himself recorded in his diary the
day before the compromise article was adopted, the conservative
spokesman James Duane had indicated that he "had his Heart sett"
upon "asserting in our Bill of Rights, the Authority of Parliament to
regulate the Trade of the Colonies." Duane favored basing that
authority, moreover, upon colonial consent as well as necessity. The
final clause adopted by the Congress came very close to satisfying
Duane's wishes.[95]

The achievement of a compromise over the declaration of rights occupied the delegates for an amount of time disproportionate to the ultimate importance of the issue. Within a few months, mutual trade boycotts and the beginning of war effectively scuttled parliamentary
regulation of colonial trade, just as it decisively ended congressional
reluctance to proceed with military preparations.

Yet the debates over the issues of military preparedness and parliamentary authority give some important indications of the political in-

clinations of the delegates. On neither did the delegates have much specific popular direction. In this sense, the issues resembled the military and administrative decisions they would face after they assembled as a government in 1775, and they differed from those actions they had taken as a convention in response to popular demands in 1774. The debates over these issues exhibit certain features of later congressional activity. Here, for example, one sees the divisions that were to characterize the Congress after 1775. Radicals, moderates, and conservatives clearly differed over both the legitimate extent of parliamentary authority and the question of the preparation for war. Here also one begins to discern the strength of the congressional moderates on issues upon which the delegates were relatively unconstrained by popular opinion.

The First Continental Congress can best be understood by differentiating between those actions that the delegates took as members of a crisis-inspired convention and those that begin to resemble acts of a legal government. The two roles are related, of course, for the authority gained by the immensely popular convention was transferred to and exercised by the government long after the Congress had lost the popular guidance, and ultimately the popular support, that it had gained in 1774.

As a convention, the Congress was enormously successful. The delegates responded actively to almost every popular demand that had been voiced during the summer of 1774, and they did so with a remarkable degree of speed and unity. Thus, a week after the Congress opened, the delegates made a strong statement of support for Boston; less than a month later they agreed upon a continental plan of commercial opposition to Great Britain. Less compelling popular demands for action to meet the immediate crisis were satisfied as well with the petition to the king and the declaration of rights. In responding to these popular demands, the delegates used the political authority that had tentatively been vested in their unprecedented and extralegal body in precisely the manner their constituents had hoped and expected that they would.

A convention, however, is by definition a temporary assembly. If the Congress was to become an institution that would survive the crisis (and there were many indications in 1774 that it would), then it would have to become a continental government, the members of which responded less to immediate constituent directions and more to their own political preferences and those of the provincial political factions they represented. For clues to the direction in which Congress would move as a government, one must examine those few issues upon which the delegates could conduct their business according to both their divergent private political views and the views of their provincial constituents.

On those issues upon which the delegates were not constrained by the demands of the 1774 crisis, they displayed a degree of moderation at variance with the view that the First Congress was a body dominated by radicals. The radicals, of course, had little cause to complain of the results of the Congress, for they had achieved their most important goals, a strong statement that Boston's suffering was a common cause, and a Continental Association. But in assessing the great enthusiasm that greeted the publication of the results of the Congress, one must also remember that the moderates, and even the conservatives, also had had their victories. Thus, although the delegates demonstrated strong support for Massachusetts on September 17, they clearly indicated in subsequent weeks that they would countenance no extreme military or civil measures by the Bostonians. Similarly, attempts to make the petition to the king a vehicle for radical plans and radical rhetoric were turned aside, and the document was carefully written to give no offense to its intended recipient. Finally, the statement of rights conceded to the conservatives the key point regarding the parliamentary power, if not the right, to regulate colonial trade. The congressional moderates and conservatives thus displayed considerable strength on almost every issue upon which the charged political atmosphere of 1774 did not dictate a specific congressional response. The real strength of these men has been obscured in large measure by an overdependence on the recollections of Joseph Galloway. But his position at the Congress was unique; one should not infer from his failure a similar failure for the congressional conservatives and moderates in general. In fact, the Jays, the Duanes, the Rutledges and their ideological colleagues exercised important influence on a wide range of issues in 1774.

The subtlety of congressional action and the care with which the delegates steered their course between the Scylla of war and the Charybdis of inaction was entirely lost upon two audiences. Immediately after the Congress dissolved and published its proceedings, colonial Tories pronounced it an illegal body whose actions had been rash and probably treasonous. More fatal to hopes for reconciliation, the British ministry quickly announced a similar position, basing its indictment of congressional radicalism largely on the body's approval of the Suffolk Resolves and pointedly ignoring the conciliatory aims of the petition and the statement of rights.

But the strength of the congressional moderates and conservatives was not lost upon one constituency. Congressional moderation appealed to moderates and conservatives in every colony who, though opposed to British policies, were fearful of the social and political disorder that their political views conditioned them to expect from any situation of upheaval. In the actions taken by the First Congress, they saw the possibility of a "prudent" continental resistance to British measures, one that was monitored and constrained by men who shared their political views and who acted through an institution that had the potential to serve their ends.

CHAPTER 4

The Association of 1774

Everyone has his Eyes & thoughts fixt just now upon Congress, anxious to know what they have done—what they have said, and what they have thought.
                                                    —Jared Ingersoll, October 24, 1774

The Connecticut man expressed the thoughts of many of his fellow colonists in the autumn of 1774. Because one of the primary reasons for the Congress had been the need to design and coordinate a plan of commercial opposition, most Americans anxiously awaited the.end of the session, when they would learn the details of the plan the delegates had agreed upon. Support for a continental commercial boycott had not, like the call for a congress itself, emerged immediately upon receipt of the news of the Port Bill. Rather, it had surfaced slowly in the spring of 1774 and had increased steadily through the summer. By September it had become irresistible.

As soon as the news of the ministry's action reached the colonies in late April 1774, the radicals on the Boston committee of correspondence sought to obtain firm commitments from their colleagues in the other major port towns for the immediate inception of a commercial boycott of Great Britain.[1] While they supported the call for a general congress, they realized that logistics alone would prevent any such meeting until at least the late summer of 1774. The purpose of a commercial boycott, however, was the speedy relief of Boston, whose port, by the terms of the Port Act, would close on June 1. A general congress simply could not act swiftly enough—or so Samuel Adams and many of his brethren believed. This analysis of the situation led the committee into its one major blunder of 1774. The members attempted in June 1774 to push the country towns of Massachusetts into adopting their own provincial boycott agreement prior to and irrespective of action taken by either the other major ports or a general congress. The attempt to promote the adoption of this "Solemn League and Covenant" by the Massachusetts towns was a failure.[2]

The radical effort, however, helped to promote the attitude toward a commercial boycott adopted by many moderates and conservatives[3] in the spring and summer of 1774, an attitude that fostered the consensus in favor of such a boycott that had developed by September. Rather than oppose the idea of economic coercion, they simply suggested that the specifics of any plan would best be settled by the impending Congress. In the words of one contributor to Draper's *Massachusetts Gazette* (the major "court" press in Boston), a commercial agreement could never procure "effectual Relief" for Boston unless it became "general in the other Colonies." The details of any such plan, he wrote, could be most "equitably fixed upon by the united Wisdom of the Whole Continent at the approaching Congress; to whose Determination every Measure of so great Importance ought to be submitted."[4] Similarly, attempts by South Carolina radicals to procure an immediate boycott agreement in July 1774 were frustrated by moderates, who argued that it would be more proper if South Carolina's continental delegates were to agree with their congressional colleagues upon any such agreement. One author in the *New-York Journal* even apologized to his readers for discussing a commercial boycott, since the entire question was "and solely ought to be" left to "the discretion and management of the general congress."[5]

Through the summer, the general discussion of a commercial boycott hardened into the expectation and desire that the impending Congress would draw up an agreement that would bind all the colonies. Out of a sample of ninety-three local and provincial meetings held during the summer of 1774, only 26 percent were vague in their directions to the delegates; they called upon them to adopt an unspecified plan or "wise measures" to deal with the crisis. Such terms may have implied commercial opposition, but not necessarily. By contrast, 66 percent of these resolutions specifically requested that the delegates draw up a nonimportation plan, and 50 percent called for the adoption of the far more controversial policy of nonexportation.[6] The most compelling policy demand that Americans made of the delegates to the 1774 Congress, therefore, was for the adoption of a plan of commercial opposition.

Significantly, the demand for such action becomes more imperative the higher one looks in the hierarchy of resistance institutions. Of the twelve provincial conventions or meetings of assemblies held prior to the Congress, nine indicated support for a continental commercial boycott, and one (Pennsylvania) resolved to acquiesce in such a plan if the Congress thought fit to adopt one. Moreover, two colonies actually adopted fully articulated boycott plans prior to the adoption of any continental agreement.[7] While all these plans were made subject to congressional additions and alterations, the fact remains that even had the Congress failed to agree on a continental plan, several of the larger colonies were prepared to proceed on their own, as they had done during the Townshend Acts crisis.

Perhaps the best evidence that some congressional economic boycott plan was inevitable comes from those who would be most intimately affected. Several Philadelphia merchants, for example, who had been hopeful in May that nonimportation could be avoided, were by early August predicating their business decisions on the expectation that Congress would adopt at least a nonimportation agreement. Some, of course, were patriots as well as merchants and welcomed the boycott despite the apparent harm to their immediate interests. Samuel Patterson, for example, insisted that all must "enter into the non Importation again" for "no way Else will bring them wicked Jack Asses to a Sense of their Proceedings in the Common[s]." For others, impending nonimportation was simply an unpleasant fact of business life to which they must adjust. Thomas Wharton reported in mid-August that the sentiment for nonimportation was so "strongly prevalent in most of the Colonies" that he thought it inevitable "that the Congress will be Compelled to Adopt the Measure."[8]

In the South as well, merchants and factors were taking what proved to be accurate readings on the political environment. Since it was "the Life of Business to know how things go on," one Virginian informed his London colleagues in early July that he was "clearly of opinion from the spirit and resolution of the Different Governments all Importation from you will be stopt in a short time." He also believed, moreover, that "all Exportation to you will not continue long." Another correspondent was even more definite. It was to be depended on, he wrote to his London contacts, that the Virginia Association would be adopted by the Congress, whose alterations would extend no further than changes "in respect to time when the Non Importation and Non Exportation is to take place."[9] British officialdom, too, had received accurate information from trusted sources about the strong probability of a renewed commercial boycott. Long before the Congress had met and actually adopted the Association, the administration had begun to plan its response.[10]

The expectations proved accurate. The Association, adopted by the delegates on October 20, 1774, was the culmination of the American search for a "perfect" means of resistance that had begun in 1765. Since the time of the Stamp Act boycotts, proponents of resistance had argued that commercial opposition would have been completely successful in 1765, or in 1768, if only the agreements had been continental in scope, if only the timing had been uniform, if only provisions for nonconsumption as well as nonimportation and nonexportation had been included. The Association was the result of this decade-long search; it was a commercial plan at last purged of all the mistakes and miscalculations that had plagued its predecessors. But it was also the beginning of another movement, the aim of which was not to alter British policy but to replace British authority. The structure of commercial opposition organized by the continental delegates in 1774 provided a clear authorization for new or existing local governments. The Association committees, which in some places duplicated and in others replaced existing bodies, soon became not only the new revolutionary institutions of local government but also the means by which the policies of the new continental authority were implemented at the local level.

Precedents for the Association

Although the delegates' adoption of some kind of commercial plan was probably inevitable by the time they assembled in Philadelphia, the precise form such a plan would take was not clear. The delegates did, however, have considerable experience with both private associations and economic boycotts, and this both guided and constrained their efforts to agree upon a continental commercial plan. They could and did draw, in a general way, on their familiarity with the technique of private association that had been used throughout the colonies to accomplish public goals independently of public institutions. More immediately, the delegates were all familiar with, and most had participated in, the various commercial boycott agreements that had first been adopted as a resistance technique during the Stamp Act crisis.

The American disposition to "join," or to associate privately to solve common problems, long preceded Alexis de Tocqueville's celebrated remarks on this trait in the early years of the American republic. In every colonial city, workingmen's associations, tradesmen's clubs, and private fire, hospital, and library companies were commonplace responses to perceived needs. Benjamin Franklin's organizing activities were unique only in scale, not in scope.[11]

Given the wide spectrum of Americans who were members of such private associations, it is not surprising that when the most urgent common problem appeared to be political, as it did in 1764 and 1765, the old associational bonds were transferred almost wholesale to accomplish the new political purposes. This was true at all levels of the social scale. Thus the old North and South End mobs in Boston, with their leadership and ritual structure intact, were drawn directly into the opposition to the Stamp Act. Similarly, the middle-class private fire company in Charleston became the nucleus of that city's Sons of Liberty. In like manner, the formal and informal merchants' exchanges and clubs that existed in every major seaport town provided the institutional structure in 1765 for the organization and implementation of the new resistance technique of commercial boycott.[12]

Whether the tactic of economic coercion originated in the need of some colonial merchants to reduce debts and inventories or in the more purely political motives of effecting changes in British policy is not relevant to the present inquiry.[13] For whatever reasons merchants first adopted the technique of an organized stoppage of colonial trade, by 1770 it had come to concern a much wider segment of the colonial community.

The tactic of commercial boycott had originated in 1765 as private agreements between merchants in several colonial cities. The political assumptions underlying this tactic showed the profound colonial commitment to the imperial system. By adopting this tactic, the colonial merchants (and the political groups that later came to support the policy) agreed to work within the existing British political system, in which "interests" received ample representation in Paliament even though certain political entities (like the colonies) were excluded. The theory behind the boycott was simple: By withholding colonial commerce, American merchants would indicate to their British colleagues that certain of their interests required political redress, and British merchants, who shared common economic interests with the Americans, would use their considerable influence in Westminster to secure the redress. Through the common economic interests of the Atlantic mercantile community, this theory implied, Americans could indeed be "represented" in Parliament.[14]

The realization of such theories began in late October 1765, only days before the Stamp Act was scheduled to go into effect, as merchants began to organize commercial boycott agreements. The first such agreement came in New York City, where on October 31 some two hundred merchants agreed in a general meeting to withhold future orders for British goods until the Stamp Act was repealed. A week later, more than four hundred Philadelphia merchants signed a similar agreement, and they added a significant proviso that advanced the tactic to a more sophisticated plane. Not only did the Philadelphians agree not to import British goods until repeal, but they appointed a standing committee from among their number to assure that all associating members strictly adhered to the agreement. By December, 250 Boston merchants had agreed to similar restrictions.[15]

The 1765 commercial agreements never went beyond these rather narrow, merchant-based agreements. They did not go into effect until after the arrival of the fall importations in 1765, and while they probably caused a certain decrease in the following spring's orders, the repeal of the Stamp Act in March 1766 soon removed the raison d'être of the 1765 agreements. Nevertheless, the tactic of economic coercion was not in the least discredited by the brief 1765 experience. Compared with the rioting and disorder that had characterized resistance efforts in several major towns, to middle- and upper-class Whigs the tactic appeared to be an effective and safe method of resisting future British encroachments.[16] The true test of the commercial boycott did not come in 1765, however, but rather in the period 1768 through 1770, when it became the primary colonial method of resistance to the Townshend duties of 1767. The lessons of the Townshend Acts boycotts were to influence decisively the Continental Association of 1774. Thus it is useful to sketch in a general way the patterns of resistance that emerged during the commercial boycotts of the late 1760s.

While the news of renewed British taxation evoked a variety of protest movements throughout the colonies, the major resistance efforts were soon concentrated in the nonimportation agreements adopted by merchants in the leading seaport towns. Through the late 1760s these narrow merchants' agreements expanded in two ways, socially and geographically. Political or quasi-political organizations like the Sons of Liberty, Boston's Loyal Nine, and the New York Tradesmen's Association gradually were drawn into the mercantile movement. At first they functioned as enthusiastic supporters of the merchants; later they became the ultimate enforcers of agreements that they came to believe were binding not only on the original associators but on all patriotic members of the community. As the social base of the movement widened in the North, the boycott movement also spread geographically as one by one the agricultural provinces of the South adopted their own commercial agreements.

Boston merchants began organized resistance to the Townshend duties in March 1768, when, after several meetings at their coffeehouse, they agreed not to import British manufactured goods for one year or until repeal of the duties, provided that merchants in Philadelphia and New York adopted similar agreements.[17] As the movement spread, the merchants of each town borrowed from and improved upon the earlier agreements until all the features that later came to characterize the Association in 1774 were incorporated into one or more of the local plans.

The agreement signed on August 27, 1768, by almost all the merchants and traders of New York, for example, was the first to term nonassociators "Enemies to their Country." This indicated that the associating merchants conceived of themselves as acting for their entire community and not for the commercial interests alone. Their action gained credibility a few days later when, in a significant innovation in the enforcement procedure, a group of tradesmen agreed to back the merchants' efforts by refusing to trade with any merchant so stigmatized or with one who refused to sign the agreement.[18] The Philadelphia merchants, who could not agree upon a plan until March 1769, carried the enforcement mechanism a step further. Their agreement was policed, as it had been in 1765, by a committee of the trade. But this time the names of nonassociators were to be published in the newspapers, presumably to be suitably ridiculed and boycotted, if not worse, by patriotic Philadelphians.[19]

As the movement spread into the southern colonies in 1769, important alterations in the northern pattern of commercial opposition occurred, owing mainly to the differing economic structures of the two regions.[20] In the North, the merchants were native, numerous, wealthy, and powerful. They were independent members of large urban communities, and even the more radical urban patriots conceded that matters of trade must be chiefly the concern of those with the power, interest, and expertise—that is, the merchants. Thus, although some Boston radicals attempted in 1768 to foreclose the merchants' options by circulating a short-lived nonconsumption agreement among the Massachusetts country towns, even they finally agreed that the success of any commercial boycott depended upon the willingness of the large import merchants to cancel their orders. The efforts of the patriotic nonmercantile members of the northern communities were directed, therefore, chiefly toward stiffening the resolve of the well-disposed merchants and punishing backsliders. While these tasks became increasingly important as time went on and the merchants showed growing reluctance to continue the boycotts, nevertheless the original agreements—the provisions, the exceptions, and the timing—had all been devised by the experts, that is, by the merchants.

In the South, however, a different pattern emerged. Here, mercantile leadership did not equate with political leadership. The merchants of Norfolk, of Annapolis, and of Wilmington, were largely outsiders, many of them first-generation Scots immigrants who had scarcely begun to be integrated into the planter-dominated societies.[21] Only in Charleston and to some degree in Baltimore did the pattern differ significantly, and even in such places merchants like the Laurens, whose position was solidified by wealth and years, were often planters as well. Furthermore, trading patterns were such that wealth depended primarily upon agriculture rather than commerce. In the late 1760s this meant that nonimportation (as opposed to nonexportation) agreements were more of an economic boon to debt-conscious planters, or an occasion for virtuous self-denial, than the economic sacrifice they represented to some northern traders.[22]

These general economic differences were reflected in the boycott agreements that southerners adopted in late 1769 and early 1770, which varied considerably from those adopted in the North. First, the southern agreements were generally devised by political and economic community leaders and then offered to the merchants, as to all members of the community, for their approval and participation. Thus, for example, the Virginia Non-Importation Association was drawn up in 1770 by the members of the House of Burgesses in consultation with leading merchants, who then "earnestly recommend[ed] this our association to the serious attention of all Gentlemen, merchants, traders, and other inhabitants of this colony."[23]

Second, the responsibility for enforcing the basically nonconsumption agreements adopted by the southerners was placed upon the community at large rather than the merchants. This was made clear in the enforcement mechanism the southerners chose. In drawing up their agreements, of course, the southerners benefited from the experiences of the northern cities where enforcement had, officially and unofficially, begun to include all members of the community, not just the merchants. The southern agreements, first in Maryland, then in Virginia and the two Carolinas, provided for the election of committees of inspection, whose membership would not be drawn from "the trade" but from the community at large. The members were empowered to enforce the provisions of the commercial agreements upon all who signed them.[24] These enforcement committees could not be considered governmental, for their duties were strictly limited to enforcing the terms of what were still private agreements, and their powers extended only to signers of these agreements. Nevertheless, the southern committees were clearly more akin to governmental institutions than had been the merchant-dominated committees of the trade that had initiated the policy of commercial boycott in 1765.

With the adoption of the South Carolina agreement on July 22, 1769, the high point of the Townshend Acts boycotts was reached.[25] The partial repeal of the Townshend duties in April 1770 gave the increasingly reluctant merchants an opportunity to alter or rescind the stringent agreements they had entered into, in some cases, two years previously. One by one—first in New York, then in Philadelphia, Boston, and Charleston—merchants voted to retain a boycott only upon the still-dutied commodity of tea and otherwise to resume importations.[26]

The Townshend Acts agreements ended in a welter of mutual recrimination and resentment, as merchants and politicians in each colony accused their colleagues in other provinces of bad faith. Nevertheless, one should not be misled by such accusations into a belief that the Townshend Acts experience had discredited the commercial boycott tactic. It had not done so, for several important reasons. First, commercial boycotts had proved themselves effective in damming the flow of British goods into America on an individual colony basis. In New England, for example, imports were almost halved during the 1768–1769 period, which was the heart of the agreement in that region (see Table 4-1). The achievement of the Philadelphians was even more impressive. From a total importation of over £440,000 into Pennsylvania in 1768, imports dropped to a little over £200,000 in 1769 and to barely £140,000 in 1770. New York's record was perhaps the best; for the 1768–1769 period, imports from Britain shrank from about £490,000 to

TABLE 4-1
Imports to the Colonies from Great Britain, 1766–1776
(official sterling values)

Year	New England	New York	Pennsyl- vania	Virginia and Maryland	Carolinas	Georgia	Total
1766	419,415	332,917	334,168	519,729	308,502	67,268	1,981,999
1767	416,186	423,979	383,121	652,672	268,671	23,481	2,168,110
1768	430,807	490,673	441,829	669,523	300,925	56,562	2,390,319
1769	223,694	75,931	204,979	714,943	327,084	58,340	1,604,971
1770	416,694	480,220	139,634	997,157	168,500	59,330	2,261,535
1771	1,435,837	655,150	747,469	1,223,726	442,967	71,795	4,576,944
1772	844,422	349,464	525,941	1,015,570	479,653	95,673	3,310,723
1773	543,165	295,953	435,940	589,427	380,878	67,102	2,312,465
1774	576,651	459,638	645,625	690,066	412,466	59,023	2,843,469
1775	85,114	1,469	1,366	1,921	6,780	123,705	220,355
1776	55,955	0	365	0	0	0	56,320

SOURCE: Jacob M. Price, "A New Time Series for Scotland's and Britain's Trade with the Thirteen Colonies and States, 1740 to 1791," in *WMO*, 3rd ser., 32 (1975): 325.

a little over £75,000. The record of the southern colonies was generally much poorer, but for the year in which the South Carolina agreement was in effect, the value of British imports into the two Carolinas dropped from about £327,000 to £168,000.

Clearly, the figures show a dramatic drop in the value of British manufactured goods arriving in the associating colonies. But they also point out a less comforting fact. Each colony withdrew its trade for different periods of time, and therefore through the two years the agreements were in effect, British manufacturers were never subjected to a complete stoppage of American trade. Total British exports to the colonies were never seriously diminished for any one period of time, although individual English merchants undoubtedly suffered. This experience almost guaranteed that in the future those who wished to renew a commercial boycott would try to obtain a uniform agreement that would go into effect simultaneously throughout the colonies.

Second, if the boycott tactic continued to develop as it had during these years, future agreements would be devised and executed by representatives of entire colonial communities rather than one segment of

those communities, that is, the merchants.[27] In the North, enforcement had clearly passed out of the merchants' hands by 1770. In Boston, for example, action against nonassociators was first undertaken
by mobs, by political organizations like the Loyal Nine, and ultimately
by the official town political institution, the town meeting and its appointed committees.[28] Similarly, in New York and Philadelphia various political organizations, some descendants of the old Sons of Liberty, had become the ultimate enforcers of agreements that the
merchants had originally devised.[29] In the South, the pattern was even
clearer. In the Maryland, Virginia, and North and South Carolina
agreements, community participation was institutionalized in local
enforcement committees that were, deliberately, not to be limited to
the trade. As George Mason explained, he did not see any way of enforcing nonimportation in Virginia except by "appointing Committees
in the County." While these committees might well include well-disposed merchants, the plan would not achieve the necessary respect
unless they were primarily composed of acknowledged community
leaders—"the most respectable men poss[ible]."[30] The conclusion that
a political problem of concern to all could not be solved by one segment of the community reached perhaps its most sophisticated form
in the last major Townshend Acts agreement, that of South Carolina.
There, initial efforts to organize an agreement, although led by a merchant (Christopher Gadsden), purposely excluded the merchants
from the matter on the theory that the virtuous body of mechanics and
planters must be at the heart of any strong agreement. The "Importers
of European goods," Gadsden declared, must be excluded, since most
of the merchants were "strangers, many of them of a very few years
standing in the province," whose "natural affection to the province is,
too plainly, not to be depended on."[31] In the end, the South Carolina
agreement, adopted in a general meeting on July 22, 1769, was carefully drawn up to include the entire community. The enforcement
committee, consisting of thirty-nine men, was carefully composed to
include exactly thirteen planters, thirteen merchants, and thirteen
mechanics.[32]

The widening community participation that characterized the
Townshend Acts boycotts also affected the methods for carrying out
future boycotts, particularly in placing a renewed emphasis upon nonconsumption. The Townshend Acts agreements had apparently collapsed in 1770 because the merchants, deciding that they could no
longer bear the damage to their private interest whatever the effect

upon the public, had rescinded their agreements. Realistic politicians like Samuel Adams took the merchants' decision almost philosophically. In writing to the English radical Stephen Sayre, he noted that the merchants had held to their agreements "much longer than I ever thought they would or could." It had been "a grand Tryal which pressd hard upon their private Interest."[33]

It is not surprising that to prevent such a collapse in the future, men like Adams turned to the nonconsumption provisions that had been common in the southern agreements. Nonconsumption was not now seen, as it had been in 1765, as a replacement for nonimportation but rather as a means by which patriotic communities far from the major seaports could demonstrate their support for resistance. They would supplement the nonimportation efforts of the major towns. The political virtue of the yeomanry, as Adams observed, would stiffen the resolve of wavering merchants, who would see that identification with the political goals of resistance was spread throughout the backcountry.[34]

Thus the Townshend Acts boycotts had taught politically conscious colonists several important lessons. The tactic of commercial opposition had proved effective; even in an imperfect form, it had brought about partial repeal of the Townshend duties. All that seemed to be needed to achieve total success in the future was the correction of those few faults that had led to the premature collapse of the 1768–1770 agreements. Future boycotts would be likely to take up where the Townshend Acts agreements had left off, in the direction of unanimity, simultaneity, and involvement of all segments of the colonial communities.

Congress Reaches Agreement

Given the universal calls for a renewed commercial boycott in 1774 and the abundant experience that Americans had had with the tactic, the speed and unanimity with which the congressional delegates agreed to a continental plan is not surprising. While the delegates spent time debating the specifics of their plan—primarily in reconciling the economic interests of the various colonies and in settling the details of timing and exceptions—the major points of the Continental Association occasioned little discussion.

There was no question, for example, that the 1774 plan would be continental. No one wanted a repeat of the Townshend Acts experience, in which two years had gone by before all the colonies had come into an agreement. Thus the delegates never considered the idea of merely recommending to the colonies that they adopt the form of boycott best suited to their local circumstances. Nor was there much discussion of the basic outlines of the plan. Virtually all agreed that any continental agreement would have to include the nonimportation and nonconsumption of British goods. Although there was more controversy over nonexportation, most believed that some form of nonexportation ought to be included in the continental plan. Finally, there was virtually no debate over what in hindsight appears to be the most controversial article in the Association, the provision that it was to be enforced by local committees elected in every town or county throughout the associating colonies. While questions of timing, exceptions, and geographic extent of the plan engendered considerable and occasionally acrimonious debate, never did any member seriously doubt that when the Congress broke up, the delegates would have devised a continental commercial boycott of predictable dimensions.

The first indication that the delegates expected to prepare such a plan came on the opening day of the Congress. The Grand Committee appointed on September 6 was charged not only with stating American rights and listing colonial grievances but also with finding "the means most proper to be pursued for obtaining a restoration" of American rights.[35] The third task was put aside, however, through most of September, in part because logic dictated that rights and grievances be stated before a method of seeking redress was designed, and in part because the delegates anticipated few problems in reaching an agreement upon such a plan and therefore saw no need to set aside large blocks of time to consider the subject. So certain were the delegates that a plan would be adopted that on September 22, before the subject of nonimportation was ever debated in Congress, the delegates unanimously agreed to warn merchants that as a continental nonimportation agreement was imminent, they would be well advised to stop sending any further orders for goods and to cancel any orders then being filled in Europe.[36]

The delegates formally took up the question of a commercial plan late on Saturday, September 24. Having failed to reach agreement on the troublesome problem of detailing American rights, they turned with relief to a topic upon which they expected little controversy. Such expectations were, in general, realized. The following Monday, September 26, when debate was resumed, Richard Henry Lee introduced a motion for a nonimportation agreement. By the end of the day, as Samuel Ward noted cryptically in his diary, the delegates had "agreed upon non Importation & adjourned." A resolution was delayed, however, until September 27, as the delegates wrangled with problems of extent and timing.[37] There was no question about barring goods of English and Irish manufacture, whether imported directly from the British Isles or transshipped through a West Indian or neutral port. Thomas Mifflin did suggest, however, that the political point of the Association might be sharpened if the Congress agreed to bar any item of whatever place of origin that bore a parliamentary duty stamp. Despite protests that such a provision would, as Pendleton pointed out in a later debate on the subject, "hang out to all the World our Intentions to smuggle" (for duties items like Madeira wine had been, and undoubtedly would be, imported without a customs stamp), this provision was incorporated into Article 1 of the Association.[38]

The nagging worry about providing speedy relief to Boston showed up in the debate over timing. Those who had been actively promoting immediate aid to Boston argued that nonimportation had already been delayed too long, since it had had to await the meeting of Congress. No "honest orders were sent after the first of June," Mifflin argued; as far as he was concerned, any merchant who had ordered goods after the closing of Boston's port deserved to lose those goods. He felt that November 1, the date the Virginia Association had specified for the commencement of nonimportation, was the very latest date the Congress should adopt. He was supported by Lee and Gadsden and by the worried Massachusetts delegates, whose position was summed up by Cushing. He was, he announced, "For a Non Importation, Non Exportation and Non Consumption, and immediately."[39]

The delegates wished to conciliate the merchants, however, many of whom, they knew, had ordered large supplies of English goods that would be arriving during the traditional months of the fall importations, October and November. As a gesture of this concern, Patrick Henry moved that December 1 be specified as the date to commence nonimportation. "We don't mean to hurt even our Rascalls," he explained, "if We have any." The committee appointed to draw up the association was to add tangible proof of the delegates' concern for merchant interests, as three of its five members were merchants.[40]

The delegates found it more difficult to reach agreement on nonexportation. The question was debated on September 27, after agreement had been reached on nonimportation. After a day's suspension of debate during which the delegates considered the Galloway plan, the delegates resumed discussion on September 29 of both the nonimportation of dutied goods and nonexportation. On September 30 the delegates appointed a committee balanced geographically, ideologically, and professionally to draw up a "plan for carrying into effect, the non-importation, non-consumption, and non-exportation resolved on."[41]

Nonexportation caused far greater difficulty throughout the session than nonimportation. The question was debated at various times through October and at the last moment created the sole threat of a colony walking out of the Congress. Despite agreement on the basic issues, the debate on nonexportation shows the difficulties under which the delegates labored in reconciling the political and economic necessities of twelve varied societies.

As with nonimportation, the timing of nonexportation was the key problem. The dilemma consisted of reconciling the urgent political necessities of Massachusetts with the equally important economic concerns of the southern agricultural colonies. For Massachusetts, of course, time was the most important consideration. With its major port closed and British troops in the capital, the New Englanders urgently required, as Lynch emphasized, "not only Redress, but speedy Redress." "Boston and New England cant hold out," Gadsden warned. "The Country will be deluged in Blood, if we don't Act with Spirit." Since the use of force had been ruled out for the present, commercial pressure was the method chosen to bring about this speedy redress. This being the case, nonexportation was a far more powerful weapon than nonimportation in bringing immediate distress to British merchants, since they were dependent upon the almost £2 million worth of agricultural products, primarily tobacco, that Americans exported annually to the mother country. Immediate withdrawal of these products would hit British merchants, Dyer of Connecticut predicted, "like a Thunder Clap." But delayed nonexportation would allow these merchants to make alternative arrangements. "A Non Exportation at a future day," Chase stated flatly, "cannot avail us."[42]

But Virginia, richest and most powerful of the southern colonies, indicated that a delayed nonexportation would have to do. Her delegates were adamant that the province's economic situation demanded it. Tobacco took a full year to mature; an entire crop had been planted in the spring of 1774, and it could not be harvested until 1775. Virginians were willing to sacrifice future crops, difficult as that would be, but they would not allow the 1775 crop to rot in the ground. Nonexportation would have to be delayed until the 1775 crop had been marketed in England. On this point the Virginians, following their convention's instructions, would not yield.[43] The Virginia stand drew accusations of selfishness. Other colonies, some argued, would also lose their markets, yet they seemed willing to make the sacrifice. Gadsden, perhaps carried away with his own rhetoric, suggested that the delegates agree to immediate nonexportation with or without Virginia—a possibility that was dismissed as patently absurd.[44] In the end, the will of the powerful Virginians prevailed; the Association provided that nonexportation would commence on September 10, 1775.

But the Virginia claim of economic necessity opened the door for other colonies to make similar claims, while those who had opposed Virginia attempted to secure an immediate, if partial, nonexportation of certain selected goods.[45] Both attempts caused the debate on nonexportation to continue right up to October 20, the day upon which the delegates finally adopted the Continental Association.

The most serious case of special pleading came at the end of the discussions, when on October 12 the draft Association was laid before the full Congress. The South Carolinians had watched with interest as the Virginians secured for themselves a year in which to export with impunity. They bided their time, however, awaiting the draft Association and other congressional documents. South Carolinian John Rutledge later explained that he had favored a total nonexportation, to Europe as well as to Britain, but this had been thwarted by the middle colonies, which had a thriving "flour and fish trade" with Europe. But under prevailing trade laws South Carolina's staples, rice and indigo, were "enumerated commodities" and could be legally exported only to Britain. He waited until the end of the session to plead South Carolina's case, however, because had Congress agreed in the declaration of colonial rights to deny Parliament's authority to regulate colonial trade, South Carolina could, with ostensible continental backing, attempt to market their crops in Europe. But Congress did not deny Parliament's authority over colonial trade, and thus the Carolinians insisted that an exception for their products be written into the

Association. When their colleagues demurred, they walked out. To preserve unanimity, although clearly unhappy about contravening, even by implication, the Navigation Acts, the delegates gave in to part of the South Carolina demand. They amended Article IV of the Association (which mandated a general nonexportation to Great Britain) to allow South Carolina to export rice, but not indigo, to Europe.[46]

By thus securing South Carolina's agreement, no further obstacles remained to the "unanimous" approval of the Continental Association on October 20.[47] The delegates clearly modeled their Association on the Virginia Association of August 1774, which in turn had been taken largely from the resolves of Fairfax County, Virginia. The Virginians, not surprisingly, had drawn heavily upon their own experiences during the Townshend Acts boycott. The Continental Association, then, was a lineal descendant of the southern pattern of the Townshend Acts agreements.[48]

The Association was a relatively short document containing fourteen articles. While all were adopted with care and each has considerable significance, of primary concern here are those clauses that specified the enforcement mechanism of the continental boycott.[49] The Association marked the culmination of the entire colonial nonimportation movement; all the perceived faults of previous agreements were rectified, all the problems of enforcement were apparently solved. The provisions for nonimportation and nonexportation were to go into effect simultaneously throughout the colonies (Articles I and II), and enforcement was to be in the hands of local committees, the members of which were to be elected by enfranchised citizens from among the most respectable members of their communities (Article XI).[50] These local Association committees survived far longer than the commercial boycott they were organized to implement. But the delegates who devised the program were not thinking in terms of creating new institutions. They were primarily concerned with the immediate effectiveness of the commercial program they had devised.

Effectiveness of the Association

Despite the revolutionary potential of Article XI of the Association, many delegates hoped that the agreement would have such an immediate effect upon British merchants that its domestic political implications would never be realized. Benjamin Franklin, writing from London, was a major source of optimism; he wrote letter after letter assuring his correspondents that a continental commercial boycott, faithfully adhered to, would bring down the ministry and secure redress from its successor. On the basis of such reports, Richard Henry Lee confidently predicted that "the same Ship which carried home [the Association] . . . will bring back the Redress." Even the prudent merchant Samuel Patterson of Philadelphia was willing to "Stake [his] Life" that "a non Importation will do in 12 months."[51] Fortunately for him, Patterson made no such wager. By the end of 1774, changes in both British public and official opinion doomed colonial hopes of influencing British policy through commercial pressure. Thus the Association must be regarded as a strategic failure in the sense that it did not succeed in securing its major objective—alterations in British policy. As a tactical matter, however, the Association was the most successful instrument of economic coercion that the colonists managed to devise. The nonimportation provisions of the 1774 agreement were far more successful than those of any preceding plan (see Table 4-1). In all twelve associating colonies, with the exception of Massachusetts, imports from Britain dropped in 1775 to a fraction of the 1774 totals. These figures confirm the perception of many Whigs in early 1775 that the Continental Association was enthusiastically welcomed throughout the colonies and its terms generally adhered to.[52]

One must judge the immediate effectiveness of the Association on its nonimportation, rather than its nonexportation, provisions. Since nonexportation was not scheduled to go into effect until late 1775, by which time the outbreak of war and the British blockade caused greater alterations of trading patterns than did the Association, nonexportation as conceived by the 1774 delegates was never really attempted. The figures on gross exports in 1775 (Table 4-2) indicate that they were not much affected by the impending ban, although individual merchants undoubtedly altered their plans to take advantage of expected scarcities in areas like the West Indies.

The wider economic effects on both Britain and America of such a dramatic trade disruption as that brought about by the Association must have been considerable. An assessment of these effects is, however, beyond the scope of this study. To give a true picture of the effect of the 1774 boycott even on the colonies, one would have to integrate new information about colonial trade patterns with institutional studies of a variety of colonial mercantile firms. Certainly, for example, the

TABLE 4-2

Exports from the Colonies to Great Britain, 1766–1776 (official sterling value)

Year	New England	New York	Pennsyl-vania	Virginia and Maryland	Carolinas	Georgia	Total
1773	132,078	78,550	36,652	1,055,278	484,662	99,963	1,887,183
1774	123,798	83,480	69,611	1,037,672	464,682	67,673	1,846,916
1775	128,175	196,222	176,720	1,247,041	605,427	103,477	2,457,062
1776	762	2,318	1,421	155,004	13,742	12,569	185,816

SOURCE: Jacob M. Price, "A New Time Series for Scotland's and Britain's Trade with the Thirteen Colonies and States, 1740 to 1791," in *WMQ*, 3rd ser., 32 (1975): 323.

impact of a stoppage would be vastly different upon a northern merchant specializing in grain exports than upon one whose business depended on dry-goods imports, and both would have interests at variance with those of a southern colleague who dealt exclusively in the West Indian or tobacco trade.[53] In like manner, the precise economic effects of the nonconsumption provisions of the Association cannot be determined without such detailed analysis. One can suggest, however, in general terms, that judging from the vain attempts of the Association committees to combat violations of the price-fixing provision of the Association (Article XIII), prices of British imported goods probably rose rapidly after 1774. If rising prices can be taken as a sign of higher demand, it appears that the nonconsumption clauses of the 1774 agreement were not having their intended effect.[54]

One important factor contributing to the tactical success of the Association was the ability of the delegates to secure for their plan the acquiescence of many importing merchants. While this adherence was to some degree secured by coercion from the enforcement committees, many merchants supported the boycott freely. It is difficult to generalize about the reasons for such support, because they varied from colony to colony according to the nature of the trade and prevailing economic conditions. Nevertheless, Egnal and Ernst offer persuasive explanations for the discontent of many large merchants in the major port cities with the imperial economic system. In their view, the period between 1745 and 1775 was one of rapid economic expansion, causing strain and a divergence of economic interests between colonial mer-

chants and important economic interests in Britain. As British manufacturing expanded, so did the desire for increased colonial markets.
Large merchandising houses in the colonies were induced by new financing methods to import ever-increasing amounts of British goods,
amounts they could never hope to sell at a profit. As a result, colonial
debts to British holders of colonial commercial paper mounted. At the
same time, the bitterness of many large colonial houses was increased
by the new trading practice of "dumping," by which British manufacturers bypassed established colonial importing firms to ship their
goods to the colonies for sale by public auction directly to retailers.
Their discontent was exacerbated by disastrous British currency legislation that artificially contracted the colonial money supply just as
merchants scrambled for the means to repay their British creditors.
This caused the merchants, in turn, to call in their own debts within
the colonies, thus worsening the currency shortage while at the same
time contracting the domestic market for unsold British goods. Finally,
colonial attempts to turn to domestic manufactures as a means of al-
leviating the currency shortage and generating an internal market
were thwarted by imperial regulations restricting such manufactures.
The economic problem was magnified by the deep depression of the
early 1770s, which, according to Egnal and Ernst, may well have been
the worst of the colonial period. As a result, they conclude, many merchants had sound economic reasons for seeking greater autonomy, or
"economic sovereignty" with respect to the British imperial system.
The Congress and its Association may have appeared to be the means
by which this could be brought about.[55]

The sheer number of prominent merchants who were zealous adherents of the resistance movement and of the Revolution would tend
in an intuitive way to support this thesis, even apart from the impressive evidence marshaled by Egnal and Ernst to support their view.[56]
Whether because economic self-interest demanded participation in
the resistance movement or because many in the trade were committed Whigs as well as merchants, the fact remains that merchants were
second only to lawyers (and in the South, planters) in the number of
members they provided to the major resistance organizations.[57]

For whatever reasons, the pattern of behavior displayed by many
merchants in the years prior to 1774 had been consistent. Except for a
very short period of control in the earliest days of the commercial boycott movement, merchants had been content to participate in, but not

necessarily to control, a movement that coincided with their economic interests and, for many, their political beliefs. The growing British practice of dumping surplus manufactured goods and flooding the major colonial markets increased the incentive of merchants in the larger northern towns to participate in the nonimportation movements, which seemed to be the most feasible means not only of securing short-term relief from such practices but also of achieving their long-range goal of greater economic autonomy.[58]

It is not surprising, therefore, that many merchants continued to support economic coercion in 1774, especially as responsibility for the boycott movement had passed into the hands of a new continental authority composed of the most respectable men in the colonies. Whether this predisposition of many merchants to cooperate with resistance would continue after 1774 would depend on the apparent reasonableness and prudence of the delegates in considering their immediate economic interests while at the same time working toward the major political and economic reorganization of the British empire that for many merchants, as for other Americans, had long been the goal of resistance. In addition, the merchants' disposition to support the boycott, like that of other Americans of a moderate disposition, depended on the apparent ability of the new institutions to foster political order, the threat to which many viewed as the major deterrent to wholehearted participation in resistance.[59]

The concern of the delegates to draw up a reasonable commercial agreement had been evident early on. Although the full Congress voted on the basic outlines of a commercial plan, it was left to a committee of experts—merchants and planters from the most interested provinces—to draw up the details of the plan.[60] Certainly the full Congress itself had demonstrated its own concern for the immediate interests of merchants by deliberately choosing the date for the commencement of nonimportation to allow importing merchants to receive the last of their fall orders.

The fall importations were of considerable importance to many importing merchants, whatever their political views. Whether economically prudent or not (given the large stocks of English goods already in America), the fact remains that many importers had attempted to take advantage of the delayed inception of nonimportation by ordering large new supplies from England. These increased orders, along with speculative British cargoes, caused a large number of ships to set sail from Britain bound for America in the late summer of 1774. In August a Bristol merchant informed an American colleague that it would be hard to fill his order, since the number of ships loading cargoes for America "makes Freights very Scarce." Around the beginning of September, the goods began arriving in America, and the heavy arrivals continued through the fall. In late September, one congressional delegate informed his merchant brother that "every Body say[s] half the Quantity of Dry Goods never was before imported, as now are, and likely to be this fall."[61]

The causes of this increased importation are various. A business recovery from the severe depression of the early 1770s and the continued British practice of sending large orders to America on easy credit, or on speculation, certainly were among them. But the fact remains that many American merchants swelled this flow of importations with inflated orders of their own, orders that they were anxious to receive. The deliberate delay in the inception of nonimportation, along with the large supply of stocks on hand, allowed many merchants to secure a sufficient stock of British goods to enable them to carry on their business almost unaffected by the boycott for at least a year after nonimportation began.[62] This only applied to those merchants (undoubtedly the bulk of those involved in the trade) whose goods arrived prior to December 1. In fact, only a mishap at sea or an unusually late order could have resulted in a fall shipment arriving after December 1.[63] But the delegates, anxious to preserve unity by keeping within the Whig ranks as many of the merchants who were moderates as possible, made reasonable provision even for latecomers.

The terms of this provision appear harsh at first glance. Article x of the Association provided that cargoes arriving after December 1, 1774, but before February 1, 1775, were either to be reshipped or sold at public auction by the local Association committee, the choice to be made by the owner of the goods. The proceeds of the sale were to aid the "poor inhabitants of the town of Boston." One hopes that Boston's poor did not have to depend upon such profits, for the pickings would have been slim indeed. In fact, Article x effectively delayed the inception of nonimportation until February 1, 1775. In colony after colony, the practice developed of the owners of late-arriving cargoes buying their goods back at auction for exactly the price they had paid for them. No one bid against the owners, apparently with the collusion of the local committee, and thus the only extra charge paid by the owners was the 1 percent auctioneer's fee. If the importer or the committee felt patriotic, a further 1 percent might be added for Boston's poor. Thus, in a typical sale in Wilmington, North Carolina, five importers, whose cargoes were valued at £5464 3½d. "bought" back their goods for £5464 2s. 1d., which meant that if there were no other charges, Boston's poor would have received the munificent sum of 1s. 9½d.[64]

Despite the failure of the Association to achieve its major objective of securing a change in British policy, most Whigs judged the Association to be a success. As they had hoped, it had eliminated the technical problems that had plagued past boycotts. Moreover, since Whigs throughout the colonies enthusiastically complied with the provisions of the improved boycott, for a few months in 1775 the Association brought about an unprecedented stoppage of British goods into the twelve associating colonies. Furthermore, in drawing up the provisions for implementing the continental boycott, the delegates had shown themselves to be prudent, moderate men who were anxious to conciliate as much as possible such important groups within the colonial polity as the merchants. They had begun to prove themselves to be worthy governors.

Political Ramifications of the Association

In the long run, the economic consequences of the Association proved to be far less important than its political consequences. Although in drawing up the agreement the delegates had drawn entirely upon past plans, in the circumstances of 1774 the system they devised was to become something entirely new. The Association committees did not become, as the delegates had hoped, the framework for an efficient system of economic coercion. Rather, the committees formed the nuclei of a new system of government in which the Congress authorized the creation of these local representative institutions, which in turn became reliable instruments for garnering local support for continental policy and then for implementing continental policy at the local level. The Association, the culmination of the resistance movement, thus also marked the beginning of the Revolution. The new Association committees drew their authority jointly from the people who elected the members and from the Congress that had authorized them. They were the beginning of a new structure of local political authority that was entirely independent of royal authority.

It is not surprising that radicals welcomed these developments. Many of them realized, at some point after 1774, that the continuation of the struggle against Britain would require an independent structure of political authority. The erection of such a system thus became their goal from an early day. Their adherence to the system devised by the Congress, therefore, requires little explanation. Even had they been dissatisfied with some aspects of congressional policy (as some were), they could not allow such qualms to surface since they had no realistic alternative but to support the Congress.[65] But further discussion is merited of the ability of this illegal and potentially revolutionary body to secure and keep the support of many moderates and conservatives—who could have continued, as many did, a reluctant allegiance to Britain—because this factor permanently affected the composition of the revolutionary polity.

When the proceedings of the Congress were published in late October 1774, Whigs throughout the continent received the results with great enthusiasm. "God bless the Congress," exclaimed one future North Carolina delegate. "Surely they were inspired!"[66] Perhaps more important for the future authority of the Congress, the major request for action that the delegates had issued—namely, that localities elect Association committees—met with remarkable compliance. Between November 1774 and January 1775 newspapers in every colony were full of announcements of local committee elections. Such notices were usually couched in extravagant terms, emphasizing the local body's dependence upon the Congress for authorization and guidance. In James City County, Virginia, for example, the newly elected committee promised "that the resolutions of the GENERAL CONGRESS should be resorted to on every occasion of difficulty, and that those resolutions ought to be considered by the committee, and the whole country, as the *sole rule of their conduct.*" By January, one merchant reported, committees had been chosen throughout Virginia, and they had universally promised to "conform themselves exactly agreeable to the laws of our Congress."[67] Compliance with the congressional mandate also extended to the reauthorization of many existing committees that had been elected during the spring and summer of 1774. As the committee of Chester County, Pennsylvania, explained, since the Congress had recommended the appointment of local committees to carry out the terms of their "well concerted plan . . . for the preservation of their dearest RIGHTS and LIBERTIES," they had determined to resign their places and call for the election of a new committee on the basis of the new grant of authority.[68]

The widespread election of Association committees wrought great changes in the colonial political scene. The immediate result, lauded by adherents of economic coercion, was to expand participation in active resistance activity into areas never before directly involved in the movement. "The Multiplication of Committees *out* of the Sea-Ports, to see the Execution of the Resolutions of the General Congress," wrote a Massachusetts man, "gives a finishing Damp to the Spirits of Messrs the Importers."[69] But the expansion had a far greater political effect than this. The election of local enforcement committees greatly increased the number of colonists who were actively involved with resistance. A recent study estimates that the process of local committee elections brought fully 7,000 Americans into positions of local resistance leadership.[70] When that number is multiplied by the number of colonists who expressed active support for the movement either by participating in local elections or later by signing copies of the Association, the dimensions of the political mobilization represented by the committee elections become clear. Yet, at the same time that active participation in the movement was thus expanded numerically and geographically, it was simultaneously contracted. As opposed to the "freeholders and other inhabitants" who had participated in the meetings to elect delegates to the provincial conventions in the summer of 1774, the Congress limited the franchise for Association committee elections to those electors already qualified to vote for members of the provincial legislatures.[71] The 1774 delegates neither contemplated nor countenanced an expansion of the social base of resistance in the committee election process.

Furthermore, the Association defined the limits of the authority of each local committee. The enforcement powers of the local committees were clearly limited by Article XI. They were "attentively to observe the conduct of all persons touching this association," and if a majority found a violation, they were to "cause the truth of the case to be published in the gazette," whereupon all patriots were directed to "break off all dealings with him or her." Far from chafing under these restrictions, the new committees proudly announced their willingness to conform exactly to the congressional mandate in every particular. The committee of Richmond, Virginia, unanimously resolved, that since "the assuming to ourselves unlimited power in our proceedings may be in the end dangerous to and subversive of, the just rights and privileges of our electors, that we will therefore confine ourselves literally within the line of duty marked out to us by the Continental Congress." Such pledges were brought home to committees by constituents dissatisfied with their committeemen's behavior. A Maryland man, for example, asked pointedly whether a particular action of the Anne Arundel County committee had been "warranted by any thing established by the continental congress."[72]

The question remains as to why the community leaders who, especially outside of the large port towns, took their places on many of the local boards, should have chosen to submit to restrictions from a new continental institution of dubious legality.[73] One obvious answer to this, as has been noted, is that since 1765 many of these men had agreed on the efficacy of commercial boycotts to bring about desired changes in British policy, and, for many of them, their economic interest coincided with their choice of political strategy. In addition, in the troubled situation of 1774, many sober men saw the renewal of a boycott as the only alternative to war.[74] But these local leaders may also have seen in the Association a means for ensuring that resistance would continue to be orderly, both in areas like New England, with its long experience with the movement, and in areas newer to resistance, where they feared disorder would break out.

The political disruption of the continent after the arrival of the news of the Port Bill had been both welcomed and feared by moderates. Of course, they welcomed the feverish round of meetings and resolutions as evidence of widespread support for Boston and a general detestation of British coercive measures. Moderates were, on the whole, proud of the remarkable degree of order that the New Englanders had preserved under the severest provocations. The long tradition of local autonomy and the early institutionalization of resistance had contributed to a situation in which, as the *Boston-Gazette* often noted, every care was taken by local leaders for the protection of life and property.[75] Despite complaints by Tories that in 1774 Massachusetts had dissolved into anarchy,[76] even the most violent of the measures undertaken by the infuriated Whigs—securing the resignations of the mandamus councilors, for example, or closing the Berkshire County Court—were accomplished with minimal destruction of property and no loss of life.[77] Clearly, the established institutions (the town meetings and committees of correspondence) demonstrated throughout 1774 their concern for curbing disorder while pursuing resistance.

Despite these efforts, however, disturbing signs had emerged that gave reason for reflection among colonial moderates, steeped as they were in Whig warnings of man's probable behavior in the absence of restraint by a government. Though he thought "the Experiment Must be tryed," even John Adams worried how long men, even men as virtuous as his fellow New Englanders, could continue to display such self-control in the absence of government. In Connecticut, a series of particularly violent mobbings of Anglican clergymen caused a good deal of soul-searching among leading Whigs as to the possible direction of the resistance movement. Simon Deane, brother of continental delegate Silas Deane, wrote that "for my own part [I am] very sorry to see so much petty mobbing and disorder." "Mr. Deane, for Gracious sake tell me what is your opinion of these times," pleaded fellow delegate Titus Hosmer, "should Mobism take place instead of good Government among ourselves?" In Philadelphia, even those merchants who supported the Congress urged correspondents to keep their letters close at hand, as "the temper of the people is such that misconstructions are put on the most innocent expressions" by "those who call themselves the Assertors of American Freedom."[78]

Even the new committeemen were not immune. In several as yet minor and scattered incidents, they saw their authority challenged by the very people who were, after all, the source of their power. Such challenges were experienced first in Massachusetts, where local committees of correspondence had been established in 1773. In Marblehead, for example, after the local committee had supported the building of a smallpox inoculation hospital, a mob of angry townsmen burned it down. The committee, apprehensive of similar mob action in the future, "resolved no more to act." Samuel Adams quickly wrote to Elbridge Gerry of the Marblehead committee in order to smooth over the affair, and the members began to meet again. In York (in what is now Maine) after the arrival of some suspect tea, the town committee ordered it stored "till further discovery could be made." But the following evening a number of "Packwacket Indians" broke into the store and destroyed the tea, despite the committee's injunctions to the contrary.[79]

Threats to committee authority began to trouble the new boards in the middle colonies as well. Through the summer of 1774, the New York Committee of Fifty-One was forced to defend its authority against radicals who claimed that their activities were as legitimate as those of the committee, since they were equally countenanced by the people. The Philadelphia mechanics, disturbed at what they considered the dilatory tactics of their Committee of Forty-Three, informed John Dickinson that "the People begin to assemble in companies to consult what they ought to do." If the committee continued in its present course, they warned "it will certainly produce a Riot."[80]

Even in the South, where committee membership often coincided with established political leadership, there were disturbing incidents. The committee of Gloucester County, Virginia, faced a situation with a tea shipment that was similar to that faced by the committee of York. The committee resolved to consult the burgesses at Williamsburg about the proper course of action. But before the legislators could give their advice, the tea was "hoisted . . . out of the hold" and thrown into the river.[81]

Perhaps the most famous example of a challenge to local committee leadership came in Annapolis, Maryland, in late October 1774, when the ship *Peggy Stuart* was burned. The Anne Arundel committee had decided, upon learning that the owners of the ship had imported tea in the *Peggy Stuart*, that the offending weed should be removed from the vessel and burned. Radicals, however, led by the Hammond brothers, insisted that a mass meeting be called to decide the issue. Cued by town radicals, enraged countrymen flooded into Annapolis for the meeting. Although they constituted only a quarter of the crowd, by threatening to tear down the owner's house and store they frightened the merchant into "voluntarily agreeing" to burn "the vessel and the tea in her." As an English official recorded the event, the moderates on the committee had been willing to accept the owner's recantation and the destruction of the tea alone, but the "frantic zealots among the multitude" had "pushed matters to extremities." Far from voluntarily burning the ship, as the Whig *Maryland Gazette* reported, the owner "destroyed property of great value to prevent worse consequences."[82]

Thus, in the midst of the satisfaction caused by the patriotic upsurge of resistance activity in the summer and fall of 1774, and the pride in the political virtue demonstrated by Americans in the absence of government, there were also disturbing signs of the disorder that Whig theory warned would be the result of too long an absence of governmental restraint. If the situation had thus far given cause for mutual self-congratulation, no prudent man would wish it to continue one hour longer than was absolutely necessary. The dilemma (whether real or imagined) was resolved by Article xi of the Association. The authority of the local committees was no longer solely dependent upon those who had elected the members. Henceforth, the committeemen would derive their authority not only from their constituents but also from a second source.[83] Congressional authority was legitimate because it was derived from the people, but it was superior to the wishes of the various localities since the Congress spoke for the constituents of all the delegates. It was the new "sovereign representative" of *all* the people, and thus the articulator and arbiter of the common good.

This may help explain the alacrity with which the local committees placed themselves under continental authority, and the exaggerated loyalty they expressed toward the new continental institution. Some of the new Association committees proceeded to use their new authority to reassert firm control and quell tendencies toward irregularity and disorder. The committee of Hanover, New Jersey, for example, could add to the customary injunction to "discourage all unlawful, tumultuous, and disorderly meetings of the people" and to "prevent any violence offered to the person or property of any one," that such action was mandated by their sworn duty to "comply with, and enforce every article of the Association of the General Continental Congress." Similarly, the York County Congress in Maine, perhaps reflecting upon past problems, resolved that "Riots, Disorders or Tumults" were "in their nature and tendency subversive of all civil government" and "destructive to the . . . present plan proposed and recommended by the Continental Congress for our deliverance." The members thus ordered that no violence or damage be done to the person or property of anyone, and that information regarding offenders should be promptly delivered to the committee so that punishment might proceed according to the "mode established by the Continental Congress."[84]

The Association, by specifically defining the limits of permissible resistance activity, gave moderates a yardstick against which perceived excesses could be measured and condemned. Thus the Maryland Convention "earnestly recommended" in December 1774, "that no persons, except members of the committees, undertake to meddle with or determine any question respecting the construction of the association entered into by the Continental Congress." The New York Provincial Congress (which took the place of a local committee for New York City) resolved in June 1775, "That whensoever doubts shall arise, with respect to the . . . Resolutions of the Continental Congress, . . . in the minds of private persons, it is the duty of such persons, to apply to this Board for an explanation, thereof." The New Yorkers condemned "any attempts to raise tumults, riots, or mobs, . . . under colour of a dubious interpretation of such . . . Resolutions" as "a high infraction of the General Association."[85]

Ironically, even local Tories benefited from the establishment of the new structure of authority. They thenceforth had an authority—the Continental Congress and its Association—that was higher than their local enemies and to which they could and did appeal when faced with threats of immediate local action. A Virginia "Associator," for example, queried whether the price fixing of his local committee was not "a stretch of power in a committee, and contrary to the sense of the ninth article of the general association?" Similarly, a Maryland man acknowledged that he had violated a clause of the provincial association but pleaded his case on the ground that "he had not thereby violated the Continental Association," to which he proposed to adhere. He could not be condemned, he believed, since the continental articles were "superior" to those of the Provincial Convention, "which . . . was only intended to carry the Resolves of the Continental Congress into execution." And when a committee in North Carolina condemned a man for not signing a copy of the Association, he pointedly replied that since "the resolves of the Congress did not command a signing of the association," the committee had no authority to condemn him for not doing so.[86]

The establishment of the local committees proved to be the most revolutionary act authorized by the First Congress, if by revolutionary we mean instrumental in supplanting British institutions in the colonies. The committees, so careful in 1774 to keep strictly within the limits of the Association, soon became the new local governments and executors of continental policy at the local level. As the war expanded the functions of the Congress, so too the powers of the local committees were stretched. They became local recruitment offices, promoters of local manufactures, jailors of prisoners of war, gatherers of ordinance and supplies, local loyalty boards, and agents for trapping spies and eliciting information.[87] The committees were soon to become so powerful that Tories equated their power with the worst of tyrannies.[88] But this growth of power was unforeseen in 1774 when the committees were still Association committees, and thus limited in function and authority. The expansion of committee authority was due to the same event that swelled congressional authority and changed the continental institution decisively from a resistance organization into a government—the coming of the war.

CHAPTER 5

Congress and Protection

People here almost universally agree with you. . . . They say that Names do not alter the Nature of Things: that the Moment we determin'd to defend ourselves, by arms against the most injurious Violence of Britain we declar'd for Independence. . . . They say, that this defensive War on the Part of the Colonies was enter'd into & has been supported under the Countenance & Encouragement of the Continental Congress—that the People . . . relied on the Wisdom & Magnanimity of that Assembly, and the Confidence they saw ev'ry Where so justly placed in it.
—Samuel Cooper, April 18, 1776

The mood in the Second Continental Congress was somber as it assembled in Philadelphia in May 1775. The First Congress had broken up only seven months previously, and the delegates had left Philadelphia with high hopes for the success of their conciliatory efforts. Many of the same men returned to Philadelphia with those hopes dashed. King and Parliament had contemptuously tossed aside the 1774 petition to the king, and the Association had been construed as rebellion. Most alarming of all, any possibility of conciliation appeared to have been ended by the outbreak of hostilities at Lexington and Concord in April 1775.

The news of Lexington and Concord had led to military preparations not only in Massachusetts but throughout the colonies. Many of the provinces had requested that the Congress supervise their military and naval efforts and direct them for the common defense. The Massachusetts request that Congress assume the command of the troops before Boston was the most important instance of a general disposition to refer all military matters to the delegates in Philadelphia. By June 1775, Congress had yielded to the general demand and accepted the responsibility for the Massachusetts army, which thenceforth became the Continental Army. By the following fall the delegates had authorized, with more reluctance, the creation of a continental navy. The appointment of Virginia's George Washington to command the New England troops symbolized congressional acceptance of the old royal responsibility for protecting the continent. Even a cursory glance at the official congressional journals between 1775 and 1776 indicates that no issue, not even independence, occupied the delegates more constantly than carrying out this function. Raising troops; providing for them; paying them; appointing officers; commissioning, manning, and provisioning ships—these were the matters upon which the delegates lavished their time and effort. The policies they adopted provide excellent evidence of the direction in which they hoped to move the new continental institution. Unlike the situation in 1774, the delegates were rarely guided by overwhelming public sentiment in their deliberations over military affairs. In 1775 their constituents demanded only that the Congress undertake the responsibility for protecting the continent; in few instances did they specify how this could best be accomplished.

This lack of constraint allowed the delegates to follow personal preferences and the guidance of provincial political leaders. Perhaps as a result, serious sectional and philosophical divisions surfaced in Congress over military policy, reflecting deep differences over political and social goals. From the beginning a majority of delegates supported Washington's conservative military views, and the Continental army was shaped accordingly in the image of the British army.

Naval affairs occupied far less of the delegates' time than did army matters, and indeed the navy as an institution carried far less ideological baggage than did the army. In some senses, congressional assumption of responsibility for naval affairs is therefore quite straightforward: The delegates were at first reluctant to accept the responsibility thrust upon them with increasing urgency by provinces threatened by British seapower. When, however, economic need, military necessity, and fears of social dislocation at last moved the delegates to act, they created a navy that, as an institution, differed little from their army. The Continental Navy, like the army, was modeled directly upon the British navy.

The Army

On the morning of June 23, 1775, George Washington, former Virginia delegate to the Continental Congress, left Philadelphia and hastened north toward Boston.[1] His proper title was now General Washington, for on June 16 his fellow delegates had appointed him commander-in-chief of the new Continental Army.[2] The lofty title contrasted sharply with the desperate reality of his situation. The "army" that Washington was to command consisted of a body of untrained and ill-equipped New Englanders raised by the Massachusetts Provincial Congress after Lexington and Concord. This army had taken up positions surrounding Boston, which housed almost 10,000 of His Majesty's best troops. The situation was explosive, and the new commander rushed toward the beleaguered town, praying that nothing would happen before he arrived. Washington's emotions were mixed as he made hasty preparations to leave Philadelphia and his civilian status. "I am Imbarked on a wide Ocean," he wrote on the eve of his departure, "boundless in its prospect, and from whence, perhaps, no safe harbour is to be found."[3]

The shift of the Massachusetts Army from provincial to continental control not only altered the chain of command but also changed the philosophy that had hitherto guided military affairs. Whig[4] theoreticians had long contended that principled citizens, not regular soldiers, were the only proper defenders of liberty. The Massachusetts Army was impermanent, egalitarian, and governed only by such rules as were suitable for free men. While not a militia, as an institution it conformed closely to Whig military ideals. Washington's earliest correspondence from Cambridge, however, clearly indicated his reservations about the Massachusetts Army. His military philosophy, shaped by his earlier career and his social predilections, was conservative[5] and conventional; he could see no way to fight the British regular army except with an American force organized along similar lines. Through the early years of the war, Washington was consistently supported by a majority of congressional delegates, who were ultimately responsible for converting his preferences into reality.

Yet alternatives were available. Whig writings, of course, presented a coherent theory of a military structure widely at variance with the regular army Washington envisioned. In reality, a force that embodied Whig military ideals lay encamped around Boston in 1775, having just proved its mettle during the siege of Boston and at Bunker Hill. Eminent military men, like General Charles Lee, urged Congress and its commander to draw upon these successful experiences as guides for future American military endeavors. Perceptive English officers worried that such advice would be followed, for they realized they had no way of combatting such tactics. But Washington and his congressional supporters never seriously considered such alternatives in their efforts to shape American military policy after June 1775.

Although no wartime army could be a true "standing army," which by definition is a permanent peacetime force, Washington and his congressional supporters worked tirelessly from 1775 to turn the citizen army that had been bequeathed to them into a regular army that embodied the social hierarchy and separation from civilian life and values that characterized that Whig anathema, the "standing army." Only such a force, they believed, could save American liberties. The delegates' military philosophy, like that of Washington, mirrored and reflected their views on civil society. As Shy has noted, the "conventional" military policy they chose to follow was one factor that prevented the Revolution from turning "sharply leftward."[6]

The Citizen Army

When the Congress assumed the duty of protection in June 1775, the citizen army was at the height of its prestige. On June 17, 1775, as Washington rode through New York and Connecticut to take up his command, the Massachusetts Army was fighting the British almost to a standstill at Bunker Hill. Though the ground was ultimately gained by the British, the New Englanders had exacted such a price for it that one English general concluded that another such "dear bought victory" would have "ruined us." The British, showing their contempt for American military skill, had chosen a frontal assault on the hill. The strategy cost them 1,054 casualties to the Americans' 441. Perhaps more important, the redcoats sustained a casualty rate of 53 percent. As one English official observed upon hearing this news, "We certainly [were] victorious in this Engagement, . . . but if we have eight more such victories there will be nobody left to bring the news of them." General Thomas Gage's bitter report of the battle attests to the skill and determination of the untrained Americans. "These People shew a Spirit and Conduct against us," he wrote, that "they never shewed against the French."[7]

The troops who fought the British regulars to a standstill at Bunker Hill constituted a true citizen army. Whig theorists had written extensively about the proper organization of the military in a free society. It was not surprising, therefore, that the American forces raised to defend Whig concepts of liberty should have been modeled on Whig military ideals.

English Whigs, with long memories of Cromwell and fresher ones of James II, had developed a considerable body of literature that emphasized the danger to liberty of a "standing army." As two of the most eminent Whig writers asserted at the end of the seventeenth century, "If we look through the World, we shall find in no Country, Liberty and an Army stand together."[8] Legitimate defense requirements, these Whigs insisted, could best be satisfied by a "citizen army," or militia. The militia system had been formally established in England in 1285. Thenceforth, generations of Englishmen professed to believe that in war a well-regulated militia would perform as well as a regular army and in peace would be far less of a threat to liberty.[9]

The militia, Whigs theorized, would make up in bravery and zeal what it lacked in formal training. Its ranks were to be filled by citizen soldiers—hardy yeoman who "thought themselves sufficiently paid by repelling Invaders; that they might with freedom return to their affairs." Ideally, the citizen soldier would be a landowner whose respect for private property would curb the soldierly instinct for plunder. Because the citizen soldier was a man of substance, he would have no incentive to follow the schemes of ambitious superiors to subvert the constitution. And because the militiaman had strong family ties in the community, he would have no incentive to linger in arms and every motive to rush home to his family and his land. Liberty would be safe, Whigs contended, with such defenders.[10]

Americans shared the traditional English hatred of standing armies and the accompanying faith in the militia.[11] Seventeenth-century Americans had imported the militia along with the other English institutions upon which they based their society and government. Certain characteristics were common to militia organization in all the colonies. Though the officers were formally commissioned by the governors, most units elected their own subalterns. Militia units were paid for exercise days as well as for days spent in actual service. These companies were rarely engaged in extended campaigns; the citizen soldier's service time was usually computed in days or weeks, and it was a rare expedition that took him far from home. On the exceptional occasions when militia units were needed for extended periods of time, bounties were paid to encourage reenlistment, especially in New England. And, because niggardly pay would not attract the sons of comfortable yeomen, militia pay rates for the lower ranks generally far exceeded those paid in the British army.[12]

In the seventeenth century the colonial militia met certain urgent defense needs by providing protection against Indian attack and serving as a first line of defense against the French and Dutch. But in the eighteenth century its function changed. The colonial forces that served as auxiliaries to the British regular troops in the eighteenth-century wars with France were usually specially recruited "marching forces" raised from the same segments of the population and governed and paid in much the same way as the regular army troops. The purpose of the militia was therefore no longer primarily to provide external defense but rather to maintain internal order. In most colonies, the militia could be mustered, in conjunction with the *posse comitatus*, to quell civil disorder. This was of course only possible where the disorder did not reflect widespread popular discontent, for in such cases the militiamen were likely to be part of the problem and thus unable to serve as a solution. In the South, however, where the white population was constantly apprehensive of slave insurrection, the militia retained important functions in controlling the black population.[13]

Despite such functions, the colonial militia might have gone the way of its moribund English counterpart had the British government not made the fatal mistake of attempting to enforce its policy decisions in the late 1760s and early 1770s by means of regular troops stationed in the concerned colonies.[14] The fresh colonial experience with resident troops resurrected and sharpened all the old Whig warnings about standing armies. The British troops in Boston and New York demonstrated only too clearly that regular soldiers soon bullied and harassed the helpless citizenry among whom they were stationed. The Boston Massacre in 1770 both confirmed and heightened American fears of standing armies, and it renewed the colonists' conviction that the only safe means of defending a free people was by a militia. As one American reiterated the Whig creed in 1769, "The well disciplining [of] the militia renders useless that dangerous power and grievous Burden, a *Standing Army*."[15]

The object lesson taught by the British troops continued to dominate American military thinking up to the eve of the Revolution. Thus, in the Boston Massacre Oration of 1774, John Hancock warned his countrymen to depend only upon the militia: "From a well regulated militia we have nothing to fear; their interest is the same with that of the state." So ingrained was the American distrust of regular military establishments that it did not recede after 1775 when the troops involved were American rather than British. "History is dyed with blood," warned a Pennsylvanian in 1775, "when it speaks of the ravages which standing armies have committed upon the liberties of mankind." Whatever the nationality of the soldiers, he begged his fellow citizens to "beware of standing armies."[16]

As the crisis between England and the colonies grew worse, it is thus not surprising that Americans turned first to the institution upon which the best Whig authorities and bitter recent experience had taught them to depend—the militia. Embroiled in the Gaspee and Judge's Salary disputes, Massachusetts men felt the need to reorganize their defenses as early as 1773.[17] But the arrival of the news of the Port Bill in the spring of 1774 touched off the first concerted effort throughout New England to strengthen defense capabilities. The Massachusetts militia had continued in existence throughout the eighteenth century, but its usefulness to Whigs in 1774 was limited by the fact that a majority of the higher officers commissioned by the royal governor had little sympathy for the patriot cause. The earliest efforts of the patriots were therefore directed toward removing these officers. By the summer of 1774, militia companies throughout Massachusetts had begun to require their officers to renounce royal commissions. In early September both the Suffolk and Worcester county conventions resolved that all militiamen should refuse to serve under officers who retained royal commissions. The companies ought to choose in their places, the Boston men resolved, those "who have evidenced themselves to be inflexible friends to the rights of the people." Soon after the Provincial Congress assembled, it adopted these proposals on behalf of the entire province. The efforts of the provincial authorities were given support when, on October 3, the Continental Congress advised "that [as] the militia, if put upon a proper footing, would be amply sufficient for their defence in time of peace; that they are desirous to put it on such a footing immediately."[18]

Through the fall of 1774, militia units began to drill actively throughout New England. "The Militia in all the New England Governments have been training," a Virginia newspaper informed its readers in late October, "and are thought to be as expert and well disciplined Soldiers as any Country can produce." Even more heartening to patriots, the feverish round of military activity was proceeding according to impeccable Whig principles. For example, New Englanders proudly read that a group of ancient Watertown men had organized themselves into a company and had chosen an eighty-eight-year-old captain to lead them, for "so general and *divine* [was] the spirit for liberty that men of all ages and denominations in the country engage in military exercises."[19]

The first test of Yankee zeal came in early September 1774, when the rumor spread through New England that General Gage had shelled Boston. Almost immediately, citizen soldiers from all over New England grabbed their arms and a few days' food and headed toward Boston. "It is probable that ten thousand men" of various towns "were yesterday on their march toward Boston," Colonel Gurdon Saltonstall of Connecticut informed Silas Deane on September 5. The response to the rumor showed "the spirit and situation of the people in that part of America," Richard Henry Lee wrote on September 20, "for we have good intelligence that 50,000 Men were in Arms in the Massachusetts Government and Connecticut, and that 30,000 were on march, well armed and provided, to Boston." "By letters from Connecticut," the editors of the *Massachusetts Spy* assured their readers, they had learned that "there were not less than 40,000 men in motion." Caesar Rodney reported that his "late very authentick acc[oun]ts" had tallied "upward of 50,000 men well-armed."[20] However many men really did rise to the occasion, the experience helped reassure Americans of the zeal of their freshly trained citizen soldiers.

While most Americans were relieved that the 1774 alarm had not touched off a general conflict, the war scare awakened many in the middle and southern colonies to the imminent danger and exposed how unprepared those provinces were for battle. Bolstered by the authority of the October 3 resolution of the Congress, the southern colonies began to join their northern brethren in strengthening their militia. As early as December 1774 the Maryland Convention resolved to reorganize the militia. Maryland's move produced "great Anxiety" among conservatives, since, as James Duane noted, "it is the first publick Act out of the pale of New England which indicates a preparation for war & denounces its near Approach." The Virginia Convention reorganized its militia in March 1775, and independent companies were formed in Delaware.[21] Even before the momentous events of April 1775, therefore, many Americans—primarily in New England, but also in several southern colonies—had foreseen the possibility of war and had resolved to rely on the militia.

As events moved toward armed conflict in late 1774 and early 1775, Americans desperately needed assurance that their faith in the citizen soldier was well placed. Many colonists harbored doubts, sometimes expressed openly, that untrained American troops would prove a match for British professionals.[22] Colonial confidence was bolstered immeasurably by the publication in November 1774 of Charles Lee's pamphlet *Strictures On A Pamphlet, Entitled "A Friendly Address To All Reasonable Americans."* Lee was uniquely qualified to diminish American fear of the vaunted British regular. A lieutenant colonel in the British army whose political opinions had effectively curtailed further prospects for advancement, Lee had accepted an offer to serve in the Polish army with the rank of major general. In 1774 he toured the colonies, and during the trip he displayed prominently both his eccentric character and his violently Whig political opinions. He managed during this trip to be introduced to, or to introduce himself to, all the major radical politicians from South Carolina to Massachusetts.[23]

To counter the fears he had heard expressed throughout the colonies, and to answer an influential Tory essay by Thomas Bradbury Chandler, Lee wrote his pamphlet. Chandler's piece, *A Friendly Address to All Reasonable Americans*, had magnified American apprehension that any resistance was doomed to failure because, in the end, the trained British army would quickly dispose of any hastily raised American force. Lee proceeded to reassure the colonists that their forces were more than equal to the task of defeating the British regulars.[24] He first called their attention to the vast pool of American manpower and contrasted it with the paltry numbers Britain could transport across the ocean. Furthermore, he argued (drawing upon Whig theory) that there was every reason to doubt "that 7,000 very indifferent troops, composed of the refuse of an exhausted nation, . . . should be able to conquer 200,000 active vigorous yeomanry, fired with the noble ardour we see prevalent through the continent," especially since the Americans were "all armed, all expert in the use of arms, almost from their cradles." He noted the poor quality of the British soldiery, and then scoffed at Chandler's assertion that no more than 40,000 Americans could be brought into the field. Lee estimated that total American manpower would be no less than 500,000 men, "for every man in America, firmly united, would not amount to less."[25] Perhaps most important, he assured Americans with all the expertise of a trained regular officer that war was a relatively simple business. He did not "mean to insinuate, that a disorderly mob are equal to a trained disciplined body of men," but only "that all the essentials, necessary to form infantry for real service, may be acquired in a few months." Lee detailed exactly which maneuvers were necessary to be learned "to prevent confusion" and insisted that all the others that the regulars could execute with such precision were merely "the tinsel and show of war," necessary only for "puerile reviews" in Hyde Park.[26] Through early 1775, Lee's arguments were echoed all over the continent, feeding American hopes that their virtuous legions of citizens were, or with a few months training could be, the military equal of British professionals.[27]

On April 19, 1775, the British regulars and the citizen soldiers of New England at last came to blows. On the evening of the eighteenth, Gage had dispatched a small force from Boston to secure colonial supplies and to arrest several prominent patriot leaders. The detachment was met early the following morning by several "minute" companies of the Massachusetts militia, first at Lexington and then at Concord Bridge. Radical groups quickly spread the news of the skirmishes through the colonies. "Expresses are hastening from town to town," wrote a Massachusetts physician on April 21, ". . . spreading the melancholy tiding and inspiriting and rousing the people *To Arms! To Arms!*"[28]

In New England the effect of the news was predictable. The hordes of armed men who had crowded the roads to Boston the previous September again took to the highways. But New England had always been forward in military preparations. The animating effect of Lexington and Concord is more surprising in the supposedly more moderate colonies to the south. "The Province of N. York is at last alarmed," exulted Richard Henry Lee. So alarmed were the New Yorkers that for a week after the news arrived New York City was in the hands of a patriot mob that forced open the arsenal and distributed six hundred muskets among the "active" citizens. In Virginia, Thomas Jefferson was informed, "every rank and denomination [is] full of marshal notions." Perhaps most surprising of all, pacific Pennsylvania was also aroused. "It is impossible," wrote an amazed southern delegate to the Congress, "to describe the Spirit of these people and the alteration they have undergone since I left them in December last."[29]

This outburst of emotion was soon channeled into what radical patriots considered constructive avenues. Military organizations sprouted throughout the middle and southern colonies. "By accounts from *all parts* of the country," reported the *Pennsylvania Journal*, we find that Americans "are every where learning the use of arms, and seem determined on *Liberty* or *Death*."[30] The feverish military activity in the spring of 1775 made the preparations of the previous winter seem almost lethargic by comparison. Several colonies went beyond a reorganization of the militia and proceeded to raise provincial forces and to commission officers. The Virginia Convention, for example, resolved to raise 3,000 troops. In June the South Carolina Provincial Congress approved the enlistment of men in both militia units and independent companies, and a military association was circulated for universal signature. By the middle of the month, South Carolina had authorized the raising of two provincial regiments of horse and one of foot.[31] The North Carolina delegates to the Continental Congress chided their constituents in mid-June that "North-Carolina alone remains an inactive spectator of this general defensive armament." They need not have worried, however, for by August the North Carolina provincial authorities had united the inhabitants in a military association similar to that of South Carolina and had proceeded to raise two regiments of foot and one of horse. New York as well joined the general movement when her provincial congress ordered the inhabitants "to use all diligence to perfect themselves in the military art, and . . . to form themselves into Companies for that purpose."[32] Even Pennsylvania sprouted numerous independent, militialike companies called Associations. Friend Christopher Marshall, a fervent patriot, informed a London friend on June 24 that Pennsylvania "Glow[s] and is enflamed" with a "Spirit of freedom and resolution, for daily and all most hourly the sound of drums Trumpets and Fifes is heard in our Ears." The conservative Pennsylvania Assembly yielded to popular sentiment and formally approved the Associator companies and assumed responsibility for their support and regulation.[33]

Not surprisingly, Lexington and Concord spurred the most extensive military efforts in Massachusetts itself. Many of the militia units and individuals from all over New England who had hurried to Boston in late April had remained encamped on the outskirts of the city to help prevent further British encroachments. The Committee of Safety, the executive arm of the hastily reassembled Provincial Congress, attempted first to feed the men, then to pay them, and finally to put them under some form of military organization. Thus was born the Massachusetts, or New England, Army.[34] The Massachusetts Army exemplified Whig military ideals. Though not a militia, the ideal characteristics of the citizen army were amply displayed by the Massachusetts forces. First, the army was impermanent. Patriotism had sent the troops hurrying toward Boston at the end of April, but little more than a laudable zeal for liberty kept them there. To be sure, the Committee of Safety did its best to induce the men to sign eight-month enlistment papers that would have kept them in camp until the end of 1775. But only ten to twelve thousand men actually signed papers, and even these enlistments were predicated upon a free and easy furlough policy and the proximity of the men's home towns. Though the Provincial Congress had resolved on April 23 to raise a force of 30,000 men, no one could say with any certainty exactly how many men were in the Massachusetts Army. The camp, noted James Warren, was "in such a shifting, fluctuating state as not to be capable of a perfect regulation." The men were "continually going and coming," making it most "difficult to say what Numbers our Army consists of." For "if a return could be had one day, it would by no means answer for the next."[35]

Second, the Massachusetts Army was egalitarian. Though the officers were appointed, they might just as well have been elected, for the men refused to serve under officers of whom they did not approve. When the Provincial Congress attempted to reorganize the army into companies of uniform size, for example, widespread protests forced the legislators to abandon the plan. The amalgamation of companies would force the men to serve under officers they did not know, and this they refused to do. To keep the men in camp, the Provincial Congress took great pains to commission those officers whom the men had chosen.[36] The pay scale established by the Provincial Congress on April 23 and 29 also demonstrates the egalitarian spirit that pervaded the citizen army. In sharp contrast to the yawning gap between the pay of officers and enlisted men in the British army (and in the eighteenth-century provincial "marching forces"), in 1775 a Massachusetts sergeant and an ensign were separated by a mere fourteen shillings a month, and the commander-in-chief of the army was paid a salary only ten times as great as that of the lowliest private soldier.[37]

Finally, the Massachusetts Army was subject to lenient military rules. As a matter of principle, the provincial authorities chose to rely upon the character and dignity of the men for such discipline and order as might be required. As the Massachusetts Provincial Congress stated, their army had no need of "such severe articles and rules . . . and cruel punishments as are usually practised in standing armies." Instead, "having great confidence in the honor and public virtue of the inhabitants of this colony, that they will readily obey the officers, chosen by themselves," the citizen soldiers needed only "such rules and regulations as are founded in reason, honor and virtue."[38]

The citizen army proved its mettle at Bunker Hill, and praise of the gallant New Englanders echoed through the continent and beyond. The victory appeared to confirm all hopes about the worth of the citizen soldiers. As one diarist observed, the Yankees had "marched to the field as an undisciplined, inexperienced body of yeomanry, rather than as professed warriors" and had contended "with an army of disciplined veterans." The glorious performance of the Americans, he concluded, "must tend greatly to increase" colonial confidence in their forces, and convey "a serious impression that we are favored with the smiles of Heaven." Bunker Hill had proved, newspaper readers were assured, that the Massachusetts Army was an excellent "martial school, which has already advanced us centuries in the military art," had "made the soldier of the citizen," and had "conveyed the knowledge of war to the inhabitant of the village, and the cottager of the mountain."[39]

But the optimism generated by the feats of the citizen soldiers might have been tempered had the army's problems been as widely publicized as its achievements. By the end of May, disturbing indications began to appear in the correspondence of Massachusetts leaders that all was not well with their army. These men, convinced as they were of the advantages (in theory) of a citizen army, nevertheless were somewhat alarmed at the particular army assembled near Boston. The changed attitude of Joseph Warren, the man most closely associated with Massachusetts military affairs until his death at Bunker Hill, is interesting in this respect. On May 17, he wrote Samuel Adams that although it was necessary to put the army under greater control, he thought that the matter "must be managed with great Delicacy." "Our Soldiers," he wrote rather proudly, "will not yet be brought to obey any Person of whom they do not themselves entertain an High Opinion." Though Warren realized that "Subordination is absolutely necessary in an Army," yet he hoped that "the Bands of Love & Esteem" would be "principally relied on" to handle the high-spirited Yankees.[40] Ten days later, however, Warren's tone had altered. The Continental Congress, he warned, must immediately authorize and strengthen civil government, "otherwise our Soldiery will lose the Ideas of Right & Wrong & will plunder instead of policing the inhabitants." "*Inter nos*," he added ominously, "this is but too evident already." He assured his friend that "unless some Authority to restrain the Irregularities of this Army is established we shall very soon find ourselves involved in greater Difficulties, than you can well imagine." Giving some hint as to what may have caused his change of heart, Warren fumed that "the least Hint from the most unprincipled Fellow who has perhaps been reproved for some criminal Behaviour is quite sufficient to expose the fairest Character to Insult & Abuse." Unfortunately, Warren concluded, "it is with our Countrymen as with all other Men, when they are in arms, they think the military should be uppermost."[41] Elbridge Gerry, who was also closely associated with the army, remarked on the same problems. "The people are fully possessed of their dignity from the frequent delineation of their rights," he wrote. Indeed, "they now feel rather too much their own importance, and it requires great skill to produce such subordination as is necessary. This takes place principally in the army," he observed, where the men ". . . affect to hold the military too high." What Massachusetts needed, Gerry wrote grimly, was "a regular general to assist us in disciplining the army."[42]

Such were the fears that, when added to the intolerable expense of paying and feeding the troops, led the Provincial Congress on May 16 to write to the Second Continental Congress, which had just assembled in Philadelphia. The Massachusetts Army, they noted, had been collected from the different colonies "for the general defence of the rights of America." The Provincial Congress therefore asked the continental body to take over "the regulation and general direction" of their army, "that the operations may more effectually answer the purposes designed."[43]

The Regular Army

The worsening military situation constituted the first order of business for the Congress. As soon as the delegates convened, on May 10, 1775, they were overwhelmed with requests that poured into Philadelphia, begging their direction and advice on the military crisis. "Such a vast Multitude of Objects . . . press and crowd upon Us so fast," John Adams lamented, "that We know not what to do first."[44] The Massachusetts delegates had come to Philadelphia convinced that the only solution to their compounding military difficulties was for the Congress to "immediately . . . adopt the Army in Cambridge as a Continental Army." Accordingly, from May 16 on they were indefatigable, as John Adams later remembered, in urging the delegates to "Appoint a General and all other Officers," and to take responsibility for "the Pay, Subsistence, Cloathing, Armour and Munitions of the Troops."[45] The arrival of the formal Massachusetts request on June 2 emphasized the urgency of the problem and caused the New Englanders to redouble their efforts to bring about decisive congressional action.

But despite the anxiety of the New England delegates to direct the attention of their colleagues to the situation in Massachusetts, a sudden crisis in New York pushed that province to the fore and claimed most of the delegates' time and effort through May and early June. The strategic position of New York was obvious both to the British and to the colonists. As both sides realized, if the British in Canada could successfully link up with a British force moving up the Hudson River, New England would be completely isolated from her allies to the south, and the entire northern frontier would fall into British hands. Thus, when the New York authorities advised the Congress on May 10 that a large body of British reinforcements was expected in the province and requested their "advice and direction" regarding "the conduct to be observed . . . toward any Troops that may arrive here," the urgency of the request was immediately apparent. The delegates responded swiftly. The New York Provincial Congress, they resolved on May 15, must immediately raise a sufficient number of troops to protect the citizens of the province from "insult and injury." But the expected British troops were not to be molested as long as they remained "peacefully in barracks."[46]

No sooner had the delegates disposed of this problem than a far more alarming situation developed in the same area. Provincial authorities in Connecticut and Massachusetts were especially sensitive to the strategic importance of northern New York. Fearing an imminent attack from Canada's capable royal governor, Sir Guy Carleton, the New Englanders had dispatched a force under the joint command of Ethan Allen and Benedict Arnold to counter the expected British moves in the region. Without specific authorization, the small band of Yankees attacked and captured the vital British posts at Ticonderoga and Crown Point on May 9 and 10.[47] News of the attack arrived in Philadelphia on the evening of May 17, carried by John Brown. Brown had been sent into Canada the previous February as an agent of the Massachusetts Provincial Congress. In his subsequent report, he had emphasized both the strategic importance of Ticonderoga and the weak state of its defenses. He had participated in the capture of the fort, and on May 18 he related the details of the affair to the full Congress. Ethan Allen, so legend has it, had claimed possession of the posts "in the name of the great Jehovah and the Continental Congress." Perhaps more to the point, neither Massachusetts nor Connecticut was willing to accept the awesome responsibility of holding two of the king's forts. By default, therefore, the delegates in Philadelphia found themselves in charge of two strategic sites in northern New York that commanded the gateway to Canada.[48]

The delegates refused to accept the responsibility. They knew that the situation of the small New England force was precarious. Nearby, at St. Johns, was a small English garrison and with it a small fleet that effectively controlled the lakes. Should Carleton prove resolute, they feared, Ticonderoga and Crown Point might be retaken as easily as they had been taken. Should this happen, the Americans would lose not only the forts and their defenders but also the precious military supplies and ordnance that they contained. Rumors that Carleton was stirring up the Indians made the captured supplies even more vital. Besides, a month had passed since Lexington without further conflict around Boston; the chance remained that Britain might yet pull back from the brink. On May 18 the delegates resolved, therefore, that as the forts had been taken by "several inhabitants of the northern colonies" (thus dissociating the act from any government authorization), they "earnestly recommend[ed]" that the New York and Albany committees oversee the removal of the stores to the southern end of Lake George. The forts themselves were to be abandoned. Moreover, an "exact inventory" was to be kept of all such supplies, "in order that they may be safely returned when . . . the former harmony between Great Britain and these colonies" had been restored.[49]

Events, however, overtook this cautious strategy. As the delegates deliberated, Arnold raided St. Johns and captured the small British fleet based there. At a stroke, any immediate threat of recapture was removed. Moreover, the delegates from New Hampshire, Connecticut, Massachusetts, and New York, who were most concerned in the matter, began receiving earnest pleas that they work to have the May 18 resolution rescinded. The importance of Canada to the American cause appeared self-evident to those colonies. The continental delegates themselves had recognized this in 1774 and had addressed an impassioned plea to the inhabitants of Canada to join the common cause. Massachusetts, as noted, had gone farther, and in February 1775 the Provincial Congress had commissioned Brown to go into Canada and sound out the possibility that the Canadians—or a suitable number of them—would accede to the Association. Anyone who looked at a map could see the reason for New England's anxiety, for Canada's strategic location posed a threat to New England quite as serious as that to New York. Moreover, British tactics in any such campaign would inevitably involve their allies, the Indians, a prospect that caused fear throughout the northern frontier. Should such a plan succeed, all New England would be effectively isolated from the other colonies and exposed to Indian attack. The key to the success of any such plan lay in the strategic forts of Ticonderoga and Crown Point—the very forts that the Congress had ordered abandoned.[50]

With Arnold's success at St. Johns, the delegates acceded to New England's pleas, rescinding the May 18 resolution. In its place, on May 31 the delegates adopted a resolution to keep the forts and asked that the governor of Connecticut send reinforcements and supplies to the forces there. The next day, however, they emphasized their reluctance to go further, insisting "that no expedition or incursion ought to be undertaken or made, by any colony, or body of colonists, against or into Canada," and they pointedly directed that the resolve "be immediately transmitted to the commander of the forces at Ticonderoga."[51]

The problem in New York effectively turned congressional attention away from Massachusetts through the entire month of May. As Silas Deane noted on June 3, "Our Business has run away with Us." The "Northern Expedition" had received general support, "yet the Resolutions necessary to be formed" unfortunately had prevented "the forming a general plan of Operation."[52] Such a general plan, with the Massachusetts Army at the heart of it, had been John Adams's goal since the Congress had opened. In the short intervals since May 10 when his colleagues were not occupied with events in New York, Adams had steered the debate to the need for a continental defense plan. From the opening days of debate, the delegates had generally agreed upon the basic outlines of such a plan. As early as May 21, Adams had assured James Warren that the Congress would indeed "do some thing in Time." He accurately predicted that the delegates would organize one army to be "posted in New York, and another in Massachusetts, at the Continental Expence." But he chafed under the slow pace of congressional deliberation. The continent, he wrote on June 10, was "a vast, unwieldy machine," with which the Yankees could not "force events," but he was hopeful that all would come to the conclusion he had reached long before, that "powder and artillery are the most efficacious, sure, and infallible conciliatory measures we can adopt."[53]

By June 14, however, Adams later recalled, he could bridle his impatience no longer. Before the Congress opened that day, he paced about the State House yard with his cousin Samuel, earnestly discussing the reluctance of their colleagues to adopt the Massachusetts Army. He realized that the press of business in New York was only one of the reasons that had caused the delegates to delay acting on the Massachusetts request. A good part of the inertia, he knew, was due to fears of New England's military power on the part of colonies farther south. A powerful "Southern Party" existed in the Congress made up of delegates from the middle and southern colonies who were determined not to have the continent defended by "a New England Army under the Command of a New England General."[54] As Eliphalet Dyer, a Connecticut delegate, wrote, they were worried "lest an Enterprising eastern New England Genll proving Successfull, might with his Victorious Army give law to the Southern & Western Gentry." Such fears, Adams realized, would have to be allayed if the continental assumption of the army was to be accomplished.[55] As they discussed the situation, John told Samuel that when the day's session opened he would make a fresh attempt to win support from without New England for adopting the Massachusetts Army. He planned to introduce a resolution that would compel the reluctant delegates to "declare themselves for or against something." Realizing from his previous discussions with delegates, especially from the South, that they would feel safe from New England military power only if a southern general, preferably Washington, was given the command of any army that the Congress adopted, John Adams offered a motion that satisfied the needs of New England and the fears of the colonies to the south. He proposed that Congress should not only "Adopt the Army at Cambridge," but also that it should appoint a general, for which position he promptly suggested George Washington.[56]

As Adams had hoped, the nomination and unanimous election of Washington broke the congressional logjam. Having named the commander of the new Continental Army, the delegates proceeded in the hectic weeks that followed to create that army. The size and general disposition of the forces had never been in dispute, and with little debate the delegates resolved that the Continental Army would consist of 15,000 men—10,000 to be posted in Massachusetts and 5,000 in New York. By late June the Congress had agreed on the organization of this force, adopted a uniform pay scale for it, appointed and commissioned all the general officers, and prepared detailed instructions for Washington that authorized him to take the offensive against the British both in Boston and New York. Nor was this all. By the time the delegates adjourned on August 2 they had provided a rudimentary supply organization, authorized the emission of bills of credit to fund the army, devised continental articles of war, and prescribed uniform regulations for all the provincial militias. "We are almost exhausted," wrote the Connecticut delegates on July 28, "May Heaven Succeed our Imperfect Endeavours."[57]

A bare three months after the Second Continental Congress had assembled, therefore, the delegates found themselves solely responsible for the protection of the continent and in charge of an army capable of fulfilling their new responsibility. "Every Idea of partial and colonial Defence" had been dismissed, wrote Nicholas Cooke, governor of Rhode Island, for the Congress had been vested with the "supreme superintending Power to exert and direct the Force of the whole for the Defence and Safety of all."[58]

Although Adams's compromise had enabled the delegates to unite in organizing the Continental Army, sharp differences of military philosophy continued to divide them. The New Englanders hoped that the Continental Army would not much differ from the Massachusetts Army it replaced; they desired a change in jurisdiction and, most particularly, in funding, but not in the military philosophy that had dominated the army. Many delegates from the southern and middle colonies, however, whose firm views on military matters Adams had detected from the start, were committed to replacing the citizen army with a hierarchical army of regular troops. This shifting congressional coalition, consisting of those who supported Washington's views on the proper structure of the army, was to grow in influence through the early years of the war as even fervent Whigs were converted by what appeared to them to be absolute military necessity.[59]

New Englanders realized that their views of the proper structure of the army differed significantly from those that prevailed in other sections. John Adams commented on the different social philosophies of New England and the South. The common people of the South, he observed, unlike the New England yeomen, were "very ignorant and very poor," while the southern gentlemen were "accustomed, habituated to higher Notions of themselves and the distinction between them and the common People, than We are." Not surprisingly, one may trace these social ideas in the military sphere. Southern militia officers, one northerner observed, were traditionally "gentlemen possessed of much property," whereas the privates were poor whites to whom "thirty-nine lashes wou'd be but a light breakfast." The social distinctions that prevailed in the southern militia are apparent from the provincial pay scales, which provided for substantial differences between the pay of officers and men. (See Table 5-1.) Thus, when the delegates chose Washington of Virginia to command the army, they chose not only a general but a regional social philosophy as well.[60]

Washington and his congressional supporters believed that a hierarchical social philosophy would best suit the regular army that they hoped to build. Although the Massachusetts citizen army had been waging a successful war against British authority since April 1775, Congress and its commander chose to fight the British in a more respectable way, by carrying on a war of maneuver, campaigns, and set battles. To execute this essentially conservative military strategy, a regular army was absolutely necessary.[61]

The result of the assumption that the British regulars could only be fought on their own terms has been to surround the creation of the American regular army with an aura of inevitability. Thus, from the premise that the war must be fought by using conventional strategy follows the conclusion that military necessity is a sufficient explanation for the creation of an army fit to fight such a war; the Americans simply had no choice. But in fact they did have a choice. There were alternative military policies to the conservative and conventional ones that Washington chose to follow. Aside from Whig theories (with which, one might argue, the hard realities of war forced Americans to dispense), experienced military men presented cogent arguments for the retention of the citizen army concept. They pointed out the difficulties of raising and training disciplined troops in a short period of time and argued that the only way to assure an American victory was to continue to rely on the guerrilla tactics that had successfully penned up the British in Boston and had stopped the regulars at Concord Bridge and at Bunker Hill. Charles Lee was the primary articulator of such a strategy. "If the Americans are servilely kept to the European Plan," he wrote, "they will make an awkward Figure, be laugh'd at as a bad Army by their Enemy, and defeated in every Rencontre which depends on Manoeuvres." His views were vindicated in the Saratoga campaign and in the campaigns of experienced frontier fighters like Daniel Morgan and tacticians like Benedict Arnold and Nathanael Greene.[62]

Perhaps the best proof of the viability of the alternative that men like Lee sketched is the horror with which British military men viewed the possibility that the Americans might accept such advice. While experienced British soldiers had no doubt that they could defeat any hastily raised American regular troops in open battle, they greatly feared the possibility that Americans might generally adopt the strategy that had been so successful in 1775 and abandon their seaport towns. They envisioned Americans retreating into the fertile hinterland and wreaking havoc upon any British force foolhardy enough to risk long supply lines to root them out. The British adjutant general, General Edward Harvey, wrote in 1775 that an attempt to "conquer [America] internally by our land force is as wild an idea as ever controverted common sense." As Hutchinson noted in his diary after a dinner with a number of British officers, many military men thought "it would be to no purpose to send forces to subdue" the Americans in their own territory. The Massachusetts Tory, Jonathan Sewall warned General Haldimand that once the Americans had "got seated" in the backcountry, they could "defend their strong holds, & . . . guard the passes & defiles of the Country," until they had "wear[ied] the patience of all the Nations of Europe." It was just such a strategy, advocated by men like Lee and feared by the British, that was later carried on with such success at Saratoga and in the southern campaign of Nathanael Greene.[63]

But Washington and his congressional supporters virtually ignored Lee. As one historian has noted, Washington "did not visualize himself as a guerrilla leader, a will-o'-the-wisp harassing the stolid British like some brigand chief." It is important to emphasize that Washington pursued his goal of creating a regular army out of the Massachusetts citizen army not after any defeat had shown the New England forces to be deficient but immediately after Bunker Hill, when the Massachusetts Army was at the height of its prestige. It is true that the commander's ideas seemed to be confirmed by later disasters that befell the New England troops, but they were not formed by those experiences. Furthermore, Washington's military preferences merely echoed those of his congressional supporters, who, like their commander, were unwilling to contemplate the social dislocation that they feared might ensue from the policies advocated by Lee. They wanted and chose "a commander who could raise and direct an army on the European model."[64]

Washington did not disappoint his supporters. From the first he attempted to eradicate exactly those characteristics of the citizen army that differentiated it from a regular army—lack of discipline, egalitarianism, and impermanence. By moving the army away from its citizen-army origins and attempting to model it on the regular armies of Europe, Washington hoped to secure for America a reliable, hierarchical military organization that would preserve the social distinctions and regularity that he thought essential to any well-ordered society. Although the end of the war came before Washington could fully accomplish all his goals, the direction in which he moved tells us much about the desires of a majority of the delegates, who supported his efforts.[65]

Discipline

As soon as Washington arrived in Cambridge, he attempted to rectify what he considered to be the scandalous lack of discipline in the Massachusetts citizen army. Washington's military training on the fringes of the British regular army had bred in him an admiration for the strict discipline that characterized the king's troops. It is not surprising, therefore, that as soon as he arrived in camp he informed the men of the change he proposed. "It is required and expected that exact discipline be observed, and due Subordination prevail thro' the whole Army," Washington explained in an early order, "as a Failure in these most essential points must necessarily produce extreme Hazard, Disorder and Confusion." He stated this theme again and again in his General Orders and emphasized it in his reports to Philadelphia. "My great concern is to establish Order, Regularity & Discipline," he wrote to Hancock on July 20, "without which our Numbers would embarrass us and in case of an Action, general confusion must infallibly ensue."[66] Washington soon moved from exhortation to example, and increasing numbers of surprised Yankees found themselves hauled before courts-martial for theft, plunder, conversing with the enemy, and insubordination.[67]

The New England officers, the commander believed, were more responsible than the men for the lack of discipline he found in the army. If they could be upgraded, Washington felt, the men's behavior would improve. New Englanders themselves had alluded to the poor figure cut by their officers. As an army physician later recalled, the men's choice of officers often "did not fall on the most respectable and meritorious, but on those who were most popular among the lower class; and these too frequently proved unqualified to discharge their military duties in a manner creditable to themselves and advantageous to the public service." Even Lee complained that "these N. England men are so defective in materials for officers that it must require time to make a real good army out of 'em." Washington himself could not mask his disappointment in his New England officers. They were, he observed, "the most indifferent kind of People I ever saw."[68]

The early apprehensions of the continental high command as to the character and probable combat performance of the citizen officers of New England proved all too justified. As soon as the new continental forces and the British met in battle, first in Canada and then in New York, the prejudices of the officers from the southern and middle colonies appeared to be confirmed. The view of these men that only a regular army could defeat the disciplined troops of the king gained support in Congress and in the army as disaster after disaster befell the untrained American forces.

Much had happened since the delegates had resolved on June 1 to prohibit Arnold from attacking Canada. Bunker Hill had removed any lingering hopes that open warfare could be avoided, and the delegates had worked feverishly through June to man, equip, and provision the army they had adopted to fight that war. The threat that the Continental Army in New England would be isolated by a British attack on New York from Canada was thus more compelling than it had been before. The New Englanders had been emphasizing, throughout the month, that the best way to meet the threat was to eliminate the source—that is, to conquer Canada before Carleton received the reenforcements he needed to launch his attack. On July 27, as part of the organization of the Northern Department of the Continental Army, the newly appointed major general, Philip Schuyler of New York, was ordered to Ticonderoga, from where, if he found it "practicable, and that it will not be disagreeable to the Canadians," he was authorized to attack Canada.[69]

Schuyler, however, did not mount the necessary expedition until the late summer of 1775. The American strategy was one of a two-pronged attack. A large detachment under Richard Montgomery, a former British officer, was to move up through the Champlain valley and capture the forts at St. Johns and Chambly before passing on to Montreal and Quebec. Benedict Arnold was to lead a smaller force through the Maine wilderness to the St. Lawrence and Quebec. It was essential for the success of the plan that it be executed before the onset of the severe Canadian winter. Though Montgomery was initially successful in taking St. Johns (after a long siege) and Montreal, and Arnold's march through the wilderness became a classic in military annals, the campaign met with ultimate defeat at Quebec on December 31. American reinforcements (New Englanders under John Thomas) rushed to the scene in early 1776, but by this time Carleton had also been reinforced. By July, Washington was prepared to concede virtual defeat on the Canadian front.[70]

Canada was, from the first, a New England operation. The troops there were supplied by New Englanders, and most of the men who fought in the area were Yankees. Thus, the dismal failures in Canada confirmed Washington's previously formed notions of the worth of these citizen soldiers. Moreover, it made their faults manifest to many delegates in Philadelphia as well. Although initial newspaper accounts insisted that all was well in Canada, in mid-1776 a series of disturbing incidents began to cause doubts. Complaints began to filter to

Philadelphia that a scandalous lack of discipline among the soldiers was a major cause of the military failures. After receiving word of the American defeats at the Sorel River, Hancock informed Schuyler that "the Congress are greatly hurt at the Misconduct of a Part of the Troops," and hoped "they will take the earliest opportunity to obliterate their Disgrace," for it was the delegates' "earnest Wish, that the strictest Discipline be observed."[71]

But instead of obliterating early disgraces, the New England troops compounded them. They forced Montgomery and Arnold to mount an unsuccessful assault on Quebec at an unpropitious time by threatening to return home the next day when their enlistments were up. Montgomery was killed in the attempt on Quebec, and without his able hand, affairs in Canada swiftly moved toward disaster. Smallpox devastated the ranks, the virulence of the disease compounded by the general disregard of Arnold's strict orders that inoculation be carried on in a safe and orderly manner. A second attack on Quebec in May 1776 resulted in a rout of the American troops, who fled in unseemly panic. What could have been "the reason of their running away," queried a despairing New Hampshire delegate, ". . . and leaving their cannon and sick and every thing behind without firing one musket[?]"[72] The cause of the disgrace was well reported by the Pennsylvanians and Jerseymen on the scene. "There is not even the Shadow of Discipline amongst the new England troops," wrote one such officer, for they were "by much the greatest Part of them . . . low dirty fellows." Pennsylvanian William Irvine wrote home of the "Shocking Situation," with "all in confusion[,] Everybody Running away . . . except the Pennsylvanians & perhaps some Jersy men." "In short, gentlemen," summarized one officer, the Americans in Canada had "commissaries . . . without provisions; quartermasters without stores; generals without troops; and troops without discipline, by G–d." In Congress these reports stirred deep consternation. A committee was sent to investigate and brought back the whole dismal story.[73]

Following on the heels of the Canadian debacle came the Battle of New York in August and September 1776. Again reports circulated about the abysmal behavior of the citizen soldiers of New England. At Kip's Bay and at Harlem the New England militia (upon whom Washington had called to reinforce his depleted army) panicked and ran. As Nathanael Greene described the fiasco, the "miserable disorderly retreat from New York" had been entirely the fault of the New England militia, "who ran at the appearance of the Enemies advance Guard" and left Washington almost alone on the field "within Eighty Yards of the Enimy, so vext at the infamous conduct of the Troops that he sought Death rather than life."[74] This behavior was compared by many with the spirited performance of the Pennsylvania, Delaware, and Maryland continental regiments on Long Island. Joseph Reed acidly noted that the spirit of "desertion, cowardice, plunder, and shrinking from duty when attended with fatigue or danger" was "conspicuous" in only "one part of the army." To such a low point had the reputation of the citizen soldiers of New England sunk that a court-martial composed of officers from the southern and middle colonies acquitted a Virginian accused of speaking disrespectfully of a New England superior. "In so contemptible a light were the New-England men regarded," Alexander Graydon recalled, "that it was scarcely held possible to conceive a case which could be construed into a reprehensible disrespect of them."[75] Such reports confirmed preexisting prejudices and greatly distressed New Englanders within and outside of Congress. "Some of our military gentlemen," wrote a chastened Samuel Adams, "have, I fear disgraced us." Perhaps the news was most difficult for John Adams to bear. "We have so many Reports here of the infamous Cowardice of the New England Troops . . . that I am ashamed of my Country." He begged to know the truth, "whether there is less Courage in the Northern than Southern troops?"[76]

The Yankee's tenacious faith in the citizen army was at last shaken by events in New York. Only a month before the battle, John Adams had been writing philosophically that "Altho it may cost us more, and we may put now and then a Battle to a Hazard" by relying on citizen-soldiers, "yet We shall be less in danger of Corruption and Violence [by relying on them than] from a standing Army." After New York, however, "Discipline, Discipline," had become his "constant topick of discourse . . . in and out of Congress" to cure the "dissipation and Idleness, . . . Confusion and distraction" in the army.[77] Washington, of course, had been sending explicit descriptions of the lack of discipline of the New England troops and predicting that dire military consequences would ensue from their behavior, from the time he had reached the camp in Cambridge. When his predictions appeared to be borne out by events, beginning with the Canadian debacle, the delegates began to cast about for a remedy. One such remedy was a thorough revision of the Articles of War.

In June 1775, when Congress had organized the army, it also had adopted a set of rules for the government of the army. As the delegates had adopted the existing Massachusetts army, so they also adopted, almost word for word, the articles of war that the New England governments had agreed upon. The purpose of these regulations, as the Connecticut articles stated, was "to preserve order, good government, and discipline in the Army, agreeable to the mild spirit of our Constitution," but ". . . not according to the severities practised in Standing Armies."[78]

The Continental articles were taken directly from the rules adopted by Massachusetts on April 5. Although in form the New England articles resembled the British articles of war, the small number of triable offenses (twenty-three) and capital crimes (three) demonstrated how far these rules were, in spirit, from the severe British regulations. Furthermore, corporal punishment was limited to the Mosaic standard of thirty-nine stripes per offense, a punishment the "bloody-backed" British regular would have considered relatively lenient. The Continental articles of war were, by design, "not much differing from those Established by the New England Colonies."[79]

Among other revelations, the campaign in Canada had shown the Continental articles to be wholly inadequate. Washington later termed them "Relaxed, and unfit . . . for the Government of an Army." The delegates had begun to consider the general's disciplinary problems the previous June, when the Committee on Spies had been requested to consider a revision of the articles of war. Not until August 1776, however, did the committee—consisting of John Adams, Thomas Jefferson, and Edward Rutledge—report its findings to the Congress.[80] Scrapping the idea of a minor revision, the committee recommended that the delegates substitute the British articles of war for the old Massachusetts rules. In other words, "the severities practised in Standing Armies" were thenceforth to regulate the American army. As Adams wrote, "It was an Observation founded in undoubted facts that the Prosperity of Nations had been in proportion to the discipline of their forces by Sea and Land." To secure such discipline, Adams (with the concurrence of Jefferson and Rutledge) reported the British articles to Congress word for word. Congress considered the recommendations on August 13 and 19 and on September 19 before adopting the British rules on September 20.[81]

The new articles were considerably harsher than the old. Capital offenses rose from three to thirty, while the permissible corporal punishment was raised to 100 lashes. The revised articles represented a deliberate attempt on the part of the delegates to support Washington's efforts to build a reliable regular army. "The Congress . . . are Anxious to promote discipline and Subordination in their army as much as Possible," John Hancock explained, and it was precisely for this purpose that the delegates had "Repeald the System of military Law they at first Adopted, & Instituted in its Room a more Severe and Rigorous one, as better Calculated to Introduce Obedience and Regularity among the Troops."[82]

Equality

Many believed that the root cause of the lack of discipline that plagued the army was the lack of social distinction between the officers and men that the New England tradition fostered. As a New York doctor observed, after reviewing some ill-behaved Connecticut troops, the cause of their unmilitary bearing was the "popular form of Government & equality of condition," which had reduced all men in the New England provinces "to such a level of sentiment and familiarity, that little or no discipline or subordination . . . exists among them."[83]

Many visitors to the Cambridge camp from the southern and middle colonies, too, were aghast at the prevailing equality between officers and men. Upon entering the camp, Marylander James Wilkinson recalled, he had been struck with the familiarity between the officers and the men. "From the colonel to the private," he had "observed but little distinction." Even more distressing, in Alexander Graydon's opinion was the fact that the officers did not seem to want the situation changed but rather sought "to preserve the existing . . . equality." Such visitors shocked each other with examples of the lack of social distinction. Joseph Reed saw a captain shaving one of his men; John Marshall recalled that some officers pooled their pay with the men in their units. In short, sighed Reed, it was simply "impossible for any one to have an idea of the complete equality which exists between the officers and men who composed the greater part of our troops."[84]

The result of such equality, these observers believed, was that the officers were afraid to exert their authority and thus encouraged the lack of discipline that plagued the continental forces. As Washington's aide, Stephen Moylan, complained, the Yankee officer "must shake every man by the hand, and desire, beg, and pray, do brother, do my friend, do such a thing; whereas a few hearty damns from a person who did not care a damn for them, would have a much better effect." The equality between the officers and the men that was thought to be so subversive of the good order of a regular army was another characteristic of the citizen army that Washington attempted to eradicate, for he believed that as long as the men considered and treated their officer "as an equal; and . . . regard[ed] him no more than a broomstick," there could be "no order, nor no discipline" in his army.[85]

One cause of the odious equality, Washington asserted, was a lack of sufficient differential between the pay of the officers and that of the men.[86] The initial pay scale agreed upon by Congress on June 16, 1775, was almost identical to that adopted by Massachusetts, which strongly reflected the New England preference for relative equality between officers and men (see Table 5-1).[87] A Massachusetts lieutenant, for example, was paid only twice as much as a private. A far different philosophy had prevailed in the southern militia. Thus, a South Carolina militia lieutenant had been paid almost five times as much as a South Carolina private. Even more revealing were the differentials between the field officers and the men. A New England colonel's pay was only six times that of a private. In the South, colonels were paid anywhere from ten to nineteen times a private's pay.

The original continental pay scale, adopted on June 14 and 16, reflected the delegates' hesitation about altering the terms upon which the men had enlisted in the former Massachusetts Army. Thus, the original congressional pay scale, of necessity, virtually duplicated the egalitarian Massachusetts scale for all ranks below that of general.[88] For the newly appointed continental generals, however, the delegates were bound by no previous agreements. In the pay voted for these officers, the Congress deviated significantly from the Massachusetts model. The salary of the new commander-in-chief was set at seventy-five times that of a continental private, while major generals and brigadiers received similarly generous salaries. (The commander-in-chief of the New England army had been paid only ten times a private's salary.) John Adams worried that "our people will think it extravagant, and be uneasy." He noted that Samuel Adams, Robert Treat Paine, and he had "used our utmost endeavors to reduce it, but in vain." They had lost the battle, he wrote, because "those ideas of equality, which are so agreeable to us natives of New England, are very disagreeable to many gentlemen in the other colonies." Since those

TABLE 5-1

Pay Rates of Colonial and British Military Forces, 1775–1776

Ratios: Pay of Higher Ranks to Private's Pay

Rank	Continental Army			Massachusetts		R.I.	Md. Aug. 1775	Va.	S.C.	British Army
	June 1775	Nov. 1775	Oct. 1776	April 23 1775	April 29 1775					
Private	1	1	1	1	1	1	1	1	1	1
Corporal	1.1	1.1	1.1	1.1	1.1	1.1	1.22	1.25	—	1.5
Sergeant	1.2	1.2	1.2	1.2	1.2	1.2	1.35	1.5	.8	2.25
Ensign	1.5	2.0	3.0	1.75	1.75	1.75	3.24	2.25	—	4.5
Lieutenant	2.0	2.7	4.0	2.0	2.0	2.0	4.05	3.0	3.5	6.0
Captain	3.0	4.0	6.0	3.0	3.0	3.0	4.86	4.5	5.4	15.0
Major	5.0	5.0	7.5	5.0	4.0	5.0	6.5	7.5	7.0	17.5
Lt. Colonel	6.0	6.0	9.0	6.0	4.8	6.0	8.65	9.25	—	25.5
Colonel	7.5	7.5	11.3	7.5	6.0	7.5	10.8	18.6	9.3	36.0
Brig. General	18.8	18.8	18.8	7.5	7.5	—	—	—	—	—
Major General	25.0	25.0	25.0	8.0	8.0	—	—	—	—	—
Commander-in-chief	75.1	75.1	75.1	10.5	10.5	—	—	—	—	—

TABLE 5-1 (contd.)
Pay Rates of Colonial and British Military Forces, 1775–1776

Ratios: Pay of Higher Ranks to Private's Pay

Actual Pay: Provincial, Continental, Sterling Currency, per Month

Rank	Continental Army June 1775	Nov. 1775	Oct. 1776	Massachusetts April 23 1775	April 29 1775	R.I.	Md. Aug. 1775	Va.	S.C.	British Army
Private	$ 6⅔	$ 6⅔	$ 6⅔	£2	£2	£2	£1 17s.	£2	£20	£1
Corporal	7⅓	7⅓	7⅓	2 4s.	2 4s.	2 4s.	2 5	2 10s.	—	1 10s.
Sergeant	8	8	8	2 8	2 8	2 8	2 10	3	25	2 5
Ensign	10	13⅓	20	3 10	3 10	3 10	6	4 10	—	4 10
Lieutenant	13⅓	18	27	4	4	4	7 10	6	69 15s.	6
Captain	20	26⅔	40	6	6	6	9	9	108 10	15
Major	33⅓	33⅓	50	10	8	10	9	15	139 10	17 10
Lt. Colonel	40	40	60	12	9 12	12	12	18 10	—	25 10
Colonel	50	50	75	15	12	15	16	37 5	186	36
Brig. General	125	125	125	15	15		20			
Major General	166	166	166	16	16					
Commander-in-chief	500	500	500	21	21					

SOURCES: JCC; Lincoln, ed., *Journal Prov. Congress of Mass.*; Proceedings of the Rhode Island Assembly and Maryland and Virginia Conventions, in Force, ed., *American Archives*; David Cole, "Outline of the South Carolina Militia," S.C. Hist. Soc., *Proceedings* (1954), pp. 14–23; Curtis, *British Army*, p. 158.
NOTE: Massachusetts pay is by lunar month; South Carolina is base pay minus perquisites. British pay scale is taken from Regiment of Foot, full pay.

gentlemen had such "a great opinion of the high importance of a continental general," they had been "determined to place him in an elevated point of light."[89]

Even though circumstances had dictated the adoption of the New
England pay scale for the lower ranks, the congressional supporters of
the regular army never accepted the June pay scale as either proper or
final. They continued to feel, Adams observed, that "the Massachusetts establishment [was] too high for the privates, and too low for the
officers." Although the Massachusetts pay scale would be allowed to
stand for the time being, Adams informed his friends at home that the
question of army pay had occasioned much debate. He and his colleagues continued to think that the pay of the continental officers was
"amazingly high. But the Southern Genuis's think it vastly too low."[90]

The next round in the pay battle was not long in coming. The enlistments authorized by the Massachusetts Provincial Congress were due
to expire on December 31, 1775. Thus by November the delegates in
Philadelphia again were arguing over a proper pay scale, this time for
the army for 1776. Washington had been pleading with his superiors to
change the June pay scale ever since he had arrived in Cambridge. In
September he had forwarded to the Congress a petition of the subalterns praying for a pay increase. Washington recommended the petition to the Congress, as he was "of Opinion the [present] allowance is
inadequate to their rank," and even worse, the low pay was "one great
source of that Familiarity between the Officers and Men, which is in-
compatible with Subordination and Discipline."[91] The supporters of a
new pay scale hoped to work through the Camp Committee that Congress had appointed on September 29 to confer with Washington on
the impending reorganization of the army. The committee consisted of
Benjamin Harrison of Virginia, Thomas Lynch of South Carolina, and
Benjamin Franklin of Pennsylvania. The committee was thus dominated by southern and middle colony men. Even had the members not
themselves been committed to a new pay scale, the instructions drawn
up for the Camp Committee specifically charged the members to recommend a reduction in the men's pay. A special provision was also
included that instructed the committee to insist that all pay be by the
calendar month. The provision was of great importance, for the Massachusetts Army had been paid by the lunar month, and the implementation of the committee's instructions would mean a month's pay
reduction per annum.[92]

Washington fully agreed with the members of the Camp Committee that the existing pay scale would not do. But, although he was philosophically committed to reducing the pay of the lower ranks and raising that of the subalterns, as a practical man he wished to defer the matter until the new army had been enlisted. On November 2 the committee returned to Philadelphia and informed the Congress of the general's views. Although the delegates respected Washington's judgment and appreciated his difficulties, nevertheless they did not believe it prudent to delay the long-overdue pay alterations any longer. A majority succeeded in pushing through a hidden pay reduction for the lower ranks (payment by calendar month) and went beyond the recommendation of the Camp Committee in voting a significant pay increase for subalterns.[93]

The delegates who supported the establishment of a regular army were cheered by their victory, and Washington himself was pleased with the results, if not the timing. Lynch wrote jubilantly to the commander that he would no longer suffer the mortification of seeing his officers "sweep the Parade [with] the Skirts of their Coats or bottoms of their Trowsers, to cheat or mess with their Men." "In short," Lynch observed, "being now [better] paid they must do their Duty & look as well as act like Gentlemen." Washington, in reporting the new pay scale to the army, observed happily that the lower officers would now be able "to support the Character and Appearance of Gentlemen and Officers."[94]

To New Englanders, however, the November pay resolves forecast the eventual doom of their egalitarian citizen army. The town of Harvard, Massachusetts, protested to the Council that the Congress had made a dangerous alteration in the traditional New England equality of officers and men. Though the petitioners were "ready to consecrate" their all for the cause, they beheld with pain anything that undermined "the unanimity of *America*," such as "the large stipends granted to officers, . . . in the *American* service, which stipends, at the lowest, were so high, that the knowledge thereof, much chilled the spirits of the commonality."[95]

In the army itself, discontent welled up to the point of mutiny. A great tumult arose in some of the regiments, according to one diarist, "wherein there was manifested great uneasiness about yr being paid in Kalender months." These "brave men" were "led to be pecuniary," noted Elbridge Gerry, by suspicions that "they are not treated with the generosity exercised towards officers . . . that might be exercised also to them."[96] New Englanders wrote worriedly to their delegates about the detrimental effect the changes were having on efforts to persuade the men to reenlist. "If your Congress don't give better encouragement to the Privates," warned Joseph Hawley, ". . . You will have No Winter Army" in 1776. The problem was due, he believed, to the "Strange Mistaken Opinion" that "Obtains among the Gentlemen of the Army from the Southward, and if I mistake Not in your Congress, that our Privates have too high wages and the officers too low." The widespread discontent with the pay alterations and the subsequent reenlistment problems strengthened the conviction of Washington and his congressional supporters that a citizen army was too unreliable an instrument to be trusted with the salvation of American liberty.[97]

In October 1776, following the New York campaign, the supporters of a regular army consolidated their achievements of the previous year. As part of the same series of decisions that brought a revision of the Articles of War, Congress also agreed upon yet another alteration of the pay scale. By comparing the new continental scale with the military pay scales of the southern colonies (Table 5-1), the significance of the changes becomes apparent. In alterations even more sweeping than those enacted in November 1775, the delegates substantially raised the pay of *all* continental officers, not just the subalterns. The pay of the enlisted men was not touched. Clearly, by the end of 1776, Congress had abandoned the egalitarian pay scale suitable for a citizen army and had opted instead for a hierarchical pay scale suitable for the regular army its commander was endeavoring to create.[98]

Impermanence

Washington's efforts toward greater discipline and a more distinct hierarchy occasioned the first major crisis for the army, the enlistment crisis of the fall of 1775. The causes and consequences of this crisis proved to the general and his congressional supporters that their early fears about the instability of the citizen army had been all too justified. Further, the crisis strengthened their determination to create an army of regulars from the unreliable band of citizen soldiers.

In the wake of Lexington and Concord, there had been confident predictions that hundreds of thousands of citizens would flock to defend the cause of liberty. In the spring of 1775 such predictions appeared to be realized as a more-than-adequate number of men crowded into the Cambridge camp. But, although the men had responded well when they had perceived imminent danger, they proved reluctant to sign enlistment papers that would have ensured their presence in camp. Thus the most prominent characteristic of the Massachusetts Army was its impermanence. Men were constantly coming and going—rushing in before Bunker Hill but dribbling home when camp life began to pall.

The recruiting difficulties of the Massachusetts Army were not widely publicized; only the provincial leaders were fully aware of the men's unwillingness to commit themselves to a definite period of service. Thus, when Washington received the first accurate returns in early July, he was truly shocked. Instead of the 30,000 men the Provincial Congress had ordered raised, the new commander found that he could not "estimate the Present Army at more than 14,500 Men Capable of Duty." As a stopgap measure until the new army was formed in 1776, Washington asked his superiors to begin enlisting regiments in the southern and middle colonies without delay.[99]

Washington hoped that the situation would change for the better when the 1776 army was recruited. The Massachusetts leaders, who had conceived of the war as a series of Bunker Hills, had not been unduly alarmed at the prospect of a fluctuating, impermanent army. Washington, however, thought in terms of long campaigns, for which a regular army committed for an extended period of service was an absolute necessity. But his hopes for building such an army were dampened in the fall of 1775 when the citizen soldiers in the Cambridge camp refused to sign one-year enlistments in the new army. "The situation of the army at this time is critical," Elbridge Gerry wrote, with "the men declining to inlist on the terms profferred by the General." The New Englanders did not like their reduced pay, they did not like the fact that their elected officers were often displaced,[100] and they especially did not like the refusal of Congress to offer them their customary reenlistment bounty. Every week, Washington passed on to Philadelphia the depressing reenlistment figures. By November 28 the army had only enlisted 2,540 men for 1776, and the total was only 5,253 by December 11.[101]

Washington's problems were compounded when the Connecticut militia, following the usual militia practice, marched out of camp on December 11 the moment their enlistments expired. The American camp was thereby denuded of men until militia units from the rest of

New England were hastily summoned to help fill the gap between December 11 and January 1. Washington's frustration and despair as he helplessly watched his army melt away in the early winter of 1775 colored all his future thoughts concerning a volunteer citizen army.[102] The enlistment crisis convinced him that an American regular army was absolutely necessary. He hoped that the new army would be large enough to obviate the need for militia reinforcement, but he insisted that it must be made up of soldiers engaged for a sufficient length of time to preclude recurrent reenlistment crises.

In February 1776 Washington begged his superiors in Philadelphia to institute a policy of long enlistments. He could not take the offensive, he explained, until he was relieved of his anxiety about the fluctuating state of his army. How could he plan a campaign when he could not be sure how many men would be in camp when the day of battle arrived? Perhaps even more important than the inconvenience, he wrote, was the impossibility of training disciplined soldiers in a few short months. "To expect . . . the same Service from Raw, and undisciplined Recruits as from Veteran Soldiers," he warned, "is to expect what never did, and perhaps never will happen." Expanding upon a familiar theme, he explained that "Men engaged for a short, limited time only, have the Officers too much in their power; for to obtain a degree of popularity, in order to induce a second Inlistment, a kind of familiarity takes place which brings on a relaxation of Discipline, . . . by which means, the latter part of the time for which the Soldier was engaged, is spent in undoing what you were aiming to inculcate in the first." From his knowledge of "all the Evils we have experienced in this late great change of the Army," Washington recommended that in the future it would be "infinitely better" if the men were engaged not for one year but "during the War."[103]

Congress, however, was engaged in disputes over trade and independence through the spring of 1776, and the delegates did not wish to take up yet another controversial question about enlistments, so Washington's advice went unheeded. In the fall of 1776, therefore, the commander faced a replay of the 1775 enlistment crisis, but with a significant difference. The army for 1777 would have to be enlisted during the heat of battle in New York and New Jersey. The "fatal system of short inlistments," Washington complained, had again left him with but "the least shadow of an Army." In mid-December he confessed to his brother that "*the game* [is] *pretty near up*," owing primarily

"to the accursed policy of short Inlistments, and placing too great a dependence on the Militia."[104] Washington's pleas for a permanent army
indicate how completely he had divested himself of any lingering
Whig doubts. He had come to the firm conclusion that there simply
was "no opposing a standing, well disciplined Army, but by one upon
the same plan." The "evils to be apprehended" from such an army he
considered to be remote, but the "consequence of wanting one," he
warned, was "certain, and inevitable Ruin."[105]

Some New Englanders with strong ties to the citizen-army ideal
were slow to accept Washington's conclusions, given the Yankee's
deep concern about the evils of a standing army. But the dire military
situation in late 1776 caused even staunch Whigs to accept the need for
long enlistments. On September 16, 1776, the delegates agreed to offer
a bounty of twenty dollars and 100 acres of land to those men who
would enlist for the duration of the war. On October 8, at Washington's urging, the offer was sweetened with the additional inducement
of an annual suit of clothes.[106] The glorious ideal of a short-term army
crashed, with so many other cherished myths, in the rubble of the
New York campaign.

Congress would not have succeeded in creating a true regular army
in 1776, however, had it merely ensured the relative permanence of
the continental forces. Unless the new army was of sufficient size to
carry on a campaign without militia reinforcement, Washington
would still have to depend upon the unreliable citizen soldiers of the
provincial militia units. When Congress had organized the Continental army in 1775, the militia had been included in all strategic calcula-
tions. The army was to have consisted of 15,000 troops, later raised to
20,000. Such an army clearly was too small to face the heavily reinforced British forces without substantial militia assistance. The reorganization of the provincial militia had been one of the earliest actions
ordered by the delegates, therefore, and Washington had been encouraged to depend on local units for reinforcements in the event of
major battles.[107] The early role of the militia thus was the one that
Charles Lee had sketched for it in 1775. The militia was to consist of
the vast manpower pool of the nation, which could be called out at any
time to turn the tide of battle by enthusiasm, patriotism, and sheer
overwhelming numbers.

Had Washington fought a different kind of war, the kind of war
most Whigs had envisaged, the militia would probably have been ad-

equate, as it was at Concord Bridge, on Bunker Hill, and on Dorchester Heights. The militia, remember, was designed for local defense, and when the units were called upon to fight near their homes for short periods of time, they usually acquitted themselves well. But Washington had long since committed his army to the traditional European style of warfare, and this decision made his disillusionment with the militia inevitable.[108]

The general's relations with the Yankee militia units had begun ominously when he was deserted by the Connecticut troops in December 1775. Desertion by the militia in time of danger was to become habitual and was a prime cause of Washington's desire to be free of any dependence on them. "From former experience," he wrote to Reed in March 1776, "we have found it equally practicable to stop a torrent as these people, when their time is up." In September 1776, after the Battle of New York, Washington summarized his views on the worth of the citizen soldier in a long letter to his superiors in Philadelphia. In the year since he had assumed command, he wrote, he had become convinced that the militiaman's short service rendered him impervious to discipline and subordination, and the constant coming and going of the units made planning a campaign impossible. This experience had proved to him that the militia was inadequate to perform the duties that Congress had assigned to it. "Men accustomed to unbounded freedom, and no controul," he explained, "cannot brook the Restraint which is indispensably necessary to the good order and Government of an Army." "To place any dependence upon Militia," he wrote, "is, assuredly, resting upon a broken staff."[109]

The New York campaign brought a majority in Congress to accept the commander's assessment. Thenceforth, the delegates decided, the strategic place then occupied by the militia must instead be filled by a regular army of sufficient size to preclude the need for any militia reinforcement. Thus the reenlistment resolves of September 16 were coupled with a decision greatly to augment the number of men in the Continental Army. In September 1776 the delegates resolved to place 75,000 men on the continental rolls. "You will perceive that the Congress have come to a Determination to augment our Army . . . and to engage the Troops to serve during the Continuance of the War," Hancock wearily informed Schuyler at the end of the month. They had done so, he explained, "being thoroughly convinced by repeated Instances . . . that our Militia is inadequate to the Duty expected of them."[110]

The deficiencies of the militia that the New York campaign had brought to the surface completed the cycle begun in 1774. Whig predictions about the ability of an armed citizenry to overwhelm the British regular army one by one had been proved false in the Canadian wilderness, in New York, and in New Jersey. Events had proved that a hierarchical regular army was necessary to fight the European style of war that Congress and its commander had resolved to fight, and by 1776 the delegates had created the outline of such an army.[111]

The Navy

The navy, as an institution, carried far fewer negative ideological connotations than did the army. Americans had long considered their protection by the British fleet to be one of the most tangible benefits of royal protection, and they saw the threat of withdrawal of that protection to be one of the most fearsome consequences of resistance.[112] Perhaps as a result, the delegates proved more reluctant to create a Continental Navy than they had been to adopt a Continental Army. Besides, in the spring of 1775 a majority of delegates were still hopeful that the coming of hostilities might yet bring the ministry down. Their adoption of the army beseiging the "ministerial troops" in Boston could be viewed as a defensive move; the creation of a navy, which was almost by definition an offensive force, was a different matter entirely.[113]

There were, of course, some delegates who had given up the idea of reconciliation from the opening day of hostilities, if not before. To them, a navy was an absolute necessity for carrying on the war. Christopher Gadsden, a former Royal Navy officer, believed an American navy to be not only necessary but easily obtainable. "He Says We can easily take [British] sloops, Schooners and Cutters, on board of whom are all their best Seamen," John Adams informed Elbridge Gerry, "and with these We can easily take their large Ships, on board of whom are all their impress'd and discontented Men. He thinks the Men would not fight on board the large ships with their fellow subjects, but would certainly kill their own officers."[114]

Gadsden's desire for a navy, if not his strategy for obtaining one, was shared by many New Englanders, whose coasts had been subject to the ravages of the British fleet since the opening of hostilities. Such a force might also provide the means, many New Englanders hoped, of relieving their desperate shortage of military supplies, for it would enable the colonists to capture the British supply vessels that were entering New England waters in increasing numbers. John Adams, one of the earliest advocates of a continental navy, received a steady stream of letters through the spring and summer of 1775 urging him to press for the creation of such a force. "As the whole Continent is firmly united," Josiah Quincy hinted, "why might not a Number of Vessels of War be fitted out, & judiciously stationed, so as to intercept any Supplies going to our Enemies?"[115] No such plan was presented in Congress, however, and one must assume that the New Englanders sensed that there was insufficient support among their colleagues. Far from assuming continental responsibility for naval defense, the delegates in fact did just the opposite. On July 18, as part of the plan for reorganizing the colonial militias, the delegates resolved

> That each colony, at their own expence, make such provision by armed vessels, or otherwise, as their respective assemblies, conventions, or committees of safety shall judge expedient and suitable to their circumstances and situations, for the protection of their harbours and navigation on their sea coasts, against all unlawful invasions, attacks, and depredations, for cutters and ships of war.[116]

During the summer of 1775, individual colonies, seeking to protect their exposed coasts and to secure military supplies, authorized a variety of naval enterprises. Rhode Island, with its coasts threatened by the patrols of the aggressive Captain Wallace aboard H.M.S. *Rose*, was the first to act. On June 2 the Rhode Island Assembly commissioned two armed vessels and a commander, who was authorized to take offensive action against any force that "shall attempt . . . the Destruction, Invasion, Detrimant or Annoyance of the Inhabitants of this Colony."[117] The Connecticut Assembly similarly authorized the fitting out of two armed vessels, and efforts were made, with less success, in the Massachusetts Provincial Congress. Even more extensive enterprises were undertaken farther south. In Pennsylvania, Franklin persuaded the Pennsylvania Assembly to fund a small fleet of row galleys to protect the Delaware basin. In South Carolina, Gadsden was equally successful. Relying on the July 18 resolution of Congress, the Committee of Safety commissioned an armed sloop and authorized its captain to intercept British supply ships headed for Saint Augustine and the Bahamas.[118]

In fact, colonial ventures at sea were not limited to those authorized by provincial authorities. Increasingly, armed ships manned by zealous individuals with no commissions began to range along the New England coast, preying on isolated British supply ships and occasionally upon colonial vessels as well.[119] Such piecemeal naval efforts pleased neither the New Englanders nor their allies in Philadelphia. "I lament with you the Want of a naval Force," Benjamin Franklin wrote to Silas Deane on August 27, "I hope the next Winter will be employ'd in forming one."[120]

The question of creating a Continental navy came before the Congress almost as soon as the delegates returned to Philadelphia after the short summer recess. Their consideration of the issue proceeded along two separate but parallel lines. On the one hand, the delegates debated and appeared to reject decisively a straightforward proposal for the creation of a Continental navy, and on the other, short-term decisions taken in response to immediate military situations brought such a force into existence. The general proposal came from Rhode Island. On August 26 the Rhode Island Assembly resolved that, as "the building and equipping of an American fleet, as soon as possible, would greatly and essentially conduce to the preservation of the lives, liberty and property of the good people of these Colonies," the Rhode Island delegates were "to use their whole influence at the ensuing congress, for building at the Continental expense a fleet of sufficient force for the protection of these colonies." On October 3, as Samuel Ward recorded in his diary, he and his colleagues "Presented our Instructions for carrying on the War effectually & building an American fleet." It was tabled, because the delegates were in the midst of an extended debate over colonial trade.[121] On October 7 the resolution was again brought before the full Congress, which was still engaged in the trade debate. This time, the Rhode Island proposals were considered, perhaps because the connection between trade and navy was so direct. With the coming of war, it was clear that the trade policy of 1774 would have to be altered. The Association represented a political strategy: Colonial trade was to be stopped in order to increase the political pressure upon the British government. By 1775, however, the strategy was the military one of carrying on a war. For this, the colonists needed military supplies and the funds to pay for them.[122] For these purposes, they would have to trade somewhere. The question was, where? The traditional American trade with the West Indies might be reopened, and the Association broken, or at least its provisions significantly altered.

Alternatively, Americans might send their ships to Europe. Finally, Congress might open American ports to the ships of all nations. All these steps, and especially the last, would strike at the heart of the British imperial system and would invite swift retaliation from the British fleet. As Zubly of Georgia warned:

> Nations as well as Individuals are sometimes intoxicated. It is fair to give them Notice. If We give them Warning, they will take Warning. They will send Ships out. Whether they can stop our Trade, is the Question. N. England I leave out of the Question. N.Y. is stopped by one Ship. Philadelphia says her Trade is in the Power of the fleet. V[irginia] and Maryland, is within the Capes of Virginia. N. Carolina is accessible. Only one good Harbour, Cape Fear. In G[eorgia] We have several Harbours, but a small naval Force may oppose or destroy all the naval Force of Georgia.
>
> The Navy can stop our Harbours and distress our Trade. Therefore it is impracticable, to open our Ports.

If, therefore, Americans were to seek trade abroad, either in their own ships or by opening their ports, they must find some way of defending both those ships and their own harbors. That way was, New Englanders believed, the creation of an American fleet.[123] The mission of such a force would not, therefore, be the destruction of the powerful British fleet, but rather the more modest task of protecting a reopened American trade. "To talk of coping suddenly with G.B. at Sea would be Quixotism indeed," John Adams realized. "But, the only question with me is can we defend our Harbours and Rivers? If we can We can trade."[124]

Considered as an adjunct of the controversial trade debate, however, the issue of an American navy aroused considerable opposition. This was particularly so in areas like Maryland and Virginia, whose trade passed through easily blockaded channels like the Chesapeake and Delaware bays. As Adams recognized, the circumstances of such colonies "distinguish them quite from New England, where the Inlets are innumerable and the Navigation all their own." The southerners acknowledged, he observed, "that a Fleet would protect & secure the Trade of New England but deny that it would that of the Southern Colonies." Moreover, the benefits of creating such a fleet, in the form of employment for mechanics to build the ships and seamen to man them, would also go disproportionately to New England. Adams feared, therefore, that it would "be difficult to perswade them to be at the Expence of building a Fleet, merely for N. England."[125]

Such sentiments, when joined to the awe with which the Royal Navy was regarded, led the delegates simply to dismiss the Rhode Island proposal when it was debated on October 7. "It is the maddest Idea in the World," sputtered Chase of Maryland, "to think of building an American fleet." Even Gadsden was "against the Extensiveness of the Rhode Island Plan." Still, he believed, "some Plan of Defence by Sea should be adopted." Even the mild suggestion that a committee be appointed to estimate the cost of the Rhode Island proposal, however, was quickly defeated. Hopkins of Rhode Island, shrewdly assessing congressional sentiment, withdrew the plan. He had, he noted, "no Objection to putting off the Instruction from Rhode Island, provided it is to a future day."[126]

While the delegates rejected the Rhode Island plan, with no apparent sense of contradiction they simultaneously undertook a series of actions that rendered such approval unnecessary. On October 5, in the middle of the stalled trade debate, letters arrived from London with intriguing news. Two brigs loaded with military supplies had sailed on August 11 without convoy and bound for Quebec. The desperate colonial shortage of arms and ammunition might be resolved at one fell swoop by a lucky interception at sea.[127] A committee of three was immediately appointed to consider the best course of action. The committee was composed of strong supporters of a Continental navy: John Adams, Silas Deane, and John Langdon. The committee reported back to the full Congress within the hour. It recommended that letters be sent requesting that all the New England colonies with armed vessels at their disposal immediately dispatch those ships to intercept the brigs. By the end of the day, expresses were speeding northward, carrying the Congress's request to the governors of Connecticut and Rhode Island and to the Massachusetts Provincial Council. While on this mission, Hancock informed the provincial authorities, the commanders were to regard themselves and their vessels as "on the Continental risque and pay."[128] The Committee of Three did not stop with this recommendation. The next day they also proposed that Congress itself outfit two armed vessels and that it commission them for a three-month cruise to intercept such British supply vessels as they might encounter. While this was a considerably more modest proposal than that of Rhode Island, it too was tabled.[129]

When the question was again considered in the Congress, however, it was not the extensive Rhode Island plan that was the subject, but rather the modest committee proposal. The presentation of a scaled-down plan, which contemplated little more than congressional authorization for a limited privateering voyage, may have been a deliberate strategy on the part of the congressional advocates of a Continental navy. "I think We shall soon think of maritime affairs," John Adams later informed Elbridge Gerry, "No great Things are to be expected at first, but out of a little a great deal may grow."[130] If this was a deliberate plan, it proved successful. On October 13, Congress voted to outfit and arm two vessels, each to carry eighty men, whose mission it would be to engage on a three-month cruise "for intercepting such transports as may be laden with warlike stores and other supplies for our enemies and for such other purposes as the Congress shall direct." Perhaps even more important, a committee of three, consisting of Deane, Langdon, and Gadsden (in place of Adams), was appointed for the limited purpose of selecting the vessels and preparing estimates of the cost of the enterprise.[131] Adams, far from disappointed at being left off this committee, was buoyed by the developments. The Quebec supply brigs, although they were never taken, had given the naval advocates a chance to recoup the losses they had suffered at the beginning of the month. "We begin to feel a little of the Seafaring Inclination here," he informed James Warren. "The Powder at Quebec, will place us all upon the Top of the House." At the same time, he clearly indicated that the modest beginning represented by the October 13 resolution was to be regarded as just that—a beginning. He advised Warren that he should arrange to have two prominent Massachusetts captains "put into continental service immediately" although, as yet, the only such service was the Continental Army.[132]

Sometime in late October the committee report, prepared by Deane, was laid before the Congress.[133] Deane had ably carried out the limited mandate of the Congress, and the report contained detailed estimates of the cost of a three-month cruise by two vessels. But Deane also presented estimates for a similar cruise of up to ten such vessels, along with extensive arguments in favor of such an expanded force. First, he believed that the expense could be considerably lessened by taking into service the armed vessels already possessed by the various New England colonies. Such a force would nearly equal the naval forces that Britain currently had deployed in North American waters and, given the advantage of surprise, it would have a good chance of capturing enough British ships to virtually pay for itself.[134] But Deane also went on to present what he considered to be the most urgent reasons in favor of setting on foot "a Naval Force under proper regulations" even were this not to prove true. The reasons he presented, interestingly enough, said nothing about the military necessity of such a force, or its role in protecting resumed colonial trade. It is possible that he believed that all such arguments were familiar to the delegates, from the extensive trade debates. Deane, however, elaborated at length upon the civil consequences of leaving naval policy in its present unregulated state. "At least Ten Thousand Seamen are thrown out of employ in the Northern Colonies," Deane noted, and neither they nor "their Owners, & the various mechanics, dependent on this extensive branch of Business" would "long rest easy, in their present destitute, distress'd Situation." What they would do, he warned, was to "pursue the only Method in their power for indemnifying themselves, and Reprisals will be made. This will at best be but a kind of Justifiable piracy & subject to No Law or Rule." As such, Deane predicted, "the Consequences may be very pernicious." Instead, he suggested:

> Is it not more prudent, where the Loss can, at most, be so trifling to Turn this Spirit, this Temper, this Necessity of the Times down its right & proper Channel, and reduce it while in its infancy to Rule & Order before it become thro Want of Regulation, unmanageable? This will be, not only preventing, a Licentious roving, or piracy, but will be turning Our Enemies Weapons upon him.
>
> Should private Adventurers take up the M[atter], every one will soon make his own Laws & in a few Years, No Law will govern, the mischief will grow rapidly & Our Own property will not be safe.
>
> Such Adventures are already entered upon, Witness several Captures made by the provincials without order or direction.
>
> This calls upon Us to be taken up & regulated at the first setting out. It will afterward be out of Our power. Our Coasts will swarm with roving adventurers, who if they forbear plundering of Us or Our immediate Friends, may thro Necessity invade the property of the Subjects or those with whom We wish to stand well, & bring Accumulated Mischief on these Colonies.[135]

To obviate such consequences, Deane proposed that Congress itself appoint a committee authorized to select and outfit a suitable number of vessels. More important, the committee ought to "have power to Commission proper persons to command the same and to Constitute such rules, Ordinances, & directions as they shall judge best for the well regulating such Naval force."[136]

Deane was suggesting the establishment of a true Continental navy, as opposed to plans for continental authorization of independent privateering voyages. His proposal was laid on the table sometime in mid-October, and debated toward the end of the month. At this point, however, John Adams's heretofore indefatigable note taking appears to have flagged, for we have no record of those debates. We do, however, know the result. On October 30 the delegates approved the basic outlines of the Deane report. Although they authorized a far smaller initial force than Deane had proposed (only four ships, as opposed to ten), nevertheless, those ships were to form the basis of a permanent Continental navy.[137] Certain factors make it clear that the delegates intended the October 30 resolution to mark a change from prior policy. First, the mission of the Continental vessels was altered. While the October 13 resolution had authorized them to intercept British supply ships, and their mission was limited to a three-month cruise, the ships commissioned under the October 30 resolution were to be used "for the protection and defense of the united Colonies, as the Congress shall hereafter direct." To emphasize the permanent nature of the force, Deane's committee was made a standing committee, and it was authorized to supervise the new naval force. The committee, henceforth known as the Naval Committee, was enlarged to seven members to enable it to perform its ongoing responsibilities.[138]

The October 30 resolution and the appointment of the Naval Committee mark the end of the delegates' hesitancy about creating a true navy. As Samuel Ward informed his brother, when the Rhode Island proposal had first been introduced, less than a month earlier, "it was looked upon as perfectly chimerical." A month's debate on trade, the specter of British naval forces terrorizing both the New England coast and southern waters and Deane's alarming report regarding the social consequences of declining to organize the continent's naval forces had brought a decisive change. "Gent[leme]n now consider it," Ward wrote, "in a very different Light."[139]

The proposals of the Naval Committee swiftly came before the full

Congress in the early weeks of November and were just as swiftly adopted. On November 2, almost immediately after news arrived of the burning of Falmouth, in what is now Maine, Congress authorized $100,000 for the use of the Naval Committee and granted it power to engage officers and men to serve in the new Continental service. On November 10, Congress authorized the raising of two battalions of marines to serve aboard the Continental vessels. The marines were to serve, as Washington was at that moment attempting to enlist his army to serve, "for and during the present war."[140] On November 25 the Congress finally satisfied Washington's request that it establish regular judicial procedures for adjudicating naval prizes. The move was necessary, the delegates resolved, to ensure that the efforts of some "good people" to secure, by self-help, some reparations for the acts of British warships, did not result in the "suffer[ing]" of those "who ha[d] not been instrumental in the unwarrantable violences."[141] On November 28 the final step in the creation of the navy was taken, and it reveals much about the delegates' purpose in organizing the service and their preferences regarding its structure. The "Rules for the Regulation of the Navy of the United Colonies," drafted by John Adams, were an almost verbatim copy of the statutes, regulations, and disciplinary rules that governed the Royal Navy.[142]

In almost every modern revolution, strong movements for political and social change have emerged from the revolutionary military forces. From Cromwell's New Model Army to the sailors on the battleship *Potemkin* and to the forces of Mao Tse-Tung, the military has served as the cutting edge of the revolution and, in many instances, has trained the leaders who carried the revolution on in the civil sphere after the end of hostilities.[143] Notable exceptions were the Continental military forces during the American Revolution. Despite early indications that the army that gathered around Boston in 1775 would build upon Whig military theories and become such a force, and despite the welcoming of such developments by military radicals like Charles Lee, the Massachusetts Army did not become a truly revolutionary military body. Once it passed under continental control, its tendencies toward radicalism were arrested or reversed.

It can hardly be argued that colonial military forces were unlikely vehicles for radical social change. Even had the example of the 1775 Massachusetts Army not been so clear, the reforming zeal that has marked

other revolutionary forces was abundantly in evidence in many provincial military entities, like the military Associations of Pennsylvania
and the Committee of Privates, which played such a large role in realizing the radical Pennsylvania constitution of 1776.[144] It was not that
the Continental Army could not have become such a radical force, but
rather that Washington, with the support of a majority of congressional delegates, labored diligently to ensure that it did not.

There can be no doubt that the policy of Washington and his supporters to turn the Massachusetts Army away from its radical Whig
origins and to shape it into a traditional military institution was a deliberate one. As soon as the new commander arrived in Cambridge, he
began to restructure the army to make it conform to his preconceived
notions of a respectable military force. A majority of delegates will-
ingly carried through the general's efforts to ensure discipline not by
appeals to reason and virtue but by means of harsh punishment, to increase the social distance between officers and men by alterations in
the pay scale, and to achieve stability and reduce contact between the
military and civil spheres by lengthening the period of military service
and thus virtually disqualifying from Continental service the "substantial yeomen" whom Whigs envisioned as the ideal defenders of a
free people. The Continental Army that Washington and his congressional supporters created by 1776 embodied the very values that characterized the British army that they were fighting.

While the navy figured much less prominently in Whig ideology
than did the army, nevertheless the delegates assumed control of the
navy under circumstances and for purposes consistent with those that
shaped their attitude toward the army. Like the army, the navy was
organized, in part, to counter threats of social dislocation in major
ports, and it, too, was modeled directly on the very institution it was
organized to fight.

The organization and administration of the Continental military
forces were the first major administrative tasks of the Congress, and
they remained so throughout the years of revolution. While the First
Congress had been occupied with the ambiguous task of choosing appropriate methods of resistance, the Second Congress, as soon as it assembled, was immediately and without controversy entrusted with
the unquestionably governmental task of directing the continent's military affairs. The delegates were given little guidance on military matters, so they were relatively free to organize their forces, to staff them,

to provision them, and to send them to fight how and where they chose. In exercising this first overtly governmental power, the ideological and regional divisions among the delegates that were to characterize the latter years of the Continental Congress began to surface, and the strength of the congressional moderates and conservatives began to tell. If one accepts the idea that a nation's military forces reflect the civilian society that they serve, then the Continental forces that a majority of delegates had created by 1776 reflected the goal of these congressional leaders not to use the Revolution to restructure American society but to preserve as much of that society as possible within a revolutionary context, old ideals of order, deference, and stability.

CHAPTER 6

Problems of Unity

If common Rights, common Interests, common Dangers and common Sufferings are Principles of Union, what could be more natural than the Union of the Colonies.
—*James Wilson, February 18, 1776*

In February 1776, James Wilson of Pennsylvania was commissioned by Congress to draft an address that would strengthen the American commitment to the war. One of Wilson's aims in writing his "Address to the Inhabitants," quoted above, was to convince the colonists that neither British troops nor British schemes could destroy the union of the colonies upon which the patriot cause depended. Wilson's task was a difficult one because, despite his rhetoric, he himself realized that a durable American union was neither inevitable nor "natural." Prior to 1776, American unity had been tenuous. The colonies were, of course, connected by a common heritage, culture, and language. Since 1765 they had also begun to forge institutional links between themselves in order to devise common strategies of resistance to British policy. But as the impending crisis approached the breaking point, the only acknowledged legal tie binding the colonies together was still their allegiance to a common sovereign.[1] Despite prior attempts to find alternatives, the only durable links that had ever united the colonies had, in fact, been those forged under the aegis of royal authority. The possibility of a lasting colonial union without some authority that could duplicate the authority that had been exercised by the British Crown seemed dangerously remote. The colonists had little basis for optimism that such a replacement could be found. Most Americans realized that previous attempts to achieve a greater degree of unity than that provided by allegiance to a common sovereign had been unsuccessful. This was as true of efforts sponsored by the British as it was of those the colonists themselves had initiated.

This realization pressed heavily upon the minds of American Whigs after 1774, for they realized that unanimity of colonial action was essential for a successful resistance. To solve this dilemma of past failure and current necessity, Americans turned to the Continental Congress. Yet the Congress, despite early optimism, was unable to agree on a plan of confederation that could secure the approval of the new states.[2] This failure had many causes. On one level, early congressional consideration of a plan of confederation was delayed for tactical political reasons. Just as a confederation was pursued by congressional radicals eager to hurry what they viewed as a corollary of independence, it was correspondingly opposed by conservatives, who sought to retard any such movement.[3]

But Congress's inability to reach agreement on confederation had a much wider significance. The plans for confederation put forward in the period before and immediately following independence represent the colonists' earliest attempts to grapple with the great theoretical problems that would frustrate their attempts to frame a federal union for many years to come. In the debates over these plans, the colonists first discussed what would prove to be the great questions of federalism: Whom did the national government represent? What were the powers appropriate to it? Where were the boundary lines between the national government's powers and those that belonged to the sovereign states?[4] In analyzing these early attempts, it is useful to distinguish between those issues that so divided the delegates as to doom early hopes for agreement upon a plan of confederation and those issues upon which there was substantial agreement. The divisions, one finds, concerned issues at the core of federalism—the basis for the authority of the new national legislature, and the boundary between its authority and that of the states. It was over these issues that the delegates argued again and again, and it was upon these shoals that early hopes for a confederation were wrecked. Yet the delegates easily reached agreement regarding other issues. Almost without discussion and with little controversy, the delegates agreed to confide in the new national government very substantial executive and administrative powers. While some debate occurred, for example, over the extent of congressional control over state military forces or over Indian affairs, all the early plans of confederation reflected substantial agreement regarding the appropriate executive and administrative functions of a legitimate central government. These powers conformed closely to those imperial powers performed by, or under the authority of, the king, and they mirrored, to a great extent, those that had been exercised by the Congress over the past year.

Until Americans resolved the great questions regarding the extent and nature of the national legislative authority, there could be no durable frame of national government. Such agreement, as events were to prove, did not come easily. Yet a functional union of the colonies could be achieved that was sufficient to carry Americans to independence and beyond, based on the extensive executive powers vested, without controversy, in the Congress.

The Colonies and Union: A Rope of Sand

Americans had rarely questioned the king's role as the legal tie that bound the empire together. In a 1773 essay, a Virginian had presented as a political maxim the proposition that "the People of both Countries are united in the King, who is the Head of the Empire."[5] The next year, a "Philadelphian" expressed no more than a political cliché when he observed that Britain's monarchs were "the Umpires of our Disputes and the Center of our Union."[6]

Because most Englishmen, and most American Tories, discounted the possibility of a durable colonial union in the absence of the king, from 1774 British policy was based directly on the assumption of American disunity. The English had only to withdraw their troops, Daniel Dulany suggested, "and trust to the probable internal convulsions among the Americans." Even if England were to be "well beaten," predicted an English merchant, it was his firm opinion that once the British "quit America," "the colonists would have fine work amongst yourselves." "It is said," summarized one Pennsylvanian, that "the moment we become free from a foreign master, we shall fall to cutting the throats of each other."[7]

Apprehensions of colonial disunity were not limited to Tories and Englishmen. In 1774 some American Whigs as well were pessimistic about the possibility of a durable American union. Philip Livingston predicted that "if England should turn us adrift we should instantly go to civil Wars among ourselves to determine which Colony should govern all the rest." As late as 1776, John Dickinson pleaded with his fellow delegates in Congress to put aside thoughts of independence because of the civil strife that removal of British authority inevitably would entail. "The restraining power of the king . . . is indispensable to protect the colonies from disunion and civil war," he avowed. In fact, Dickinson thought "the most cruel hostility which Britain could wage against" the colonists would be to leave them "a prey to their own jealousies and animosities." The Pennsylvanian reminded his colleagues that "even when supported by the powerful hand of England," the colonists had "abandoned themselves to discords, and sometimes to violence." Remove the "counter-poise of monarchy," Dickinson warned, and "province would rise against province, city against city, and the weapons . . . assumed to combat the common enemy would turn against themselves."[8]

This belief that the Americans, if independent of British authority, could never unite among themselves, was based upon a realistic acknowledgment of the failure of all past attempts to bring about a colonial union. From the end of the seventeenth century, when the military dangers from the French became apparent, British and colonial leaders had urged the necessity of a colonial union for defense. In 1698 proposals were put forward by both William Penn and Charles Davenant calling for a colonial congress (under British supervision) that would have the power to coordinate and conciliate intercolonial affairs.

Such plans became the model for similar schemes that were periodically presented throughout the early and middle eighteenth century. As the French danger increased during this period, the plans of union placed before the colonial legislatures and the Board of Trade proliferated. The most famous, and perhaps the most promising, of all the early proposals to unite the colonies, was Benjamin Franklin's Albany Plan of Union. It should be remembered, however, that Franklin's plan, presented at the 1754 Albany conference called to treat with the powerful New York Indian confederation, differed little from plans presented about this time by such disparate figures as Archibald Kennedy, a New York royal official, and Governor Robert Dinwiddie of Virginia.[9]

The Albany Plan of Union called for a continental government that would consist of a legislature—the Grand Council—whose members would be chosen by the colonial assemblies, and an executive—the President General—who would be appointed by the king. The Grand Council was given extensive responsibilities for colonial defense, including the management and regulation of Indian trade, treaties, and land purchases. To meet these responsibilities, it was empowered to levy taxes and issue currency. All measures of the Grand Council, however, were to be subject to the veto of the appointed President

General. Franklin's plan thus envisioned a relatively strong central government with broad powers to devise, fund, and execute continental policy. Although accepted by the Albany conferees, the plan suffered the same fate as had all previous attempts to link the American colonies in formal union. As Franklin himself described the fate of his Plan of Union, not one colonial assembly adopted it, "as they all thought there was too much prerogative in it," while "in England it was judged to have too much of the democratic," and "the Board of Trade therefore did not approve of it."[10]

These early failures were not merely unfortunate accidents. Some considered the inability of the American colonies to unite among themselves to be an inevitable result of the very real differences between them—in form of government, in religion, in economic base, and in life style. Such differences, many Americans believed, were sufficient to permanently preclude any lasting colonial union independent of the Crown. "Massachusettensis" [Daniel Leonard] observed that "there is perhaps as great a diversity between the temper and habits of the Carolinians" and those of his fellow Yankees "as there subsist between some different nations." Nor need one look so far south, he asserted; such differences existed even among the supposedly homogeneous New England colonies. "Most of the colonies are rivals to each other in trade," he continued. "Between others there subsist deep animosities . . . and the sword of civil war has been more than once unsheathed, without bringing these disputes to a decision." It was clear, he concluded, "that so many discordant, heterogeneous particles could not suddenly unite and consolidate into one body."[11] John Adams, Leonard's bitter opponent on almost all other issues, agreed with him on this. "The Characters of gentlemen in the four New England colonies, differ as much from those in the others," he noted, "as that of the Common People differs, that is, as much as several distinct Nations almost." "We are an infant Country," feared a Virginian, "unconnected in Interest, & naturally disunited by inclination." "Our Forms of Government differ egregiously," he observed, "but our religious Tenets still more so. Our Modes of Life vary, & our Articles of Commerce interfere prodigiously." "Nor," he added, "are we naturally more disjointed in Situation than in Temper."[12]

These differences were encapsulated in a series of stereotypes with which Americans of one section habitually characterized the inhabitants of other sections.[13] New Englanders, for example, were disliked and feared for their supposed grasping, unscrupulous natures and their suspected republicanism. Although "national or Provincial reflections are generally illiberal," wrote a New York doctor to John Dickinson, he could not help noting that the Bostonians had "exhibited an appearance of artfulness, duplicity or behavior twistical" on too many occasions "to merit the entire faith and confidence of their neighbours." Josiah Quincy, Jr., reported after a journey through Pennsylvania that there was "a general disliking, not to say antipathy among the Quakers against N[ew] England, and the aversion has its influence in their judgment on the men and things of that country." Frequently, he reported, they recalled and retold "little anecdotes of the severities used toward their ancestors" in New England.[14] Southerners distrusted New England politics as much as they did the Yankee character. A notion prevailed throughout the middle and southern colonies that New Englanders were, by tradition and preference, republicans.[15] One of the first impressions William Eddis received of "the political disposition of the colonists" upon his arrival in Annapolis in 1769 was that "in the northern provinces a republican spirit evidently prevails." As one merchant bluntly put it, "We are well aware of the intentions of the New England Men, they are of the old King Killing breed." Tory pamphleteer Thomas Bradbury Chandler drew upon such preconceptions in 1775. The "real sentiments" of the New Englanders, he observed, were of "a *peculiar* complexion." They had been inherited from their ancestors, who had "imported with them an aversion to the *regal* part of our Constitution." These old Puritans, he avowed, were "inveterate enemies" to "every species of monarchy" and could not even bear "to read the word *King* in their *Bibles*."[16]

Given this history of distrust, it is not surprising that apprehensions of the motives and dark designs of the Yankees deepened as the crisis with Britain grew graver. New Englanders were naturally domineering, some southerners and middle-colony men believed. Should English authority be removed, some feared an attempt to establish a New England hegemony over the other colonies. When Josiah Quincy, Jr., visited South Carolina in 1773, one gentleman complained over dinner "that the Massachusetts were aiming at sovereignty over the other provinces." "You may depend upon it," he warned his companions, "if the Colonies shake themselves clear" of British authority, the rest of the provinces "will have governors sent you from Boston; Boston aims at nothing less than the sovereignty of the whole continent; I know it." Such fears were particularly likely to occur to classically trained minds who may have seen in modern Massachusetts the reincarnation of the militarily expansive republican Rome.[17]

The Massachusetts delegates to the Continental Congress had their hands full trying to eradicate such views. There was a great "jealousy" among the southerners, Samuel Adams wrote to his friend Joseph Warren, that "we shall in time overrun them all." This fear had not diminished by 1776. "The Province of New York is not without her Fears & apprehensions from the Temper of her Neighbors," Carter Braxton noted darkly, "their great Swarms & small Territory." Such thoughts caused the distrust with which John Adams had to contend of an army made up chiefly of New Englanders. The southerners, he complained, had "a Secret Fear . . . that New England will soon be full of Veteran Soldiers and at length conceive Designs unfavourable to the other Colonies."[18]

Southern distrust of New England was matched by the Yankees' distaste for southerners, whom they viewed as dissipated because of their economic system and sunk in luxury and sloth. The inhabitants of South Carolina, wrote Josiah Quincy, Jr., might all be categorized as either "opulent and lordly planters, poor and spiritless peasants [or] vile slaves." "Their fiercer passions," he noted, did not burn for liberty but rather "seem to be employed upon their slaves and here to expend themselves." "The luxury, dissipation, life, sentiments and manners of the leading people," Quincy believed, naturally tended to make them "neglect, despise, and be careless of the true interests of mankind in general."[19] New England opinions of the middle colonies were not much higher. New York's servility and lukewarmness in the cause of liberty was a continuing topic of New England censure. And the Pennsylvanians, the Yankees believed, thought only of their pocketbooks and were incapable of more elevated conceptions.[20]

Americans feared that such stereotypes, and the intercolonial distrust that spawned them, were too deeply implanted to allow for any permanent colonial union independent of Britain. Previous attempts to unite the colonies in a common course of resistance at the time of the Stamp and Townshend Acts added to American doubts. These efforts to achieve united colonial action had not been designed to bring about a permanent union, but rather to concert colonial measures against specific British actions. Even with this circumscribed objective, the results of early efforts at independent colonial union were limited. Participation in the Stamp Act Congress was not universal, and the meeting had few concrete results. The opposition to the Townshend Acts, which had never been coordinated either in timing or purpose, collapsed in colony after colony and left a bitter residue of recrimination and distrust. By 1774, then, previous attempts to unite the colonies in opposition to Great Britain, like those efforts toward closer colonial union under the aegis of British authority, had achieved no durable results.[21]

Those of a more optimistic temper, however, could find cause for hope in recent events. Despite the considerable differences between the colonies, they *had* been able to achieve a remarkable degree of unity since 1774 regarding the measures necessary to resist British policy. The Congress had become both the symbol of that unity and the institution responsible for coordinating and directing a common resistance policy.

The necessity for a united policy of resistance was apparent to American Whigs from the inception of the final crisis. Only by united action in support of Boston, they realized, could the effects of British tyranny be cast off. All over the colonies, writers stressed the absolute necessity of unity. "An UNION of the colonies," asserted "A Philadelphian," "like an electric rod, will render harmless the storms of British vengeance and tyranny." "Our preservation, as a people," wrote another, "depends upon our Union." "Without Unity," Philip Livingston feared, "America is undone." In short, a New England minister concluded, "unanimity in all orders and ranks of people, is necessary at the present alarming crisis, to give weight, force and strength to all attempts to save this sinking land." "They who endeavor artfully to divide," he declared, "are attempting to destroy us."[22]

Because unity was so essential to a successful opposition, it is not surprising that Whigs insisted that, whatever the previous history of colonial discord, now the colonists *were* united. This unity was at first portrayed as of a spontaneous, almost a providential, origin, having arisen simultaneously within towns, cities, and provinces all over America.[23] Internal unanimity within each colony was matched, Whigs claimed, by the emergence of a widespread and unprecedented intercolonial unity. "The whole continent seems inspired by one soul," reported the *New-York Journal*, "and that soul a vigorous and determined one." The colonists' unprecedented "Union of Sentiment and Conduct," exulted "A British American," was an unmistakable sign "that Heaven designs they shall be free."[24]

Whig newspapers began to emblazon their mastheads with symbols of the new unity, and patriots informed English correspondents that traditional colonial divisions were at an end. "Tell our good friend [Dr. Price]," wrote Franklin to Joseph Priestly, that "his doubts and despondencies about our firmness" were misplaced, for "America is determined and unanimous." As Joseph Howe summarized the remarkable spirit of 1774, "The same plans [were] formed, the same modes of executing" were adopted all over the continent "without consulting each other. The Determinations of every Colony anticipate the wishes of the rest.—One soul activates the whole."[25]

However heartening such sentiments were, patriots began to seek a secure, institutional basis for the unity of action that was so vital to the success of their endeavors.[26] Not surprisingly, they looked to the Congress. As John Witherspoon wrote in 1774, many thought "that the great object of the approaching Congress should be to unite the colonies and make them as one body."[27] To a remarkable extent, the Congress had fulfilled such expectations and had devised a united plan of resistance that had commanded widespread support.[28] By 1775, with the coming of the war, however, it had become clear that Congress would have to continue in existence for the indefinite future and to perform governmental functions of increasing variety and complexity. It seemed only logical, therefore, that the delegates would attempt to institutionalize and define Congress's role in securing colonial unity. As Benjamin Franklin noted in introducing the first proposal for a plan of confederation that came before the Congress in 1775, "Great Britain had now rendered an opposition by arms necessary" and he thought there ought accordingly to be "some bond of union, in writing, that each colony might know how far it stood engaged, and for what purposes, and how far it had a right to rely on its sister colonies."[29]

Confederation, 1775–1776

The earliest proposal introduced in Congress for institutionalizing a colonial union was that introduced by Joseph Galloway in 1774. Galloway's plan, however, had both presupposed and been premised upon the continuation of the colonies within the empire, and its goal was to remove the points of controversy regarding Parliament's right to legislate for the colonies.[30] From early 1775 on, however, congressional radicals had begun to conceive of a permanent colonial union that had as its purpose the perpetuation of coordinated colonial resistance to British policy. Thus Samuel Ward proposed in December 1774 that whatever the British ministry did in the winter of 1774–75, the colonies ought still to send delegates to an annual colonial congress. "Many new Regulations of Commerce Manufactures &c., may be adopted for the general Good of the Colonies," he noted, "and should the Ministry be inclined to make any new Attempts upon Us our being united & on our Guard would be the most probable Means of preventing them." While such men thought it possible that their united resistance might be pursued from within the empire, they were also prepared to contemplate that it might have to be pursued from without. Thus Silas Deane, in corresponding with Patrick Henry in January 1775, reflected upon the old New England Confederation of 1643–85. He noted:

> I need not mention to you what would have been the Consequences had this Confederation have continued untill now, and the other Colonies early acceded to it—it is not too late to form such an one that will suit Our present Circumstances & which being varied as future Contingences arise may last forever. Something of this kind appears most absolutely necessary, let Us turn which way We will. If a reconciliation with G Britain takes place, it will be obtained on the best terms, by the Colonies being united, and be the more like to be preserved, on just and equal Terms; if no reconciliation is to be had without a Confederation We are ruined to all intents and purposes. United We stand, divided We fall, is our motto and must be. One general Congress had brought the Colonies to be acquainted with each other, and I am in hopes another may effect a lasting Confederation which will need nothing, perhaps, but time, to mature it into a complete & perfect American Constitution, the only proper one for Us, whether connected with Great Britain, or Not.

Because confederation (as those like Deane conceived of it) presupposed, or at least contemplated, independence, the issue (like independence) was not widely discussed prior to Bunker Hill. With the coming of the war, however, the necessity for an extended period of armed resistance made the need for a formal colonial union more apparent.[31]

This was the ostensible basis upon which Benjamin Franklin, an old advocate of colonial union, laid his proposed articles of confederation before the Congress on July 21, 1775. Franklin clearly did not intend his plan—a hastily drawn product containing thirteen vaguely worded articles—to do anything more than induce the delegates to consider the issue. He labeled his personal copy of the plan a "sketch," and he presented it to his colleagues as a tentative draft, "to be moulded" by them "into any shape [they] thought proper, and merely to set the thing a-going."[32] But, however tentatively presented, Franklin's plan was a coherent, if ill-defined, outline of a relatively strong national government.[33] The government was to consist of a national legislature—the Congress—whose executive and administrative functions were to be undertaken by both the Congress itself and, when it was in recess, by an executive council. The delegates to the Congress were to be elected by each colony by an unspecified process. The number of delegates allotted to each colony was to be proportionate to the male population, and the expenses of the confederation were to be apportioned on a similar basis. The powers and duties of the national government were summarized in one terse article. They would extend to

> determining on War and Peace, to entring into Alliances, the Settling all Disputes and Differences between Colony and Colony if such should arise; and the Planting of new Colonies when proper. The Congress shall also make such general Ordinances as tho' necessary to the General Welfare, particular Assemblies cannot be competent to; viz. those that may relate to our general Commerce; to the Establishment of Posts; and the Regulation of Forces. The Congress shall also have the Appointment of all Officers civil and military, appertaining to the general Confederacy, such a General Treasurer Secretary, &c.

Aside from such large discretionary powers ceded to the national government, each colony was to "enjoy and retain as much as it may think fit of its own present Laws, Customs, Rights, Privileges, and peculiar Jurisdictions within its own Limits" as it saw fit. As to duration, Franklin's plan clearly reflected the rationale upon which he introduced it. The union of the colonies would last until the British government accepted the "Terms of Reconciliation" proposed by Congress. Failing this, however, "the Confederation is to be perpetual."[34]

Franklin read his proposals aloud before the Congress sitting as a committee of the whole. As Benjamin Harrison later recalled the delegates' reception of his work, "the congress refused to enter into any consideration of it, to send it to the conventions for their approbation, to have it printed for public perusal, to have any entry made in their journals of such a paper being offered, or in any manner to make any order which should imply either approbation or disapprobation of it; it was simply permitted to lie on the table."[35]

After July 1775 the subject of confederation virtually disappears from the *Journals* until almost the eve of independence. The silence in the *Journals* is misleading, however. Although Congress did not officially consider the issue until the following June, it was discussed at length both by the delegates and their constituents, and copies of Franklin's plan were widely circulated among the delegates and the provincial legislatures.[36]

Confederation, in fact, remained a subject dear to radical hearts during the summer and fall of 1775. It was clearly a hot topic in Massachusetts during this period. "It appears plain to me," Joseph Hawley informed the newly elected continental delegate Elbridge Gerry, "that no vigorous and effectual operation for general defence will be carried on until a firm and well digested Confederation be formed and communicated by the Congress." "Where are the Articles of Confederation," James Warren asked John Adams in November, "I want to see some settled Constitution of Congress."[37] The delegates continued to refuse to consider confederation, however, despite continuing efforts to bring the issue before the Congress. Confederation was clearly of considerable interest to the Connecticut delegates. In early December 1775 they informed Governor John Trumbull that they had "not as yet been able to lay before the Congress" the "draught of Articles of Confederation," for "Business of every kind, & from every Quarter" was "thickening fast at this Season."[38] The articles to which they referred were probably an expanded version of proposed articles of confederation prepared by Silas Deane, perhaps in consultation with his colleagues Roger Sherman and Eliphalet Dyer.[39]

Deane's proposed articles were, in substance, very similar to those suggested by Franklin, and, like them, they were quite short and quite vaguely worded. While he suggested that Congress be invested with considerable executive and administrative powers, Deane, unlike Franklin, did not propose that Congress create a separate executive and administrative arm. Like Franklin, Deane proposed that the number of delegates to be allotted to each colony be proportional to population, but he also proposed that the manner of ascertaining congressional decisions be varied according to the substantive importance of the issue involved. Thus, he suggested that "in determining on Supplies of Men, or Money, . . . & other Concerns of a Lesser Nature there must be a Majority of Numbers represented in Congress, independent of particular Colonies," whereas "in determining on Warr, or peace, on the privileges of the Colonies in General, or of any one in particular, there must be, . . . a Majority both of Colonies, and Numbers." Also, like Franklin, Deane suggested that broad powers be ceded to Congress, proposing, for example, that Congress possess extensive power to appoint provincial officials, as well as the power to lay customs duties for the benefit of the Continental treasury.[40]

The Connecticut proposal, while interesting as an early conception of a relatively strong central government, was never introduced in Congress, and its primary author, Deane, had little to do with the subsequent debate over confederation. Deane was, in fact, near the end of his term in Congress when in January 1776 Franklin, in league with Samuel Adams, again tried to move his colleagues to consider his own plan of union. On January 15, 1776, Samuel Adams informed his cousin John that he and Franklin had agreed to bring the issue of confederation before the Congress again. His patience was almost at an end, he noted; if the Congress continued to ignore the subject of confederation, he and Franklin had agreed that it would have to "be done by those [colonies] that inclind to it." For his part, Samuel Adams promised to "endeavor to unite the New England Colonies in confederating, if *none* of the rest would joyn in it." Franklin had agreed that if he succeeded, he "would cast in his Lot among us."[41] True to this plan, on the following day Samuel Adams and Franklin attempted to get a definite date set for debate on the question of confederation. As Edward Tilghman, an observer of the Philadelphia political scene who was unfriendly to Adams, informed his father, Adams ("Judas Iscariot") had "made a motion . . . [which] tended towards a *closer confederacy*." The motion, he noted, had caused such a stir, "that whole Colonies have threatened to leave the Congress." Richard Smith, a more impartial observer, recorded in his diary that "considerable Arguments" were engendered by the proposal and that "William Hooper, John Dickinson, and others had asserted themselves against it. The proposal was thereupon "carried in the Negative."[42]

Through the winter, the advocates of confederation continued to press the issue, both in and out of Congress. In the face of the stubborn refusal of his colleagues in Congress even to consider the question, Franklin began to sound the possibility of creating a New England confederation independent of any action by Congress. Samuel Ward, who was an early and continuing supporter of confederation, agreed with his brother Henry "upon the immediate Necessity of a Confederation." "I am daily in Pursuit of it & never intend to loose sight of it," he wrote, but he believed that the "unhappy Jealousy" of New England that prevailed in Congress was a major factor that "retards it." Although there were "many important Considerations on both Sides of the Question," he was beginning to agree with Franklin that if the four New England colonies agreed to confederate among themselves and invited all to join them, "this would be the surest Way to induce the other Cols. to join Us." Others, like John Adams, continued to pin their hopes on Congress. Thus, in a list Adams drew up, probably in mid-February, regarding the "Measures to be Pursued in Congress," he included "The Confederation to be taken up in Paragraphs," and he prepared a draft resolution (never introduced) that the Congress appoint a committee "to prepare a Draught of a firm Confederation," which would be sent to the "several Assemblies and conventions of these united Colonies, to be by them adopted, ratified and confirmed."[43]

Those who supported confederation viewed the measure from the beginning as an essential step toward their cherished goal of independence. Opponents of independence shared this view. Because they also saw independence and confederation as inherently linked, they worked against the latter primarily because they abhorred the former.[44] As Samuel Adams explained the political alignments in Congress on the issue to James Warren in early January 1776, "You ask me, 'When you are to hear of our Confederation'? I answer, when some Gentlemen . . . shall 'feel more bold.' . . . Are you sollicitous to hear of our Confederation? I will tell you, It is not dead but sleepeth," its progress retarded because "the timid sort of men" feared that "the People without Doors would [not] follow the Congress passibus aequis, if such Measures as *some* called spirited, were pursued."[45]

As the spring wore on, the opponents of independence shifted their position regarding confederation. Thus, although men like Dickinson had opposed the efforts to bring the issue before the Congress in January, by late spring a declaration of independence appeared all but inevitable. With their great goal of reconciliation rapidly fading from view, the opponents of independence began to view confederation not as a precursor of independence but as a necessary precondition. While they still opposed a declaration of independence, they began to argue that, if it must come, it at least ought to be delayed until the colonies had agreed among themselves upon a plan of confederation. As "J.R." of Connecticut wrote in May 1776, "to make a Declaration of Independency before a proper foundation is laid by the union of the Colonies for it to rest upon, is like beginning at the top." Edward Rutledge observed that "the Sensible part of the House" (those who thought as he did) did not object to a confederacy, but "a Man must have the Impudence of a New Englander" to proceed to independence "in our present disjointed state." Carter Braxton declared in April 1776 that if independence "was to be now asserted, the Continent would be torn in pieces by intestine Wars & Convulsions." He too believed that prior to independence . . . "a grand Continental League must be formed & a superintending Power also." Thus John Dickinson, in his final speech against independence, argued, "Not only Treaties with foreign powers but among Ourselves should precede this Declaration; We should know on what Grounds We are to stand with Regard to one another."[46]

For different reasons, therefore, and with different objectives, by June 1776 all the factions agreed that the Congress ought to begin work on a plan of confederation. As Josiah Bartlett reported on July 1, "the whole Congress are unanimous for forming a plan of Confederation of the Colonies."[47] Thus, when the Congress agreed on June 11 to appoint committees to draft a declaration of independence and to prepare a draft treaty with foreign powers, it also agreed to appoint a committee "to prepare and digest the form of a confederation to be entered into between the colonies." Unlike the other two committees, the Confederation Committee was to consist of one member from each colony.[48]

The committee deliberated almost continuously for the next two weeks. On July 1, Josiah Bartlett wrote that his committee "have been upon it for about a fortnight at all oppertunities; last Saturday the Committee spent the whole Day on it, this Day after Congress we are to meet again." The dominant figure in these deliberations was none other than John Dickinson.[49] Debate in the committee was intense, particularly regarding those clauses of Dickinson's draft (Articles xviii and xix of the committee draft) that delineated the powers and function of the national legislature.[50] But as Dickinson later told the full Congress, "The Committee on Confederation dispute almost every Article," causing "some of Us totally [to] despair of any reasonable Terms of Confederation." For Edward Rutledge, a major reason for the struggle lay in the Dickinson draft from which the committee was working. "It has the Vice of all his Productions to a considerable Degree," he declared, "I mean the Vice of Refining too much." "Unless it is greatly curtailed it can never pass," Rutledge predicted, "as it is to be submitted to Men in their respective Provinces who will not be led or rather driven into Measures which may lay the Foundation of their Ruin."[51]

On July 12 the committee draft was placed before the full Congress, and eighty copies were ordered printed, under strict admonitions of secrecy, for distribution to the delegates.[52] The committee draft was considerably more elaborate, and considerably more specific, than any of its predecessors. It consisted of twenty densely written articles. The national government proposed by the committee, like all previous proposals, consisted of a national legislature—the Congress—which was, as Franklin had proposed, empowered to appoint an executive council of state to consist of one delegate from each colony. The council was given executive and administrative responsibility for carrying on the business of government during congressional recesses and taking certain emergency military actions. In addition, the Congress was empowered to appoint all civil officers it believed necessary to carry out the duties and functions entrusted to the national government.[53] Those powers are specified, for the most part, in Article xviii, by far the longest of all the draft articles.

The exclusive powers vested in the Congress included that of determining war and peace, including war and peace with the Indian nations except in cases of actual Indian attack. To this end, Congress was also given the exclusive power to order the respective colonies to raise specified land forces, to itself raise naval forces, to commission higher officers, and to equip and regulate the armed forces. Conversely, no state was permitted to keep a standing army. The national government had the exclusive power to regulate foreign affairs, including the power to send and receive ambassadors and to enter into treaties and alliances. To emphasize the exclusivity of this power, the states were expressly forbidden to do that which Congress was empowered to do. Congress also had the exclusive power to "Settl[e] all Disputes and Differences now subsisting, or that hereafter may arise between two or more Colonies concerning Boundaries, Jurisdictions, or any other cause whatever." Congress had the exclusive power, as well, to regulate the Indian trade and manage all Indian affairs, with the exception noted above. Congress was additionally vested with such administrative tasks as setting up a national post office, coining and valuing money, and devising a uniform system of weights and measures. Perhaps most important, the committee would have given Congress the power to create a national domain by giving the national government the exclusive power both to purchase land from the Indians and to limit the western boundaries of those colonies that had clauses in their charters granting them land from sea to sea. Power over trade policy, however, was not made exclusive. Instead, any individual colony was allowed to "assess or lay such Imposts or Duties as it thinks proper, on Importations or Exportations," so long as "such Imposts or Duties do not interfere with any Stipulations in Treaties" that Congress had entered into with foreign powers. Aside from such specified congressional powers, however, each individual state was to "retain and enjoy as much of its present Laws, Rights and Customs, as it may think fit, and reserves to itself the sole and exclusive Regulation and Government of its internal police, in all matters that shall not interfere with the Articles of this Confederation." The expenses of the national government were to be supplied out of a common treasury, with the contribution of each colony to the treasury to be proportionately assessed upon the basis of "the Number of Inhabitants of every Age, Sex and Quality." In determining all questions to come before the Congress, however, Article xvii tersely provided that "each Colony shall have one Vote."[54]

Congress, sitting as a committee of the whole, began its consideration of the committee draft on July 22. The debates went on almost daily until August 2, despite a multitude of other pressing business. After a short hiatus to deal with urgent military matters, the subject of confederation was again taken up from August 6 through 8, and then put aside until the end of the month.[55] While some had expressed optimism, it was clear to most at the beginning of the debate that substantive agreement on confederation would be difficult to reach. Near the end of the arduous committee deliberations, Josiah Bartlett wrote that he did not know when the full Congress "will model it to their minds." Although it was "a Business of the greatest importance to the future happiness of America," he thought his correspondent might "Easily see the Difficulty to frame it so as to be agreable to the Delegates of all the Different Colonies & of the Colonial Legislatures also." As the debates in the full Congress dragged on, the pessimism regarding an ultimate resolution increased. By August 9, Samuel Chase despaired of an agreement. "When we shall be confederated States," he sighed, "I know not. I am afraid the Day is far distant." Three days later William Williams wrote that although Congress labored hard over the confederation, he feared "a permanent one will never be settled."[56]

The pessimism was the result of major substantive disagreements that had surfaced during the course of the long committee deliberations and the longer congressional debate. John Adams summarized the issues that divided the delegates again and again through July and August. They argued over "how We shall vote. Whether each Colony shall count one? or whether each shall have a Weight in Proportion to its Numbers, or Wealth, or Exports and Imports, or a compound Ratio of all?" Another important question was "whether Congress shall have Authority to limit the Dimensions of each Colony, to prevent those which claim, by Charter, or Proclamation or Commission to the South Sea, from growing too great and powerfull, so as to be dangerous to the rest."[57] These questions concerned the nature and functions of the national legislature that the delegates were endeavoring to create—the basis for representation within it, the powers appropriate to it, and the appropriate boundary between those powers and the powers that belonged to the states. These were precisely the questions that had torn the empire asunder as the colonists and the British sought to define and allocate legislative authority between the colonial legislatures and the imperial parliament. After independence, these issues formed the basis of the enduring contradictions of federalism, so it is not surprising that they did not prove amenable to easy solution in 1776.[58]

The difficulties regarding the basis of representation within the national legislature had been apparent from the opening day of the First Congress.[59] At that time, the delegates had agreed to the voting procedure that allocated an equal vote to all colonies only because the crisis was so pressing and the statistical basis for ascertaining an equitable proportional representation was lacking. But the solution, in which each colony was simply given one vote, was clearly not intended to be final.[60] Thus, in Franklin's draft articles of July 1775, he proposed instead a proportional mode of representation; delegates in Congress were to be allocated according to the adult male population of a colony. Fairness and symmetry were to be preserved by allocating responsibility for continental expenses by precisely the same formula.[61] Franklin's proposal quickly drew protest from an observer who, on his copy of Franklin's articles, scribbled in the margin next to this provision, "the delegates from each colony should be changed. . . . I believe that if each colony had but one vote in the present manner of voting it would be a more equal government." He added prophetically that "much may be said on the Subject; it requires consideration." Silas Deane also proposed to allocate delegates according to population. But he proposed a compromise on the voting procedure that in another form became the basis for the ultimate compromise reached in 1787. He suggested that certain important issues, such as determining war and peace, were to be resolved by a majority vote "both of Colonies and Numbers." By December, Samuel Ward was debating the issue with his brother Henry at the same time that he was urging the absolute necessity of a confederation:

> You say Representation ought to be as equal as possible. Agreed, but what is to be represented—not the Individuals of a particular Community but several States, Colonies or Bodies corporate. All Writers agree that a Nation is to be considered as one Person, one moral accountable Person having a Will of its own &c. Your Proposition allows to the larger Colonies several Wills [i.e., several delegates] & to the smaller not one, that is not one entire and compleat Will, & thereby makes the smaller wholly dependent on the larger.[62]

When Dickinson originally drafted his articles, he left this provision blank, realizing that it would be subjected to intense debate. He was correct. The committee notes show that the members widely canvassed the practices of existing confederations, such as that of the United Provinces of the Netherlands, as well as Franklin's old Albany Plan. In the end, however, the committee draft suggested that the Congress retain its existing voting procedure—one vote for each colony, with each colony left to decide how many delegates it wished to send to Congress.[63]

The debates on Articles xi and xvii (the voting and expense articles) show how bitterly divisive these intertwined issues were. They took place on July 30, 31, and August 1, and the lines were drawn early. Chase immediately called attention to the importance of the debate. The article over voting procedure, he observed, "was the most likely to divide us of any one proposed in the draught under consideration. That the larger colonies had threatened they would not confederate at all if their weight in congress should not be equal to the numbers of people they added to the confederacy; while the smaller ones declared against an union if it did not retain an equal vote for the protection of their rights." Chase thereupon proposed a compromise very much along the lines of Deane's proposals. He suggested "that a discrimination should take place among the questions which would come before Congress," and that some of them ought to be settled by a majority vote of the states, and some by a majority of delegates. Franklin, ostensibly seconding Chase, instead reiterated his unwavering conviction that "the votes should be so proportioned in all cases." He thought it extraordinary that the small states should say, in effect, that "they would not confederate with us unless we would let them dispose of our money." Connecting the voting issue squarely with that of expenses, he added, "Certainly if we vote equally we ought to pay equally; but the smaller states will hardly purchase the privilege at this price."[64] To this, Witherspoon answered that if "an equal vote be refused, the smaller states will become vassals to the larger; & all experience has shewn that the vassals & subjects of free states are the most enslaved."[65]

The debate was not, however, really about economic fairness, for all agreed that the larger states ought to continue to pay a larger share of the Continental expenses than the smaller ones, with the argument coming primarily over how that share ought to be calculated. Neither was it over the possible hegemony of the larger states, for, as Wilson noted, the large states of Virginia, Pennsylvania, and Massachusetts had such divergent interests that they were much more likely to disagree than to conspire to deprive the small states of their liberty.[66] The underlying issue was much more fundamental, and the delegates were quite explicit about this. The argument was really over whether the new national legislature represented the people as individuals or the states as separate political bodies. John Witherspoon argued for the latter; for him, Congress clearly was the exclusive agent of the states as corporate entities. He concluded that "the colonies should in fact be considered as individuals; and that as such in all disputes they should have an equal vote. That they are now collected as individuals making a bargain with each other, & of course had a right to vote as individuals." For analogies he looked not to Parliament but to the Belgian confederacy and, more revealingly, to the "East India Company [where] they voted by persons, & not by their proportion of stock." Witherspoon admitted that equality of representation was an excellent principle but believed that it must be "of things which are co-ordinate; that is, of things similar & of the same nature: that nothing relating to individuals could ever come before Congress; nothing but would respect colonies." Such was also the view of Roger Sherman, who stated succinctly, "We are rep[resentative]s of States not Individuals."[67]

Benjamin Rush's conception of the Congress could not have been more different. For Rush, the delegates were representatives of the people, not ambassadors from the states. While it was true, he admitted, that "the members of the congress . . . are app[ointe]d by States," he believed that they "repres[ented] the people—& no State hath a right to alienate the priviledge of equal rep[resentatio]n," which, he noted, was "the found[ation] of liberty." He continued: "The Objects before us are the people's rights, not the rights of States. Every man in America stands related to two legislative bodies—he deposits his prop[ert]y, liberty & life with his own State, but his trade [and] Arms, the means of enriching & defending himself & his honor, he deposits with the congress." "It has been said," noted James Wilson, that "Congress is a representation of states; not of individuals," but "I say that the objects of it's care are all the individuals of the states. . . . As to those matters which are referred to Congress, we are not so many states; we are one large state. We lay aside our individuality whenever we come here."[68]

Such a fundamental divergence of views over the basis of Congress's authority could not be easily resolved. In the August 20 draft Articles that were distributed to the states, Article xvii remained unchanged. The disgust of the advocates of proportional representation was palpable. Despite his longstanding commitment to the principle of confederation, Franklin drafted a proposal that the Pennsylvania Assembly dissent from the articles precisely because of the inequitable voting procedure. John Adams worried about the consequences of the inequitable system agreed upon by the delegates, in which "R.I. will have an equal Weight with the Mass. The Delaware Government with

Pensilvania and Georgia with Virginia." In adopting this principle of representation, he feared, "We are sowing the Seeds of Ignorance[,] Corruption, and Injustice, in the fairest Field of Liberty, that ever appeared upon Earth, even in the first Attempts to cultivate it." It was, he thought, "poor Consolation, under the Cares of a whole Life Spent in the Vindication of the Principles of Liberty, to See them violated, in the first formation of Governments, erected by the People themselves on their own Authority." For Jefferson as well the Articles were a disappointment. They were, he wrote to Richard Henry Lee as soon as he had read the committee draft, "in every interesting point the reverse of what our country would wish."[69]

Of particular distress to the Virginians and to other colonies whose colonial charters gave them unlimited title to western lands (the so-called "sea to sea" clauses) were the clauses in Articles xiv and xviii of the committee draft that gave Congress the power to limit "the Bounds of those Colonies, which by Charter or Proclamation, or under any Pretence, are said to extend to the South Sea, and ascertaining those Bounds of any other Colony that appear to be indeterminate." With the land thus detached from existing colonies, and that which the Congress obtained by purchase from the Indians (to which it was given exclusive right by Article xiv), Congress was authorized to create and define the boundaries of new states and sell the land therein for the benefit of the Continental treasury.[70]

The delegates debated these issues on July 25 and on August 2, and again the debates revealed very deep divisions. At one level, the cause of the controversy and the positions of the parties were obvious. Those colonies, like Virginia and Connecticut, that had "sea to sea" clauses in their charters had no intention of ceding this potential source of wealth to the continent. Those colonies that did not have such clauses had no intention of uniting on such unequal terms with the colonies that did. As Samuel Chase of Maryland asserted bluntly, "no colony has a Right to go to the S[outh] Sea. They never had—they can't have. It would not be safe to the rest." His colleague, Thomas Stone, reiterated at the end of the debates that "the small Colonies have a Right to Happiness and Security. They would have no Safety if the great Colonies were not limited." Furthermore, he noted, these western lands would be secured only by the common efforts of all in the struggle against Great Britain; in fairness, all should share the gain.[71]

Benjamin Harrison of Virginia answered with a question. "How came Maryland by its Land?" The answer was obvious: "by its Charter." Thus, he observed, how could Maryland dispute the claims of Virginia, for by "its Charter Virginia owns to the South Sea." He ended, however, with an assertion. The delegates, he stated, "shall not pare away the Colony of Virginia." Wilson attacked the legality of the clauses themselves. Any such claims were "extravagant," he argued, in that such "Grants were made upon Mistakes," as the grantors were "ignorant of the Geography." While he acknowledged that Pennsylvania had "no Right to interfere in those claims," she did have "a Right to say, that she will not confederate unless those Claims are cut off."[72]

The issue, however, had another dimension, for implied in the assertion that Congress had a right to limit the boundary of a sovereign state was the premise that Congress, as an institution, was superior to the states, and that it could, if necessary, alter the frames of government that the people of the states had adopted or created. This was the argument made explicitly by Huntington of Connecticut. He admitted that Virginia presented a danger, but, he asked, did it "follow that Congress has a Right to limit her Bounds?" The consequence of not doing so, he realized, might be the failure of the confederation, "but as to the Question of Right, We all unite against mutilating Charters. . . . A Man's Right does not cease to be a Right because it is large." Jefferson, for his part, "protest[ed] vs. the Right of Congress to decide, upon the Right of Virginia."[73]

Virginia and its allies triumphed in the short run. In the August 20 draft circulated to the states, virtually every provision that gave the Congress the power to create and administer a national domain was deleted. Thus in the struggle to delineate the relative powers of the national legislature and the states in the critical area of the western lands, where conflict was most likely to arise, the rights of the national legislature were subordinated to those of the states.[74] But the victory of the "sea to sea" states on this issue, like that of the smaller states on the issue of representation, was a pyrrhic one, because the positions taken in the debates over these issues, and the readiness that the delegates displayed to maintain these positions at the expense of a confederation, showed how far they were from resolving the basic dilemma of federalism. They simply could not find an easy or quick solution to the problem of how to divide the sovereignty derived from the people between their representatives in the state legislatures and those in the national legislature. By the end of July, this was evident to those on all sides of the debate. "Much of our time is taken up in forming and debating a Confederation for the united States," wrote Joseph Hewes. "What we shall make of it God only knows," but he was "inclined to think we shall never modell it so as to be agreed to by all the Colonies."[75]

Yet these differences, fundamental as they were, do not tell the whole story regarding the prospects for national union. Although the debates showed clearly that the delegates could not agree upon the composition and authority of the national legislature, they also evidenced substantial agreement regarding the executive and administrative powers that were to be vested in the new national government. While these powers engendered disagreement and discussion, there was in all the various proposals for confederation a substantial consensus regarding powers that would later become essential components of a strong national government. In this sense, the issues upon which the delegates agreed were as important as those upon which they did not.

All the drafts granted to the central government the authority to conduct all relations with foreign powers. In the committee draft, this power was, apparently without debate, made exclusive, for the colonies were expressly forbidden to "enter into any Treaty, Convention or Conference" with any foreign power.[76] Similarly, full powers over the military forces of the colonies were also vested in the Congress. According to the committee draft, Congress was to determine the size of the land forces the continental service required, and to pay them, regulate them, and appoint the general officers to command them. Furthermore, Dickinson's draft strengthened continental control of the military forces by specifically limiting those of the states. Thus the states were prohibited from keeping a standing army in peacetime, except for those forces that Congress decided were necessary to guard the state's frontier against Indian attack. This considerable limitation upon the authority of the states was also retained both by the committee and by the whole Congress in the August 20 draft.[77] It is important to note that Continental control of the land forces was not exclusive, for the states remained the agents responsible for raising the forces that Congress requisitioned, and they retained the power to appoint inferior officers. But such qualifications show only that there was nothing instinctive or foreordained regarding the extensive executive powers confided to the central government; rather, the delegates made a deliberate decision to institutionalize congressional practice over the past year in raising and regulating Continental land forces. The power granted to Congress to raise and regulate naval forces, however, was made exclusively Continental, and this, too, reflected the practice of the preceding year.[78]

Similarly uncontroversial were the considerable administrative powers granted to Congress to guarantee the internal union of the colonies. Thus, the central government was empowered to organize a post office, to issue and value a Continental currency, and to devise and administer a uniform system of weights and measures.[79] Despite the failure to retain central power over the western lands, the August 20 draft did retain the powers given to Congress to adjudicate boundary disputes between colonies.[80] Additionally, and again without controversy, Congress was vested with extensive powers to appoint such civil officers as it thought necessary to carry out its executive and administrative responsibilities.[81]

Virtually the only executive responsibility vested in the Congress that gave rise to recorded debate was the provision in Article XVIII that gave the Congress the exclusive right to regulate trade and all other affairs with the Indians.[82] The clause was briefly debated on July 26. The South Carolina delegates objected to giving control of the lucrative Indian trade to the Congress, especially given the expense to which the colonies were put in defending their frontiers against the Indians. Yet the controversy seems muted when compared to the violence of the debates over representation and the national domain. "No lasting Peace will be with the Indians, unless made by one Body," Wilson argued, and a "perpetual War would be unavoidable, if every Body was allowed to trade with them."[83] His argument was apparently successful, for continental control over Indian affairs was retained in the August 20 draft, and the issue did not surface subsequently as a major source of controversy.

The implicit model that guided the delegates' choices becomes clearer when one compares the decision regarding trade with the Indians with that regarding trade with foreign powers, for Congress was not given the power, grudgingly conceded to Parliament in 1774, to regulate and coordinate national trade policy with foreign nations. Instead, the committee draft gave each state the power to "assess or lay such Imposts or Duties as it thinks proper," except where such imposts would "interfere with any stipulations in Treaties hereafter entered into by the United States assembled" with foreign powers.[84] Thus, although the powers given to Congress by the draft Articles of Confederation were not explicitly divided into legislative, executive, or judicial, it seems safe to say that the delegates had considerably less trouble confiding the executive functions formerly exercised by the king to Congress than they did in allocating the legislative authority formerly exercised or claimed by Parliament to the new central government.

One may gain a clearer understanding of the extensiveness of the executive authority confided to the national government by the draft Articles of Confederation when that authority is compared with the powers later granted to the executive branch by the Convention of 1787. Virtually every power, except that of pardon, allotted to the executive in Article II, Section 2, of the Constitution, was also allotted to the national government by all the drafts of the Articles of Confederation.[85]

The model that so decisively influenced the shape of the national executive was that of the British Crown.[86] Many of the basic imperial powers exercised by the king had been thrust upon a reluctant Congress from 1775 on. When the first debates over confederation took place, Congress had been exercising those powers for over a year. Until the great problems of federalism were resolved, there would be no frame of government that would guarantee the union of the colonies. Yet Congress could be the instrument of a functional union sufficient to carry the colonists over the Rubicon of independence and beyond, if it were based upon the extensive executive and administrative functions it had assumed from the vacating British Crown. "We want a confederation you will say," wrote John Adams, an early advocate of confederation, to like-minded James Warren on the eve of independence. "True. This must be obtained. But we are united now they say— and the difference between Union and confederation is only the same with that between an express and implied Contract."[87]

CHAPTER 7

Congress and Unity: Foreign Affairs

My Idea of the Congress's Power was that She was to make Peace or War, say how much each Province was to find or sink of the Taxes necessary, conclude Alliances, make Laws regulating the whole where the Jurisdiction of the Colonies were unequal to the Task such as a Contention between Colonies about Limits or any other Quarrell between them &c.
                                              —*Benjamin Rumsey, June 3, 1776*

Thus did a Maryland legislator articulate his conception of the legitimate extent of congressional authority. Rumsey was a province man by choice, with limited knowledge of the momentous events then transpiring at the Congress in Philadelphia. Yet his independent assessment of the desirable extent of congressional power differed little from that of most continental delegates. In fact, Rumsey's comments reflect a general agreement on the nature of congressional power that is evident in all the drafts of the Articles of Confederation considered through the early years of the Revolution. In all of them, the exclusive power to regulate the foreign affairs of the confederating colonies was confided, without debate, in the Congress. In fact, the Articles merely reflected the events of the previous two years. From 1774 on, at the insistence of their constituents, the delegates assumed the exclusive responsibility not only to conduct all negotiations with Great Britain but to direct relations with all foreign powers as well. While at first the delegates responded to clearly expressed constituent desires, those desires reflected the delegates' own views. For they soon began to assert, quite self-consciously, their own exclusive power over Continental foreign affairs.

External Union: Relations with Great Britain

In 1774 the "foreign affairs" of the colonies (if intra-imperial relations could thus be called) referred solely to relations with the mother country.[1] Early congressional efforts beyond the Atlantic, therefore, exclusively concerned colonial relations with Great Britain. Initial congressional activity in this area was directed toward stating a united colonial position on the disputes between the colonies and the mother country and presenting this position publicly. The methods employed by the delegates clearly show their conception of the proper congressional role. As an extralegal convention attempting to influence the policies of a colonial power, the Congress directed many of its early documents beyond the British government directly to the people of Great Britain. Convincing the British people of the rectitude of the colonial cause was the purpose behind such efforts as the *Address to the People of Great-Britain* of October 21, 1774, a similar address of July 8, 1775, and the *Address to the People of Ireland* of July 28, 1775.[2]

But the delegates were also moving toward becoming a legitimate central government authorized to negotiate on a government-to-government level with all external powers. This newer and ultimately dominant conception becomes clearer when one examines the process by which the delegates assumed responsibility for carrying on negotiations with the mother country. This authority was initially thrust upon them by colonial assemblies asked to respond to Lord North's 1775 peace initiative. But the delegates also took upon themselves the responsibility not only to respond but also to initiate negotiations with Britain, and they increasingly claimed that the power to do so was vested exclusively in their body.

In late February 1775, Parliament approved the reconciliation plan that Lord North had introduced on February 20.[3] North offered, in sum, that if the colonial legislatures would guarantee to provide an adequate and permanent revenue to the Crown sufficient to meet the needs of colonial defense and civil administration, Parliament would in turn give up its claim of a right to tax the colonies.[4] According to a circular letter by Lord Dartmouth to the royal governors, the plan was to be presented by each governor to his legislature, and the governors were authorized to call special sessions of the legislatures for the purpose of considering the North plan.[5] All the colonial legislatures to which the plan was presented, however, reacted uniformly; as the plan implicated matters of general colonial concern, they concluded that the Congress was the proper body to form an appropriate response. Thus on May 1, 1775, Governor John Penn called the Pennsylvania Assembly into special session in order to consider the plan. "As you are the first Assembly on the Continent to whom this Resolution has been communicated," Penn noted, "much depends on the moderation and wisdom of your counsels." Only two days later the Assembly issued a ringing reply penned by John Dickinson. "If no other objection to the plan proposed occurred to us," he wrote, "we should esteem it a dishonorable desertion of sister Colonies, connected by General Counsels, for a single Colony to adopt a measure so extensive in consequence, without the advice and consent of those Colonies engaged with us by solemn ties in the same common cause."[6]

New Jersey quickly followed Pennsylvania's lead. The royal governor, William Franklin, laid the plan and Dartmouth's letter before the Assembly on May 16. Along with it he presented his own carefully considered statement of the plan's merits. After four days of consideration, the Assembly answered. "As the Continental Congress is now sitting to consider of the present critical situation of *American* affairs; and as this House has already appointed Delegates for that purpose," they wrote, they would have been glad had Franklin postponed presenting the plan to them until such time as the Congress acted. "Until [the] opinion [of the Congress] is known, we can only give your Excellency our proper respect to, and abide by, the united voice of the Congress on the present occasion." The Assembly accordingly forwarded the plan to their Continental delegates and instructed them to lay it before Congress.[7]

Lord Dunmore of Virginia also called a special session of the Assembly, which met on June 1. Peyton Randolph, the President of Congress, gave up his Philadelphia post to take up his position as Speaker of the House of Burgesses. Yet Dunmore received no greater response from Virginia's proud Assembly than had his colleagues to the north. As soon as news of North's plan arrived in America, Richard Henry Lee wrote his brother, Francis Lightfoot Lee, regarding the course he hoped the burgesses would follow. "You should, after making [. . .] proper spirited observations on the folly, injury and insidiousness of the proposition; refer him [Dunmore] to the united opinion of N. America in Congress."[8] Lee's suggestions were followed precisely. The House resolved (in resolutions written by Jefferson) that, as the plan did not concede any material point, it could offer no substantive basis for negotiations, and even if it could, it was procedurally incorrect for an individual assembly to respond. "Because the proposition now made to us involves the interest of all the other Colonies," Jefferson wrote, and as "we are now represented in General Congress by members approved by this House, where our formal union, it is hoped, will be so strongly cemented, that no partial application can produce the slightest departure from the common cause," the Burgesses considered themselves "bound in honour, as well as interest" to share the fate of the other colonies. Having declared their opinions on this "important subject," therefore, "final determination we leave to the General Congress, now sitting, before whom we shall lay the papers his Lordship has communicated to us. To their wisdom we commit the improvement of this important advance. . . ."[9]

The plan's fate in Congress was foreordained, for from the time news of it had arrived in the colonies it had not been considered a serious effort, as it conceded nothing regarding the right of the colonial assemblies to control their own revenues. Not until July 22 did the delegates, preoccupied with other matters, finally appoint a committee to prepare a formal response to the plan. The committee reported on July 25, and its report was adopted with little change on July 31. In substance, the delegates' response closely resembled that of the House of Burgesses, which is hardly surprising, since Jefferson wrote both documents.[10] Procedurally, however, the resolution had considerable significance, for it represented the delegates' acceptance of the responsibility to formulate and present the united colonial response to a British proposal to open negotiations.

Control over relations with the mother country involved not only the right to respond but also the right to initiate. The process by which the delegates assumed this responsibility becomes clearer when one compares the petitions that the Congress sent to the king in 1774 and 1775.[11] Petitioning, of course, was the traditional "constitutional" method of dealing with the mother country, and the delegates' initial endeavors in government-to-government negotiations were directed toward centralizing all colonial petitioning efforts. Separate petitions by individual colonial legislatures had long been the rule, but in the past the petitions by individual colonies had consistently failed to achieve any significant change in British policy.[12] By 1774, therefore, many skeptical Whigs believed that the only possibility for a successful petition rested with a petition of the united colonies, and there was little surprise when the First Congress devised the October 1774 petition to the king.[13]

What was new in 1774 was a growing feeling that the congressional petition should be the *sole* petition to the mother country. Congressional control of external relations, however, was as yet uncertain in 1774, and both the New York and New Jersey legislatures followed up the congressional document with petitions of their own. This greatly troubled many English, as well as American, Whigs, and correspondingly delighted the Tories, who had so much to gain from colonial disunion. "Two days since a Petition arrived here from N. Jersey," Arthur Lee informed John Dickinson in April 1775. He "could have wished" that "every Assembly had desisted from such a measure till it was approved by the general Congress." The absence of separate colony petitions, Lee believed, would "have manifested the foremost union" and demonstrated the determination of the colonies to look to the Congress "as their shield and guide."[14]

In 1775, with the adoption of the Olive Branch Petition, the delegates were able to stop any similar efforts by individual colonies. The Olive Branch Petition was part of a complex plan conceived of by John Dickinson for opening negotiations with Britain while at the same time carrying on a vigorous defensive war. With the adoption of the petition, which encompassed major portions of Dickinson's plan, the delegates concentrated exclusive authority over negotiations with Britain in the Continental Congress.

Historians have rarely dealt sympathetically with the Olive Branch episode. In part this is due to the nature of the surviving evidence, much of which comes from those who opposed both Dickinson and his plan. John Adams in particular worried that efforts to seek peace in May 1775 would compromise the military preparations upon which he believed the fate of Massachusetts rested; he termed the Olive Branch Petition a "measure of Imbecility." Thomas Jefferson also recalled the petition as a faintly ridiculous effort. The delegates had adopted it with scarcely an amendment, he wrote, merely to indulge John Dickinson, whose great but waning influence still procured for him this small measure of respect.[15]

In fact, the delegates took the Olive Branch plan far more seriously than these accounts would have it. The moderates,[16] led by John Dickinson, with the support of conservatives like James Duane, closely linked their reconciliation plan with the defense measures that the radicals ardently desired; they would not support the latter unless assured of the former.[17] The Dickinson-Duane group proved strong enough to impose much of their plan upon their colleagues. As a result of their Olive Branch effort, they also achieved an agreement among the delegates that exclusive authority over negotiations with Britain belonged to the Continental Congress.

When the Second Continental Congress assembled in May 1775, Dickinson was ready with a plan that he hoped would deal with the new situation created by Lexington and Concord. His proposals were complex and went through several revisions, but the basic outline of his plan was simple. For the next two months Dickinson consistently sought measures that would bring about "accomodation[,] Reconciliation, [and] pacification." Lexington and Concord had convinced every thinking man, he believed, of the urgent necessity of vigorously preparing for war.[18] He suggested, therefore, that the Congress immediately consider what measures were necessary for "putting these Colonies immediately into the best State of Defense." Under this head he proposed that the delegates discuss ways and means for raising men and money, and even suggested the immediate dispatch of ships to Holland and France to procure arms and ammunition.[19]

But at the same time that the colonies were preparing for war, Dickinson insisted that they must pursue every possible means to achieve peace. Although he recognized that the ministry had obdurately refused to consider previous peace proposals, he reasoned that the shock of Lexington and Concord might move the administration to consider negotiations, much as it had convinced many colonists of the need for such discussions. He therefore proposed that the king be petitioned yet again. But the 1775 petition was not to be an end in itself. In Dickinson's mind the Olive Branch Petition would be a means to achieve his desired goal of opening negotiations. He proposed that the Congress authorize several congressional delegates to carry the Olive Branch Petition to the king. These delegates, unlike the colony agents to whose sole care the 1774 petition had been confided, were to be fully instructed by Congress as to the concessions they might make and were to be generally authorized to do whatever was necessary to reach an accommodation.[20] Under the guise of another petition, Dickinson suggested nothing less than the dispatch of fully authorized congressional peace commissioners. Their mission would be to negotiate with one sovereign state on behalf of what was, in all but name, another.

In order to increase the commissioners' standing in England, Dickinson also suggested a substantial—and as it proved to be, permanent—extension of congressional authority. He proposed that all the individual colonies pledge themselves to be bound by the outcome of the congressional negotiations. After the Congress had agreed upon the terms to be sought and had fully instructed the commissioners, Dickinson would have had every colony solemnly agree to "associate and confederate with one another" to abide by the congressional terms and on no account to "accommodate or treat of an Accommodation but jointly with all the Colonies represented in this Congress."[21]

Dickinson's plan was the first overt proposal that Congress assume one of the most public attributes of sovereignty: the authority to appoint, accredit, and instruct ambassadors. He claimed for the Congress not only the full but the exclusive authority to conduct the external affairs of all the colonies.[22] Ironically, this constituted as much a declaration of independence as anything John Adams was proposing at the time. As Dickinson himself argued the next year, the authority to conduct such matters was "one of the highest Powers of Sovereignty—There can not be a Sovereignty without it." If such power was "not lodged in the Crown or King of G.B.," he stated, "the Sovereignty is not vested in him; it is vested in Us."[23]

The moderates succeeded in their plan of forcing simultaneous consideration of the Dickinson proposals and urgent defense measures.[24] In one of the "warm and long debates" on the subject that stretched from late May through mid-June, Dickinson recorded the price the radicals would have to pay for moderate acquiescence in the continental takeover of the army: "As to rais[in]g armies, That Recommendation must go pari passu with Measure of Reconciliation. We must know the one Measure will be taken before We assent to the other." "If We will go on with Measure of War," Dickinson told his opponents, they "must go on with Measure of Peace." "If some of Us cannot go as far as others[,] let them not strain us too far—to put us out of breath[,] to discourage us."[25]

The success of Dickinson and his allies, while not complete, was substantial.[26] On May 25, James Duane introduced a series of resolutions that incorporated much of Dickinson's plan. After two days of heated debate, the delegates adopted several resolutions that either specifically or generally incorporated Dickinson's major proposals.[27] First, the delegates agreed that Gage's attack upon the New Englanders had rendered it imperative that "these colonies be immediately put into a state of defense," and they therefore made specific provisions for the defense of New York. Second, they agreed that in order to restore harmony to the empire, "an humble and dutiful petition be presented to his Majesty." Finally, although specific plans for a peace commission were not adopted, the delegates agreed that "measures be entered into for opening a Negotiation, in order to accommodate the unhappy disputes . . . and that this be made a part of the petition to the King." On June 3 a committee was appointed to draft a petition. The committee reported a draft on June 19, which the full Congress deferred until July 4, debated for two days, and finally signed on July 8.[28]

Although the petition as adopted followed Dickinson's draft closely, nevertheless the peace plan it embodied differed from that which Dickinson had originally proposed. The most important alteration concerned the dispatch of congressional delegates as peace commissioners. Dickinson's reference to such commissioners (who were to explain the colonial position "more fully & at large") was struck from the rough draft of the document and a clause inserted giving the king the responsibility of "direct[ing] some mode" for opening negotiations.[29] Despite this change, which Dickinson later claimed had been intended as a conciliatory move, the final petition was clearly intended to be a vehicle for opening negotiations between Congress and the British government.[30] To emphasize this, the Olive Branch Petition was not simply confided to the care of the several colony agents in London, as the 1774 petition had been.[31] Instead, Richard Penn, the respected former governor of Pennsylvania, was given the task of presenting the petition and, perhaps, peace proposals, "on behalf of the Congress." Although the delegates requested that the colony agents accompany him, it was Penn himself who was entrusted with an entirely new role, that of the authorized representative of an American central government to a sovereign power.[32]

Whatever the merits of the Dickinson plan and the petition that resulted from it, several aspects of the effort mark the beginning of a new concept of the delegates' role in conducting the continent's external affairs. First, the Olive Branch Petition, while still clouded with ambiguity in the sovereign-subject relationship, was the first congressional attempt to open negotiations with a sovereign state on a government-to-government level. Second, the 1775 petition marked the end of the legitimacy of separate negotiations by individual colonies. Dickinson made the first overt claim that the Congress, and only the Congress, was empowered to conduct the external affairs of the united colonies, and furthermore that congressional determinations on foreign policy were binding upon all the individual colonies.[33] The delegates began to act upon this new conception of the congressional role almost as soon as Penn sailed for England.

Since late 1774 many colonists had questioned the wisdom (if not the right) of individual colonies to petition the king, just as they had felt obliged to spurn British overtures to open separate negotiations in connection with North's 1775 reconciliation plan. They affirmed that it was the responsibility of the Congress, not of individual provinces, to conduct all negotiations with Britain. The actions of the New York Provincial Congress in June 1775 contrasted sharply with those of the province's assembly the previous year. While the 1774 session of the Assembly had directed a New York petition to the king, the Provincial Congress, after drafting a full reconciliation plan, transmitted the New York proposals to the colony's delegates in Philadelphia. Any action on their plan, the provincial legislators observed, must come from "that august body of which you are members."[34]

The delegates themselves did not hesitate to assert and insist upon their sole responsibility for negotiating with Britain. Thus, when the New Hampshire Provincial Congress resolved to send a separate petition in May 1775, John Sullivan and John Langdon hurriedly wrote home to forestall the action. "We Earnestly Entreat you to prevent our General Court from making any application to Great Britain," they wrote. Such an action "would Draw the Resentment of all America upon our Province[,] it being agreed that no one Shall make terms without the advice & Consent of the Whole." Their plea was successful; New Hampshire sent no petition.[35]

By December the delegates were no longer relying on such informal appeals. On December 4, after learning that Governor William Franklin was urging the New Jersey Assembly to consider a petition, the delegates unanimously resolved "That in the present situation of affairs, it will be very dangerous to the liberties and welfare of America, if any Colony should separately petition the King or either House of Parliament." To back up this resolution, they dispatched Dickinson, George Wythe, and John Jay to New Jersey to dissuade the Assembly. "The Assembly had it in their Intentions to petition his Majesty again," Franklin informed Lord Dartmouth in early January. "But after the draft of an address was prepared . . . a Committee of the general Congress at Philadelphia" had come in "great haste" to Burlington, where they "harangued the House for about an Hour . . . and persuaded them to drop their Design."[36]

Dickinson presented the views of the delegates to the Jerseymen in the strongest possible terms, affirming that "*Nothing would bring Great Britain to reason but our Unity & Bravery. That all Great Britain wanted was to procure Separate Petitions,* which we Should avoid" since such a course "would *break our Union,*" and "we would be *a Rope of Sand.*" The tactic was successful, and the New Jersey Assembly followed the New Hampshire authorities in deferring to the Congress.[37]

By the spring of 1776, therefore, Congress was in control of the nascent foreign policy of the colonies as it related to Great Britain. Thus, when Lord Dunmore attempted in early 1776 to interest some Virginia conservatives in opening separate negotiations, Edward Pendleton pointedly reminded him through an intermediary that "The Continental Congress have, in their last Petition to the Throne, besought His Majesty to point out some mode for such negociation," which suggestion the British could still embrace. "At all events," he continued, "any other steps to be taken must proceed from the Representatives of the Continent, and not from us," since the Virginia legislators were not authorized or inclined to meddle in the mode of negotiation.[38]

Congressional control over relations with Britain was at no time more severely tested than in the winter and spring of 1776, when moderates and conservatives, anxious to avert a declaration of independence, redoubled their efforts to bring about a reconciliation. Thus, in the late winter of 1776 some delegates proved willing not only to listen to, but to negotiate seriously with, a self-appointed mediator, Lord James Drummond.[39] Drummond, a Scots nobleman resident in New York since 1768 and an acquaintance of several moderate provincial leaders, had shuttled between the colonies and England in 1774 and 1775 bearing the outlines of his own plan of accommodation.[40] In late December 1775 he arrived in Philadelphia and let it be known that although he was a private citizen, he had engaged in extensive conversations with the ministry, and he was ready to speak, unofficially of course, to colonial leaders, also in their private capacity.[41] The Pennsylvania Committee of Safety, its suspicions aroused, asked permission to arrest Drummond. Not only did Congress refuse to sanction his arrest, but several delegates engaged in extensive and completely unauthorized negotiations with him, despite the shadow such unofficial deliberations cast on Congress's newly claimed authority to be the sole official negotiating body for the colonists.[42] As Richard Smith later described these contacts, "It appeared that Ld. Drummond had conversed with several Delegates . . . on the Subject of Pacification and, [although Drummund was] unauthorized by the Ministry, [he] had thrown out his own Ideas of what the Ministry would concede and expect and had endeavoured to draw from those Members what Congress would demand & accede to on their Part."[43] These negotiations apparently reached the point of substantive agreement on the outlines of a peace plan and also on the method of moving the negotiations to an official plane. The delegates with whom Drummond spoke agreed that Congress should appoint commissioners—a variation on Dickinson's 1775 proposal—while Drummond agreed to serve as hostage for their safety. Despite the fact that neither the plan nor the commissioners had ever been proposed, much less adopted, by Congress, Drummond left Philadelphia in late January convinced that he had succeeded. He went so far as to apply to the British commander in Boston for safe conduct for the American peace delegation. When Drummond's letter came before Congress, the delegates were forced to consider the unauthorized activities of several of their number.[44] Despite the implications of such private efforts for Congress's tenuous authority over foreign affairs, a majority of the delegates refused to disavow the effort. By a vote of eight colonies to three, they refused to adopt a resolution offered by George Wythe "import[in]g that no Public Bodies or private Persons other than the Congress or the People at large ought to treat for Peace." They also refused to summon Drummond before them to explain his conduct.[45] But, while they refused to disavow such private ventures, the delegates did not follow up on the Drummond initiative. By March, when his plan came before Congress, hopes for opening negotiations had shifted, because the colonists were anticipating the arrival of the official British peace commissioners, news of whose authorization had reached the colonies in late February.[46]

As independence appeared almost inevitable in the spring of 1776, moderates and conservatives clung with ever more determination to the will-o'-the-wisp of reconciliation, with their hopes now centered on the peace commissioners. On April 6, Robert Morris impatiently wrote to Horatio Gates (unaware that peace commissioners had not yet even been appointed), "Where the plague are these Commissioners, if they are to come what is it that detains them." "It is time," he avowed, "we shoud be on a Certainty & know positively whether the Libertys of America can be established & Secured by reconciliation."[47]

The radicals had opposed Dickinson's 1775 plan to centralize the authority to negotiate in the Congress not because they opposed the assumption of such authority by Congress but because they opposed its object—a petition and an attendant reconciliation plan.[48] In 1776, however, it was the British who offered, officially, to negotiate, but only if the colonists were willing to forego claims that Congress was the sole negotiating agent for the colonies. In March 1776, William Hooper reported that most delegates were of the opinion that the expected commissioners "have instructions to bring about a negociation with the several assemblies of the provinces, nay to condescend to treat with Counties, Towns, particular associations but to avoid, if possible any Correspondence with the continental Congress, lest by any act of theirs they should recognize the legality of that body."[49] The radicals therefore became the strongest defenders of congressional authority over foreign affairs, and they opposed the Howe peace commission as a threat to that authority.[50] Congressional power over negotiations with the mother country had only recently been asserted, and it was not, after all, formally vested in the Congress. With the Drummond episode fresh in their minds, the radicals were worried that the desire for reconciliation would overwhelm the desire for union and that the individual colonies would avail themselves of the British offers.[51]

Their apprehensions, however, proved groundless, and the episode of the peace commissioners only proved the strength of congressional control over relations in Britain. The peace commission's chief member, Lord Howe, had the background and impeccable Whig connections for his role.[52] As a credible peace commissioner, however, his circumstances in 1776 were absurd. For not only was he a peace commissioner but a "war commissioner" as well, charged with the command of the huge body of British military reinforcements that arrived off Sandy Hook, New York, on July 12, 1776.

Lamenting the fact that he had not arrived a week sooner, prior to the proclamation of independence, Howe immediately plunged into his pacific duties, attempting to open negotiations with individual provinces and provincial leaders. He sent off a proclamation and a circular letter to all the royal governors, explaining his mission and powers, and he bolstered his efforts by distributing letters of recommendation he had brought with him from British respected Whigs to colonial leaders like Franklin and Joseph Reed. Howe was most interested in publicizing his peaceful intentions, and he deliberately left his packets unsealed so that their contents would be made public. He was not disappointed, but the means by which his documents were made public was not much to his liking. Many of his letters and proclamations were intercepted by congressional agents, and the personal letters were voluntarily laid before Congress by their recipients.[53] From the beginning, Howe's efforts to open separate negotiations with individual colonies and individual colonial leaders were thus thwarted. The matter was quickly brought within the sole purview of the Congress, and the vigorous debate that ensued as to the proper course of action was centered in the congressional arena alone. Not one of the new states rose to Howe's bait.[54]

The resolution of the states not to meddle in foreign negotiations was not severely tried on this occasion, for all parties agreed that the limited extent of Howe's authority (which had become clear from the letters and proclamations) was patently inadequate to the peace commission's ostensible task. The powers that Howe was permitted to reveal prior to securing a colonial surrender extended only to the granting of pardons to those persons willing to "return to their duty."[55] So paltry did these powers appear when measured against the colonists' earlier expectations of what they would be that the radicals realized that the best way to reconcile all Americans to the harsh measures ahead was to publish Howe's papers for all to read. "Lord Howe's proclamation," wrote Josiah Bartlett, "has now convinced every body that no offers are to be made us but absolute submission." He thought it "very happy for America that Britain has insisted on those terms for had she proposed a Treaty and offered some concessions there would have been danger of divisions."[56]

Howe tried again in September, using the captured American general John Sullivan as an emissary, in the hope that the military disasters in New York might have softened congressional attitudes. But the results were as negligible as they had been in the spring. Although the Congress sent a committee consisting of Adams, Franklin, and Rutledge to confer with Howe, in the ensuing polite conversations both sides revealed that nothing had changed. The committee report caused only greater resentment at Howe's continued refusal to recognize the authority of Congress as a sovereign government. The only result of Howe's second initiative was to consolidate and confirm the complete authority of the Congress over negotiations with the mother country.[57]

External Relations: Relations with Foreign Powers

Relations with Britain, however, constituted only half of American foreign policy. An independent nation must conduct business with all the world. As soon as the dispute with Britain reached the point of open warfare, the question of foreign alliances came up in Congress. Although the delegates continued to insist in public declarations to the people of Great Britain and Ireland that America would rely upon her own resources, no Englishman and few colonists doubted that in dire circumstances the Congress would seek aid from abroad.[58]

The first overt expression of this possibility came in Jefferson's Declaration of the Causes of Taking up Arms, of July 1775. Americans would triumph, the Virginian boldly declared, because not only were their "internal resources . . . great," but "if necessary, foreign assistance" was "undoubtedly attainable." This assertion was quickly followed, however, by a disclaimer, "lest this declaration . . . disquiet the minds of our friends and fellow-subjects." "Necessity," Jefferson assured his audience, "has not yet driven us into that desperate measure."[59]

Although the idea of foreign assistance was in American minds from the beginning of the armed conflict, John Adams, in October 1775, was the first to ask specific questions about the feasibility of obtaining such help. As Adams saw it, the problem was threefold. First, could foreign nations be induced to deliver to the colonies, clandestinely if necessary, the tools of war? Second, supposing that the united colonies assumed an "intrepid Countenance," and actively solicited diplomatic relations with foreign powers, was there "a Probability, that our Ambassadors would be received[?]" Furthermore, he asked, "on what terms would nations openly treat with the colonies? Would commercial treaties suffice, or would the nations seek a sovereignty over the colonies." "Would not," he worried, "our Proposals and Agents be treated with Contempt?"[60]

Adams's colleagues shared these concerns. In the fall of 1775 they initiated a secret two-pronged effort that marked the beginning of

American efforts to establish relations with foreign powers. On September 18, Congress appointed a nine-man committee, thereafter called the Secret Committee, to contract for clandestine arms importations from abroad. On November 29 the delegates appointed a sister Committee of Correspondence (designated, after January 30, 1776, the Committee of Secret Correspondence) "for the sole purpose of corresponding with our friends in Great Britain, Ireland, and other parts of the world."[61] The two committees are often confused, partly because of their overlapping membership[62] but also because of their related missions—in the eighteenth century, trade and alliance presupposed one another.[63] Thus, though one committee dealt with information and the other with clandestine trade, the missions of the two committees were intertwined. Both were entrusted with negotiating with foreign powers on behalf of the united American colonies.

The first efforts of the Committee of Secret Correspondence were directed toward procuring information about the attitudes of foreign powers toward the American cause. On December 12, a bare two weeks after the committee's appointment, Franklin wrote to Arthur Lee in London on behalf of his colleagues. "It would be agreable to Congress," he stated, "to know the Disposition of Foreign Powers towards us, and we hope this Object will engage your Attention." He cautioned Lee that "great Circumspection and impenetrable Secrecy are necessary," and he promised that Congress would compensate Lee for his trouble and expense. Even before this, on December 9, Franklin assured the committee of a steady flow of information from The Hague, "where ambassadors from all the courts reside," by confiding similar tasks to his old friend C.W.F. Dumas. According to his commission, Dumas was to make use of his strategic position to discover, if possible, "the disposition of the several courts with respect to . . . assistance or alliance, if we should apply for the one, or propose the other." Franklin authorized Dumas to use his letter as a credential when conferring with foreign ambassadors, only cautioning him to keep the knowledge of his mission from the English ambassador.[64] The committee, in effect, commissioned Lee and Dumas to act as accredited, if secret, agents of the united colonies. While they were not yet ambassadors, they were certainly more than the colony agents had been.[65]

The country that interested the Secret Committee most, of course, was France, England's traditional and most powerful adversary. Not surprisingly, the French were equally interested in sounding out American intentions. In August 1775 the French minister, the Comte de Vergennes, dispatched an agent, Julien de Bonvouloir, to Philadelphia to gain information about the colonists' plans and to report home on their prospects. Bonvouloir's mission encouraged Congress to appoint its own agent to the French court, and on March 2 the delegates commissioned Silas Deane to proceed to Paris, "there to transact such business commercial & political, as we have committed to his Care, in Behalf of & by Authority of the thirteen United Colonies."[66]

The instructions of the Committee of Secret Correspondence to Deane were, of course, more explicit than those in his commission. Since Bonvouloir's mission had been secret, there was no indication that Vergennes desired as yet to move beyond covert contacts with the Americans. Respecting these wishes, Deane was instructed to retain "the Character of a Merchant" among the French in general, "it being probable that the Court of France may not like it should be known publickly, that any Agent from the Colonies is in that Country." They further instructed him to seek an audience with Vergennes to broach the topic of obtaining arms from France. Deane was to intimate that independence was imminent and to enlarge upon the commercial advantages Britain had always derived from her colonies. If Vergennes responded favorably to these soundings, Deane was to inquire whether, in the event that the colonies did declare independence, France would acknowledge them as an independent state, "receive their Ambassadors," and "enter into any Treaty or Alliance with them, for Commerce, or defense, or both."[67] By virtue of his commission and instructions, Deane became the first American ambassador. Four months prior to declaring independence, Congress was exercising the power of accrediting and instructing emissaries to conduct relations and negotiations with foreign powers, the results of which were to be binding on all the colonies.

But Deane's mission was still a secret one. To assume full authority over foreign policy, the delegates had to move from covert control of such matters to overt action. The French alliance being pursued by the Committee of Secret Correspondence was becoming an open topic of conversation in Congress as independence approached. On February 16, in the midst of a debate regarding the opening of American ports to ships of foreign nations, George Wythe averred that "the Colonies have a Right to contract Alliances with Foreign Powers." About the same time, John Penn reached the conclusion that Britain would seek foreign assistance to aid her struggle with the colonies. "Must we not do something of the like nature?" he wondered. "Can we hope to carry on a war without having trade or commerce somewhere?"[68]

By June 1776 the close connection between foreign alliances and independence was clear to all parties in the Congress. While timing was in dispute, virtually no one doubted that eventually both steps would have to be taken.[69] On June 12, therefore, the day on which a committee to draw up a plan of confederation was appointed, Congress also designated Dickinson, Franklin, Adams, Harrison, and Morris as a committee "to prepare a plan of treaties to be proposed to foreign powers."[70]

Adams had been musing over the terms upon which the colonies might ally with France since early March, when Deane had left for Paris. "What Connection may We safely form with her?" he wondered. He scribbled the answer in cryptic notes to himself:

"1st. No Political Connection—Submit to none of her Authority— receive no Governors, or officers from her.
2nd. No military Connection—receive no Troops from her.
3rd. Only a Commercial Connection, i.e. make a Treaty, to receive her Ships into our Ports. Let her engage to receive our Ships into her Ports—furnish Us with Arms, Cannon, Salt Petre, Powder, Duck, Steel."

On June 23 he reiterated his thoughts. "I am not for soliciting any political Connection, or military assistance. . . . I wish for nothing but Commerce, a mere Marine Treaty."[71] Thus when the committee reported Adams's draft treaty on July 18 it proved to be a strictly commercial agreement based on traditional seventeenth-century treaties of amity and commerce. His draft also showed that a French alliance was uppermost in his colleagues' minds, for he proposed "a firm, inviolable, and universal Peace, and a true and sincere Friendship between the most serene and mighty Prince, Lewis the Sixteenth . . . and the United States of America." Its terms contemplated mutual trading privileges, mutual protection for each other's ships while in port, and mutual support of each other's ships against the Barbary pirates while at sea. It differed from previous commercial treaties only in the extent of the freedom to trade that Adams wished to see the treaty protect. The closest the treaty came to a modern concept of alliance lay in the provisions that neither party would assist Great Britain in carrying on war (Articles 7 and 8), that France would not seek to regain its Canadian possessions in case of any war with Great Britain, and that if France should regain any West Indian islands as a consequence of such a war, Americans should be permitted to trade there (Articles 9 and 10).[72]

On September 17, 1776, the Adams draft was accepted by the delegates with almost no alteration. On September 24, Congress proceeded formally to instruct agents to lay the draft before the French king, and two days later Franklin, and still later Arthur Lee, were added to Deane (who was already in France) as commissioners empowered to execute this instruction. Although French dismay at American military defeats prevented the final execution of the treaty until May 1778,[73] the Adams draft was virtually identical to the French Treaty of Amity and Commerce of 1778, and indeed it was to be the model for all American commercial treaties until 1800.[74]

Congressional assumption of authority over the foreign affairs of the United States proceeded precisely in the manner of its assumption of other vacated functions of the king. The ineffectiveness of early attempts to conduct separate colonial negotiations with the mother country through individual colony petitions led to a general demand, from 1774 on, that the united power of the continent as exercised by the Continental Congress be brought to bear on such negotiations. By 1776 the authority to conduct all such deliberations with Britain had been delegated to the Congress so firmly that strong British efforts to open negotiations with individual colonies were doomed to failure.

Control of relations with foreign powers, as well as with the mother country, was also concentrated in the delegates' hands during this period. With virtually no controversy, the Congress began in 1775 to conduct covert trade and intelligence operations throughout Europe, directing its major efforts toward securing the aid of France. By 1776, when the approach of independence legitimized American approaches to foreign nations, the question of formal alliances came exclusively before the Continental Congress, where it was dispatched with little debate. By 1776, then, the Congress had been conducting the external relations of the American colonies for almost two years, exercising its power in this area, moreover, for the same purposes and in the same manner as did all eighteenth-century powers.[75]

CHAPTER 8

Congress and Internal Union

Previous to Independence all disputes must be healed & Harmony prevail. A grand Continental League must be formed & a super-intending Power also. When these necessary Steps are taken & I see a Coalition formed sufficient to withstand the Power of Britain or any other, then am I for an independent State & all its Consequences, as then I think they will produce Happiness to America.
—Carter Braxton, April 14, 1776

For Carter Braxton, the moment to declare independence had not yet arrived, for Congress had not as yet agreed upon a formal plan of continental government. But for others the form of a continental government was not as urgent as the reality of it. When they considered the Congress in 1776, they saw an institution that for almost a year had been carrying on the basic administrative functions that had been essential to internal imperial harmony. Thus, since the beginning of the war the Congress had, on behalf of all the colonies, supervised trade and treaties with the Indian nations; it had organized, operated, and financed a continentwide system of internal communication; and perhaps most important, it had begun to serve as the forum for adjudicating intercolonial disputes. Thus, before the Articles of Confederation had been ratified, Anthony Wayne congratulated Benjamin Franklin on the Congress's success. "The settling the Boundaries of the respective States is an event that has given the highest Satisfaction to every thinking Gent[lema]n," he wrote. Such actions were "truly worthy of the Congress."[1] Thus, while agreement on the Articles of Confederation proved impossible to achieve in 1776, a functioning confederation did not. Its existence provided a comforting assurance that should independence be forced upon the colonies, they would not be without an effective "superintending Power" to preserve the internal unity of the new American states.

The Indians

Control of the western Indians had long been a recognized prerogative of the Crown. The Indian trade itself was lucrative, and there was the possibility of gaining control of new western lands by treaty. The potential for intercolonial conflict over these valuable privileges was therefore enormous. In addition, the Indians (especially the powerful Confederation of the Five Nations centered in upper New York) were important for general colonial defense, because they had been traditional English allies in the wars with France. The Indian alliances, however, required constant negotiation and periodic treaties. To minimize the potential for conflict and to centralize defense functions, therefore, by the eighteenth century the ultimate responsibility for all matters concerning the Indians had become the Crown's responsibility.[2]

At the beginning of the conflict between America and England, Americans viewed the Crown's traditional control of the western Indians with alarm, since the warriors who had proved so effective against the French could now be directed against them.[3] Total control of Indian affairs was therefore placed quickly, if tacitly, in the hands of the Congress. The issue of Indian affairs first came before Congress in June 1775 as an adjunct of the growing defense problems in northern New York. The New York Provincial Congress, worried about the influence the Johnson family (who were Tories)[4] would have over the northern Indians, requested aid from Congress.[5] On June 16, 1775, in response to New York's request, Congress charged a committee of five with the task of reporting "what steps, in their opinion, are necessary to be taken for securing and preserving the friendship of the Indian nations."[6] By June 30 this committee was referred to as the Committee for Indian Affairs.[7] On June 26 the committee brought in its report. The Congress was then in the middle of its grand efforts to create an American army, and the consideration of the report was postponed. However, on June 30 Congress indicated its increasing disposition to take charge of the Indian problem by instructing the committee to prepare a form to be used for treaties with the various Indian tribes. Heretofore such treaties were the unquestioned province of the Crown. The next day, the delegates went even further. In a reflection of their concern over the influence of the Johnson family, the Congress resolved that if Britain entered into an Indian alliance directed against the colonists, "the colonies ought to avail themselves of an Alliance with such Indian Nations as will enter into the same, to oppose such British troops and their Indian Allies." This warning issued, and overwhelmed with other business, Congress continued to delay consideration of the committee's report, though a sign of the delegates' growing inclination to accept responsibility for a common Indian policy appeared on July 10. Congress then agreed to appoint a committee to consider the purchase of a considerable quantity of goods suitable for the Indian trade. This could only mean that they were prepared to enter into the second aspect of a common Indian policy, which was related to, but separate from, defense.[8]

After a day's debate in committee of the whole, all these indications were confirmed. On July 12 Congress agreed to appoint permanent commissioners "to superintend Indian affairs in behalf of their colonies" under the authority and supervision of the Congress. They proceeded to divide the colonies for this purpose into Northern, Middle, and Southern departments and to authorize the appointment of commissioners for each department. The commissioners' object, they further resolved, was to "treat with the Indians in their respective departments in the name, and on behalf of the united colonies" in order to preserve their friendship and neutrality. The Congress then approved a carefully contrived speech for the commissioners to read to the various Indian tribes, explaining (from the colonial viewpoint) the disputes between England and America. Commissioners were appointed for the Northern and Middle departments and provision was made the following week to allow the South Carolina Committee of Safety to appoint three of the southern commissioners. Moreover, the commissioners were empowered "to take to their assistance gentlemen of influence among the Indians, in whom they can confide, and to appoint Agents, residing near or among the Indians, to watch the conduct of the [king's] superintendants and their emissaries" and, if need be, to arrest the royal superintendents on behalf of the Congress. Considerable sums of money were then authorized to be paid out of the continental treasury for necessary expenses and presents. Finally, to emphasize that the Continental control of Indian affairs was to be permanent, the commissioners were ordered to "exhibit fair accounts of the expenditure of all monies by them respectively to be received for the purposes aforesaid, to every succeeding Continental Congress, or committee of Congress, together with a general state of Indian affairs, in their several departments; in order that the colonies may be informed, from time to time, of every such matter as may concern them to know and avail themselves of, for the benefit of the common cause."[9]

With the appointment and instruction of the commissioners, Congress stepped directly into the king's vacated role as supreme arbiter of relations with the Indians, and it continued to exercise its new responsibility in this area for almost a year by supervising the activities of the Indian commissioners on an ad hoc basis. On April 30, 1776, however, the finishing touches were put on congressional authority over Indian affairs. A standing committee was appointed that thenceforth supervised the commissioners and served as the executive body ultimately responsible for the conduct of Indian affairs.[10]

Not until July 1776 did the delegates debate whether this power really ought to reside in a central body. The occasion was the debate over Article VIII in the committee draft of the Articles of Confederation, which gave Congress the exclusive right to regulate the Indian trade, and manage all other affairs with the Indians.[11] Edward Rutledge and Thomas Lynch raised the objection that the Indian trade was profitable and that the profits ought accrue to the states. Moreover, they pointed out, the individual provinces had heretofore borne the burden of maintaining frontier defenses and ought therefore obtain the benefit. Thomas Stone believed that the power would cause discord between the states and the Congress, each struggling for control. Roger Sherman, however, moved "that Congress may have a Superintending Power, to prevent injustice to the Indians or Colonies." James Wilson, in support of Sherman's motion, spoke for the majority of the delegates and explained the basis upon which Indian affairs had been tacitly confided to the Congress for over a year, and why the delegates would do so formally in the Articles of Confederation. "No lasting Peace will be with the Indians," he argued, "unless made by some one Body. . . . No powers ought to treat, with the Indians, but the united States. . . . None should trade with the Indians without a License from Congress. A perpetual war would be unavoidable if every Body was allowed to trade with them."[12] In the committee draft, and all subsequent drafts of the Articles of Confederation, control of Indian affairs was left firmly in congressional hands.

The Post Office

A similar sequence of events is evident regarding the post office. British control of the post office had long been a sore point with American Whigs, because the British were fond of using American acquiescence in post office charges as a precedent for the internal taxation of the colonies. If they did not object to post office charges, the British argued, why should the Americans be so adamant about the Stamp Act and Townshend duties? As Arthur Lee admitted to Samuel Adams in early 1774, though the post office charges were "not a tax in its principles, it is in its operation." The revenue to Britain from this source was about £3000 yearly, he continued, and "it is hourly increasing." Therefore, he thought, "it is our duty to frustrate, by all means, so pernicious an institution." The manner of doing so was simple, Lee believed. "Let the Merchants of Boston, New York, & Philadelphia support Carriers by Subscription, who shall deliver all Letters post free," he explained, and "the imposition must inevitably fall."[13]

Willing hands were not lacking to carry out such a scheme, and two of the most willing belonged to William Goddard, a printer from Providence, Rhode Island, who by 1773 was publishing a newspaper in Philadelphia.[14] Early in 1774, Goddard, with the support of local Whigs, established his "Constitutional Post" to ply between Philadelphia and Baltimore. He also took a tour of New England, hoping to interest the northerners in his scheme. He took with him fervent letters of recommendation from Whigs all along his route. The New York committee, for example, wrote to the Boston committee, "recommending, in the strongest terms, the proposals which Mr. Goddard has to make, and our earnest desires to cooperate with you, and the rest of the friends of *just government* in carrying this *glorious plan* into *immediate* execution." They assured their New England allies that "The friends of Liberty in the southern colonies . . . you may depend will establish riders, upon the *new plan* . . . [as] soon as they obtain information on the concurrence and approbation of the town of Boston." With backing like this, it is not surprising that the New Englanders enthusiastically embraced Goddard and his plan when he arrived in March 1774. They hailed the scheme's supposed success farther south and indicated that a delay in establishing the Constitutional Post in New England was tantamount to backwardness in the cause of liberty. "The noble example set for us in Maryland, seconded by Philadelphia,

and adopted by New-York" should immediately be followed, one letter exhorted. Since the new post was already established farther
south, the author had no doubt that New England would follow this
noble example. Thus, he asserted, "a large sum annually extorted
from us by way of revenue and applied to injure and distress, if not
destroy us, will be wrested out of the hands of our enemies," and, he
added practically, "two thirds perhaps" will "be saved, and the residue applied to purposes advantageous to OURSELVES."[15]

Goddard's scheme was given a hefty push when, in the middle of
his New England visit, word arrived that the royal deputy postmaster-
general, Benjamin Franklin, had been removed from his place by the
ministerial clique in London. Previously some ardent patriots, although convinced of the necessity for an American postal service, had
hesitated to support Goddard's scheme because of the injury such a
move would do to the respected Dr. Franklin, who had largely been
responsible for organizing the royal post in the colonies. Now this fear
was gone. "The Removal of Dr. Franklin," the *Boston Gazette* asserted,
". . . has added fresh Spirit to the Promoters of this salutary Plan, as
several viewed an Opposition to his Interest, at a Time when he had
signally served the Cause of America, as a very disagreeable Object."[16]

Despite all the optimistic projections, however, Goddard's post, although it was set up in the middle and New England colonies, did not
succeed in supplanting the efficient royal postal system.[17] Throughout
early 1775, the vast majority of colonial mail continued to be carried by
the king's riders.[18] The failure to fully implement Goddard's plan in
1774, however, added to the chaos of 1775. Zealous local committees
succeeded where Goddard had failed and busily went about putting
an effective end to the royal post. In a burst of patriotic fervor, royal
post riders were stopped and the mail they carried examined. By mid-
1775, therefore, a situation was rapidly approaching where no reliable
post existed, either royal or patriot.[19] Instead of attempting to resurrect
Goddard's private post office plan, however, many colonists looked to
Congress in hopes that the Continental body would set up a new
government post, preferably one as much like the old royal post as
possible.

As with the other functions assumed by the Congress, pressure to
establish a Continental post office came from the outside and gathered
steam on the eve of the meeting of the Second Congress in May 1775.
When in May the royal postmaster of New York abruptly closed down

the office and fired his riders, the *New York Journal* predicted that "An office for the necessary business, will doubtless be put under proper regulations by the Continental Congress, and no more be permitted to return to the rapacious hands of unauthorized intruders." The New York committee, vindicating the *Journal*'s prophecy, proceeded to hire the royal riders and set up a temporary post with Ebenezer Hazard as postmaster until, they said, the matter could be put into the hands of the Congress.[20] Without waiting for any such Continental action, on May 8 Goddard again announced he was setting up his Constitutional Post-Office "on the ruins of the Parliamentary one, which is just expiring in convulsions." Recognizing that public sentiment favored a congressional, rather than a private, institution, he hastened to add that there was no doubt "but the institution will be patronised and properly regulated by the Continental Congress." By the end of May, all the New England governments had announced themselves in favor of a Continental post office, and most had proceeded to organize their own systems, which were to be in effect, as the Massachusetts Provincial Congress ordered on May 13, "until the Continental Congress . . . shall make some further order relative to the same."[21]

Congress responded to this pressure, aware, in the wake of Lexington and Concord, of the military necessity of keeping lines of communication open and cognizant generally of the urgent necessity of preserving the unity of colonial action. On May 29 the delegates resolved that as "the present critical situation of the colonies renders it highly necessary that ways and means should be devised for the speedy and secure conveyance of Intelligence from one end of the Continent to the other," a committee was to be appointed "to consider the best means of establishing posts for conveying letters and intelligence through this continent." The guiding spirit of the committee appointed in consequence of this resolution was Benjamin Franklin. On July 25 the committee brought in its report, which was accepted with little debate the next day.[22]

The Continental Post Office set up in accordance with the committee's recommendations had little in common with the private subscription post that Goddard had originally set up. The new Continental post, like its royal predecessor, was a government institution whose deficits would "be made good by the United Colonies," and, more hopefully, whose profits would be paid to the Continental treasury. The new plan was, in fact, a mirror image of the old royal post—not surprisingly, since the unanimously elected postmaster general was none other than the author of both the old royal and the new Continental systems, Benjamin Franklin.[23]

Pushed by necessity and general expectations, then, the Continental Congress succeeded in establishing a new, unifying post office, which, except for its source of authority, recreated the old royal post. "As the constitutional post now goes regularly," Francis Lightfoot Lee wrote in late October, "we may with a safe conscience say how d'ye to each other." In the spring of 1776 the editors of a South Carolina newspaper informed their readers that "regular Constitutional Posts are now established under Authority of the Congress, throughout all the United Colonies," and that "the Post Offices are put in the care of Gentlemen of Honour and Fidelity, so that there may, in future, be the greatest Confidence in Correspondence."[24]

The establishment of a colonial post office and the centralization of the management of Indian affairs are excellent illustrations of the manner in which Congress took over the vacated unifying functions of the king. Both of these functions contributed to colonial unity, though neither was essential to it. What *was* essential was the transferal of the Crown's authority to provide a forum for the resolution of disputes between colonies and thereby to preserve peace and harmony among them. Congress assumed the authority to adjudicate intercolonial disputes by much the same pattern as described above; it was not sought by the delegates, it was thrust upon them. Thus, just as the king had exercised unquestioned authority as "sovereign umpire" to resolve all intra-imperial disputes, so the Congress was compelled to step into his vacated position in order to preserve the fragile union of the colonies. Because the issue is so important to an understanding of the way in which Congress assumed authority over the vacated executive powers of the Crown, it is useful to examine the process in some detail.

Boundary Disputes

Longstanding conflicts over boundaries were a primary cause of Whig doubts about the possibility of a colonial union. Such controversies embroiled colony with colony in extended litigation at the highest courts in the empire and in violent confrontations at the contested sites. These boundary conflicts had rarely been settled by intercolonial arbitration, although there had been many attempts to settle them. Instead, the explosive conflicts were referred for settlement to the "sovereign umpire," the king-in-council. The contesting parties usually (but not always) acquiesced in royal decisions, albeit often after extended appeals. Whatever the ultimate decision in a particular case, however, all parties invariably agreed that only the king or the institutions vested with his authority could constitute a legitimate forum in which to adjudicate intra-imperial disputes. Removal of this critical element of royal power, Tories contended, was an invitation to civil war.[25]

Many Whigs shared this apprehension about the explosive potential of intercolonial disputes. They feared that individual colonies could not be expected to renounce self-interest consistently in order to negotiate settlements between themselves. It was much safer, therefore, to recreate a superior authority charged with protecting the general interest and preserving the common good, to whom all would submit disputes that threatened to disturb intercolonial harmony. If there was to be a new "sovereign umpire," most Americans agreed, it could only be the Continental Congress. Article xviii of the draft Articles of Confederation, which gave the power to the Congress to resolve all disputes between colonies, merely codified existing practice. The contending provinces had already entrusted the Congress with the authority to reconcile intercolonial disputes.[26]

Congressional Reluctance: The Pennsylvania-Virginia Controversy

The initial boundary dispute that came to the attention of the Congress, in the spring of 1775, was that between Pennsylvania and Virginia over the contested region at the forks of the Ohio River around modern Pittsburgh. Unable to reach a settlement among themselves, Pennsylvanians and Virginians sought congressional aid in reaching an equitable solution. The continental delegates, however, refused to accept responsibility for reconciling the dispute and referred the conflict back to the contending parties. Their response exemplifies the delegates' reluctance to accept the former royal powers pushed upon them by provincial authorities. In the end, the Pennsylvania-Virginia dispute was settled without reference to the Congress, indicating clearly that there was nothing preordained or inevitable about congressional succession to the old royal authority to adjudicate intercolonial disputes.

The possibility of a Virginia-Pennsylvania boundary dispute was present from at least the 1750s, when settlers from both colonies had begun to move into the rich lands of the Monongahela valley. After the Treaty of Fort Stanwix of 1768 reduced the danger from the western Indians, colonists from both provinces poured into the region. By the early 1770s there were two distinct groups of settlements, the Virginians having taken most of the land in the Monongahela valley, and the Pennsylvanians having settled farther east around Hannastown. Both groups of claimants held their lands under title from their respective governments, which made a jurisdictional conflict almost inevitable, though as yet neither Virginia nor Pennsylvania had laid claim to the unsettled lands. The inhabitants themselves, protected by the royal garrison at Fort Pitt, did little to disturb the situation by raising questions of jurisdiction.[27]

In 1772, two events occurred that increased the potential for conflict. First, in an economy move, the royal garrison was removed from Fort Pitt, creating a power vacuum in the region. Second, James Murray, earl of Dunmore, an aggressive Scots peer with a taste for speculation in western lands, was appointed royal governor of Virginia. When Lord Dunmore visited the western frontier in 1773 he met Dr. John Connolly, a contentious leader of the Virginia settlers who was to become Dunmore's trusted agent in asserting Virginia's claims to the area. Dunmore's decision to act quickly was strengthened when, on February 26, 1773, the Pennsylvania authorities incorporated the disputed area into the Pennsylvania county of Westmoreland. In retaliation, Lord Dunmore commissioned Connolly as the Virginia militia commandant of the area, a commission that Connolly proceeded to nail to the walls of Fort Pitt in early January 1774. On the basis of this authority, he and his band of Virginians took over the fort and commanded all area residents to report there and be embodied a militia company under Virginia authority. Responding to this challenge, a Pennsylvania magistrate of the new Westmoreland bench, Arthur St. Clair, ordered Connolly's arrest. The Pennsylvanians managed to secure Connolly but soon released him, trusting in the good doctor's pledge to return to Hannastown for trial at the next meeting of the Westmoreland County Court. As scheduled, Connolly appeared at the Pennsylvanians' county seat in April 1774, but he brought with him an armed force of several hundred men. Connolly promptly turned the tables on his judges, arrested them, and carried them off to Fort Pitt.

Alarmed by the violent turn of events, the governor of Pennsylvania, John Penn, sent a delegation of Pennsylvanians to Williamsburg to settle on a temporary boundary line with Dunmore. Largely due to Dunmore's intransigence, no agreement was reached, and by July the region was convulsed by a savage Indian war precipitated and prosecuted by the Virginians. Dunmore personally commanded his troops in what became known as Lord Dunmore's War. On the march west, he stopped at Fort Pitt (now renamed Fort Dunmore) and there formally laid claim to all land west of the Laurel Hill Mountains, which he proceeded to incorporate into the Virginia district of West Augusta. On October 12, 1774, Governor Penn issued a counterproclamation and the battle lines were drawn.[28]

Throughout the early part of 1775, the situation on the forks of the Ohio was chaotic, with two jurisdictions, each with a complete set of subordinate officers, claiming authority over the same territory. Magistrates under both governments imprisoned their opposite numbers at every opportunity, and claimants under both governments were dispossessed of land by their rivals. After Lexington and Concord, the settlers under both jurisdictions met separately and pledged their support to the patriot cause. Soon, an uneasy coalition of the two groups of settlers was formed. One resistance committee was organized for the area (the West Augusta Committee) and one defense association (the Westmoreland Association). But the two separate civil jurisdictions continued, as did violent confrontations between Pennsylvanians and Virginians. In May 1775 the unsettled state of affairs led the West Augusta Committee to apply to the Continental Congress for assistance.[29] The settlers' application mainly concerned not the disputed jurisdiction, however, but relations with the neighboring Indians. After fighting had begun in Massachusetts, Connolly had proved himself to be as committed to Dunmore's policy of supporting British authority as he was to the governor's efforts to establish Virginia hegemony on the Ohio. Establishing firm Indian alliances was the key to securing the frontier for the British. Since the settlers under both Virginia and Pennsylvania were committed patriots, Connolly realized that he would soon have to flee the area, but before he left he was determined to prepare the way for an eventual return by securing the necessary alliances. Accordingly, he called for an Indian council to be held at Fort Dunmore, the object of which was to obtain their pledges of support for the British.[30]

Connolly's move alarmed the settlers, who petitioned the Congress to appoint commissioners to attend the council. The Continental delegates had no hesitation about complying with this request. The petitions were referred to the delegates from Virginia and Pennsylvania, who quickly arranged to have the necessary agents dispatched to forestall Connolly. In addition, the settlers had complained that "the uncertainty of the Boundaries between Virginia & Penna. is the Cause of Great uneasiness," and therefore they requested in their petition that the continental delegates settle a temporary line to quiet the discontent in the district. This request was clearly a proper one, a Pennsylvanian wrote, since such a boundary was "undoubtedly a prudent & necessary thing."[31] The continental delegates, however, refused to accept the responsibility for drawing such a boundary line. In the late spring of 1775 they were working furiously both to organize and to reconcile the struggle that had begun on Lexington Green. It is not surprising, therefore, that on the same day the delegates refused to widen the scope of the war by countenancing further incursions into Canada, they also refused to accept the old royal authority to settle (even temporarily) an intercolonial boundary dispute. While they did not hesitate to use their good offices to help the interested parties reach an agreement, they would by no means accept the responsibility, however temporary, for adjudicating the dispute. Accordingly, when referring the settlers' petition back to the Virginia and Pennsylvania delegates, they carefully deleted all reference to the requested boundary line.[32]

In referring the petition back to the Virginians and Pennsylvanians, the Continental delegates certainly hoped that the interested parties themselves could reach at least a temporary solution. The Virginia and Pennsylvania delegates complied with the wishes of their colleagues and attempted to appeal to the settlers' spirit of unity, in the hope that old feuds could be buried in the post-Lexington avalanche of patriotism. They urged the settlers under both governments "that all animosities, which have heretofore subsisted among you" would, in time of danger, give way to unity and harmony. But the delegates' plea was in vain, and the conflict at the forks of the Ohio continued.[33]

Problems again arose in the area the following September. After Connolly's conference had ended in the spring, the settlers had called for a new Indian conference to be held in the fall, the purpose of which would be to commit the Indians to the patriot cause. The new congressional Indian commissioners for the Middle Department, Thomas

Walker and Lewis Morris (accompanied by James Wilson) arrived for the conference to find that Virginia militiamen had already taken over the site of the conference (the erstwhile Fort Pitt), had harassed the Pennsylvania settlers, and were generally hindering the delicate negotiations with the Indians. Wilson and Morris wrote back to Philadelphia concerning the precarious situation and again petitioned Congress to fix a temporary boundary line, which they hoped would quiet the contention. On September 25, Thomas Willing presented the Wilson and Morris letters to the full Congress. The request occasioned two days of debate during which, according to Richard Smith, the question of a boundary line was "agitated but Nothing determined."[34]

This was the end of congressional involvement in the dispute. Further developments in the controversy concerned only the interested colonies and had much to do with politics and little to do with the merits of the respective claims. The Pennsylvanians assumed an intrepid patriot stance and prepared to use the frontier settlements on the Ohio as a base to attack British trading posts (primarily Fort Detroit) in the west.[35] The Virginia leader, Connolly, joined his master, Dunmore, aboard a British warship and was eventually captured and imprisoned by the Congress.[36] Virginia's claim to the area suffered from the taint of toryism and in the ensuing boundary negotiations, which were carried on between the new Pennsylvania and Virginia state governments, Virginia eventually ceded jurisdiction over the area.[37]

Congress, however, had nothing to do with the ultimate resolution of this dispute. In their first encounter with the ticklish problem of intercolonial disputes, the delegates displayed only hesitation, reluctance, and an intense desire to remove themselves from the position of responsibility that was being thrust upon them. But the problem of intercolonial disputes, which for decades had taxed the king's authority, could not be avoided by the successor to that authority. Before long an even more explosive boundary dispute than that between Pennsylvania and Virginia was laid before the Congress.

Congressional Involvement:
The Susquehannah Company Dispute

No boundary controversey was of longer duration or had more volatile potential than that between Connecticut and Pennsylvania over an area (the Wyoming Valley) now in northeastern Pennsylvania on the

Susquehanna River.[38] This dispute first directly engaged the Continental Congress in the problem of boundary disputes and established the precedent for its authority over these matters.

In theory, the Pennsylvania-Connecticut boundary dispute began in 1681, when the Pennsylvania charter was granted, because the grant of land to Penn was in direct conflict with the clause in the Connecticut charter by which that colony's boundaries were designated as being "from sea to sea." Connecticut, however, did not protest the Penn grant, nor did it lay claim to lands within the boundaries of Penn's grant until the middle of the eighteenth century.[39] Connecticut expansion into the area began in earnest around 1750, when the Susquehannah Land Company was organized. A burgeoning population and a fixed land base made for a ready supply of Yankees willing to take up the company's offer of cheap land. The pace of Connecticut settlement in the area increased greatly after 1768, when the Treaty of Fort Stanwix secured the area on the Susquehanna River for peaceful settlement. But peace with the Indians by no means insured tranquillity in the region. Between 1768 and 1771 the battles between the Yankees and the "Pennamites" (settlers who had claimed their land under Pennsylvania authority) became legendary. In the early 1770s, Connecticut towns along the river assumed the aspect of armed camps. Not until 1772 were the Connecticut settlers in secure possession of the lands on which they had settled.

Possession, however, was not the same thing as jurisdiction. The Pennsylvania proprietors might not have opposed the Yankee settlements on their frontier had the Connecticut men been prepared to acknowledge Pennsylvania jurisdiction over the area. But the Yankees and the Connecticut-chartered Susquehannah Company were not willing to accept Pennsylvania sovereignty over the Susquehannah lands, even though the Connecticut government had never, prior to 1771, indicated any interest in pursuing a claim to the region. For the Connecticut settlers, the jurisdictional problem was severe. With no acknowledged government, problems of disorder (endemic in any frontier community) soon arose. Leaders of the Connecticut settlers attempted to control their constituents by informal agreements and associations, but they realized that until the Connecticut government incorporated the area within its boundaries, their property would not be secure against either internal disorder or the claims of the Pennamites. Through the early 1770s, therefore, the Yankee settlers consistently appointed agents to attend each session of the Connecticut General Assembly. The agents presented pleas from the inhabitants that Connecticut government be extended to the Susquehanna.

The Susquehannah Company, of course, was not a disinterested bystander in the contest. The company's land claims could never be secure until the Connecticut Assembly assumed jurisdiction over the area, so it was forced to enter the complex realm of Connecticut provincial politics. So involved did the company become in the political affairs of the colony, in fact, that on the eve of the First Continental Congress the primary factional division in Connecticut was along pro- and anti-Susquehannah Company lines.[40] And the company's involvement in politics proved successful. In May 1771, Connecticut formally laid claim to the Susquehanna lands, and by the spring of 1773 (after having obtained favorable opinions from several prominent English attorneys), the Connecticut legislators were vigorously pursuing their case in London before the Board of Trade.

The same political pressures that led Connecticut to lay formal claim to the Susquehanna lands also rendered its assembly receptive to the continuing petitions from their settlers there for Connecticut government. When, in late 1773, an Assembly attempt to negotiate with the Pennsylvania proprietors failed, the pro-Susquehannah faction in the Connecticut Assembly was strengthened.[41] In January 1774, therefore, the Connecticut Assembly narrowly voted to incorporate the disputed area as the Connecticut town of Westmoreland, a decision that created a town with a larger area of land than the entire mother colony.[42] The assembly's action strengthened the Pennsylvanians in their determination to pursue their claims in England, and in 1773 they appealed their case before the highest imperial court, the king-in-council, but by the middle of 1775, there was still no sign of a decision from England.[43]

So matters stood when the Continental Congress, gradually assuming other executive powers through 1775, was drawn into the complicated Wyoming dispute as well. The victory of the Susquehannah faction in the Connecticut elections in late 1774 encouraged both speculators and migrants to begin laying out new towns on the Wyoming lands. The Connecticut Assembly encouraged these efforts by widening the already-swollen boundaries of the Town of Westmoreland to include the Pennamite lands on the west branch of the Susquehanna River. It appeared, therefore, that the Connecticut men would not be content even to stay within their former settlements on the east branch of the Susquehanna but were determined to move into new territory on the west branch.

In late July 1775, almost immediately prior to the summer recess of the Second Continental Congress, the Pennsylvanians laid two petitions protesting the Connecticut expansion before the Congress. The journals record only that the consideration of the affair was ordered postponed until the delegates reconvened in September.[44] The postponement was due to the extreme discomfort that the Pennsylvania-Connecticut quarrel was causing in the Congress. On the one hand, Congress was looked to as the guarantor of colonial unity, and after Lexington and Concord the preservation of that unity was more important than it had ever been before. The dispute between Pennsylvania and Connecticut had reached the point of open warfare in the Susquehanna valley, threatening to give potent evidence of the colonial disunion upon which the English depended.[45] So, despite the delegates' reluctance to assume new authority, powerful reasons impelled them to try to foster a settlement. Yet the delegates were still actively pursuing the goal of reconciliation with England and were therefore extremely reluctant to step into a role that they acknowledged was legally in the province of the king. The monthlong postponement, therefore, represented their attempt to deal with the Pennsylvania-Connecticut differences as they had previously dealt with the Pennsylvania-Virginia controversy. Congress again chose to preserve an official silence on the subject, while the delegates attempted to foster negotiations by the involved colonies during the congressional recess.[46]

The response of the delegates from those colonies was not promising. In their consultations, Silas Deane recalled, both the Connecticut men and the Pennsylvanians showed "some warmth." Nevertheless, they agreed that the union of the colonies was the primary concern, and thus each side undertook to urge their respective claimants "to remain peaceably, on the Lands they had taken up" for the duration of "the present Contest."[47] But there were early indications that such an approach would not be successful. By midsummer, despite the public and private pleas of the Connecticut delegates that further Yankee expansion be halted, the Connecticut leaders on the scene continued to lay out new towns on the west branch and in early August 1775, William Judd (a Connecticut magistrate) led a large, quasi-military group there from Connecticut. They arrived on September 23 and promptly began to build fortifications. On September 25 they were defeated by a superior force of Pennamites, and several were taken prisoner (including the Connecticut leaders) and were marched off to jail in Philadelphia.[48]

The expedition infuriated the Pennsylvanians, the Continental delegates, and even the Connecticut delegates, who throughout the summer had been writing of the necessity of avoiding just such an encounter. On September 30 the Pennsylvania Assembly instructed its Continental delegates to lay the whole matter before the Congress, praying that it devise some method of preventing further intrusions until the conflict could be finally determined by the king-in-council. Pennsylvania's delegates, Richard Smith recorded on September 30, "moved for [the Congress] to interfere in the Dispute between Connecticut & Pennsa. for that there is immediate Danger of Hostilities between them on the Susquehannah."[49]

The Assembly's request was formally presented to the full Congress by George Ross on October 7. In the debate that followed, Thomas Willing clearly indicated the role he envisioned for the Congress. In the absence of the king, Willing intimated, it would have to serve as an umpire between the contending colonies. But the delegates were not ready to accept such a role; they were still reluctant to adjudicate, that is, to hear evidence on the merits of each side's case and render a final decision. Instead, the delegates referred the matter to their Connecticut and Pennsylvania colleagues.[50]

The continental delegates, recognizing that those most closely involved with the dispute imminently expected violence, called for the Pennsylvanians and the Connecticut men to report back almost immediately. But all that the delegates from the interested provinces could agree upon was that Congress must take some action, and on October 14 they resubmitted the matter to the full Congress. Although they themselves had been unable to reach agreement, they recognized that the gravity of the situation on the Susquehanna was such that some action would have to be taken. They recommended, therefore, that the Congress appoint a committee from among their disinterested colleagues to deal with the matter.[51]

On October 17 the committee was chosen. The members were charged with reporting "what in their opinion is proper to be done by Congress" to reconcile the bitter contest on the Susquehanna River. With the appointment of this committee, the Congress finally took upon itself at least a part of the king's authority, for they agreed at least to consider whether the Congress might play a role in resolving the dispute. The fact that the conflict had now moved into the continental sphere, rather than remaining in provincial hands, was symbolized by the personnel chosen for the committee: John Rutledge of South Carolina, Samuel Chase of Maryland, Thomas Jefferson of Virginia, James Kinsey of New Jersey, and Stephen Hopkins of Rhode Island. No committee of Congress was more studiedly continental. Nor is this surprising, since the committee was to report on a matter that was newly accepted as a continental responsibility.[52]

The delegates' acceptance of this new responsibility was far from a complete takeover of the old royal authority to decide intra-imperial disputes. With the appointment of the committee, the delegates had only agreed that they, not the contesting provinces, must find a way to prevent future contentions. They still had not accepted the power to decide the contest. This distinction was clear in the minds of the committeemen as they began their work. They heard evidence from both sides "with great Patience and Candour," but they cautioned that ". . . it was not the Intention of the Congress to take upon themselves the Decision of any Matters touching the Merits of the Controversy. They had only been charged, they protested, with finding a way in which the "Authority of Congress may be reasonably interposed for keeping the Peace till a Decision of this Matter."[53] They agreed that the Congress might serve as a mediator; they had not yet concluded it ought be an adjudicator.

Meanwhile, the situation on the Susquehanna grew steadily worse. The Pennsylvania land claimants (many of them wealthy Philadelphians) were at last exasperated by the inaction of their assembly and the slow pace of congressional deliberations. They began to take matters into their own hands. They formed a militant land claimants' association, which began recruiting men and gathering material for a major expedition against the Yankees. Their aim was either to drive the Connecticut men from the Susquehanna valley once and for all or to have the Yankees acknowledge Pennsylvania authority over the region. By the middle of November, rumors had spread about the size and destination of the Pennsylvania expedition. About the only certainty, as one Pennsylvanian wrote, was that there would "be a Scuffle."[54]

The continental delegates were forced by the imminent danger of armed conflict to drop their last vestiges of hesitation; they reluctantly accepted the full authority to adjudicate an explosive dispute that threatened to realize Tory predictions of intercolonial civil war. The altercations must "be quieted by the Honble Congress," Jonathan Trumbull of Connecticut wrote bluntly, for they could not be resolved by the colonies themselves. On November 27 the delegates finally asked their Susquehanna committee to begin "to hear evidence on the possession and jurisdiction of the lands in dispute," and to lay the results before the full Congress, where appropriate action would be taken. Authority not only to mediate the conflict but to decide it was now in continental hands.[55] On December 18 the Connecticut delegates, who had been hearing alarming reports about the progress of the Pennsylvania expedition, demanded that the inconclusive committee deliberations be halted, and that the full Congress investigate the situation and take immediate action to end hostilities. Faced with this urgent request, the delegates could no longer postpone making a decision that they had agreed the previous November 27 was theirs to make.[56]

A temporary solution to the conflict had never been hard to find, at least in theory. If both parties of settlers had been content to stay peaceably upon the lands already settled, the east branch of the Susquehanna River would have formed an admirable boundary line between Yankee and Pennamite. Such a line had, in fact, been suggested previously by the Connecticut delegates. For the Pennsylvanians, however, such a line was a less-than-ideal solution; its acceptance would have given up a major point in contention, that of jurisdiction. The Pennsylvanians had always balked at conceding even temporary jurisdiction to the Yankees, and they continued to protest vehemently against such a solution. Yet the Congress was not, at this point, favorably disposed toward the Pennsylvanians, for the delegates were angered by the Pennamite armed expedition. In any case, given the urgent need for action, the range of alternatives available to the continental delegates was limited. On December 20, therefore, by the narrow margin of six colonies to four, they set the east branch of the Susquehannah River as a temporary boundary line and thus granted temporary jurisdiction of east branch settlements to the Yankees.[57]

The Pennsylvanians "were very angry & discontented with this Determination of Congress," and the delegates quickly moved to placate them. The Pennsylvanians had long wished to see Connecticut migration to the area curbed, for this would effectively stop Yankee expansion. To avoid hostilities, the Connecticut Assembly had in fact already voted to halt migration until such time as the Assembly ordered. On December 23, by another narrow vote, Congress voted to substitute itself for the Assembly as the body responsible for determining when Connecticut migration might resume. This move displeased the Connecticut delegates, but in some measure it encouraged the Pennsylvanians to acquiesce in a settlement that was, on the whole, contrary to their interests.[58]

The solution was a weak one, however, that did not (as it was not meant to) finally resolve this troublesome dispute.[59] The December 20 resolution is probably more important for what it said, therefore, than for what it did. In it, the delegates accepted responsibility for establishing an equitable, if temporary, boundary line. Furthermore, they gave every indication that they expected their jurisdiction over the dispute to continue. Although their solution was to last only until "a legal decision can be had on such dispute," nevertheless, the alternative to such a settlement was stated to be: "or this Congress shall take further order thereon."[60] Furthermore, the delegates clearly expected their decision to be accepted as final. When, on December 29, a petition of Pennsylvania residents was presented in Congress "intimating that they will not obey the Recommendations of Congress in the Wyoming Affairs," the petition, one diarist reported, "gave much Offence."[61] Ultimately, the congressional decision was reluctantly accepted by both parties, despite considerable discontent. Neither side was prepared to challenge the only institution that, in the place of the discredited king, had sufficient authority to preserve intercolonial union. An uneasy quiet settled on the Susquehanna valley, "where they are peaceble at present," Carter Braxton wrote in mid-1776, "only thro the Influence of the Congress."[62]

The Pennsylvania-Connecticut dispute has been discussed in detail because it was the occasion on which the colonies involved thrust upon a reluctant Congress the responsibility to serve as the "sovereign umpire" of intercolonial quarrels. The Susquehanna conflict set a precedent. Henceforth, other longstanding disputes were brought, on the initiative of the contesting parties, from the council table in London to the new institution in Philadelphia.

The Limits of Congressional Authority: The New Hampshire Grants

An epic confrontation over the area that became the state of Vermont had long poisoned relations between the two original claimants, New

York and New Hampshire.[63] New York's 1664 charter gave that province complete jurisdiction over lands up to the Connecticut River.
Complaints over New York's jurisdiction might have been expected
from Massachusetts and Connecticut, whose "sea to sea" clauses were
in conflict with the Duke of York's patent, but Yorkers certainly looked
for no trouble from tiny New Hampshire, which had no definitive
charter until 1679 and which had no comprehensive "sea to sea"
clause. But New Hampshire was to prove a source of endless trouble
for the New Yorkers. The conflicts began in 1741 when Benning Wentworth became the royal governor of New Hampshire. For the next
twenty-five years Wentworth proceeded to make grants of land in territory west of the Connecticut River that, by almost any criteria, was
within New York's boundaries. Land-hungry New Englanders scrambled into the grants around the Green Mountains, hoping that possession would make up for the legal deficiencies of their titles, and by the
spring of 1764, New Hampshire had incorporated 128 townships in
the disputed territory.

Both New York and New Hampshire began litigating their conflicting claims to the area in 1750 and both agreed to grant no more land
until a settlement was reached. New York was as scrupulous about
keeping her part of the bargain as New Hampshire was diligent in ignoring hers. For fifteen years the two claims were pressed in London
until finally in 1764 a decision was reached. In the summer of 1764, the
king-in-council sustained New York's case, and the boundary was
declared thenceforth "to be" the Connecticut River.[64]

New York, which had kept its side of the bargain of 1750 and had
refrained from granting lands west of the Connecticut River (probably
in the correct expectation that its legal case was good and eventually
would be upheld) now began to make grants in the area. Its grants
(which, like those of New Hampshire, were often to wealthy speculators) conflicted in many instances with Wentworth's old New Hampshire grants. The problem was intensified by the fact that in the years
between 1750 and 1764 the area had acquired a considerable number
of settlers under New Hampshire titles. This fact perhaps would not
have been very important had New Hampshire not decided to continue litigation. Seizing on the phrase in the Board of Trade's letter to
the effect that the boundary between the provinces was henceforth "to
be" the Connecticut River, the New Hampshire men wondered if the
phrase did not mean that prior to 1764 the Connecticut River had *not*

been the boundary, and therefore perhaps the New Hampshire grants made prior to 1764 were valid. To decide this shaky point, the case went back to England, and it was only "on the eve" of settlement ten years later.

The ten-year period between 1764 and 1775 was one of turmoil and bitterness in the area henceforth known as the New Hampshire Grants. As New York attempted to impose its authority on the area (based on the 1764 decision), the large Yankee landholders like the Allen brothers (Ira, Heman, and Ethan) and Seth Warner began to organize the settlers under the New Hampshire titles. The New England men, soon known as the Green Mountain Boys, were chiefly concerned with discouraging Yankee settlers from seeking New York confirmation of their land titles and preventing New Yorkers from entering the area to make surveys or to settle. New York authority, though ostensibly acknowledged by the settlers, was often nullified on the scene by the mistreatment of Yorker magistrates. The charges, countercharges, and periodic eruptions of violence continued on both sides despite an attempted truce fostered by Governor Tryon of New York in late 1772. By 1775, although Ethan Allen and Seth Warner (the Green Mountain leaders) had been declared outlaws by New York in a futile gesture of rage, effective New York authority over the area had virtually come to an end.[65]

Congress became entangled with the dilemma of the New Hampshire grants in mid-1775. Its initial involvement, however, stemmed from the area's strategic location and the delegates' growing defense responsibilities rather than the continental body's new jurisdictional authority. Ethan Allen, worried by the vulnerability of the New Hampshire Grants to the British forts of Ticonderoga and Crown Point but countenancing no authority other than his own intrepid spirit, led his Green Mountain Boys in a successful attack on the British garrisons on May 9 and 10, 1775.[66] On June 23, the news of their exploit arrived in Philadelphia, and although Congress was reluctant to consider either the military or jurisdictional consequences of the attack, they were most anxious to prevent discord between the conquerors of Ticonderoga (outlaws, remember, under New York law) and the newly aroused provincial authorities of New York. Congress therefore gave Allen and Warner leave to organize their men into a regiment and choose their own officers but specified that the new regiment was to be under New York authority.[67]

Rumors were circulating, spread by New Yorkers, that the Allens had ulterior motives for seizing Ticonderoga. "Their design appears to be," a Connecticut man reported, "to hold those places [Ticonderoga and Crown Point] as a security to their lands [the New Hampshire Grants], against any that might oppose them." To defuse such reflections and to demonstrate their patriotism, the Green Mountain Boys agreed to a condition to which they had never before, or ever would again, consent. They acquiesced in the congressional decision and placed themselves under New York authority. When, as Ethan Allen wrote to the New York Provincial Congress in July 1775, he reflected on "the unhappy controversy which hath [for] many years subsisted between the Government of *New-York* and the settlers on the *New Hampshire Grants*" and contrasted it with the "friendship and union that hath lately taken place between the Government and those its former discontented subjects," he could not "but indulge fond hopes of reconciliation." Allen specifically noted "your respectful Treatment, not only to Mr. *Warner* and myself, but, to the *Green Mountain Boys* in general, in forming them into a battalion." He pledged, "as soon as opportunity may permit" to "hold [himself] in readiness to settle all former disputes and grievances on honorable terms."[68] The congressional effort to secure harmony in the troubled area of the New Hampshire Grants, therefore, was initially successful. But a deeply rooted controversy over conflicting property rights could not be so easily settled on the peripheral issue of military organization. In May 1776 the question of jurisdiction over the New Hampshire Grants was presented to the Congress for settlement in its newly established role as the continent's "sovereign umpire."

As independence approached, the inhabitants of the Grants began to question whether the Crown's decision of 1764, the basis of New York's asserted authority over them, remained valid. If present tyranny nullified the king's past authority, they reasoned, could they not reunite with New Hampshire? And if such a reunion were not possible, the Allen brothers and their ally, Jonas Fay, were pushing hard for the alternative solution of incorporating the area into a completely independent jurisdiction that acknowledged no superior authority but that of the Continental Congress. On January 16, 1776, a convention of New Hampshire grantees had been held at Dorset. The delegates resolved to petition Congress regarding New York's refusal to recognize their land titles and to request that their service to the common cause might henceforth be rendered independent of any New York authority. The resulting petition, drafted in the spring of 1776, was presented to Congress on May 8, 1776, by Captain Heman Allen of Seth Warner's battalion.[69]

The petition, signed by Joseph Woodward, "Chairman of the Committee of the New Hampshire Grants," is a remarkable document. It contains a full recapitulation of the grantees' legal position and a representation of "the many intervening and unhappy disputes which have since happened between those Land-Traders of New York and your Petitioners." The petitioners earnestly assured the Congress that "we are entirely willing to do all in our Power in the General Cause, under the Continental Congress," but were no longer "willing to put ourselves under the honorable provincial Congress of New York in such manner as might in future be detrimental to our private property," as would be the case if they continued to take certain oaths entailed by military service under New York authority. Therefore the grantees "prayest your Honors to take our case into your wise consideration, and order that for the future your petitioners shall do Duty in the Continental service . . . as inhabitants of said New Hampshire Grants, and not as inhabitants of the province of New York." The approval of this petition would have indicated congressional acquiescence in the dismemberment of New York, a course that, given the military situation of May 1776, the delegates were especially reluctant to take. Yet the military situation in Canada was also deteriorating. To retrieve it, the aid of the Green Mountain Boys was thought to be essential. The disposition of the problem was laid before a committee of five, who were directed to hear out Allen's presentation of the grantees' case.[70]

On May 30 the committee reported to Congress. Its recommendations amounted to a complete, if interim, vindication of New York's position and, one historian has suggested, may have contributed to a more favorable calculation by the Yorkers of the possible advantages of independence.[71] The petitioners' main request to serve the continent as independent inhabitants of the New Hampshire Grants was denied completely, and they were asked "for the present, to submit to the government of New York, and contribute their assistance, with their countrymen" under that authority. On June 4 a disgusted Allen requested and obtained leave from Congress to withdraw his petition, "he representing that he has left at home some papers and vouchers necessary to support the allegations therein contained."[72] Allen returned home in time to report to the next convention, which met at Dorset on July 24, 1776. As the 1764 decision of the Crown had not been accepted as final, neither were the hardy men of the New Hampshire Grants inclined to accept the May 30 resolution as the delegates' final word on the subject. The grantees' pretensions were enhanced, moreover, by Allen's report of his progress in Philadelphia. He suppressed any references to the committee report and emphasized that "sundry members of Congress and other Gentlemen of distinction" had advised the grantees to proceed on their own "to associate and unite the whole of the Inhabitants of said Grants together." Moreover, there were some grounds for his argument that the continental delegates had countenanced separate action by the grantees, for, as a by-product of military developments in Canada, Seth Warner had ultimately received a continental commission independent of New York's authority. The Dorset convention of July 1776 proceeded to form a New Hampshire Grants Association independent of New York and resolved to apply "to the Inhabitants of said Grants to form the same into a separate district."[73] Independence was in the air, and the New Hampshire grantees partook of the spirit.

In January 1777, pursuing the course decided upon the preceding July, the Convention of the New Hampshire Grants voted themselves "a new and separate state" and dispatched a committee to Philadelphia to petition Congress for recognition. On June 30, 1777, Congress's decision on the matter came down, and it was as categorical as it had been the previous year. It disavowed the new government and denied that Colonel Warner's commission had given any sanction to such proceedings as had been indulged in by the Dorset conventions. New York had again triumphed in the Congress. As James Duane, one of the leading New York proprietors, jubilantly wrote to a colleague, "I own I feel no small satisfaction in contemplating our Success."[74] Duane's euphoria was, of course, short-lived. The grantees regarded Congress's decision in this case as no more final than they had its previous answer to Heman Allen. In July 1777, on the eve of the Battle of Bennington, the Convention of Windsor either in ignorance of or in spite of the June 30 resolution, adopted a sweepingly democratic constitution modeled on that of Pennsylvania, as well as the name of "Vermont," and the new state proceeded to govern itself. In 1790 New

York finally accepted its defeat, and acquiesced in Vermont's formal admission to the union.[75]

The controversy over the New Hampshire Grants points up the limits of congressional authority in jurisdictional disputes, limits that had circumscribed the Crown's authority as well. The decision of 1764 never had been accepted by the tenacious Green Mountain Boys, and the commonly held opinion of everyone familiar with the dispute was that if the king had finally given judgment for New York, the decision could only have been enforced by British troops.[76] The Congress, on the other hand, had brought about the only example of voluntary Green Mountain acquiescence in New York authority when in 1775, Warner's battalion had been placed under the control of the New York provincial authorities.

As important as any final settlement, however, is the fact that both parties repeatedly brought the dispute before Congress and argued their cases in that forum, both obviously regarding the Congress as the only proper arbiter for such disputes. It is not surprising that the petitions drawn up by both sides drew heavily on, and closely resembled, their prior petitions to the king-in-council. Furthermore, when the Vermonters in 1777 finally did proceed on their own without continental approval, they did so with great temerity, acutely aware that they lacked the sanction of the one institution whose authority they recognized. In 1780 Ira Allen recalled that he and his colleagues never did submit the July 1777 constitution to the people for ratification, for it was "very doubtful whether a majority would have confirmed it, considering the resolutions of Congress, and their influence at the time."[77] The power that the draft Articles of Confederation granted to Congress of "deciding all disputes and differences now subsisting, or that hereafter may arise between two or more States concerning boundaries, jurisdictions or any other cause whatever" was therefore merely another recognition of existing practice.[78] Since 1774, interested jurisdictions themselves had been transferring disputes submitted for final settlement from the Privy Council in London to the new authority in Philadelphia.

Whether Congress actually succeeded in settling a dispute, or whether longstanding conflicts defied congressional attempts at solution, it is interesting to note that the alternative course of action—that the colonies undertake to settle their disputes between themselves—

met with little enthusiasm and less success. The ultimate unity of the empire had always been guaranteed by the existence of a "sovereign umpire" charged with the responsibility and authority to guarantee intra-imperial unity by providing the superior authority before which all sides agreed to argue their case. To recreate this authority, rather than to substitute new procedures, Americans turned to the Continental Congress as the guarantor of the internal unity of the new American state.[79]

By mid-1776, Americans could have some confidence that internal strife, disunion, and civil war would not follow inevitably upon the removal of the unifying authority of the British Crown. The growth of this comforting belief was due largely to the success of the Continental Congress in stepping into the king's vacated place as unifier of the empire. The first task it assumed was to insure that the external policy of the empire was directed in a unified manner toward the achievement of goals that would enhance the common good. The king had also been the guarantor of the empire's internal unity through his authority to adjudicate internal disputes and to provide the administrative machinery that would serve common goals. The king's "abdication" forced the colonists to look elsewhere for the performance of these functions, and many of them began to push these responsibilities upon their reluctant continental delegates. By the time independence appeared to be inevitable, Congress was performing enough of those functions with sufficient success to enable Americans to view it as a legitimate de facto continental government. Many of the new provincial governments, however, had yet to be seen in this light.

CHAPTER 9

Congress Grants Authority
for Government

I have ever Thought it the most difficult and dangerous Part of the Business Americans have to do in this mighty Contest, to contrive some Method for the Colonies to glide insensibly, from under the old Government, into a peaceable and contented submission to new ones.

—*John Adams, April 16, 1776*

On this spring evening in 1776, John Adams was explaining to his old friend Mercy Warren the problems with which he and his fellow delegates struggled. The note of caution in his letter is somewhat surprising, since Adams had been the first to urge the formation of new provincial governments as an essential step toward independence. Yet as the goals toward which Adams and his allies worked approached fruition in 1776, he paused to consider the implications for the internal peace of the colonies of the drastic steps he had been recommending. He was not alone. From 1775 on, some in Congress and in the provinces had in part forestalled a declaration of independence because they feared the consequences of such a step. Independence meant the formation of new provincial governments—and changes in governments, they knew, were rarely accomplished without enormous political and social upheaval. Yet by late 1775 and early 1776 new provincial governments appeared to be not only inevitable but necessary. The structure of political order that the Continental Congress had begun to build in 1774 was itself collapsing by late 1775. The military threat, present or imminent, strained the resources and authority of improvised provincial government structures. As a consequence, these congresses, conventions, and committees found it increasingly difficult to prevent disorder, to protect property, and to inspire a sense of "due subordination" to government. In short, they appeared incapable of performing the essential tasks of legitimate government. Faced with the real, or feared, consequences of such a lack of regular government, conservatives[1] and moderates in every colony began to join earlier radical demands for the formation of new, authoritative provincial governments. As a New Yorker admitted in 1776, "A well formed civil government is . . . necessary . . . to keep all things in order during the war."[2]

But how were such governments to be formed? For some, like John Adams, the answer was clear. With the king's abdication, legitimate governing authority had reverted to the people: it was now up to them to gather in each province and form new governments that would be based solely upon popular authority.[3] Just such answers, however, increased moderate and conservative apprehension of the political (and perhaps social) experimentation that might follow independence. Aside from the ideological implications, the practical problems of implementing solutions such as those suggested by Adams seemed insurmountable. All around them, moderates saw the turmoil brought about by war and civil discord, with established institutions from assemblies to courts everywhere under attack. Under such circumstances it seemed unlikely that the badly divided population of each province could unite to form a government that could command the acquiescence of the majority of the citizens. Yet if such legitimate governments could not be formed quickly, the only two alternatives—either anarchy or the use of force to uphold the new governments—seemed too terrible to contemplate.[4]

A similar situation had developed in 1774, when the establishment of committee authority had been at issue, and the decisions the provincial leaders made in 1776 closely resembled those they had made two years previously. An examination of events within those provinces that were forced by the events of the war to organize new provincial governments reveals a pattern.[5] When a worsening military situation began to threaten the ability of the interim provincial governments to function—to control their own troops, to raise money, or to meet internal or external military threats—moderate provincial leaders turned to the Continental Congress for assistance. In response, the Congress issued grants of authority that enabled them to organize new, authoritative governments.

It is important to emphasize that the new provincial governments could not possibly have been based solely upon congressional authority, and it is inconceivable that the continental delegates would have attempted to dispatch constitutions and governors from Philadelphia.[6] To be legitimate, these new provincial governments (like all governments) had to draw their authority from the people they governed. The continental delegates were careful to word all congressional authorizations to form new governments so that the officers and constitutions of these governments would be chosen by the people of each province. But it is also clear that neither the delegates nor the provincial leaders considered such popular sanction sufficient to ensure the legitimacy of the new governments. If they had, they would not have endured the hardship and frustration entailed by congressional hesitation and delay. In several provinces, military and civil difficulties threatened to overwhelm harassed provincial leaders as they cajoled, pleaded, and argued with the continental delegates for the authority to form new governments. No province proceeded to organize a new government before such congressional authority was received.

For the most part, the purposes for which Congress issued these grants of authority are also clear. The delegates did so not in response to early pleas that such grants would hasten the pace of independence but in response to urgent representations from provincial leaders that their ability to maintain control within their provinces was threatened. With one important exception, provincial leaders used the congressional authority for basically conservative political and social purposes: to control what they perceived as disorder and to forestall, to the extent possible, the political experimentation towards which radical provincial leaders wished to move. All but one of the new provincial governments formed under the grants of congressional authority issued in 1775 and 1776 closely resembled the old governments they replaced.

Authority for Government: The Particular

Massachusetts, the initial target of British vengeance, was the first province to experience the trials of a "state of nature." The necessity of forming government anew was therefore discussed in the Bay Colony from the opening days of the controversy.[7] When the royal government virtually ceased to function in mid-1774, after the arrival of the Massachusetts Government Act, the demand to resume government became general throughout the colony.[8] By the fall of 1774, on the eve of the meeting of the First Continental Congress, counties, towns, and individuals throughout the province were clamoring for a new government independent of royal authority. The most practical way to achieve this end, many believed, was to resume government under the old charter of 1629. As John Pitts observed, British tyranny had deprived the people of Massachusetts of any "government whatever, consistent with an idea of the English constitution." It was obvious, therefore, that if the people wished to "avoid . . . the general inconvenience of a state of nature," they must quickly act to "constitute a government." It was "the general opinion," he reported, that the new government should closely resemble that of the old charter, which had provided for a virtually republican form of provincial government.[9] This "general opinion" was strongest in the western areas of the province. In August 1774 the delegates to the Worcester Convention resolved that since Britain had dissolved the government, they recommended that a provincial congress be held "to devise proper ways and means to reassume our original mode of Government."[10] In September, Samuel Adams received reliable information that the backcountry was united in its determination to resume the old charter, and Joseph Warren put his old friend on notice that many eastern men agreed with their western brethren.[11]

On October 6, Paul Revere delivered to the delegates in Philadelphia a September 29 letter of the Boston committee of correspondence that detailed the compounding problems in the Bay Colony and that requested authority to resume the old charter. The Congress sidestepped the entire issue and on October 11 admonished the Massachusetts men to "peaceably and firmly persevere in the line they are now conducting themselves, on the defensive."[12] The reluctance of the continental delegates to countenance a resumption of the old charter relieved many moderates in Massachusetts, who felt that the action taken by the Boston committee had been precipitate. Armed with the authority of the Continental Congress, these moderates succeeded (for the time being) in forestalling efforts to assume a new provincial government. The first Massachusetts Provincial Congress, which met in October 1774, took no action on the matter, despite the strong sentiment among the western delegates and their eastern allies for the immediate resumption of charter government. This inaction infuriated people like John Adams, who saw no reason for delay. "We have no Council, No House, No Legislature, No Executive," he fumed to James Burgh in December 1774. "Not a Court of Justice, has Sat Since the Month of September—Not a debt can be recovered, nor a Trespass redressed, nor a Criminal of any kind, brought to Punishment."[13]

The degree to which the Massachusetts provincial leaders bowed to continental advice was shown on April 1, 1775, less than a month before Lexington. Rumors circulated that the royal governor, Thomas Gage, was about to issue writs for the election of a new assembly to be held in early May. Instead of denying Gage's authority to issue the writs and recommending a boycott of the election (the reaction favored by the radical-dominated Committee of Safety), the provincial delegates did just the opposite. They pushed aside their own previous call for a spring meeting of a provincial congress and resolved that if Gage issued his writs, "the several towns in this colony ought to obey such precepts, and choose their members as usual," save only that "the members ought transact no business" with the appointed Council. Only if Gage were to dissolve the Assembly, they stipulated, were the members thus elected "to meet in a Provincial Congress, for the purpose of considering and transacting the affairs of this colony."[14]

The battles of Lexington and Concord and the resulting confusion in the province ended the calm of early April. The necessity of raising an army and controlling it convinced even the reluctant eastern moderates that some more authoritative form of government than committees and congresses must be formed. As early as March, Colonel Ephraim Doolittle had complained that Massachusetts was "in a most lamentable situation, for want of a sanction of Government on our [military] establishments." He would have been "exceedingly glad" to hear that Massachusetts' continental delegates had laid "the difficulties we labour under for want of a Civil Constitution" before Congress, and obtained "their voice in justification of this Province in establishing one." The problem had worsened by early May as the hastily reconvened Provincial Congress struggled to cope with the flood of volunteers, regulate the army, and keep panic from spreading through the countryside. James Warren wrote to John Adams that the efforts to regulate the army were "attended with many difficulties, under the present Circumstances of our Government, in which recommendations are to supply the place of Laws," and in which the Congress was "destitute of coercive power, exposed to the Caprice of the

People, and depending entirely on their virtue for Success." By the end of May, Joseph Warren, soon to die at Bunker Hill, saw "more & more the Necessity of establishing a civil Government here, and such a Government as shall be sufficient to controul the military Forces not only of this colony, but also such as shall be sent to us from the other Colonies."[15]

The Massachusetts radicals, whose patience had been severely tried by the pacific advice of the First Continental Congress, saw in the changed situation of April 1775 an opportunity to undermine the provincial delegates' policy of acquiescing in that advice. If they had considered the assumption of a new government desirable in 1774, they believed it to be obligatory by the spring of 1775. Accordingly, on May 4 the radicals on the Committee of Safety, led by the rabid supporter of independence James Warren, launched an attack on the policy of acquiescence. In their morning meeting, the committeemen adopted a resolution that stated bluntly that "the public good of this colony requires, that government in full form ought to be taken up immediately," and they ordered a copy of the resolution transmitted to the Provincial Congress, then sitting in Watertown. When the Provincial Congress assembled the next afternoon, this explosive resolution, and thus the whole question of the assumption of government, was before the harried delegates. With evident satisfaction, Warren informed John Adams of the committee's action three days later. "The extream want of the Exercise of a fixt settled Government is sufficiently felt here at this time," he wrote, that the Provincial Congress had agreed to take up the matter on May 9. On that date, Warren predicted, the delegates would "vote to assume a Government."[16]

Warren's confidence, however, was premature. The moderates realized that Warren was attempting to take advantage of the military emergency to push the Provincial Congress into an immediate resumption of the old charter. They worried that Warren and his western allies meant to agree on "a plan of Government," and "put it into execution immediately without consent of the Congress at Philadelphia." This plan, one observer noted, "has given some little uneasiness to the moderate Wiggs of the Province," who thought it necessary that the continental delegates give "their Sanction to a Form of Government for us." The moderates therefore resolved upon a policy of delay. On May 8, the day before the Committee of Safety resolution was scheduled to come up for debate, the moderates moved that con-

sideration of the resolution be postponed until May 12. They succeeded, and the next day they defeated a radical motion "that an earlier day be assigned for that purpose."[17] On May 12 the moderates'
victory was completed. Rather than assuming an independent provincial government under the charter of 1629, the Provincial Congress
voted to appoint a committee to draft an application to the Second
Continental Congress, then assembling in Philadelphia, for permission "to take up and exercise civil government, as soon as may be,"
and that the application be based on "the necessity of the case." The
application to the Continental Congress, dated May 16, pointedly reminded the continental delegates that Massachusetts, "though urged
thereto by the most pressing necessity, to assume the reins of civil government," had no wish to take such a drastic step without the "advice
and consent" of the Congress. The situation in the Bay Colony, however, had grown critical after Lexington and Concord had compelled
the provincial leaders to raise an army. The delegates trembled, they
wrote, "at having an army, . . . without a civil power to provide for
and control it." They therefore humbly hoped the Continental Congress would "favor us with your most explicit advice, respecting the
taking up and exercising the powers of government, which we think
absolutely necessary for the salvation of our country." Armed with
this plea, Benjamin Church was dispatched to Philadelphia to present
the case of Massachusetts Bay.[18]

For weeks, Massachusetts waited for the return express from Philadelphia that would bring the continental answer. Meanwhile, the situation in the province grew steadily worse. On May 18, James Warren
fidgeted that "it will no longer . . . do to delay a question that should
have been determined 6 months ago." Elbridge Gerry pleaded with
the Massachusetts delegates in Philadelphia to hurry the matter along,
for the grave problems in the province would brook no delay. "Government is so essential," he wrote, "that it cannot be too soon
adopted," for the people felt "rather too much their own importance,"
and it required "great skill to produce such subordination as is necessary." In early June, James Warren impatiently wrote to John Adams
that "the public Expectation to hear from the Congress is great." The
people wondered, he complained, "that the Congress should sit a
month without their receiving something decisive with regard to
us."[19] On June 11 the Provincial Congress sent a somewhat frantic letter to the continental delegates requesting their immediate attention to

the plight of Massachusetts. "The situation of any colony, or people, perhaps was never before such as made it more necessary for fully exercising the powers of civil government," they wrote. They alluded to such "alarming symptoms" as the declining sense "in the minds of some people, of the sacredness of private property," the cause of which was "plainly assignable to the want of civil government." These problems, they noted, had "necessitated the sending a special post to obtain your immediate advice upon this subject."[20]

While the anxious Massachusetts men fretted, the delegates in Philadelphia struggled to cope with the torrent of business that came before them as soon as they assembled on May 10. The urgent problems of organizing the Continental Army occupied nearly all their efforts during this period. But the urgent situation in the Bay Province, particularly the need to control the army, finally forced the delegates to act. On June 2 the Massachusetts application was laid before the full Congress.[21]

The Massachusetts delegates, especially John Adams, had been chafing at the delay in responding to their state's message. As Adams later remembered, the matter had lain "with great Weight upon my Mind as the most difficult and dangerous Business that We had to do." When the May 16 letter came before the delegates, therefore, Adams "embraced the Opportunity to open myself in Congress" on the important subject of the formation of government. During the early June debate, Adams emphasized that sooner or later new governments would be necessary in every colony. They must, he later remembered insisting, be instituted on impeccable Whig principles, that is, "by Conventions of Representatives chosen by the People in the several Colonies, in the most exact proportions." But Adams labored in vain. Though a few delegates heard his "new, strange and terrible Doctrines" with pleasure, the majority listened politely and proceeded to deal with the specific problem of Massachusetts in a very different manner than Adams and his colleagues desired.[22]

On June 3 a conservative-dominated committee of five was appointed to take the Massachusetts request into consideration. Four days later the committee brought in its report, which was accepted by the full Congress on June 9. The long-awaited congressional recommendations, which were to be the basis for Massachusetts government until 1776, simply provided for the resumption of government under the royal charter of 1691 and rejected the plea to organize a semirepublican government under the old charter of 1629. The Congress agreed with the Massachusetts moderates that the province needed a regular government. But to organize such an authority the Congress simply resolved that the offices of the royal governor and lieutenant governor should be considered vacant and that otherwise Massachusetts was to conform "as near as may be, to the spirit and substance of the [1691] charter." In the absence of a "constitutional" governor or lieutenant governor, the executive of the new government was to be provided by an elected council, as the charter specified. The assembly and council were to continue to govern the province, the resolution went on, "until a Governor, of his Majesty's appointment, will consent to govern the colony according to its charter."[23]

Resumption of the 1691 charter was about the last recommendation the Warren faction in Massachusetts desired from the Congress. As far back as 1774 they had chafed under the restraints of the royal charter. "Charters have become bubbles—empty shadows without any certain stability or security," the town of Leicester had resolved, and its delegate to the Provincial Congress in 1774 had been instructed to oppose any moves "for patching up" the 1691 charter and allowing it to serve as a new frame of government. In early May 1775, when the question of the future government of Massachusetts was presented to the Continental Congress, Joseph Warren had voiced his specific objections to the 1691 charter. "We cannot think, after what we have suffered for a Number of Years," he complained to his friend Samuel Adams, "that you will advise us to take up that Form established by the last Charter."[24]

But resumption of the 1691 charter was precisely what the Continental Congress had recommended, and despite the apprehensions and dissatisfactions that radicals had been expressing on this vital question of internal policy since 1774, the edict of the continental body was not disputed. As Joseph Warren wrote, "We have . . . submitted. & are sending out our Letters. & shall Express our Gratitude." On June 20 the Provincial Congress proceeded to thank the continental delegates "for that compassion, seasonable exertion, and abundant wisdom, evidenced in your recommendation to this people," and promised to apply themselves "with all diligence, to fulfil your benevolent intentions, and establish the form of government recommended by your honors; that so, order and government may be restored to this disturbed community."[25]

The best evidence of the continental body's ability to compel obedience to its decisions on the vital question of the formation of government was the alacrity with which its advice was followed. Although immersed in the expanding military difficulties, the Massachusetts Provincial Congress immediately complied with the June 9 resolution. On July 20 it ordered copies of the resolve printed and circulated to all the towns in the province, and it accompanied the copies with its own letter, modeled directly on the old royal election writs. A new assembly was to be elected, the Provincial Congress specified, "In observance of the foregoing resolve of the Hon. Continental Congress." The new governing body of Massachusetts convened on July 19, and it adopted all the usages of the old General Assembly. The term "Provincial Congress" was dropped forever, and "House of Representatives" resumed. The new representatives chose councilors, as the charter of 1691 provided, and their approval henceforth was deemed necessary for the completion of any legislative action. The results of this new assembly were termed "Acts" rather than "resolves" or "recommendations." And the first Act of the new assembly was "An ACT to confirm and establish the Resolves of the several Provincial Congresses of this Colony." In early August, Benjamin Church reported that the new government was nearly completed and that the province was beginning to emerge from a state of nature."[26] Massachusetts continued to govern itself in the anomalous manner provided by the Continental Congress until, on May 15, 1776, the Congress granted authority for the Bay Province, among others, to assume a more congenial form of government.[27] No more striking evidence exists of the desire to entrust the Congress with the authority to institute government than Massachusetts' adherence to its truncated charter government through one of the most difficult years of its history.[28]

Massachusetts was the first province to be given leave to assume government, and although the continental response had been tailored specifically to the situation in the Bay Colony, it began to set a pattern. In the future, as in the case of Massachusetts, a situation of internal disorder and confusion would lead moderates within a colony to appeal to the Congress for assistance. Despite urgent internal problems, these provincial leaders would wait, as the Massachusetts leaders had waited, for continental advice before they proceeded with the important step of forming a new government. In no other colony did the continental recommendations cause as much difficulty as they had in

Massachusetts, however, for the Continental Congress henceforth granted authority for government in terms general enough to allow each colony to take up the form of government that best suited its internal needs and circumstances. As with other powers assumed by the Congress, the impetus for the assumption came not from the continental delegates but from provincial leaders who pushed their notion of the legitimate authority of a central government upon their reluctant and hesitant continental colleagues. But once the delegates in Philadelphia had issued the authority to assume government in one instance, they found it much easier to respond to the request of a second province.

New Hampshire's difficulties became apparent later than those of Massachusetts, and it did not share the happy political situation of its sister New England colonies of Rhode Island and Connecticut, whose charters rendered them virtually independent. New Hampshire, unlike Massachusetts, was a royal province, so the legality of all governmental actions in the colony depended directly upon the king's writs and the instructions sent out with each individual governor at the beginning of his term. The royal governor in 1775, John Wentworth, though American-born, was a confirmed king's man, and by late June he had removed himself to the royal fort in Portsmouth harbor, protected by the guns of H.M.S. *Scarborough*. Along with Governor Wentworth and his family went all legal authority in the province. Since New Hampshiremen were notorious for resisting *any* government demands upon them (whether issued by the legitimate authorities or not), the problem facing the delegates to the Provincial Congress in 1775 was a distressing one. How could they command obedience, which in the particular situation of 1775 meant compelling the payment of taxes, when the Provincial Congress itself had no legal basis, no coercive power, and thus no way of dealing with the constituents' traditional resistance to the demands of even established government?[29]

After Lexington and Concord, New Hampshire found it necessary to raise troops, both to respond to the appeals of the Bay Province and to cope with problems of internal defense. Raising and arming troops requires money, however, and money was the root of serious political difficulties in the province. The province's poverty was, in fact, very much on the minds of the provincial delegates as they began to raise troops in May 1775. They were looking to the Continental Congress for help, they wrote on May 23, since British America had been "trusted to your wisdom" that "as by a pole star, it may steer in the tempest occasioned by the . . . unnatural attacks of the *British* Ministry." To their representatives in Philadelphia, John Sullivan and John Langdon, the provincial delegates were blunter. Since they had no alternative, they were organizing the necessary forces. But "how shall we pay them," the delegates added pointedly, "you are sensible must now be our Question."[30]

New Hampshire's money problems were a symptom of a larger difficulty. The Provincial Congress could not collect money because it could not gain widespread acceptance as the legitimate successor to royal authority. In midsummer the New Hampshire authorities admitted that the problem was a general one. "The affairs of this Colony . . . at this time . . . is in some confusion," the Committee of Safety informed the province's continental delegates, for the people did not suffer "things to proceed in their former manner." The colony's situation caused the delegates to "greatly desire some . . . Regulations," but they could not proceed, they wrote, without direction from Philadelphia.[31] What the New Hampshiremen specifically desired from the Congress was an authorization (similar to its June 9 resolution regarding Massachusetts) to assume a new provincial government. Only such a grant of authority, the provincial leaders believed, could resolve the governmental crisis that was fostering disorder and undermining the provincial war effort. On September 1, therefore, the Provincial Congress of New Hampshire, following the example of Massachusetts, directed its continental delegates to seek this authority from the Congress. "We would have you immediately use your utmost endeavours," the provincial leaders wrote, "to obtain the Advice & Direction of the Congress, with respect to a Method for our Administring Justice and regulating our civil Police." They pressed the delegates "not to delay this matter, as, its being done speedily . . . will probably prevent the greatest confusion among us."[32]

Despite this plea for speed, the New Hampshire delegates in Philadelphia (by this time Sullivan had been replaced by Josiah Bartlett) decided that a question of such import should not be thrust without warning upon the continental delegates. They themselves favored the application and had been urging the Provincial Congress for some time to petition Congress on the subject. John Sullivan, then a New Hampshire delegate, had been one of the few who had heard John Adams's June 2 remarks "with apparent Pleasure." But the delegates cautiously decided to prepare the ground by conducting private discussions before presenting their September 1 instructions formally to the full Congress. By October, Bartlett and Langdon were ready to move. On October 18 they laid New Hampshire's request to assume a new government before the full Congress.[33]

The New Hampshire request quickly became the subject of vigorous debate. As the New Hampshire delegates reported, "The Arguments on this Matter . . . were Truely Ciceronial." John Adams remembered that he had "embraced with Joy the opportunity of harranguing on the Subject at large." In fact, he wanted much more than a specific authorization for New Hampshire. Adams urged Congress to adopt "a general recommendation to all the States to call Conventions and institute regular Governments." Such a step was necessary, he argued (with reasoning calculated to appeal to his more moderate colleagues), because of the danger to the people's morals arising "from the present loose State of Things and general relaxation of Laws and Government through the Union." Adams had first presented these views (he later recalled) during the debates the previous June on the Massachusetts resolution. Although he found that the opposition in October, "was still inveterate," he also found that "many Members began to hear me with more Patience." On October 26, however, after a week's delay, a committee of five was appointed to report to the Congress on the question of New Hampshire's request to assume government.[34]

On November 2 the members of the committee brought in a report favorable to the province's application. By this time bold steps had been legitimized by the arrival of news that the king had rejected the Olive Branch Petition. With the option of reconciliation all but foreclosed, a determined and united Congress proceeded to take up the committee report. After extensive debate, on November 3 Congress adopted the committee's draft resolution. The delegates agreed

> that it be recommended to the provincial Convention of New Hampshire, to call a full and free representation of the people, and that the representatives, if they think it necessary, establish such a form of government, as, in their judgment, will best produce the happiness of the people, and most effectually secure peace and good order in the province, during the continuance of the present dispute between G[reat] Britain and the colonies.[35]

The New Hampshire resolution went much farther than did that of Massachusetts. Rather than specifying a particular form of government for the province, the continental delegates left provincial authorities free to establish the form of government they thought appropriate. The distinction was made necessary in part by the form of government then in existence in New Hampshire. As it lacked a charter, the province could hardly be advised, as Massachusetts had been, to organize a government based upon a pre-existing constitution. Nevertheless, the broad language of the resolution cheered the province's continental delegates, who pointed out to Matthew Thornton, the president of the Provincial Congress, that the power granted by Congress was "ample and full, even to the Choice of Governor," although they recognized that the permission was "Limited to the Present Contest to ease the minds of Some few persons, who were fearful of Independence."[36]

The New Hampshire Provincial Congress, meanwhile, had been waiting anxiously for the outcome of the deliberations in Philadelphia. On November 14, unaware that the Congress had granted the request, the provincial delegates issued writs for the election of a new Provincial Congress. They were careful to add, however, that "in case there should be a recommendation from the Continental Congress for this Colony to assume Government in any way that will require a House of Representatives," that the new Provincial Congress would "be empowered to resolve themselves into such a House as may be recommended." Having thus proceeded as far as they felt authorized to go, the delegates dissolved the current Provincial Congress on November 16.[37]

The diffidence of the Provincial Congress in mid-November contrasts sharply with the burst of activity it exhibited in early December after news arrived of the November 3 resolution. The New Hampshire legislators obviously believed that they could not proceed to organize a new provincial government until they had received specific continental authority to do so, although they thought that such a government was urgently needed. As John Sullivan noted on December 11, he could now begin to think about the best form of government for New Hampshire, since "the Continental Congress has given our Province a power to assume government."[38] The form of government chosen by the provincial delegates, which was to govern the province until 1783, was exactly that which Congress had prescribed for Massachusetts—a house of assembly, and an elected council to fill the place of the abdicated royal executive.[39] This new constitution was simply declared to be in effect by the Provincial Congress. No convention was called to form the government, and it was not submitted to the people for ratification. The authority for this plan of government was dual in nature, as the delegates to the Provincial Congress expressly stated in their proclamation of January 5, 1776. The new government derived its authority both from the "Free Suffrages of the People" who had chosen the provincial delegates, and from "a Recommendation to that Purpose" from the Continental Congress.[40]

The day after Congress granted leave to assume government to New Hampshire, it granted similar leave, in identical language, to South Carolina. There, as with Massachusetts and New Hampshire, a worsening military situation combined with a crumbling royal government to cause moderate and conservative leaders to seek a solution from the Continental Congress. Since 1775, South Carolina, in effect, had been governed by a Provincial Congress, with executive power vested in a committee called first the General Committee and later the Committee of Safety. A merchant-planter aristocracy centered in Charleston dominated both the Provincial Congress and the executive committees, as they had the colonial assembly. The patriot leadership denied the backcountry a proportional representation in the new revolutionary bodies, thus continuing the chronic underrepresentation of the frontier areas that had been traditional under royal rule.[41]

But the exclusion of the backcountry did not guarantee the harmonious conduct of South Carolina's affairs by her new rulers, for the eastern merchant-planter aristocracy itself had been bitterly divided since 1774 over questions of tactics and timing. The supporters of independence, led by Christopher Gadsden and William Henry Drayton, were for the strongest possible measures in opposition to Britain. But their headlong course was checked at every turn by conservatives and moderates—like John Rutledge, Rawlins Lowndes, and Henry Laurens—who believed that the opposition should proceed at a slower pace and in an orderly manner. Although the moderates had controlled the major revolutionary bodies since 1774 (Laurens himself had been elected president of the General Committee in 1775), signs were proliferating by late 1775 that their power was eroding. The Second Provincial Congress, which assembled on November 1, 1775, elected William Henry Drayton as chairman.[42]

Factional disputes alone, however, are not sufficient to explain the extreme disquiet of the South Carolina conservatives in the late summer and early fall of 1775. These aristocrats had always felt uneasy as revolutionaries. Their position was made intolerable by their feeling that they were governing the colony with absolutely no authority that they considered legitimate. The members of the Committee of Safety, according to one historian, seemed always to have the uncomfortable feeling that they were treading perilously close to the line that separated lawful resistance from treason.[43] Where that business involved organizing resistance, primarily by enforcing the provisions of the Association, the irregular nature of the provincial resistance organizations caused few problems. This was at least in part because established government in South Carolina had not ceased to function. The provincial leadership had developed an acceptable working arrangement with Lord William Campbell, the last royal governor of South Carolina, who had arrived in the province on June 18, 1775. Campbell had attempted, with some success, to work with the Whig leadership in carrying on the business of government and to this end had kept the Assembly in regular session. Most of the provincial leaders were members of the Assembly, and they were content to remain in their legislative positions while simultaneously serving in the resistance organizations. This anomalous arrangement was perhaps epitomized by the commissions that Campbell signed for the officers of the volunteer companies that were raised by the Provincial Congress.[44] As South Carolina was at such a great distance from the primary theater of war, this situation might have continued had not indigenous loyalism brought the war closer to home.

In the late summer and early fall of 1775, armed conflict broke out in the backcountry, which had a long history of conflict with the eastern planter elite. On July 12, 1775, in obedience to the directions of the Council of Safety, backcountry patriots seized royal military stores in Fort Charlotte and moved them to the frontier settlement of Ninety-Six. Moses Kirkland, a local man who had taken a commission in the Whig volunteer companies, abruptly changed sides and incited backcountry loyalists to retake the powder and arrest local Whig leaders. The Council of Safety, alarmed at its lack of control over events in the region, dispatched two agents, William Henry Drayton and William Tennant, to set up Whig headquarters at Ninety-Six and to organize the Whig militia in the area. By this time the Tories had found an able indigenous leader, Thomas Brown, and were pursuing a similar course. Both sides attempted to enlist the aid of the Cherokee Indians, while accusing the other of barbarism for doing the same. By the middle of September, bloody skirmishes were taking place throughout the region, and organized armed forces were encamped on opposite banks of the Saluda River.[45]

The ominous events in the backcountry destroyed the fragile accommodation between the Whig leadership and the royal governor in Charleston. The patriot leadership suspected Campbell of inciting and aiding the backcountry Tories. Taking advantage of the governor's accessibility, they now dispatched a Whig agent to engage him in extended conversation regarding his policy toward the backcountry. To draw the governor out, the agent espoused fervently Tory views. As Charles Drayton later informed his brother William Henry Drayton, "His trepanned Lordship advises the back Country people not to take up arms unless they think they are full strong enough," but "if they think they are they may; & that they will be soon relieved by troops expected to be here soon."[46] The agent's report to the Committee of Safety ended any hope of continued cooperation between the provincial leaders and the governor. That evening, Campbell sent orders to H.M.S. *Tamar*, a man-of-war stationed with a small fleet of attendant vessels in Charleston Harbor, to send a detachment to dismantle the cannon at Fort Johnston, which commanded the harbor. The next day, September 15, Campbell dissolved the Assembly and moved his government to the *Tamar*. The captain's log recorded that this day "came on board his Excellency Lord William Campbell for the Safety of his Person."[47]

As South Carolina, like New Hampshire, had no charter, with the departure of the royal governor and the dissolution of the Assembly went the only legitimate government in the province. The effects of the vacuum were soon felt. As Henry Laurens, the president of the Council of Safety, described the situation to his son, "Lord William is gone on board the *Tamar* Man of War, . . . the House of Assembly [is] dissolved—the Judges have shut up their Courts of Law—the Custom House will probably Soon follow the example."[48]

Just when the established institutions of the government collapsed, however, the need for such institutions became more urgent, because of the deteriorating military situation that followed in the wake of the governor's departure. With the governor aboard the man-of-war, the situation in the province changed abruptly, for now there was nothing to prevent an attack by the British warships on the rebellious town of

Charleston. The key to any such attack, as the governor had seen immediately, was Fort Johnston, situated offshore and guarding the entrance to the harbor. The guns of the fort, if turned on the British fleet, would prove a powerful weapon to defend the town; if the guns remained under British control, however, the harbor also belonged to the British. The Council of Safety was, like the governor, aware of the fort's strategic importance. On the night of the fourteenth, it dispatched a force of some 150 men to Gadsden's Wharf, where they were taken on board two packets. Once under way, the men were told the mission—they were to take Fort Johnston.[49] The surprise was complete and the mission was successful, although the cannon they found there had been damaged by the British detachment. The next day, September 16, Governor Campbell sent his secretary, Captain Alexander Innes, to the fort. Innes made clear the fragile authority under which the provincial authorities were operating. He had come, he said, by authority of the governor to demand of the provincials what manner of troops they were, and by "what Authority [they had taken] possession of this Fort." They were American troops, they answered, and their authority had been "the express Command of the Council of Safety." Whatever legitimate authority the council lacked, however, it did not lack energy. Determined to hold the fort, it dispatched reinforcements the next day. By the evening of September 16, some five hundred troops held Fort Johnston in the name of the Council of Safety.[50]

Thus, within a few short days the council had gone from a resistance organization working in uneasy truce with the royal government to the de facto government of the province, responsible both for directing military operations in the backcountry and facing a more immediate threat from British warships in the harbor. As a letter from Charleston dated September 15, 1775, reported, "Our people have taken possession of Fort Johnston, where there are now between five and six hundred of our Provincials, who are in daily expectation of an attack from the man of war, one armed vessell, and two packets armed, which are now in the road," meaning Rebellion Road, the entrance to the harbor. Moreover, as Arthur Middleton informed William Henry Drayton on the same day, "It is confidently said [troop] Transports & Frigates will be here soon."[51]

At this juncture Laurens took advantage of a favorable opportunity to send news of the events in Charleston to the province's continental delegates. The Council of Safety had, he wrote, "business of very great importance to lay before you, which we think will merit the consideration of the Representatives of the United Colonies." He proceeded to relate to the delegates the "recent transactions of a most dangerous tendency in the interior parts of this Colony," and more particularly "the treachery of our Governor," of whom they had "for some time entertained suspicions." Lord Campbell's actions, both in the backcountry and in Charleston harbor, had created a situation that rendered "this application for your advice & assistance absolutely indispensable." First, Laurens related the events that had led to Campbell's departure and the necessity the council had been under of taking the fort. "We also intend to fortify the Harbour as effectually as our circumstances will admit of," he added, but in doing so, "'tis possible the Man of War may interrupt our proceedings, in such Case we shall be under a necessity of attempting to take or destroy her.—here we are at a loss to know to what lengths each Colony will be warranted by the Voice of America in opposing & resisting the King's Officers in general & the British Marine." Next, Laurens related the great difficulties the council had had in organizing the provincial military forces. The previous June they had raised two provincial regiments and had specified that the officers of those regiments were to take precedence over militia officers when on active service. But the need to engage in active service had engendered great dissension, as the militia officers refused to recognize either the authority of the provincial officers or, indeed, any superintending authority at all. The situation had given rise to "no inconsiderable degree of ferment & dissatisfaction." "To this untoward circumstance," Laurens continued, "add the unfavourable accounts which we have received from the Indians, the danger which we are always exposed to & more especially at this time from domestic [i.e., slave] Insurrection[,] the expectation of British Troops & Ships of War with other incidents . . . & you will agree that we have before us a very unpleasant prospect." For the protection not only of South Carolina but of North Carolina and Georgia as well, the province therefore urgently required that the Continental Congress not only authorize the province to raise Continental troops, "at the general Charge of the Colonies," but also that it organize and regularize the structure of all the provincial military forces. Finally, Laurens noted, civil government in the province was at an end: "the Judges have refused to do business in their departments, hence the Courts are shut up, the Custom House may soon follow the example." In such a situation, the council therefore urgently entreated the continental delegates "to consider of proper measures for the keeping the Militia in due subordination & procuring a strong recommendation, on this head from the Congress." In addition, the council noted, the party who conveyed its letter and the supporting documents also carried "a verbal message which cannot be so well imparted in any other manner."[52]

On November 2, the day upon which the report of the New Hampshire Committee was brought in, "on Motion made," the Congress resolved "that the Congress will to Morrow take into consideration the state of S[outh] Carolina." The next day, after agreeing to the New Hampshire resolution, the Congress "taking into consideration the state of South Carolina, and sundry papers relative thereto, being read and considered," appointed a committee of five to consider "what, in their opinion, is necessary to be done." The committee, although dominated by southerners, did not include a representative from South Carolina.[53] Nevertheless, it is clear from the resolutions agreed to the next day that the impetus for the move had been Laurens's letter and its accompanying documentation. On November 4 the South Carolina Committee brought in, and the Congress adopted, no fewer than nine resolutions regarding South Carolina, in stark contrast to the New Hampshire resolution, which had solely concerned the assumption of government. Most of the resolutions dealt specifically with the deteriorating military situation that Laurens had described. Thus, for example, the province was authorized to raise, at continental expense, three battalions of foot, which were to be paid and regulated as was the Continental Army. For this purpose, the dispatch of blank commissions, signed by the president of the Congress, was also authorized. To solve the problem of precedence to which Laurens had referred, the Congress specified that the continental officers were to take precedence over provincial forces, and that the provincial forces were in turn to take precedence over the local militia. Also in response to Laurens's request, the Congress resolved that "the town of Charleston ought to be defended against any attempts that may be made to take possession thereof by the enemies of America," and that the Council of Safety was authorized to build such fortifications as it thought necessary to defend the town. Furthermore, if the provincial authorities thought it "expedient for the security of that colony, to seize or destroy . . . any ship or vessel of war, this Congress," the delegates resolved, "will approve of such proceeding." The final resolve in this list, in the same language as that used for New Hampshire, was a resolution authorizing the Convention to assume a new provincial government.[54]

The reasons for this last resolution must remain obscure, because there is no surviving contemporary evidence that explains the delegates' decision to act, and the South Carolina authorities had not, as had those in New Hampshire, asked for such authorization in so many words, although we cannot know what requests were contained in the verbal message carried by the Council of Safety's messenger. Nevertheless, the context of the resolution, and the request of the Council of Safety that was the occasion for Congress's consideration of events in South Carolina, do permit some speculation. It is clear that the Council of Safety considered the lack of established institutions of government to be one of the most serious problems caused by the governor's departure and that it was particularly worried about its ability, absent some superior authority, to keep its increasing military forces subordinate to civilian authority. Such problems would have weighed heavily upon the mind of John Rutledge, one of South Carolina's more prominent continental delegates.[55] Rutledge was one of only two men to have been a member of both the committee appointed to consider the Massachusetts request to take up government and the similar committee appointed to consider the request of New Hampshire. The New Hampshire Committee was appointed on October 26, and the debates on the resolution were thus occurring just as the letters from South Carolina arrived in Philadelphia. It is possible, therefore, that Rutledge saw in such congressional authorization—the arguments regarding which were so fresh in his mind—a solution to the problems of South Carolina that had been so graphically chronicled by his friend and ally Laurens.[56] Whatever the case, it is clear that the sudden vacuum of civil authority that occurred simultaneously with the need for expanded military endeavors caused the conservative provincial authorities to look to the Continental Congress for a solution. Part of the solution suggested by the Congress was the assumption of a new civil authority.

Additional clues to Rutledge's motives for seeking such authorization may be discerned in the interpretation of the meaning of the congressional resolution that he carried home with him when he left Philadelphia in December 1775. In early February 1776, Rutledge introduced the continental resolution in the South Carolina Provincial

Congress. Rather than call the "full and free representation of the people" recommended by Congress, the Provincial Congress simply took the task upon itself. The broad-based committee chosen to consider the resolution brought in a report on February 10. The debate over the committee report showed a wide divergence of opinion in the province over the meaning of the congressional grant of authority.[57] Gadsden, speaking for the radicals, adopted the position of his friend John Adams and that of Thomas Paine, whose new pamphlet, *Common Sense*, he had brought home with him. Elaborating on ideas that Adams had been advocating in Philadelphia and that Paine had newly espoused, Gadsden asserted that the only proper way to implement the November 4 resolution was to call for a convention of the people to institute their own government. Surely, he asserted, the new government should not simply be concocted and "pronounced" by the Provincial Congress.[58] Rutledge, however, immediately rose and denounced Gadsden's notions as treasonable. The November 4 resolution, as he had every reason to know, had been intended only to authorize the means by which the provincial authorities might preserve order until a reconciliation with Britain could be achieved. He saw no need to call a special convention and frame a government to achieve these limited ends. The authority of the Provincial Congress, he believed, bolstered as it was by the resolution of the Continental Congress, was perfectly adequate.[59]

Rutledge's views were apparently shared by a majority of his colleagues in the Provincial Congress. They resolved that since many regulations were needed "for securing peace and good order during the unhappy disputes between Great Britain and the colonies," it was the duty of the Provincial Congress (as pointed out by the continental delegates) to provide such regulations as would secure the "well governing" of "the good people of the colony." The regulations adopted by the Provincial Congress were embodied in the South Carolina Constitution of 1776, a document that, except for the nomenclature and the source of authority, duplicated the royal government of South Carolina.[60] Despite grumblings among the radicals and their Charleston supporters, the "new Constitution, agreed on by our Congress, by the Approbation of the Continental Congress," was simply declared to be in effect by the Provincial Congress in early March. It was never submitted to the people for ratification. Fittingly, John Rutledge was chosen to be the first president of South Carolina under the new frame of government.[61]

The New Hampshire and South Carolina resolutions, with that of Massachusetts, formed the pattern that characterized the congressional resolutions granting authority to assume new governments in individual provinces. A deteriorating military situation combined with a vacuum in civil authority caused by the vacating royal government would cause moderate provincial leaders to seek a solution from Congress. The Congress would respond to such requests with military assistance but also with a grant of authority to assume new provincial governments should the provincial authorities find such a step necessary. While some provincial leaders expressly requested such advice, others, such as those in South Carolina, may not have done so. Nevertheless, by late 1775, in contrast to the hesitation that had marked their initial response to the overtures from Massachusetts, the continental delegates had themselves begun to see the assumption of new provincial governments as an essential step for preserving internal order in war-torn provinces. The situations in Massachusetts, New Hampshire, and South Carolina had made it clear that no province would proceed to organize a new government before receiving continental authorization to do so. The news of the Proclamation of Rebellion and the rejection of the Olive Branch Petition rendered it likely that the armed conflict would be long and the outcome uncertain. As Congress authorized large and increasing military establishments to cope with threats spreading throughout the colonies, civilian governments possessed of sufficient authority to control those establishments appeared to be ever more necessary to "keep things in order during the war." To other provinces in crises brought on by military developments and compounded by loosening civil authority, the continental delegates displayed no further hesitation in prescribing, as part of the solution, a reorganization of provincial governments.

This was clearly the case in Virginia, the next colony to receive continental authorization to assume a new government. A worsening military situation and the collapse of legitimate civil government soon led the moderate leadership of Virginia to seek a solution from the Continental Congress. As was the case in South Carolina, the Congress's prescribed solution was a combination of military aid and an authorization to assume a new civil government.

Since August 1774, Virginia's resistance efforts had been conducted by moderates and conservatives—men like Edmund Pendleton, Richard Bland, and Robert Carter Nicholas—who dominated both the local county committees and the Virginia Convention. Their chief concern lay in keeping the situation in the colony as peaceful as possible while an orderly resistance to British measures was pursued.[62] Through the early months of 1775 they had perfected radical plans for a large military establishment and a new tax system to support it. Similarly, in April 1775 they had managed to contain a situation that posed almost as serious a threat to peace as the British march on Concord. When Governor Dunmore rashly seized the colony's gunpowder reserves and stored them aboard a British warship, the colony leaders, through adroit negotiation, contrived to head off an armed confrontation between the governor and an angry band of backcountry men led by Patrick Henry.[63]

Many of Virginia's leaders, like those of South Carolina, were reluctant revolutionaries. A major difference between their situation and that of the South Carolinians, however, lay in the personality of the royal governor, John Murray, earl of Dunmore. Lord Dunmore had succeeded two extremely popular governors and he had himself begun his tenure auspiciously by undertaking a highly popular expedition against the western Indians in 1774.[64] When, therefore, Dunmore appeared to open the way for compromise by issuing writs for a new assembly, the provincial leaders were willing to comply, and they gathered in Williamsburg on June 1 in obedience to the royal summons. Even Peyton Randolph, who was then presiding over the Congress in Philadelphia, concluded that the governor's summons took precedent over his continental duties, and he hurried home to take his place as speaker of the Virginia House of Burgesses.[65]

It was unfortunate for the cause of reconciliation, however, that a man of Dunmore's personality and politics occupied the beautiful Governor's Palace in Williamsburg during this critical period. He was of a very different temper than Lord William Campbell, or Robert Eden, the capable royal governor of Maryland. For while his courage was never in question, Dunmore's judgment always was. Throughout the latter half of 1775, the governor invariably chose a course of action that undermined his slender base of support within the colony while it united the great mass of Virginians against him.[66] In early June, while the House of Burgesses he had summoned was still meeting in Williamsburg, Dunmore suddenly removed himself, his family, and his effects aboard H.M.S. *Fowey*. In explanation of his unexpected departure, Dunmore alleged that he had received assassination threats, a charge most Virginians regarded as ridiculous.[67] Once on board the British warship, Dunmore abandoned all pretense of caution and prudence. After issuing a highly inflammatory threat to free and arm the slaves (a threat he was soon to make good), he proceeded to wage a terrifying war of raids on coastal settlements, plying up and down Virginia's waterways with his little fleet of ships and tenders.[68]

His actions forced the reluctant planter elite into action. The Convention created the Committee of Safety, a body that came to have near-dictatorial powers over Virginia's military and civil affairs. The Convention leaders also ordered a vast increase in the colony's military forces to cope with the governor's attacks. The necessity of dealing with Dunmore's threat had forced the Virginia leaders out of the role they preferred, that of legally resisting citizens, and into one they disliked, that of illegal governors. That fall the Convention, in an obvious attempt to bolster the legality of its measure, began to adopt "the Style & Form of Legislation." This was done, explained George Mason, because the Convention leaders felt most uncomfortable relying "upon Resolves & Recommendations" and urgently wished "to give obligatory Force to their Proceedings."[69]

By the late fall, despite the belated activity of the Convention and the Committee of Safety, the military and civilian situation in Virginia had grown critical. Dunmore, under the cover of his ships' guns, had established a land base for his troops in the vicinity of Norfolk, in Princess Anne County, traditionally a Tory stronghold. He had succeeded in securing pledges of allegiance from a considerable portion of the population, and his strategic position was such that with little effort it appeared likely that he would acquire complete control not only of the Norfolk area but of the entire Accomac peninsula across the bay.[70]

Dunmore's successes were having a disturbing effect upon the peace and good order of the colony, for the moderates and conservatives who ruled Virginia appeared to be unable to check his progress. In October, Pendleton, now president of the Committee of Safety, wrote sorrowfully to the colony's continental delegates of the "degrading and mortifying Accounts from Norfolk." As the traditional leaders failed to cope with Dunmore and related problems, new leaders appeared at the local level to challenge their dominance. One study has indicated that in the local committee elections of late 1775, the entrenched leaders in counties and towns all over the province lost their seats to newcomers. Established provincial leaders perceived such events as disorder and confusion, and they seemed to have arrived in the wake of Dunmore's ships.[71]

The governor was not loathe to press his advantage. In the last weeks of October, he received some of the reinforcements he had been eagerly awaiting, and he immediately proceeded to make a series of landings on the patriot-held shore, routing the local militia units. To meet this renewed activity, the Committee of Safety sent a large detachment of colony troops hurrying from Williamsburg toward Norfolk. They arrived just in time to meet Dunmore, who landed at Norfolk on November 7 with 150 regulars and a handful of loyalists and blacks. The governor met and defeated the patriot force at Kempsville, taking the two colonial commanders prisoner.[72]

In the aftermath of this victory, which raised loyalist spirits all over the colony and correspondingly demoralized the patriots, Dunmore made his supreme bid to recover his power in Virginia. In imitation of Charles I, Dunmore erected the royal standard at Kemp's Landing and issued his famous, or infamous, proclamation. First, declaring that "the ordinary Course of the civil Law" was insufficient to return the colony to good order, the governor proclaimed martial law over all of Virginia. Second, noting that he had erected the royal standard, he required every man capable of bearing arms to rally to it "or be looked upon as Traitor to his Majesty's Crown and Government." Having branded most of the adult white population of the province traitors, Dunmore concluded by taking a step that Virginians dreaded above all others. In a move that caused his proclamation to be called (by an ironic twist of history), Dunmore's Emancipation Proclamation, the governor declared that "all indented Servants, Negroes, or others (appertaining to Rebels)" were henceforth free, provided that they were "able and willing to bear Arms" and that they immediately joined His Majesty's forces.[73]

Dunmore's proclamation infuriated and united the Whigs as nothing else could have done. The governor coupled in one announcement the two most odious acts imaginable. First, he had voided Virginia's civil constitution and plunged the inhabitants into anarchy. Second, and equally as distressing, he had made manifest the deepest fear of most white Virginians, that of a slave uprising. Virginians, like most southerners, had traditionally overreacted to even the slightest threat of a slave revolt. Now Dunmore proposed not only to free their blacks but to arm them, organize them, and turn them loose against their former masters. Nothing could have united the white population against the governor quite as effectively as Dunmore's Emancipation Proclamation. "The Inhabitants," one young minister reported, were "deeply alarmed" at Dunmore's "infernal Scheme," which had served to strengthen them in their resolution "to overpower him . . . at every Risk." "Lord Dunmores unparalleled conduct in Virginia has . . . united every Man in that large Colony," wrote Richard Henry Lee. "If Administration had searched thro the world for a person the best fitted to ruin their cause, . . . they could not have found a more complete Agent than Lord Dunmore."[74]

While the Whigs' anger was kindled, so was their fear, because as a result of Dunmore's military victory the governor had gained control of a large part of the Accomac peninsula. The situation was particularly precarious on the small part of the Accomac peninsula that remained in patriot hands. On November 25 a desperate Committee of Northampton County sent out urgent requests for aid to the Committee of Safety and, because reinforcement was only possible from the north, to the Continental Congress as well. After relating the terrible progress of Dunmore, culminating in his proclamation, the committee depicted its own lamentable situation. The patriots in Northampton were totally cut off from reinforcement by Chesapeake Bay and were surrounded by the Tories in Princess Anne County and Norfolk. Due to Dunmore's success at Kempsville, the committee had "reason to believe Lord *Dunmore* will soon pay us a visit here," and the inhabitants were "totally unprepared at present to receive him." In this predicament they prayed for "such immediate assistance and direction as you, in your great wisdom, shall think the importance of the case requires." The committee particularly wished to call the delegates' attention to the fact that "troops (in case you should judge it necessary to send any here) can be drawn much quicker and with more safety from the northward than from the western shore of *Virginia*."[75]

The Northampton petition was read in Congress on Saturday, December 2. The emergency nature of the request was clear, and Congress took swift action to avoid the threatened disaster on the Accomac peninsula. The delegates directed the Naval Committee immediately to dispatch an armed vessel, currently in harbor, "for the purpose of taking or destroying the cutters and armed vessels in Chesapeake Bay, under Lord Dunmore." They then sent Benjamin Harrison on an emergency mission to Maryland to engage and outfit as many other ships as he could find already on the Chesapeake for similar service.[76] The Congress also dealt with the larger problem presented by Dunmore's proclamation and military progress. As far back as November 4, the governor's actions had aroused sufficient alarm to cause the delegates to appoint a committee "to enquire into the state of the colony of Virginia, to consider whether any, and what provisions may be necessary for its defence." The committee had not, as of December 2, reported to Congress. The Northampton petition and its accompanying documents were therefore laid before the preexisting Virginia Committee for immediate action.[77] That evening, all the Virginia delegates appeared before the committee. Of late, the Virginians had themselves been receiving alarming news from Virginia. On November 27, Edmund Pendleton had informed Richard Henry Lee of Dunmore's victory at Kempsville and of his proclamation. "Letters mention that slaves flock to him in abundance," Pendleton wrote, although he "hope[d] it is magnified." He then mentioned the colony's impending application to the Congress for assistance. John Page had informed Jefferson on November 24 that Dunmore had made "a compleat Conquest of Princess Ann and Norfolk and Numbers of Negros, and Cowardly Scoundrels flock to his Standard." "So defenceless" was the province, Page informed Richard Henry Lee the following week, "that I am persuaded that a couple of Frigates with a few Tenders & only one Regiment might at this Time make as compleat a Conquest of all the lower Counties of Virginia as L[ord] D[unmore] has made of Princess Ann & Norfolk."[78] Francis Lightfoot Lee had written home from Philadelphia that such reports, coupled with the Northampton petition, gave "great concern to all the real friends of America," who were convinced by the documents that "Fatal consequences may follow if an immediate stop is not put to that Devil's career." The dangers disclosed in the letters had convinced his colleagues, Lee believed, that it would "require very vigorous efforts, to put a stop to the proceedings of Lord Dunmore." Since Lord Dunmore, by his proclamation, had torn apart civil authority, Lee thought the Convention would have to take some action "to establish the present Laws and Judges."[79]

It is likely that the Virginia delegates, during their evening meeting with the committee, disclosed this information, as well as their views regarding the actions they wished the delegates to take in order to meet the crisis. They must have expounded on the urgency of the situation, for, in contrast to their previous inaction, the Virginia Committee reported to Congress the next day. First, dealing with the military situation, the delegates ordered three Pennsylvania battalions to proceed immediately to the aid of the Northampton committee. Next, the delegates responded to the vacuum of civil authority caused by Dunmore's proclamation. The delegates recommended that the Virginians "resist to the utmost the arbitrary government intended to be established" by Dunmore. And as Dunmore, by his late proclamation, "has declared his intention to execute martial law, thereby tearing up the foundations of civil authority and government within the said colony," Virginia was given leave to assume a new provincial government.[80]

Uncharacteristically swift as the Congress's response to the Virginia emergency had been, by the time news of the December 4 resolution reached Virginia the military situation that had prompted the resolution had been completely reversed. Colonel William Woodford's Second Virginia Regiment, which had been ordered to Norfolk by the Committee of Safety, decisively defeated the governor's forces at the Battle of Great Bridge on December 9, 1775. Almost overnight the military situation had been turned around, and Dunmore was forced out of Norfolk and back onto his ships.

The alteration in military affairs had brought about a changed civil situation. The need for a more authoritative government, which had seemed so imperative a few weeks previously, had become less urgent. The Virginia Convention, which met in early December, therefore decided not to act immediately on the congressional resolution, which in any case had only advised the Convention to take up government, if they found it necessary. As an interim measure, the already-great powers of the Committee of Safety were confirmed. The Virginia leadership evidently hoped that the less threatening military situation would make it possible to secure order in the province without assuming a new government.[81]

Virginia did, however, avail itself of the congressional grant of authority at the next Convention, held in May 1776. Again, a sense of disorder—variously described as confusion, anarchy, or chaos—led the colony's moderate leaders to the conclusion that a more authoritative form of government would have to be organized. "It makes me uneasy to find from yr. Letr.," Francis Lightfoot Lee wrote to Landon Carter in early April, "that licentiousness begins to prevail in Virg[ini]a." "The old Government being dissolved, & no new one being substituted in its stead," he continued, "Anarchy must be the consequence." Lee reminded Carter that Congress had foreseen this and had already granted Virginia leave to take up government. He pointed to the examples of New Hampshire and Massachusetts, which had been "getting into the utmost disorder; but upon their assuming Government, by the advice of Congress, they are restored to perfect harmony & regularity." "The Southern Colonies by delaying the remedy," would, he feared, "have violent symptoms to encounter." He hoped that the next Convention would follow the example of New England; should they not, he dreaded the consequences. John A. Washington wrote to Richard Henry Lee at the end of the month that it was certain that Virginia could "no longer do without a fixed form of government." Indeed, he felt, "that we have done as well under our present no-form is astonishing to every reflecting mind and not to be accounted for but by Providence." Richard Henry Lee shrewdly framed an appeal to conservative Robert Carter Nicholas in much the same language. Lee asked whether Nicholas did not see "the indispensable necessity of establishing a Government [at] this Convention." "How long popular commotions may be suppressed without it, and anarchy be prevented," he observed, "deserves intense consideration."[82]

Perhaps John Page best expressed the reasoning of Virginia's moderate leaders on the subject of a new government. At the end of April he wrote a worried letter to his friend Jefferson. Virginians, he believed, had thus far "exhibited an uncommon Degree of Virtue" in "behaving so peaceably and honestly as they have when they were free from the Restraint of Laws." "But," he wondered, "how long this may be the Case who can tell?" "To prevent Disorders," he counseled, "in each Colony a Constitution should be formed as nearly resembling the old one as Circumstances, and the Merit of that Constitution" would admit of. As Edmund Pendleton flatly stated to the Convention in his opening address in May, since government had been "now . . . suspended for almost two years," it would become the delegates "to reflect whether we can longer sustain the great struggle we are making in this situation."[83]

The Convention, heeding this advice, assumed a new provincial government in June 1776, making Virginia the fourth colony to avail itself of a congressional grant of authority to take up government. Once again a grant of authority from the Continental Congress had been used by provincial conservatives and moderates to secure their vision of peace and good order.[84]

Authority for Government: The General

Until May 1776 congressional authority to take up government had been conferred piecemeal in response to pleas for aid from particular colonies. No colony proceeded to assume government prior to receiving a congressional grant of authority to do so.[85] On May 10, 1776, the Congress abandoned this approach and adopted a broad resolution that "recommended to the respective assemblies and conventions of the United Colonies, where no government sufficient to the exigencies of their affairs have been hitherto established," that they "adopt such government as shall, in the opinion of the representatives of the people, best conduce to the happiness and safety of their constituents in particular, and America in general."[86] Five days later, Congress adopted a startling preamble to this resolution. Since the colonists were at war with the tyrant George III, the preamble noted, "it appears absolutely irreconcilable to reason and good Conscience, for the people of these colonies now to take the oaths and affirmations necessary for the support of any government under the crown of Great Britain." It was therefore "necessary that the exercise of every kind of authority under the said crown should be totally suppressed."[87]

These steps were hailed by John Adams (who, with his cousin Samuel, had been instrumental in bringing them about) as "an Epocha" and "a decisive Event." Adams, of course, had good reason to cheer the May 15 resolution (as the May 10 resolution with the preamble came to be called). He had been urging, bullying, and haranguing his colleagues on the subject of new provincial governments since June 1775. "It was a measure," he later recalled, "which I had invariably pursued for a whole Year."[88] As Adams later remembered the series of events that had led to the May 15 resolution, he had worked so tirelessly to procure such a resolution because he feared that independence, his ultimate goal, would be impossible without the organization of new governments purged of royal authority. After news arrived in April 1776 that the king had dispatched a large force of German mercenaries to fight in America, Adams judged that the time was right for renewed efforts regarding provincial governments. In early May, he recalled, he procured the appointment of a committee whose purpose was "to prepare a resolution recommending to the people of the States to institute Governments. The Committee of whom I was one requested me to draught a resolve which I did and by their Direction reported it." "Opposition was made to it," he recalled, "but on the 15th of May 1776 it passed." "Millions of Curses were poured upon me," for this act.[89]

Here, however, Adams was melding together two distinct events; the resolution, reported on May 10, and the far more controversial preamble, adopted on May 15. In fact, no committee was ever appointed to draft the May 10 resolution. Since early May, the *Journals* reveal, much congressional business on a variety of topics was being transacted, on a day-to-day basis, in committee of the whole. It was from one such session, probably that of May 9, that the delegates reported the text of the resolution that was adopted the next day.[90] Further, the May 10 resolution caused little of the outrage and indignation that Adams later recalled. It had, in fact, as Adams himself accurately reported at the time, passed "with remarkable Unanimity." Nor is this lack of controversy surprising when one considers the delegates' record concerning the assumption of new governments. Whenever provincial leaders had informed their continental leaders of a deteriorating military situation and a vacuum in civil authority, the delegates had responded by supplying those leaders not only with military assistance but with congressional authority to assume a new provincial government. With the news of the coming of 20,000 foreign troops, coupled with the Prohibitory Act, it appeared that the entire continent would soon be facing threats similar to those that had caused crises in the individual colonies. It would be folly, many agreed, to face the massive British military danger without strong, stable governments. Such reasoning had particular force for the New York delegates, whose province was soon to bear the brunt of the British attack. Thus, William Floyd wrote in early May that, given the enormous military force that would soon be arriving, it was "Necessary that all Collonies Should be in a Situation best Calculated to Exert its whole Strength." He therefore thought that "it Cannot be long before our provencial Congress will think it necessary to take up Some more Stable form of Government than what is now Exercised in that provence." John Jay had already come to the same conclusion. Since it now seemed that "the Sword must decide the Controversey," the first thing that Jay thought ought to be done was "to erect good & well ordered Governments in all the Colonies, and thereby exclude that Anarchy which already too much prevails." Similar sentiments were expressed by delegates from other colonies as well. Such a step, Caesar Rodney observed, was necessary "that the several Colonies may be Competent to the opposition now making, and which may tend to the good Order and well-being of the people." Even Dickinson, leader of the conservative faction striving to avoid a declaration of independence, was himself now "an Advocate for Colony Government[s]," John Adams reported on May 12. As Jefferson explained, the ensuing campaign "would simply require greater exertion than our unorganized powers may at present effect."[91]

Given these views, many moderates and conservatives saw no compelling reason to object to, and many saw reason to support, the May 10 resolution, which recommended the assumption of new governments only in those provinces that had none "sufficient to the exigencies of [their] affairs." The moderate tenor of the May 10 resolution was also evident in the implementation procedure recommended by the Congress. In contrast to the individual colony resolutions, which had recommended that the provincial conventions "call a full and free representation of the people" in order to frame a new government, the May 10 resolution merely directed the "respective assemblies and conventions" to themselves "adopt such government" as they deemed necessary to enable their respective provinces to meet the coming British threat.[92]

Dickinson perhaps epitomized the conservatives' reaction to the May 10 resolution. Since the resolution referred only to provinces without a functioning government, he concluded that it could not possibly apply to his native Pennsylvania, whose Assembly was functioning and whose conservative leadership had won a hard-fought election victory only two weeks previously. He therefore supported the measure, the purpose of which, he believed, was to strengthen the forces of order in needy provinces. Many of his congressional allies shared this view. Carter Braxton, a Virginia conservative and certainly no ally of the Adamses, explained, that the assumption of government was so patently necessary that conservatives had made little Objection to the resolution. John Adams had therefore been accurate when he informed James Warren of the "remarkable Unanimity" with which the May 10 resolution had passed. John Dickinson, having given his blessing to a measure he believed to be necessary, if regrettable, left Philadelphia immediately after the vote for a few days of rest on his Delaware estate.[93]

But Dickinson's vacation would prove costly. John Adams had not been pleased with the conservative cast given to the May 10 resolution, and the reasons for his dissatisfaction were close at hand—in fact, they were just up the stairs of the Pennsylvania State House, where the Pennsylvania Assembly sat. Adams and his colleagues had for months been thwarted in their drive toward independence by the adamant refusal of the Assembly to alter the instructions against independence that John Dickinson had written the previous November.[94] Pennsylvania's intransigence was thus a prime force retarding the movement toward independence, and Adams and his allies clearly intended the May 10 resolution to be the weapon that would bring down the Assembly, and with it the hated instructions.[95] But the resolution was clumsily drawn for such a purpose and, as Dickinson had shown, was as amenable to an anti-independence as to a pro-independence construction.

Undeterred, Adams tried again. On May 10 he arranged the appointment of a committee, upon which he and Richard Henry Lee were to serve, in order to draft a preamble to the resolution. Such a preceding paragraph was customarily added to congressional documents intended for public consumption, and Adams's move, apparently a formality, aroused little opposition. As James Duane, who had supported the resolution, informed John Jay on May 11, the resolution "waits only for a preface and will then be usherd into the world."[96]

The committee brought in a draft preamble the following Monday. Its language was in stark contrast to that of the resolution itself. While the latter had relied on a wholly pragmatic rationale for the assumption of new governments—necessity—the rationale of the preamble was entirely ideological. Given the king's exclusion of his subjects "from the protection of his Crown," it began, and his numerous acts of tyranny, it was therefore "irreconcilable to reason and good Conscience, for the people of these colonies now to take the oaths and affirmations necessary for the support of any government under the crown of Great Britain." In such a case, it had become "necessary that the exercize of every kind of authority under the said crown should be totally suppressed, and all the powers of government exerted, under the authority of the people of the colonies." Whereas the resolution had allowed the various provinces, should their assemblies or conventions deem it necessary, to reorganize and strengthen their governments in order to be better prepared to fight, the preamble virtually ordered the people to tear down any existing institutions based on royal authority. As Duane himself noted when sending Jay the resolution with its preamble, "the Resolution itself first passed and then a Committee was appointed to fit it with a preamble. Compare them with each other and it will probably lead you into reflections which I dare not point out."[97]

When the preamble was read, it touched off a furious debate that lasted for two days. As Adams had hoped, the opponents of independence had been caught off guard. With Dickinson gone, they were leaderless and disorganized. "Why all this Haste? Why this Urging? Why this driving?" queried a worried James Duane. He read aloud his instructions from the Provincial Congress, which mandated that he vote against independence. The preamble, connoting as it did the destruction of all royal authority in the colonies, was, he said, a declaration of independence, to which he was not authorized to agree. What right did Congress have, with such a resolution, to interfere with the oaths taken, or procedures followed, by provincial authorities? Congress had no right to pass such a resolution, "any more than Parliament has." He vehemently protested against "this Piece of Mechanism, this Preamble."[98]

Many delegates clearly understood the import of the preamble. James Wilson, who tried to hold the conservatives together in Dickinson's absence, was one of those. He reminded his colleagues that the preamble took the question of new governments far beyond the grounds on which the delegates had previously dealt with it. Those colonies in which governments had previously been authorized had been in anarchic situations, royal colonies stripped of authoritative governments. As "they could not subsist without some Government," he had supported those resolutions. For similar reasons, his delegation had supported the May 10 resolution. But the preamble to the resolution, Wilson believed, was a complete departure from previous practice. It was specifically directed against the existing government in Pennsylvania, a government that had proved itself capable of keeping the province in order and capable of contributing its full share to the war effort—in short, "sufficient to the exigencies of [its] affairs." The effect of the preamble, he warned, would be to subvert completely the stabilizing purpose of the resolution, at least in Pennsylvania. The province would likely be subject to "an immediate Dissolution of every Kind of Authority," and "the People will be instantly in a State of Nature."[99]

The preamble passed by a narrow margin. As Thomas Stone explained the failed tactics of those who opposed it, they had done "everything to prevent the destructive Precipitancy which seems so agreeable to the Genius of some. Further delay could not be obtain[ed,]" although "there was the strongest reason for it. Two colonies being unrepresented & a representation expected shortly." Nevertheless, he reported, "the Majority of Colonies attending was known to be for the Proposition & the opportunity [was] not to be let slip," so it was "vain to reason or expostulate." Carter Braxton also expressed dissatisfaction with the radical gloss that the preamble had put upon the May 10 resolution. "You will say [the resolution] falls little short of Independence," he observed unhappily to a friend. "It was not," he protested, "so understood by Congress."[100]

It was, however, so understood by provincial radicals in Pennsylvania, whose allies in Congress had, in all probability, crafted the language of the preamble in order to aid the radicals' campaign to bring down the Pennsylvania Assembly.[101] The Pennsylvania radicals (still chafing from their electoral defeat two weeks previously) interpreted the resolution entirely in terms of the preamble, which mandated the suppression of all royal authority. Since the Pennsylvania Assembly drew its authority from the colony's royal charter, they reasoned, it must be overthrown. Yet, as supporters of the Assembly pointed out, the Connecticut and Rhode Island assemblies were also authorized by royal charter. Did the preamble also mandate the destruction of these assemblies, as well as the Pennsylvania Assembly? Moreover, as a troubled Caesar Rodney later informed his brother, the May 10 resolution "was certainly meant to go to the Assemblies" for execution "where there were such who had authority to Set." The Pennsylvanians "having Taken the matter up upon other Grounds," he complained, "had occasioned very great disturbance."[102]

Whatever the majority of congressional delegates had intended, however, in Pennsylvania the preamble to the May 15 resolution was clearly used by provincial radicals exactly as their congressional allies had hoped and intended it would be used—to bring down the conservative Pennsylvania Assembly. It was an effective, if drastic, measure by which to change the province's vote on independence. On the day the resolution passed, a Philadelphia radical recorded in his diary that he "went to the Philosophical Hall to meet a number of persons to consider what steps might be necessary to take, on the dissolution of

Government." The radical conclave agreed to call immediately for a convention on the basis of the May 15 resolution, and to protest against "the present Assembly doing any business in their house until the sense of the Province is taken in that Convention." On May 18, the Philadelphia committee decided to anticipate the convention and called for a mass meeting to be held on May 20 "in order to take the sense of the people respecting the resolve of Congress of the Fifteenth instant." Despite a downpour, from four to five thousand people gathered in the State House Yard and agreed to protest any further action by the Assembly, since, contrary to the May 15 preamble, it had been elected only "by such Persons . . . as were either in real or supposed Allegiance to the . . . King" and was therefore unqualified "for framing a new Government." It is important to note that the protest of the mass meeting was based almost entirely on the wording of the preamble, not on the resolution itself.[103]

The Pennsylvania Assembly was still dominated by conservatives who perhaps had thought that their problems had been solved by their electoral victory over the radicals. The victors of that closely contested election moved as if in a daze, unwilling or unable to cope with the radical storm that was about to burst upon their heads. The members had assembled on May 20, the day of the mass meeting, but radical members had prevented them from obtaining a quorum. They were able to proceed to business on May 22, when they received the protest drawn up by the radical-dominated Philadelphia committee. In response, the Assembly merely appointed a committee to take the matter under consideration. The committee was instructed to draw up a memorial that would explain to the radicals, and to Congress, how seriously the provincial radicals had misinterpreted the meaning of the congressional resolution. Specifically, it would make clear that it was "the Assemblies and Conventions, now subsisting in the several Colonies," who were "the Bodies, to whom the Consideration of continuing the old, or adopting new Governments" was referred by the Congress.[104]

While the Assembly was correct in its interpretation of the motivation of most congressional delegates, it was caught in a web spun during a long history of partisan politics in the province, and its fate was not to be determined by the technical correctness of its interpretation of congressional intentions. The Assembly, torn apart by the debate over independence, was simply not equipped to withstand the superb radical organization that had gone into action after May 15. As the conservatives struggled day after day to obtain a quorum (which radical members often prevented them from obtaining), the radicals proceeded with their plans for the Convention, which was to assemble on June 18. On June 14, after withdrawing the instructions against independence, the Assembly adjourned until mid-August. By the time it attempted to meet again, a new Pennsylvania constitution had been drawn by the Convention, and the Convention itself had taken effective control of provincial affairs.[105]

Historians have speculated that the significance of the May 15 resolution lay in the results it brought about in Pennsylvania. As noted, radicals like the Adams cousins had been in long and intimate contact with the radicals of the Philadelphia committee and shared their concerns about the refusal of the Pennsylvania Assembly to instruct its continental delegates to support independence. After the elections of early May registered a decisive radical defeat, an attractive course open to the provincial radicals and their congressional allies was that of circumventing the Assembly by using the authority of the Continental Congress. Undoubtedly, then, the Pennsylvania situation was uppermost in the minds of such delegates as Samuel and John Adams and Richard Henry Lee as they pushed the preamble through a balky Congress.[106]

But to assert that the majority of continental delegates, as opposed to the Adamses and their allies, voted for the May 10 resolution because of the Pennsylvania situation is to ignore the whole history of congressional action regarding the assumption of government, and it is to ignore the fact that Pennsylvania's congressional delegation itself favored the May 10 resolution. In truth, the success of the radicals on the Philadelphia committee in using congressional authority to overthrow the Assembly did not come because a majority in the Congress deliberately passed the May 15 resolution to facilitate this end, for the resolution did not necessarily apply to Pennsylvania, and even the preamble, when read in conjunction with the resolution, was subject to varying interpretation. Rather, the Pennsylvania radicals succeeded because superior organization enabled them to use the resolution of Congress to accomplish their ends, while the Assembly, whose interpretation of congressional intentions was probably more accurate, was too weak and divided to take advantage of the theoretical superiority of its position.

The intentions of the continental delegates in passing the resolution can be more clearly distinguished if we extend our view beyond Pennsylvania to consider the effect of the congressional mandate on the various other colonies that, like Pennsylvania, had not yet instituted a new government prior to May 15, 1776.[107] In Delaware, for example, matters proceeded very differently after May 15 than they had in Pennsylvania. The military situation there had grown increasingly serious through the spring of 1776. The Delaware Tories, concentrated in Sussex and Kent counties, were numerous and active. Armed insurrection broke out in the spring, and the local militia, aided by continental troops, was barely able to contain it. The problem reached crisis proportions in late March when H.M.S. *Roebuck* entered Chesapeake Bay. Delaware's geography left the province almost defenseless against naval attack. The threat grew more serious when the *Roebuck*, joined by H.M.S. *Liverpool*, began cruising up and down the bay, menacing exposed coastal settlements and the shipping upon which the province depended. Despite a defeat of the British naval forces in early May, Delaware's harassed patriot legislators continued to fear a junction between the Tory units on land and the king's ships in the bay. For them, the May 15 resolution appeared to provide a means by which they might bolster their authority against internal and external threats, and they heartily supported the resolution.[108]

To understand the extent of that support, one must note that many of Delaware's moderate leaders were apprehensive that the military crisis would inevitably have serious repercussions on political stability within the province. On May 17, Caesar Rodney fully set out these considerations. "You will find published in the next paper . . . a matter of such importance as ought and no doubt will, Command your serious Attention," he wrote to John Haslet. "It is No less than a Resolution of Congress Recommending it to the Assemblys or Conventions of all those Colonies . . . to Assume Regular Government." Compelling necessities urged compliance with the resolution for taking up a new government, which, Rodney was careful to observe, ought not to differ much from the present government.[109] Rodney then put forward the standard conservative rationale in favor of assuming new governments: "Nothing will lead more to Ensure Success in the prosecution of the war; because there is nothing so conclusive to vigour, Expedition, secrecy, and every thing advantageous in War, as a well regulated Government." "Confusion and perplexity accompany us, in almost every department," he observed, but the Province was in particular need "of a Good Executive."[110] After expounding on these difficulties, Rodney revealed his deepest apprehensions. No one could tell how long the war would last, he wrote, and it was evident that "no prudent man would choose to Trust himself long, without the Security of a Regular Established Government." Without such a government, the laws would "grow into disuse and Contempt" and "All the Evils of Anarchy" would then "prevail, and the most Wanton depredations be Committed." To correct such abuses, "and for Want of Laws and Magistrates, Whose Authority is Acknowledged and Respected," he feared that "recourse may be had to Military power."[111] Even more dangerous, in the long run, were the licentious habits into which the people might fall if left too long without a regular government. "When the people are accustomed to irregular Government," he warned, "it is Exceedingly difficult to recover them to the love of order, and obedience to those Laws which are the Essential bonds of Society," for "Bad habits in the political, as well as the Natural Body, are Verry Easy to be acquired and verry hard to be Eradicated." "These things," he observed, "to men of penetration Wear a Serious aspect, and Seem Urgently to demand a Speedy remedy, which is only to be found in the Establishment of a Regular Constitution."[112]

Rodney spoke eloquently for all those moderate men who saw in the May 15 resolution not an invitation to social upheaval but an opportunity to reimpose political and social order on dangerously disordered societies. The assumption of government in Delaware proceeded along the moderate path that had been blazed by those provinces that had earlier received congressional grants of authority. The recommendation of Congress went to the royally chartered Delaware Assembly, as the continental delegates had intended, and the existing Assembly proceeded to implement it. On June 14, Thomas McKean formally presented the May 15 resolution to the Assembly, and the provincial delegates promptly approved it unanimously. On July 27 the Assembly, "taking into consideration the Resolution of Congress of the 15th of May" called for a constitutional convention (to be elected by qualified electors of assemblymen) to meet at Newcastle on August 27, there to draw up a new frame of government.[113]

The new constitution produced by the August Convention almost duplicated the royal government of Delaware, as Rodney had hoped it would. It was written by George Read, the province's leading conservative, who had been elected chairman of the Constitutional Convention. Not until 1792 did Delaware choose a frame of government that significantly differed from the old pattern.[114] The transfer of governmental authority in Delaware was accomplished smoothly and with minimal upheaval, since every step, as the legislators were quick to point out, had been authorized by the Continental Congress. The May 15 resolution was used in Delaware, therefore, for almost exactly the opposite purposes to those to which the radical Pennsylvanians had put it.

The problems faced by the Delaware provincial leaders were magnified in New Jersey. Not only were the domestic Tories active there, but their spirits were raised by expectations of the imminent arrival of large British reinforcements under Lord Howe. In preparation for Howe's arrival, provincial legislators had ordered the arrest of William Franklin, the last royal governor in America. With Franklin, however, as with all the royal governors, went the last vestiges of legal government in New Jersey.[115]

A new Provincial Congress had been elected in May and it assembled in Burlington on June 10, 1776. On June 21, it "went into the consideration of the propriety of Forming a Government &c.," and with remarkable speed unanimously resolved that afternoon "That a Government be formed for regulating the internal police of this Colony, pursuant to the recommendation of the Continental Congress of the 15th of *May* last."[116] On June 24 a ten-member committee was chosen to prepare a new frame of government. Proceeding swiftly, the committee laid a draft constitution (largely the work of John Witherspoon) before the Provincial Congress two days later, and it was approved on July 2. This conservative frame of government, which was to govern the province for the next sixty-eight years, differed little from the prior royal government and was promptly presented to the people of New Jersey and simply declared to be in effect.[117]

A revealing preamble clearly stated the authority on which the delegates had proceeded to draw up this instrument. No one doubted the necessity of a new government, the preamble began, for Great Britain had left the province "in a state of nature" and in this "deplorable situation" "some form of Government" was "absolutely necessary . . . for the preservation of good order." Happily, the provincial delegates continued, legitimate authority had been issued for assuming a new government by the "honourable the Continental Congress, the supreme council of the *American* colonies" on the previous May 15. Based as it was on the authority of Congress, the New Jersey constitution, like the other early state constitutions, was never ratified.[118]

Across the Hudson River, New York's legislators were also considering the implications of the May 15 resolution. New York, like Pennsylvania, was governed in the spring of 1776 by a legislative body (the Third Provincial Congress) dedicated to delaying a declaration of independence as long as possible. Given this similarity of political opinion between the political leaders of the two provinces, the effect of the May 15 resolution in New York might have been expected to produce a parallel situation to that in Pennsylvania. On the contrary, however, events in New York followed the general pattern. That is to say, in New York, as in its sister provinces, the authority of the Continental Congress was used by moderates and conservatives to reimpose their vision of order and regularity on a situation that threatened their ability to control provincial affairs.

From the beginning of the crisis in 1774, the revolutionary organs in New York had been torn between the radicals, centered in New York City and headed by men like Isaac Sears and Alexander McDougall, and the conservatives, whose power was concentrated in the successive ruling committees in New York City and subsequently in the Provincial Congress. The New York delegates in the Continental Congress were chosen by, and reflected the views of, the intermittently dominant conservative faction in the Provincial Congress.[119] But the ruling faction had never been secure in its leadership. Not only did urban mechanics constantly threaten from the left, but the pressure from the right—from the Tories—was nowhere more severe than in New York. Upstate, Provincial Congress's control was tenuous at best, for it was constantly tested by the Tories, who were led by the powerful Johnson family and who had consistent support from the British in Canada, and by the Green Mountain Boys, who were seeking an independent state. Ringing New York City itself, Tories in Westchester, Queens, Kings, and Suffolk counties also disputed patriot leadership, as they had done from the beginning of the crisis.[120]

The Provincial Congress, aware of its own weakness, had never dared to test its authority by attempting, for example, such traditional governmental acts as levying taxes or raising troops. Thus a typical report from Dutchess County at a critical period in 1776 impressed the moderates in the Provincial Congress with a sense of their lack of authority. "You cannot command the Militia throughout the County," the legislators were informed, "for Your Government is not firmly enough established for the people to yield a willing obedience."[121] By 1776 this lack of control assumed decisive importance, because New York was faced with the greatest military threat to any province since Massachusetts' trials in 1775—the landing of British forces on Staten Island.

The arrival of the May 15 resolution was therefore the sound of opportunity knocking for New York's ruling conservatives. Their reaction certainly differed markedly from that of their ideological colleagues in Pennsylvania, because, as one historian has explained, their situation differed markedly from that of the Pennsylvanians. In Pennsylvania, which faced no imminent military threat, the conservatives tied their increasingly unpopular stand against independence to an established institution of government, the Assembly. When urban and rural radicals combined against that policy (not being distracted by any need to unite against a British military threat), they also brought their combined strength to bear against the Assembly itself. In New York, by way of contrast, the military threat in 1776 could not have been more imminent, and it called radical leaders like Sears and McDougall away from provincial politics and into active military service. Moreover, the New York conservatives had not made their political base the colony's Assembly (which had not met since the crisis began) but rather had gained control of the Provincial Congress, the established resistance institution, and it was from within the Provincial Congress that they waged their campaign to delay independence. The conservative leadership—a coalition of merchants, urban professionals, and Whig landlords—had "a coherent sense of itself," and was all the more confident because the radicals they faced were divided and leaderless. The New York City radicals, on the other hand—the mechanics—had simply been unable to forge the same links with like-minded colleagues in the backcountry that their counterparts had forged in Pennsylvania. In such a situation, the prospect of organizing a new government was one that, if properly managed, could serve to consolidate and perpetuate conservative control of the province.[122]

The New Yorkers thus faced the prospect of assuming a new government with considerable equanimity. Robert R. Livingston, in a letter to his son-in-law, John Jay, clearly alluded to the different attitudes toward the May 15 resolution in New York and in Pennsylvania. The resolution, he noted on May 17, had "occasioned a great alarm" in Pennsylvania among "the cautious folks" who were "very fearful of its being attended with many ill consequences." But "our people," he noted, were "satisfied of the necessity of assuming a new form of government" and he hoped Jay would keep him informed "in what channel it will probably run."[123] Jay agreed with Livingston. On May 29 he wrote to James Duane that the resolution had been necessary because of the "great . . . inconveniences resulting from the present mode of Government." Jay assured Duane that New York undoubtedly would "almost unanimously agree to institute a better [government], to continue till a peace with Great Britain may render it unnecessary." To Livingston himself, Jay was blunt. It was essential, he believed, "to institute a better government than the present which," in his opinion, "will no longer work any thing but mischief."[124]

Conservative reasons for welcoming the May 15 resolution were explained by "Columbus" in the *New York Journal* of June 12, 1776. "Columbus" began by asserting that no rational man could doubt the necessity of assuming a new government in New York. He requested those who objected to the plan "to consider that, at present, no Government exists here" because of the absence of the royal governor. "Must not, then, our courts of justice, and, indeed, the whole course of the law, stand still," he queried. "Can Congress of Committees" be equal to the tasks of regular government? "They cannot," he answered, and thus "without a new legal Government, universal disorder must ensue."[125] He held up to his audience a vision drawn by a conservative quill of the immediate future of New York, should a new government not be formed. He spoke of a time "when the most ambitious man, or set of men, heading a lawless multitude, shall direct our councils, by his or their mere will and pleasure; when tyranny, anarchy, and confusion, shall pervade this once peaceful land; when, for want of Government, the strong shall lord it over the weak." Happily, "Columbus" continued, God had given such abundant "wisdom to the conductors of our publick affairs" in the Continental Congress as to have left New Yorkers with another alternative. The Congress had given the colonies authority to assume government anew by means of the May 15 resolve, which was "of the most glorious and interesting nature." Since New Yorkers could have "no happiness or safety as a people" without a new government, and since the Continental Congress "have directed us to the measure," it was "absolutely necessary" to comply with the "directions of the Congress."[126]

The May 15 resolution came before New York's Third Provincial Congress on May 24. Despite the opinion of some that the authority of the Congress was a sufficient basis upon which to proceed, internal politics made a delay attractive to the conservative leadership. They argued, therefore, that they had no political mandate to organize a government, and that a new congress, in which they hoped their position would be even stronger, was necessary. The Provincial Congress therefore appointed a committee on May 24 to determine whether a special election ought to be held to give the representatives specific authorization for implementing the May 15 resolution. On May 26 the committee reported that since the old government had been dissolved by the fact of British tyranny, "it hath become absolutely necessary for the good people of this Colony to institute a new and regular form of internal government and policy." They therefore recommended the calling of an election that would specifically authorize the existing delegates or their replacements to implement the congressional resolution. Until that time, however, they resolved (as had the Delaware Assembly) that the present Congress "ought to continue in the full exercize of their present Authority." On May 31, acting on the committee report, the Provincial Congress authorized the election of a new congress specifically empowered to draw up a new constitution, such congress to meet on the following July 9. The authorization for this action was clearly set forth by the Provincial Congress in their proclamation calling for the election. They first cited the temporary nature of the present government "by Congress and Committees," and "the many and great inconveniences" that attended "the said mode of Government." They then quoted the May 15 resolution in full and called for the election of deputies who were "to take into consideration the necessity . . . of instituting such new government as in and by the said resolution of the Continental Congress is described and recommended," and "to institute and establish such a government."[127]

As Edward Countryman has concluded, "the conservative leaders handled things exactly as they should, from their point of view" during this period, because "by the time the new congress did convene, the imminence of a British invasion had neutralized the mechanics as a political force. The immediate danger of a radical solution like Pennsylvania's had been averted."[128] Thus in New York as well, a conservative provincial leadership had used the authority conferred by the Congress to help strengthen their control of provincial affairs.

Congress thus assumed a fourth, and perhaps most critical, function of the vacating royal government. Like all the powers that found their way into continental hands, the delegates had neither sought nor initially accepted the power to authorize the assumption of new provincial governments. Thus, the delegates had virtually ignored the early pleas of the Massachusetts radicals who wished to assume a new government in the interest of hastening independence from Britain. When deteriorating military situations and resultant vacuums of civil authority threatened to undermine the ability of provincial leaders to maintain order, however, the delegates responded with grants of authority that would enable conservative and moderate provincial leaders to assume new provincial governments. These provincial leaders, one province excepted, used these grants of authority for the intended purpose; they established governments that, at the time of independence, differed little from the vacating royal governments they replaced. The new governments were, as Caesar Rodney hoped the new Delaware government would be, "similar at present to the one we now have Except as to the derivation of Authority."[129]

CHAPTER 10

A National Executive or

a National Legislature

*I will here take an Opportunity to observe upon what must strike
the Observation of every Gentleman acquainted with our publick
Affairs. It is that a Body such as the Congress is inadequate to the
Purposes of Execution. They want that Celerity & Decision upon
which depend the Fate of Great Affairs.*

—*Gouverneur Morris, 1778*

Gouverneur Morris's gloomy observation, made in the midst of a
lengthy proposal for administrative reform in 1778, contrasts sharply
with the universal expressions of sentiment in 1774 and 1775. Then,
Congress had been portrayed as the savior of American liberties, a
body that had only to decide upon the course of action that the common cause required for its decisions to be put into effect by provincial
or local authorities. It is important to note, however, that pessimistic
as Morris was, he did not criticize the nature of the governmental functions that had been given to the Congress, but rather he questioned
the ability of the Congress to perform those functions.

When in 1774 the colonists had first perceived a need to concert their
resistance to British aggression, they had harbored no thoughts of creating a government capable of answering the "purposes of Execution." The Congress met in 1774 not to replace the English government but to protest, on behalf of the united colonies, against the
excesses of that government. When Americans spoke of "government" in 1774, in fact, they were still largely referring to the institutions of British imperial authority—that is, to the king personally, to
the crown institutionally, and to deputed subordinate magistrates.
Eighteenth-century American Whigs depended on this government
for the protection of their lives and property and for the preservation
of the political and social stability upon which they might predicate the
orderly conduct of life's affairs. It is thus of more than passing signifi-

cance that they habitually prefaced the noun "government" with the possessive "His Majesty's."

As has been noted, the king retained important functions in the eighteenth-century imperial constitution, the performance of which complemented the legitimacy of his government. First among those functions—indeed, the function upon which the governmental contract and thus the consent of the governed to his rule depended—was that of providing protection. Second, the king united the disparate parts of the empire both by regulating relations among the provinces and by managing imperial relations with foreign states. Finally, Whigs acknowledged that the king's authority gave legal status to acts taken under its aegis or by his warrant. In a very real sense, that authority made the government work, for by virtue of the king's discretionary, or prerogative, powers, administrators were appointed, boards created, corporations chartered, currency printed, and officers commissioned.[1]

Yet between 1774 and 1776 the colonists' continued allegiance to George III was rendered impossible, many believed, by the king's tyrannical behavior. American Whigs, thoroughly schooled in the Whig theory of kingship, drew the inevitable conclusion that by 1776 George III had irrevocably breached the Coronation Oath and had broken the governmental contract that bound king and colonist together. He had therefore abdicated his American thrones. In such a situation, the colonists had few alternatives. They could (as they were later to do in many of the states) alter drastically their conception both of the basis and functions of a continental government, but to do so they would have to forge new institutions that would fulfill these new visions. Suggestions along these lines were made regarding both the appropriate procedure for forming a new continental government and the powers appropriate to that government. Thus, for example, John Adams believed that a new continental frame of government ought to be formed by representatives of the people sitting in conventions called specifically for that purpose.[2] There were those who suggested that the powers of the new central government ought to be expanded and that it ought to have considerable discretionary authority to appoint provincial officers, to legislate on any subject that the rulers perceived to be related to the general welfare, or to levy direct taxes on all inhabitants.[3] On the other hand, others thought that a continental treaty of commercial and military alliance was all that was necessary, for the people already had governments sufficient to their needs—their new provincial authorities.[4] But Americans chose none of these courses. Instead, they virtually remade the resistance organization of 1774, the Continental Congress, into a true continental government by molding it into as close a replica as circumstances would allow of the old imperial executive.

Executive versus Legislative

The model that guided the delegates' choices regarding the allocation of continental authority becomes clearer when one briefly notes the powers that the delegates did *not* assign to the central government and compares them with those that they did. For the powers that Congress did not assume were fully as essential to the creation of a strong central authority as those that they did, and, in fact, some of the powers that Congress did not assume bore a close logical relationship to those that they did. For example, while Congress was charged with the responsibility of paying, provisioning, and directing the military forces of the United Colonies, it was not charged with the responsibility of directly raising the money to pay for defense. While Congress was given broad latitude in resolving intercolonial disputes regarding "any Cause whatever," it was not given the authority to regulate intercolonial commercial relations. While Congress had broad discretion to negotiate with foreign powers, it could not prevent the states from imposing such commercial trade barriers as they saw fit. Finally, in sharp contrast to the broad discretion given to Congress in the exercise of its executive responsibilities, it was given almost no discretion regarding the objects for which it might legislate.

Almost as soon as Congress had taken on the responsibility of overseeing the continental defense, it also decided on the method it would follow, throughout the war, to finance those efforts. On June 3, 1775, the delegates appointed a committee of five "to bring in an estimate of the money necessary to be raised" should it decide to assume control of the Massachusetts Army.[5] The issue of finance was thus debated in the committee of the whole simultaneously with the host of other issues involved in the decision to adopt the Massachusetts Army. On June 22, having appointed most of the high command of what thenceforth became the Continental Army, Congress decided how the troops were to be paid. The delegates resolved that Congress would emit "a sum not exceeding" two million dollars, "for the defence of America," and that "the twelve confederated colonies be pledged for the redemption of the bills of credit, now directed to be emitted."[6] On July 29 the delegates agreed on the means by which the bills were to be redeemed. Treasurers were appointed, to reside in Philadelphia, who would be empowered to sign and issue such bills as Congress saw fit to issue. Meanwhile, each colony was to "provide ways and means to sink its proportion of the bills ordered to be emitted by this Congress, in such manner as may be most effectual and best adapted to the condition, circumstances, and usual mode of levying taxes in such colony."[7] By the end of 1775, Congress had issued $6,000,000 in continental bills. Throughout the war, as the need for funds increased and the value of the continental bills decreased, Congress simply printed more bills.[8]

Yet there was nothing surprising about the mode of finance Congress had chosen, although its disastrous potential looms so large in hindsight. Individual colonies had emitted similar bills throughout the colonial period, secured only by the faith of the colony, or by its land, until the practice was curbed by the Crown. Yet the critical difference was that the individual colonies had the unquestioned authority to levy the taxes or duties necessary to fund their debts. Indeed, one of the first acts of the new provincial governments, prior to the assumption of almost all other powers of government, had been to secure their tax bases by directing that any taxes be paid to them, not to royal officials.[9] The colonies, both individually and in concert, had bitterly fought all attempts by Parliament to encroach upon the exclusive taxing power of the individual provinces. Had Congress attempted to assume any such power, it would not only have been politically unwise, but it would have been without constitutional foundation until the issue of whether Congress represented the states or individuals was resolved.[10] Until then, the power to tax lay with the individual provincial assemblies, not with any imperial legislature, be it Parliament or Congress. Thus, in Benjamin Franklin's draft of the Articles of Confederation, which generally granted broad powers to the national government, Article VI specified that all of the expenses of the confederacy were to be proportionately assessed, "the Taxes for paying that proportion to be laid and levied by Laws of each Colony." The same formula was followed in all subsequent drafts of the Articles.[11] The question of why the Confederation Congress lacked the power to levy direct taxes does not so much illuminate the debate between the nationalists and the advocates of the states as it illustrates the point that not until Congress was conceived of as primarily a national legislature, rather than an executive and administrative body, would prevailing constitutional thought allow it to be charged with the power to levy direct taxes.

Similarly conceived of as inappropriate powers for the Continental Congress to wield were all matters that touched upon the internal governments of particular colonies. All the drafts of the Articles contained clauses asserting that each state reserved the right to "retain and enjoy as much of its present Laws, Rights & Customs, as it may think fit, and reserves to itself the sole and exclusive regulation and Government of its internal Police in all Matters that shall not interfere with the Articles of this Confederation."[12] The strength of this conviction was demonstrated by the fate of Dickinson's proposed Article 4 of the draft that he submitted for the consideration of the Confederation Committee. Dickinson hoped the Confederation would be the vehicle by means of which religious liberty would be guaranteed to each citizen of the United Colonies. It is significant that it is the only clause in his draft that begins with the phrase, "No person in any Colony . . ." rather than "No Colony or colonies. . . ." Yet, with no recorded comment or discussion, the committee simply rejected Dickinson's proposal out of hand. It was deleted from the committee draft, and, in fact, it was never heard of again. Religion, like taxation, was a matter to be regulated by the individual state legislatures.[13]

Several less obvious powers were also considered by the delegates to relate to "internal police," and therefore not to be fit subjects for continental regulation. Thus, Dickinson's original proposals envisioned that Congress would have a supervisory power over interstate commercial relations, for his original Article 8 would not only have guaranteed reciprocal privileges and immunities among all citizens of the confederating states but would also have forbidden any state to burden interstate commerce by imposing duties or imposts. Dickinson would have allowed the states neither to "assess or lay any Duties or Imposts on the importation of the productions or manufactures of another Colony, nor settle or establish any fees for Entries, Clearances, or any Business whatever relative to Imports." But this proposal also failed to meet with continental approval, despite its arguably primary relation to the regulation of commercial relations *between* states, as opposed to its interference with internal matters *within* states. The committee draft deleted Dickinson's prohibition on duties on internal commerce, while the full Congress deleted the proposed guarantee of reciprocal privileges and immunities as well.[14]

Perhaps the clearest example of the implicit model guiding the delegates as they struggled to allocate power between the Congress and the states was that regarding trade with foreign nations. As we have seen, Congress assumed control over continental foreign policy very early. All the early drafts of the Articles reveal that this practice reflected settled conviction; in all of them, the power to negotiate with foreign sovereigns was given, exclusively and explicitly, to Congress. It is also clear that the power to negotiate treaties thus given to Congress was primarily a power to conclude *commercial* treaties, for it was the commercial status and treatment of their new nation, not its military relations, that most concerned Americans.[15] Yet all the drafts of the Articles bifurcated this supposedly natural, almost inherent, power of the new central government by allowing the states to continue to "lay any imposts or duties" upon foreign commerce, except where such impositions interfered with the treaties negotiated with Congress. Such an arrangement was bound to cause clashes between national and state authority, for the Articles did not even specify which body was to have the authority to decide when a state impost and a congressional treaty were inconsistent.[16] It is also clear that the delegates were familiar with alternative solutions, for Silas Deane's proposals on confederation had proposed that *only* the Congress (to which he would have given exclusive authority to negotiate treaties) would have the power to lay commercial duties, and that such duties were to be paid into the continental treasury.[17]

Finally, the Articles granted markedly different discretionary powers to the national government when acting in its executive capacity than it did to the same government when exercising its legislative powers. Thus, for example, Congress was empowered, in very broad language indeed, to regulate the Indian trade and manage all other affairs with the Indians, to negotiate on all subjects with foreign nations, and to decide in an unspecified manner "all disputes and differences" between colonies regarding "any . . . Cause whatever." Furthermore, Congress had the power to appoint any and all "such Committees and Civil Officers as may be necessary for managing the general affairs of the United States."[18] Benjamin Franklin had proposed a similarly broad grant of discretionary legislative power to the Congress. In Article v of his proposed Articles, he would have given Congress the authority to "make such Ordinances as tho' necessary to the General Welfare, particular assemblies cannot be competent to," with the Congress to decide what those areas of the "General Welfare" might be.[19] No subsequent draft of the Articles, however, had any comparable grant of discretionary legislative authority.

There are, of course, exceptions to the model presented here. Thus, the states, not Congress, succeeded to the royal power to choose provincial executives and judicial officers. All the drafts of the Articles granted, without controversy, full discretionary powers to Congress to appoint such "civil Officers as may be necessary for managing the General Affairs of the United States."[20] Yet, an early suggestion by Silas Deane that the Congress assume the Crown's power to appoint governors and lieutenant governors in former royal colonies was, like Dickinson's religious toleration clause, never seriously debated.[21] One explanation is that the power of appointment had so recently been used as an instrument of coercion—in the Massachusetts Government Act—that the colonists were reluctant to vest a possible instrument of tyranny in a new central government. A more likely explanation, however, is to be found in the distinction between intrastate and interstate power that has been described here. The power to appoint provincial officials was not essential to the king's *imperial* role, but rather had its most direct impact upon the internal politics of individual colonies. Both the delegates and the provincial leaders had tacitly agreed to insulate the internal politics of individual colonies against continental control, and within these entities John Adams's "new, strange and terrible Doctrines" of popular sovereignty were to transform American politics.[22] It is not surprising, however, that the Crown's power that most directly concerned the colonies as individual political entities, and that least directly related to the imperial links between them, was not assumed by the Congress.

Despite such exceptions, it has here been argued that the most obvious model guiding the delegates' allocation of powers between the national government and the states was that of the old empire. For the most part, I have argued, the executive and administrative responsibilities that had been exercised by or under the aegis of the king's authority were confided to the successor to his authority, the Congress.

Those powers that were exercised or claimed primarily by Parliament, however—the power to tax, to regulate trade both among the colonies and with foreign nations, and to design or alter the internal constitutions of individual colonies—were just as firmly allocated to the states.

The Decline of the Executive

This allocation of functions, which would decisively influence the powers of the executive branch in the final form of an American continental government, nevertheless helped to seal the fate of the first such government. From 1774 on it had been clear that the Congress was inappropriately constituted to serve as an executive institution. Whigs had been quite explicit regarding the advantages of an executive that rendered it indispensable to good government. As Richard Price had written, the reason an executive was an essential component of any constitution was that it provided the government with "wisdom, union, dispatch, secrecy, and vigour."[23] Congress, however, was institutionally incapable of meeting all, or even most, of these requirements. It was too large to act either with dispatch, secrecy, or unity, and it lacked men of expertise who could carry on their responsibilities competently and efficiently. As the Connecticut delegates explained the slow pace of the Congress in 1774 to their provincial superiors, "we . . . confess Our anxiety for greater dispatch of the Business before Us, than it is in Our power, or perhaps in the Nature of the Subject, to effect," given the nature of "an Assembly like this, though it consists, of less than Sixty Members, yet coming from remote Colonies, each of which, has some modes, of transacting public Business, peculiar to itself some particular provincial rights and Interests to guard, & secure." Although the delegates wished to act with dispatch, however, they did not wish to do so at the expense of unity, and securing unanimity among a group of lawyers, for whom scanning for details was their life's work, was no easy task. As John Adams later explained the problem, after what must have been a particularly exasperating day, he had "the Pleasure of inclosing" to his correspondent, "a Declaration. Some call it a Manifesto. And We might easily have occasioned a Debate of half a Day whether it should be called a Declaration or a Manifesto."[24]

These problems, serious enough at the deliberative assembly of

1774, were nearly disastrous when the Congress met in 1775, for almost all of the delegates' business consisted of executive and administrative affairs. "Our Assembly is scarcly numerous enough for the business," John Adams wrote. "Every body is engaged, all Day in Congress and all the Morning and evening in Committees." "We are lost in the Extensiveness of our Field of Business," he wrote to another correspondent. Silas Deane simply concluded that "Our Business has run away with Us." Indeed, so busy had Samuel Ward become, with congressional business increasing so fast, that he gave up trying to keep minutes of the proceedings.[25] The problems caused by the multitude of business were compounded by the inexperience of many of the delegates about the matters that they were called upon to consider. "It is a vast and Complicated System of Business which We have gone through," Adams worried, "and We were all of us, unexperienced in it."[26]

The effect of congressional inexperience and increasing business was exacerbated by its own procedures. Congress dealt with the business that came before it in two ways. One was for Congress to resolve itself into a committee of the whole. As Adams later recalled the procedure, all sorts of matters, diverse in subject matter and importance, would be debated and discussed all at once. Thus, for example, the committee of the whole might take up dispatches from Washington, Indian affairs, revenue requirements, "and twenty other Things, many of them very trivial" that were "mixed, in these Committees of the whole, with the Great Subjects of Government, Independence and Commerce." "We could only harrangue against the misapplication of time," he remembered, which was particularly futile, for "harrangues consumed more time."[27]

The second major way of conducting business was by appointing ad hoc committees of delegates. The delegates very quickly moved to a system of standing committees, however, which were to be responsible on a continuing basis for the matters referred to their care. By the end of 1775 there were seven standing committees.[28] While the standing committees were an improvement over the prior method, they nevertheless had serious deficiencies. First, the membership of Congress was constantly in flux, and the attendance of those delegates who were appointed was erratic. This meant that the members of the standing committees had little opportunity to develop the expertise that was so sadly lacking. Second, because the membership of the standing committees was drawn from among the delegates only, there was a limited, and shrinking, pool of bodies able and willing to fill the committee seats. Competent men of business, like Adams and Wilson, served on dozens of committees, some of them simultaneously, and they were often torn between the call of their committee business and their duties on the floor of Congress itself. "Everybody is engaged, all Day in Congress and all the Morning and evening in Committees," Adams wrote home. A surprisingly cheerful Silas Deane wrote home in September 1775: "Am in my old usual way Committeeing it away, and busy." Yet the diligence of some delegates could not overcome the basic deficiencies in the system itself. Caesar Rodney explained to a colleague in 1776 why he was unable to leave Philadelphia: "The state of the public business in Congress has been such that I cou'd not leave this place with propriety for these two days past tho truly little has been done in them particularly the Marine Committee is so wanting in Attending Members that for 2 Evenings past we could not procure a sufficient Number to proceed to business." The state of affairs had not changed materially when Josiah Bartlett informed John Langdon some two years later that "our commercial, marine and treasury affairs are in a very bad Situation and will never be otherwise while they are managed by Committees of Congress who are many of them unacquainted with the business and are continually changing and by that time they begin to be acquainted with the business they quit, others come in who know nothing that has been done: thus we go on from time to time to the great loss of the public."[29]

As early as 1775, jokes were being made about the slow pace of Congress's dispatch of executive business. Thus when Benjamin Harrison explained to Washington that there would be a delay in dispatching the bills of credit Washington needed to pay his army, he added, "What has Occasion'd a Delay of this Article I know not" but he thought that the continental treasurers might have acted in "Imitation of the Congress," in which body "Slowness has become fashionable." But from at least the time of the Canadian campaign of 1775–1776, it had become clear that there was little to laugh about regarding congressional inefficiency.[30] Most of the officers who participated in the campaign had seen firsthand that a major cause of the disaster had been the inability of Congress to ensure prompt and regular ordinance and supplies. Not only were the numbers of troops inadequate, one Pennsylvania officer informed James Wilson, but the troops "were in want of every thing and had no Body to command them." Samuel Chase, a member of the committee sent by Congress to investigate the whole dismal affair, concluded that some major changes in congressional procedure were necessary. The Canadian debacle had proved, Chase wrote, that "the Congress are not a fit Body to act as a Council of War. They are too large, too slow, and their Resolutions can never be kept secret." The solution Chase suggested was simple: "Pray divide your business into different Departments, a War Office, a Treasury Board, et et."[31]

Chase's suggestion was not novel. As early as March 19, 1776, Richard Smith had recorded in his diary that Johnson of Maryland had proposed for consideration "the Propriety of establishing a Board of Treasury, a War Office, a Board of Public Accounts and other Boards to consist of Gentn. not Members of Congress." By December 1776 the cry had been taken up with increasing insistence by Robert Morris, one of the premier men of business in Congress. "I will not enter into any detail of our Conduct in Congress, but you may depend on this that so Long as that respectable body persist in the attempt to execute as well as to deliberate on their business it never will be done as it ought & this has been urged many & many a time by myself & others." "I say mismanagem[en]t," wrote Morris, reaching the core of the issue, "because no Men living can attend the daily deliberations of Congress & do executive parts of business at the same time."[32]

By December 26, 1776, a majority of delegates agreed. A committee of five was appointed "to prepare a plan for the better conducting the executive business of Congress, by boards composed of persons, not members of the Congress." An exultant James Wilson informed Morris that "Congress see, at last, the Propriety of distributing the executive Business of the Continent into different Departments, managed by Gentlemen, not Members of Congress, and whose whole Time and Attention can be devoted to the Business committed to their Charge."[33] The euphoria would be short-lived, however, for not until 1781 did Congress create executive departments with unitary heads for finance, foreign affairs, war, and marine matters.[34]

The practice of separating out Congress's executive from its legislative functions had clearly begun in the months immediately following independence, however. These executive departments would ultimately effect a considerable improvement in the competence with which Congress performed its executive functions.[35] But it was a competence that was acquired at a very high price, for the creation of separate executive departments had the unintended side effect of overtly bifurcating Congress's functions. Eugene Sheridan and John Murrin have concluded that "once Congress provided executive bodies distinct from itself, virtually every instinct of eighteenth-century political thought compelled contemporaries to think of it as a legislature whose will the department heads would execute."[36] Thus, after these departments were created only one role was left to Congress, that of a national legislature. In this role, however, Congress appeared weak and incompetent, for it obviously lacked the most essential powers of such a legislature: the power to tax, to regulate internal and external trade and commerce, and to exercise its discretion to create new legislative solutions to emerging problems.

Once Congress began to be viewed primarily as a legislature rather than an executive, an additional and perhaps fatal weakness became increasingly apparent. As a national legislature, Congress simply lacked legitimate authority when measured against criteria that had been developing through the 1770s and early 1780s. Congress could no longer demonstrate, as the newly sovereign states so palpably could, that its constituents had consented to its exercise of legislative authority. In 1774 and 1775 it had been the Congress that had possessed the attributes of legitimate government, as both individuals and provincial governments explicitly and extravagantly expressed their consent to congressional decisions. But by the late 1770s the positions were reversed. The process of constitution making in the states had created new ways of legitimizing the new state constitutions: conventions of "the people" called specifically for the purpose gave these documents, and the state governments formed under them, the most overt stamp of approval by the governed that has yet been devised. But the national frame of government, from which Congress drew its authority, had no such imprimatur. It had been written by delegates elected for purposes other than the formation of a national government, and it had been ratified, not by the sovereign people solemnly convened, but by the ordinary state legislatures.[37] Thus, while the new state governments were undoubtedly legitimate, it was no longer so clear that the Congress was. As a delegate to the 1787 Convention noted pointedly: "*State constitutions* [were] formed at an early period of the war, and by persons *elected by the people* for that purpose. . . . The *confederation* was formed . . . and had its ratification not by any *special appointment* from the people, but from the several assemblies. No judge will say that the *confederation* is paramount to a State constitution.[38]

The mission of the delegates to the Constitutional Convention of 1787 was to devise a frame of government that would remedy such perceived deficiencies of the old Confederation. The document that the delegates devised completely restructured the relationship between the national government and the states, transformed the composition and power of the national legislature, and created a national judiciary. The delegates did not, however, significantly alter the executive and administrative powers allocated to the central government. The powers of the national executive under the Constitution were basically those that had been exercised by the Congress since 1775, and before that by the king. The institutional structure of the executive, however, *was* altered in 1787, for the Congress had proved to be palpably incapable of carrying out the executive functions with which it had been charged. The executive institution devised by the delegates to replace the Congress also had its roots, at least in the minds of some, in an earlier institution. "Let us now consider what our constitution is," John Adams wrote in 1789, "and see whether any other name can with propriety be given it, than that of a monarchical republic, or if you will, a limited monarchy."[39]

A Note on Terminology

Anyone who chooses to write about the American Revolution is tempted to use the terms "radical," "moderate," and "conservative" to characterize various persons and policies. I, too, have succumbed.

I am aware, however, that in the rapidly changing stream of events that characterize any revolution, the meaning of such terms changes quickly, so that one year's radical becomes the next year's conservative. In addition, these terms are somewhat chameleonlike in their imprecision, for they acquire different meanings according to the particular context in which they are used. The potential for confusion is therefore considerable. An example of changing meaning over time is Thomas Lynch of South Carolina. On almost any scale, Lynch must be termed a political radical in 1774. A veteran of South Carolina's radical politics and the Stamp Act Congress, Lynch had long corresponded with the Massachusetts delegates, and he worked in close contact with them at the First Continental Congress. Yet by February 1776 Lynch was actively involved in negotiations with the shadowy British emissary Lord Drummond, trying desperately to foster a reconciliation with Britain. He did so primarily because he viewed the alternative— a declaration of independence and the establishment of American republican governments—as a recipe for disaster. By 1776, then, Lynch had become a political moderate or conservative.

A similar case in point, illustrating the importance of context as well as change over time, is the celebrated "Pennsylvania Farmer," John Dickinson. For some purposes, Dickinson should be termed a radical in provincial politics, for in 1774 he battled the entrenched forces of the conservative Speaker of the Assembly, Joseph Galloway. Yet by 1776 Dickinson had become the foremost opponent of independence. Even at their most politically radical, however, neither Dickinson, a wealthy lawyer and gentleman farmer, nor Lynch, a similarly wealthy merchant and planter, sought to effect substantial changes in social structure, as did, for example, the Pennsylvania radicals James Cannon and Timothy Matlack.

Yet, though the precise meaning of the three terms changes with the context and the time, there are valid reasons for employing them. First, they are stylistically convenient, and they avoid the use of very cumbersome qualifying phraseology that I am reluctant to impose upon any reader. Second, the terms do have *some* meaning; the trick is to ensure that the meaning the reader draws from them is that which the author wishes to convey. The solution I have adopted is that devised by Richard A. Ryerson in his fine work *The Revolution Is Now Begun: The Radical Committees of Philadelphia, 1765–1776* (Philadelphia, 1978). Ryerson carefully defines the meaning of his terms in a note at the outset of every chapter. I have tried to do the same. The disadvantage of this approach is that if the unwary reader misses the critical footnote, he or she will be all the more confused. *Caveat lector!*

Local and Provincial Resolutions, 1774

Province	Number	Locality	Date
New England			
New Hampshire	1	New Hampshire Provincial Congress	July 21
Connecticut	13	Farmington (town)	May 19
		New Haven (town)	May 23
		Connecticut House of Representatives	May 30
		Lebanon (town)	June 2
		Norwich (town)	June 6
		Preston (town)	June 13
		Middletown (town)	June 15
		Wethersfield (town)	June 17
		Hartford (town)	June 20
		Glastonbury (town)	June 23
		Windham (town)	June 23
		East-Windsor (town)	August 3
		Hartford, New London, Windham, and Litchfield counties	September 15
Rhode Island	4	Westerly (town)	May 16
		Providence (town)	May 17
		Newport (town)	May 20
		Rhode Island General Assembly	June 15
Middle Colonies			
New York	10	South Haven, Suffolk County	June 13
		East Hampton, Suffolk County	June 17
		Huntington, Suffolk County	June 21
		Orange Town (town)	July 4

Province	Number	Locality	Date
		New York County inhabitants	July 6
		New York Committee of 51	July 19
		Poughkeepsie, Dutchess County	August 10
		Rye, Westchester County	August 10
		Westchester (town)	August 20
		Palatine District, Tryon County	September 27
New Jersey	11	Lower Frederick, Monmouth County	June 6
		Essex County	June 11
		Morris County	June 24
		Bergen County	June 25
		Hunterdon County	July 8
		Middlesex County	July 15
		Salem County	July 15
		Sussex County	July 16
		Gloucester County	July 18
		Monmouth County	July 19
		New Jersey Convention	July 21
Pennsylvania	12	Lancaster (borough)	June 15
		Philadelphia (town)	June 18
		Chester (town)	June 18
		Northampton County	June 21
		York (town)	June 24
		Berks County	July 2
		York County	July 4
		Bucks County	July 9
		Lancaster County	July 9
		Cumberland County	July 12
		Chester County	July 13
		Pennsylvania Provincial Convention	July 15–21
Delaware	5	New Castle County	June 29
		Kent County	June 30
		Sussex County	July 23
		Lewestown (town)	July 28
		Delaware Convention	August 1

Province	Number	Locality	Date
South			
Maryland	11	Chestertown (town)	May 18
		Talbot Court House (town)	May 24
		Annapolis (town)	May 26
		Queen Anne County	May 30
		Baltimore County	May 31
		Anne Arundel County	June 4
		Hartford County	June 11
		Frederick County	June 11–20
		Charles County	June 14
		Caroline County	June 18
		Maryland Convention	June 22
Virginia	30	Prince William County	June 6
		Frederick County	June 8
		Dunmore County	June 16
		Westmoreland County	June 22
		Spotsylvania County	June 24
		Richmond County	June 29
		Prince George's County	June 29
		James City County	July 1
		Norfolk (town)	July 6
		Culpepper County	July 7
		Essex County	July 9
		Fauquier County	July 9
		Nansemond County	July 9
		New-Kent County	July 12
		Chesterfield County	July 14
		Gloucester County	July 14
		Caroline County	July 14
		Henrico County	July 15
		Middlesex County	July 15
		Surry County	July 16
		York County	July 18
		Fairfax County	July 18
		Hanover County	July 20
		Stafford County	July 20
		Elizabeth City County	July 25
		Albemarle County	July 26
		Accomack County	July 27
		Princess Anne County	July 27

Province	Number	Locality	Date
		Buckingham County	July 28
		Virginia Convention	August 1–6
North Carolina	9	Wilmington (town)	July 21
		Rowan County	August 8
		Johnston County	August 12
		Pitt County freeholders	August 15
		Granville County	August 15
		Anson County	August 18
		Chowan County	August 22
		Halifax (town)	August 22
		North Carolina Convention	August 24
South Carolina	1	Charleston (town and province)	July 6–8
Georgia	1	Georgia Convention	August 10
Totals by region:			
New England (excluding Massachusetts)			18
Middle Colonies			38
South			52
			108

The sample listed above is culled from the proceedings of local and provincial meetings that occurred during the summer of 1774 and that were first published in contemporary newspapers and later by Peter Force in *American Archives* and in various published provincial records. While the sample is comprehensive enough to reflect opinion in every colonial region concerning the 1774 crisis, I do not claim that it includes every such proceeding that occurred during the period in question.

As the regional tabulation indicates, the sample is weighted toward those rural areas, especially in the southern and middle colonies, that were newly politicized during the 1774 crisis. Opposition opinion in New England (and especially in Massachusetts) had been expressed through established institutions like town meetings and through the newer town committees of correspondence prior to April 1774. Perhaps as a result, the New England resolutions in the sample were the shortest and least elaborate of those included, sometimes referring simply to "our previously expressed sentiments." The resolutions of the middle and southern colonies, on the other hand, were often the first such local statements made there and were more directly related to the crisis brought on by the Port Bill. They thus closely reflect the crisis sentiment that brought the Congress into existence. Part of this bias toward the southern and middle colonies is due to my decision to exclude from the sample any Massachusetts resolutions. I did this because one goal of the study is to examine opinion in the other colonies toward dealing with the crisis in Massachusetts, because this opinion helped shape policy in Congress. Assuming that sentiment in New England in 1774 was more radical (in the sense of desiring stronger measures against England) than that to the south, then the sample is, as a result, biased in a conservative direction. Given this fact, the considerable support for Boston and for a trade embargo is all the more remarkable. (It should be noted, however, that the New England resolutions in the sample do not differ in any significant way from those of the middle or southern colonies.)

The sample does not, of course, reflect the sentiments of those colonists who did not attend the meetings, whether for reasons of apathy or disapproval. Little contemporary disapproval of the meetings surfaced, however, even in those journals, like Hugh Gaine's *New-York Gazette*, that were open to such opinion. (This paucity is in direct contrast to the flood of Tory pieces, in press and pamphlet form, that appeared after November 1774 opposing the actions of the Congress.) Furthermore, I made a reasonably diligent search in conservative journals like Gaine's for proceedings of meetings held during the summer in which Boston's actions were condemned or British measures approved, but I could find none to include in the sample, though a number of such meetings did occur, especially in Massachusetts and New York, after November 1774. The sample, therefore, excludes no colonial sentiment toward the 1774 crisis that was published in radical, moderate, or conservative journals.

TABLE A-1

Analysis of Local and Provincial Resolutions

1. *Political Attitudes*
   Of 98 resolutions that contain some statement of political attitude:

Aver loyalty to George III	62	(63%)
Demand rights of Englishmen	49	(50%)
Demand to be taxed only by consent	54	(55%)
Abhor parliamentary revenue taxes	63	(64%)
Abhor Coercive Acts	90	(92%)
Discern ministerial conspiracy	35	(36%)
Ask for "restoration of rights"; "establishment of rights of permanent foundation," or use similar language	65	(66%)

2. *Support for Boston*

Aver Boston suffers in "common cause"	82	(76%)
Raise subscription for Boston	47	(44%)
Ask payment for tea	2	(—)

3. *Goals of Resistance**

Redress of unspecified grievances	62	(57%)
Repeal of Coercive Acts	55	(51%)
Restoration of harmony	24	(22%)

4. *Sentiment Favoring Congress*

Congress called for	72	
Congress called for by inference	<u>21</u>	
	93	(86%)

   Of 93 resolutions calling for a Congress:
   (a) Authority of Congress:

agreement in advance to comply with congressional decisions	45	(48%)

   (b) Methods of resistance to be pursued by Congress

unspecified plan or "wise measures"	27	(29%)
petition	7	(8%)
declaration of rights**	4	(4%)
nonimportation/nonconsumption	61	(66%)
nonexportation	46	(49%)

5. *Expectations of Continued Need for Resistance*

appointment of officers to take further action	95	(88%)
appointment of new local committees	58	(54%)

6. *Expansion of Political Process*

Of the 95 local resolutions:

Attendees limited to freeholders and/or "gentlemen"	24	(25%)
Attendees include "freeholder" and "other inhabitants"	71	(75%)

NOTE: Unless otherwise specified, percentages refer to total sample of 108 local and provincial resolutions.

* Several state two or more goals.

** But note that 65 of 98 resolutions asked for "establishment of rights on permanent foundation," which comprehends a declaration of rights.

Notes

Introduction

1. On Pownall's ability and analytical effort, see John Shy, "The Spectrum of Imperial Possibilities: Henry Ellis and Thomas Pownall, 1763–1775," in *A People Numerous & Armed* (London, 1976), pp. 37–72.

2. The term derives from the classical Latin *legitimus*, meaning lawful or according to law; Dolf Sternberger, "Legitimacy," *International Encyclopedia of the Social Sciences*, 9:244. Definitions and analyses of the concept abound; they are to be found in almost every classic work of politics, from the writings of St. Augustine to the work of John Locke and Jean-Jacques Rousseau. Modern theories of legitimacy derive from Max Weber's classic work, *The Theory of Social Organization* (New York, 1957; orig. publ. 1922). Weber posited that in all political systems the quality of legitimacy is based on the beliefs and values of the ruled and that its primary characteristic is its ability to command the obedience of the ruled. Weber created a typology in which he attempted to distinguish among the various types of legitimacy: the traditional, the charismatic, and the rational. While this typology has been criticized, most modern analyses adopt Weber's thesis of the basically subjective quality of legitimacy. See, for example, Carl J. Friedrich, *Man and His Government: An Empirical Theory of Politics* (New York, 1963), pp. 232–46; Friedrich, "Political Leadership and the Problem of Charismatic Power," *Journal of Politics* 23 (1963): 3–24; and R. A. Dahl, *Modern Political Analysis*, 3d ed. (Englewood Cliffs, N.J., 1976), p. 60. For criticism of the subjective school, see J. G. Merquior, *Rousseau and Weber: Two Studies in the Theory of Legitimacy* (London, 1980), pp. 6–9. The following draws heavily upon Friedrich's analysis.

3. Sternberger, "Legitimacy," p. 244.

4. Dahl, *Modern Political Analysis*, p. 61.

5. Friedrich, *Man and His Government*, pp. 233–34; Dahl, *Modern Political Analysis*, p. 60. See also Ted R. Gurr, *Why Men Rebel* (Princeton, N.J., 1970), p. 115, where he also defines legitimacy as a government's ability to induce obedience through means other than coercion.

6. Sternberger, "Legitimacy," p. 244. On the power of consecration to legitimize kingship, see, for example, Ernst H. Kantorowicz, *The King's Two Bodies: A Study in Mediaeval Political Theology* (Princeton, N.J., 1957). On magic, see Marc Bloch, *Les Rois Thaumaturges* (Paris, 1961), and J. G. Frazer's classic work *The Golden Bough: A Study in Magic and Religion*, 3d ed., 12 vols. (London, 1919–22).

7. Sternberger, "Legitimacy," pp. 245, 247; Burke, "Speech on Representation," May 7, 1782, cited in Friedrich, *Man and His Government*, p. 235 n. 5.

8. Friedrich, *Man and His Government*, pp. 236, 244.

9. Gordon Schochet, "Patriarchalism, Politics, and Mass Attitudes in Stuart England," *Historical Journal* 12 (1969): 414; Friedrich, *Man and His Government*, pp. 221–23. On the habitual dimension of legitimacy, see also Richard M. Merelman, "Learning and Legitimacy," *American Political Science Review* 60 (1966): 548–61. It is the fear that such habitual, unreflective obedience cannot survive a transfer from one form of government to another that causes apprehensions regarding the process of revolution, however desirable its goals. See Andrew C. Janos, "Authority and Violence: The Political Framework of Internal War," in Harry Eckstein, ed., *Internal War: Problems and Approaches* (New York, 1964); and Robert A. Nisbet, *Tradition and Revolt: Historical and Sociological Essays* (New York, 1968), pp. 82–83. The colonists' references to such apprehensions were couched in terms of expressions of fear that revolution would bring with it a loss of "due subordination." See Chapter 9.

10. Thus, for example, much documentary material cited in Chapter 1 dates from the time of George III's coronation, as well as the years of crisis after 1774.

11. See Chapter 1.

12. See Chapter 2.

13. Sternberger, "Legitimacy," p. 244.

14. See, for example, Daniel Boorstin, *The Americans: The Colonial Experience* (New York, 1958). Important new work has traced the long-term differentiation of American society and institutions from those of Great Britain. See Chapter 1, n. 9, and sources cited therein.

15. Only one American constituency, that which later became the state of Vermont, seriously attempted to return to British authority, although many individual American Tories, of course, favored such a course. See Chapter 9 and Peter S. Onuf, *The Origins of the Federal Republic: Jurisdictional Controversies in the United States, 1775–1787* (Philadelphia, 1983), pp. 103–45.

16. The now-classic works of the imperial school of historians, which detail the institutional basis of British authority in the colonies, include such works as Leonard Labaree, *Royal Government in America* (New Haven, 1930); Charles M. Andrews, *The Colonial Period of American History*, vol. 4, *England's Commercial and Colonial Policy* (New Haven, 1938); and volume 9 of Lawrence Henry Gipson's monumental work *The British Empire before the American Revolution*, entitled *The Triumphant Empire: New Responsibilities within the Enlarged Empire, 1763–1766* (New York, 1956). More specialized studies include Carl Ubbelohde, *The Vice-Admiralty Courts and the American Revolution* (Williamsburg, Va., 1960); and Evarts B. Greene, *The Provincial Governor in the English Colonies of North America* (New York, 1898).

17. On British conduct of the war with the colonies, see Piers Mackesy, *The War for America, 1775–1783* (Cambridge, Mass., 1964).

18. See, for example, that collected in Arnold M. Pavlovsky, "Between Hawk and Buzzard: Congress as Perceived by its Members, 1775–1783," *Pennsylvania Magazine of History and Biography* 101 (1977): 349–64.

19. See Chapter 3.

20. See Chapter 6.

21. The idea of the success or failure of a political institution only has meaning in terms of the comparison chosen and the criteria used to judge. Thus, how one decides to frame the question predetermines the answer.

22. See Chapter 10.

23. William Hooper to James Iredell, Apr. 26, 1774, in William L. Saunders, ed., *The Colonial Records of North Carolina* (Raleigh, N.C., 1886–90), 9:985.

Chapter 1

1. Margaret Hutchinson to Elizabeth Hutchinson, Oct. 19, 1774, Thomas Hutchinson Papers, Egerton Manuscripts, vol. 2659, fol. 109, British Museum.

2. Charles L. Hansen, ed., *A Journal for the Years 1739–1803 by Samuel Lane of Stratham, New Hampshire* (Concord, N.H., 1937), p. 38; Abigail Adams to John Adams, May 14, 1776, in Lyman H. Butterfield, ed., *The Adams Papers*, ser. 2, *Adams Family Correspondence* (Cambridge, Mass., 1963–), 1:408. On the American reverence for the king up to the eve of revolution, see William D. Liddle, " 'A Patriot King, or None': Lord Bolingbroke and the American Renunciation of George III," *Journal of American History* 65 (1979): 951; see also Peter Shaw, *American Patriots and the Rituals of Revolution* (Cambridge, Mass., 1981), p. 14.

3. On the use of the term "radical," see "A Note on Terminology." The term "Whig" is defined below in note 13. The term "radical Whig," as used in this chapter, refers to those who shared the ideas sketched in the next section of this chapter.

4. "A.Z.," *Massachusetts Gazette and the Boston Post-Boy and Advertiser*, Nov. 15, 1773; Mercy Otis Warren to John Adams, Sept. 1785, in Worthington C. Ford, ed., *Warren-Adams Letters: Being Chiefly a Correspondence among John Adams, Samuel Adams, and James Warren*, Massachusetts Historical Society, *Collections* (Boston, 1917–25), 2:260 (hereafter cited as Ford, ed., *Warren-Adams Letters*); "Journal of Josiah Quincy, Jun., During the Voyage and Residence in England from September 28th, 1774, To March 3d, 1775," Massachusetts Historical Society, *Proceedings* 50 (1916–17): 445; Charles Thomson to John Dickinson, July 29, 1776, in Paul H. Smith, ed., *Letters of Delegates to Congress, 1774–1776* (Washington, D.C., 1979–), 4:562 (hereafter cited as Smith, ed., *LDC*).

5. On antimonarchism in the Federalist era, see Louise B. Dunbar, *A Study of Monarchical Tendencies in the United States from 1776 to 1801*, University of Illinois Studies in the Social Sciences, 10:1 (Urbana, Ill., 1922), pp. 99–101, 116–26; Donald H. Stewart, *The Opposition Press of the Federalist Period* (Albany, N.Y., 1969), pp. 487–90; Marshall Smelser, "The Jacobin Phrenzy: The Menace of Monarchy, Plutocracy and Anglophilia, 1789–1798," *Review of Politics* 21 (1959): 239–58. On the continuing attraction of the idea of a "patriot king," see Liddle, " 'A Patriot King or None,' " pp. 969–70.

6. Williamson in Max Farrand, ed., *The Records of the Federal Convention of 1787* (New Haven, Conn., 1911), 2:101. On Hamilton, see, for example, his speech to the Federal Convention, June 4, 1787 (Madison version), in Harold C. Syrett and Jacob E. Cooke, eds., *The Papers of Alexander Hamilton* (New York,

1961–), 4:192–94. Gouverneur Morris to Robert Walsh, Feb. 5, 1811, in Anne C. Morris, ed., *The Diary and Letters of Gouverneur Morris* (New York, 1888), 2:526; and Gerald Stourzh, *Alexander Hamilton and the Idea of Republican Government* (Stanford, Calif., 1970), pp. 46, 107. On Washington, see Thomas Jefferson to Dr. Walter Jones, Jan. 2, 1814, in Paul L. Ford, ed., *The Works of Thomas Jefferson* (New York, 1904–5), 11:377–78. The Franklin comment is in his speech to the Federal Convention, June 2, 1787 (James Wilson reading), in Farrand, ed., *Records of the Federal Convention*, 1:83. For an extensive discussion of this theme, see Jeremy Belknap to Ebenezer Hazard, Feb. 27 and Mar. 3, 1784, in *The Belknap Papers*, Massachusetts Historical Society, *Collections*, 5th ser. (Boston, 1877), 2:307, 315.

7. See, for example, Gordon S. Wood, *The Creation of the American Republic, 1776–1787* (Chapel Hill, N.C., 1969), p. 93: "this ease of transition into republicanism remains remarkable and puzzling even today." Some scholars, however, do not see the transition from monarchy to republic as either easy, smooth, or inevitable. See, for example, Liddle, "Patriot King." A provocative study by Burrows and Wallace finds the abandonment of the imperial "family" and the father-king to have caused considerable psychological upheaval for many colonists. See Edwin Burrows and Michael Wallace, "The American Revolution: The Ideology and Psychology of National Liberation," *Perspectives in American History* 6 (1972): 167–306.

8. On the characteristics of the "old society," see Harold Perkin, *The Origins of Modern English Society, 1780–1880* (London, 1969), pp. 17–62; and Peter Laslett, *The World We Have Lost* (New York, 1965), pp. 23–199. Particular studies on the growing American divergence from this pattern include, for example, Stephanie G. Wolf, *Urban Village: Community and Family in Germantown, Pennsylvania, 1683–1800* (Princeton, 1976), and Richard L. Bushman, *From Puritan to Yankee: Character and the Social Order in Connecticut, 1690–1765* (New York, 1967). Gary B. Nash demonstrates how, throughout the eighteenth century, great economic and social changes in the northern seaport towns created politically conscious lower classes whose goals and views caused them not only to oppose British authority but to seek to use the resistance movement to achieve their own social agenda; *The Urban Crucible: Social Change, Political Consciousness, and the Origins of the American Revolution* (Cambridge, Mass., 1979). See also Richard D. Brown, "Modernization and the Modern Personality in Early America, 1600–1865: A Sketch of a Synthesis," *Journal of Interdisciplinary History* 2 (1972): 201–28.

9. On the gradual disengagement of American political elites and political institutions from the English imperial system, see James Kirby Martin, *Men in Rebellion: Higher Governmental Leaders and the Coming of the American Revolution* (New York, 1973), and Jack P. Greene, *The Quest for Power: The Lower Houses of Assembly in the Southern Royal Colonies, 1689–1776* (Chapel Hill, N.C., 1963). On the Whig opposition movement in England and the colonies as a potent force molding American opinion and directing American effort toward the final break, see Pauline Maier, *From Resistance to Revolution: Colonial Radicals and the Development of the American Opposition to Britain, 1765–1776* (New York, 1972).

On the basic disequilibrium of American and British political institutions within the imperial context, see the excellent summary by Jack P. Greene, "An Uneasy Connection: An Analysis of the Preconditions of the American Revolution," in Stephen G. Kurtz and James H. Hutson, eds., *Essays on the American Revolution* (Chapel Hill, N.C., 1973), pp. 32–80.

10. An alternative historiographical school finds American politics and society developing throughout the eighteenth century in a direction that moved the colonies closer to the English pattern. The foremost articulator of this "Anglicization" thesis is John Murrin. See his "Anglicization and Identity: The Colonial Experience, the Revolution, and the Dilemma of American Nationalism" (Paper presented at the Seventy-Seventh Annual Meeting of the Organization of American Historians, Denver, Colorado, 1974) and, with Rowland Berthoff, "Feudalism, Communalism and the Yeoman Freeholder: The American Revolution Considered as a Social Accident," in Kurtz and Hutson, eds., *Essays on the American Revolution*, pp. 256–88. For the development of eighteenth-century colonial society in the direction of hierarchy and growing inequality, see, for example, James A. Henretta, "Economic Development and Social Structure in Colonial Boston," *WMQ*, 3d ser., 22 (1965): 75–91; Kenneth Lockridge, "Land, Population, and the Evolution of New England Society, 1630–1790," *Past and Present* 39 (1968): 62–80; James T. Lemon and Gary B. Nash, "The Distribution of Wealth in Eighteenth-Century America: A Century of Change in Chester County, Pennsylvania, 1683–1782," *Journal of Social History* 2 (1968): 1–24. See also Burrows and Wallace, "The American Revolution: The Ideology and Psychology of National Liberation." Burrows and Wallace, like Murrin, note the increasing colonial admiration for and emulation of British culture and institutions in the eighteenth century (pp. 276–78). Their psychological explanation for this phenomenon posits, first, a genuine psychological attachment to the imperial "family"—"mother" country, "father" king. They also discern, however, a darker side to this phenomenon, noting that "individuals placed in precarious or insecure positions, or situations in which they are made to feel helpless and inferior, will mimic the traits and styles of whoever holds authority over them—not out of affection, but rather out of the unconscious transformations of inexpressible frustration and hostility" (pp. 278–79).

11. The most comprehensive study of serious monarchist plots in the early years of the republic is Dunbar, *A Study of "Monarchical" Tendencies*. Americans who secretly favored an American monarchy (but did not actually plot to overthrow the republic) may have been more numerous, but they were still on the fringe of Federalism; see David H. Fischer, *The Revolution of American Conservatism: The Federalist Party in the Era of Jeffersonian Democracy* (New York, 1965), pp. 22–23. It is important to note, however, the vast range of political alternatives that were encompassed by the eighteenth-century conception of the term "republican," including, for example, a unitary, life-tenure executive possessed of extensive discretionary powers. Good republicans could and did advocate the continued performance of old royal functions by new institutions only marginally different from the old monarchical ones. On the wide political

variations comprehended by the term "republican," see Stourzh, *Alexander Hamilton*, pp. 44–75.

12. On the fear among committed republicans regarding the fragility of republican institutions, see John R. Howe, Jr., "Republican Thought and the Political Violence of the 1790s," *American Quarterly* 19 (1967): 154–63; and the monumental study by Gordon Wood, *The Creation of the American Republic, 1776–1787*, pp. 413–25.

13. For the wide range of sources from which Americans drew their political theory, see Clinton Rossiter, *Seedtime of the Republic: The Origin of the American Tradition of Political Liberty* (New York, 1953), pp. 356–61. See also the selective library lists collected in H. Trevor Colbourn, *The Lamp of Experience: Whig History and the Intellectual Origins of the American Revolution* (Chapel Hill, N.C., 1965), pp. 199–232; and the catalogue of Thomas Jefferson's library, which was unique in scale and scope; E. Millicent Sowerby, ed., *The Catalogue of the Library of Thomas Jefferson* (Washington, D.C., 1952).

The term "Whig," although universally used by contemporaries from the late seventeenth century on, is a very loose term and could be used to denote very different men and ideas in 1670, 1689, 1715, 1750, or 1776. It is used in this chapter in the broadest sense, to denote all those English political writers whose basic political principle was adherence to the Revolution Settlement of 1689. While such a definition leaves very few writers out, such all-inclusiveness is useful because it emphasizes the wide range of "acceptable" political theorists from whom Americans drew congenial political ideas. See John M. Werner, "David Hume and America," *Journal of the History of Ideas* 33 (1972): 439, 447.

14. For the existence of such a Whig political spectrum, see Stourzh, *Alexander Hamilton*, pp. 66–67; and Nash, *Urban Crucible*, pp. 340–42.

15. The dominant influence of the radical Whig world view upon colonial political thought has been established by Caroline Robbins, *The Eighteenth-Century Commonwealthman: Studies in the Transmission, Development and Circumstance of English Liberal Thought from the Restoration of Charles II until the War with the Thirteen Colonies* (Cambridge, Mass., 1959), and Bernard Bailyn, *The Ideological Origins of the American Revolution* (Cambridge, Mass., 1967).

16. It is clear that theorists like Blackstone, Hume, and Ferguson influenced American thought on the nature and functions of authoritative government. Their work is thus of considerable relevance to the present study. In order to discuss these authors as a group, I have termed them "establishment Whigs," a term that is not entirely satisfactory. J.G.A. Pocock, in his monumental study of the transmission of Renaissance civil humanism to the Anglo-American political tradition, detected the development in England of a world view that countered that of the radical Whigs. He used the dichotomy of Court and Country to denote the two strains of thought. (See his consideration of the work of Hume and Ferguson in *The Machiavellian Moment: Florentine Political Thought and the Atlantic Republican Tradition* [Princeton, 1975], pp. 486–88, 493–505.) Although this terminology is illuminating, the term "Court" has too many pejorative connotations for it to be applied neutrally to a study of Amer-

ican politics—hence, "establishment Whigs." The term "establishment" is not intended to convey any religious meaning; rather, it is meant to convey the idea that the political theorists of the late eighteenth century were the beneficiaries of the changed political circumstances in England after 1689. As opposed to their earlier, more radical colleagues, who were often religious as well as political outsiders, men like Blackstone (Professor of English Law at Oxford) and Hume (although a Scot, the holder of various government posts) were participants in, and generally approved of, the changes that had transformed English politics and society in the eighteenth century. They differed from the radicals in their disposition to defend rather than to attack, to champion the present rather than to seek a return to a virtuous past or a plunge into a glorious future.

The term "Whig" is used as defined above (see note 13). The term may be questioned when applied to men like Hume and Blackstone. The first volume of Hume's *History of England* was considered by some radicals to be an apology for the Stuarts, and as a result, Hume was labeled a Tory by some (see Werner, "David Hume and America," p. 443). But Hume considered himself to be a Whig (see Hume to Henry Home, Feb. 9, 1748, in J.Y.T. Grieg, ed., *The Letters of David Hume* [Oxford, 1932], 1:111), and he certainly shared many of the political opinions that characterized Whig politics, including a clear defense of the right of revolution. See Hume to David Hume the Younger, Dec. 8, 1775, ibid. 2:30; and, in general, Duncan Forbes, "Politics and History in David Hume," *Historical Journal* 6 (1963): 280–95. Similarly, Blackstone, ever the champion of Parliament, continued to be one during the crisis of the 1770s, and in this view one may trace what Stourzh has termed "the cliché of Blackstone's 'Toryism.' " Gerald Stourzh, "William Blackstone: Teacher of Revolution," *Jahrbuch für Amerikastudien* [West Germany] 15 (1970): 184, 199–200.

Nevertheless, such labels ought not obscure the very real contributions these men made to colonial political thought. Although there has been no systematic study of the thought of them as a group, it is clear from individual studies that the works of the theorists considered here—William Blackstone, David Hume, and to a lesser extent Adam Ferguson—greatly influenced the thought of many leading colonial political theorists. It did so both in general and in particular regarding subjects of great relevance to the present study— the nature of executive power and its functions, the contract between ruler and ruled, and the right of resistance to unjust authority.

William Blackstone was perhaps the most influential of the three men. He was widely read in the colonies both before and after the publication in 1765 of his masterful *Commentaries on the Laws of England* (ed. Joseph Chitty, new ed. [London, 1826]). The first American edition of Blackstone's *Commentaries*, in 1771–72, had an advance subscription of 1,587 sets, a truly astonishing number. Catherine S. Eller, "The William Blackstone Collection in the Yale Law Library," Yale Law Library *Publications*, 6 (1938): 37, cited in Stourzh, "William Blackstone," p. 199 n. 40. More important than circulation, however, was the influence Blackstone had upon the colonists who read him. In an impeccable study, Stourzh has traced several of Blackstone's ideas and in some instances his very language to such influential colonial pamphlets as William Henry Drayton's *A Letter from Freemen of South-Carolina, to the Deputies of North-America* (August 1774), James Wilson's *Speech Delivered in the Convention for the Province of Pennsylvania* (January 1775), and Alexander Hamilton's *A Full Vindication of the Measures of Congress* (December 1774) and *The Farmer Refuted* (February 1775). See Stourzh, "William Blackstone," and *Alexander Hamilton*, pp. 13–24. On Blackstone's citation as absolute authority by a wide variety of colonial writers, see Rossiter, *Seedtime of the Republic*, p. 360; Colbourn, *Lamp of Experience*, pp. 19, 92, 109, 119; Ernest Barker, "Blackstone on the British Constitution," in *Essays on Government* (Oxford, 1945), p. 123.

Hume's influence on colonial thought was similarly great. His works, especially his *Essays Moral, Political, and Literary* (ed. T. H. Green and T. H. Grose, new ed., 2 vols. [London, 1889]), was widely circulated in the colonies. Werner, "David Hume and America," pp. 444, 453. Hamilton "closely read and cherished" them; Stourzh, *Alexander Hamilton*, p. 19. As Werner documents, Franklin corresponded regularly with Hume through the 1760s and early 1770s; Benjamin Rush met him when he studied in Edinburgh and continued to correspond; Josiah Quincy, Jr., Daniel Dulany, and John Dickinson relied in their revolutionary writings on the authority of, as Dickinson put it, "this great man whose political speculations are so much admired." Quoted in Werner, "David Hume and America," p. 453. Jefferson's debt to Hume is noted in Lucia White, "On a Passage by Hume Incorrectly Attributed to Jefferson," *Journal of the History of Ideas* 37 (1976): 133–35; and Hume's decisive influence on Madison has been established by Douglass Adair, "That Politics May Be Reduced to a Science: David Hume, James Madison, and the Tenth Federalist," in Trevor Colbourn, ed., *Fame and the Founding Fathers* (New York, 1974), pp. 75–106.

Similarly, Adam Ferguson, Professor of Moral Philosophy at the University of Edinburgh, influenced Americans who studied in Edinburgh (James Wilson, for example) as well as those who were educated in the colonies, for the "Moral Philosophy" curriculum at most colonial colleges was drawn from Ferguson's lecture notes, as well as those of others of the "Scottish school." George M. Dennison, "The 'Revolution Principle': Ideology and Constitutionalism in the Thought of James Wilson," *Review of Politics* 39 (1977): 157; Douglass Adair, "James Madison," in *Fame and the Founding Fathers*, p. 128; and Gladys Bryson, *Man and Society: The Scottish Inquiry of the Eighteenth Century* (Princeton, N.J., 1945), p. 31.

17. See, for example, Hume, *Essays* 1:116; Adam Ferguson, *Principles of Moral and Political Science . . .* (Edinburgh, 1792), 2:487; James Burgh, *Political Disquisitions; or, An Inquiry Into Public Errors, Defects, and Abuses* (London, 1774), 1:5; citation from [John Trenchard and Thomas Gordon], *Cato's Letters, or Essays On Liberty, Civil And Religious, and Other Important Subjects* (New York, 1969; orig. publ. London, 1753), 1:261. For an American example in which this dichotomy is presented as a political maxim, see the article by "Philomates" entitled "Of Liberty and Government" in the *Massachusetts Calendar* (Boston, 1772), n.p., Jacob Cushing Diaries Collection, Force Collection, series 8D, Library of Congress.

18. Trenchard and Gordon, *Cato's Letters* 1:262; Burgh, *Political Disquisitions* 1:1–2. For similar views, see Hume, *Essays* 1:118; Ferguson, *Principles* 1:1–2, and, for an American example, "Junius Cato," *Massachusetts Spy; or, Thomas's Boston Journal*, Feb. 4, 1773.

19. The necessity for restraining those entrusted with power is a recurrent theme of the radical Whigs. See, for example, Trenchard and Gordon, *Cato's Letters* 1:185, 255, 259, 2:228–31; and [Thomas Gordon], *The Character Of An Independent Whig* (London, 1720), p. 14.

20. The earliest conceptions of the governmental contract held that the king was "elected" by the people, in return for which he provided protection, both magical and real. See Fritz Kern, *Kingship and Law in the Middle Ages*, trans. S. B. Chrimes (New York, 1956; orig. publ. Tübingen, 1914), pp. 12, 25–26; and William A. Chaney, *The Cult of Kingship in Anglo-Saxon England* (Manchester, Eng., 1970), pp. 15–17.

21. Locke's exposition of his version of the original contract is in *The Second Treatise of Government*, ed. Thomas P. Peardon (Indianapolis, 1952; orig. publ. 1690), pp. 44–74. On the American preoccupation with the contract between ruler and ruled, see Thad Tate, "The Social Contract in America, 1774–1787—Revolutionary Theory as a Conservative Instrument," *WMQ*, 3d ser., 22 (1965): 376, 378; Locke, *Second Treatise*, p. xv. Stourzh claims that "the kind of contract referred to most often, whose violation was charged most often, was the governmental contract between ruler and ruled. However, this contract is *not* part of Locke's system. It is, on the other hand, part of the formula the Convention of 1689 found for declaring the abdication of James II and the vacancy of the throne." "William Blackstone," p. 196. See also Stourzh, *Alexander Hamilton*, pp. 24–30. Be that as it may, Americans still owed their conception of the consensual, as opposed to the patriarchal or the divinely inspired, basis of political obligation to Locke. See Burrows and Wallace, "Ideology and Psychology of National Liberation," pp. 176–77; John Dunn, "Consent in the Political Theory of John Locke," *Historical Journal* 10 (1967): 153–82.

22. Trenchard and Gordon, *Cato's Letters* 2:25; Robert Viscount Molesworth, *The Principles of a Real Whig; Contained in a Preface to the Famous Hotoman's Franco-Gallia . . .* (London, 1775; orig. publ. London, 1721), p. vii; Blackstone, *Commentaries* 1:366–67.

23. John Adams Diary, Dec. 21, 1765, in Lyman H. Butterfield, ed., *The Adams Papers*, ser. 1, *Diary and Autobiography* (Cambridge, Mass., 1962), 1:270; [Joseph Galloway], *A Candid Examination Of The Mutual Claims of Great-Britain, And The Colonies: With A Plan of Accommodation, On Constitutional Principles* (New York, 1775), p. 18; John Tucker, *A Sermon Preached At Cambridge, Before His Excellency Thomas Hutchinson Esq. . . .* (Boston, 1771), p. 28; Andrew Eliot, *A Sermon Preached Before His Excellency Francis Bernard . . .* (Boston, 1765), p. 40; James Wilson, "Speech to the [Pennsylvania] Convention in January 1775," in James Wilson Papers, Historical Society of Pennsylvania, Philadelphia, reprinted, with marginalia included as note b, in Robert G. McCloskey, ed., *The Works of James Wilson* (Cambridge, Mass., 1967), 2:754 and note b.

24. David Hume, *A Treatise of Human Nature . . .* , ed. L. A. Selby-Bigge (Oxford, 1958; orig. publ. 1739), p. 563; Wilson, draft "Address to the Inhabit-

ants," [Feb.] 1776, Dickinson Papers, box 2 (cited portion struck out); see also Ferguson, *Principles* 2:484. Radical Whig assertions of the right of resistance were, of course, even more vehement than those of the establishment theorists. See, for example, Burgh, *Political Disquisitions* 1:4, and Benjamin Hoadley, *The Original And Institution Of Civil Government Discus'd* (London, 1710), p. 168. American assertions of the lawfulness of their resistance, based upon contract theory, were numerous. See, for example, "Mutius Scaevola," *Boston-Gazette and Country Journal*, March 4, 1771; "Vox Vociferantis in Eremo," July 8, 1774, *Boston-Gazette*, Aug. 15, 1775; and, in general, Tate, "Social Contract in America," and sources cited therein. The establishment Whigs, while recognizing the right of resistance, were more likely to emphasize that it ought to be exercised only in extreme cases. See, for example, David Hume, *History of England* (Oxford, 1826; orig. publ. 1757–62), pp. 130–31. As an American echoed this caution, "much, very much ought to be borne, before the people can be justified in restoring [*sic*] to their natural power, in the reclaiming of which so much disorder and confusion must necessarily arise." "Civis," Dixon and Hunter's *Virginia Gazette* (Williamsburg), Apr. 29, 1775.

25. [John Allen], *An Oration, Upon the Beauties of Liberty; or, The Essential Rights of the Americans* (Boston, 1772), p. 60. The idea that the tyrant loses his right to rule is very old; see Kern, *Kingship and Law*, pp. xxiii, 103, 115, 196. For the implications of this theory in America, see below, Chapter 2.

26. Blackstone, *Commentaries* 1:233, 244, and, in general, pp. 233–34. See also, [Robert Viscount Molesworth], *An Account of Denmark As It Was In The Year 1692* (London, 1738), p. xvi. The establishment Whigs were, in general, more skeptical about trusting their liberties to a theoretical contract, so they were even more likely than the radicals to rely on the precedent of 1688. See, for example, Hume, *Essays* 1:445–60, and Ferguson, *Principles* 2:218–25, 232–35. On the importance of Blackstone's codification of the "precedent" of 1688 to American political theorists, see Stourzh, "William Blackstone."

27. Peter Whitney, *The Transgressions of a Land punished by a Multitude of Rulers . . .* (Boston, 1774), p. 19. See also "Americanus," *New-York Journal; or, The General Advertiser*, Nov. 24, 1774; "A Friend to Liberty and the Constitution," Rind and Pinkney's *Virginia Gazette* (Williamsburg), July 20, 1775.

28. The Coronation Oath of 1689, sworn to by all subsequent British kings, pledged the king to rule according to law, to judge fairly and wisely, and to uphold the Protestant religion. The text is in Percy E. Schramm, *A History of the English Coronation*, trans. L. G. Wickham-Legg (Oxford, 1937), pp. 225–26. On the significance of the oath, see ibid., pp. 210–13, 219, 224; and Kern, *Kingship and Law*, pp. 76–78.

29. Blackstone, *Commentaries* 1:234. American political writers frequently reminded the king of his duties toward them by referring to the coronation oath. See, for example, "Scipio," *Pennsylvania Journal; and the Weekly Advertiser* (Philadelphia), Oct. 5, 1775; "W. D.," *New-York Gazette; and the Weekly Mercury*, Aug. 12, 1776; "Amicus Constitutionis," *New-York Journal*, Oct. 19, 1775.

30. Richard Price, *Additional Observations on the Nature and Value of Civil Liberty, and the War with America* (London, 1777), p. 8; and Price, *Observations on*

the Nature of Civil Liberty, the Principles of Government, and the Justice and Policy of the War with America (London, 1776), p. 12.

31. Hume, *Essays* 1:116-17.

32. Thus Hume worried during the Wilkesite disorders in London about the destruction of balanced government by an excess of liberty. "Our Government has become a Chimera; and is too perfect in point of Liberty, for so vile a Beast as an Englishman, who is a Man, a bad Animal too, corrupted by above a Century of Licentiousness." But the danger was, he realized, "that this Liberty can scarcely be retrench'd without Danger of being entirely lost." Hume to Gilbert Eliot, Feb. 21, 1770, in Greig, ed., *Letters of Hume* 2:216.

33. Ferguson, *Principles* 2:458-59; Burgh, *Political Disquisitions* 1:2.

34. Blackstone, *Commentaries* 1:250. Blackstone was here echoing the justification for magistracy laid down half a century earlier by Trenchard and Gordon. See *Cato's Letters* 2:245.

35. Yves R. Simon, *Philosophy of Democratic Government* (Chicago, 1951), p. 59.

36. Ferguson, *Principles* 2:463. One Hume scholar concluded that "rather than rely on the current vocabulary of class and its broad fluid conceptions of social division, Hume used the eighteenth-century terms of 'rank, distinction, and character' which connote a rather fixed and stable social order by placing individuals in definite ranks in the social hierarchy with fixed positions within the community." Stephen Wallech, "The Elements of Social Status in Hume's *Treatise,*" *Journal of the History of Ideas* 45 (1984): 207. See also Henry Home, Lord Kames, *Sketches of the History of Man*, 2d ed. (Glasgow, 1802), 2:221. The belief that man tended to organize his social and political relations in a hierarchical pattern was shared by many radicals, although they were anxious to assure that the distinctions between the ranks did not become too great. See Trenchard and Gordon, *Cato's Letters* 2:71. Even the eighteenth-century Commonwealthmen, Caroline Robbins noted, were not egalitarians, but rather accepted the inevitability of the hierarchical society in which they lived. See *Eighteenth-Century Commonwealthmen*, pp. 16, 90. On the continuity of this conviction among American political leaders, see J. R. Pole, *Political Representation in England and the Origins of the American Republic* (London, 1966), p. 342; Jeremy Belknap to Ebenezer Hazard, Mar. 3, 1784, *Belknap Papers*, Mass. Hist. Soc., *Collections*, 5th ser., 2:313-14. On the characteristics of English society, see Perkin, *Origins of Modern English Society*, pp. 24-26, 37-62.

37. Blackstone, *Commentaries* 1:271; Ferguson, *Principles* 2:463.

38. Benjamin Throop, *Religion and Loyalty, The Duty and Glory Of A People . . .* (New London, Conn., 1758), p. 17. See also Jonathan Mayhew, *Two Discourses Delivered November 23d 1758 . . .* (Boston, [1758]), p. 47; Tucker, *A Sermon*, p. 28; Samuel Cooke, *A Sermon Preached At Cambridge, In The Audience Of His Honor Thomas Hutchinson, Esq. . . .* (Boston, 1770), p. 12.

39. See, for example, [Richard Wells], *The Middle Line, or, An Attempt To Furnish Some Hints For Ending the Differences Subsisting Between Great-Britain and the Colonies* (Philadelphia, 1775), pp. 12-13, 25; [Silas Downer], *A Discourse Delivered in Providence, In the Colony of Rhode-Island, . . . At The Dedication of the Tree*

of Liberty . . . By a Son of Liberty (Providence, 1768), pp. 8, 15; "An Anxious By-Stander," *Pennsylvania Gazette* (Philadelphia), Jan. 4, 1775.

40. *New-York Gazette*, Oct. 3, 1774; William Smith, *A Sermon On The Present Situation Of American Affairs. Preached in Christ Church, June 23, 1775 . . .* (Philadelphia, 1775), p. 29; Alexander Hamilton, *The Farmer Refuted, or, A more impartial and comprehensive View of the Dispute between Great-Britain and the Colonies* (1775), in Syrett and Cooke, eds., *Papers of Hamilton* 1:98.

41. Hume, *Essays* 1:115.

42. Blackstone, *Commentaries* 1:246. See also Trenchard and Gordon, *Cato's Letters* 1:94. Another convention that helped to assure political stability was the king's constitutional immortality, which was expressed in the ritual language used to announce the death of a sovereign: "The king is dead, long live the king." For the origin of this convention, see Kantorowicz, *The King's Two Bodies*, pp. 13, 312–16.

43. "An Antiministerial Loyalist," *Boston-Gazette*, Aug. 24, 1774; [Richard Wells], *A Few Political Reflections Submitted To The Consideration Of The British Colonies, By A Citizen of Philadelphia* (Philadelphia, 1774), letter 3, p. 35.

44. John Carmichael, *A Self-Defensive War Lawful, Proved In A Sermon, Preached at Lancaster, before Captain Ross's Company of Militia . . .* (Lancaster, [1775]), p. 23. See below, Chapter 2.

45. Blackstone, *Commentaries* 4:127. The king's role as father of the national community was an ancient one that found perhaps its fullest expression and political significance in seventeenth-century England. See Gordon J. Schochet's thoughtful and significant study, *Patriarchalism in Political Thought: The Authoritarian Family and Political Speculation and Attitudes Especially in Seventeenth-Century England* (New York, 1975), and Jerrilyn G. Marston, "Gentry Honor and Royalism in Early Stuart England," *Journal of British Studies* 13 (1973): 21–43.

46. Mayhew, *A Discourse*, p. 7; "On Smuggling," Nov. 24, 1767, in Albert H. Smythe, ed., *The Writings of Benjamin Franklin* (New York, 1970; orig. publ. New York, 1905–7), 5:63.

47. [John Allen], *The American Alarm; or, The Bostonian Plea, For the Rights, and Liberties, of the People . . . By The British Bostonian* (Boston, 1773), king's address, p. 4.

48. As Michael Walzer has argued, a symbolic construct—for example, the "body politic" or the "imperial family"—is "a pervasive world-view, which cannot in its time be denied, though its parts can certainly be manipulated. Thus symbolic systems set (rough) limits to thought, supporting certain ideas, making others almost inconceivable." Walzer cautions, however, that "just as religious symbols need to be ritually acted out if they are fully to be felt, and just as the symbols change when the rituals do, so in the world of politics there is a continuous interaction between symbolic formation and enactment. . . . The king will not long be acknowledged as head or father, for example, if he fails convincingly to act out the parts, or if other actions become more significant in communal life than the rituals of headship or fatherhood." Michael

Walzer, "On the Role of Symbolism in Political Thought," *Political Science Quarterly* 82 (1967): 191–204, 195–96, 200. See also Burrows and Wallace, "Ideology and Psychology of National Liberation," pp. 270–74. They contend that "once a symbol has come into existence, it becomes a social datum with a life and coercive authority of its own" (p. 272). On the importance of symbolic constructs in maintaining authoritative government, see Friedrich, "The Political Myth, Its Symbols and Utopian Order," *Man and His Government*, pp. 94–105.

49. See Burrows and Wallace, "Ideology and Psychology of National Liberation." For Burrows and Wallace, the familial analogy

> enabled all parties to the controversy to struggle with a new and extraordinarily complex issue without losing their ideological bearings. Almost no one doubted that relations between England and the colonies were to be governed by mutual rights and responsibilities, but no one had ever before been obliged to work out the precise content of those rights and responsibilities. To argue that the empire was just like the natural family embedded in contractualist theory was not, in the context, to indulge in idle and empty rhetoric. It was, rather, to create a conceptual model or paradigm of the imperial bond that gave clear meaning to the flow of events and allowed men on all sides to find ideological justification for political action in the principles of natural law. For English Tories, Whigs, and radicals the correspondence between imperial and parental authority was indispensable for legitimizing their respective conclusions that the colonial "children" should be coerced into submission as unnatural ingrates, enticed back to obedience by a return to policies of leniency and affection, or given their independence for having at last come of age. For colonial Americans the same analogy provided the chief rationale for dependency by delineating a status in nature distinct from outright slavery. But while some ultimately saw in it a justification for inviting imperial repression, others exploited its flexibilities, first to assert their natural right of dissent and opposition to unjust authority, then to claim the higher right to break the imperial connection and achieve national autonomy. (pp. 250–51)

Winthrop Jordan has also argued that the familial metaphor had deep psychological importance for Americans, finding in this the tremendous liberating effect of Thomas Paine's *Common Sense*, which he views as a ritual killing of the father-king turned tyrant. See Winthrop Jordan's "Familial Politics: Thomas Paine and the Killing of the King, 1776," *Journal of American History* 60 (1973): 294–308.

50. Mercy Otis Warren to John Adams, Sept. 1785, in Ford, ed., *Warren-Adams Letters* 2:260. For the psychological importance of monarchical grandeur, see Ernest Jones, "The Psychology of Constitutional Monarchy," in *Essays in Applied Psychoanalysis* (London, 1951), 1:232; and Percy Black, *The Mystique of Monarchy* (London, 1953), pp. 25–26.

51. This description is compiled from accounts of the event published in *Rivington's New-York Gazetteer; or, The Connecticut, New-Jersey, Hudson's River and Quebec Weekly Advertiser*, Aug. 29, 1773; Purdie and Dixon's *Virginia Gazette*, July 15, 1773; and Rind's *Virginia Gazette*, Sept. 9, 1773.

52. Ferguson, *Principles* 2:487; Blackstone, *Commentaries* 1:241.

53. Unsigned letter, *Pennsylvania Gazette*, Mar. 8, 1775. See also Blackstone, who often referred to the king as "the representative of his people"; see, for example, *Commentaries* 1:252–53. The problem of who was entitled to represent the people preceded modern conceptions of "representative" government by centuries. As Hobbes, the first theorist to deal systematically with the concept of representation, noted, "Men who are in absolute liberty, may, . . . give Authority to One man, to represent them every one, as well as give Authority to any Assembly of men whatsoever." Thomas Hobbes, *Leviathan* (London, 1934; orig. publ. 1651), 2:19, 97. When this idea was coupled with the equally hallowed notion that legitimate kingship rested upon the actual or tacit election by the people, it becomes easier to understand the survival into the eighteenth century of the king's role as representative of the entire national community. On the king's election, see Kern, *Kingship and Law*, pp. 12, 25–26; Franklin Le V. Baumer, *The Early Tudor Theory of Kingship* (New Haven, Conn., 1940), p. 166; and for the use of the idea in the colonies, see Whitney, *Transgressions of a Land*, p. 20; and "Scipio," *Pennsylvania Journal*, Oct. 5, 1774.

Parliament's claim to represent the colonies "virtually" was a constitutionally advanced position, for by making such a claim the members claimed for themselves the king's traditional right to represent the entire nation. On the king's role as sovereign representative, see Louise F. Brown, "Ideas of Representation from Elizabeth to Charles II," *Journal of Modern History* 11 (1939): 23–40; Alfred De Grazia, *Public and Republic: Political Representation in America* (New York, 1951), pp. 15, 17; and Hannah Pitkin, *The Concept of Representation* (Berkeley, Calif., 1967), pp. 2, 23.

54. The king's legitimate authority rested on his theoretical ability to represent the common good rather than private or group interest. As a modern scholar notes, "The mantle of authority naturally falls, . . . on whatever serves to represent and uphold the public claim amid the strife of private interests." Charles W. Hendel, "An Exploration of the Nature of Authority," in Carl J. Friedrich, ed., *Authority*, Nosmos 1 (Cambridge, Mass., 1958), p. 9.

The king's role as imperial unifier was also symbolic and stemmed from his personification or embodiment of the nation as a whole. Walzer has explained the importance of the personification of a symbol of national unity: "In a sense, the union of men can only be symbolized; it has no palpable shape or substance. The state is invisible; it must be personified before it can be seen, symbolized before it can be loved, imagined before it can be conceived." "Symbolism," p. 194. See also Burrows and Wallace, "Ideology and Psychology of National Liberation," p. 271.

55. "America Solon," *Boston-Gazette*, May 18, 1774. The evocative "body politic" metaphor was still commonly used to convey the mutuality of interest between subject and prince. See, for example, Samuel Cooke, *A Sermon*

Preached At Cambridge . . . (Boston, 1770), p. 10; Allen, *American Alarm*, Governor's Address, p. 4.

56. Ferguson, *Principles* 2:487; Franklin, "Tract Relative to the Affair of Hutchinson's Letters," [1774], in William B. Willcox, ed., *The Papers of Benjamin Franklin* (New Haven, 1959–), 21:418; [James Wilson], *Considerations On The Nature And The Extent Of The Legislative Authority Of The British Parliament* (1774) in McCloskey, ed., *Works of Wilson* 2:745; Hamilton, *Farmer Refuted*, in Syrett and Cooke, eds., *Papers of Hamilton* 1:98–99.

57. "S.X.," *A Letter Concerning Prerogative* (Dublin, 1755), pp. 18–19; Wells, *Political Reflections*, letter 3, p. 40. The matter was stated authoritatively by Blackstone: "With regard to foreign concerns, the king is the delegate or representative of his people." The king was "a centre" in which "all the rays of his people are united." *Commentaries* 1:252.

58. [Richard Wells], *The Middle Line; Or, An Attempt To Furnish Some Hints For Ending the Differences Subsisting Between Great Britain and the Colonies* (Philadelphia, 1775), p. 34; "A Philadelphian," *Pennsylvania Gazette*, May 18, 1774.

59. On boundary disputes, see Chapter 8. On Tory expectations of disunity, see, for example, [Samuel Seabury], *The Congress Canvassed: or, An Examination Into the Conduct of the Delegates, At Their Grand Convention* . . . (New York, 1774), p. 26; Speech of Joseph Galloway (Notes of John Adams), Sept. 28, 1774 in Butterfield, ed., *Adams Papers* 2:141–44.

60. Trenchard and Gordon, *Cato's Letters* 2:245; Ferguson, *Principles* 2:484.

61. See note 23.

62. Blackstone, *Commentaries* 1:262; Hamilton, *Farmer Refuted*, in Syrett and Cooke, eds., *Papers of Hamilton* 1:91.

63. Jonathan Mayhew, *A Discourse Occasioned by the Death of King George II and the Happy Accession of his Majesty George III* . . . (Boston, 1761), p. 33. On Dettingen, see, for example, Samuel Cooper, *A Sermon Upon The Occasion of the Death of Our Late Sovereign, George the Second* (Boston, 1761), p. 31. On George III, see "Sketch of the mode of living observed by their Majesties during their summer residence at their Royal Palace at Kew," Dixon and Hunter's *Virginia Gazette*, Dec. 16, 1775; Wolfe is quoted in Charles E. Everett, ed., "Boyle's Journal of Occurrences in Boston, 1759–1778," *New England Historical and Genealogical Register* 84 (1930): 147.

64. See Chapter 2.

65. Cooper, *Sermon on George II*, p. 35; Thomas Foxcroft, *Grateful Reflections on the signal appearances of Divine Providence for Great Britain and its Colonies in America, which diffuse a general Joy* (Boston, 1760), p. 32.

66. James Duane, "Speech to the Committee on Rights," Sept. 8, 1775, in Smith, ed., *LDC* 1:52; Wells, *Political Reflections*, letter 1, p. 15; [Samuel Seabury], *Free Thoughts, On The Proceedings of The Continental Congress, Held at Philadelphia Sept. 5, 1775* . . . ([New York], 1774), p. 9. See also Speech of Joseph Galloway (Notes of John Adams) Sept. 28, 1774, in Butterfield, ed., *Adams Papers* 2:143–44.

67. On radical Whig assertions that original political power resided in the body of the people, see, for example, Hoadley, *Original and Institutional*, p.

168; and Burgh, *Political Disquisitions* 1:3. While members of Parliament were considered to be the popular element in the constitution, after 1689 there was an increasing tendency to resurrect the old concept of the king's election, and hence his similar dependence upon the people. See, for example, the assertion of "Old Friend" in 1773 "That the Rights of the Prince are the *Gift of the People.—*He can have no legal Prerogative but what *they* give him" (*Boston-Gazette,* February 8, 1773, 1:236).

68. Blackstone, *Commentaries* 1:249; Hume, *Essays* 1:124; Blackstone, *Commentaries* 1:236.

69. *Letter Concerning Prerogative,* p. 11; Judah Champion, *Christian And Civil Liberty And Freedom Considered And Recommended: A Sermon, Delivered Before The General Assembly . . .* (Hartford, Conn., 1776), p. 19; [Trenchard and Gordon], *Cato's Letters* 1:91. Locke defined prerogative in much the same way, as "*nothing but the power of doing public good without a rule*" (*Second Treatise,* p. 95). As Stourzh explained, "Sovereign power is by definition absolute. Yet since sovereign power is also by definition legitimate power, the use of power in arbitrary or illegitimate ways divests it of the quality of sovereignty. One of the biggest obstacles to our understanding of the political theory of the American Revolution has been the tendency to confuse absolute with arbitrary power." *Alexander Hamilton,* p. 22.

70. This is a vital, if vague, element of political legitimacy. Only when the sovereign king was finally replaced by what Sir Ernest Barker has termed "the sovereign constitution" were the ambiguities over the ultimate repository of sovereignty resolved. As Stourzh notes, the impact of any sovereign power depends upon the "title of legitimacy attached to it." In the United States only the Constitution, which embodied the sovereign power of the people and thus stood above individual legislators, could replace a system in which only acts receiving a royal assent achieved the status of law. Ernest Barker, *Traditions of Civility* (Cambridge, 1948), p. 341; Stourzh, *Alexander Hamilton,* pp. 60–61. On the speed with which the Constitution achieved its sovereign status, see Lance Banning, "Republican Ideology and the Triumph of the Constitution, 1789 to 1793," *WMQ,* 3d ser., 31 (1974): 167–88.

71. Throop, *Religion and Loyalty,* p. 25; Blackstone, *Commentaries* 1:271, 266.

72. Blackstone, *Commentaries* 1:270, 272.

73. Arthur Lee to Samuel Adams, June 1773, in Samuel Adams Papers, photostat, vol. 8, Library of Congress. See also Hamilton, *Farmer Refuted,* in Syrett and Cooke, eds., *Papers of Hamilton* 1:108–22.

74. "Obadiah," *New-York Journal,* Sept. 21, 1775.

75. See Caroline Robbins, "European Republicanism in the Century and a Half before 1776," in *The Development of a Revolutionary Mentality,* Library of Congress Symposia on the American Revolution (Washington, D.C., 1972), pp. 31–55.

76. David Hume to David Hume the Younger, Dec. 8, 1775, in Greig, ed., *Letters of Hume* 2:306; Hume, *Essays* 1:126; Trenchard and Gordon, *Cato's Letters* 3:159. See also Thomas Lynch, who told William Smith that he believed a republic was a form of government that "reads better than it looks. It is best in

Idea, bad in Experiment," Diary of William Smith, Feb. 4, 1776, cited in Smith, ed., *LDC* 3:199.

77. Trenchard and Gordon, *Cato's Letters* 2:192; Hume, *Essays* 1:126; "Diary of Josiah Quincy, Jun.," Aug. 27, 1765, Massachusetts Historical Society, *Proceedings*, 1st ser., 4 (1858–60): 50.

78. The tendency to cling to symbols of authority in the midst of revolutionary turmoil is one that radical patriots recognized and feared. As a modern scholar has explained the phenomenon: "People . . . naturally react through a kind of self preservation, towards anything that disrupts the familiar order and leaves them lost, helpless, and exposed. . . . Thus men look to authority as the saving power in their existence. This welcoming of authority as a means of salvation can happen . . . whenever people feel grave insecurity and the threat of the destruction of hearth and home" (Hendel, "Exploration of Authority," in Friedrich, ed., *Authority*, p. 9). For a similar analysis of the American situation in 1776, see Caesar Rodney to John Haslet (?), May 17, 1776, in George H. Ryden, ed., *Letters to and from Caesar Rodney, 1756–1784* (Philadelphia, 1933), pp. 79–80.

79. Elbridge Gerry to Boston Committee of Correspondence, June 4, 1775, in Elbridge Gerry Papers, box 1, Library of Congress; Whitney, *Transgressions of a Land*, p. 53; John Adams to Abigail Adams, July 3, 1776, in Butterfield, ed., *Adams Family Correspondence* 2:28.

80. "Hampden," Dixon and Hunter's *Virginia Gazette*, Apr. 20, 1776.

81. Caesar Rodney to John Haslet (?), May 17, 1776, in Ryden, ed., *Rodney Letters*, p. 80.

82. The classic explanation of the process by which Whig political theory was shaped into a republican ideology that was realized in new political institutions is Gordon Wood, *The Creation of the American Republic, 1776–1787*. On the process of political experimentation in the states, see Jackson Turner Main, *Political Parties before the Constitution* (New York, 1973), and the older study by Elisha P. Douglass, *Rebels and Democrats: The Struggle for Equal Political Rights and Majority Rule during the American Revolution* (Chapel Hill, N.C., 1955). For an excellent study of such a process in one colony, see R. A. Ryerson, *The Revolution Is Now Begun: The Radical Committees of Philadelphia, 1765–1776* (Philadelphia, 1978).

83. The most modern definition of "revolution" in the *Oxford English Dictionary* is "an instance of great change or alteration in affairs" or "a complete overthrow of the established government in any country or state by those who were previously subject to it." An older definition, now classified as rare or obsolete, is "the return or recurrence of a point or period in time." On the change in the definition of "revolution," which events first in America and then in France helped bring about, see J. H. Elliott, "Revolution and Continuity in Early Modern Europe," in Lawrence Kaplan, ed., *Revolutions: A Comparative Study* (New York, 1973), p. 56.

84. These men may have more in common with premodern than with modern revolutionaries, which renders them particularly inaccessible to historians. As Elliot asks, "how far can historians accustomed to look for *innovation*

among revolutionaries, enter into the minds of men who themselves were ob-
sessed by *renovation*—by the desire to return to old customs and privileges,
and to an old order of society?" "Revolution and Continuity," p. 60.

Chapter 2

1. For an account of the Howe peace mission of 1776, see Chapter 7.

2. Speech of Gouverneur Morris [May 1776], in Jared Sparks, *The Life of Gouverneur Morris, With Selections From His Correspondence And Miscellaneous Papers
. . .* (Boston, 1832), 1:106–7.

3. There are problems in chronology in asserting that many Americans in
1774 still remained attached to the king. Some, of course, did not. For the disaffected, the events of the late 1760s and early 1770s had effectively ended the
affectionate tie between subject and sovereign, although it had not as yet
ended the formal obligation of allegiance (see note 7). It is the contention of
this chapter, however, that habits of loyalty and affection were not easily broken, and moreover, that the colonists' constitutional position forced many of
them to subordinate their suspicions about the king's intentions to their desire
to remain within the empire.

4. Wolcott to Samuel Lyman, May 16, 1776, in Smith, ed., *LDC* 4:17. As Arthur Lee declared in his introduction to Thomas Jefferson's 1774 pamphlet *A
Summary View*, the colonists' submission to the king was so habitual that it
could not "easily be dispensed with." "Do them but *justice*," he pleaded with
the king, and Americans would "esteem it an *act of Grace*"; "To the King,"
[Thomas Jefferson], *A Summary View Of The Rights of British America. Set Forth
In Some Resolutions Intended For The Inspection Of The Present Delegates Of The People Of Virginia. Now In Convention . . .* (Williamsburg, [1774]), p. xv. Jefferson's
annotated copy with Lee's introduction is in the Rare Book Room of the Library of Congress. It is reprinted without introduction in Julian P. Boyd et al.,
eds., *The Papers of Thomas Jefferson* (Princeton, 1950–), 1:121–37.

5. For a sympathetic account of George III's education and abilities, see John
Brooke, *King George III* (New York, 1972), pp. 26–72; see also Stanley Ayling,
George the Third (London, 1972), pp. 27–54.

6. See, for example, *Pietas et Gratulatio Collegii Cantabrigiensis Apud Novanglos*
(Boston, 1761), a collection of extravagant tributes to the new king written by
students at Harvard. See also the sermons preached on the occasion, as, for
example, Mayhew, *A Discourse Occasioned By The Death of King George II*. In general, see William Liddle, " 'A Patriot King, or None': American Public Attitudes toward George III and the British Monarchy, 1754–1776" (Ph.D. diss.,
Claremont Graduate School, 1970).

7. On the close relationship between American radicals and the English
Whig opposition to George III, see Maier, *From Resistance to Revolution*, pp.
163–227; John Sainsbury, "The Pro-American Movement in London, 1769–
1782," *WMQ*, 3d ser., 35 (1978): 423. As Maier notes, the movement reached a
peak during the extended Wilkes affair, during which Americans petitioned

the king as often and as enthusiastically as did their English colleagues. The king's cold response to the petitions, she concludes, implicated the king in a conspiracy that in colonial minds had previously included only corrupt ministers and legislators. For early denunciations of the king, see, for example, "An American," *Boston Gazette*, Dec. 16, 1771; Allen, *American Alarm*, p. 19; "RULES for KINGS," Rind's *Virginia Gazette*, Jan. 21, 1773. On the Wilkes petition movement, see Pauline Maier, "John Wilkes and American Disillusionment with Britain," *WMQ*, 3d ser., 20 (1963): 373–95. On the basis of a survey of the colonial press, however, Liddle discounts the influence of the Wilkes affair in increasing colonial enmity towards the king. He concludes that "there was no significant colonial indictment of the king in the crimes of the ministry during the years 1767–1773." Liddle, "Patriot King," *JAH* 65: 962–63. According to Shaw, "despite overwhelming evidence of George III's complicity in policies that were driving them toward revolution, Americans of all classes on the patriot side sustained their loyalty to the king throughout the period from 1760 to 1776" (*Rituals of Revolution*, p. 14). Darrett Rutman, "George III: The Myth of a Tyrannical King," in Nicholas Cords and Patrick Gerster, eds., *Myth and the American Experience*, 2nd ed. (New York, 1978), pp. 94–98. Rutman contends that through the crises of the 1770s, all evidence suggests the sincerity of the colonists' professions of loyalty.

8. Although vicious diatribes against the king were often published in the English opposition press and republished in American Whig newspapers, Americans did not begin to match the level of English invective until very late in 1775 and did not vilify him with regularity until after the publication of *Common Sense* in January 1776. See note 21.

9. Stourzh, *Alexander Hamilton*, pp. 40–41.

10. Franklin to William Franklin, Oct. 6, 1773, in Willcox, ed., *Papers of Franklin* 20:437. Such positions had been hinted at as soon as Americans began to deny the legislative authority of the British Parliament; see Richard Bland, *An Inquiry Into The Rights Of The British Colonies . . .* (Williamsburg, 1766), pp. 20–21.

11. Wilson, *Considerations on the Authority of Parliament*, in McCloskey, ed., *Works of Wilson* 2:742–45. Galloway ridiculed such attempts to deny the legislative authority of Parliament. "The Charters of Settlement have all been granted . . . under the Authority of the *Great Seal* and by the subsequent Kings in their Politic, not private Capacity, and as the Sovereign Representative of the politic Body of the whole State. . . . There is no Exemption in any of them, save one, . . . from the Legislative Authority of the Parliament: and had there been such an Exemption in all of them it would have been an Excess of the Royal Authority & void." Joseph Galloway to Samuel Verplanck(?), Dec. 30, 1774, in Smith, ed., *LDC* 1:286–87.

12. Hamilton, *Farmer Refuted*, in Syrett and Cooke, eds., *Papers of Hamilton* 1:90–91, 99. The theme was also central to Jefferson's *Summary View* and to John Dickinson, *An Essay On The Constitutional Power Of Great-Britain Over The Colonies In America . . .* (Printed in Philadelphia, reprinted in London, 1774), pp. 93–95.

13. "To the Parliament of Virginia," *New-York Journal*, Nov. 4, 1773.

14. [Moses Mather], *America's Appeal To The Imperial World . . .* (Hartford, Conn., 1775), p. 20; *Pennsylvania Gazette*, Jan. 4, 1775. See also "Americanus," *New-York Journal*, Dec. 16, 1773; Downer, *Discourse-Liberty Tree*, p. 3; Allen, *American Alarm*, p. 14. One scholar has suggested that the model of imperial government developed here—that is, one in which legitimate imperial authority was defined by the king's prerogative powers—helped to shape American conceptions regarding the legitimate functions of their new continental government. See Peter S. Onuf, *Origins of the Federal Republic*, p. 16.

15. In this chapter, the terms "radical," "moderate," and "conservative" are defined entirely in terms of the imperial crisis. The focus of the chapter is on England, not the colonies, and thus the following general definition will suffice. On the colonial side, radicals were those who, after the passage of the Coercive Acts, had abandoned any hope that either the king *or* Parliament could resolve the crisis peacefully and who distrusted the king and his ministers and did not distinguish between them. They generally distrusted and opposed efforts toward reconciliation (for example, the 1774 petition to the king), and they supported steps toward military preparedness. Moderates were those who did distinguish between the king and Parliament and between the king and his ministers. They blamed the latter for the Coercive Acts, which they abhorred. They supported most measures of Congress, including the Continental Association of 1774 but were enthusiastic supporters of reconciliation attempts like the 1774 petition, and they appeared to believe such efforts had a chance of success. In return for a real reconciliation, some were prepared, of necessity, to accept parliamentary sovereignty over colonial trade, but they refused any further acknowledgment of the authority of Parliament over the colonies. Conservatives were those who opposed the Coercive Acts and supported many measures of Congress; in this they may be distinguished from Tories. They saw no alternative to parliamentary sovereignty over colonial trade, and because of this, they saw no possibility that the colonies might prosper outside the British empire. They were fearful of colonial disunion and suspected "radical" New Englanders of creating a crisis in order to further a scheme of independence.

On the English side the definitions are simpler, for virtually no one distinguished between the king's authority over the colonies and that of Parliament. Instead, British radicals are those who believed from 1774 that the Americans were right to resist the authority of a corrupt Parliament and viewed Americans as the true defenders of English liberty. They were part of a tiny minority in England who opposed the Coercive Acts. Richard Price is a good example of this group of "pro-Americans." (See John Sainsbury, "Pro-American Movement in London," and Bernard Donoughue, *British Politics and the American Revolution* [London, 1964], pp. 146–61.) Moderates were those who thought the Americans were wrong to resist the authority of Parliament but who favored all attempts at reconciliation and opposed coercive measures. The archetype moderate within the cabinet was Lord Dartmouth. See Donoughue, *British Politics*, p. 38. Outside of the government, this group included men like

David Hume, who believed coercion to be futile and American independence to be all but inevitable. Conservatives were those who thought, on the contrary, that the only alternative to an independent America was an America subordinate to the authority of Parliament, and they believed coercion was the only effective means of bringing about American submission. In the cabinet, Lord Suffolk exemplifies this view, as, indeed, does the king.

16. Speech of Lord North, Oct. 26, 1775, in Thomas C. Hansard, ed., *The Parliamentary History of England: From the Earliest Period to the Year 1803* (London, 1806–20), 18:771; Report from London, March 10, 1774, *South-Carolina and American General Gazette* (Charleston), May 20–27, 1774.

17. On the continuing desire for reconciliation, see the anxious anticipation of the arrival of the 1776 peace commissioners described in Chapter 7. The American theorists were in fact arguing for a form of the "responsible government" later outlined in the famous Durham Report on Canada in 1839. This became the basis for the present British Commonwealth. On the Canadian solution to the problems of imperial federalism, see Nicholas Mansergh, *The Commonwealth Experience* (London, 1969), pp. 30–58; Chester New, *Lord Durham's Mission to Canada* (Ottawa, 1963); and the report itself in C. P. Lucas, ed., *Lord Durham's Report on the Affairs of British North America*, vols. 2 and 3 (Oxford, 1912).

18. Stourzh, *Alexander Hamilton*, p. 28. But, as Darrett Rutman writes, "the king would not accept the role assigned to him by the colonists. He would not be their father and protector. . . . In the situation, the position of the colonists was somewhat unique and certainly difficult. The king was the only link to England and empire which they were prepared by this time to admit, yet the king refused to serve as such a link. As a consequence this last link had to be severed." Rutman, "Myth of a Tyrannical King," p. 99.

The account of the events in England that follows is written from a colonial perspective, for its purpose is to trace American disillusionment with the king during the final years of the crisis. As such, it portrays the king in a far more malevolent light than is fair or true, because that is the light in which Americans came to view him. Although some attempt is made to explain how a combination of the king's personality, his political perceptions, and events led him to take the actions that the colonists abhorred, one may not contend that this is a neutral portrait. The best, and most balanced, account of George III's personality and reign is in Brooke, *King George III*.

19. King's Speech, Jan. 13, 1774, in Hansard, ed., *Parliamentary History* 17:932–40. The most complete account of the crisis engendered by the Tea Act, considered from the English viewpoint, is Donoughue, *British Politics*, upon which the following account draws heavily.

20. Alan Valentine, *Lord North* (Norman, Okla., 1967), 1:313–15; Lord Dartmouth to General Frederick Haldimand, Feb. 5, 1774, Haldimand Papers, Additional Manuscripts, vol. 21695, fol. 68, British Museum. See also Thomas Gage to Thomas Hutchinson, Feb. 2, 1774, Hutchinson Papers, Egerton Manuscripts, vol. 2659, fol. 69, British Museum; and George III to Lord North, Feb. 4, 1774, in Sir John Fortescue, ed., *The Correspondence of King George the Third*

from 1760 to December 1783 (London, 1928), 3:59. As the king's most sympathetic biographer writes, George III "could conceive of no middle way for the colonies between independence and unconditional submission. He saw politics as an extension of morals and always in terms of black and white." Brooke, *King George III*, p. 175.

21. See, for example, the author in the *St. James Chronicle* who "looked upon all the Kings of England," and commented that they made "a choice collection" of "weak, wicked, cruel, and worthless wretches" (reprinted in the *Boston Gazette*, Sept. 18, 1775). Another scribe, this time in the *London Chronicle* traced George III's ancestry back to William the Conqueror, who, he noted pointedly, was "a ——— SON OF A WHORE" (reprinted in the *Massachusetts Spy*, May 5, 1774). The most famous English attacks on the king came from the pens of "Junius," "The Scourge," and the author of "The Crisis" series, all reprinted in American newspapers through the early 1770s. Rarely did American authors match these English authors in invective; see Jordan, "Familial Politics," p. 295 n. 3; and Liddle, "Patriot King," *JAH* 65:962–63.

22. B. Franklin to William Franklin, July 14, 1773, in Willcox, ed., *Papers of Franklin* 20:308; Izard to Edward Rutledge, Nov. 15, 1774, in Anne I. Deas, ed., *Correspondence of Mr. Ralph Izard, of South Carolina, From the Year 1774 to 1804; With A Short Memoir* (New York, 1844), 1:29. See also Arthur Lee to S. Adams, June 11, 1773, S. Adams Papers, vol. 8. Lee, author of the "Junius Americanus" letters, was deeply involved in English opposition politics, and his attacks on the king resembled those of his English colleagues. See A. R. Riggs, "Arthur Lee, a Radical Virginian in London, 1768–1776," *Virginia Magazine of History and Biography* 78 (1970): 268–80.

23. I have studied 108 town, county and provincial resolutions written during the period of greatest resentment to British coercive measures. Of these, 62 still begin with a ritual statement of loyalty to George III. See Appendix a.

24. "As for courage," writes Ayling, "for George III it represented the most important of all virtues," *George the Third*, p. 179. See also Brooke, *King George III*, pp. 56–66, 260–62. On the darker side of the king's character, see Frank A. Mumby, *George III and the American Revolution*, vol. 1 (London, 1923). See also Donoughue, *British Politics*, p. 43: "George III was an inflexible and priggish man, who frequently mistook obstinacy for courage. As a monarch he was extremely conscious of the dignity of Crown and Parliament, and of the delicate balance of legislative and executive powers in the British Constitution. He was also completely certain that by the Constitution the American Colonies were subordinate, and he believed it was his duty to maintain that subordination."

25. Brooke, *King George III*, pp. 175–76; George III to Lord North, Sept. 10, 1775, in John Fortescue, ed., *The Correspondence of King George the Third From 1760 to 1783* (London, 1927–28), 3:1709.

26. Brooke, *King George III*, pp. 171–72. Lord Germain told his Undersecretary, William Knox, that the king had told him he reproached himself only for one action he had taken during his life—that of changing his ministers in 1766 and consenting to the repeal of the Stamp Act. Cited in Donoughue, *British Politics*, p. 43 n. 1.

27. George III to Lord North, July 1, 1774, in Fortescue, ed., *Correspondence of George III* 3:116; Hutchinson's account of his interview with the king is in his diary under the date of July 1 and in a letter to Thomas Gage, July 4, 1774, in Peter O. Hutchinson, ed., *The Diary and Letters of His Excellency Thomas Hutchinson, Esq. . . .* (Boston, 1884), 1:157–75, 175–76. See also Bernard Bailyn, *The Ordeal of Thomas Hutchinson* (Cambridge, Mass., 1974), pp. 277–78. The original of the diary, after being accurately copied by Peter Hutchinson, was deposited in the British Museum, Egerton MSS, vol. 2662. Hutchinson's letterbook for this period, which Peter Hutchinson excerpted, is in the same depository; Egerton MSS, vol. 2661. Donoughue notes that "assuming that Hutchinson and the king were honest in their reporting, it does seem that there was a basic misunderstanding of what Hutchinson actually said." *British Politics*, p. 163.

28. George III to Lord North, May 6, Sept. 11, 1774, Mar. 6, 1775, in Fortescue, ed., *Correspondence of George III* 3:104, 131, 184.

29. Hutchinson to Jacob Green, Aug. 27, 1774, in Hutchinson, ed., *Diary and Letters of Hutchinson* 1:230. See also Hutchinson to Thomas Hutchinson, Jr., July 6, 1774, and Hutchinson to Mr. Lee, Aug. 2, 1774, Hutchinson Letterbook, Egerton, MSS, vol. 2661, fols. 30, 40. As Donoughue notes, while differences over American policy sharply divided the cabinet, "in the early months, after the news of the Tea Party, they were completely blurred by the indignation which everyone felt. All were united in accepting the legality of an undivided British sovereignty over the Colonies." *British Politics*, p. 71. Hutchinson's diary and letters during the period after his arrival in England on June 29, 1774, and prior to Bunker Hill provide exceptionally good sources for divining ministerial intentions toward America. As a respected former governor with intimate knowledge of Massachusetts, most members of the government continually sought his advice and informed him of cabinet discussions. This information he diligently conveyed to correspondents in Massachusetts and to his diary. After Bunker Hill, when government interest shifted away from colonial politics and toward military matters, both his influence and his access to information declined.

30. It is interesting (and ironic) to note that the cabinet's first response to the crisis was to deal with it exclusively through executive action—for example, by directing Governor Hutchinson to move the capital from Boston. Only after considering the political effect of such a course—it "might have raised the ghost of prerogative to haunt the sleep of English Whigs"—did the cabinet resolve to seek legislation. On the development of a wholly executive plan to deal with the crisis, see Donoughue, *British Politics*, pp. 51–64. On the development of the plan as presented to Parliament, see ibid., pp. 66–71.

31. Lord Dartmouth to Hutchinson, Mar. 9, 1774 (marked "Secret & Confidential"), copy, Haldimand Papers, Additional MSS, vol. 21695, fol. 84. The entire administration program for coercing Boston was foreshadowed in the king's speech; see Hansard, ed., *Parliamentary History* 17:1159.

32. George III to Lord North, May 6, 1774, in Fortescue, ed., *Correspondence of George III* 3:104. On the development of the legislation, see Donoughue, *Brit-*

ish Politics, pp. 73–126; Ian R. Christie and Benjamin W. Labaree, *Empire or Independence* (New York, 1976), pp. 183–96.

33. The ministry sent the text of the acts to Gage almost immediately. They were dispatched on June 3. Donoughue, *British Politics,* p. 102. See below, Chapter 3, and David Ammerman, *In the Common Cause: American Response to the Coercive Acts of 1774* (Charlottesville, Va., 1974), pp. 19–34.

34. Josiah Quincy, Jr., *Observations On The Act of Parliament Commonly Called The Boston Port-Bill; With Thoughts On Civil Society and Standing Armies . . .* (Boston, 1774), p. 11.

35. "A Scotchman," Purdie and Dixon's *Virginia Gazette,* Oct. 11, 1774; "Phocian," Rind's *Virginia Gazette,* Sept. 15, 1774.

36. On British expectations that their coercive measures would be effective, see Donoughue, *British Politics,* pp. 163, 167–68, 175–76.

37. The Congress met from September 5 through October 26, 1774. See Chapters 3 and 4.

38. George III to Lord North, Nov. 18, 1774, in Fortescue, ed., *Correspondence of George III* 3:154; Hutchinson to Samuel Quincy, Nov. 1, 1774, Hutchinson letterbook, Egerton MSS, vol. 2661, fol. 73.

39. Hutchinson, ed., *Diary and Letters of Hutchinson* 1:232. Donoughue, *British Politics,* pp. 172–73. Dartmouth's attitude toward Congress was expressed in a letter to Lord Hardwicke on Aug. 29, 1774:

> Such a meeting is undoubtedly illegal but as it has been adopted with too much precipitation to be prevented . . . and will certainly take place, I am not without hopes that some good may arise out of it, and illegal as it is, if it should chalk out any reasonable tone of accommodation, or make any moderate or temperate proposal, I should in my own private opinion think it wise in government to overlook the irregularity of the proceedings, and catch at the opportunity of putting our unhappy differences into some mode of discussion that might save those disagreeable consequences which must arise to everyone of us either from open rupture and hostility with our fellow subjects, or from the no less calamitous interruption of our commercial intercourse with them.

Dartmouth to Hardwicke, Aug. 29, 1774. Additional MSS, vol. 35612, fol. 43. See also Christie and Labaree, *Empire or Independence,* pp. 214–34.

40. Oct. 28, 1774, Hutchinson, ed., *Diary and Letters of Hutchinson* 1:272. On October 2, 1774, General Gage's dispatches, written on June 26, 1774, arrived in England, and they described the heated colonial reaction to the Port Bill; Donoughue, *British Politics,* pp. 168–69. On congressional approval of the Suffolk Resolves, see below, Chapter 3.

41. See Chapter 3.

42. Haldimand to Lord Barrington, Sept. [Oct.] 5, 1774, Haldimand Papers, Additional MSS, vol. 21696, fol. 118. See also Thomas Ramsden to Charles Jenkinson, Nov. 2, 1774, Liverpool Papers, Additional MSS, vol. 38208, fol. 111.

43. Nov. 1, 1774; Hutchinson to ?, Nov. [1–2], 1774, in Hutchinson, ed., *Diary and Letters of Hutchinson* 1:273, 284. This seems an appropriate point to

briefly describe the men who comprised the cabinet during the critical period. The Cabinet consisted of seven members who regularly met and decided on American policy. As Donoughue describes them (pp. 36–44), they were: Frederick, Lord North, First Lord of the Treasury and Chancellor of the Exchequer, who presided over the cabinet but who was not yet a true prime minister in the modern sense of the term. He was by temperament inclined to the moderate position, as defined above, and as exemplified by his stepbrother, William Legge, Earl Dartmouth, Secretary for the American Department until November 1775, when he resigned to become Lord Privy Seal. Dartmouth was a correspondent of American leaders like Benjamin Franklin and Joseph Reed. North was forced, however, to conciliate the powerful "hawkish" members of the faction led, until his death in 1771, by John Russell, fourth duke of Bedford. Another "hawk" was John Montague, fourth earl of Sandwich, First Lord of the Admiralty, who was a notorious libertine but an efficient naval administrator. Also counted among the Bedfordites was Granville Leveson-Gower, second Earl Gower, later Marquis of Stafford, Lord President of the Council. An old adherent of Lord Grenville, who by the 1770s was (not surprisingly) a supporter of coercion, was Henry Howard, twelfth earl of Suffolk, Secretary of State for the Northern Department. Also supporting coercion was William Zuylestein, fourth earl of Rochford, Secretary of State for the Southern Department. He resigned from the cabinet in the fall of 1775. Last, and definitely least, was Henry Bathurst, Baron Apsley, of whom Donoughue has written "politically he was a nonentity."

As Donoughue describes their relative positions: "Suffolk, Gower and Sandwich were then the most aggressive coercionists in the Cabinet, and in the Closet they were more than matched by the king. Dartmouth and North were more moderate, and they held crucial ministerial posts, but neither had the courage to insist on a policy against the wishes of their royal master and their Cabinet colleagues. . . . The remaining two ministers, Rochford and Apsley, were of no great political consequence and were happy to go along with the punitive policy." Donoughue, *British Politics*, pp. 44–45. The cabinet personnel are described on pp. 36–44. See also his description of the subordinates of these ministers, who played important policy-making roles (pp. 45–46).

44. George III to Lord North, Nov. 18, 1774; "Memoranda by the King," [1774, wrongly dated ?1773 by Fortescue], in Fortescue, ed., *Correspondence of George III* 3:153, 48. As Donoughue notes, "The King was almost relieved that the die was cast. . . . George III had never appreciated the refinements of constitutional wrangles. His mind was simple and puritanical. Those who were not for him were against him; and the sooner the people made up their minds the happier was the king. . . . the king almost welcomed the prospect of a decision by blows. It was a form of contest which he understood and which he felt that England was certain to win." *British Politics*, p. 221.

45. By December 12 the latest American newspapers to have reached London were those of October 17. See Hutchinson Diary, Dec. 12, 1774, Hutchinson, ed., *Diary and Letters of Hutchinson* 1:323. On the election, see Don-

oughue, *British Politics*, pp. 177–200. It should be noted that Donoughue cautions against drawing too much significance regarding national policies from the election results, since in the 1774 elections, as in all Parliamentary elections, many results turned on purely local issues. See also Valentine, *Lord North* 1:333–38. On the king's personal interest, see, for example, Fortescue, ed., *Correspondence of George III* 3:125–26, 132–47.

46. Nov. 10, Dec. 14, 1774, Hutchinson, ed., *Diary and Letters of Hutchinson* 1:291–92, 324.

47. The proceedings of the Congress arrived on December 13, and the petition was not included in them. See Dec. 13, 21, 1774, ibid., 323, 329.

48. King's Speech, in Hansard, ed., *Parliamentary History* 18:34; Hutchinson to Mr. Turall, Dec. 10, 1774, Hutchinson Letterbook, Egerton MSS, vol. 2661, fol. 89.

49. Abigail Adams to Mercy Warren, [Feb. 3? 1775], in Butterfield, ed., *Adams Family Correspondence* 1:183.

50. Jan. 25, 1775; and Hutchinson to Thomas Flucker, Jan. 20, 1775, in Hutchinson, ed., *Diary and Letters of Hutchinson* 1:363, 359; Hutchinson to I. Pemberton, [Dec. 1774], and to Robert Auchmuty, Feb. 14, 1775, Hutchinson Letterbook, Egerton MSS, vol. 2661, fols. 92, 120.

51. Administration activity during the winter and early spring of 1775 is recorded in Donoughue, *British Politics*, pp. 219–65. See also Valentine, *Lord North* 1:349–61; Ammerman, *Common Cause*, pp. 125–38.

52. Hutchinson to ?, Feb. 1775, Hutchinson Letterbook, Egerton MSS, vol. 2661, fol. 124. David Hartley, an opposition member of Parliament, accurately foretold American reaction to the proposal. "To say, Give me as much money as I wish, till I say enough, or I will take it from you, and then to call such a proposition conciliatory for peace, is insult added to oppression." Feb. 27, 1775, in Hansard, ed., *Parliamentary History* 18:350. On the fate of the two plans for reconciliation offered by Lord Chatham and Edmund Burke, see Donoughue, *British Politics*, pp. 255–64, 232–38.

53. Sept. 21, 1774, Hutchinson, ed., *Diary and Letters of Hutchinson* 1:256. See also Hutchinson to Mr. Lee, Sept. [20–29], 1774 (not sent), Hutchinson Letterbook, Egerton MSS, vol. 2661, fol. 54. It is clear that the king had also concluded that a British blockade would be one proper response to the colonial embargo. See "Memoranda by the King" [1774], in Fortescue, ed., *Correspondence of George III* 3:48.

54. Donoughue, *British Politics*, pp. 223–30; Valentine, *Lord North* 1:354–55.

55. Hansard, ed., *Parliamentary History* 18:298–300, 411. Gage's specific orders were to use his forces to secure the countryside surrounding Boston. He was ordered to "arrest and imprison the principal actors & abettors in the [Massachusetts] Provincial Congress." See Clarence E. Carter, ed., *The Correspondence of General Thomas Gage with the Secretaries of State, and with the War Office and the Treasury, 1763–1775* (New Haven, Conn., 1931–33), 2:179–83. Lord Dartmouth's orders arrived in Boston on April 14, 1775, scarcely a week before the battles of Lexington and Concord. The connection between the ministry decisions in January and the beginning of the war is clear. See John R. Alden,

General Gage in America: Being Principally a History of His Role in the American Revolution (Baton Rouge, La., 1948), pp. 233–44. On the progress of the administration plan through Parliament, see Donoughue, *British Politics*, pp. 231–65. The "Message for an Augmentation of the Forces," Feb. 10, 1775, is in Hansard, ed., *Parliamentary History* 18:298.

56. Hutchinson to Robert Auchmuty, Feb. 14, 1775; and to Mr. Clarke, Mar. 4, 1775, Hutchinson Letterbook, Egerton MSS, vol. 2661, fols. 120, 128; Mar. 29, 1775, Hutchinson, ed., *Diary and Letters of Hutchinson* 1:419; George III to Lord North, Nov. 18, 1774, in Fortescue, ed., *Correspondence of George III* 3:153.

57. See, for example, his speech to Parliament, Nov. 30, 1774, in Hansard, ed., *Parliamentary History* 18:33–34; his contemptuous rejection of a City of London petition praying for a change in the administration's American policy, in Peter Force, ed., *American Archives: Consisting Of A Collection of Authentick Records, State Papers, Debates, And Letters And Other Notices of Publick Affairs, The Whole Forming A Documentary History Of The Origin And Progress Of The North American Colonies; Of The Causes And Accomplishment Of The American Revolution . . .* , 4th ser. (Washington, D.C., 1837–53), 1:1853–56; Jefferson to William Small, May 7, 1775, in Boyd, ed., *Jefferson Papers* 1:165.

58. Samuel Stillman to Patience Wright, Nov. 13, 1774, in "Letters to Josiah Quincy, Jr.," Mass. Hist. Soc., *Proceedings* 50 (1916–17): 475. See also Samuel Ward to John Dickinson, Dec. 14, 1774, Logan Branch, Philadelphia Free Library. One must remember that, concurrent with reports of the king's malevolence, Americans were still receiving dispatches from England that supported the idea that the ministers, not the monarch, were responsible for the coercive measures. See, for example, "Extract of a Letter from a Gentleman in London to his friend in Virginia," July 1, 1775, in Force, ed., *American Archives*, 4th ser., 2:1518.

59. Dr. John Jones to John Dickinson, Oct. 15, 1774, John Dickinson Papers, item 25-2, Library Company of Philadelphia; Arthur Lee to Izard, Feb. 19, 1775, in Deas, ed., *Correspondence of Izard* 1:48.

60. For the genesis of the mutual atrocity stories, see Don Higginbotham, *The War of American Independence: Military Attitudes, Policies, and Practices, 1763– 1789* (New York, 1971), pp. 62–63. For examples of the charges against the British, see William Lincoln, ed., *Journal of Each Provincial Congress of Massachusetts in 1774 and 1775, And of the Committee of Safety* (Boston, 1858), pp. 661–94; John Winthrop to Richard Price, June 30, 1775, in *Letters to and From Richard Price* (Cambridge, Mass., 1903), p. 33.

61. Matthew Patten, *The Diary of Matthew Patten of Bedford, N.H., from Seventeen Hundred Fifty-four to Seventeen Hundred Eighty-eight* (Concord, N.H., 1903), p. 361.

62. It is not surprising that the Congress, for policy reasons, continued to distinguish between the king and the British troops, who were described as agents of the ministry. See, for example, Jefferson and Dickinson's Declaration of the Causes of Taking Up Arms, July 6, 1775, in *JCC* 2:128–57. It is more of a sign of how habitual was the practice of shielding the king that people like George Washington and Abigail Adams continued to use the phrase "minis-

terial army" in private correspondence. See, for example, Washington to George W. Fairfax, May 31, 1775, in John C. Fitzpatrick, ed., *The Writings of George Washington . . .* (Washington, D.C., 1931–44), 3:291; Abigail Adams to John Adams, Mar. 16, 1776, in Butterfield, ed., *Adams Family Correspondence* 1:357.

63. The official was Charles Jenkinson; May 10, 1775, Hutchinson, ed., *Diary and Letters of Hutchinson* 1:441; Hutchinson to Foster Hutchinson, May 25, 1775, Hutchinson Letterbook, Egerton MSS, vol. 2661, fol. 153.

64. Hutchinson to Thomas Hutchinson, Jr., May 31, 1775, in Hutchinson, ed., *Diary and Letters of Hutchinson* 1:456.

65. June 10, 1775, ibid. 1:466.

66. Edward Gibbon to J. B. Holroyd, June 17, 1775, in J. E. Norton, ed., *The Letters of Edward Gibbon* (London, 1956), 2:75; June 19, 1775, Hutchinson, ed., *Diary and Letters of Hutchinson* 2:472; [Suffolk] to William Eden, June 20, 1775, Auckland Papers, Additional MSS, vol. 34412, fol. 339.

67. George III to Lord North, July 5, 1775, in Fortescue, ed., *Correspondence of George III* 3:233. For the cabinet's reaction to the news of the battles of Lexington and Concord, see Valentine, *Lord North* 1:367–80.

68. George III to Lord North, July 26, 1775; Lord North to George III, July 26, [1775], in Fortescue, ed., *Correspondence of George III* 3:235, 234; Hutchinson to Thomas Hutchinson, Jr., July 26, 1775, Hutchinson, ed., *Diary and Letters of Hutchinson* 1:503. The effect of Bunker Hill upon British military strategy is discussed by John Shy, "The American Revolution: The Military Conflict Considered as a Revolutionary War," in *Essays on the American Revolution*, pp. 129–33.

69. Gibbon to J. B. Holroyd, Aug. 1, 1775, in Norton, ed., *Letters of Gibbon* 2:82. See Rodney Atwood, *The Hessians: Mercenaries from Hessen-Kassel in the American Revolution* (Cambridge, Eng., 1980), pp. 23–24.

70. Capt. Francis Hutcheson to Haldimand, Oct. 7, 1775; Haldimand to Lord Harrington, Sept. [Oct.] 5, 1774, Haldimand Papers, Additional MSS, vol. 21680, fol. 34, and vol. 21696, fol. 199. The policy was also suggested by a knowledgeable American. See Jonathan Sewall to [Haldimand], May 30, 1775 (copy), ibid., vol. 21695, fol. 122. The Secretary of War, Lord Barrington, was convinced that he would be unable to raise the 20,000 troops thought necessary to prosecute a land war and favored a wholly naval strategy; Donoughue, *British Politics*, p. 277. The naval strategy that was followed, however, was to use the fleet to support the land forces, and this entailed operations that increased American enmity towards Britain. See discussion below.

71. Lord Dartmouth to Haldimand, Apr. 15, 1775, Haldimand Papers, Additional MSS, vol. 21695, fol. 68.

72. Lord Suffolk to Eden, July 30, 1775, Auckland Papers, Additional MSS, vol. 34412, fol. 243. The most complete accounts of British efforts to engage German and Russian troops are in Atwood, *The Hessians*, pp. 22–57; and in Nikolai N. Bolkhovitinov, *Russia and the American Revolution*, trans. C. Jay Smith (Tallahassee, Fla., 1976), pp. 6–9. See also the older account in Bancroft, *History* 7:347–48, 8:100–7, 147–56, 250–71. The means by which the foreign troops were engaged was by "treaty of subsidy." Sovereign A agreed, by treaty, to

pay a certain designated subsidy to Sovereign B; Sovereign B, in turn, engaged to put trained troops at the disposal and command of Sovereign A. See Atwood, *The Hessians*, pp. 22–23 on the legal basis for this arrangement.

73. J. Pownall to Gov. Carleton, Sept. 8, 1775, Haldimand Papers, Additional MSS, vol. 21697, fol. 107; Lord Suffolk to Eden, June 20, 1775, Auckland Papers, Additional MSS, vol. 34412, fol. 339; Catherine is quoted in Bancroft, *History* 8:152.

74. George III to Lord North, Aug. 1, 1775, in Fortescue, ed., *Correspondence of George III* 3:237.

75. Feb. 29, 1775, in Hansard, ed., *Parliamentary History* 18:1175. See also the Protest of the Nineteen Lords, Oct. 26, 1775, ibid., 728. Also, see pp. 798–831 for the November 1775 debates on the employment of foreign troops and pp. 1156–1228 for the debates on the ratification of the German treaties. On the negotiations with Hesse, see Atwood, *The Hessians*, pp. 23–29.

76. See Mather, *America's Appeal*, p. 49; and "Obadiah," *New-York Journal*, Sept. 21, 1775.

77. American intelligence was remarkably accurate. Thus, on October 7, 1775, the Congress received information from London about the embarkation of the Hanoverians in a letter dated July 26, 1775, indicating that it had been sent just as the ministry was deciding the matter; Force, ed., *American Archives*, 4th ser., 3:944. See also Arthur Lee to Izard, July 28, 1775, and Izard to Thomas Lynch, Sept. 8, 1775, in Deas, ed., *Correspondence of Izard* 1:107–8, 124, also, Samuel Adams to James Warren, Oct. 7, 1775, and John Hancock to Philip Schuyler, Oct. 7, 1775, in Smith, ed., *LDC* 2:138, 139–40.

78. Josiah Bartlett to John Langdon, May 19, 1776, in Smith, ed., *LDC* 4:39; "Armatus," *Boston Gazette*, June 24, 1776.

79. Gerry to S. Adams, Oct. 9, 1775, in James T. Austin, *The Life of Elbridge Gerry, With Contemporary Letters* (Boston, 1828–29), 1:118; Purdie's *Virginia Gazette*, Mar. 29, 1776.

80. Joseph Shippen to Edward Shippen, Jan. 15, 1776, Shippen Papers, Force Coll., ser. 8D.

81. William Hooper to Samuel Johnston, Dec. 2, 1775, in Smith, ed., *LDC* 2:425.

82. Speech, Nov. 20, 1775, in Hansard, ed., *Parliamentary History* 18:984. On the British and the Indians, see Jack M. Sosin, "The Use of Indians in the War of the American Revolution: A Re-assessment of Responsibility," *Canadian Historical Review* 46 (1965): 101–21; and on Dunmore, see below, Chapter 9. This is not to say that American fears were not justified by the private views of some British officers. Thus, the Scots general James Grant bluntly stated, "a few scalps taken by Indians . . . would operate more upon the minds of those deluded distracted people than any other loss they can sustain." Quoted in Ayling, *George the Third*, p. 248. See also Lord Dartmouth to Gage, Aug. 2, 1775, in Force, ed., *American Archives*, 4th ser., 3:6.

83. "An American," Purdie's *Virginia Gazette*, Jan. 26, 1776.

84. Donoughue, *British Politics*, pp. 204–5.

85. Graves was, by all accounts, an indecisive and timid man whose quies-

cence during the early months of 1775 disappointed his superiors and gave
hope to the colonists, who feared, above all, the might of the British fleet. As
one commentator notes, "Because he [Graves] did not receive direct orders
from the Admiralty to act offensively against colonial shipping and colonial
ports until September [1775], Graves remained semi-neutral. This astonishing
attitude—as if the army were at war while the navy was not—could hardly
have been anticipated by the government in London—or by the colonists!"
Nathan Miller, *Sea of Glory: The Continental Navy Fights for Independence, 1775–
1783* (New York, 1974), p. 23. A more balanced assessment, however, is given
by Fowler: "For several months he [Graves] had to operate in a quasi-war situation with little or no direction from the ministry or Admiralty on how to conduct himself in this uncertain state of belligerency. . . . If the admiral appeared
at times to be unsure and vacillating, he was in great measure simply reflecting
the indecision of those above him." William M. Fowler, Jr., *Rebels under Sail:
The American Navy during the Revolution* (New York, 1976), p. 32. On the British
mission, see ibid., pp. 32–33, and Miller, *Sea of Glory*, pp. 25–27.

86. The incidents are recounted in Captain John Linzee to Graves, Aug. 10,
1775; Journal of H.M.S. *Rose*, Capt. James Wallace, Oct. 8, 1775; Dr. Ezra Stiles
Diary, Oct. 10, 1775; and Letter from Bristol, R.I., Oct. 12, 1775, in William B.
Clark, ed., *Naval Documents of the American Revolution* (Washington, D.C.,
1966), 1:1110–11, 2:362–63 (hereafter cited as Clark, ed., *NDAR*).

87. Graves's instructions were dated July 6, 1775, but did not arrive until
October 6. They authorized him "to carry on such operations upon the sea
coasts of the four governmen[ts] in New England as he should judge most
proper for suppressing the rebellion now openly avowed and supported in
those colonies." Narrative of Vice Admiral Samuel Graves [Oct. 4, 1775], in
Clark, ed., *NDAR* 2:292, 323–24.

88. Captain Henry Mowatt to the People of Falmouth, Oct. 16, 1775, ibid.,
471; Miller, *Sea of Glory*, pp. 46–48; Fowler, *Rebels under Sail*, pp. 33–34.

89. Letter from Jacob Bailey, Oct. 18, 1775, in Clark, ed., *NDAR* 2:500. Bailey's account and other eyewitness accounts were quickly sent to Washington's headquarters in Cambridge, and he sent the dispatches to Philadelphia
via a congressional committee consisting of Thomas Lynch, Benjamin Franklin, and Benjamin Harrison that was at that time in Cambridge. The Congress
ordered the account of the burning copied and sent to the various colonies.
See Committee of Conference to John Hancock, Oct. 24, 1775; Samuel Ward
Diary, November 1, [1775], in Smith, ed., *LDC* 2:244, 283. The documents are
reprinted in Force, ed., *American Archives*, 4th ser., 3:1151–55.

The burning of Falmouth became almost a catch phrase for British brutality.
As Benjamin Franklin wrote to Anthony Todd, the secretary of the British post
office, "Do you think it prudent by your Barbarities to fix us in a rooted Hatred
of your Nation, and make all our unnumerable Posterity detest you? Yet this
is the Way in which you are now proceeding. Our Primers begin to be printed
with Cuts of the Burnings of Charlestown, of Falmouth, of James Town, of
Norfolk with the Flight of Women & Children from those defenceless Places,
some Falling by Shot in their Flight." Franklin to Anthony Todd, Mar. 29,
1776, in Smith, ed., *LDC* 3:462.

At the same time that Graves turned the navy to offensive action in New England, Lord Dunmore, operating a much smaller "fleet" of boats attached to H.M.S. *Fowey*, was conduiting a terrifying series of coastal raids along Virginia's shoreline. See Chapter 9. See also Bancroft's lively, if biased, account of Dunmore's depredations in his *History* 8:212–79. Although Dunmore acted without official instructions, Americans attributed his raids to the same policy as that followed in New England. See John Hancock to George Washington, Jan. 16, [1776], in Smith, ed., *LDC* 3:99.

90. James Warren to John Adams, Oct. 20, 1775, in Ford, ed., *Warren-Adams Letters* 1:154; Benjamin Franklin to Richard Bache, Oct. 24, 1775, in Smith, ed., *LDC* 2:246. See also Samuel Adams to Elizabeth Adams, Nov. 7, 1775, ibid. 3:3. Franklin's views predated the attack on Falmouth. On September 12 he wrote to David Hartley, "The Burnings of Towns, and firing from Men of War on defenceless Allies and Villages filled with Women & Children . . . are by no means Acts of a legitimate Government. They are of barbarous Tyranny and dissolve all Allegiance." Ibid. 3:4.

91. "Johannes in Eremo," *Boston Gazette*, July 17, 1775; Oliver Wolcott to Mrs. Wolcott, May 16, 1776, in Smith, ed., *LDC* 4:17 n. 1.

92. An excellent account of the circumstances leading up to the proclamation of rebellion is in Frothingham, *Rise of the Republic*, pp. 403–55.

93. George III to Lord North, Aug. 18, 1775, in Fortescue, ed., *Correspondence of George III* 3:248.

94. The proclamation is in Force, ed., *American Archives*, 4th ser., 3:240–41.

95. On the Olive Branch Petition, see Chapter 7 and Charles J. Stillé, *The Life and Times of John Dickinson, 1732–1808* (Philadelphia, 1891), pp. 157–58.

96. Bancroft, *History* 8:130–33.

97. George III to Lord North, Aug. 18, 1775, in Fortescue, ed., *Correspondence of George III* 3:248. The City of London petition and the king's answer are in Force, ed., *American Archives*, 4th ser., 1:1853–54.

98. John Pitts, Nov. 12, 1775, S. Adams Papers, vol. 7; "Extract of a letter from Rhode Island," Nov. 27, 1775, in Force, ed., *American Archives*, 4th ser., 3:1686; James Warren to J. Adams, Nov. 15, 1775, in Ford, ed., *Warren-Adams Letters* 1:184.

99. On November 3 and 4, Congress authorized both New Hampshire and South Carolina to organize new governments; on November 29, the Committee of Secret Correspondence was appointed and charged with opening negotiations with foreign powers; *JCC* 3:319, 326–27, 392.

100. Hansard, *Parliamentary History* 18:696. To ensure that the coercive policy would be carried out by ministers fully committed to it, the cabinet was reshuffled at this time. The most important change was the removal of Lord Dartmouth as Secretary of State for the Colonies. He became Lord Privy Seal, replacing the duke of Grafton, who was dismissed by the king on November 9. Dartmouth was replaced by the bellicose Lord George Germaine. Lord Rochford was also replaced as Secretary for the Southern Department by Lord Weymouth. See Mackesy, *War for America*, pp. 46–47.

101. See the debates on the American Prohibitory Act in Hansard, ed., *Parliamentary History* 18:992–99, 1028–41, 1056–1106.

102. Lord North's speech was on November 20, 1775; see also speeches by Edmund Burke (Nov. 20); Thomas Walpole (Dec. 1), and Charles Fox (Dec. 8), in ibid., 992–93, 999, 1029–31, 1058–60.

103. It was a major cause, for example, of Congress's decision to open American ports to foreign shipping; see *JCC* 4:229–33, and William Whipple to Joshua Brackett, April 11, 1776, in Smith, ed., *LDC* 3:509.

104. John Adams to Horatio Gates, March 23, 1776.

105. Robert Alexander to Maryland Council of Safety, Feb. 27, 1776, in Smith, ed., *LDC* 3:431, 307. See also William Whipple to Joshua Bracket, Mar. 17, 1776; and Joseph Hewes to Samuel Johnston, March 20, 1776, in ibid., pp. 395, 416. The printed text of the bill reached the colonies by February 13, 1775; see John Hancock to Thomas Cushing, Feb. 13, 1776; Joseph Hewes to Samuel Johnston, Feb. 13, 1776; North Carolina Delegates to North Caroline Council of Safety, Feb. 13, 1776; and John Penn to Thomas Person, Feb. 14, 1776, ibid., pp. 244, 247, 250–51, 254–55.

106. See, for example, Nathanael Greene to Jacob Greene, Dec. 20, 1775, in Force, ed., *American Archives*, 4th ser., 4:367.

107. As a Virginian queried in May 1776, "Considering the perfidy and obstinacy of the King, is not a declaration of independence of the Crown as just a measure now as a declaration of an independence upon the parliament was some years ago?" From "Serious QUESTIONS addressed to the Congress . . . ," Purdie's *Virginia Gazette*, May 10, 1776. See also Christopher Marshall to "J.B.," Christopher Marshall Letterbook, Hist. Soc. Pa., Philadelphia.

108. Thomas Paine, *Common Sense* (1776), in Philip S. Foner, ed., *The Complete Writings of Thomas Paine* (New York, 1945), 1:41. On the psychological significance of *Common Sense*, see Jordan, "Familial Politics," pp. 432–33, n. 49.

109. John Penn to Thomas Burke, June 28, 1776, Thomas Burke Papers microfilm Reel 1, Southern Historical Collection, University of North Carolina Library, Chapel Hill; Edward Rutledge to Izard, Dec. 8, 1775, in Deas, ed., *Correspondence of Izard* 1:168; Henry Laurens to John Laurens, Feb. 3, 1777, Colonial Office, 5/50, Public Record Office, London.

Chapter 3

1. Robert Treat Paine, Diary, Aug. 29, 1774, in Smith, ed., *LDC* 2:13.

2. June 17, 1774, Proc., Mass. House of Representatives, in Force, ed., *American Archives*, 4th ser., 1:421–22. The emissary was Thomas Flucker, the Province Secretary; see Benjamin W. Labaree, *The Boston Tea Party* (New York, 1964), p. 237. There were also other early calls for a congress; see David Ammerman, "The First Continental Congress and the Coming of the American Revolution" (Ph.D. diss. Cornell University, 1966), pp. 22–34. This material was excised from Ammerman's subsequently published monograph *Common Cause*, an elegant and insightful study that is the best available work on the First Continental Congress.

3. June 17, 1774, Proc., Mass. House of Representatives, in Force, ed., *American Archives*, 4th ser., 1:421.

4. Force, ed., *American Archives*, 4th ser., 1:331n; S. Adams to James Warren, Mar. 31, 1774, in Cushing, ed., *Writings of Adams* 3:93.

5. S. Adams to James Warren, May 14, 1774; and to Charles Thomson, May 30, 1774, in Cushing, ed., *Writings of Adams* 3:112, 122. A good account of the reaction of the Boston committee of correspondence to the Port Bill is in Richard D. Brown, *Revolutionary Politics in Massachusetts: The Boston Committee of Correspondence and the Towns, 1772–1774* (Cambridge, Mass., 1970), pp. 185–89.

6. Boston Committee of Correspondence to Committee of Correspondence of Philadelphia [and others], May 13, 1774, in Cushing, ed., *Writings of Adams* 3:110. The committee also requested the immediate institution of a commercial boycott; see Chapter 4.

7. The express riders from Boston delivered the plea of the Boston committee, where possible, to the legislatures of the various colonies, to their legislative committees of correspondence, or to established committees in the major cities. Royal governors attempted to prevent the legislative bodies from responding to Boston's plea by dissolving sitting legislatures or simply not calling recessed bodies into session. In response, individual legislative leaders, "rump" legislative meetings (as in Virginia), or the committees in the major cities (as in South Carolina) called upon the towns to meet and select delegates to provincewide meetings that were to be held to deal with the crisis. The major purpose of the local gatherings, therefore, was to elect delegates to the provincial conventions. The resolutions the localities adopted were a byproduct. See notes 20–22.

8. A list of the 108 resolutions used in the following analysis is found in the Appendix. Table A-1 presents a fuller view of the results of the survey, which are only summarized in the following section. The importance of these resolutions has also been recognized by Jack N. Rakove, *The Beginnings of National Politics: An Interpretive History of the Continental Congress* (New York, 1979), pp. 27–34. Although this work was published after the study described here was completed, its conclusions are generally consistent with those described below.

9. In this chapter, radicals, moderates, and conservatives continue to be defined in purely political terms, that is, in terms of the positions they took on the political issues that faced the Congress in 1774. Radicals tended to believe that the time for reconciliation had passed, both because events in Massachusetts had gone too far and because they had lost all faith in the British government's capacity to effect meaningful reforms. Thus their first priority was to rally continental support for Massachusetts' resistance to Gage, both in the province's military preparations and in its attempts to resume civilian government. They also supported military preparations throughout the continent. Consistent with their view of the inevitability of armed conflict, they thus viewed any conciliation toward Parliament on the question of regulating colonial trade to be unnecessary and wrong, and they believed that the traditional means of effecting reconciliation, such as a petition to the king, to be futile distractions. See, for example, Samuel Ward to Mary Ward[?], Oct. 10, 1774, in Smith, ed., *LDC* 1:171. While most radicals had supported immediate commercial nonintercourse in May 1774, by the time the Congress met in Septem-

ber they had begun to doubt that such tactics alone could bring Boston the immediate relief it required. They nevertheless supported the Continental Association. See, for example, John Adams to William Tudor, Sept. 29, 1774, ibid., p. 130. This group is exemplified by Christopher Gadsden of South Carolina, Richard Henry Lee of Virginia, and Samuel Adams of Massachusetts.

Moderates, on the other hand, believed that reconciliation was still possible, and all their efforts at the Congress were directed toward adopting policies that could bring it about while at the same time keeping a lid on the explosive situation in Massachusetts. They were willing to make some real concessions to Britain, chiefly in the acknowledgment of parliamentary authority to regulate colonial trade. Although they supported traditional means to bring about reform, such as a petition to the king, they put their greatest faith in commercial nonintercourse and the resulting pressure English merchants would put on the ministry for a change in policy. This strategy needed time to work, however, and in the meantime their policy toward Massachusetts was one of caution; they opposed anything that might cause the situation in the province to degenerate into armed conflict. On the other hand, there were clear limits to the lengths to which they would go in order to achieve a reconciliation. They would not abandon Massachusetts, and thus they favored public expressions of support for the province, and they would not countenance Parliament's authority to regulate the internal affairs of the colonies. This group was exemplified by Benjamin Harrison and Richard Bland of Virginia, and later by John Dickinson of Pennsylvania.

Conservatives were those who thought a reconciliation to be not only desirable but absolutely necessary, for they feared that there would be no colonial trade to worry about without the protection of the British navy, and they feared that colonial disunion would follow the withdrawal of British authority. They also viewed the alternative to reconciliation—armed conflict with the mother country—as suicidal, given Britain's advantage in troops, training, and firepower. They were fully prepared to acknowledge parliamentary authority over colonial trade, not as a tactical concession but rather because it accorded with their concept of the proper imperial relationship. Toward Massachusetts they were ambivalent. They opposed British policy and therefore sympathized with and supported Massachusetts as its target. They suspected, however, that the Bostonians had made their own bed by precipitate action. James Duane of New York and John Rutledge of South Carolina epitomized this viewpoint. See, for example, James Duane to Samuel Chase, Dec. 29, 1774, in Smith, ed., LDC 1:277–80, for a full explanation of the conservative position.

On these divisions, see also H. James Henderson, Party Politics in the Continental Congress (New York, 1974), p. 46. While his categories are generally consistent with the positions sketched above, he does not include a separate "moderate" category, and therefore those who are here termed moderates fall into Henderson's "conservative" group.

In using my own definitions, I must emphasize how ephemeral they are. In some cases they did not survive the winter of 1774, for events moved too quickly. See Chapter 5.

10. Force, ed., *American Archives*, 4th ser., 1:331.

11. The proceedings were those of Fairfax, Virginia (chaired by George Washington), and Middlesex County, Virginia, the latter meeting issuing the most conservative resolutions in the sample; ibid., pp. 587–602, 551–52.

12. If proceedings included a desire for the "united action of the colonies," or referred to the "united wisdom of the colonies" (common synonyms for the Congress), they were included in the twenty-one resolutions that implied that they wanted a congress to be called. For localities that contemplated immediate action at the local or provincial level, see, for example, the proceedings of Stafford and Fauquier counties, Virginia, and Easthampton, New York, in ibid., pp. 618, 528, 420.

The fact that a local meeting did not call for a congress by no means indicated that the area leaned toward toryism. In most cases it meant just the opposite. Thus, of the fifteen resolutions in the present sample that did not call for a congress, ten demanded the immediate or imminent adoption of a trade embargo. Furthermore, although Massachusetts has been excluded from the sample for reasons explained in the Appendix, the call of the Boston committee of correspondence for an immediate commercial boycott in May 1774 was deliberately made independent of any congress. See S. Adams to Charles Thomson, May 30, 1774, in Cushing, ed., *Writings of Adams* 3:122–24. The meeting of a congress was made more probable, of course, by the call for such a session by the Massachusetts House of Representatives. See note 2 and accompanying text.

13. Proc. of Committee of Lancaster County, Pa., July 9, 1774, postscript, *Pennsylvania Gazette*, July 20, 1774. Although the political authority that these local proceedings delegated to the Congress was extralegal, it satisfies modern definitions of political authority that equate it with sufficient power, whether coercive or persuasive, to carry out political decisions. See William A. Gamson, *Power and Discontent* (Homewood, Ill., 1968), p. 21; and David Easton, *The Political System* (New York, 1953), p. 132.

14. Force, ed., *American Archives*, 4th ser., 1:727. Twenty-nine percent of the resolutions calling for a congress ask only that the assembly adopt "wise measures" or an unspecified plan to bring about the desired alterations in British policy.

15. The conventions were those of Delaware, Pennsylvania, Georgia, and the Rhode Island Assembly.

16. In Massachusetts, which does not appear in these figures, it is clear that considerable sentiment existed in favor of a commercial boycott. See Brown, *Revolutionary Politics*, pp. 200–208. In addition, those localities favoring a boycott but not a congress are also not included in the 66 percent. Given the sample's bias toward the middle and southern colonies, the 66 percent figure given here is almost certainly a conservative estimate of sentiment favoring a boycott. See also the estimates of Ammerman in *Common Cause*, pp. 36–47, which indicate similarly substantial sentiment for some kind of trade embargo.

17. The desire of the Massachusetts towns to await a congressionally devised boycott helped to doom the hopes of the Boston committee for an im-

mediate embargo in June 1774. See Brown, *Revolutionary Politics*, pp. 201–2.

18. The best studies of political mobilization in New England and in the large urban centers are Brown, *Revolutionary Politics*; Maier, *From Resistance to Revolution*; and Ryerson, *Revolution Is Now Begun*. It is clear, however, that right up to the eve of the Revolution these efforts had barely penetrated the backcountry, which made the activities of the Boston committee among the Massachusetts towns so unique. See Rakove, *Beginnings of National Politics*, p. 29.

19. This mobilization process was enhanced by the election of the local Association committees after November 1774. See Chapter 4 and Ammerman, *Common Cause*, pp. 103–9.

20. The best general study of the selection of the delegates to the First Congress is Ammerman, "First Continental Congress," pp. 44–75, upon which the following account draws heavily. The selection of delegates figured prominently in the developing revolutionary movements within several colonies. The full significance of the process, therefore, cannot be understood without consulting such works as R. A. Ryerson, *Revolution Is Now Begun*, pp. 39–64; and Carl Becker's classic account of the battles in New York in *The History of Political Parties in the Province of New York: 1760–1776* (Madison, Wis., 1968; orig. publ. 1909).

My survey of the local, county, and provincial meetings that preceded the congress revealed that at least forty-seven of the fifty-six continental delegates participated in them. Of the nine who did not, four were members of Galloway's delegation, and the other five were the Rhode Island and Connecticut delegates appointed by the Provincial Assembly and the Assembly Committee of Correspondence, respectively.

21. See Ammerman, "First Continental Congress," pp. 44–46. In Pennsylvania, the delegates to the First Congress were also chosen and instructed by the Assembly under the firm hand of the conservative Speaker, Joseph Galloway. Galloway's initial success, however, should not obscure the fact that a parallel process, sparked by the crisis of 1774, was transforming Pennsylvania politics. Thus, the radical Philadelphia Committee of Forty-Three, after unsuccessfully petitioning the royal governor, Thomas Penn, to call a special Assembly session in order to select continental delegates, issued a call to the various counties to elect delegates to an extralegal provincial convention that would select and instruct delegates. By the time the convention met on July 15, however, Governor Penn had called a regular Assembly session and thus the convention simply drew up a set of proposed instructions for the continental delegates that the Assembly would select. The Convention also suggested to the Assembly that John Dickinson, James Wilson, and Thomas Willing would make splendid continental delegates. Speaker Galloway completely ignored both the proposed delegates and the proposed instructions. His triumph was short-lived, however, for in provincial elections held in the fall of 1774, Galloway lost control of the Assembly, Dickinson was elected member from Philadelphia, and the reconstituted Assembly voted to add him to the Pennsylvania delegation. See Ryerson, *Revolution Is Now Begun*, pp. 39–64, 91–93.

In Massachusetts, the delegates were chosen by the regularly constituted legislature, but only because that body physically resisted the governor's efforts to dissolve it. See note 2.

22. In most colonies, only the obstructionist tactics of royal governors prevented the assemblies from taking a larger role in the delegate selection process than they did. Thus, for example, in New Hampshire, Governor Wentworth dissolved the Assembly, whereupon the members of the legislature's committee of correspondence, meeting after the dissolution, issued a call for the towns to elect representatives to a provincial convention, which was held on July 21. In Delaware and Virginia, the Speakers of the respective assemblies issued similar calls, after the royal governors there also prevented regular assembly sessions. See Ammerman, "First Continental Congress," pp. 47–48, 61–62, 64–68. In South Carolina, although the delegates were elected by a provincial convention called into being by a circular letter of the Charleston committee, the election of the delegates was formally approved by a regular session of the Assembly, which also voted funds to defray the expenses of the continental delegates. See E. Stanly Godbold, Jr., and Robert H. Woody, *Christopher Gadsden and the American Revolution* (Knoxville, Tenn., 1982), pp. 116–20.

The situation in New York was *sui generis*. Two rival committees, the moderate Committee of Fifty-one and the radical Committee of Twenty-five battled through the summer, in a series of public meetings, to control the appointment of the continental delegates. Ultimately, the New York City delegation consisted of the slate favored by the Committee of Fifty-one. Perhaps because of the depth of the factional struggles, there was no provincial convention in New York. Instead, several upstate counties either elected their own delegates or voted to accept the New York City delegates as their representatives. See Becker, *Political Parties in New York*, pp. 112–41. On the accreditation of the New York delegates, see Duane, "Notes of Debates," Sept. 5, 1774, in Smith, ed., *LDC* 1:26, 37.

Only in Georgia did the process fail to result in the election of continental delegates. Although a "general meeting" was held in Savannah on August 10 and a number of resolutions were adopted, no delegates were elected. Only one parish, St. John's, supported the idea of sending delegates to Philadelphia. See Force, ed., *American Archives*, 4th ser., 1:700, 766–67. Georgia was therefore not represented at the First Congress.

23. Diary, August 29, 1774, in Butterfield, ed., *Adams Papers* 2:114.

24. Proc. of the Monmouth County, N.J., Committee, *New-York Journal*, Sept. 1, 1774; "B.N.," *New-York Journal*, Aug. 4, 1774.

25. Appellation taken from "Extract of a Letter from Boston . . ." Rind and Pinkney's *Virginia Gazette*, Oct. 27, 1774.

26. Diary, Sept. 5, 1774, in Butterfield, ed., *Adams Papers* 2:122–24; James Duane, Notes of Debates, Sept. 5, 1774, citation from Deane to Mrs. Deane, Aug. 31-Sept. 5, 1774, in Smith, ed., *LDC* 1:25–26, 20; Notes of Debates, Sept. 6, 1774, in Butterfield, ed., *Adams Papers* 2:124–26; Sept. 5–6, 1774, *JCC* 1:13–14, 25–27.

Whenever one speaks of the delegates' "unanimity" in the First Congress, it must be with trepidation. First, there were no roll-call votes. Next, the voting procedure adopted on September 6 meant that each delegation would decide for itself how the province's vote would be cast. Dissension within a delegation therefore would not be evident in the final tally. Finally, no goal was more important to the delegates in 1774 than unity, or at least the appearance of unity. As Paul Smith notes, "the delegates aspired at the outset to secure passage of their resolutions 'unanimously in the affirmative,' to present them to the outside world 'N.C.D.' (nemine contradicente), without dissent" (Smith, ed., *LDC* 1:xx).

27. Duane, "Notes of Debates," Sept. 6, 1774, in Smith, *LDC* 1:30.

28. Ibid., pp. 30–31.

29. John Adams, "Notes of Debates," Sept. 6, 1774, ibid., p. 28. See also remarks of Richard Bland in Richard Henry Lee there.

30. Ibid.; Duane, "Notes of Debates," Sept. 6, 1774, in ibid., p. 31. See also *JCC* 1:25.

31. The committees were proposed on September 6 and appointed on September 7; *JCC* 1:26–29. The manner in which the members were appointed to the Grand Committee demonstrates the great concern for unity. Lynch, who had been proposing most of the procedural motions favored by the radicals, moved that members of the Grand Committee be chosen by the delegates "out of the Members at large without Regard to Colonies." This method might well have excluded some conservatives from this vital committee. But the motion "occasioned much debate," chiefly over the difficulty of adequately representing the views of each colony if each province did not choose its own members. Lynch's motion was defeated, the only early motion he offered to suffer this fate. The delegates then voted by "a great majority" to have the members of each individual delegation choose two of their number to serve upon the Grand Committee. When it became clear that the work of the committee would be long and arduous, three delegations (Massachusetts, Pennsylvania, and Virginia) were allowed to choose an additional member each. Duane, "Notes of Debates," Sept. 7, 1774, in Smith, ed., *LDC* 1:35–36; Sept. 7, 19, 1774, *JCC* 1:27–29, 41.

32. For a good summary of the "conspiracy" theme, see, for example, Edmund C. Burnett, *The Continental Congress* (New York, 1941), pp. 47–50; John C. Miller, *Origins of the American Revolution* (Boston, 1943), pp. 380–81.

33. See Ammerman, *Common Cause*, pp. 89–94.

34. Joseph Galloway to William Franklin [Sept. 5, 1774], in Smith, ed., *LDC* 1:27.

35. Galloway's accounts of the congressional proceedings were published in 1775 and during his exile in England in 1779; see note 83. It is ironic, as Ammerman points out, that in this particular instance the views of the "losers" have triumphed, for subsequent treatments of the Congress have relied heavily upon Galloway's partisan statements; see *Common Cause*, p. 90.

36. Samuel Ward Diary, Sept. 3, 1774; Joseph Galloway to William Franklin, Sept. 3, 1774, in Smith, ed., *LDC* 1:14, 24. A rough tabulation of the contacts that the Massachusetts delegates had with their future colleagues on the trip

to Philadelphia and during the week preceding the Congress demonstrates that between August 10 and September 5 they met with Connecticut delegates seven times, with Rhode Island delegates six times, with New Hampshire delegates four times, with New York delegates ten times, and with South Carolina delegates nineteen times. They met the late-arriving Virginians nine times between September 1 and September 5, and with the similarly tardy Delawarians three times. They even squeezed in a visit with the Maryland delegates, who arrived on September 3. Their contacts with the Pennsylvanians provide an interesting contrast. Although they met with Galloway's enemies—Thomas Mifflin and John Dickinson—eight times, they saw Galloway only twice, both times by accident. They did not encounter the rest of the Pennsylvania delegation at all, despite the fact that Philadelphia hosted the Congress. From the above tabulation it is obvious that the Massachusetts men were by no means limiting their contacts to the supposed radicals among the delegates. Yet, they did not seek out the man whom historians have pictured as the leader of the congressional conservatives, Galloway. See Diary, Aug. 10–Sept. 4, 1774, in Butterfield, ed., *Adams Papers* 2:97–122.

It is important to emphasize that the other delegates may have been meeting their future colleagues as furiously as the Massachusetts men. The evidence we have from sources like Silas Deane's extensive letters to his wife and Samuel Ward's sketchy diary indicates a level of interaction among the other delegates similar to that of the Massachusetts men. See, for example, Deane to Mrs. Deane [Aug. 31–Sept. 5, 1774], and Samuel Ward Diary, Aug. 31–Sept. 3, 1774, in Smith, ed., *LDC* 1:13–14, 15–23. In contrast to this general activity, Galloway's isolation, and that of his Pennsylvania allies, is striking. On the isolation of the Galloway men from the precongress socializing, see Burnett, *Continental Congress*, p. 27. This isolation was not shared by those who are generally considered to be Galloway's ideological colleagues, such as Duane and Jay of New York, or John Rutledge of South Carolina. Ryerson attributes Galloway's isolation to a combination of political miscalculation and personal arrogance, and he contrasts it with the behavior of Galloway's arch rivals, Thomas Mifflin, whom Galloway had not been able to exclude from the Pennsylvania delegation, and John Dickinson, whom he had. According to Ryerson, "Joseph Galloway assumed that congressmen from most other colonies would, like him, be constitutionally conservative and tactically cautious, and as delegates arrived in Philadelphia, neither he nor Pennsylvania's other conservative congressmen sought out their new colleagues to present their views." Galloway's rivals, Ryerson notes, "were not so foolish." *Revolution Is Now Begun*, p. 90.

37. J. Adams to Timothy Pickering, Aug. 6, 1822, in Charles Francis Adams, ed., *The Works of John Adams, Second President of the United States* . . . (Boston, 1854), 2:512n. Adams here names the "warners" as Thomas Mifflin, Benjamin Rush, and John Bayard. Also, see the warning delivered by Alexander Macdougall, the New York radical; Diary, Aug. 22, 1774, in Butterfield, ed., *Adams Papers* 2:106. S. Adams to Joseph Warren, Sept. 25, 1774, in Smith, ed., *LDC* 1:100.

38. On the day the Massachusetts delegates arrived in Philadelphia, they conversed with Lynch, among others. They met with him again on each of the following two days and again dined in his company on September 2. Undoubtedly, some plans were laid during the course of these visits. Diary, Aug. 29, 30, 31, Sept. 2, 1774, in Butterfield, ed., *Adams Papers* 2:114, 116, 117, 119.

One must note, however, that Lynch, a veteran of the Stamp Act Congress, was too important a figure to be a "puppet" of the Adamses. If anything, the situation was reversed; in such esteem was Lynch held that on September 7 conservative James Duane nominated him for the chairmanship of the Grand Committee. When Lynch declined and nominated Stephen Hopkins in his stead, Hopkins was promptly elected. Duane, "Notes of Debates," Sept. 7, 1774; Silas Deane to Mrs. Deane, Sept. 7, 1774, in Smith, ed., *LDC* 1:34, 37. It is as reasonable to suppose that Lynch, who had arrived in Philadelphia early, had settled upon a course of action with other like-minded delegates, which he then communicated to the approving Massachusetts delegation in the days before the Congress opened, as it is to assume the opposite. Whatever the case, it is important to remember that the Massachusetts delegates had come to the Congress as supplicants in dire need of continental assistance as well as martyrs in the cause of liberty. They did not believe that they would have things all their own way.

39. Diary, Aug. 30, 1774, in Butterfield, ed., *Adams Papers* 2:115. It is likely that the coalition of Pennsylvanians headed by Dickinson and Mifflin had chosen the Carpenters' Hall as the site of the Congress sometime in the middle of the summer. The provincial convention that they had sponsored had met in the hall in mid-July, and on July 18 a slip of the pen by the clerk of the Carpenter's Company indicated that the choice of the hall as the site of the upcoming Congress may have been known to officials of the company. See Richard Tyler, *"The Common Cause of America": A Study of the First Continental Congress*, Historic Resource Study, Independence National Historical Park (Denver, 1974), pp. 102–3 and n. 141. If Galloway's political opponents did choose the Carpenters' Hall, they had ample occasion to convey the decision to Adams before he took his walk on August 30, for Mifflin had been among the men who met the Massachusetts delegation at Frankford. Furthermore, Galloway probably meant the Dickinson-Mifflin faction when he observed that the early decisions of the Congress had been "privately settled by an Interest made out of Doors," and thus the phrase refers to factionalism within Pennsylvania, and not, as it had usually been interpreted, to factionalism within the Congress. On the relationship between the policies of the Congress and factionalism within Pennsylvania, see Ryerson's meticulous study, *Revolution Is Now Begun*, especially pp. 89–115.

40. Ammerman, *Common Cause*, p. 994.

41. See, for example, R. H. Lee to John Dickinson, July 25, 1768, in James C. Ballagh, ed., *The Letters of Richard Henry Lee* (New York, 1911), 1:29. The immediate result of the movement to concert resistance was the formation of an intercolonial network of corresponding committees, most of them appointed by the colonial assemblies. By 1774 this network was virtually complete. See Ammerman, *Common Cause*, p. 21; Tyler, *Common Cause*, pp. 34–48.

42. See, for example, "PROPOSALS for the good of the AMERICAN Colonies, made and offered by a PHILADELPHIAN," *Boston Gazette*, Mar. 15, 1773; "TIME and JUDGEMENT," *Boston Gazette*, Aug. 2, 1773; "Observation," *Boston Gazette*, Sept. 27, 1773, reprinted in the *Pennsylvania Journal*, Oct. 13, 1773; and Purdie and Dixon's *Virginia Gazette*, Nov. 11, 1773.

43. Thus Caesar Rodney, a Delaware delegate, wrote to his brother from New York on October 20, 1765: "You . . . perhaps are surprised to think We should Set So Long When the business of our Meeting Seemed only to be the Petitioning the King and Remonstrating to both houses of Parliament" in Ryden, ed., *Rodney Letters*, p. 25. Colden is quoted in Frothingham, *Rise of the Republic*, p. 185: for lack of newspaper coverage, see Claude H. Van Tyne, *The Causes of the War of Independence* (Boston, 1922), p. 182, and on the meeting in general, Edmund Morgan and Helen Morgan, *The Stamp Act Crisis: Prologue to Revolution*, 2d ed., rev. (New York, 1962), pp. 138–54.

44. The members of both congresses were Eliphalet Dyer (Conn.), Philip Livingston (N.Y.), John Dickinson (Pa.), John Morton (Pa.), Thomas McKean (Pa.), Caesar Rodney (Del.), Thomas Lynch (S.C.), Christopher Gadsden (S.C.), and John Rutledge (S.C.). See Morgan and Morgan, *Stamp Act Crisis*, pp. 139–40 n. 42; Aug. 29, Notes of Debates, Sept. 3, 5, 1774, in Butterfield, ed., *Adams Papers* 2:115, 121, 123.

45. "B.I.," *Pennsylvania Gazette*, Mar. 8, 1775; *Pennsylvania Journal*, June 14, 1775. See also Izard to Cadwallader Colden, Sept. 10, 1775, in Deas, ed., *Correspondence of Izard* 1:128.

46. Duane, Notes of Debates, Sept. 5, 1774, in Smith, ed., *LDC* 1:25; Notes of Debates, Sept. 6, 1774, in Butterfield, ed., *Adams Papers* 2:125. Two years later, when the Congress bore little resemblance to the convention of 1774, the delegates were still making the analogy. See "Address to the Inhabitants of the Colonies," Feb. 13, 1776, in *JCC* 4:137.

47. Rakove similarly emphasizes the delegates' consensus as to the major goals to be accomplished in 1774; *Beginnings of National Politics*, pp. 42–62.

48. Duane, Notes of Debates, Sept. 6, 1774; Robert Treat Paine Diary, Sept. 6, 1774; and Samuel Ward Diary, Sept. 6, 1774, in Smith, ed., *LDC* 1:32–33.

49. Deane to Mrs. Deane [Sept. 7, 1774], in Smith, ed., *LDC* 1:34; J. Adams to A. Adams, Sept. 8, 1774, in Butterfield, ed., *Adams Family Correspondence*, 1:150.

50. Deane to Mrs. Deane, Sept. 8, 1774, in Smith, ed., *LDC* 1:50.

51. See Reed to Lord Dartmouth, Feb. 10, 1775, in William B. Reed, ed., *Life and Correspondence of Joseph Reed . . .* (Philadelphia, 1847), 1:94. Ammerman concludes that "the report of an attack on Boston undoubtedly affected the subsequent debates. It probably contributed to the later endorsement of the supposedly radical resolutions submitted by Suffolk County, and it certainly reminded the members of Congress that almost any incident might touch off events that could lead directly to war." *Common Cause*, p. 74.

52. The Suffolk Resolves are in *JCC* 1:32–39. For an analysis of the Suffolk Resolves emphasizing their similarity to resolves adopted by other Massachusetts county conventions, see Stephen E. Patterson, *Political Parties in Revolutionary Massachusetts* (Madison, Wis., 1973), p. 98; and Brown, *Revolutionary*

Politics, pp. 230–31. The letters between the Massachusetts delegates and the Boston committee of correspondence suggest "that a preplanned flow of news from Boston was maintained to sustain an air of crisis and to generate support in Congress for vigorous measures in behalf of Massachusetts." Editor's note, Smith, ed., *LDC* 1:72 n. 1.

53. See S. Adams to the Boston Committee, Sept. 14, 1774, in Cushing, ed., *Writings of Adams* 3:154; and *JCC* 1:39–40. The official *journal* of the Congress wrongly dated the approval of the resolves as "Saturday, September 18." Congress did not sit on Sunday and undoubtedly acted on the Resolves on Saturday, September 17. See *JCC* 1:39 n. 1. Peyton Randolph to Joseph Warren, Sept. 17, 1774, in Smith, ed., *LDC* 1:76 n. 1.

54. *JCC* 1:32–39. The civil provisions of the Resolves were precipitated by Gage's attempt to implement the new form of "royalized" government mandated by the Massachusetts Government Act.

55. On the effect of the approval of the Suffolk Resolves upon English public and official opinion, see Chapter 2. For Tory opinion, see, for example, [Harrison Gray], *The Two Congresses Cut Up, or, A Few Remarks Upon Some Of The Votes and Resolutions of the Continental Congress* . . . (New York, 1775), p. 7; "Mary V.V.," *A Dialogue Between a Southern Delegate and His Spouse* . . . (New York, 1774), p. 5; "Grotius," *Pills For The Delegates* . . . (New York, 1774), p. 5.

56. Diary, Sept. 17, 1774, Butterfield, ed., *Adams Papers* 2:134–35. Adams's interpretation of the significance of the Resolves has often been reiterated. See, for example, Arthur M. Schlesinger, *The Colonial Merchants and the American Revolution, 1763–1776* (New York, 1968; orig. publ. 1916), pp. 412–13; and Becker, *History of Political Parties in New York*, pp. 147–50. This view also appears in such standard works as Van Tyne, *Causes of the War of Independence*, pp. 440–42; and Burnett, *Continental Congress*, pp. 44, 46; and in more recent accounts, such as Merrill Jensen, *The Founding of a Nation: A History of the American Revolution, 1763–1776* (New York, 1968), p. 496; and is strongly implied in Henderson, *Party Politics*, p. 38. Ammerman, however, offers a different interpretation (and one that I find persuasive, for the reasons stated in the text). See *Common Cause*, p. 92. Rakove also finds that in substance the Suffolk Resolves were "neither as belligerent or provocative as they have often been portrayed." *Beginnings of National Politics*, p. 46.

57. Read to Mrs. Read [Sept. 18, 1774], in Smith, ed., *LDC* 1:82. The delegates' understanding that their response to the Suffolk Resolves was in the nature of an immediate reaction to an explicit request for advice from the "war zone" is also made explicit in Thomas Cushing to Richard Devens and Isaac Foster, Jr., Sept. 18, 1774:

> We have received your Favor of the 5th Instant inclosing a Copy of the Proceedings of the Comttee from the Several Towns & districts in the County of Middlesex and communicated them to the Congress. The Members of the Congress were highly pleased with your Resolutions & much applaud The Wisdom, temperance and Fortitude of your Conduct but as at the time your Proceedings came to hand the Congress were very

Busy & several large Committees were closely engaged upon matters of great Importance there was then no opportunity particularly to take under Consideration the State of the Province of the Massachusetts Bay. However on the 16 Instant an Express arrived & brought us the Resolutions of the County of Suffolk and as in the Letter Accompanying them there was an express application to the Congress for advice, The affairs of the Massachusetts were immediately taken up & several Resolutions passed, which I now Inclose, approving of the Wisdom and Fortitude with which our People in general had Conducted the opposition to the late ministerial Measures. And we trust, they will strengthen the hands & Comfort the hearts of the Freinds to American Liberty as well as Confound & Discomfit its Enemies. (Ibid., p. 83)

See also Rodney to Thomas Rodney, Sept. 17, 1774 in ibid., pp. 77–78. It is interesting that Rodney interpreted the key phrase in the Resolves to mean that the Bostonians were "determined not [to] Injure the General [Gage] or any of the Kings Troops, Unless Compelled thereto by an Attack made by the Troops on them." This defensive interpretation of the Resolves, which many of the delegates may have shared, was entirely lost on English officialdom (see Chapter 2). The phrase in the Resolves that occasioned the most controversy concerned the Bostonians' statement that their newly trained militia would continue to act on the defensive only "so long as such conduct may be vindicated by reason and the principles of self-preservation, but no longer." *JCC* 1:35.

Read, Rodney, and Cushing's contention that the Bostonians specifically requested that the Congress act immediately upon the Suffolk Resolves is supported by comparing the delegates' response in this case with that of the Middlesex Resolves, which arrived on September 14. Although the latter resolves were read with "high Applause," no action was taken on them. See S. Adams to Boston Committee of Correspondence, Sept. 14, 1774, in Cushing, ed., *Writings of Adams* 3:154. See also Cushing to Devens and Foster, in Smith, ed., *LDC* 1:83.

58. See Rodney to Thomas Rodney, Sept. 17, 1774, in Smith, ed., *LDC* 1:77–78; Rakove, *Beginnings of National Politics*, p. 47.

59. John Adams to Richard Cranch, Sept. 18, 1774, in Smith, ed., *LDC* 1:81.

60. Joseph Hawley, "Broken Hints To be communicated to the Committee of Congress for the Massachusetts," [Aug. ? 1774], in Robert J. Taylor, ed., *Papers of John Adams* (Cambridge, Mass., 1977), 2:135. Christopher Leffingwell to Deane, Aug. 22, 1774, "Correspondence of Silas Deane, Delegate to the First and Second Congress at Philadelphia, 1774–1776," Conn. Hist. Soc., *Collections* 2 (1870): 140. On the need for military preparations, see, for example, reports dated Norwich, Conn., September 15, in the *Boston Gazette*, Sept. 19, 1774, and the *New-York Gazette*, Sept. 26, 1774. The Massachusetts delegates received a steady stream of letters through the fall that emphasized the absolute necessity of undertaking military preparations. See, for example, William Tudor to John Adams, Sept. 17, 1774; and Benjamin Kent to same, Sept. 23,

1774, in Taylor, ed., *Papers of Adams* 2:167, 170–71; Thomas Young to S. Adams, Aug. 19, 1774, S. Adams Papers, vol. 6.

61. J. Adams to James Warren, July 17, 1774, in Ford, ed., *Warren-Adams Letters* 1:29.

62. Adams quickly assessed Henry to be an ally on military matters. When he read him a copy of Hawley's "Broken Hints," Henry declared, "I AM OF THAT MAN'S MIND," in Niles, ed., *Principles and Acts*, p. 324; *JCC* 1:53. The committee consisted of Richard H. Lee, Patrick Henry, John Adams, and the conservatives, John Rutledge and Thomas Johnson.

63. The pretext for including Lee's resolution in the petition was that strong colonial militias would enable the colonists to protect themselves, thus obviating the need for parliamentary defense taxes. Lee's resolution is in *JCC* 1:54 n. 1; see also Silas Deane Diary in Smith, ed., *LDC* 1:133.

64. Oct. 3, 1774, Silas Deane Diary in Smith, ed., *LDC* 1:138–39.

65. Ibid.; *JCC* 1:53–54 n. 1.

66. *JCC* 1:102.

67. Oct. 24, 25, 26, 1774, *JCC* 1:103, 104, 115–21; John Dickinson to George Logan, Sept. 15, 1804, in Stillé, *Life of Dickinson*, p. 145. On the petition, see Edwin Wolf II, "The Authorship of the 1774 Address to the King Restudied," *WMQ*, 3d ser., 22 (1965): 189–224.

68. J. Adams to William Tudor, Sept. 29, 1774, in Smith, ed., *LDC* 1:130.

69. Boston Committee of Correspondence to Continental Congress, Sept. 29, 1774, in *JCC* 1:55–56.

70. The agitation for resumption of the charter was precipitated by the Massachusetts Government Act, by the terms of which courts were closed and the legislature reconstituted. See Chapter 9.

71. On the desire to take up the old charter, see Patterson, *Political Parties in Massachusetts*, pp. 117–20; Brown, *Revolutionary Politics*, pp. 231–33, and below, Chapter 9. See also Thomas Young to S. Adams, Sept. 4, 1774; and Joseph Warren to S. Adams, Sept. 1774, S. Adams Papers, vol. 6; S. Adams to Joseph Warren, Sept. [24], 1774, in Smith, ed., *LDC* 1:95; and John Palmer to J. Adams, Sept. 14, 1774, in Niles, ed., *Principles and Acts*, pp. 322–23.

72. Oct. 8, 10, 1774, *JCC* 1:58–60; J. Adams to William Tudor, Sept. 29, 1774, in Smith, ed., *LDC* 1:130.

73. J. Adams to William Tudor, Oct. 7, 1774, ibid., p. 157; Oct. 8, 1774, *JCC* 1:58.

74. Oct. 10, 11, 1774, *JCC* 1:59–62. The delegates did, however, vote to support Massachusetts' efforts to *repel* any attack by Gage; see Oct. 8, 1774, *JCC* 1:58.

75. John Andrews to William Barrall, Oct. 19, 1774, in Winthrop Sargent, ed., *Letters of John Andrews, Esq. of Boston, 1772–1776* (Cambridge, Mass., 1866), p. 65. The Lee motion, offered on either October 7 or 8, is in *JCC* 1:59n. The plan of the Bostonians to evacuate the town, for which Lee's motion would have gained continental approval, was entirely serious (as events in 1775 were to prove) and was well known to the Massachusetts delegation. See Benjamin Church to S. Adams, Sept. 29, 1774, Adams Papers, vol. 6; Samuel Cooper to J. Adams, Oct. 16, 1774, in Niles, ed., *Principles and Acts*, p. 324.

76. Quoted in Stephen Collins to Paine, Jan. 14, 1775, Robert Treat Paine Papers, Massachusetts Historical Society, Boston. On the defeat of radical efforts to secure continental approval for a "preemptive strike" against Gage, see John Drayton, *Memoirs Of The American Revolution, From Its Commencement To The Year 1776, Inclusive; As Relating To The State of South Carolina* . . . (Charleston, 1821), 1:165.

77. On the Galloway plan, see Julian Boyd, *Anglo-American Union: Joseph Galloway's Plans to Preserve the British Empire, 1774–1778* (Philadelphia, 1941). The plan is in *JCC* 1:49–51 under the date of its introduction, September 28, 1774.

78. See, for example, Wharton to Thomas Walpole, May 31, 1774, Thomas Wharton Letterbook, Hist. Soc. of Pa., Philadelphia; Thomas Clifford to Thomas Frank, June 21, 1774, Clifford Correspondence, vol. 29, Hist. Soc. of Pa., Philadelphia.

79. See, for example, Burnett, *Continental Congress*, pp. 47–50; Henderson, *Party Politics*, p. 39.

80. *JCC* 1:101. Galloway also sat on the Grand Committee, but he was selected for this committee by his own delegation.

81. On the structure of Assembly politics in Pennsylvania on the eve of the Revolution, and on political events in Philadelphia during the late spring and summer of 1774, see Ryerson, *Revolution Is Now Begun*, pp. 89–115.

82. Ammerman is the first to note that Galloway offered his plan as a solution to the question of parliamentary authority and not, as has often been assumed, as a substitute for a trade embargo. See *Common Cause*, p. 58.

83. Notes of Debates, Sept. 28, 1774, in Butterfield, ed., *Adams Papers* 2:143–44; Ammerman, *Common Cause*, pp. 58–60. Galloway's account of his plan's reception in Congress is in [Joseph Galloway], *The Examination of Joseph Galloway, Esq.; Late Speaker of the House of Assembly of Pennsylvania. Before the House of Commons, In A Committee On The American Papers* (London, 1779), p. 48.

84. Ammerman has made the most comprehensive study of the Statement of Rights and Grievances adopted by the First Congress, a document upon which, he noted, the delegates spent fully half of their session. The following account draws heavily upon Ammerman, *Common Cause*, pp. 53–71. See also Rakove, *Beginnings of National Politics*, pp. 52–60.

85. Of the local resolutions examined, only York County, Virginia, and Pitt County, North Carolina, specifically called upon the Congress to devise a statement of rights. The Pennsylvania and North Carolina provincial conventions voiced similar demands. However, 66 percent of the attitude sample did call for the "establishment of colonial rights on a permanent foundation," or made a similar demand in slightly different language. Rakove interprets such statements, or similar statements rejecting Parliament's authority over colonial legislation, as a mandate for a congressional statement of rights and grievances. *Beginnings of National Politics*, p. 32.

86. Diary, Oct. 24, 1774, in Butterfield, ed., *Adams Papers* 2:156. It was a project, moreover, with great appeal to the thirty-two lawyers who constituted the dominant occupational group among the delegates. See Tyler, *Common Cause*, p. 114, Table G.

87. Sept. 6, 1774, *JCC* 1:26; Samuel Ward Diary, Sept. 9, 1774, in Smith, ed., *LDC* 1:59. The membership of the subcommittee is uncertain, but it included at least John Adams, James Duane, John Rutledge, and Samuel Ward. The other tasks were to devise a means of redress (which became the Continental Association) and to draft a list of grievances. Subcommittees were also formed to deal with these matters. See Samuel Ward Diary, Sept. 14, 1774, in Smith, ed., *LDC* 1:72.

88. Autobiography, in Butterfield, ed., *Adams Papers* 3:309.

89. Samuel Ward Diary, Sept. 9, 1774, in Smith, ed., *LDC* 1:59. See Notes of Debates, Sept. 8, 1774, in Butterfield, ed., *Adams Papers* 2:128–30; and James Duane, "Speech to the Committee on Rights," Sept. 8, 1774, in Smith, ed., *LDC* 1:53–55.

90. Notes of Debates, Sept. 8, 1774, in Butterfield, ed., *Adams Papers* 2:128. For Jay as a conservative, see Henderson, *Party Politics*, p. 46. In the debates of September 8, those in favor of including the law of nature were R. H. Lee, Sherman, Livingston, Pendleton, and Jay. In Henderson's radical–conservative scale, Sherman and Lee are listed as radicals, Pendleton and Jay as conservatives, and Livingston (who is not listed on the 1774 table) emerges as a moderate on the 1775–1776 table. See *Party Politics*, pp. 46, 72.

91. Diary, Sept. 14, 1774, in Butterfield, ed., *Adams Papers* 2:133.

92. Ibid., p. 148.

93. Autobiography, in Butterfield, ed., *Adams Papers* 3:309–10. In this memoir, Adams claims for himself the authorship of the key compromise phraseology. In this, as in other cases, his memory may have been faulty. Burnett believed that Duane had as much responsibility for the key wording as did Adams. See Edmund C. Burnett, ed., *Letters of Members of the Continental Congress* (Washington, D.C., 1921–36), 1:47n, and his *Continental Congress*, p. 14. Burnett's interpretation is supported by a comparison of the language of the final compromise resolution with that of a speech made by Duane on the subject during the debates in the full Congress on the Declaration. The Declaration of Rights and Grievances as adopted includes the statement:

> But from the necessity of the case, and a regard to the mutual interest of both countries, we cheerfully consent to the operation of such acts of the British parliament, as are bona fide, restrained to the regulation of our external commerce, for the purpose of securing the commercial advantages of the whole empire to the mother country, and the commercial benefits of its respective members; excluding every idea of taxation, internal or external, for raising a revenue on the subjects in America, without their consent.

Duane's speech includes the very similar statement:

> They [the British Parliament] exercise the right [to regulate colonial trade] and none mean to dispute it. Our interest will be served by admitting it under restrictions (to wit) *that it be conducted bona fide, with a just regard to the interest of the respective members of the Empire excluding every idea of taxation internal and external for the purpose of raising a revenue without our consent.*

Declaration of Rights and Grievances, Oct. 14, 1774, in *JCC* 1:68; and James Duane's Notes for a Speech in Congress [Oct. 13, 1774], in Smith, ed., *LDC* 1:190 (emphasis in original). On the debates in the subcommittee, see Samuel Ward Diary, Sept. 14, 15, 16, 1774, in Smith, ed., *LDC* 1:72, 75; and Sept. 22, 1774, in *JCC* 1:42. The subcommittee on grievances had considerably less trouble than that on rights. Its report was laid before the full Congress on September 24; see *JCC* 1:42.

94. Samuel Ward Diary, Oct. 12, 13, 14, 1774; Robert Treat Paine's Notes of Debates; Samuel Ward's Notes for a Speech in Congress; James Duane's Notes for a Speech in Congress; and Notes of Debates, in Smith, ed., *LDC* 1:181–83, 184–89, 189–91, 191–92, 194–96. Diary, Oct. 13, 1774, in Butterfield, ed., *Adams Papers* 2:151. The compromise was embodied in Clause 4 of the Statement of Rights and Grievances; *JCC* 1:68–69. See above, note 93, for the text.

Some delegates may have considered the compromise as conceding to Parliament the right as well as the power. See, for example, Edward Rutledge to Izard, Oct. 29, 1774, in which he notes, "We have formed a bill of Rights by which we insist . . . that the Parliament of Great Britain, has, of necessity, a right to regulate trade." Smith, ed., *LDC* 1:252.

95. Autobiography, and diary entry of Oct. 13, 1774, in Butterfield, ed., *Adams Papers* 3:310, 2:151. See also James Duane, Notes for a Speech in Congress, in Smith, ed., *LDC* 1:189–91, and note 93 above. Adams also noted that when the compromise was first suggested, John Rutledge, another conservative, announced that he had "a great Opinion" of grounding parliamentary authority in "the Necessity of the Case" and was "determined against all taxation for revenue." Autobiography, in Butterfield, ed., *Adams Papers* 3:309. Adams, on the other hand, was worried about how the compromise would be accepted, and he seemed surprised that his constituents approved it heartily. "Pray, write me, as often as possible, and let me know, how, the fourth Resolution in our Bill of Rights, is relished and digested, among the Choice Spirits along the Continent. I had more Anxiety about that than all the rest. But I find it is extreamly popular here [in Massachusetts]." John Adams to Edward Biddle, Dec. 12, 1774, in Smith, ed., *LDC* 1:266.

Chapter 4

1. Brown, *Revolutionary Politics*, pp. 185–86. The letters of the Boston committee of correspondence are in Cushing, ed., *Writings of Adams* 3:109–10.

2. S. Adams to Charles Thomson, May 30, 1774, in Cushing, ed., *Writings of Adams* 3:123; Brown, *Revolutionary Politics*, pp. 191–209. Samuel Adams's explanation of the radical attempt (under the pseudonym "Candidus") is in the *Boston-Gazette*, June 27, 1774; the relevant documents are in Force, ed., *American Archives*, 4th ser., 1:397–98. On the league, see Rakove, *Beginnings of National Politics*, pp. 23–27.

3. This chapter spans several periods. Thus, prior to November 1774 the definitions used in the prior chapters are still appropriate. The publication of the

proceedings of Congress in November 1774 and the need to enforce the Association, however, necessitate different definitions. From November 1774, therefore, it becomes possible to speak meaningfully of Whigs and Tories. Whigs supported the measures of Congress; Tories, most vociferously, did not. Rivington's *New-York Gazetteer* was the premier Tory press and contained many diatribes against Congress from November on.

Where I wish to distinguish between Whigs, I again use the terms radical, moderate, and conservative. As the scene has now shifted from the delegates themselves to the reception of Congress's measures in the colonies, the terms refer both to the delegates and their constituents. Radicals were those who favored the most vigorous enforcement of the Association, without consideration of the economic impact of such behavior upon individuals. They enthusiastically supported all committee attempts to enforce the boycott through ostracism and stigmatization, and some supported coercion if it proved necessary to ensure support of the Association. They were also supporters of expanded powers for local committees beyond those specified by the Association, especially in the area of military preparations. If the decision of a particular local committee conflicted with radical perceptions of what vigorous enforcement of the Association required, radicals would oppose the action of the local committee in the name of vigorous enforcement of the Association.

Moderates were strong supporters of the Association, but although they claimed to be "literalists" in its enforcement and spoke of confining themselves strictly to the forms prescribed by Congress, they were more likely to bend the rules in order to accommodate the interests of local merchants and planters (see, for example, note 64 and the accompanying text). Moderates, who often dominated local committees, were reluctant to add to the powers confided to the committees by the Association.

Both radicals and moderates enthusiastically proclaimed support of the Congress and its measures, and both condemned all tendencies toward mob rule and disorder. Radicals, however, thought American resistance had, almost miraculously, been characterized by the absence of any such behavior; moderates were more likely to view radical attempts to vigorously enforce the Association as first steps toward such behavior.

Conservatives are distinguished from moderates chiefly by their attitude toward the Congress. Conservatives did *not* enthusiastically support the Congress's measures, and they were particularly suspicious of the Association. However, they did welcome some efforts, such as the petition and the Declaration of Rights, and because they opposed British policy, most were willing to sign their local Association agreements, by which means they bound themselves to abide by its terms.

4. Draper's *Massachusetts Gazette; and the Boston Weekly News-Letter*, June 23, 1774.

5. John Drayton, *Memoirs of the American Revolution* 1:127–30; "Anglus Americanus," *New-York Journal*, July 7, 1774. See also Deane to Samul H. Parsons, Apr. 13, 1774, in "Deane Correspondence," Conn. Hist. Soc., *Collections* 2 (1870): 130. See Rakove, *Beginnings of National Politics*, pp. 26–27.

6. See Appendix. For a full colony-by-colony analysis of the development of a consensus favoring a commercial boycott during the summer of 1774, see Ammerman, *Common Cause*, pp. 35–51. See also Rakove, *Beginnings of National Politics*, pp. 49–50.

7. Virginia and North Carolina. See Appendix for a list of conventions and assembly meetings. Connecticut, Massachusetts, and Rhode Island, whose assemblies adopted spirited, if general, resolutions, have been included in the ten also on the basis of the more specific resolutions of their principal towns. See Ammerman, *Common Cause*, p. 47 and n. 40. On the reticence of the Pennsylvania Convention, see Ryerson, *Revolution Is Now Begun*, pp. 57–60.

8. Patterson to Levi Hollingsworth, May 19, 1774, Hollingsworth Papers, Correspondence, box 7, Hist. Soc. of Pa., Philadelphia; Wharton to Thomas Walpole, Aug. 20, 1774, Thomas Wharton Letterbook, Hist. Soc. of Pa., Philadelphia. See also Henry Drinker for firm of James and Drinker to Nathan Hyde, Sept. 16, 1774, Henry Drinker Letterbook, Hist. Soc. of Pa., Philadelphia; Thomas Clifford and Sons to Thomas Frank, Sept. 16, 1774, Clifford Correspondence, vol. 29, Hist. Soc. of Pa., Philadelphia. The harm may have been more anticipated than actual. See below, notes 55 and 60–62 and accompanying text.

9. William Carr to Russell, July 6, 1774, James Russell Papers, bundle 2, Alderman Library, Univ. of Va., Charlottesville; Thomas Fisher to Russell, Aug. 27, 1774, ibid., bundle 6.

10. William Franklin to Lord Dartmouth, May 31, 1774, *Documents Relating to the Colonial History of New Jersey*, in Archives of the State of New Jersey, 1st ser. (Newark, 1886), 10:457–58; Haldimand to Lord Barrington, Sept. [Oct.] 5, 1774, Haldimand Papers, Additional MSS, vol. 21696, fol. 119; Hutchinson to a Mr. Lee [not sent], Sept. [20–29] 1774, Hutchinson Letterbook, Egerton MSS, vol. 2661, fol. 54.

11. Alexis de Tocqueville, *Democracy in America*, edited by J. P. Mayer and Max Lerner (New York, 1966), Book 2, Part 2, Chap. 5, pp. 485–88; Carl Bridenbaugh, *Cities in Revolt: Urban Life in America, 1763–1776* (New York, 1955), pp. 156–63. Examples of the rich associational life in colonial towns may be found, for example, in G. B. Warden, *Boston, 1689–1776* (Boston, 1970), p. 156; Richard Walsh, *Charleston's Sons of Liberty: A Study of the Artisans, 1763–1789* (Columbia, S.C., 1959), pp. 29–31; Carl Bridenbaugh and Jessica Bridenbaugh, *Rebels and Gentlemen: Philadelphia in the Age of Franklin* (New York, 1965), pp. 86–93, 225–62, 321–22, 334–39.

12. Warden, *Boston*, pp. 152, 156, 163–68; Morgan and Morgan, *Stamp Act Crisis*, pp. 159–61, 244–45; Maier, *From Resistance to Revolution*, pp. 85–86; Walsh, *Charleston's Sons of Liberty*, pp. 30–33, 38–39; Carl Bridenbaugh, *Cities in the Wilderness: The First Century of Urban Life in America, 1625–1742* (New York, 1955), p. 340n; Bridenbaugh, *Cities in Revolt*, p. 364; Roger J. Champagne, "Liberty Boys and Mechanics of New York City, 1764–1774," *Labor History* 8 (1967): 119–20.

13. The controversy on this point began with Arthur Schlesinger's now-classic work, *The Colonial Merchants and the American Revolution, 1763–1776*.

Schlesinger, a Progressive historian, argued for purely economic motives behind the nonimportation movement, a position that was challenged by such
"neo-Whigs" as Maier (*From Resistance to Revolution*, pp. 51–76). The case for
economic causation has been made in a most sophisticated manner by Marc
Egnal and Joseph Ernst, "An Economic Interpretation of the American Revolution," *WMQ*, 3d ser., 29 (1972): 3–32.

14. There was a basis in reality for such an optimistic analysis of the British
system. For years, West Indian sugar planters, formally unrepresented in Parliament, had obtained all the political action they desired in Westminster. See
Lewis B. Namier, *England in the Age of the American Revolution*, 2d ed. (New
York, 1961), pp. 234–41.

15. Schlesinger, *Colonial Merchants*, pp. 78–80.

16. Maier, *From Resistance to Revolution*, pp. 116–20. On the inability of mid-
dle- and upper-class Whigs to retain control of resistance to the Stamp Act, see
Nash, *Urban Crucible*, pp. 292–311.

17. Schlesinger, *Colonial Merchants*, pp. 114–15. The Philadelphia merchants
proved reluctant to follow the Boston lead, and each city eventually organized
independent nonimportation agreements. See Ryerson, *Revolution Is Now Begun*, pp. 26–33.

18. Schlesinger, *Colonial Merchants*, pp. 115, 124; Becker, *Political Parties in
New York*, p. 63. Nash notes that, given severe unemployment in the major
seaport towns during the depression of the early 1770s, artisan and tradesman
support of a boycott strategy was rooted in economic self-interest, because
damming the flow of imports would naturally increase the market for American manufactures; *Urban Crucible*, pp. 321, 332–37.

19. Schlesinger, *Colonial Merchants*, p. 130. It should be noted that all the
agreements differed in detail in matters of timing and exceptions. Compare
the enforcement powers given to the Association committees in 1774 in Article
XI of the Association, *JCC* 1:79.

20. The distinction used here follows that of Egnal and Ernst, "Economic
Interpretation of the Revolution," pp. 11–12, where they distinguish between
"those areas in which the distribution of British goods was handled by an urban center controlled by a strong native merchant community" and those regions where the distribution "occurred within a decentralized marketing and
credit structure" characterized by a nonnative mercantile community. If one
excepts Charleston and later Baltimore from the latter category, the division
corresponds roughly to a regional one between North and South. For the sake
of succinctness, the regional designations will be employed here.

21. Ibid., pp. 25–28.

22. But see notes 55, 58, 61–64 and accompanying text regarding the economic interest of northern traders in supporting commercial boycotts.

23. Virginia Nonimportation Association [June 22, 1770], in Robert A. Rutland, ed., *The Papers of George Mason, 1725–1792* (Chapel Hill, N.C., 1970),
1:121.

24. Schlesinger, *Colonial Merchants*, pp. 201–2, 208; Maier, *From Resistance to
Revolution*, pp. 116–17. On the social expansion of the enforcement mechanism in Philadelphia, see Ryerson, *Revolution Is Now Begun*, pp. 29–33.

25. Edward McCrady, *The History of South Carolina under the Royal Government, 1719–1776* (New York, 1899), pp. 650–51; Walsh, *Charleston's Sons of Liberty*, pp. 45–50; Godbold and Woody, *Christopher Gadsden*, pp. 82–96.

26. Becker, *Political Parties in New York*, pp. 88–93; Warden, *Boston*, pp. 239–44; Walsh, *Charleston's Sons of Liberty*, pp. 54–55.

27. Schlesinger, in *Colonial Merchants*, viewed the widening social base of the nonimportation movement as detrimental to the merchants' economic interests. Having lost control of nonimportation, he theorized, they turned against resistance in 1774. The point emphasized here is that merchant control was illusory almost from 1765, as wider elements of the community sought to accomplish political as well as economic purposes through nonimportation. See Maier, *From Resistance to Revolution*, p. 117; Ryerson, *Revolution Is Now Begun*, pp. 32–33. Furthermore, the short- and long-range economic interests of many merchants may have continued to be served by nonimportation whether they controlled such movements or not. See notes 55, 58 and 61–64 and accompanying text.

28. Nash, *Urban Crucible*, pp. 292–300; Maier, *From Resistance to Revolution*, pp. 116–17.

29. Becker, *Political Parties in New York*, pp. 89–90. Charles S. Olten, "Philadelphia's Mechanics in the First Decade of Revolution, 1765–1775," *Journal of American History* 59 (1972): 322–23. See also Richard A. Ryerson, "Political Mobilization and the American Revolution: The Resistance Movement in Philadelphia, 1765–1776," *WMQ*, 3d ser., 31 (1974): 563–88.

30. Mason to R. H. Lee, June 7, 1770, in Rutland, ed., *Papers of Mason* 1:117.

31. "Pro Grege et Rege" [Christopher Gadsden], *Timothy's South-Carolina Gazette* (Charleston), June 22, 1769. In the South, many importing merchants were recently immigrated Scotsmen.

32. A list of members is in McCrady, *Royal Government in South Carolina*, p. 651.

33. S. Adams to Stephen Sayre, Nov. 16, 1770, in Cushing, ed., *Writings of Adams* 2:58. See also, S. Adams to Peter Timothy, Nov. 21, 1770, ibid., p. 65; James Bowdoin to John Temple, May 9, 1772, "The Bowdoin and Temple Papers," Mass. Hist. Soc., *Collections*, 6th ser., 9 (1897): 292. Gadsden to S. Adams, June 6, 1774, in Richard Walsh, ed., *The Writings of Christopher Gadsden, 1746–1805* (Columbia, S.C., 1966), p. 94.

34. S. Adams to R. H. Lee, July 15, 1774, in Cushing, *Writings of Adams* 3:139. See also Gerry to S. Adams, June 21, 1773, in Gerry Papers, box 1; and John Collins to Samuel Ward, July 17, 1774, Gratz Coll., case 1, box 4, Hist. Soc. of Pa., Philadelphia.

35. *JCC* 1:26.

36. Ammerman, *Common Cause*, p. 56; *JCC* 1:41.

37. Notes of Debates [Sept. 26–27, 1774], in Butterfield, ed., *Adams Papers* 2:137; Samuel Ward Diary, Sept. 26, 1774, in Smith, ed., *LDC* 1:107; *JCC* 1:43.

38. Notes of Debates, Sept. 26–27, Oct. 6? 1774, in Butterfield, ed., *Adams Papers* 2:138, 147.

39. Ibid., pp. 137–39.

40. Ibid., p. 139; see below, note 41.

41. *JCC* 1:53. The committee consisted of:

Thomas Cushing	Mass.	merchant/politician
Isaac Low	N.Y.	merchant
Thomas Mifflin	Pa.	merchant/politician
Richard Henry Lee	Va.	planter
Thomas Johnson, Jr.	Md.	lawyer

Of Johnson, John Adams noted in his diary that he had "a clear and a cool Head, an Extensive Knowledge of Trade as well as Law." Oct. 10, 1774, in Butterfield, ed., *Adams Papers* 2:150.

42. See Table 4-2. Notes of Debates, Sept. 26–27, 1774, in Butterfield, ed., *Adams Papers* 2:138–39.

43. See "Instructions by the Virginia Convention to their Delegates in Congress, 1774," in Boyd, ed., *Jefferson Papers* 1:141–43; and Remarks of R. H. Lee, in Notes of Debates, Sept. 26–27, 1774, in Butterfield, ed., *Adams Papers* 2:139.

44. See, for example, "QUERIES proposed to AMERICA," Rivington's *Gazetteer*, Oct. 13, 1774; Notes of Debates, Sept. 26–27, 1774, in Butterfield, ed., *Adams Papers* 2:139, especially the remarks of Chase, Hooper, and Edward Rutledge.

45. On October 5 a "Mr. Adams" moved to debate the issue of an immediate nonexportation of flaxseed. See Silas Deane Diary, [Oct. 5, 1774]; Samuel Ward to Joseph Wharton, Oct. 3, 1774; Robert Treat Paine, "Notes for a Speech in Congress" [Oct. 5, 1774]; and Silas Deane Diary, [Oct. 6, 1774], in Smith, ed., *LDC* 1:141, 143–49, 153–54. After the debate began to elicit suggestions as to which specific goods each colony would agree to stop, it became clear that agreement would be impossible. As Benjamin Harrison argued, "the Measure cannot be carried into Execution & will defeat the Whole." Silas Deane Diary [Oct. 6, 1774], ibid., p. 153. Thereupon, as Samuel Ward recorded, "Non Exportation of particular articles dropped." Ibid., p. 154.

46. *JCC* 1:62–63. The only account of this episode comes from the report the South Carolina delegation made to their provincial congress on January 11, 1775. It is reprinted in Drayton, *Memoir of the American Revolution* 1:168–76, from which source it was reprinted in Smith, ed., *LDC* 1:292–95. See also Ammerman, *Common Cause*, pp. 82–83. The conduct of the delegates caused bitter political battles in South Carolina. On the debate over Parliament's right to regulate colonial trade, see Chapter 3.

47. On the supposed unanimity, see Samuel Ward Diary, [Oct. 20, 1774], in Smith, ed., *LDC* 1:222 n. 1, in which Smith notes that, at least according to Galloway, "some delegates signed the association although opposed to it."

48. The Fairfax County Resolves, of July 18, 1774, are in Force, ed., *American Archives*, 4th ser., 1:597–602; the Virginia Association, of August 1–6, 1774, is in Boyd, ed., *Jefferson Papers* 1:137–40.

49. For interesting discussions of the nonconsumption, domestic manufacturing, and "moral regeneration" clauses of the Association, largely ignored here, see Rhys Isaac, "Dramatizing the Ideology of Revolution: Popular Mobilization in Virginia, 1774 to 1776," *WMQ*, 3d ser., 33 (1976): 374–75; Ammer-

man, *Common Cause*, pp. 114–18; Edmund S. Morgan, "The Puritan Ethic and the American Revolution," *WMQ*, 3d ser., 24 (1967): 3–43.

50. Article XI of the Association provides:

That a committee be chosen in every county, city, and town, by those who are qualified to vote for representatives in the legislature, whose business it shall be attentively to observe the conduct of all persons touching this association; and when it shall be made to appear, to the satisfaction of a majority of any such committee, that any person within the limits of their appointment has violated this association, that such majority do forthwith cause the truth of the case to be published in the gazette; to the end, that all such foes to the rights of British-America may be publicly known, and universally contemned as the enemies of American liberty; and thenceforth we respectively will break off all dealings with him or her.

51. See, for example, B. Franklin to William Franklin, to Peter Timothy, and to Thomas Cushing, June 30, Sept. 3, 7, 1774, in Willcox, ed., *Papers of Franklin* 21:235, 280, 291; Diary, Sept. 3, 1774, in Butterfield, ed., *Adams Papers* 2:120; and Patterson to Levi Hollingsworth, July 6, 1774, Hollingsworth Papers. See also Rakove, *Beginnings of National Politics*, p. 50.

52. Examples of claims of the immediate adherence to the terms of the Association may be found in Samuel Ward to Dickinson, Dec. 14, 1774, in Smith, ed., *LDC* 1:269; John Jones to Dickinson, Mar. 20, 1775, Dickinson Papers, items 25-2, 360, Library Company of Phila.; *Boston-Gazette*, Mar. 27, 1775. The major port of Massachusetts was, of course, under effective British occupation during this period.

53. See, for example, Edward Papenfuse's meticulous study of the way in which Annapolis merchants both adapted to and profited from the changed trading patterns brought about first by the Association and then by the war. *In Pursuit of Profit: The Annapolis Merchants in the Era of the American Revolution, 1763–1805* (Baltimore, 1975).

54. Although rising prices clearly contravened Article XIII of the Association, they did not necessarily mean that consumers were actually buying contraband goods, that is, those that had been imported contrary to the terms of the Association. Most 1775 advertisements offering British goods were careful to state that goods had been imported "last fall," although a few intrepid importers, perhaps from habit, began their list of such offerings with the phrase, "just imported." See, for example, the advertisement of William Ross, shoemaker, *Pennsylvania Gazette*, Feb. 1, 1775. For "imported last fall" examples, see advertisements of Thomas Lawrence and Joseph Dean, *Pennsylvania Journal*, Apr. 12, June 14, 1775.

55. See Egnal and Ernst, "Economic Interpretation of the Revolution," pp. 1–32; Joseph A. Ernst, *Money and Politics in America, 1755–1775: A Study in the Currency Act of 1764 and the Political Economy of Revolution* (Chapel Hill, N.C., 1973). See also Nash, *Urban Crucible*, pp. 316–18. The southern planters in the tobacco-growing regions, as well as the South Carolina exporters of rice and

374 NOTES TO PAGES 119–121

indigo, had their own reasons for discontent. The financing mechanism of the tobacco trade involved high levels of planter indebtedness to large Scots trading houses, which was increasingly difficult to repay as tobacco prices declined through the 1770s. See Egnal and Ernst, "Economic Interpretation of the Revolution," pp. 24–28. For the ideological implications of the desire for "economic sovereignty," see Joyce Appleby, "The Social Origins of American Revolutionary Ideology," *Journal of American History* 64 (1978): 935. On the structure of trade in the tobacco regions, see Jacob M. Price, *Capital and Credit in British Overseas Trade: The View From the Chesapeake, 1700–1776* (Cambridge, Mass., 1980).

56. Although some merchants opposed the resistance movement in 1774, in almost every colony many prominent men of trade were in the forefront of the movement. A few examples will suffice to illustrate the geographical and ideological range of patriot merchants: John Hancock and Thomas Cushing of Massachusetts, Isaac Low of New York, Thomas Mifflin and George Clymer of Pennsylvania, Samuel Purviance, Sr., of Maryland, and Christopher Gadsden and Henry Laurens of South Carolina.

57. See, for example, Tyler, *Common Cause*, Table G, p. 114. Studies of the social composition of the resistance movement in Philadelphia conclude that while the relative importance of the merchants in the resistance committees declined, in absolute terms they remained, even after 1774, the largest single occupational bloc on the committees. See Table 2 and Fig. 2, in Ryerson, "Political Mobilization," *WMQ*, 3d ser., 31 (1974): 586–87; Robert F. Oaks, "Philadelphia Merchants and the First Continental Congress," *Pennsylvania History* 40 (1973): 157.

58. Egnal and Ernst, "Economic Interpretation of the Revolution," pp. 15–24; Ernst, *Money and Politics*, pp. 357, 360; Nash, *Urban Crucible*, pp. 316–18.

59. The failure of many Tory merchants to support the Revolution, it has long been contended, stemmed from a fear of social and political dislocation. See Schlesinger, *Colonial Merchants*, pp. 591–92; and Leonard W. Labaree, *Conservatism in Early American History* (New York, 1948), pp. 144–51, 162–64. What has not been so well understood, however, was the ability of many conservatives to participate in the resistance movement by either suppressing such fears or subordinating them to immediate political and economic goals, or simply by retaining sufficient confidence in their ability to maintain control. See Egnal and Ernst, "Economic Interpretation of the Revolution," p. 30.

60. See note 41.

61. Thomas Frank to Thomas Clifford and Sons, Aug. 27, 1774, Clifford Correspondence, vol. 5; Caesar Rodney to Thomas Rodney, Sept. 24, 1774, in Smith, ed., *LDC* 1:97. See also, Caesar Rodney to Thomas Rodney, Sept. 9, 12, 1774, in ibid., pp. 58, 67; William Fitzhugh to Russell, Oct. 18, 1774, Russell Papers, bundle 6; Champion to Willing & Morris, Sept. 30, 1774, in Guttridge, ed., *Letters of Champion*, p. 29; Israel Mauduit to Charles Jenkinson, Sept. 15, 1774, Liverpool Papers, Additional MSS, vol. 38208, fol. 100; Hutchinson to Foster Hutchinson, Aug. 6, 1774, Hutchinson Letterbook, Egerton MSS, vol. 2661, fol. 43.

Contemporary observations that ships from England were crowding into American harbors, particularly New York and Philadelphia, in the later months of 1774, are borne out by a comparison of the sheer numbers of ships that newspapers reported were entering these ports from England in the first and last halves of 1773 (a year of trade depression, one must remember) and in the same periods of 1774:

	Jan.–July		July–Dec.	
	1773	1774	1773	1774
Philadelphia	31	31	62	81
New York	34	37	32	48

Source: Customshouse entries, 1773–74, *Pennsylvania Journal*, *Pennsylvania Gazette*, *New-York Gazette*, Rivington's *Gazetteer*.

62. Estimates of the sufficiency of the fall importations, when added to goods already in the country, varied. The goods would be sufficient:

"for a year" [Philadelphia] (Zachariah Flood to Russell, Sept. 10, 1774, Russell Papers, bundle 8)

"to serve us two years" ("A Friend to LIBERTY," Rind and Pinkney's *Virginia Gazette*, Jan. 12, 1775)

"to supply the wants of all Virginia for two years" (Thomas Nelson, "Address to the People," July 18, 1774, in Force, ed., *American Archives*, 4th ser., 1:596)

"[for] a considerable time" [Philadelphia] (Joseph Reed to Lord Dartmouth, Dec. 10, 1774, in Reed, *Life of Reed*, 1:88).

63. See, for example, the saga of the *Chalkeley*, owned by the Philadelphia Tory firm of James & Drinker. The ship's captain, Edward Spain, had great difficulty finding a cargo in England, given the great number of other American vessels vying for the same goods, and when he finally did, his ship was further delayed by bad weather on the passage to America. These circumstances, which caused the *Chalkeley* to arrive in Philadelphia after December 1, may be traced in James and Drinker to Capt. Edward Spain, Sept. 18, 1774; James and Drinker to Pigou and Booth, Oct. 1, 1774, July 5, 1775; James and Drinker Letterbook, Foreign, Henry Drinker to Pigou and Booth, Jan. 31, 1775, and to Brown and Finley, Apr. 7, 1775, Henry Drinker Letterbook.

64. On none of the five cargoes, which were sold separately, was the difference between the invoice value and the auction price greater than 18*s*. Proceedings of the Committee of Wilmington, Dec. 30, 31, 1774, in Saunders, ed., *Colonial Records of North Carolina* 9:1103–4. See also the case of the Virginia doctor who was persuaded by the local committee to offer his late-arriving medicines for auction by assurances from his local committee that "there has never been an instance . . . of the inhabitants bidding against the proprietors." Similarly, Henry Laurens assumed when his cargo of personal effects arrived late that he would receive "the usual indulgence of buying them in myself." See

also the factor who bluntly stated about his tardy goods, "I shall Buy them myself, without paying anything to the distressed Bostonians." "In Committee-Chamber," Feb. 7, 1775, Norfolk, Rind and Pinkney's *Virginia Gazette*, Feb. 16, 1775; Henry to John Laurens, Feb. 6, 1775, *South Carolina Historical and Genealogical Magazine* 4 (1903): 276–77; William Carr to James Russell, Jan. 24, 1775, Russell Papers, bundle 2.

65. For radical dissatisfaction with certain elements of congressional policy, see Chapter 3. For efforts to create new provincial governments, see Chapter 9.

66. William Hooper to J. Duane, Nov. 22, 1774, in Smith, ed., *LDC* 1:262.

67. Rind's *Virginia Gazette*, Dec. 1, 1774; William Carr to James Russell, Jan. 24, 1775, Russell Papers, bundle 2. See also the resolution of the Massachusetts Provincial Congress, Dec. 5, 1774, in Lincoln, ed., *Journal Prov. Congress of Mass.*, p. 58.

68. *Pennsylvania Gazette*, Dec. 7, 1774. See also the proceedings of Bucks County, Pennsylvania and Burlington County, New Jersey, committees in *Pennsylvania Journal*, Nov. 30, 1774, and *Pennsylvania Gazette*, Jan. 11, 1775; and of the Northampton, Prince William, and Richmond City, Virginia, and Charles City County, Maryland, committees in Rind and Pinkney's *Virginia Gazette*, Jan. 12, 19, 1775; and Dixon and Hunter's *Virginia Gazette*, Jan. 14, 1775.

69. James Lovell to Josiah Quincy, Jr., Nov. 25, 1774, "Quincy Letters," Mass. Hist. Soc., *Proc.* 50 (1916–17): 477–78.

70. Ammerman, *Common Cause*, p. 109. His estimates of the expansion on a colony-by-colony basis are on pp. 103–9.

71. Of the 95 local resolutions considered, 71 stated that the attendees to the general meetings included "freeholders and other inhabitants," while 24 noted that participants included only "gentlemen" and/or "freeholders." The provision is in Article xi of the Association; *JCC* 1:79.

72. *JCC* 1:79; Purdie's *Virginia Gazette*, Dec. 29, 1774; "A Friend to Liberty and Moderation," *Maryland Gazette* (Annapolis), Jan. 19, 1775. The best account of the enforcement activities of the Association committees is Ammerman, *Common Cause*, pp. 111–24.

73. See, for example, Larry Bowman, "The Virginia County Committees of Safety, 1774–1776," *Virginia Magazine of History and Biography* 79 (1971): 333; Dale E. Benson, "Wealth and Power in Virginia, 1774–1776: A Study in the Organization of Revolt" (Ph.D. diss., University of Maine, 1970), pp. 284–94; Ammerman, *Common Cause*, pp. 109–10.

In the larger cities with a longer history of resistance committees, the established leaders had begun by 1774 to be joined by newer, less socially elevated and more politically radical committee colleagues. See Ryerson, "Political Mobilization," pp. 574–77, 581; Becker, *Political Parties in New York*, pp. 165–68.

74. See Chapter 3.

75. For the care shown by early resistance organizations to maintain order, see Maier, *From Resistance to Revolution*, pp. 74–76, 96–100, 123–25, 280–83.

76. Examples of the Tory complaints are Andrews to William Barrall, Sept.

21, 1774, in Sargent, ed., *Letters of John Andrews*, p. 51; Copley to Isaac Clarke, Apr. 26, 1774, in "Letters and Papers of John Singleton Copley and Henry Pelham, 1739–1776," Mass. Hist. Soc., *Collections* 71 (1914): 217–19; and Anne R. Cunningham, ed., *Letters and Diary of John Rowe, Boston Merchant, 1759–1762, 1764–1779* (Boston, 1903), p. 261.

77. The accounts of these events in the patriot press all stress the orderliness of the proceedings. See, for example, *Massachusetts Spy*, Sept. 22, 1774; *Boston Gazette*, Sept. 12, 1774; and "Mr. Frye's frank and generous Declaration," *Massachusetts Spy*, Sept. 1, 1774. The "mandamus councilors" were those whom the governor was authorized to appoint by the terms of the Massachusetts Government Act. Previously, members of the Council had been elected, as provided in the Charter of 1691.

78. John Adams to A. Adams, Sept. 20, 1774, in Butterfield, ed., *Adams Family Correspondence* 1:161. On the attacks on Anglican clergymen, see, for example, the treatment of Col. Fitch and the Rev. Peters in *New-York Gazette*, Sept. 5, 1774. The Deane and Hosmer statements are from Simon Deane to Silas Deane, Oct. 15, 1774, and Titus Hosmer to Silas Deane, Sept. 4, 1774, in "Deane Correspondence," Conn. Hist. Soc., *Collections* 2 (1870): 191, 156; Joseph Jacob to Daniel Mildred, Jan. 3, 1774, Cox-Parrish-Wharton Papers, vol. 11, Hist. Soc. of Pa., Philadelphia.

79. S. Adams to Gerry, Mar. 24, 1774, in Austin, *Life of Gerry* 1:38; Report from Portsmouth, N.H., Sept. 22, 1778, *South-Carolina and American General Gazette* (Charleston), Oct. 14–21, 1774.

80. Becker, *Political Parties in New York*, pp. 105–41; "Address of the Mechanicks" to Dickinson, June 27, 1774, Dickinson Papers, item 156, Library Company of Phila.

81. Rink and Pinkney's *Virginia Gazette*, Nov. 24, 1774.

82. David C. Skaggs, "Maryland's Impulse Toward Social Revolution: 1750–1776," *Journal of American History* 54 (1968): 761; *Maryland Gazette*, Oct. 20, 1774, William Eddis to ?, Oct. 26, 1774, in Aubrey C. Land, ed., *Letters from America* (Cambridge, Mass., 1969), pp. 90–97. See also John Galloway to Thomas Ringgold, Oct. 20, 1774, in "Account of the Destruction of the Brig 'Peggy Stuart' at Annapolis, 1774," *Pennsylvania Magazine of History and Biography* 25 (1901): 250.

83. See, for example, Ryerson's conclusion that the congressional decision to entrust the enforcement of the Association to local committees had put Philadelphia's resistance movement "on a semi-official and quasi-governmental basis." The "congressional mandate solved the question of the committee's institutional status." "Political Mobilization," *WMQ*, 3d ser., 31 (1974): 570. What was done with the authority, of course, reveals the political persuasion of the authorizing institution. In Philadelphia, the Association Committee was the nucleus of institutions through which the radicals triumphed in Pennsylvania. See Ryerson, *Revolution Is Now Begun*, pp. 89–115; also, see below, Chapter 9.

84. Proc. of the Committee of Hanover, N.J., Feb. 15, 1775, in Force, ed., *American Archives*, 4th ser., 1:1240–41; Proc. of York County Congress, *Boston-Gazette*, Dec. 5, 1774. See also Ammerman, *Common Cause*, pp. 122–23.

85. Proc. of the Maryland Convention, Dec. 8, 1774, *New-York Gazette*, Jan. 5, 1775; Proc. of New York Provincial Congress, June 7, 1775, *New-York Journal*, June 8, 1775.

86. Rind and Pinkney's *Virginia Gazette*, Feb. 9, 1775; Proc. of the Committee of Prince George's City, Maryland, Apr. 10, 1775, in Force, ed., *American Archives*, 4th ser., 2:308; "To the GENTLEMEN of the COMMITTEE for the County of HALIFAX," Rind and Pinkney's *Virginia Gazette*, Jan. 26, 1775.

87. See, for example, on recruitment: Oct. 4, 1775, Dec. 2, 1775, *JCC* 3:275, 400–401; on manufactures: Oct. 20, 1774, Nov. 4, 1775, ibid., 1:78, 3:322–23; on prisoners: Dec. 6, 18, 1775, Jan. 27, 1776, ibid., 3:408, 435, 4:95; on supplies: June 10, 26, Nov. 1, 1775, ibid., 2:85–86, 108, 3:314; on loyalty: Oct. 6, 1775, Jan. 9, 11, 1776, ibid., 3:280, 4:42, 49.

88. See, for example, "A SPEECH delivered on Long-Island . . . ," *New-York Gazette*, Oct. 14, 1776; Charles Inglis to Joseph Galloway, Dec. 12, 1778, Tory Letters, "Brother Jonathan," Force Coll., ser. 8D; "A Real Churchman" to [John] Vardill, May 2, 1775, Egerton MSS, vol. 2135.

Chapter 5

1. *JCC* 2:91–92.

2. Francis V. Greene, *The Revolutionary War and the Military Policy of the United States* (New York, 1911), p. 5.

3. Washington to John A. Washington, June 20, 1775, in Fitzpatrick, ed., *Writings of Washington* 3:299. The best account of Washington's ride to Boston is in Douglas Southall Freeman, "Planter and Patriot," in *George Washington: A Biography* (New York, 1951), 3:460–77.

4. In this chapter, "Whig" refers to the late seventeenth- and early eighteenth-century opponents of a standing army.

5. Where I wish to indicate only that a particular delegate supported Washington's policies, or supported the establishment of a continental navy, I use the restrictive terms, "Washington's supporters," and "advocates of a navy." This group fluctuated throughout the period 1775–1776 with which this chapter deals, usually according to the fortunes of war. Where I wish to emphasize that the support for (or opposition to) a particular military policy reflected certain views toward the military's role in effecting social change or in mirroring the overall stability of society, I use the terms "radical," "moderate," and "conservative." Radicals favored using the military as a vehicle for social change. An extreme example of a military radical would be Timothy Matlack of the Pennsylvania Committee of Privates. Conservatives, on the other hand, favored hierarchy, order, and discipline in the military, because this, they believed, reflected the proper structure of society at large. Washington exemplified this view. The moderates, as ever, stood in between. In theory, they favored relying on a militia, and the values it embodied, as the military institution of choice. In practice, they were willing to defer to Washington's

presumed expertise, especially when his views on the need for a regular army appeared to be borne out by military misfortunes on the battlefield. Benjamin Franklin, the ultimate pragmatist, is an example of a military moderate.

6. John Shy, "American Strategy: Charles Lee and the Radical Alternative," in *A People Numerous and Armed: Reflections on the Military Struggle for American Independence* (London, 1976), pp. 161–62.

7. One of the best of the numerous accounts of the Battle of Bunker Hill is still Richard Frothingham, *The Siege of Boston* (Boston, 1851), pp. 121–206. For a modern summary, see Higginbotham, *War of Independence*, pp. 68–77. General Henry Clinton is cited in Allen French, *The First Year of the American Revolution* (Boston, 1934), p. 254; William Eden to [North], [Aug.] 1775, Auckland Papers, Additional MSS, vol. 34412, fol. 340; Gage is cited in French, *First Year*, p. 258; casualty estimates are from Greene, *Revolutionary War*, p. 12. Although the battle was fought on Breed's Hill, not Bunker Hill, I shall continue to employ the more familiar name.

8. [John Trenchard and Walter Moyle], *An Argument Shewing, That A Standing Army Is Inconsistent With A Free Government, And Absolutely Destructive To The Constitution Of The English Monarchy* (London, 1697), p. 11. The most important pamphlets on Whig military philosophy were those published near the end of the seventeenth century during the controversy over the small army that William III attempted to maintain after the Treaty of Ryswick in 1697. They included, in addition to the above: [John Trenchard], *A Short History of Standing Armies In England . . .* (London, 1698); and [Andrew Fletcher], *A Discourse On Government With Relation to Militia . . .* (London, 1698). The best accounts of the controversy are by Lois G. Schwoerer, "The Literature of the Standing Army Controversy, 1697–1699," *Huntington Library Quarterly* 28 (1965): 187–212; and Schwoerer's *"No Standing Armies!" The Antiarmy Ideology in Seventeenth-Century England* (Baltimore, 1974). An especially interesting interpretation of the significance of these arguments for the development of eighteenth-century Whig thought on corruption is J.G.A. Pocock, "Machiavelli, Harrington, and English Political Ideologies in the Eighteenth Century," *WMQ*, 3d ser., 22 (1965): 558–64. The importance of this literature to the military attitudes of the American revolutionaries has been extensively examined in Lawrence D. Cress, *Citizens in Arms: The Army and the Militia in American Society to the War of 1812* (Chapel Hill, N.C., 1982), pp. 15–33.

9. See, for example, Trenchard and Gordon, *Cato's Letters* 2:321; James Burgh, cited in Schwoerer, "Standing Army Controversy," 210. See generally Cress, *Citizens in Arms*, pp. 16–25.

10. Comte de Guibert, quoted in Orville T. Murphy, "The American Revolutionary Army and the Concept of *Levée en masse,*" *Military Affairs* 32 (1969): 14. See also Trenchard and Moyle, *An Argument*, pp. 20–21; [Trenchard], *Standing Army*, p. 42, and, in general, Fletcher, *A Discourse*, and Cress, *Citizens in Arms*, pp. 20–21.

11. English faith in the militia was largely theoretical in the eighteenth century, because the trained bands, from long disuse, had deteriorated into little

more than county social organizations. On the English militia during this period, see John R. Western, *The English Militia in the Eighteenth Century: The Story of A Political Issue, 1660–1802* (London, 1965).

12. Much good work has been done on the American colonial militia. This brief sketch is drawn from some of these studies, including: David Cole, "A Brief Outline of the South Carolina Militia System," S.C. Hist. Soc., *Proceedings*, 1954:14–25; E. Milton Wheeler, "The Development and Organization of the North Carolina Militia," *North Carolina Historical Review* 41 (1965): 307–23; John R. Anderson, "Militia Law in Revolutionary Jersey: The Beginnings, 1775–1776," and "Militia Law in Revolutionary Jersey: 'Men Not Money,' 1777–1781," N.J. Hist. Soc., *Proceedings*, n.s., 76 (1958): 280–96, and 77 (1959): 9–21; Jack S. Radabaugh, "The Militia of Colonial Massachusetts," *Military Affairs* 18 (1954): 1–18; French, *First Year*, pp. 32–39. For a most interesting general theory, see John Shy, "A New Look at the Colonial Militia," *WMQ*, 3d ser., 20 (1963): 175–85. For a recent survey of the function and practice of the eighteenth-century militia, see Cress, *Citizens in Arms*, pp. 4–8.

13. Cress, *Citizens in Arms*, pp. 4–8. For studies that emphasize the declining military importance of the eighteenth-century militia, see Shy, "Colonial Militia," 181–82; John M. Murrin, "Anglicizing an American Colony: The Transformation of Provincial Massachusetts" (Ph.D. diss., Yale University, 1966).

14. See John Shy's pathbreaking study, *Toward Lexington: The Role of the British Army in the Coming of the American Revolution* (Princeton, 1965), pp. 191–231, 267–320.

15. [Thomas Pickering], *Essex Gazette*, Jan. 31, 1769, quoted in Charles K. Bolton, *The Private Soldier under Washington* (Port Washington, N.Y., 1964), p. 31 n. 3. See also "A Carolinian," Timothy's *South Carolina Gazette*, Aug. 23, 1774; Benjamin Rush to Catherine Macaulay, Jan. 18, 1769, in Butterfield, ed., *Rush Letters* 1:70; "Caius," *Pennsylvania Journal*, Oct. 5, 1774. Pickering's phrasing was typical and appeared in most of the colonial militia resolutions; the reference to the militia in the second amendment to the Constitution is a variation on this theme. See Robert E. Shalhope, "The Ideological Origins of the Second Amendment," *Journal of American History* 69 (1982): 599. On the importance of the troops, see Shy, *Toward Lexington, passim*; Cress, *Citizens in Arms*, pp. 34–44.

16. Quoted in Richard H. Kohn, *Eagle and Sword: The Federalists and the Creation of the Military Establishment in America, 1783–1802* (New York and London, 1975), p. 6; "Caractacus," "On Standing Armies," Dunlap's *Pennsylvania Packet; or, The General Advertiser* (Phila.), Aug. 21, 1775. Some of the more important patriot pamphlets of 1774 develop this theme. See, for example, Jefferson, *Summary View*, and Josiah Quincy, Jr., *Observations on the Boston Port-Bill*. Charles Royster has characterized the legacy of radical Whig treatises, and the experience with the troops in Boston, as follows:

> The most prevalent wartime legacy of the ingrained suspicion of a standing army was not ideological but emotional. The revolutionaries felt a strong distaste for an army in repose, an army as an institution, an army

as an organ of the state. Nothing surpassed their admiration for soldiers in combat, and no degree of admiration could allay their intuitive conviction that an officer corps must tend to subvert self-government. We scarcely overstate the revolutionaries' concern by saying that they felt that when the army was not attacking the British, it must be doing some mischief to the revolutionaries.

This is from *A Revolutionary People at War: The Continental Army and American Character, 1775–1783* (Chapel Hill, N.C., 1979), p. 36.

17. See, for example, "PROPOSALS for the good of the AMERICAN Colonies made and offered by a Philadelphian," *Boston-Gazette*, Mar. 15, 1773.

18. French, *First Year*, pp. 35–40; Proc. of Suffolk and Worcester County Conventions, Sept. 6, 1774, and Proc. of the Provincial Congress, Oct. 26, 1774, are in Lincoln, ed., *Journal Prov. Congress of Mass.*, pp. 33–34, 604, 636; *JCC* 1:54. (This was the resolution that had so disappointed R. H. Lee; see Chapter 3.) See also, Gerry to Boston Committee of Correspondence, Apr. 4, 1774, Gerry Papers, box 1.

19. Purdie and Dixon's *Virginia Gazette*, Oct. 27, 1774; "Moses and Aaron," *Massachusetts Spy*, Oct. 27, 1774. It would be interesting to know whether the elderly Watertown company ever marched beside a unit from Newport, Rhode Island, that consisted of "fifty young gentlemen, the eldest not exceeding the age of fourteen." Rind and Pinkney's *Virginia Gazette*, Feb. 23, 1775.

20. Saltonstall to Deane, Sept. 5, 1774, in "Deane Correspondence," Conn. Hist. Soc., *Collections* 2:150; R. H. Lee to William Lee, Sept. 20, 1774, and Rodney to Thomas Rodney, Sept. 19, 1774, in Smith, ed., *LDC* 1:88, 85–86; *Massachusetts Spy*, Sept. 8, 1774.

21. See Chapter 3 for the mood in Philadelphia when the war rumors of 1774 were contradicted. Proc. of the Maryland Convention, in Force, ed., *American Archives*, 4th ser., 1:1032; and Duane to Samuel Chase, Dec. 29, 1774, in Smith, ed., *LDC* 1:277; Proc. of the Virginia Convention, Mar. 5, 1775, in Force, ed., *American Archives*, 4th ser., 2:169–70; Proc. of the Newcastle, Del., Committee, *Pennsylvania Journal*, Dec. 28, 1774.

22. See, for example, James Duane to Thomas Johnson, Dec. 29, 1774, in Smith, ed., *LDC* 1:281; Royster, *Revolutionary People at War*, pp. 11–13.

23. This sketch of Lee's career is drawn from John R. Alden, *General Charles Lee: Traitor or Patriot?* (Baton Rouge, La., 1951), pp. 1–65.

24. The authorship is in dispute for *A Friendly Address To All Reasonable Americans, On The Subject Of Our Political Confusions: In Which The Necessary Consequences Of Violently Opposing The King's Troops, And Of A General Non-Importation Are Fairly Stated . . .* (New York, 1774). The standard bibliographies by Evans and Adams assign it to Thomas Bradbury Chandler, but Alden attributes it to Myles Cooper; see *Charles Lee*, p. 62.

25. [Charles Lee], *Strictures On A Pamphlet, Entitled, "A Friendly Address To All Reasonable Americans, On The Subject Of Our Political Confusions. Addressed To The People Of America . . ."* (1774), included in Charles Lee, *The Life and Memoirs of the Late Major General Lee . . .* (New York, 1813), pp. 122–24.

26. Ibid., pp. 127–30.

27. For examples of the popularity of Lee's arguments, see, for example, Charles Chauncy to Richard Price, Jan. 10, 1775, in "Letters to and from Richard Price," Mass. Hist. Soc., *Proc.*, 2d ser., 17 (1903): 276. There are reports from Rhode Island in Rind and Pinkney's *Virginia Gazette*, Feb. 23, 1775; *South Carolina and American Gazette*, Mar. 24–31, May 12–19, 1775. Benjamin Rush conceded that Lee had been useful in "inspiring our citizens with military ideas and lessening in our soldiers their superstitious fear of the valor and discipline of the British army." Quoted in Shy, "Charles Lee," in George Billias, ed., *Washington's Generals* (New York, 1964), p. 46. See also Royster, *Revolutionary People at War*, pp. 40–41.

28. James Thacher, *Military Journal of the American Revolution . . .* (New York, 1969), p. 13. A good account of the skirmishes is in Allen French, *The Day of Lexington and Concord: The Nineteenth of April, 1775* (Boston, 1925).

29. R. H. Lee to William Lee, May 10, 1775, in Smith, ed., *LDC* 1:337; Becker, *Political Parties in New York*, p. 193; George Gilmer to Jefferson [July 26 or 27, 1775], in Boyd, *Jefferson Papers* 1:238; Joseph Hewes to Samuel Johnston, May 11, 1775, in Smith, ed., *LDC* 1:342. An excellent account of the *rage militaire* in the spring of 1775 is in Royster, *Revolutionary People at War*, pp. 25–31.

30. *Pennsylvania Journal*, May 10, 1775. The delegates' letters are replete with descriptions of extensive military preparations. See, for example, Benjamin Franklin to David Hartley, May 8, 1775, R. H. Lee to William Lee, May 10, 1775; Richard Caswell to William Caswell, May 11, 1775, and Silas Deane to Elizabeth Deane, May 12, 1775, in Smith, ed., *LDC* 1:335–36, 337–38, 339–40, 345–47.

31. Purdie's *Virginia Gazette*, July 28, 1775. Proc. of the South Carolina Provincial Congress, *South Carolina and American Gazette*, June 2–9, 23–30, 1775; Drayton, *Memoirs of the American Revolution* 1:255, 258.

32. North Carolina delegates to North Carolina Committees, June 19, 1775, in Smith, ed., *LDC* 1:513. Proc. of the North Carolina Convention, Aug. 31, Sept. 1, 1775, in Saunders, ed., *Colonial Records of North Carolina* 10:185–88. North Carolina's lack of vigor, when compared with her sister colonies, was a persistent theme of her delegates. See Joseph Hewes to Samuel Johnston, May 23, 1775; and William Hooper to Samuel Johnston, May 23, 1775, in Smith, ed., *LDC* 1:397, 399. Proc. of the New York Provincial Congress, May 31, 1775, *New-York Gazette*, June 5, 1775. New York's activity, which so amazed many delegates in comparison to the province's lack of such spirit in 1774, was due in large part to the news that several regiments of British troops had been ordered to proceed to New York. See below. See also, Proc. of the New Jersey Provincial Congress, June 3, 1775, in Force, ed., *American Archives*, 4th ser., 2:261, and Land, ed., *Letters from America*, p. 113.

33. Marshall to Peter Barker, June 24, 1775, Christopher Marshall Letterbook, Hist. Soc. of Pa., Philadelphia. The votes of the Assembly on June 30, 1775, are in Charles F. Hoban et al., eds., *Pennsylvania Archives*, 8th ser. (Philadelphia and Harrisburg, 1852–1935), 8:7245–49. For the spirit in Philadelphia and the Pennsylvania backcountry after Lexington and Concord, see J[ames]

Wilson to Jaspar Yeates, May 9, 1775, Fogg Coll., Maine Historical Society, Portland; Benjamin Rush to Thomas Ruston, Oct. 29, 1775, in Butterfield, ed., *Rush Letters* 1:92; Richard Caswell to William Caswell, May 11, 1775, in Smith, ed., *LDC* 1:340. The military organization in Pennsylvania was to have immense political consequences. See Ryerson, *Revolution Is Now Begun*, pp. 117–47.

34. The decisions of the Massachusetts authorities are in Lincoln, ed., *Journal Prov. Congress of Mass.* A good narrative account of the origin of the Massachusetts Army is in French, *First Year*, pp. 47–75. Although the Massachusetts Provincial Congress was in charge of the army, troops were raised in Connecticut, Rhode Island, and New Hampshire as well as Massachusetts. See Lincoln, ed., *Journal Prov. Congress of Mass.*, pp. 148–49.

35. French, *First Year*, pp. 47–75; James Warren to J. Adams, May 7, 1775, in Ford, ed., *Warren-Adams Letters* 1:47.

36. Thus, the Committee of Safety assured the men on April 26 that "the utmost care will be taken to make every soldier happy in being under good officers." Lincoln, ed., *Journal Prov. Congress of Mass.*, p. 523.

37. For pay scales, see Table 5.1. The Massachusetts pay scale is in Proc. of the Provincial Congress, Apr. 23, 1775, in Force, ed., *American Archives*, 4th ser., 2:766, and under the date of Apr. 28, 1775, in Lincoln, ed., *Journal Prov. Congress of Mass.*, p. 163.

38. Proc. of the Provincial Congress, Apr. 5, 1775, in Lincoln, ed., *Journal Prov. Congress of Mass.*, p. 121; the Massachusetts Articles of War are in ibid., pp. 121–29. See also, "Agreement of the Wethersfield Company of Volunteers," Apr. 3, 1775, in "Deane Correspondence," Conn. Hist. Soc., *Collections* 2:216.

39. Thacher, *Military Journal*, p. 27; "Cosmopolitan," *Massachusetts Spy*, Dec. 1, 1775. See also, Benjamin Franklin to Jonathan Shipley, July 7, 1775, and Thomas Lynch to Ralph Izard, July 7, 1775, in Smith, ed., *LDC* 1:605, 609. The historian of the British army noted that insofar as Bunker Hill encouraged Americans in their "blind and fatal confidence in undisciplined troops," it was "probably a greater misfortune" to the Americans than to the British. See J. W. Fortescue, *A History of the British Army* (London, 1911), 3:162. See also, Greene, *Revolutionary War*, p. 11. Similar accounts of the victory of the untrained Americans circulated after Lexington and Concord. See, for example, Richard Henry Lee to William Lee, May 10, 1775, in Smith, ed., *LDC* 1:337–38.

40. Joseph Warren to S. Adams, May 17, 1775, S. Adams Papers, vol. 7.

41. Joseph Warren to S. Adams, May 26, 1775, ibid.

42. Gerry to the Massachusetts Delegates, June 4, 1775, in Austin, *Life of Gerry*, 1:78–79. See also, Col. E. Doolittle to J. Hancock, Mar. 21, 1775, in Force, ed., *American Archives*, 4th ser., 2:177–78.

43. Petition to the Massachusetts Provincial Congress, May 16, 1775 in Lincoln, ed., *Journal Prov. Congress of Mass.*, pp. 229–31. It also appears under the date June 2, 1775, in *JCC* 2:76–78.

44. J. Adams to James Warren, May 21, 1775, in Smith, ed., *LDC* 1:364. The New Hampshire Provincial Congress on May 23 wrote that the province "for

the present" had resolved to raise 2,000 men, though its action was only interim "untill we have the Advice of the Continental Congress, to whose Su-
perintendency we chuse to submit." Similarly, a Connecticut delegate was advised that his province's citizens "look up to the Congress for direction" and
would "proceed to any lengths they shall recommend." [Matthew Thornton],
New Hampshire Provincial Congress to Continental Congress, May 23, 1775,
Force Coll., ser. 9, box 12; Thomas Mumford to Deane, May 22, 1775, "Deane
Correspondence," Conn. Hist. Soc., *Collections* 2:235.

45. Autobiography, in Butterfield, ed., *Adams Papers* 3:315.

46. Resolution of New York Committee of 100 to New York Delegates, May
10, 1775, in Force, ed., *American Archives*, 4th ser., 2:531; New York Delegates
to New York Provincial Congress, May 16, 1775, in Smith, ed., *LDC* 1:353; the
resolution appears under the date of May 15, 1775, in *JCC* 2:49, 52–53. The
news of the British plan to send four regiments to New York was carried by
Benjamin Franklin, who arrived on May 5. See Jonathan G. Rossie, *The Politics
of Command in the American Revolution* (Syracuse, N.Y., 1975), pp. 2–3. On the
strategic importance of New York, see ibid., p. 3. A committee was appointed
on May 15 to consider further the problem of the defense of New York. This is
the first indication that the Congress would accept continuing responsibility
for advising individual colonies on military affairs. Washington was appointed to this committee, a clear indication that his colleagues valued his military expertise.

47. Silas Deane Diary [May 18, 1775], and George Read to Gertrude Read,
May 18, 1775, in Smith, ed., *LDC* 1:356, 359. The strategic importance of the
forts lay in their location. Ticonderoga and Crown Point guarded the land por-
tage between Lakes Champlain and George. An army invading New York
from Canada (or vice versa) would have to pass this point. See Rossie, *Politics
of Command*, p. 4. A good account of the affair is in Allen French, *The Taking of
Ticonderoga in 1775* (Boston and New York, 1928). The capture of the forts was
not a particularly impressive military achievement; a year earlier, British military men had commented on the "ruinous state" of both Ticonderoga and
Crown Point and recommended abandoning the latter. See Haldimand to
Lord Dartmouth, Mar. 2, 1774, Haldimand Papers, Additional MSS, vol.
21695, fol. 78.

48. Allen and Arnold sent Brown to New York City as soon as the forts were
captured. Isaac Low, chairman of the New York Committee of 100, received
the news on May 15. He "thought proper to refer the matter" to Congress, as
the New Yorkers "did not conceive ourselves Authorized to give any Opinion
upon a matter of such Importance." Low to Hancock, May 15, 1775, Force
Coll., ser. 9, box 12. Allen himself is the source of the legendary quote; see
Ethan Allen, *A Narrative of Col. Ethan Allen's Captivity*, 4th ed. (Burlington, Vt.,
1846), pp. 14–15. The British officer to whom the remark was addressed later
remembered Allen as having shouted, "Come out, you old rat." French, *First
Year*, p. 151.

49. New Hampshire Delegates to Provincial Congress of New Hampshire,
May 22, 1775, and Connecticut Delegates to William Whipple, May 31, 1775,
in Smith, ed., *LDC* 1:369, 423; *JCC* 2:55–56.

50. See French, *First Year*, pp. 153–54. On the anxiety caused by the May 18 instruction, see Sub-Committee of Albany to Provincial Congress of New-York, May 26, 1775; Assembly of Connecticut to Massachusetts Congress, May 27, 1775; Massachusetts Provincial Congress to Hancock, May 27, 1775; Joseph Hawley to James Warren, June 9, 1775, in Force, ed., *American Archives*, 4th ser., 2:712–13, 719, 944–45; Bouton, ed., *N.H. Prov. Papers* 7:488, 497–500.

51. May 31, June 1, 1775, *JCC* 2:73–5.

52. Deane to Mrs. Deane, June 3, 1775, in Smith, ed., *LDC* 1:436.

53. Adams to James Warren, May 21, 1775, in Ford, ed., *Warren-Adams Letters* 1:51; J. Adams to Moses Gill, June 10, 1775, in Smith, ed., *LDC* 1:466. As early as June 3 the delegates had resolved to borrow £6,000 for "the purchase of gunpowder for the use of the Continental Army." See *JCC* 2:79. The need for a New York army had been clear since early May, when the news had arrived of the four regiments that were to be stationed in New York City. See note 46.

54. Adams Autobiography, in Butterfield, ed., *Adams Papers* 3:321–22.

55. Dyer to Joseph Trumbull, June 17, 1775, in Smith, ed., *LDC* 1:499.

56. Adams Autobiography, in Butterfield, ed., *Adams Papers* 3:321–23. New Englanders had been discussing the possibility of Washington's appointment since early May. See James Warren to John Adams, May 7, 1775, in Ford, ed., *Warren-Adams Letters* 1:47. Butterfield assigns the probable date of June 14 to Adams's resolution. See also a letter from a Virginia delegate to an unknown addressee June 14, 1775, in Smith, ed., *LDC* 1:486.

57. June 15–17, 19, 20, 22–24, 26, 30, July 13, 14, 18, 19, 25, 29, 1775, *JCC* 2:91, 93–94, 97–101, 103–5, 106–7, 111–22, 183–84, 187–90, 191, 207, 220–23. The resolves establishing the size and disposition of the army do not appear in the *Journals* in June, although on June 18, John Adams wrote to Elbridge Gerry giving the correct figures. See Smith, ed., *LDC* 1:503. The editors conclude that the resolves were agreed to in committee of the whole at about the time of Washington's selection. The size of the northern army appears in *JCC* 2:207 under the date of July 25. On July 21 Washington was authorized to increase the size of the army in Massachusetts to 22,000 men. See *JCC* 2:202. Quote in text is from Connecticut Delegates to Jonathan Trumbull, Jr., July 28, 1775, in Smith, ed., *LDC* 1:672. On the adjournment, see Francis Lewis to Philip Schuyler, Aug. 2, 1775, in ibid., p. 694. The best description of the organization of the Continental Army is Robert K. Wright, Jr., *The Continental Army* (Washington, D.C., 1983), pp. 45–65.

58. Nicholas Cooke to Rhode Island Delegates, Jan. 21, 1776, Force Coll., ser. 9, box 15. A good narrative of the organization of the Continental Army and the appointment of the high command is in Jonathan G. Rossie, *Politics of Command*, pp. 1–30.

59. Autobiography, in Butterfield, ed., *Adams Papers* 3:321–22. The congressional coalition to which Adams referred was not, of course, a political party in the modern sense. Rather, the term connotes the fluctuating coalition of delegates who generally supported Washington's efforts to build a regular army and who may well have shared the social views that underlay those efforts. Initially there was some basis for Adams's opinion that the split between

the supporters of a regular army and those who favored a citizen army was a sectional one. The New England delegates often differed from those in the middle and southern colonies on the issues of army pay scales, the length of enlistment, and other matters. Thus, for example, in the only recorded congressional debate over military affairs in the early months of the war (which concerned the congressional appointment of officers, a move that would have undercut the quasi-election of New England officers), the sectional division holds firm. Supporting congressional appointments were James Duane and John Jay (N.Y.), George Ross (Pa.), Samuel Chase (Md.) and E. Rutledge (S.C.). Defending provincial appointments were Deane and Dyer (Conn.), Langdon (N.H.), and Ward (R.I.). See Notes of Debates, Oct. 10, 1775, in Butterfield, ed., *Adams Papers* 2:203–4; also see below. But such positions were constantly subject to change. John Adams, for example, whose military views were typical of his section in 1775, changed into an advocate of a regular army later in the war, probably as a result of his close association with military affairs as a member of various standing committees. Some New Englanders had begun to question the concept of a citizen army by the middle of 1775, if not before (see above, text accompanying notes 40 and 41).

60. J. Adams to Joseph Hawley, Nov. 25, 1775, in Smith, ed., *LDC* 2:385; John Armstrong to James Wilson, May 7, 1776, Gratz Coll., case 4, box 11. See also J. Adams to Cotton Tufts, June 21, 1775, and J. Adams to J. Winthrop, Oct. 2, 1775, in Smith, ed., *LDC* 1:529, 2:96; also, Thomas Hartly to James Wilson and George Read, May 1, 1776, Gratz Coll., case 4, box 20. On the military effects of the differing social philosophies, see Bolton, *Private Soldier*, p. 127. Adams made the comments cited above in the context of a letter explaining to Hawley why the Congress had voted to increase the officers' pay but not that of the privates. Pay scales similar to those in the southern colonies probably prevailed in the middle colonies as well. See below, Table 5-1; also, Pennsylvania Delegates to Cumberland County Committee of Correspondence, June 15, 1775, in Smith, ed., *LDC* 1:491–92.

61. Most military historians who have written on this phase of Washington's career have agreed that the general's military philosophy was a conservative one. See Marcus Cunliffe, "George Washington: George Washington's Generalship," in Billias, ed., *Washington's Generals*, pp. 11–12; Marcus Cunliffe, *George Washington: Man and Monument* (New York, 1958), p. 110; Russell F. Weigley, *Towards An American Army: Military Thought from Washington to Marshall* (New York and London, 1962), pp. 2–9; Higginbotham, *War of Independence*, p. 87; Walter Millis, *Arms and Men* (New York, 1956), p. 26; Sidney Kaplan, "Rank and Status Among Washington's Continental Officers," *American Historical Review* 56 (1951): 322. As Royster notes, Washington and his senior officers "wanted the Continental Army to become a regular army in its discipline as well as in the duration of its enlistments. When they thought of a regular army, they thought of the armies of Europe, especially Britain's, officered by gentlemen, disciplined by force, maneuvered in the field by elaborate formulas." *Revolutionary People at War*, p. 70. A good description of the characteristics of eighteenth-century warfare as fought by regular armies is in R. R.

Palmer, "Frederick the Great, Guilbert and Bulow: From Dynastic to National War," in *Makers of Modern Strategy: Military Thought from Machiavelli to Hitler*, ed. by Edward M. Earle (Princeton, 1948), pp. 49–52.

62. Cited in Shy, "Charles Lee and the Radical Alternative," in Shy, ed., *A People Numerous and Armed*, p. 154. Shy was the first to detail this "radical alternative" to the conventional military strategy adopted by Washington and has linked it to advanced military thinking then current in Europe: "[Lee] sought a war that would use the new light-infantry tactics already in vogue among the military avant-garde of Europe, the same tactics the free men at Lexington and Concord had instinctively employed. Such men could not be successfully hammered into goose-stepping automatons and made to fire by platoons, but properly trained and employed, they could not be defeated." See ibid., p. 161, and, in general, pp. 150–55, 160–62. A military treatise very popular among Americans advocated that they adopt just such strategies, arguing against, for example, fixed battles with the regulars and advocating essentially guerrilla tactics. See Lewis Nicola, *A Treatise of Military Exercise, Calculated For the Use of the Americans* (Philadelphia, 1776). See also Don Higginbotham, "Daniel Morgan: Guerilla Fighter," in Billias, ed., *Washington's Generals*, pp. 291–313.

63. General Harvey to General Irwin, June 30, 1775, quoted in Fortescue, *History of the British Army* 3:167. Oct. 30, 1774, Hutchinson, ed., *Diary and Letters of Hutchinson* 1:272; Sewall to [Haldimand], May 30, 1775, Haldimand Papers, Additional MSS, vol. 21695, fol. 122; see also Jack Weller, "The Irregular War in the South," *Military Affairs* 24 (1960): 124–36; and Robert C. Pugh, "The Revolutionary Militia in the Southern Campaigns, 1780–81," *WMQ*, 3d ser., 14 (1957): 154–75.

64. Cunliffe, "Washington's Generalship," in Billias, ed., *Washington's Generals*, pp. 11–12. See also John Shy, "The American Revolution: The Military Conflict Considered as a Revolutionary War," in Kurtz and Hutson, eds., *Essays on the American Revolution*, pp. 121–56; and Shy, "Charles Lee and the Radical Alternative," in Shy, ed., *A People Numerous and Armed*, p. 161.

65. Washington's success, however, was apparent early on. "By the summer of 1776," Cress concludes, "Congress was well on its way toward creating a military establishment that placed a premium on military expertise, avoided the use of militiamen whenever possible, and relied extensively on enlistment bonuses and bounties to fill the ranks of the chronically undermanned American Army." *Citizens in Arms*, p. 58.

66. General Orders, July 4, 1775; and, for example, General Orders, July 22, 24, 26, Aug. 1, 3, 1775; Washington to Hancock, July 20, 1775, in Fitzpatrick, ed., *Writings of Washington* 3:309, 355, 363, 366, 382, 384, 349. For a sympathetic view of Washington's efforts to impose strict discipline, see Stuart L. Bernath, "George Washington and the Genesis of American Military Discipline," *Mid-America* 49 (1967): 83–100.

67. See, for example, General Orders, July 5, 15, Aug. 21, 1775, in Fitzpatrick, ed., *Writings of Washington* 3:312, 340–41, 439.

68. Thacher, *Military Journal*, p. 59; Lee to Robert Morris, quoted in Bolton,

Private Soldier, p. 131; Washington to Lund Washington, Aug. 20, 1775, in Fitz-patrick, ed., *Writings of Washington* 3:433. See also Nathanael Greene to Jacob Greene, June 28, 1775, in Richard K. Showman, ed., *The Papers of General Na-thanael Greene* (Chapel Hill, N.C., 1976), 1:92–93; and Joseph Hawley to Wash-ington, July 5, 1775, in Force, ed., *American Archives*, 4th ser., 2:1126, 1589. On the lack of discipline, see Royster, *Revolutionary People at War*, pp. 69–76.

69. *JCC* 2:109–10; French, *First Year*, pp. 158–59; Rossie, *Politics of Command*, pp. 36–37. See also R. H. Lee to George Washington, June 29, 1775: "You will see that we have again taken up the business of entering Canada, and have left the propriety of it to Gener. Schuyler. If it can be done, in a manner agreeable to the Canadians, it will certainly shut the door against dangerous tampering with the Indians on all our Western frontiers." Smith, ed., *LDC* 1:558.

70. On American efforts in Canada, see Justin H. Smith, *Our Struggle for the Fourteenth Colony* (New York, 1907); and Gustave Lanctot, *Canada and the Amer-ican Revolution: 1774–1783*, trans. Margaret M. Cameron (Cambridge, Mass., 1967), pp. 43–148.

71. The early difficulties are narrated in French, *First Year*, pp. 383–94, 415–31; and Hancock to Schuyler, Oct. 11, 1775, in Smith, ed., *LDC* 2:163. See also, R. H. Lee to [Charles Lee], Apr. 22, 1776, in Ballagh, ed., *Letters of Lee* 1:182. For an account of the Canadian debacle that lays the blame at the door of Schuyler, see Rossie, *Politics of Command*, pp. 45–60.

72. Benedict Arnold to Deane, Mar. 30, 1776, in "Papers of Silas Deane, 1774–1790," New-York Hist. Soc., *Collections* 19 (1886): 128–29; Josiah Bartlett to John Langdon, June 10, 1776, in Smith, ed., *LDC* 4:181.

73. Arthur St. Clair to James Wilson, May 19, 23, 1776, and Irvine to James Wilson, June 1, 1776, Gratz Coll., case 4, boxes 14, 12; [Alexander Graydon], *Memoirs Of A Life, Chiefly Passed in Pennsylvania, Within the Last Sixty Years . . .* (Harrisburg, Pa., 1811), p. 126. Feb. 15, 1776, *JCC* 4:151. The members of the committee were Charles Carroll of Carrollton, Benjamin Franklin, and Samuel Chase. The fragmented and disorganized supply system devised by Congress is described in E. Wayne Carp, *To Starve the Army at Pleasure: Continental Army Administration and American Political Culture, 1775–1783* (Chapel Hill, N.C., 1984).

74. Nathanael Greene to Gov. Nicholas Cooke (R.I.), Sept. 17, 1776, in Showman, ed., *Greene Papers* 1:300.

75. Reed to Hancock, 1777, in Reed, *Life of Reed* 1:240; Graydon, *Memoirs*, p. 156. See also John Morin Scott to Jay, Sept. 6, 1776, in Henry P. Johnston, ed., *The Correspondence and Public Papers of John Jay* (New York and London, 1883–86), 1:81–82; Thacher, *Military Journal*, p. 58.

76. S. Adams to E. Gerry, Sept. 26, 1776, in Cushing, ed., *Writings of Adams* 3:226; J. Adams to William Tudor, Sept. 20, 1776, in Smith, ed., *LDC* 5:200. The reports of the infamous behavior of the New England troops filled the dele-gates' letters. See, for example, Arthur Middleton to William Henry Drayton, Sept. 18, 1776; and Caesar Rodney to Thomas McKean and George Read, Sept. 18, 1776, in Smith, ed., *LDC* 5:190–91, 197.

77. J. Adams to Samuel Parsons, Aug. 19, 1776, in Smith, ed., *LDC* 5:23; Au-tobiography, in Butterfield, ed., *Adams Papers* 3:433.

78. The Connecticut articles of war are in Force, ed., *American Archives*, 4th ser., 2:564–70.

79. The Massachusetts articles of war are in Lincoln, ed., *Journal Prov. Congress of Mass.*, pp. 120–29. The British articles of war for this period are in E. Samuel, *An Historical Account of the British Army . . .* (London, 1816), pp. 224–76; the Continental articles of war are in *JCC* 2:111–22; Roger Sherman to Joseph Trumbull, July 6, 1775, in Smith, ed., *LDC* 1:599. See also R. H. Lee to George Washington, June 29, 1775, in ibid., 558. For the legendary severity of punishment in the British army, see Edward E. Curtis, *The Organization of the British Army in the American Revolution* (New Haven, 1926), pp. 28–30. The differences between the continental articles and the Massachusetts articles were minimal. The Congress enumerated a few more triable offenses and limited somewhat the discretionary powers of courts-martial. Several articles were added that dealt with the administration of the army.

Most colonies organized their provincial forces subsequent to June 1775 and most accepted, in large part, the lenient Continental articles. See, for example, the Virginia articles of war, in Force, ed., *American Archives*, 4th ser., 3:411–18. An exception was Pennsylvania, which adopted its own "Rules and Regulations for the better Government of the MILITARY ASSOCIATION of Pennsylvania," on November 28, 1775. These rules were much milder than even the continental rules. Only eleven triable offenses were listed, none of them capital, and the only permitted punishments were degradation of rank, cashiering, and fining. It is no wonder, then, that the Pennsylvania companies were reluctant to sign the Continental articles when they were called into continental service. The Pennsylvania rules are in Hoban et al., eds., *Pennsylvania Archives*, 8th ser., 8:7369–80.

80. Washington to Hancock, Sept. 24, 1776, in Fitzpatrick, ed., *Writings of Washington* 6:111; June 14, Aug. 7, 1776, *JCC* 5:442, 636. The delegates had, in fact, slightly revised the articles as early as November 1775 in conjunction with the enlistment of the army for 1776. The revision, which entailed an increase in the number of offenses that would result in cashiering, had been discussed by Washington and the congressional "Camp Committee" that had been sent to confer with the general in September 1775. See Thomas Lynch to George Washington, Nov. 13, 1775, in Smith, ed., *LDC* 1:338. The revised articles are dated November 7, 1775, in *JCC* 3:331–34.

81. Autobiography, in Butterfield, ed., *Adams Papers* 3:409–10, 433. Edward Rutledge wrote, more accurately, that the British articles had been adopted "as far as local Circumstances will admit." Rutledge to R. R. Livingston [Aug. 19? 1776], in Smith, ed., *LDC* 5:26. The revised Articles of War are in *JCC* 5:788–807.

82. Hancock to Gen. Horatio Gates, Sept. 27, 1776, in Smith, ed., *LDC* 5:255.

83. John Jones to John Dickinson, July 6, 1776, Dickinson Papers, item 25-1, Library Company of Phila. See also Joseph Reed to Elias Boudinot, Aug. 13, 1775, Gratz Coll., case 4, box 14.

84. Wilkinson, cited in Kaplan, "Rank and Status," *American Historical Review* 56 (1951): 321; Graydon, *Memoirs*, p. 131; Reed, *Life of Reed* 1:243; John Marshall, *The Life of George Washington, Commander in Chief Of The American*

Forces During The War Which Established The Independence Of His Country, And First President Of The United States, 2d ed. (Philadelphia, 1848), 1:101–2.

85. Moylan to Washington, Oct. 24, 1775; and Washington to Hancock, Sept. 24, 1776, in Fitzpatrick, ed., *Writings of Washington* 3:508 n. 60, 6:110. See, in general, Bolton, *Private Soldier,* pp. 125–42.

86. Royster has explained the direct relationship between the pay scale and the social hierarchy: "Continental Army officers sought . . . distance from their men because they believed, as did officers in European armies, that social hierarchy sustained military hierarchy. To have the proper authority over enlisted men, they thought, an officer had to be a gentleman." But in America, Royster argues, there were not enough "real" gentlemen to go around, and therefore, for those who shared these ideas, an officer class had to be created. "By upholding standards of ostentatious conduct, with a pay scale to support it, senior officers and their allies in Congress tried to create a corps of gentlemen." *Revolutionary People at War,* pp. 86–87.

87. The values referred to in this section are ratios instead of absolute values because pay rates for the various militia and provincial forces were usually given in provincial currencies whose value relative to the pound sterling and each other was constantly in flux. Both ratios and absolute values are found in Table 5-1. The dollar, the continental currency adopted in June 1775, also fluctuated in value, although not as much during the early period as during the later war years.

88. See Samuel Ward to Samuel Ward, Jr., Aug. 15, 1775, in Smith, ed., *LDC* 1:702; *JCC* 2:89–90, 93–94. The full pay scale, which had been adopted piecemeal through June and July for the various administrative officers, was listed under the date of July 29, ibid., pp. 220–21.

89. J. Adams to E. Gerry, June 18, 1775, in Smith, ed., *LDC* 1:504.

90. Ibid.; J. Adams to Cotton Tufts, June 21, 1775, ibid., p. 529. The adoption of the Massachusetts pay scale caused problems in other colonies, where different pay scales had been the practice. The Pennsylvania delegates assured a local committee that they would do their best to see that the Pennsylvania Assembly voted additional funds to augment the salaries of the officers in any companies the committee raised. June 15, 1775, in Smith, ed., *LDC* 1:491.

91. Washington to Hancock, Sept. 21, 1775, in Fitzpatrick, ed., *Writings of Washington* 3:508.

92. *JCC* 3:265, 266, 270–72, 285. Thus, in transmitting the continental pay scale to the secretary of the New York Provincial Congress, Charles Thomson was careful to note that although "the Congress did not particularly ascertain the number of Days in a month, [he was] . . . confident they meant calendar month." Charles Thomson to John McKesson, Aug. 11, 1775, in Smith, ed., *LDC* 1:701. The delegates did not even wait for the return of the Camp Committee to begin their reformation. On October 9, when ordering the raising of two New Jersey battalions, the delegates specified that the privates were to be paid $5 per month, rather than the $6⅔ then prevailing in the Continental Army.

93. Thomas Lynch to George Washington, Nov. 13, 1775, in Smith, ed., *LDC* 2:338. See also James Bowdoin to Thomas Cushing, Dec. 9, 1775, Mass. Hist. Soc., *Proceedings*, 2d ser., 8 (1892–94): 289.

94. Lynch is quoted in Kaplan, "Rank and Status," p. 321; General Orders, Nov. 17, 1775, in Fitzpatrick, ed., *Writings of Washington* 4:95. On the significance of the pay scale, see above, note 86.

95. Petition of the Town of Harvard, Mass., Dec. 1775, Force, ed., *American Archives*, 4th ser., 4:1245.

96. "Diary of Rev. Benjamin Boardman," Mass. Hist. Soc., *Proceedings*, 2d ser., 7 (1891–92): 412; Gerry to J. Adams, Dec. 1775, Gerry Papers, box 1.

97. Hawley to J. Adams, Nov. 14, 1775, in Taylor, ed., *Papers of Adams*, 3:297. See also James Bowdoin to Thomas Cushing, Dec. 9, 1775, Mass. Hist. Soc., *Proceedings*, 2d ser., 8 (1892–94): 289; James Sullivan to John Sullivan, Dec. 6, 1775, in Force, ed., *American Archives*, 4th ser., 4:206.

98. By examining Table 5-1 one may note the impact of the successive pay alterations. A continental ensign, for example, who had been paid 1.5 times a private's pay in June 1775 and twice as much by November 1775 was making three times as much in October 1776. The October changes were even more dramatic in the case of the field officers, whose pay had not been raised the previous November. A continental colonel, for example, had his pay raised from 7.5 times a private's pay to 11.2 times as much. The October pay raises made the salaries of continental officers consistent with those of southern militia officers.

99. Washington to Massachusetts Provincial Congress, July 10, 1775; to Hancock, July 10, 1775; to R. H. Lee, July 10, 1775, in Fitzpatrick, ed., *Writings of Washington* 3:319, 326–27, 330.

100. This was due to another significant factor in the "continentalizing" of the army—the control of the appointment of officers. When Congress took over the Massachusetts Army, it also accepted the officers selected by the men and commissioned by the Provincial Congress. Washington had simply carried blank continental commissions with him to Cambridge, to be filled out upon his arrival. But he had been displeased with this arrangement almost from the day he had arrived in Cambridge, and he began urging Congress to make officer appointments and promotions a continental matter. In part this was due to his low opinion of the New England officers that the men selected. See Washington to Lund Washington, Aug. 20, 1775; and to R. H. Lee, Aug. 29, 1775, in Fitzpatrick, ed., *Writings of Washington* 3:433, 450–52. He pressed these views upon the camp committee, but on October 9 and 10, before the committee returned to Philadelphia, the issue came before the full Congress. The subject of the debate was whether Congress or the New Jersey Provincial Congress ought to appoint the officers for the two new continental battalions Congress had requested the Provincial Congress to raise. The debate was long and acrimonious, and it showed how deep the sectional divisions over military policy had become. The southern and middle colony delegates were ranged firmly on the side of congressional appointments, while those from New England strongly opposed them. See Notes of Debates, Oct. 10, 1775, in

Butterfield, ed., *Adams Papers* 2:202–4. Opposed to congressional appointment were Sherman (Conn.), Ward (R.I.), Dyer (Conn.), Langdon (N.H.), and Deane (Conn.). In favor of congressional appointment were Chase (Md.), E. Rutledge (S.C.), Duane (N.Y.), Ross (Pa.), and Jay (N.Y.). The issue was deferred until the return of the Camp Committee and, in the end, a compromise was reached. On November 7, Congress selected all officers above the rank of major for the two battalions—the men chosen, however, were those recommended by the New Jersey Provincial Congress. The precedent for continental appointment of officers under field rank, however, was set, and on December 8 a standing committee consisting of one delegate from each colony was appointed to "take into consideration the application of the several persons applying to be officers in the American army." Thus by December the control of officer appointments above the rank of captain was firmly in continental hands, a fact the New Englanders found most disturbing, for in the ensuing "continentalizing" of their regiments, many of their chosen officers were not selected or were denied promotions. *JCC* 3:285, 289, 385, 416. The best account of this process, upon which the above draws heavily, is Rossie, *Politics of Command*, pp. 69–74.

101. E. Gerry to J. Adams, Dec. 4, 1775, Gerry Papers, box 1. On the bounty, see, for example, Thomas Mumford to Deane, Dec. 18, 1775, in "Deane Correspondence," Conn. Hist. Soc., *Collections* 2:344. Congress absolutely refused to offer the customary bounty, even after Washington, in desperation, began urging the delegates to do so. See Washington to Reed, Dec. 23, 1775, and Feb. 10, 1776, in Reed, *Life of Reed* 1:137, 157. On the reenlistment crisis of 1775, see French, *First Year*, pp. 503–26.

102. Washington's views may be traced in his letters to Hancock, Nov. 11, 28, Dec. 4, 11, 1775; to Joseph Reed, Nov. 28, Dec. 25, 1775, Jan. 14, 1776; to the Massachusetts Legislature, Nov. 29, 1775; and to Nicholas Cooke, Dec. 5, 1775, in Fitzpatrick, ed., *Writings of Washington* 4:83, 121–22, 143, 158, 124, 185, 241–42, 128, 145–46.

103. Washington to Hancock, Feb. 9, 1776, in Fitzpatrick, ed., *Writings of Washington* 4:316–18.

104. Washington to Massachusetts Legislature, Dec. 18, 1776; and to John A. Washington, Dec. 18, 1776, ibid. 6:395, 398.

105. Washington to Philip Schuyler, Sept. 20, 1776; and to Hancock, Sept. 24, 1776, ibid., pp. 81, 112.

106. For continuing New England fears about the dangerous tendencies of standing armies, see, for example, Ebenezer Baldwin to Deane, Oct. 30, 1775, in "Deane Correspondence," Conn. Hist. Soc., *Collections* 2:314; Autobiography, in Butterfield, ed., *Adams Papers* 3:387–88; Joseph Hawley to Gerry, July 17, 1776, in Austin, *Life of Gerry* 1:208; and William Williams to Joseph Trumbull, Sept. 13, 1776, in Smith, ed., *LDC* 5:156.

For the bounty and the promise of a suit of clothes annually, see *JCC* 5:762–63, 855. Congress had waited too long, however, and it was eventually forced, because of the dearth of men, to offer the bounty (but not the land) to those who would enlist for three years; ibid. 6:945, 971. The English official William

Eddis clearly saw the tendency of these changes. They afforded, he wrote, "the probability of a permanent army under the most strict and regular military discipline." To Mrs. Eddis, Jan. 1, 1777, in Land, ed., *Letters from America*, p. 176.

107. For army size, see note 57, and July 18, Nov. 4, 1775, *JCC* 2:187–90, 3:324. For Washington's encouragement to depend on militia, see, for example, Instructions to the Camp Committee, Oct. 2, 1775, in Papers of Cont. Congress, reel 23.

108. Douglas Southall Freeman, *George Washington: A Biography* (New York, 1948–57), 3:40, 148. For the success of the militia in local defense, see, for example, John Page to Charles Lee, July 12, 1776, in Charles Lee, *The Life and Memoirs of the Late Major General Lee, . . . To Which Are Added His Political and Military Essays* (New York, 1813), p. 219; "Extract of a Letter from Charlestown, South Carolina," June 29, 1775, *Pennsylvania Gazette*, July 19, 1775; Tryon City Committee to New York Provincial Congress, Sept. 19, 1775, in Force, ed., *American Archives*, 4th ser., 3:737; and, in general, Shy, "Military Conflict as Revolutionary War," in Kurtz and Hutson, eds., *Essays on the American Revolution*; and Fortescue, *History of the British Army* 3:407–8.

109. Washington to Joseph Reed, Mar. 25, 1776, in Reed, *Life of Reed* 1:177–78; and to Hancock, Sept. 24, 1776, in Fitzpatrick, ed., *Writings of Washington* 6:110–11. Washington's complaints about the inadequacies of the militia fill his letters. See, for example, Washington to Putnam, Aug. 25, 1776; to New York Legislature, Aug. 30, 1776; to Heath, Aug. 30, 1776; to Hancock, Sept. 2, 4, 8, 1776; to Trumbull, Sept. 9, 1776; to Samuel Washington, Oct. 5, 1776; and to Schuyler, Oct. 22, 1776, ibid. 5:489, 499, 6:4–6, 14, 32, 39, 169, 223.

110. Sept. 16, 1776, *JCC* 5:762; Hancock to Schuyler, Sept. 27, 1776, Papers of Cont. Congress, reel 23. See also, Cress, *Citizens in Arms*, p. 58.

111. It is important to note that whatever the true nature of the army created by Washington and his congressional supporters, the Continental Army had another role, that of defining and in fact creating certain persistent traits of American character. This heroic, almost mythic, role has been analyzed, in all its inconsistencies and ironies, in Charles Royster's imaginative study, *A Revolutionary People at War*.

112. See Chapter 1.

113. William M. Fowler, Jr., *Rebels under Sail*, p. 142. The following draws heavily upon Fowler's narrative account of the development of the Continental Navy. See also the older account, Charles O. Paullin, *The Navy of the American Revolution* (Cleveland, 1906), pp. 31–60.

114. John Adams to Elbridge Gerry, June [7?], 1775, in Smith, ed., *LDC* 1:450. On Gadsden's contributions to the movement for a navy, see Godbold and Woody, *Christopher Gadsden*, pp. 138–40.

115. Josiah Quincy, Jr., to John Adams, July 11, 1775, in Clark, ed., *NDAR* 1:859. See also James Warren to John Adams, same date, ibid., p. 857.

116. *JCC* 2:189.

117. Cited in Miller, *Sea of Glory*, p. 35. On the behavior of Wallace, see above, Chapter 2.

118. On the efforts in Massachusetts and Connecticut, see French, *First Year*, pp. 364–66. See also, James Warren to John Adams, July 7, 1775, in Ford, ed., *Warren-Adams Letters* 1:78. On Pennsylvania, see John W. Jackson, *The Pennsylvania Navy, 1775–1781: The Defense of the Delaware* (New Brunswick, N.J., 1974). On South Carolina, see Arthur Middleton to William H. Drayton, Aug. 5, 1775; South Carolina Council of Safety to Lempriere, July 25, 1775; and the Journal of the South Carolina Council of Safety, July 15, 1775, in Clark, ed., *NDAR* 1:894, 966, 974, 1076.

119. In perhaps the most famous incident of this kind, the "Machias Admiral," Jeremiah O'Brien, led a little fleet of lumber sloops after the schooner H.M.S. *Margaretta*, which had sailed to northern Maine to take on supplies. The Yankees fired on, boarded, and captured the schooner, as well as a smaller ship that was accompanying her. O'Brien, liable to capture and trial by the British as a pirate, subsequently applied for and received a commission from the Massachusetts Provincial Congress as "Commander of the Armed Schooner *Diligent*, [née *Margaretta*] and of the sloop *Machias-Liberty*, now lying in the Harbour of Machias, fixed for the purpose of guarding the Sea-Coast." French, *First Year*, pp. 363–65; Miller, *Sea of Glory*, pp. 29–35. See also the account of the expedition of Captain Nicholas Broughton to Prince Edward Island in Fowler, *Rebels under Sail*, pp. 26–27. Broughton carried a commission from Washington. On the fears aroused by such enterprises, see Silas Deane, Proposals for Establishing a Navy [Oct. 16? 1775], in Smith, ed., *LDC* 2:182.

120. Smith, ed., *LDC* 1:710.

121. *JCC* 3:274; Smith, ed., *LDC* 2:106.

122. See, for example, remarks of R. R. Livingston in John Adams, Notes of Debates, Oct. [4], 1775, in Smith, ed., *LDC* 2:107, and, in general, pp. 106–10.

123. Remarks of J. J. Zubly in John Adams, Notes of Debates, Oct. 5, 1775, in Smith, ed., *LDC* 2:111, John Adams to James Warren, Oct. 7, 1775, ibid., pp. 135–38.

124. Ibid., p. 138.

125. John Adams to James Warren, Oct. 19, 1775, in Smith, ed., *LDC* 2:205–6. See, for example, remarks of Samuel Chase in Notes of Debates, Oct. 21, 1775, ibid., pp. 222–23. The southerners became more amenable to the idea of a navy as the fall progressed, however, due to Lord Dunmore's depredations along the Virginia rivers. See Chapter 9.

126. Notes of Debates, Oct. 7 [1775], ibid., pp. 130–31.

127. Fowler, *Rebels under Sail*, p. 50; Miller, *Sea of Glory*, p. 43.

128. Oct. 5, 1775, *JCC* 1:276–77, 278–79; Samuel Ward Diary, Oct. 5, 1775, in Smith, ed., *LDC* 2:121; John Hancock to Nicholas Cooke, Oct. 5, 1775; to Massachusetts Council, same date; and to George Washington, same date, in Smith, ed., *LDC* 2:114–16, 117.

129. Oct. 6, 1775, *JCC* 3:280.

130. The debate on the Rhode Island proposal took place on October 7. See Adams, Notes of Debates, in Smith, ed., *LDC* 2:130–31; Fowler believes that the decision to debate the Rhode Island proposal before that of the committee was a play by the advocates of the navy to see how much they could achieve;

Rebels under Sail, p. 51, and John Adams to Elbridge Gerry, Nov. 5, 1775, in Smith, ed., *LDC* 2:303. Adams here was referring specifically to the small naval force approved on October 30, but as Fowler notes, this may have been a continuation of the policy of "starting small." See below.

131. *JCC* 3:293–94. The limited nature of the contemplated mission, and the limited powers of the committee, are apparent from the wording of the resolution:

> The Congress, taking into consideration the report of the Committee appointed to prepare a plan, for intercepting vessels coming out with stores and ammunition, and after some debate,
>
> *Resolved*, That a swift sailing vessel, to carry ten carriage guns, and a proportionable number of swivels, with eighty men, be fitted, with all possible despatch, for a cruize of three months, and that the commander be instructed to cruize eastward, for intercepting such transports as may be laden with warlike stores and other supplies for our enemies, and for such other purposes as the Congress shall direct.
>
> That a Committee of three be appointed to prepare an estimate of the expence, and lay the same before the Congress, and to contract with proper persons to fit out the vessel.

Ibid. A second vessel was also approved that day.

132. John Adams to James Warren, Oct. 13, 1775, in Smith, ed., *LDC* 2:177. See also *JCC* 2:293 n. 2.

133. Smith assigns a tentative date of October 16 to Deane's proposals, for he believes they were included in the committee report that was read in the full Congress and recommitted on October 17. See *JCC* 3:297. Fowler, however, believes that the committee report was recommitted in order to enable the committee to prepare more detailed estimates and that Deane's estimates (as well as the rest of his report) was written in the two weeks between October 17 and the end of the month. Fowler, *Rebels under Sail*, p. 54.

134. "Silas Deane's Proposals for Establishing a Navy," [Oct. 16? 1775], in Smith, ed., *LDC* 2:182–84.

135. Ibid., p. 185.

136. Ibid., pp. 185–86.

137. In approving the October 13 resolution, the delegates agreed to outfit two ships, and on October 30, they agreed to outfit two more; *JCC* 3:311.

138. Ibid. The additional members were Hopkins of Rhode Island, Hewes of North Carolina, Lee of Virginia, and John Adams. Adams has left a vivid description of the activities of the Naval Committee in his autobiography; Butterfield, ed., *Adams Papers* 3:342–50.

139. Samuel Ward to Henry Ward, Nov. 16, 1775, in Smith, ed., *LDC* 2:355.

140. *JCC* 3:316, 348. The marines were to be "considered as part of the number which the continental Army before Boston is ordered to consist of" and their pay was set at exactly the prevailing army level; ibid., p. 384.

141. Ibid., pp. 372–73. On Washington's request for a procedure for adjudicating prizes, see George Washington to Richard Henry Lee, Nov. 8, 1775;

and George Washington to John Hancock, Nov. 11, 1775, in Fitzpatrick, ed., *Writings of Washington* 4:75, 82. On Washington's early attempts to commission ships himself in order to relieve his chronic shortage of military supplies, see Fowler, *Rebels under Sail*, pp. 21–31.

142. *JCC* 3:378–87; Paullin, *Navy of the Revolution*, pp. 47–48; Miller, *Sea of Glory*, p. 55. Adams's draft rules were laid before Congress on November 23 and debated on the twenty-fifth, before being adopted on the twenty-eighth; *JCC* 3:364, 375.

143. On the New Model Army, see C. H. Firth, *Cromwell's Army: A History of the English Soldier during the Civil Wars, the Commonwealth and the Protectorate*, 4th ed. (London, 1962), pp. 346–81. On the Chinese army, see Samuel B. Griffith II, *The Chinese People's Liberation Army* (New York, 1967). On the *Potemkin*, see Richard A. Hough, *The Potemkin Mutiny* (New York, 1961), pp. 13–97.

144. For the influence of the military in forming Pennsylvania's radical government in 1776, see David Hawke, *In the Midst of a Revolution: The Politics of Confrontation in Colonial America* (Philadelphia, 1961), pp. 149–50; 169–71; 186–89; and, in general, Richard A. Ryerson, "Philadelphia Patriots Take Up Arms: The Role of Armed Resistance in Radicalizing Pennsylvania Politics" (Paper presented at the Annual Meeting of the Organization of American Historians, Boston, 1975). Gary Nash concluded that "by the fall of 1775 the Philadelphia militia had become a school of political education, much in the manner of Cromwell's New Model army" (*Urban Crucible*, p. 379). It is important to note also that the militia ideal did not fade, at least at the state level. All of the new state constitutions made provision for its protection, and indeed glorification. See Cress, *Citizens in Arms*, pp. 60–61.

Chapter 6

1. For the king as imperial unifier, see Chapter 1. See also, Andrew C. McLaughlin, "The Background of American Federalism," *American Political Science Review* 12 (1918): 217.

2. The Articles of Confederation were not formally ratified until 1781, when Maryland finally acceded to the union.

3. Merrill Jensen was the first to note the significance of the radicals' linking of the issues of confederation and independence. See Jensen, "Idea of a National Government," *Political Science Quarterly* 58 (1943): 363; and *The Articles of Confederation: An Interpretation of the Socio-Constitutional History of the American Revolution* (Madison, Wis., 1940), pp. 109–11. Henderson argues that no discernible party positions emerged in the early debates on confederation, since votes on particular issues were more likely to depend upon how a delegate's constituents would be affected than upon his ideological preferences. While Henderson has accurately described the debates that occurred after 1776, Jensen's analysis better fits the pattern prior to that date, when the linking of confederation with independence brought an ideological dimension to the former issue that it lacked in later years. For Henderson's views, see *Party Politics*, pp. 132–42.

The terms "radical" and "conservative," when used in this chapter, however, refer solely to positions taken on independence—a radical sought to bring a declaration about quickly; a conservative, to avoid one as long as possible. Where possible, however, I do not use these terms in this chapter. Events relating to confederation took place simultaneously with those relating to the creation of new provincial governments, which is described in Chapter 9. Because the terms "radical," "moderate," and "conservative" take on a definite social connotation in the context of the latter topic that they do not have in the context of confederation, to prevent confusion I have avoided the use of the terms here.

4. The most extensive consideration of the importance of the early debates on confederation for theories of federalism and the development of a national government are in Rakove, *Beginnings of National Politics*, pp. 135–215, upon which the following section on confederation draws heavily.

5. "A PLAN to Perpetuate the Union," Purdie and Dixon's *Virginia Gazette*, Apr. 29, 1773.

6. "A Philadelphian," *Pennsylvania Gazette*, May 18, 1774. See also, Benjamin Franklin, James Wilson, and Alexander Hamilton, quoted above, Chapter 1, text accompanying note 56.

7. Daniel Dulany, "Regarding the Continental Congress, 1774," Force Coll., ser. 9, box 11; John Blackburn, Jr., to William Logan, March 13, 1775, Logan-Fisher-Fox Papers, box 2, Hist. Soc. of Pa., Philadelphia; "Antoninus," *Pennsylvania Journal*, Oct. 11, 1775.

8. Livingston is quoted in Diary, Aug. 22, 1774, in Butterfield, ed., *Adams Papers* 2:107; Dickinson is quoted in Charles H. Lincoln, *The Revolutionary Movement in Pennsylvania, 1760–1776* (Philadelphia, 1901), p. 255 n. 1.

9. A good, if older, narrative of early attempts at union is in Frothingham, *Rise of the Republic*, pp. 101–57, from which this brief summary is drawn. See also Merrill Jensen, "Idea of a National Government," p. 358. There were also regional attempts at union, the most prominent being the New England Confederation of 1643–87.

10. On the Albany Plan of Union, see Robert Newbold, *The Albany Congress and Plan of Union of 1754* (New York, 1955), and Alison C. Olson, "The British Government and Colonial Union, 1754," *WMQ*, 3d ser., 17 (1960): 22–34. The delegates recurred to the Albany Plan, among others, in drawing up their plan of confederation. See Josiah Bartlett's Notes on the Plan of Confederation [June 12–July 12, 1776], in Smith, ed., *LDC* 4:200.

11. "Massachusettensis," *Massachusetts Gazette; and the Boston Post-Boy and Advertiser* (Boston), Jan. 23, 1775. See also Galloway, *Candid Examination*, p. 45. On such disunion, see John Murrin, "Anglicization and Identity: The Colonial Experience, the Revolution and the Dilemma of American Nationalism" (Paper presented at the Annual Meeting of the Organization of American Historians, Denver, Colo., 1974), pp. 29–35.

12. Adams to Joseph Hawley, Nov. 25, 1775, in Smith, ed., *LDC* 2:385; Robert Beverley to John Backhouse, Aug. 10, 1775, Robert Beverley Letterbook, Lib. Cong.

13. The prevalence of such stereotypes had much to do with the continuing

strength of sectional and regional loyalties. Such loyalties retarded the development of an allegiance to the larger continental entity. See Murrin, "Anglicization and Identity." See, for example, the language used by Thomas Jefferson to express his disappointment with the draft of the Articles of Confederation brought in by the Confederation Committee on July 12. They were, he wrote to Richard Henry Lee, "in every interesting point the reverse of what our country would wish." July 16, 1776, in Smith, ed., *LDC* 4:470. The "country" Jefferson referred to was obviously Virginia.

14. John Jones to John Dickinson, Oct. 15, 1775, Dickinson Papers, item 25-1, Library Company of Phila., Josiah Quincy, Jr., "General Remarks and Observations on Pennsylvania," May 1773, Mass. Hist. Soc., *Proceedings* 49 (1915–16): 477.

15. Prior to 1776 the use of the term "republican" to characterize political affinity had definite pejorative connotations in certain sections of the colonies. See W. Paul Adams, "Republicanism in Political Rhetoric before 1776," *Political Science Quarterly* 85 (1970): 397–421. For an alternative view, see Pauline Maier, "Beginnings of American Republicanism," in *Development of a Revolutionary Mentality*, pp. 99–117.

16. Eddis to ?, Oct. 1, 1769, in Land, ed., *Letters from America*, p. 12; John Blackburn, Jr., to William Logan, Feb. 14, 1775, Logan-Fisher-Fox Papers, box 2; Chandler, *Friendly Address*, p. 30. See also Jonathan Sewall to [Gen. Frederick Haldimand], May 30, 1775, Haldimand Papers, Additional MSS, vol. 21695, fols. 120–25.

17. Josiah Quincy, Jr., "Journal," Mass. Hist. Soc., *Proceedings* 49 (1915–16): 445. For the aggressive model of republican Rome, see Pocock, *Machiavellian Moment*, pp. 197–99.

18. Adams to Warren, Sept. 25, 1774, in Cushing, ed., *Writings of Adams* 3:158; Braxton to Landon Carter, Apr. 14, 1776, in Smith, ed., *LDC* 3:523; Adams to James Warren, June [July] 6, 1775, in Ford, ed., *Warren-Adams Letters* 1:76–77. There was some basis for contemporary fears that overpopulation in New England would lead to Yankee expansionism. See Kenneth Lockridge, "Land, Population and the Evolution of New England Society, 1630–1790," *Past and Present* 39 (1968): 63–80.

19. Josiah Quincy, Jr., "Journal," Mass. Hist. Soc., *Proceedings* 49 (1915–16): 454–55, 476. For the political importance of luxury to minds steeped in the English "country" tradition, see, for example, Pocock, *Machiavellian Moment*, pp. 430–31; Wood, *Creation of the American Republic*, pp. 107–14.

20. On New York, see, for example, Samuel Adams to Samuel Cooper, Apr. 30, 1776, in Smith, ed., *LDC* 3:601. On Yankee conceptions of Pennsylvanians, see, for example, Silas Deane to Mrs. Deane, Sept. 8, 1775, in "Deane Correspondence," Conn. Hist. Soc., *Collections* 2 (1870): 167, 207; Diary [Oct. 9], 1774, in Butterfield, ed., *Adams Papers* 2:150.

21. On the Stamp Act Congress, see C. A. Weslager, *The Stamp Act Congress* (Newark, Del., 1976), pp. 58–168, and on reaction to the Townshend Acts, see above, Chapter 4 and notes. Pauline Maier sees the development of links between radical organizations in the major colonial cities (which occurred during

the Stamp and Townshend Acts crises) as important precursors of colonial union. This is undoubtedly true, yet during this same period, Maier notes, colonial radicals were forging similar links and engaging in extensive correspondence with British radicals. These latter contacts certainly prefigured no permanent political union, and except in hindsight it is difficult to read into the links between colonial radicals the seeds of a national government. See *From Resistance to Revolution*, pp. 77–227. The most promising institutional link, prior to 1774, was probably the development of the intercolonial network of committees of correspondence. See Ammerman, *Common Cause*, pp. 20–23.

22. "A Philadelphian," *Pennsylvania Gazette*, May 18, 1774; *Four Letters on Interesting Subjects* (Philadelphia, 1776), p. 6; Livingston to James Duane, Sept. 27, 1774, "Duane Letters," Southern History Association, *Publications* (Charleston, 1904), 8:54; Whitney, *Transgressions of a Land*, p. 66. The necessity of unanimity was constantly urged by Franklin, who, writing from London, recognized the ministry's readiness to magnify any signs of the intercolonial dissension upon which they pinned their hopes. See Franklin to Thomas Cushing, Jan. 28, 1775; and to Charles Thomson, Feb. 5, Mar. 13, 1775, in Willcox, ed., *Papers of Franklin* 21:458, 476–77, 521–22.

23. For examples of Whig insistence upon the "unanimity" that prevailed in local meetings, see, for example, *Boston Gazette*, June 20, 1774; and William Hooper to Samuel Johnston, May 23, 1774, in Force, ed., *American Archives*, 4th ser., 2:676. In many cases, such reports of unanimity accurately reflected the tremendous resentment caused by the Intolerable Acts and the general agreement that they must be resisted. It is important to note, however, that so important did the Whigs consider the image of unity that they insisted that such unity had prevailed whether it had or not. Thus, for example, regarding dissension-torn New York City, Samuel Adams informed Elbridge Gerry in May 1774 that the merchants had universally agreed to suspend trade with Britain when in fact such a policy was a major cause of the dissension. Similarly, Whig reports of the unanimity prevailing in Charleston, South Carolina, during the General Meeting of July 6–8, 1774, differed greatly from the acrimony described by observers like William Henry Drayton. See Samuel Adams to Elbridge Gerry, May 20, 1774, in Cushing, ed., *Writings of Adams* 3:119–20; "Report from South Carolina," *Boston Gazette*, Aug. 15, 1774; Drayton, *Memoirs of the American Revolution* 1:204–5.

24. *New-York Journal*, June 30, 1774; *Massachusetts Gazette and Post-Boy*, Jan. 2, 1775. For an excellent account of the unanimity of sentiment at both the local and continental level in 1774, see Ammerman, *Common Cause*, pp. 19–51. See also Chapter 3.

25. See, for example, the new masthead of the *Massachusetts Spy*, which first appeared on June 7, 1774, and that of the *New-York Journal* of June 23, 1774, both of which sported Franklin's old "Unite or Die" rattlesnake of 1754. Franklin to Priestly, Oct. 3, 1775, in Willcox, ed., *Papers of Franklin* 22:218; Howe to Samuel Adams, June 7, 1775, S. Adams Papers, vol. 7. On the "Spirit of 1774," see Chapter 3.

26. As the philosopher Yves Simon noted, a remarkable degree of unanim-

ity may appear in any society, no matter how diverse, during periods of crisis. But as the crisis continues and alternative modes of action emerge, all of which appear equally likely to achieve common goals, "unanimity is a precarious principle of united action." *General Theory of Authority*, pp. 40–41.

27. Quoted in David W. Woods, *John Witherspoon* (New York, 1906), p. 159. See also Richard Henry Lee to [William Lee], May 10, 1775, in Smith, ed., *LDC* 1:337; and James Bowdoin to Samuel Adams, Dec. 9, 1775, S. Adams Papers, vol. 7.

28. See Chapter 4.

29. Benjamin Harrison to ?, Nov. 24, 1775, in Smith, ed., *LDC* 2:381 (recalling Franklin's remarks at the time he introduced his proposals).

30. On the Galloway Plan of Union, see Chapter 3. The plan therefore belongs logically among the colonial plans of union, discussed above, that also sought to institutionalize a colonial union under the aegis of British authority.

31. Samuel Ward to Richard Henry Lee, Dec. 14, 1774; and Silas Deane to Patrick Henry, Jan. 2, 1775, in Smith, ed., *LDC* 1:271, 291. John Adams later recalled that he had been the first to refer to the matter openly in the Congress, and he assigned a very early date for such a speech, June 2, 1775. He recalled that he then suggested that the plan of confederation be prepared by the people themselves in separate colony conventions. See Autobiography, June 2, 1775, in Butterfield, ed., *Adams Papers* 3:352. There is no contemporary evidence that such a confederation speech was made at this time, however, and considering the importance of the subject, it seems unlikely that a speech on such an important topic would pass without comment. Adams clearly was, however, an early supporter of confederation. See below.

32. As reported in Benjamin Harrison to ? [Nov. 24, 1775], in Smith, ed., *LDC* 2:381.

33. Franklin's plan is reprinted in *JCC* 2:195–99. His original draft, with interlineations shown, is in Willcox, *Papers of Franklin* 22:122–25. The central government envisioned by Franklin is termed "relatively strong" primarily because of its large discretionary grant of legislative authority in the "general welfare" clause in Article v. Franklin's plan did not, however, confer taxing authority upon the central government.

34. Articles III–VII, IX, in Willcox, *Papers of Franklin* 22:122–24 (interlineations omitted).

35. Benjamin Harrison to ? [Nov. 24, 1775], in Smith, ed., *LDC* 2:381–82.

36. Boyd notes that "numerous" copies were made of the Franklin plan, and they were probably intended for circulation in the various provincial assemblies and conventions. Boyd's list of the extant copies of the draft indicates a circulation in at least Massachusetts, New York, and Virginia. On August 24, 1775, the Provincial Congress of North Carolina ordered copies of the draft circulated to the various county committees, and it was formally discussed and rejected by the Provincial Congress on September 4, 1775. See Boyd, ed., *Jefferson Papers* 1:179n–180n.; Saunders, ed., *Colonial Records of North Carolina* 10:175–79; Smith, ed., *LDC* 2:382 n. 3. On the disposition of the various copies of Franklin's articles, see ibid., 1:643n–644n.

37. Hawley to Gerry, [1776], "Hints for the Consideration of Mr. Gerry," Elbridge Gerry Papers, Mass. Hist. Soc.; James Warren to John Adams, Nov. 16, 1775, in Taylor, ed., *Papers of Adams* 3:306.

38. Connecticut Delegates to Governor Trumbull, Dec. 5, 1775, in Smith, ed., *LDC* 2:440, referring to Trumbull's letters of November 18 and 25, 1775.

39. Silas Deane's "Proposals to Congress" are printed in ibid. 2:418–19 under a date of "November ?, 1775." Rakove has traced the history of this draft; *Beginnings of National Politics*, pp. 137–39. They are discussed substantively on pp. 143–47. He believes that Silas Deane drafted very sketchy articles of confederation sometime in late July or early August, 1775 (p. 137n). He may, in fact, have done so earlier, for in his letter to Patrick Henry, written on January 2, 1775, he spoke of the need for "a lasting Confederation" and concluded, "A Sketch of this I likewise send you." See Smith, ed., *LDC* 1:291. Through the summer, Rakove documents, Governor Trumbull corresponded with the Connecticut delegates, and in this correspondence he referred several times to, and suggested several revisions in, the Deane sketch. It was this revised and expanded draft, Rakove suggests, to which Governor Trumbull referred in his letter of December 5, and this may be what he terms the "Connecticut Plan," which was printed in the *Pennsylvania Evening Post* in March 1776 but which was never presented in Congress. (For the differences between the plan as published in 1776 and that printed in *LDC*, see Smith, ed., *LDC* 1:146–47.) Rakove therefore assigns a somewhat earlier date to the Deane draft than do the editors of the *LDC*, although they also suggest that Deane may have completed his draft prior to November 1775.

40. Silas Deane, "Proposals to Congress," November ?, 1775, in Smith, ed., *LDC* 2:418–19. Rakove terms the definition of Congress's power in both plans "remarkably brief and imprecise." *Beginnings of National Politics*, p. 144.

41. Samuel Adams to John Adams, Jan. 15, 1776, in Smith, ed., *LDC* 3:94.

42. Edward Tilghman to his father, Feb. 4, 1776, quoted in Stillé, *Life of Dickinson*, p. 174; Richard Smith Diary, Jan. 16, 1776, in Smith, ed., *LDC* 3:103.

43. Samuel Ward to Henry Ward, Feb. 19, 1776, in Smith, ed., *LDC* 3:285; Diary, in Butterfield, ed., *Adams Papers* 2:231–33.

44. For examples of the linking of the issues of independence, confederation, and alliance, see Joseph Hawley to Elbridge Gerry, May 1, 1776, in Austin, *Life of Gerry* 1:176; and Joseph Hawley to Samuel Adams, Apr. 1, 1776, S. Adams Papers, vol. 8; also, Thomas Nelson to John Page, Feb. 13, 1776; William Whipple to Meshech Weare, May 11, [1776]; and John Adams to William Cushing, June 9, 1776, in Smith, ed., *LDC* 3:249, 658, 4:178.

45. Samuel Adams to James Warren, Jan. 1, 1776, in Smith, ed., *LDC* 3:52.

46. Force, ed., *American Archives*, 5th ser., 1:399. Rutledge to John Jay [June 8, 1776]; Carter Braxton to Landon Carter, Apr. 14, 1776; and John Dickinson's Notes for A Speech in Congress [July 1, 1776], in Smith, ed., *LDC* 4:174–75, 3:523, 4:355.

47. Josiah Bartlett to Nathaniel Folsom, July 1, 1776, in Smith, ed., *LDC* 4:349.

48. July 11, 12, 1776, in *JCC* 5:431, 433. The Virginia resolution calling for the

appointment of these committees was introduced on June 7, ibid., pp. 425–26. The members of the Confederation Committee were Josiah Bartlett (N.H.), Stephen Hopkins (R.I.), Samuel Adams (Mass.), Roger Sherman (Conn.), Robert R. Livingston (N.Y.), Francis Hopkinson (N.J.) (appointed June 28; JCC 5:491), John Dickinson (Pa.), Thomas McKean (Del.), Thomas Stone (Md.), Thomas Nelson (Va.), Joseph Hewes (N.C.), Edward Rutledge (S.C.), and Button Gwinnett (Ga.).

49. Josiah Bartlett to Nathaniel Folsom, July 1, 1776; and Edward Rutledge to John Jay, June 29, 1776, in Smith, ed., LDC 4:349; 338. The editors of LDC have traced the draft articles during these weeks. See ibid., pp. 251–52 n. 1. They conclude that the committee worked from a draft submitted by Dickinson very early in its proceedings, which originally left some of the most controversial articles blank, including the mode of voting. A clean copy of one of Dickinson's drafts in the hand of Josiah Bartlett (thus, the "Bartlett Draft") is printed in the left-hand columns of Smith, ed., LDC 4:233–50. The editors have also reprinted another copy of Dickinson's draft, with heavy interlineations and marginalia (the "Dickinson draft"), in the right-hand columns (pp. 233–50). This was the committee's working draft, through which the changes wrought in the course of its deliberations may most easily be traced. Finally, Dickinson prepared a clean copy of the results of the committee's deliberations, and this (the "committee draft") was submitted to the full Congress. It is reprinted under the date of July 12 in JCC 5:546–54. Where possible, I cite the committee draft, because it reflects the ultimate result of the committee's deliberations. These citations refer to the various articles by the roman numeral designations under which they appear in JCC. When I wish to refer to the progress of the draft through the committee, I cite the Bartlett draft (in which the articles are also designated by roman numerals), or the Dickinson draft, in which the articles are designated by Arabic numerals, which the editors place in brackets.

50. Articles 19 and 20 of the Dickinson draft. Smith, ed., LDC 4:252 n. 1 and p. 254 n. 17. The editors so conclude from the heavy amendments to these clauses in the course of the committee deliberations. Rakove reaches a similar conclusion; Beginnings of National Politics, pp. 154–55.

51. John Dickinson's Notes for a Speech in Congress [July 1, 1776]; and Edward Rutledge to John Jay, June 29, 1776, in Smith, ed., LDC, 4:355, 338. Some of the changes wrought by the committee clearly reflect this desire to pare down and simplify Dickinson's draft and to remove some of its redundancies. Thus, for example, in Dickinson's draft, Article 19, after granting power to Congress to appoint an executive Council of State to act in the recess of Congress "and such Committees and Officers as may be necessary for managing the general Affairs of the Union, under the Direction of Congress," he then goes on to specify further that they might appoint "a Chamber of Accounts, an Office of Treasury, a Board of War, a Board of Admiralty, out of their own Body, and such Committees out of the same as shall be thought necessary. They may appoint one of their Number to preside, and a suitable person for Secretary. The Chamber of Accounts, the Office of Treasury, the Board of War,

and Board of Admiralty, shall always act under the Direction of Congress while sitting, and in their Recess, under that of the Council of Safety." Smith, ed., *LDC* 4:244. The committee draft, in language very similar to that in the Bartlett draft and that later adopted by the full Congress, simply said that Congress might appoint "such Committees and Civil Officers as may be necessary for managing the general Affairs of the United States, under their Direction while assembled, and in their Recess, of the Council of State—Appointing one of their number to preside, and a suitable Person for Secretary . . ." *JCC* 5:551. Compare Article xiv of the August 20 draft Articles: "The United States in Congress Assembled shall have authority to appoint a Council of State, and such Committees and Civil Officers as may be necessary for managing the general affairs of the United States, under their direction while assembled, and in their recess under that of the Council of State—to appoint one of their number to preside, and a suitable person for Secretary." *JCC* 5:683. All these versions convey very full powers of appointment to Congress, sufficient to create as extensive an administrative bureaucracy as the delegates wished.

52. *JCC* 5:555. The editors of the *LDC* note that work on the draft was probably concluded on approximately July 1, however, and that the question of confederation was postponed while the Congress debated independence. Dickinson left the Congress for military service after independence was declared. He was not present, therefore, when his plan was debated and, with some amendments, adopted by Congress on August 20 and circulated to the states (the "August 20 draft"). Smith, ed., *LDC* 4:251–52 n. 1. The committee draft is also reprinted, in single-column format to facilitate comparison, under the date of August 20, 1776, along with the Articles as adopted by the full Congress on that date, in *JCC* 5:674–89.

An extensive analysis of the substantive provisions of the committee draft can be found in Jensen, *Articles of Confederation*, pp. 126–39. But Jensen's view of the Articles of Confederation as a weak framework for central government, subordinate to the states and fatally flawed from its inception as a basis for national authority, has been criticized by Rakove, who argues that the committee basically adopted both Dickinson's conception of a strong national government and the better part of his original draft, which reflected a government "whose own needs would enjoy clear precedence over the rights of the states; that would be empowered to interfere in some aspects of their internal police; and that would limit their ability to exercise powers inimical to the union." *Beginnings of National Politics*, p. 152. He cites as support for this reading, among other provisions, the proviso to Article iii, that preserves the power of the states to regulate their own affairs "in all Matters that shall not interfere with the Articles of this Confederation," the exclusive power given to Congress over foreign and military affairs, and most important, the extensive powers to create a national domain. These are discussed below. See Rakove's detailed analysis of the revision of Dickinson's draft by the committee (pp. 153–56). As he sees it, the thrust of the committee draft was fundamentally altered, however, by the debates in the full Congress, which resulted in the removal of the provision for congressional control of a national domain. For the reasons outlined below, I find Rakove's analysis persuasive. Dickinson's proposed national government, however, appears strong largely by comparison with that proposed in the August 20 draft, and especially when compared with the Articles as ultimately adopted. The early, rather vague proposals of Franklin and Deane nevertheless envisioned national governments with broader powers and more discretion than the government designed by Dickinson.

53. Articles XVIII, XIX.

54. Articles IV, VIII, IX, X, XI, XIII, XIV, XVII, XVIII.

55. July 23–26, 29–31, August 1–2, 6–8, 1776, JCC 5:603–4, 608, 609, 611, 612, 615, 616, 621–22, 624–25, 628, 635, 636, 639–40.

56. For early optimism, see, for example, John Adams to John Winthrop, June 23, 1776. The remaining statements are from Josiah Bartlett to Nathaniel Folsom, July 1, 1776; Samuel Chase to Philip Schuyler, Aug. 9, 1776; and William Williams to Oliver Wolcott, Aug. 12, 1776, in Smith, ed., LDC 4:299, 349, 644, 667.

57. John Adams to Abigail Adams, July 29, 1776, ibid. 4:556. See also Samuel Chase to R. H. Lee, July 30, 1776, ibid., 570–71. Chase separated Adams's first question into two components, "Representation," and "The Mode of Voting."

58. See Onuf, Origins of the Federal Republic, pp. 186–209.

59. The dilemma that is here treated as one controversy had several component parts, but all concerned the basic issue of the relative power of each state within the national government. The first question was the basis upon which a fixed number of delegates was to be allotted to each state. Were all the states to have an equal number of delegates? If not, were the numbers to be ascertained on the basis of population, wealth, real property, or some combination of these? If population was to be the basis, was it to be adult male population, or adult white male population? And if slaves were to be counted in calculating a state's delegates, were they also to be counted in fixing a state's proportion of continental expenses? Even assuming a proportional delegate representation, the next question was: How would the number of delegates allotted to each colony affect the weight of its vote in the Congress? That is, was each state to have an equal vote, was each delegate to have a vote, or was there to be some distinction regarding the method of voting according to the substantive significance of the issue involved?

60. See Chapter 3 and JCC 1:25.

61. Articles VI and VII, Franklin Draft Articles, in Willcox, Papers of Franklin 21:123.

62. Unidentified author, on copy found in James Duane Papers, New-York Hist. Soc., quoted in Smith, ed., LDC 1:644n; Silas Deane's Proposals, Articles 5–7 [Nov. ?, 1775], ibid. 2:418; Samuel Ward to Henry Ward, Dec. 31, 1775, ibid. 2:539.

63. Bartlett draft, ibid. 4:242; Josiah Bartlett's Notes on the Plan of Confederation, ibid. 4:199–200; Article 18, Dickinson draft, ibid. 4:242; Article XVII, committee draft, JCC 5:550.

64. Thomas Jefferson's Notes of Proceedings in Congress [July 12–Aug. 1, 1776], Smith, ed., LDC 4:441–42. The debate over Article XI (the expense arti-

cle) was mainly a bitter controversy over the basis for ascertaining a colony's share of the Continental expenses. On July 30 Chase moved that expenses ought to be apportioned on the basis of *white* male population only, arguing that slaves were property, not people. John Adams and James Wilson met this by noting that slaves contributed to a colony's wealth as much as, or more than, freemen. Lynch clearly signaled the explosiveness of the issue: "If it is debated, whether . . . Slaves are . . . Property, there is an End of the Confederation." Ibid., pp. 438–40; John Adams's Notes of Debates, July 30, 1776, ibid., p. 568. Chase had raised an issue, however, that few were willing to pursue. As Rutledge of South Carolina noted, "I shall be happy to get rid of the idea of Slavery." John Adams's Notes of Debates, July 30, 1776, ibid., p. 569. Chase's motion was defeated.

65. Thomas Jefferson's Notes of Proceedings in Congress [July 12–Aug. 1, 1776], ibid., p. 442.

66. Ibid., pp. 444–45.

67. Ibid., p. 442; John Adams's Notes of Debates, Aug. 1, 1776, ibid., p. 592.

68. Benjamin Rush's Notes for a Speech in Congress [Aug. 1, 1776]; and Thomas Jefferson's Notes of Proceedings in Congress [July 12–Aug. 1, 1776], in ibid., 4:599, 444.

69. "Protest against the First Draft of the Articles of Confederation" [before Aug. 20, 1776], in Willcox, ed., *Papers of Franklin* 22:571–75; John Adams to Joseph Hawley, Aug. 25, 1776, in Taylor, ed., *Papers of Adams* 4:496–97; Thomas Jefferson to Richard Henry Lee, July 16, 1776, in Smith, ed., *LDC* 4:470. In justification of his position, Franklin wrote that the position taken by the smaller states, "having given us in Advance this striking Instance of the Injustice they are capable of, and of the possible Effects of their Combination, is of itself sufficient Reason for our determining not to put ourselves in their Power by agreeing to this Article." "Protest," pp. 573–74.

70. Committee draft, Articles XVIII, XIV, *JCC* 5:550–51, 549.

71. John Adams, Notes of Debates, July 25, Aug. 2, 1776, Smith, ed., *LDC* 4:538–39, 603.

72. Ibid., pp. 539–603.

73. Ibid., pp. 603–4. This basic question of whether, on issues of national concern, the states were to be subordinate to Congress and whether Congress would thereby have the power to alter the governments of the individual colonies is discussed at length in a letter from Oliver Wolcott to Samuel Lyman dated April 17, 1776. At issue was a proposal by the town of Litchfield that the Continental delegates be directly elected by the people rather than by the Assembly. He had no objection to this in principle, Wolcott wrote, but he was very worried about what such a procedure might signify about the nature of Congress's authority:

Is it not one material Part of the Continental Members Duty to guard the Constitution of the Colony, ought they not therefore to be Ameniable to the Jurisdiction of the colony, and liable to be called to an Account or displaced by them whenever they Please? If the continental Delegates are

Chosen by the People at large (which I have no objection to if it does not in its Consequences absolutely destroy the Colony jurisdiction) can they ever be called to acco[unt] by the assembly or be displaced or receive any Instructions or advice from them more than from so many Individuals and would not the Colony be absolutely Bound (or rather I may say the People living within the present Lines of the Colony, for upon this Idea they could hardly be called a Colony as they would have no separate Jurisdiction) by every Act their Delegates should do, as they would have all the Authority absolutely and independently which the People could give them, as fully and compleatly as any of the present Members of Parliament have, and if they should (being thus Appointed) concurr in Adopting any Maxims intrenching never so much on the Colony Constitution, would not the People be absolutely Bound by their own Act? In a Word, would not the Consequences (if attended to) reduce in a few years the Colony Jurisdiction as low as the present Powers of our Selectmen.

Ibid. 3:552–53.

74. Rakove, *Beginnings of National Politics*, pp. 159–60.

75. Joseph Hewes to Samuel Johnston, July 28, 1776, in Smith, ed., *LDC* 4:555.

76. See Franklin Draft Articles, Article v, in Willcox, ed., *Papers of Franklin* 22:123; Silas Deane's Proposals to Congress, Article 2, in Smith, ed., *LDC* 2:418; Committee draft, Article iv, *JCC* 5:547. If anything, the full Congress expanded the prohibition. Thus the August 20 draft's Article iv prohibited the states from entering into "any conference, agreement, alliance or treaty." *JCC* 5:675.

77. See Dickinson draft, Articles 10 and 19, in Smith, ed., *LDC* 4:237, 244; Committee draft, Articles ix and xviii, *JCC* 5:548, 551; August 20 draft, Articles vii and xiv, *JCC* 5:677, 684.

78. Committee draft, Article xviii, *JCC*, 5:550–51; August 20 draft, Article xiv, ibid., pp. 681–82.

79. Ibid., pp. 551–52, 682.

80. Ibid., pp. 681–82. This power, however, did cause controversy later, and in succeeding drafts of the Articles, Congress's broad powers over boundary disputes were limited by procedures that made Congress simply the court of last resort in such disputes; see Rakove, *Beginnings of National Politics*, p. 180.

81. Committee draft, Article xviii, and August 20 draft, Article xiv, in *JCC* 5:551, 683.

82. Article xviii, ibid., p. 550. In part, the controversy was tied to that over a national domain, for Congress's full powers included that of an exclusive right to purchase Indian lands. This right, in Article xiv of the committee draft, was deleted from the August 20 draft. Ibid., pp. 549, 679.

83. John Adams, Notes of Debates, July 26, 1776, in Smith, ed., *LDC* 4:546.

84. Committee draft, Article viii, and in slightly different language, August 20 draft, Article vi, *JCC* 5:547–48, 676.

85. The ultimate *form* of the national executive was not, of course, settled in 1776. Indeed, it was in part the inappropriateness of entrusting such vast executive authority to a plural institution that led to the perceived weakness of Congress in the later years of the Confederation (see Chapter 10). It is interesting to note, however, that when the Randolph plan, with its extensive proposed revisions in the national legislature, was introduced to the federal convention in 1787, the powers proposed for the executive were as follows: "that besides a general authority to execute the National laws, it ought to enjoy the Executive rights vested in Congress by the Confederation." May 29, 1787, in Farrand, ed., *Records of the Federal Convention* 1:21.

86. In an article written in 1918, McLaughlin located the model for the American federal union in the old British empire. Specifically, he noted that "the essential qualities of American federal organization were largely the product of the practices of the old empire as it existed before 1764." Moreover, McLaughlin recognized that "the active instrument or authority of imperial government was the crown," not Parliament, which "had legislated little if at all for strictly local internal affairs of the colonies." See "The Background of American Federalism," *American Political Science Review* 12 (1918): 215, 217.

This is not to claim that Americans ignored the examples of ancient and modern republics and confederacies but simply to note that those models do not sufficiently explain the functions undertaken by successive American federal governments. On those models, see Caroline Robbins, "European Republicanism in the Century and a Half before 1776," in *The Development of a Revolutionary Mentality*, pp. 31–55.

In an imaginative reconceptualization of this theme, Peter Onuf begins with the premise that Americans recurred to the monarchy and the functions of the Crown for their model of the functions to be exercised by a legitimate central government. He thus dismisses at the outset the usefulness of republican ideology in forming American conceptions of a federal union. He then examines, by focusing on the persistent problem of boundary disputes and claims to western lands, how this conception was reconciled, during the critical period, with that of state sovereignty. Onuf, *Origins of the Federal Republic*, pp. xiv–xv, 7, 16. On this theme, see below, Chapter 8.

87. John Adams to James Warren, Apr. 16, 1776, in Smith, ed., *LDC* 3:536.

Chapter 7

1. The following discussion is concerned solely with the process by which Congress assumed authority over Continental affairs. It does not concern the uses to which the delegates put this power or the principles upon which they acted. On these questions, see Felix Gilbert, *To the Farewell Address: Ideas of Early American Foreign Policy* (Princeton, N.J., 1961) and the attacks on Gilbert's thesis by James H. Hutson, "Early American Diplomacy: A Reappraisal," and William C. Stinchcombe, "John Adams and the Model Treaty," in Lawrence

S. Kaplan, ed., *The American Revolution and 'A Candid World'* (Kent, Ohio, 1977).

2. *JCC* 1:82–90, 2:163–71, 212–18. Early congressional foreign policy thus of necessity resembled the foreign policies of modern revolutionary regimes.

3. See Chapter 2.

4. On the North plan, see Weldon A. Brown, *Empire or Independence: A Study in the Failure of Reconciliation, 1774–1783* (Port Washington, N.Y., 1966), pp. 35–57.

5. Dartmouth letter is in *New Jersey Archives*, 1st ser., 10:555.

6. Force, ed., *American Archives*, 4th ser., 2:454. For Dickinson's authorship of the response, see Ryerson, *Revolution Is Now Begun*, p. 118.

7. Force, ed., *American Archives*, 4th ser., 2:590–95; 599–600; May 26, 1775, *JCC* 2:61–63.

8. R. H. Lee to Francis L. Lee, May 21, 1775, in Smith, ed., *LDC* 1:366 (bracketed ellipsis in original).

9. Force, ed., *American Archives*, 4th ser., 2:1187, 1202.

10. See Chapter 2 and *JCC* 2:202. The committee consisted of Franklin, Jefferson, John Adams, and Richard Henry Lee; ibid., pp. 203, 224–34. Compare the Virginia resolutions in Force, ed., *American Archives*, 4th ser., 2:1200–1202. For Jefferson's authorship, and the deliberate similarity of the two documents, see *JCC* 2:225 n. 1, citing Jefferson's autobiography.

11. On the 1774 petition to the king, see Chapter 2. This account does not concern itself with the 1775 Olive Branch Petition as it related to the party divisions in Congress between the Adams radicals and the Dickinson conservatives. On this point, see Henderson, *Party Politics*, pp. 49–50. Rather, I concentrate here on the role of the petitions in the early diplomatic history of the United States. On the Olive Branch Petition in general, see Weldon A. Brown, *Empire or Independence*.

12. See Chapter 1 and Maier, *From Resistance to Revolution*, pp. 213–14.

13. Seven of the twelve provincial congresses or assemblies in 1774 expressed a desire that the Congress adopt a petition. See Chapter 3.

14. John M. Head, *A Time to Rend: An Essay on the Decision for American Independence* (Madison, Wis., 1968), pp. 14–15. Arthur Lee to John Dickinson, April 10, 1775, in Dickinson Papers, item 25–2. New York's action was considered more heinous than New Jersey's because the New York legislators had sent a separate petition and had disapproved of the proceedings of Congress, whereas the New Jersey Assembly had approved of the measures of Congress.

15. Autobiography, in Butterfield, ed., *Adams Papers* 3:321; Autobiography, in Ford, ed., *Writings of Jefferson* 1:15.

16. In this chapter, radicals and moderates are defined in terms of their positions on the reciprocal issues of reconciliation and independence, and the time frame moves back to the period preceding and following the outbreak of war in the spring of 1775. Radicals believed independence to be desirable, inevitable, and necessary for carrying on the war. They therefore favored policies that either implied or were corollaries to independence—for example,

seeking foreign alliances and opening the ports. The radicals opposed continued efforts to effect a reconciliation because they believed such efforts wasted time and deflected energy from the policies they supported. For example, they chafed when moderate desires to await the British peace commissioners in the spring of 1776 delayed the movement toward independence. Moderates, on the other hand, saw nothing to lose and everything to gain in pursuing a policy of vigorous prosecution of the war while simultaneously attempting to open negotiations with Britain. Thus they vigorously supported efforts to equip and arm the Continental military forces and supported such covert efforts to secure supplies as the activities of the Secret Committee, while at the same time they earnestly pursued all avenues, such as that opened by Lord Drummond, that raised a possibility, however slight, of bringing about peace on terms acceptable to colonial Whigs. They generally opposed independence, except as a last resort, and thought that even in the last resort such steps as securing foreign alliances, a confederation, stable state governments, and an improved military situation ought to precede, rather than follow, any declaration. See, for example, Carter Braxton to Landon Carter, Apr. 14, 1776; and Edward Rutledge to John Jay, June 8, 1776, in Smith, ed., *LDC* 3:522, 4:174–75. I have not defined these groups in terms of their position on the congressional assumption of power over foreign affairs, because radicals and moderates tended to support or oppose the expansion of congressional power over such matters according to whether the issue under consideration (for example, Dickinson's peace plan of 1775) had as its object independence or reconciliation.

I have not distinguished moderates from conservatives here. With the coming of the war, many of those previously defined as conservatives, like Joseph Galloway, dropped from the ranks of Whigs. Conservatives, at this point, were those, like James Duane, who generally supported the same policies as the moderates but who were so pessimistic regarding the consequences of independence that they continued to oppose it—and any policies that were thought of as corollaries to it—far longer into the spring than did the moderates.

17. The linking of defense and peace measures reflected the sentiments of many colonial moderates. The opening of hostilities shocked them into a sense of the seriousness of the situation and caused them to redouble their efforts to reach a settlement while they simultaneously prepared for war. Henry Ward of Rhode Island, for example, urged the delegates to pursue "decisive and vigorous" measures, by which he meant "that at the same Time we carry the Sword in one Hand we shall hold out in the other equitable Terms of Peace and Reconciliation." Henry Ward to Samuel Ward, May 30, 1775, in Bernhard Knollenberg, ed., *Correspondence of Governor Samuel Ward, May 1775-March 1776* (Providence, R.I., 1952), p. 43. See also Lady Juliana Penn to Gov. John Penn, June 18, 1775, in Thomas Penn Letterbook, vol. 10, Thomas Penn Papers, reel 3, Hist. Soc. of Pa.

18. John Dickinson, note in margin of rough draft, Olive Branch Petition, Gratz Coll., case 14, box 3, Hist. Soc. of Pa. See, for example, John Dickinson

to Samuel Ward, Jan. 29, 1775; and John Dickinson to Arthur Lee, Apr. 29, 1775, in Smith, ed., *LDC* 1:302–3, 332.

19. Two successive drafts of Dickinson's peace proposals, along with extensive notes for a speech in Congress explaining them, are in the Gratz Coll., case 14, box 3. They are undated, and I tentatively assigned them to late May or early June. My reasons were: (1) the similarity of Dickinson's draft proposals to the actions taken in Congress on May 26 (see below) and to the Olive Branch Petition in early June, and (2) the Dickinson proposal that Congress immediately "enter into Consideration" of adopting the Massachusetts Army. Since Congress adopted the army in mid-June, the Dickinson proposals were clearly offered at an earlier date. The editors of the *LDC* have meticulously reconstructed these documents from the mass of marginalia, interlineations, and Dickinson's minute handwriting. I cite the published version, except where the citation refers to interlineated material. The above quotation is found under the date "[May 23–25?, 1775]" in Smith, ed., *LDC* 1:383.

20. Ibid., pp. 383–84. Dickinson's full proposal shows how similar to authorized special envoys, or ministers plenipotentiary, Dickinson wanted the agents to be. He proposed:

That we will send Home part of our Body in behalf of themselves & the other Petitioners to present the said Petition & to treat of an Accommodation. That for this purpose, we will give Instructions to our said Agents, suited as nearly as may be to every possible State of Affairs that may exist on their Arrival in England, or may afterwards happen there, containing full & most exact Directions how they are to conduct themselves in every Part of their Behavior, and what Concessions and what Demands they are to make in every Event favorable or unfavorable that shall occurr, reserving to ourselves an Exemption from all Obligations upon Ourselves or our Constituents by any Act of our said Agents untill the same shall be ratified by this Body. (Ibid., p. 384)

21. Ibid., pp. 384–85.

22. Dickinson's conception that Congress had exclusive power over foreign policy, which is apparent in his 1775 peace proposals, may be followed directly into his 1776 draft of the Articles of Confederation, which deals with this aspect of central authority. See Article 4 of the Bartlett draft and Article 5 of the Dickinson draft in Smith, ed., *LDC*, 4:235.

23. John Dickinson, Notes for a Speech in Congress [June 8–10, 1776], in Smith, ed., *LDC* 4:166.

24. On congressional defense decisions from May through July 1775, see Chapter 5.

25. John Dickinson, draft fragment, [May 23–25? 1775], in Smith, ed., *LDC* 1:390–91. These notes appear on the last sheet of Dickinson's poposed resolutions. Several lines of them clearly appear to be Dickinson's notes on the debate over his resolutions. The quoted passage, however, seems to be Dickinson's scrawled notes in answer to those who opposed his resolution.

See Silas Deane Diary, [May 23, 24, 1775], ibid., pp. 371, 401. The sentiments expressed are entirely consistent with Dickinson's position. On this point, see Charles Thomson to William Henry Drayton [1779], in New-York Hist. Soc., *Collections* (Revolutionary Papers), 1:274.

26. It was, in fact, the success of the Dickinson group that so infuriated John Adams that at the end of July he was led to characterize his former ally as "a great Fortune and piddling Genius." The letter to James Warren in which this phrase appears fell into British hands, was published, and started a rift between Dickinson and Adams that was never healed. It is clear from Adams's autobiography that his wrath with Dickinson stemmed from the latter's performance during the debates on the accommodation plan. See John Adams to James Warren, July 24, 1775, in Ford, ed., *Warren-Adams Letters* 1:88; Autobiography, in Butterfield, ed., *Adams Papers* 3:317–20.

27. Duane's speech in defense of the resolutions is in Smith, ed., *LDC* 1:391–95. The editors assign it to the same period as Dickinson's proposed resolution, May 23–25, 1775. On Duane's introduction of the plan, see *JCC* 2:65 n. 1.

28. May 25, 26, June 3, 19, July 4, 5, 7, 8, 1775, in *JCC* 2:59, 65–66, 80, 100, 126, 157, 158. The petition is on pp. 158–62. The Petition Committee, appointed on June 3, consisted of Dickinson, Thomas Johnson, John Rutledge, John Jay, and Benjamin Franklin.

29. Rough Draft, Olive Branch Petition, in Gratz Coll., case 3, box 14; Final Draft, Olive Branch Petition, in *JCC* 2:161.

30. In a draft petition to the king written by John Jay and completely rejected by the committee, the following method was proposed:

> That they most earnestly beseech his Majesty to commission some good & great Men to inquire into the Grievances of his faithful Subjects, & be pleased to devise some Means of accommodating those unhappy Dissentions which unless amicably terminated must endanger the safety of the whole Empire and that shd. his majesty not be disposed to hear the Complaints of his American Subjects from their Representatives in Congress we most humbly beseech his Majesty to direct Com[missioner]s from their different Assemblies to convene for the Purpose.

[June 3–13, 1775], in Smith, ed., *LDC* 1:441. This draft, which Smith concluded was rejected partly because this method was perceived as "too conciliatory," clearly showed Jay's anxiety over what was, in retrospect, the boldest aspect of Dickinson's plan, the appointment of congressional "ambassadors." Dickinson later explained the delegates' dropping of the plan to appoint such "ambassadors" as a conciliatory move in which the delegates sought to obviate all objections to the procedure of the petition, as coming from an illegal body, or to the persons of the ambassadors. As he later explained,

> we carried our Reverence for the royal Character so far, that sufficiently declaring our Meaning, yet We forbore using the Word *Treaty*, least the Term should appear too harsh, when offered by subjects to their sover-

eign. Nor could we devise a more dutiful and unexceptionable Method of conveying our ardent and loyal Wishes to his Majesty, than by relying on his "wisdom" for "the Direction of a Mode" that might improve the Requests of his American subjects into a perfect accommodation. It appeared to us too, a fortunate Circumstance, that our Petition would be delivered to his Majesty by so respectable a Gentleman as the honorable *Richard Penn* Esquire late Governor of *Pennsylvania*, who had taken no Part in the present unhappy dispute.

For the same reason, he noted, the delegates had signed the petition in their private capacity, rather than as delegates. See Draft Address to the Inhabitants of America [Jan. 24? 1776], in Smith, ed., *LDC* 3:143–44. But also see Rakove, *Beginnings of National Politics*, p. 78.

31. In part, the delegates may have chosen to send the petition via a specially appointed emissary because of dissatisfaction with the conduct of the colonial agents in 1774. Only three of the six agents then accredited in London (William Bollan, Arthur Lee, and Benjamin Franklin) agreed to present the 1774 petition in London. According to Michael Kammen, this was the nadir of the steady decline of the colonial agency as an institution. See Michael G. Kammen, *A Rope of Sand: The Colonial Agents, British Politics, and the American Revolution* (Ithaca, N.Y., 1968), pp. 300–301.

32. Penn was not simply a chance messenger. Although he had long planned a trip to England, his departure was clearly delayed until the petition and accompanying Declaration of the Causes of Taking Up Arms were completed. See John Penn to Lady Juliana Penn, Jan. 30, 1775, and June 5, 1775; and Edmund Physick to Lady Juliana Penn, June 30, 1775, in Thomas Penn Papers, reel 10. Penn was considered a perfect choice to represent the Congress, as he was a firm Whig who had nevertheless taken no previous part in the controversy and so would not offend the king's dignity in the way a congressional delegate might. See Caesar Rodney to Thomas Rodney, Sept. 24, 1774; and John Dickinson, Draft Address to the Inhabitants [Jan. 26? 1776], in Smith, ed., *LDC* 1:96, 3:143.

33. The claim that Congress had sole responsibility for conducting foreign affairs was in part a necessity to counteract the British strategy of dividing the colonies and negotiating separately with each colony's legislature. See Brown, *Empire or Independence*, pp. 58–60; Notes on Delegates' Remarks to the New Jersey Assembly [Dec. 5, 1775], in Smith, ed., *LDC* 2:444.

34. New York Provincial Congress to New York Delegates, June 29, 1775, in Force, ed., *American Archives*, 4th ser., 2:1329. The deliberations on the New York accommodation plan are in ibid., pp. 1265, 1271, 1315–18, 1326–27, 1329.

35. John Sullivan and John Langdon to New Hampshire Provincial Congress, May 22, 1775, in Smith, ed., *LDC* 1:370. Thus, in proposed resolutions offered by Edmund Pendleton in the course of the debates on the means of pursuing reconciliation and defense, he proposed, first, that the delegates commit themselves to "procuring by all possible means a reconciliation" and, second, "that no terms of Accommodation which may be proposed from Great

Britain to any Colony separately, ought to be accepted or treated of by the Assembly of such Colony, but such treaty shall only be made & agreed to in a Representation of all in Genl. Congress." Smith, ed., *LDC* 1:402. This was a response to North's plan, and, as it turned out it proved unnecessary, as no assembly responded to the plan.

It is important to note that although radicals generally opposed congressional initiatives aimed at opening negotiations with Britain, they did not differ from moderates in opposing any such efforts on behalf of individual colonies. This was both because they opposed the goal and because the method reflected adversely on the colonial union. The latter sentiment is clear in Sullivan and Langdon's plea to the New Hampshire Provincial Congress.

36. *JCC* 3:404; William Franklin to Lord Dartmouth, Jan. 5, 1776, *New Jersey Archives*, 1st ser., 10:677. A full account of this episode is in Smith, ed., *LDC* 2:445 n. 1.

37. Notes on Delegates' Remarks to the New Jersey Assembly [Dec. 5, 1775], Smith, ed., *LDC* 2:444.

38. Edward Pendleton to Richard Corbin, Feb. 19, 1776, in David J. Mays, ed., *Letters and Papers of Edmund Pendleton, 1734–1803* (Charlottesville, Va., 1967), 1:153.

39. Good accounts of the Drummond episode are in Smith, ed., *LDC* 3:24–27 n. 1, and Milton M. Klein, "Failure of a Mission: The Drummond Peace Proposal of 1775," *Huntington Library Quarterly* 35 (1972): 343–80, from which the following account draws heavily.

40. Smith notes that Drummond's plan was in substance very similar to that put forward by James Duane at the First Continental Congress; *LDC* 3:24 n. 1.

41. The way in which Drummond presented himself is suggested in Thomas Lynch to George Washington, Jan. 16, 1776, ibid., pp. 101–2. Lynch noted that Lord North's public speeches had become much more conciliatory since the Americans had taken up arms, and that he now publicly offered a return to the colonies' situation in 1763:

A gentleman well known to Moyland, Ld Drummond just from England, assures me he will give much more. He tells me that he has had many Conversations with Ministry on the Subject & Shewed me a Paper approved by all of them & which he is sure will be supported in both Houses. The Substance of it is America to be declared free in point of Taxation & internal Police, Judges to be approved by the Judges of England and commissioned during good Behaviour, upon stated & sufficient support be statedly assigned them by the Colonies, all Charters to be held Sacred, that of Boston restored, Britain to regulate Trade sub modo, all Duties laid for the purpose of Regulation be paid into the Colony Treasury where they arise, applicable to its uses by its own Legislature, in Lieu of which America shall, by Duties on such Articles as will probably keep pace in its Consumption with the Rise or declention of the Colony, laid by each Legislature by permanent Act of Assembly, Grant towards the general Support of the Empire, annual Sums in proportion to £5000 Sterling for this Colony. As this sum is little more than half of what did arise by Duties heretofore paid in this place, I doubted his information, but was assured that Ministry wanted nothing but a shew of Reve[nue] to hold up to Parliament, as they are affraid [to] propose Reconciliation, without saving what the[ir] stiff old Englishmen call the Honor of the Nation.

See also William Smith Diary, cited in ibid., p. 199 n. 2.

42. By Lord Drummond's own account, he met regularly with Thomas Lynch, James Duane, John Jay, William Livingston, and Andrew Allen. He also met with Silas Deane, Edward Rutledge, and probably John Dickinson. See Lord Drummond's Notes and Minutes, Jan. 3–9?, Jan. 5, 6, 9, 10, 14, 1776, ibid., pp. 21–24, 32–33, 39–40, 69–71, 74, 91–93. The substance of the settlement supposedly agreed upon as a basis of negotiation with Britain involved an agreement by the colonial assemblies to provide a perpetual revenue for the purpose of colonial defense, while for its part Britain would give up its claim of a right to tax the colonies and would put any revenues forthcoming from its regulation of trade, after the expense of collecting it was deducted, to the use of the legislature. For a summary, see ibid., p. 24 n. 1. As such, Drummond's plan was remarkably similar to Lord North's, which had been decisively rejected the previous year.

43. Richard Smith Diary, Mar. 5, 1776, ibid., p. 335.

44. Drummond gave his letter to Thomas Lynch, with whom he conferred in New York on February 5, for transmission to Washington and thence to the British commander. Washington laid the letter before Congress. Lord Drummond's Minutes, Feb. 5, 1776; and Richard Smith Diary, Feb. 29, 1776, ibid., pp. 198–99, 311.

45. Richard Smith Diary, Mar. 5, 1776, ibid., p. 335.

46. The commissioners were Admiral Lord Richard Howe and General William Howe. The best account of the Howe peace mission is in Ira D. Gruber, *The Howe Brothers and the American Revolution* (New York, 1972), pp. 45–126. Gruber notes that the Howe peace mission was probably doomed to failure from the beginning, not because the British government wavered between a policy of conciliation and one of coercion (as older accounts had claimed), but because the British government had made a firm policy commitment to the use of coercion, and thus "North, Dartmouth and Howe were . . . running directly against prevailing British governmental opinion" when they worked toward a peace mission with wide enough powers to effect a true reconciliation (p. 87). See also, above, Chapter 2. On the Howe peace mission, see also Brown, *Empire or Independence*, pp. 75–139.

47. Robert Morris to Horatio Gates, Apr. 6, 1776, in Smith, ed., *LDC* 3:495. The reports of the coming of the commissioners and speculation about the extent of their powers began in February 1776 as soon as news of the Prohibitory Bill arrived. See, for example, Joseph Hewes to Samuel Johnston [Feb.] 13, [1776]; and Robert Morris to Charles Lee, Feb. 17, 1776, ibid., pp. 247, 269.

48. See, for example, John Adams to James Warren, [July] 6, 1775, ibid., 1:589.

49. William Hooper to Joseph Trumbull, Feb. [Mar.] 13, 1776, ibid. 3:372. Hooper continued, however, that it was hinted that "rather than return *re infecta* they are to make propositions to the Continental Congress."

50. For radical distrust of the commissioners' intentions, see, for example, Josiah Bartlett to John Langdon, Feb. 19, 1776; Oliver Wolcott to Samuel Lyman, Feb. 19, 1776; and John Adams to Abigail Adams [April 6, 1776], ibid. 3:281, 286, 492.

51. Gruber, *Howe Brothers*, p. 96. This fear was reflected in the virulent newspaper campaign that tried to bring about a total rejection of the commissioners and their proposals. "Cassandra" [James Cannon], for example, recommended that the commissioners be arrested as soon as they stepped ashore and sent under armed guard to the Congress "with the strictest injunction that they be permitted to speak with no man . . . until they arrive in Philadelphia." *Pennsylvania Packet*, Mar. 25, 1776. See also *Boston Gazette*, Mar. 11, Apr. 15, 1776; "Planter in Virginia," Pinkney's *Virginia Gazette*, Mar. 23, 1776; *Pennsylvania Journal*, Feb. 28, 1776; William Whipple to John Langdon, Apr. 2, 1776, in Smith, ed., *LDC* 3:478. The radical fears of the "lure" of the commissioners stemmed in large part from uncertainty over the extent of their powers. Thus William Hooper, in the letter cited above, speculated that the commissioners had instructions that they were, in the last resort, to treat with the Congress, and that "It is hinted that in the last instance their proffers will be liberal, & that if we resist the Allurements which parade, persuasion, venality and Corruption may turn out, the day is our own & that Britain must hold forth by her Commissioners a Carte Blanche to her injured Sons in America." Hooper to Joseph Trumbull, [Mar.] 13, 1776, in Smith, ed., *LDC* 3:372. See also Carter Braxton to Landon Carter, Apr. 14, 1776; and Robert Morris to Joseph Reed, July 21, 1776, ibid. 3:522, 4:511. John Adams worried, "We continue Still between Hawk and Buzzard. Some People yet expect Commissioners to treat with Congress—and to offer a Chart blanc." Adams to Joseph Palmer, Apr. 2, 1776, ibid. 3:473.

52. He was the brother of the revered Lord Howe who had fallen in Canada during the Seven Years War. A respected Whig, Howe had carried on extensive conversations with Franklin in London in early 1775 that had been aimed at bringing about a reconciliation. See Gruber, *Howe Brothers*, pp. 53–55.

53. Gruber, *Howe Brothers*, pp. 93–94; Brown, *Empire or Independence*, pp. 108–9. See, for example, the letter from Dennis De Berdt to his son-in-law, Joseph Reed, May 3, 1776, wherein the Englishman assures him, "Do my dear friend, let me persuade you that Lord *Howe* goes to *America* as a mediator, and not as a destroyer." Force, ed., *American Archives*, 5th ser., 1:372–73. Reed forwarded the letter to Washington and Robert Morris, and requested that it "be made use of as your good judgment may direct." Ibid., p. 415. Their good judgment directed that it be laid before the Congress. See also John Hancock to George Washington, July 18, 1776, in Smith, ed., *LDC* 4:485 nn. 1, 2; Samuel Adams to Samuel Cooper, July 20, 1776; and William Ellery to [Ezra Stiles?], [same date?], ibid., pp. 493, 497–98.

54. While there was a good deal of interest in the commissioners and their

reported powers, there was no serious discussion of negotiations by individual colonies. As Robert Morris said bluntly, he had heard that the commissioners "can only Treat with the Colonies separately & will have nothing to do with the Congress. If this be the case they may as well stay where they are." Morris to Silas Deane, Mar. 10, 1776, in Smith, ed., *LDC* 3:366.

55. Gruber notes that Howe's powers were, in fact, greater than those announced publicly (as Howe kept intimating they were). But the wide powers could not be revealed until a colonial surrender had been made, so they were useless in any attempt to bring about a shift in colonial attitudes. *Howe Brothers*, pp. 77–78.

56. July 19, 1776, in *JCC* 5:592–93; Josiah Bartlett to John Langdon, July 22, 1776, in Smith, ed., *LDC* 4:513–14.

57. Sept. 3, 17, 1776, in *JCC* 5:730–31, 765–67. John Adams gave a complete account of the September negotiations, as he later recalled them, in his autobiography; Butterfield, ed., *Adams Papers* 3:417–30. For contemporary accounts of the negotiations, see John Adams to Samuel Adams, Sept. 8, 1776; John Adams to James Warren, Sept. 8, 1776; Caesar Rodney to Thomas Rodney, Sept. 11, 1776; Caesar Rodney to George Reed, Sept. 13, 1776; John Adams to Abigail Adams, Sept. 14, 1776; John Adams to Samuel Adams, Sept. 14, 1776; and Josiah Bartlett to William Whipple, Sept. 14, 1776, in Smith, ed., *LDC* 5:121–23, 134–35, 154, 159–63. For a contemporary British account, see that of Howe's private secretary published in Paul Ford, ed., "Lord Howe's Commission to Pacify the Colonies," *Atlantic Monthly* (June 1896), pp. 758–62.

58. In fact, Englishmen may have assumed that Americans would be forced to seek foreign assistance before the colonists had themselves reached that conclusion. Thus, almost before the Congress had begun to explore seriously the possibility of foreign aid, the royal governor of New Jersey reported to Lord Dartmouth "that the Congress have well-grounded Assurances of Assistance from France." William Franklin to Lord Dartmouth ("Secret and Confidential"), Jan. 5, 1776, in *New Jersey Archives*, 1st ser., 10:679.

59. *JCC* 2:154–55.

60. John Adams to James Warren, Oct. 7, 1775, in Ford, ed., *Warren-Adams Letters* 1:126–28. The fear that France would demand political concessions in return for assistance dominated Adams's thinking on foreign policy. The refusal to grant such concessions became a key element in his position, and ultimately in American foreign policy. See Gilbert, *To the Farewell Address*, pp. 49–54.

61. *JCC* 2:253–54, 3:392. Most of the accounts of the early foreign affairs of the colonies focus on the activities of the Secret Committee rather than the Committee of Secret Correspondence. An excellent modern account is in Henderson, *Party Politics*, pp. 187–217. Much has been written on the fascinating relationship between Silas Deane (an agent of both committees), in his role as procurement officer of the Secret Committee, and Beaumarchais—playwright, adventurer, and agent of the French government charged with supplying the colonies through the ghost firm of "Hortales et Cie." See, on this, Richard W. Van Alstyne, *Empire and Independence: The International History of the American Revolution* (New York, 1965), pp. 79–11; and Van Alstyne, *The Rising American*

Empire (New York, 1960), pp. 1–78. See also A.B. Darling, *Our Rising Empire, 1763–1803* (New Haven, Conn., 1940).

I am here more interested in the Committee of Secret Correspondence, which was the precursor of the Committee of Foreign Affairs, set up by the Congress on April 17, 1777, *JCC* 7:274. The delegates abandoned, as quickly as militarily feasible, such remnants of their early revolutionary endeavors as the Secret Committee and attempted as soon as they could to conduct the new nation's affairs along accepted eighteenth-century diplomatic lines. The Secret Committee was, however, in existence until 1778.

On the day the Committee of Secret Correspondence was appointed, it wrote, through Franklin, to Arthur Lee, informing Lee of the mission, asking that he begin to gather information, and offering to pay the expense of an express packet boat should Lee have any information he believed needed instant communication. Committee (Franklin) to Lee, in Willcox, ed., *Papers of Franklin* 22:281.

62. The membership of the Secret Committee between 1774 and 1776 included Thomas Willing, Benjamin Franklin, Philip Livingston, John Alsop, Silas Deane, John Dickinson, John Langdon, Thomas McKean, Samuel Ward, Francis Lewis, Josiah Bartlett, Archibald Bulloch, and Robert Morris. The Committee of Secret Correspondence consisted of Benjamin Harrison, Benjamin Franklin, Thomas Johnson, John Dickinson, John Jay, and Robert Morris.

63. The congressional assumption of the power to regulate the trade of the colonies followed closely upon the pattern of the congressional assumption of foreign affairs. First, a common trade policy toward England was devised in the Association of 1774. Then, through 1775, exceptions to the Association were adopted by Congress as occasion demanded. Finally, on April 6, 1776, American ports were opened to vessels of all nations. *JCC* 4:257. On the connection between trade policy and the development of the navy, see Chapter 5. See Adams, Notes of Debates, in Butterfield, ed., *Adams Papers* 2:188–94, 204–17, 219–20, 229–30. On the close connection between trade and foreign policy in the eighteenth century, see Gilbert, *To the Farewell Address*, p. 46.

64. Franklin et al. to [Arthur Lee], Dec. 12, 1775, in Willcox, ed., *Papers of Franklin* 22:297; Franklin to C.W.F. Dumas, Dec. 9, 1775, in Smith, ed., *LDC* 2:466.

65. Kammen, *Rope of Sand*, p. 318.

66. On Bonvouloir's mission, see his account in Clark, ed., *NDAR* 3:279–84. See also Darling, *Rising Empire*, pp. 12–13, and Van Alstyne, *Rising American Empire*, pp. 31–33. Deane's commission is in Smith, ed., *LDC* 3:320–23. The appointment of the Secret Committee on November 30 had been in response to a motion, offered by Chase on November 29 and seconded by Adams, to send an ambassador to France. See Willcox, ed., *Papers of Franklin* 22:280n.

67. Committee of Secret Correspondence, Minutes of Proceedings, Mar. 2, 1776, in Smith, ed., *LDC* 3:320–22.

68. Richard Smith Diary, Feb. 16, 1776, in Smith, ed., *LDC* 3:267; John Penn to Thomas Person, Feb. 14, 1776, in Saunders, ed., *Colonial Records of North Carolina* 10:456.

69. See, for example, R. H. Lee to Landon Carter, June 2, 1776; and Elbridge

Gerry to John Wendell, June 11, 1776, in Smith, ed., *LDC* 4:117–18, 187–88. See also Jefferson, Notes of Proceedings in Congress, June 7–28, 1776, ibid., p. 163: "That a declaration of Independence alone could render it consistent with European delicacy for European powers to treat with us, or even to receive an Ambassador from us."

70. *JCC* 5:433, 576–89. See Elbridge Gerry to James Warren, June 11, 1776; and Rhode Island Delegates to Nicholas Cooke, June 21, 1776, in Smith, ed., *LDC* 4:187, 286. Gerry noted that although independence had been postponed until the middle-colony assemblies could empower their delegates to vote for it, "in the interim will go on plans for confederation and foreign alliance." Ibid., p. 181. Thus, when the delegates had first debated the question of foreign alliances on the eve of Silas Deane's departure for France, it became clear that nothing could be done "when it appeared that 5 or 6 Colonies have instructed their Delegates not to agree to an Independency till they, the Principles, are consulted." Richard Smith Diary, [Feb. 29, 1776], ibid. 3:311–12.

71. John Adams, Notes on Relations with France [Mar. 4? 1776]; and John Adams to John Winthrop, June 23, 1776, in Smith, ed., *LDC* 3:326, 4:299.

72. *JCC* 5:576–89. For Adams's account of drawing up the draft treaty, see Autobiography, in Butterfield, ed., *Adams Papers* 3:337–38. Adams's Model Treaty, although based upon traditional European commercial treaties, nevertheless was a milestone in the early development of a distinctively American foreign policy. As Gilbert notes, Adams's absolute refusal to make political concessions in return for French aid, and the rigorous confinement of the permanent connection between France and America solely to commercial relations, presaged all future American alliances. See Gilbert, *To the Farewell Address*, pp. 48–54. Gilbert also notes that while Adams's conception of the term "alliance" does not accord with modern conceptions of the term as encompassing mutual military obligations, this view of the term reflected standard eighteenth-century usage (p. 46). On the substance of the treaty, Gilbert notes, "agreements which regulated the commercial relations between England and France were used as patterns for the Model Treaty (p. 50).

Gilbert notes that Articles 8, 9, and 11 of the final plan of treaties, when read together, guaranteed no more than that if France's alliance with the colonies caused an Anglo-French war, the colonies agreed that they would not assist England in such a war. He terms it "astounding . . . how little the Americans were willing to offer" (pp. 52–53).

73. Also, the French insisted that there must be a treaty of political alliance to accompany the Treaty of Amity and Commerce before they would agree to either. See Gerald Stourzh, *Benjamin Franklin and American Foreign Policy*, 2d ed. (Chicago, 1969), pp. 141–46.

74. *JCC* 5:768–78, 813–17, 827. Jefferson was originally selected as one of the commissioners on September 26. Upon his declining to serve, the commission was offered on October 22 to Arthur Lee. The process of seeking formal European alliances was rounded out on December 30 when Congress resolved to send commissioners to the courts at Vienna, Madrid, and Potsdam and to the Grand Duke of Tuscany, all seeking alliances and assistance. *JCC* 6:1054. The

report of the committee to draw up instructions for the commissioners, dated September 10, 1776, is in Papers of the Continental Congress, National Archives Microfilm M-247, reel 61.

75. It should be emphasized that congressional foreign policy precisely followed the traditional eighteenth-century pattern. Although forced by circumstances in its early years to conduct a quasi-revolutionary policy of "Addresses to the People," the Congress moved as quickly as possible to assume a more traditional (and legitimate) role. By 1776 its foreign policy efforts were directed almost exclusively toward signing formal treaties of amity and commerce with the "corrupt" courts of Europe. In style, however, and in the rigorous exclusion of political considerations from foreign negotiations, the American diplomats *were* attempting something new—nothing less, according to Gilbert, than the infusion of Enlightenment ideas into the conduct of foreign policy. The tension between the old diplomacy and the new diplomacy was a major factor in the political crises that erupted periodically in the early years of the republic. See Gilbert, *To the Farewell Address*, pp. 44–75.

Chapter 8

1. Anthony Wayne to Benjamin Franklin, Oct. 3, 1776, in Benjamin Franklin Papers, Univ. of Pa.

2. For the development of the English system of Indian control, see John R. Alden, "The Albany Congress and the Creation of the Indian Superintendencies," *Mississippi Valley Historical Review* 27 (1940): 193–210; and Clarence Alvord, *The Mississippi Valley in British Politics* (Cleveland, 1917).

3. For American fears that the Indians, especially those on the Canadian frontier, would be called into British service, see Chapters 2 and 5. See also, John Hancock to Philip Schuyler, Oct. 7, 1775, in Smith, ed., *LDC* 2:139.

4. For the effectiveness of the Tory heirs of Sir William Johnson, see James T. Flexner, *Mohawk Baronet: Sir William Johnson of New York* (New York, 1959), pp. 349–51. See also, William L. Stone, *The Life and Times of Sir William Johnson, Bart.* (Albany, 1865), 2:502–28. The story of the Johnson family is a fascinating one. Sir William Johnson, of Johnson Hall, was the English commissioner for the Indians in northern New York. He had lived among them for years, had taken an Indian wife, and had enormous influence. His influence passed to his son, Sir John Johnson, at his death in 1774. Sir John's activities continued to worry the New York authorities throughout the war. See "Extract of a Letter from the Committee of Tryon County, New-York, to Col. Guy Johnson" [June 1775]; Col. Guy Johnson to the Committee of Tryon County, June 5, 1775; New York Delegates to New York Congress, June 10, 1775; and Samuel Kirkland to New York Provincial Congress, June 9, 1775, in Force, ed., *American Archives*, 4th ser., 2:879–80, 911–12, 954, 1309–10.

5. New York Provincial Congress to the Congress, June 7, 1775, in Force, ed., *American Archives*, 4th ser., 2:1281. The Provincial Congress specifically suggested that, though they did not "presume to dictate any measure to you,"

they submitted "to your consideration whether it is proper to leave the management of the numerous tribes of *Indians* entirely in the hands of persons appointed by and paid by the Crown." If not, they asked, "whether it will not be both politick and just to nominate a Continental Superintendent of *Indian* affairs." See also above, Chapter 5, for the connection between this request and the need to protect New York's Canadian frontier.

6. June 16, 1775, in *JCC* 2:93. Reflecting the New York concern that had prompted the action, the committee consisted of Philip Schuyler, James Duane, and Philip Livingston, as well as James Wilson and Patrick Henry.

7. June 30, 1775, in *JCC* 2:123.

8. June 26, 29, 30, July 1, 10, 1775, in *JCC*, 2:108, 110–11, 123, 173.

9. July 11, 12, 13, 19, 21, 1775, in *JCC*, 2:173, 174–77, 177–83, 192, 194; Silas Deane Diary, [July 13, 1775], in Smith, ed., *LDC* 1:624, 624 n. 1.

10. For subsequent congressional dealings with Indian affairs, see, for example, July 17, 1775, Nov. 8, 11, 23, 1775 (whereby, on the request of the northern Indians, the trade at Schenectady and Albany was reopened under congressional auspices), Dec. 22, 1775, Jan. 27, Mar. 16, Apr. 29, 30, 1776, in *JCC* 2:186, 3:336, 350, 366–67, 444, 4:95, 208, 318, 319. The standing committee consisted of George Wythe, James Wilson, Oliver Wolcott, Lewis Morris, and Edward Rutledge. On the Congress and Indian affairs, see Burnett, *Continental Congress*, p. 97.

11. *JCC* 5:550.

12. John Adams, Notes of Debates, July 26, 1776, in Smith, ed., *LDC* 4:546.

13. Arthur Lee to Samuel Adams, Feb. 8, 1774, Samuel Adams Papers, vol. 5, Photocopy, Library of Congress.

14. The most complete work on Goddard is Ward L. Miner, *William Goddard, Newspaperman* (Durham, N.C., 1962). Goddard was free to take on the task of organizing a postal service largely because of an imbroglio with his former publishing partner, Joseph Galloway, that almost put him out of business in Philadelphia. Goddard's account of the affair is in *The Partnership, or, The History of the Rise and Progress of the Pennsylvania Chronicle . . .* (Philadelphia, 1770). On his post office endeavors, see Miner, *Goddard*, pp. 113–36.

15. This episode is related in Miner, *Goddard*, pp. 115–33; "Extract from a Gentleman in New York," Boston, Feb. 28, 1774, *South Carolina and American and General Gazette*, Apr. 29–May 6, 1774; letter to *Massachusetts Spy*, Mar. 24, 1774. For enthusiastic references to, and confidence in, the speedy establishment of the Constitutional Post, see *Massachusetts Spy*, Mar. 17, 24, 1774; "Hortensius," *Boston Gazette*, Mar. 21, 1774; "Letter from New London," ibid., Apr. 11, 1774; ibid., May 2, 1774; Purdie and Dixon's *Virginia Gazette*, Aug. 11, 1774; *South Carolina and American General Gazette*, Apr. 29–May 6, 1774.

16. *Boston Gazette*, Apr. 25, 1774; see also, "A Pennsylvanian," *Massachusetts Spy*, Apr. 22, 1774. Goddard, in fact, attempted to interest the First Congress in taking over his system, but without success. "Editorial Note on the Founding of the Post Office," in Willcox, ed., *Papers of Franklin* 22:133.

17. The efficiency of the Royal Post in America was largely due to the efforts of Franklin.

18. Part of Goddard's problem stemmed from an unfortunate incident that occurred on April 8, 1774, when one of the patriot riders for the Constitutional Post absconded with some $558—"rode off with the cash, and has never been heard of since." The reputation of the Constitutional Post never quite recovered. *Draper's Massachusetts Gazette*, Apr. 28, 1774; see also *Massachusetts Spy*, Apr. 28, 1774. In late 1774 a Tory predicted that the new scheme of provincial congresses would "end in the same ridiculous manner as their late projects for erecting new Post-Offices. . . . The Bostonians assured us," that their plans "met with the unanimous concurrence of all the Colonies on the Continent," but it "vanished like a dream." "Substance of Several Letters from Boston," *Boston Gazette*, Oct. 24, 1774.

19. See, for example, Hugh Finlay to Lord Dartmouth, May 20, 1775: "Our riders have been stop'd in the Provinces of Massachusetts and Connecticut, and His Majesty's Mails have been opened to discover who are Friends to Government." Brit. Trans., Public Record Office, CO 5, vol. 246, copy, Library of Congress. The New York postmaster, when questioned by the New York committee as to why he had dismissed the royal riders, reported "that the last four mails between *New-York* and *Boston* have been stopped, the mails broken open, many of the letters taken out and publicly read . . . and that the riders informed him that it was not safe for them to travel with the mail." Proceedings of the New York Committee, May 3, 1775, in Force, ed., *American Archives*, 4th ser., 2:481. The result was that by 1774 many colonists were refusing to trust their letters to either post but were sending them privately. On April 27, 1775, William Williams warned Dr. Thomas Williams, "every Post is now Stopd & other mails taken." Gratz Coll., case 8, box 12, Hist. Soc. of Pa. On July 28, Ralph Wormely, Jr., of Virginia, warned George Mercer, "a private hand may now perhaps be safer than the post." Ibid., case 4, box 31. See also *Pennsylvania Gazette*, Dec. 20, 1775. Even love letters, it seems, were not exempt. Thus, a young minister away from his beloved noted in his journal of November 13, 1775, "I wrote home by the Post to Day to my dear absent Betsey. . . . I fear however their Safety as the public are so jealous of what is passing by Letter through the Country." Robert G. Albion and Leonidas Dodson, eds., *Philip Vickers Fithian, Journal, 1775–1776, Written on the Virginia-Pennsylvania Frontier and in the Army around New York* (Princeton, N.J., 1934), p. 133.

20. When Congress began to consider setting up a Continental post, they requested information from the New York authorities regarding their progress. See New York Delegates to New York Provincial Congress, May 30, 1775, in Smith, ed., *LDC* 1:419.

21. *New-York Journal*, May 4, 1775; letter from New York Committee, May 3, 1775, in Force, ed., *American Archives*, 4th ser., 2:482, 536–38; Proceedings of New Hampshire Convention, May 18, 1775, ibid., p. 651; Proceedings of the Rhode Island Assembly, June 1775, ibid., pp. 1160–61; Proceedings of the Provincial Congress of Massachusetts, May 13, 1775, in Lincoln, ed., *Jour. Prov. Cong. Mass.*, p. 223. See also the letters that William Goddard gathered in favor of his plan from the committees of Providence and Newport in Rhode Island (May 30, 31, 1775) and Stamford (May 5, 1775), Norwalk (May 7, 1775),

Middletown (May 7, 1775), Hartford (May 7, 1775), and New London (June 6, 1775) in Connecticut, in Force, ed., *American Archives*, 4th ser., 2:982–83. Willcox notes that during this period independent post offices, set up by various provincial authorities and even by individual towns, were burgeoning. Willcox, ed., *Papers of Franklin* 22:133.

22. *JCC* 2:71, 203, 208–9. The Committee recommended, and Congress adopted, a very simple expedient for ensuring that the new system would supplant the royal post. In specifying the rates that would be charged, the Congress agreed "that the rates of postage shall be 20 pr cent less than those appointed by act of Parliament." Ibid., p. 208. The delegates envisioned that the system would be self-supporting in that the deputy postmasters were allowed 20 percent of the revenues collected, "in lieu of salary and all contingent expenses." Ibid. The discounted charges were subsequently rescinded, on motion of Franklin, when it became clear that the post would not be self-supporting at the reduced rate. See Richard Smith Diary, Sept. 30 [1775], in Smith, ed., *LDC* 2:83.

23. The Congress, on the basis of the committee report, authorized an extensive postal network that was to stretch from Falmouth, Maine, to Savannah, Georgia. The head of the system, the postmaster general, was authorized to appoint as many deputies as he thought necessary. Willcox believes that without more extensive documentation, it is impossible to assign a leading role in the organization of the post office to Franklin; Willcox, ed., *Papers of Franklin* 22:134. Yet the similarity of the new Continental system to that which Franklin had set up under royal authority seems to argue for his guiding influence. It seems clear that he set to work immediately during the adjournment of Congress to organize the new institution. Thus, on August 2 he wrote to Jane Mecom, "I have now upon my Hands the Settling a new General Post Office." Willcox, ed., *Papers of Franklin* 22:143. On August 27 he reported to Silas Deane that he had dispatched the indefatigable Goddard southward "for settling the new Post-Offices all along to Georgia," and had sent his son-in-law, Richard Bache (the Comptroller of the New Post Office) "Northward on the same Business." Bache would carry orders from Franklin "to establish all the Officers in your Government that you recommend, and the new Offices and Stages that appear likely to support themselves." Ibid., pp. 183–84. The delegates continued to oversee the system. See, for example, the appointment of a committee on December 1, 1775, to see if the express system could not be speeded up; *JCC* 3:401.

24. *South Carolina and American General Gazette*, Feb. 28–Mar. 8, 1776; Francis L. Lee to Landon Carter, Oct. 21, 1775, in Smith, ed., *LDC* 2:227. Thus, when the delegates debated on October 7, 1775, whether they ought to put a stop to the royal post riders in addition to organizing their own post, Dyer argued that this was an unnecessary move as "we have already superceeded the Act of Parliament effectually." Paine also argued that, "The Ministerial Post will die a natural death. . . . It would be Cowardice to issue a Decree to kill that which is dying," as, in its last run from Boston "it brought but one Letter." John Adams, Notes of Debates, in Smith, ed., *LDC* 2:133.

25. On the king's authority to settle boundary disputes, see Chapter 1 and Onuf, *Origins of the Federal Republic*, pp. 4, 8–9. For the records of such appeals, see Joseph L. Smith, *Appeals to the Privy Council from the American Plantations* (New York, 1950). To the eve of revolution, the authority of the king to act upon such disputes was rarely challenged. In early 1774, James Wilson asserted that "The Power of determining disputes between different Provinces is vested in the Crown," and it was "that Power, which alone can make such a Decision." James Wilson to Arthur St. Clair, Jan. 14, 1774, Gratz Coll., case 12, box 14, Hist. Soc. of Pa. For a Tory prediction of civil war, see, for example, "Massachusettensis" [Daniel Leonard], *Massachusetts Gazette and Post-Boy*, Jan. 23, 1775.

26. Onuf, *Origins of the Federal Republic*, pp. 10, 13–14.

27. Good accounts of the origin, progress, and settlement of this dispute are: Boyd Crumrine, "The Boundary Controversy between Pennsylvania and Virginia, 1748–1785," Carnegie Museum of Pittsburgh, *Annals* 1 (1901): 505–24; Percy B. Caley, "Lord Dunmore and the Pennsylvania-Virginia Boundary Dispute," *Western Pennsylvania Historical Magazine* 22 (1939): 87–100; Solon J. Buck and Elizabeth H. Buck, *The Planting of Civilization in Western Pennsylvania* (Pittsburgh, 1939), pp. 156–74, 180–82; and Russell J. Ferguson, *Early Western Pennsylvania Politics* (Pittsburgh, 1938), pp. 21–28. For the respective claims of both colonies to the disputed territory, see Robert H. Foster, "The Pennsylvania and Virginia Controversy," *Pennsylvania Archives*, 3d ser., 3:485–504. The following account is largely drawn from these sources.

28. The Connecticut delegates wrote that Dunmore's action would have "occasion[ed] much greater Speculations here," had "the whole Attention of the public [not been] taken up on more important Subjects." To Jonathan Trumbull, Oct. 10, 1774, in Smith, ed., *LDC* 1:170.

29. The petition from "that part of Augusta county, . . . on the west side of the Allegeny Mountain," is found under the date of June 1, 1775, in *JCC* 2:76. See also, George Ross to Lancaster Committee of Correspondence, May 30, 1775, in Smith, ed., *LDC* 1:421–22; Buck and Buck, *Western Pennsylvania*, pp. 179–80; Ferguson, *Early Western Pennsylvania*, p. 27.

30. Caley, "Pennsylvania-Virginia Boundary," p. 98.

31. *JCC* 2:76; George Ross to Lancaster Committee of Correspondence, May 30, 1775, in Smith, ed., *LDC* 1:421; John Armstrong to James Wilson, June 6, 1775, Gratz Coll., case 4, box 11, Hist. Soc. of Pa. The Virginians also manifested a great interest in a temporary boundary line. See the Virginia Committee of Safety to the Virginia Delegates in Congress, June 17, 1776, in Boyd, ed., *Jefferson Papers* 1:388.

32. June 1, 1775, in *JCC* 2:76.

33. Virginia and Pennsylvania Delegates to Laurel Hill-West Side Inhabitants, July 25, 1775, in Boyd, ed., *Jefferson Papers* 1:234.

34. Richard Smith Diary, Sept. 15, 25, 26, 1775; and Samuel Ward Diary, Sept. 23, 1775; in Smith, ed., *LDC* 2:17, 49, 57–58, 67; James Wilson to John Montgomery, Sept. 14, 1775, Dreer Coll., Members of Old Congress, vol. 5, Hist. Soc. of Pa.; Sept. 14, 15, 22, 25, 26, Oct. 7, in *JCC* 2:251, 3:259, 262, 283;

Charles P. Smith, *James Wilson, Founding Father* (Chapel Hill, N.C., 1956), pp. 69–70. The Virginians were extremely suspicious of Pennsylvania's intentions and may well have prevented a congressional settlement of the affair. Thomas Walker wrote from Fort Pitt of "the unhappy territorial dispute between the two Colonies which has proceeded to an inconceiviable [*sic*] length" and advised Jefferson that if the Congress took up the dispute, "you and the other Virginians will object to the giving up any of the Teritory west of the Laurel hill." Sept. 13, 1775, in Boyd, ed., *Jefferson Papers* 1:245.

35. On the Detroit expedition, see Samuel Ward Diary, Sept. 14, 1775; George Ross to James Wilson, Sept. 15, 1775; John Hancock to Lewis Morris and James Wilson, Sept. 15, 1775; Richard Smith Diary, Sept. 13, 14, 1775, in Smith, ed., *LDC* 2:8–10, 15–16; Sept. 13, 14, 1775, *JCC* 2:246, 251; William Henry Smith, ed., *The St. Clair Papers: The Life and Public Services of Arthur St. Clair . . .* (Cincinnati, 1882), 1:14–15.

36. See Clarence M. Burton, "John Connolly: A Tory of the Revolution," American Antiquarian Society, *Proceedings*, n.s., 20 (1909): 70.

37. Virginia initiated the intercolony negotiations that eventually resulted in a settlement. Commenting that recent armed conflicts between Pennsylvania and Virginia settlers did "not look like neighbours and freinds [*sic*] united in a most glorious common cause," Pendleton wrote to the Virginia delegates in Congress that "surely it must be for common Interest to settle a temporary boundary, and that all Jealousies and much more hostilities should subside." Virginia thus proposed that negotiations begin between the Convention and the Pennsylvania Assembly. See Virginia Committee of Safety to the Virginia Delegates in Congress, June 17, 1776; and Edmund Pendleton to Virginia Delegates in Congress, July 15, 1776, in Boyd, ed., *Jefferson Papers* 1:387–88, 463–65. On the resolution of the dispute, see Crumrine, "Boundary Controversy," pp. 521–23, and Onuf, *Origins of the Federal Republic*, pp. 49–61.

38. The area is variously referred to as "the Susquehannah lands," "the Wyoming," the counties of "Northampton and Northumberland" (Pa.), and the town of "Westmoreland" (Conn.).

39. The early years of the controversy have been fully discussed in Julian P. Boyd, *The Susquehannah Company: Connecticut's Experiment in Expansion*, Tercentenary Commission of the State of Connecticut, Historical Publications (Hartford, 1935), and an earlier work by the same author, "Connecticut's Experiment in Expansion: The Susquehannah Company, 1753–1803," *Journal of Economic and Business History* 4 (1931): 38–69. A detailed summary of the progress of the dispute in the early 1770s is found in the introduction to Robert J. Taylor, ed., *The Susquehannah Company Papers* (Ithaca, N.Y., 1968), 5:xxi–lii. The following discussion has been drawn largely from these sources.

40. Governor Jonathan Trumbull of Connecticut, for example, had been so identified with the cause of the Susquehannah Company that in 1773 the company cited him as "the one particular Gentleman in this Colony . . . that has done Sundry Services for this Company" and granted him five hundred acres. Quoted in Boyd, ed., *Jefferson Papers* 6:476.

41. The Connecticut negotiators proposed that the west branch of the Susquehannah River be accepted by both sides as a temporary boundary line until the dispute could be finally settled in England. The Pennsylvanians absolutely refused to agree to this proposal, because such a solution would force them to cede (albeit temporarily) their claim to jurisdiction over the Yankee-held lands. These inflexible positions in 1773 were duplicated in the 1775 negotiations and precipitated congressional intervention into the dispute. See Taylor, ed., *Susquehannah Company Papers* 5:xxi–xxiii, and below.

42. The Connecticut Assembly had, in its view, acted moderately. The settlers wished their lands to be incorporated as a Connecticut county, which would have given them considerable autonomy, especially in judicial matters. This the Assembly refused to do, instead conferring the more limited governmental powers of a town upon the area. The result was the enormous land area encompassed by the Town of Westmoreland. Ibid., p. xxiv. The Connecticut action resulted in a political furor both in Connecticut and in Pennsylvania and spawned a vigorous pamphlet battle that was still raging when the First Continental Congress met.

43. Much of the correspondence between Lady Juliana Penn and Governor John Penn during this period concerned the progress of the Pennsylvania petition on the Westmoreland controversy. Only after Lexington and Concord did John Penn begin to doubt that the final solution of the dispute would take place in London. See John Penn to Lady Juliana Penn, Apr. 3, 1775, in Thomas Penn Papers, microfilm, reel 10, Hist. Soc. of Pa. The relevant correspondence is in the Thomas Penn Papers.

44. July 31, Aug. 1, 1775, in *JCC* 2:235, 238.

45. See Chapter 6.

46. Silas Deane to Thomas Mumford, Oct. [16?], 1775, in Smith, ed., *LDC* 2:188. It is interesting to note that so limited were some perceptions of congressional authority over boundaries that the Pennsylvanians who petitioned Congress regarding Connecticut expansion admitted that the attempt to foster a settlement between the Connecticut and Pennsylvania delegates was "all that honorable body could do in the affair." R. L. Hooper and Reuben Haines to J. Lowden, Aug. 13, 1775, in Taylor, ed., *Susquehannah Company Papers* 6:340. Silas Deane, however, had other ideas. Thus, one reason for his urgent request that the Connecticut settlers remain quiet was that violence would "prejudice the Colonies against Our Claim, and it is probable as things are ripening that the Colonies will be Our Judges at last." Silas Deane to Zebulon Butler, July 24, 1775, in Smith, ed., *LDC* 1:661.

47. Silas Deane to Thomas Mumford, Oct. [16?], 1775, in Smith, ed., *LDC* 2:188. The letters of the Connecticut delegates are: Silas Deane to Zebulon Butler, July 24, 1775; and Connecticut Delegates to Zebulon Butler, Aug. 2, 1775, ibid., 1:660–61, 693. The effect of this plea was undercut by Eliphalet Dyer's private advice to William Judd, a leading Connecticut settler. Dyer advised Judd not to stop Connecticut settlement on the west branch but instead to "infiltrate" with one or two Yankees, rather than going in force, and to try to con-

vince the Pennsylvania settlers, especially the "Common people and let them know as far as you can make them understand, how much better it will be for them to come in under our Colony & that they will be secured by Our Government." July 23, 1775, ibid., p. 655.

The Pennsylvania response has not been found. Since no reflections were cast upon the Pennsylvanians for noncompliance, one may assume that they did not contravene the joint decision. At any event, during this period it was the Connecticut men who were threatening to move into Pennsylvania-held territory, rendering the response of the Connecticut delegates the pertinent one.

48. Taylor, ed., *Susquehannah Company Papers* 5:xlvii–xlviii. This was, of course, precisely what Dyer had advised Judd *not* to do. See Eliphalet Dyer to William Judd, July 23, 1775, in Smith, ed., *LDC* 2:655.

49. For the response to the Judd expedition, see Silas Deane to Thomas Mumford, Oct. [16?], 1775; and Eliphalet Dyer to Zebulon Butler, Oct. 1, 1775, in Smith, ed., *LDC* 2:188, 93. For the actions of the Pennsylvania Assembly see its Proceedings, Sept. 30, 1775, in *Pennsylvania Archives*, 8th ser., 8:7296. Richard Smith's statements are from his diary, Sept. 30, 1775, in Smith, ed., *LDC* 2:83.

50. Notes of Debates, in Butterfield, ed., *Adams Papers* 2:200; *JCC* 3:283. Willing's use of the term "umpire" is of considerable importance, for it was the word characteristically used to refer to the king's role as adjudicator of intra-imperial disputes. See, for example, William Smith to William Samuel Johnson, Apr. 9, 1774, in Taylor, ed., *Susquehannah Company Papers* 6:187 and above, Chapter 1.

51. Oct. 9, 11, 14, 1775, in *JCC* 3:285, 287–88, 295.

52. Ibid., p. 297. That the geographical distribution of the membership of the committee was not an accident but an expression of congressional intent became clear on November 27 when the report of the Committee was recommitted. As Rutledge (S.C.), Chase (Md.), and Kinsey (N.J.) were absent, Hooper (N.C.), Wythe (Va.), and Jay (N.Y.) were added in their places. Ibid., p. 377. It should also be noted that the members chosen for this committee were among the most respected and talented in the Congress; clearly the Wyoming dispute was a matter of the first importance in the minds of the delegates.

53. Pennsylvania Archives, 8th ser., 8:7315. Congressional reaction to the continuing crisis points up how unsure the delegates were of the new powers they had assumed. The delegates postponed consideration of the committee report brought in on November 4, and resolved only that the respective assemblies "take the most speedy and effectual steps to prevent . . . hostilities." In adopting this resolution, the delegates fell back upon the old expedient of confiding the issue to the relevant provincial authorities. Nov. 4, 1775, in *JCC* 3:321. See and compare the proposed resolution offered by the Connecticut delegates of a cease-fire in place. This was vigorously opposed by the Pennsylvanians as an effective confirmation of the Yankees' jurisdiction over the east branch. See "Connecticut Delegates' Proposed Resolution" [Oct. 17? 1775], and note thereto, in Smith, ed., *LDC* 2:196–97.

54. Taylor, ed., *Susquehannah Company Papers* 5:xlix–lii; Edward Burd to James Burd, Nov. 1, 1775, Shippen Papers, vol. 7, Hist. Soc. of Pa.

55. Jonathan Trumbull to Connecticut Delegates, Nov. 17, 1775, in Taylor, ed., *Susquehannah Company Papers* 6:389; Nov. 27, 1775, in *JCC* 3:377. The November 27 action was formally a recommittal of the report of the October 17 committee. Consideration of the committee report had been postponed almost from day to day through November. The members apparently had decided that the Congress would have to settle a temporary boundary line, and for this they felt the need for additional evidence. Nov. 10, 15–17, 20, 23, 24, 1775, in *JCC* 3:349, 355, 357, 359, 361, 368, 369.

56. For examples of the Connecticut alarm at the progress of the Pennsylvanians, see, for example, "Extract of the Minutes of the Connecticut Council of Safety," Nov. 3, 1775; Jonathan Trumbull to a Committee of the Town of Westmoreland, Nov. 7, 1775; Jonathan Trumbull to the Connecticut Delegates, Nov. 11, 1775; and Memorial to Congress, Dec. 18, 1775, in Taylor, ed., *Susquehannah Company Papers*, 6:385, 386, 389, 414–16; Richard Smith Diary, Dec. 18, 1775, in Smith, ed., *LDC* 2:494.

57. *JCC* 3:439–40. Connecticut Delegates' Proposed Resolution [Oct. 17? 1775], in Smith, ed., *LDC* 2:196–97. For a statement of the consistent Pennsylvania position regarding jurisdiction, see Resolution of the Pennsylvania Assembly, Oct. 27, 1775, in Taylor, ed., *Susquehannah Company Papers* 6:383; Richard Smith Diary, Dec. 20, 1775, in Smith, ed., *LDC* 2:500.

58. Richard Smith Diary, Dec. 21, 23, 1775, in Smith, ed., *LDC* 2:500–501, 517.

59. The Wyoming dispute was not finally settled until 1784, when, in a famous compromise, Connecticut ceded her claims to the area in return for a rich part of the national domain thenceforth known as the Western Reserve in what is now Ohio. See Boyd, ed., *Jefferson Papers* 6:475–77. On the continuing disputes in the region, see Onuf, *Origins of the Federal Republic*, pp. 61–72.

60. Dec. 20, 1775, in *JCC* 3:439–40.

61. Petition is in *Pennsylvania Archives*, 1st ser., 4:669; Richard Smith Diary, Dec. 29, 1775, in Smith, ed., *LDC* 2:535. Robert Sherman, however, transmitted the December 20 and 23 resolves in a very different spirit. "It appears to me," he wrote, "the Honorable Congress will lay their hand upon it, and do everything needful that Justice may be done, and any future attacks on our peaceable people at that place prevented." Sherman to Zebulon Butler, Jan. 19, Feb. 19, 1776, in Smith, ed., *LDC* 3:115–16, 283.

62. Carter Braxton to Landon Carter, Apr. 14, 1776, in Smith, ed., *LDC* 3:523. The settlers were not all that "peaceble," for on April 15, 1776, the delegates were again required to caution them, in the interest of unity, against further violence; *JCC* 4:283.

63. The controversy over the New Hampshire Grants has been well documented. An excellent short account is in Dixon Ryan Fox, *Yankees and Yorkers* (New York and London, 1940), pp. 152–75. More extensive treatment may be found in Matt B. Jones, *Vermont in the Making, 1750–1777* (Cambridge, 1939). The history of the controversy from a New York viewpoint is in Edward P.

Alexander, *A Revolutionary Conservative: James Duane of New York*, New York State Historical Assn., 6th ser. (New York, 1938). Vermont's case is made by James B. Wilbur in *Ira Allen: Founder of Vermont, 1751–1814*, 2 vols. (Boston and New York, 1928), in which much valuable documentation may conveniently be found. This account has largely been drawn from these sources. The most complete collection of source material on the history of the controversy prior to 1775 is in E. B. O'Callaghan, ed., *Documents Relative to the Colonial History of the State of New York; procured . . . by John Romeyn Brodhead* (Albany, 1853–87), 7:531–1034.

64. For the bargain of 1750, see Benning Wentworth to Gov. Clinton, Apr. 25, 1750, in Jones, *Vermont*, p. 37. See also Fox, *Yankees and Yorkers*, p. 157. The letter from the Board of Trade to the king, July 10, 1764, which sustained New York's case, is in Jones, *Vermont*, pp. 397–403; the operative clause is on p. 401. This report was implemented by the king's Order-in-Council of July 20, 1764, in O'Callaghan, ed., *Docs. Rel. Hist. of New York* 4:574–75.

65. For a full understanding of the depth of the bitterness, one ought to read the charges and countercharges filed on both sides and solemnly recorded in numerous depositions to be found in O'Callaghan, *Docs. Rel. Hist. of New York*, volume 4. See, for example, John Munro to Governor Tryon, Nov. 6, 1771, p. 744; Affidavit of Charles Hutchesson, Nov. 12, 1775, p. 745; "An Account of the temper of the rioters," Apr. 14, 1772, p. 776; Deposition of Philip Nichols, Apr. 28, 1773, p. 830; and Adolphus Benzel to Gov. Tryon, Sept. 27, 1773, p. 854.

66. See Chapter 5.

67. June 23, 1775, in *JCC* 2:105.

68. Barnabas Deane to Silas Deane, June 1, 1775, in "Deane Correspondence," Conn. Hist. Soc., *Collections* 2:247; Ethan Allen to New York Provincial Congress, July 20, 1775, in Force, ed., *American Archives*, 4th ser., 2:1695–96.

69. Jones, *Vermont*, pp. 358–59; May 8, 1776, in *JCC* 4:334–35. Allen was in Philadelphia to settle accounts owed to his battalion. See Board of Treasury to New York Committee of Safety, May 7, 1776, in Smith, ed., *LDC* 3:637.

70. Petition is in Wilbur, *Ira Allen* 1:78–80; May 8, 1776, in *JCC* 4:335, 337. The committee consisted of Caesar Rodney, Benjamin Harrison, Joseph Hewes, Thomas Lynch, and Robert Alexander.

71. May 30, 1776, in *JCC* 4:405; Alexander, *Revolutionary Conservative*, p. 121. Nevertheless, the solution was to last only until "the present Troubles are at an End [and] the final Determination of their Right may be mutually referr'd to proper Judges." *JCC* 4:405.

72. Committee report cited in Jones, *Vermont*, pp. 360–62; June 4, 1776, in *JCC* 4:416; Alexander, *Revolutionary Conservative*, p. 121. See also, Robert R. Livingston to John Jay, June 4, 1776, in Smith, ed., *LDC* 4:140–41.

73. Quoted in Wilbur, *Ira Allen* 1:83. The advice brought by Allen "made a deep impression," according to Jones; *Vermont*, p. 364. Regarding Warner's commission, the New York authorities were incensed, for they were fully sensible of the uses to which such a grant of authority, however inadvertent, could be put. "The Convention are sorry to observe that by conferring a Com-

mission on Col. Warner, with authority to name the officers of a regiment to be raised independent of the legislature of this State," the president of the New York Committee of Safety wrote Hancock, ". . . Congress hath given but too much weight to the insinuations of those who pretend that your hon'ble body are determined to support these insurgents." Abraham Tenbroeck to John Hancock, Jan. 20, 1777, Force Coll., ser. 7, box 51, New Hampshire Grants.

74. The Vermont Declaration of Independence is in Wilbur, *Ira Allen* 1:92. The petition to Congress of January 15, 1777, is in Force Coll., ser. 7E, box 51. Jonas Fay, Thomas Chittenden, Heman Allen, and Reuben Jones to the Continental Congress, Jan. 13, 1777, Force Coll., ser. 9, box 19; June 30, 1777, in *JCC* 8:508–13. Strong as Congress's final report was, the initial committee report, drawn up by James Wilson, was couched in even harsher language; see James Duane to Robert R. Livingston, July 2, [1777], in Smith, *LDC* 7:280. By thus denying the right of a constituent people to formulate their own political entity, and by confirming the rights of a colonial entity (New York) to the boundaries fixed by the Crown, Congress followed a line of reasoning that, if carried to its logical conclusion, meant that "the colonies had not been in a 'state of nature' in 1776; the revolution right could be exercised only by governments that could claim to be legitimate successors to British colonial governments." Onuf, *Origins of the Federal Republic*, p. 131.

75. Jones, *Vermont*, pp. 379–93; Wilbur, *Ira Allen* 1:397–98. The full and fascinating story of the way in which the state of Vermont entered the union is in Onuf, *Origins of the Federal Republic*, pp. 103–45.

76. Alexander, *Revolutionary Conservative*, p. 91, General Haldimand to Gov. Tryon, 1773; and Lord Dartmouth to Gov. Tryon, Oct. 14, 1773, in O'Callaghan, ed., *Docs. Rel. Hist. of New York* 4:512, 518. Dartmouth settled the matter of using troops by indicating the king's unwillingness to have his troops used in such affairs of property.

77. Alexander, *Revolutionary Conservative*, p. 127; Ira Allen, cited in Wilbur, *Ira Allen* 1:111–12. See also, Onuf, who explains the precarious position in which Vermonters found themselves when Congress refused to countenance their claims; *Origins of the Federal Republic*, pp. 135–36. Thus the Vermont leaders had to carry through their opposition to congressional policy in spite of the popular belief, formed at the outset of the war, that "Congress was next to God Almighty, in power and perfection." Ira Allen, cited in ibid., p. 136.

78. *JCC* 5:681–82; Jensen, *Founding of a Nation*, p. 135; Onuf, *Origins of the Federal Republic*, p. 7. The relatively uncontroversial clause in the draft Articles of Confederation granting Congress the power to settle all intercolonial disputes should not be confused with the far more troublesome clause that assigned Congress the power of "Limiting the Bounds of those Colonies, which by Charter or Proclamation, or under any Pretence, are said to extend to the South Sea, and ascertaining those bounds of any other Colony that appear to be indeterminate." This latter clause, tied up with the whole problem of the disposition of the western lands, was, of course, one of the most difficult problems that the colonial legislators had to solve, and it was a prime cause of the

delay in the final ratification of the Articles of Confederation. See Chapter 6. It should merely be noted in this context that the debates over control of the western lands also had troubled the harmony of the old empire. The later disputes can, in fact, be viewed as a continuation of old, unresolved problems.

79. Onuf traces the attempt by Congress to re-create the old adjudicatory mechanism that had characterized proceedings before the Privy Council; *Origins of the Federal Republic*, pp. 19–20. He concludes that such elaborate mechanisms, while interesting as evidence of contemporary expectations regarding Congress's role, in fact were rarely invoked and played little role in settling interstate conflicts during the critical period. Yet, he notes, although the American states discovered various means of resolving their differences, in which Congress rarely played more than an indirect role, . . . these jurisdictional settlements would not have been achieved without the implicit acceptance of a common interest and of the legitimacy of a higher authority" (p. 20).

Chapter 9

1. The period with which this chapter deals, late 1775 through July 1776, not only saw the formation of new governments in almost all the colonies but also carried the colonists through to independence. Not surprisingly, the burning issue of independence was a major political dividing line. I here use the terms "supporters" and "opponents" of independence when I wish simply to refer to these views. Hence, John Adams was a supporter of independence, and John Dickinson was an opponent. I do this in order to distinguish the positions taken on independence from attitudes toward the new provincial governments. I reserve the terms "radical" and "conservative" to characterize provincial leaders according to their views on the purposes for which they wished to see new government assumed and the substantive policies they wished to see incorporated in the new provincial constitutions. For radicals (who were also, almost without exception, supporters of independence) the assumption of new governments presented a glorious opportunity to make society anew, to secure great changes by implementing political reforms, such as reducing or eliminating the provincial executive, as well as great social changes, such as the expansion of the franchise, or religious toleration. Pennsylvania radicals like James Cannon or Timothy Matlack epitomized this view, as did Thomas Young in Massachusetts and Alexander McDougall in New York. The conservatives, on the other hand (although some were strong supporters of independence), saw the formation of new provincial governments not as an opportunity but as a grim necessity brought on by the war and the vacuum of civil authority left by vacating royal governments. They wished to see a transition from old to new accomplished without domestic upheaval, and they wished to see, as a result, new governments that differed as little as possible from the old. Only such governments, they believed, could hope to command sufficient respect and obedience to reimpose a sense of due subor-

dination upon societies torn apart by war. John Rutledge of South Carolina and John Jay of New York epitomized this viewpoint. Moderates, like Edmund Pendleton of Virginia, simply tried to steer between these two positions. See note 62.

2. "To the Printer," *New-York Journal*, May 9, 1776.

3. Autobiography, June 2, 1776, in Butterfield, ed., *Adams Papers* 3:351–52.

4. For a discussion of the necessity of political authority under conditions of unanimity and of division, see Yves Simon, *A General Theory of Authority*, (Notre Dame, Ind., 1962), pp. 31–56.

5. The provincial governments of Connecticut and Rhode Island, whose colonial charters conferred virtually autonomous powers of self-government, never ceased to function. Because no new provincial governments were formed in those provinces, they are not part of the story told in this chapter.

6. "Inconceivable" is perhaps too strong a word, because some delegates clearly did so conceive. Thus, Richard Henry Lee suggested on May 18, 1776, regarding the Virginia resolution calling for both a declaration of independence and the assumption of independent provincial governments, that "perhaps the proviso which reserves to this Colony [Virginia] the power of forming its own Government may be questionable as to its fitness. Would not a Uniform plan of Government prepared for America by the Congress and approved by the Colonies be a surer foundation of Unceasing Harmony to the Whole?" Lee to John Adams, May 18, 1776, in Taylor, ed., *Papers of Adams* 4:194. Silas Deane also contemplated that Congress should have the power, at least in the former royal colonies, to appoint provincial governors and lieutenant governors. See Silas Deane's Proposals to Congress [Nov. 1775], in Smith, ed., *LDC* 2:418–19. See also John Adams to James Warren, October 1775, in which he parodied sentiment for the appointment of "a Continental King, and a Continental House of Lords, and a Continental House of Commons," which system would "once effected" allow "His American Majesty [to] appoint a Governor for every Province," or perhaps "condescend to permit the provincial Legislatures, or Assemblies [to] nominate two three or four persons out of whom he should select a Governor, . . . would not this do, nicely?" He assured Warren that "this is no Chimaera of my own. It is whispered about in Coffee Houses, &c. and there are [those] who wish it." In Taylor, ed., *Papers of Adams* 3:266–67.

7. See, for example, "The Dialogue . . . between the Britons and Americans," *Massachusetts Spy*, Oct. 7, 1773.

8. The act, one of the Intolerable Acts, changed the composition of the Council and the courts of the province, and with colonial resistance to these changes, the old provincial government came to an end. See Chapter 3.

9. John Pitts to Samuel Adams, Oct. 16, 1774, in S. Adams Papers, vol. 6. See also Thomas Young to Samuel Adams, Sept. 4, 1774, S. Adams Papers, vol. 6; and Col. Gurdon Saltonstall to Silas Deane, Sept. 5, 1774 in "Deane Correspondence," Conn. Hist. Soc., *Collections* 2:150–51; Benjamin Kent to R. T. Paine, Sept. 15, 1774, Robert T. Paine Papers, Mass. Hist. Soc.

The best account of Massachusetts politics during this period is Stephen E.

Patterson, *Political Parties in Revolutionary Massachusetts* (Madison, Wis., 1973). Much of the following narrative concerning the assumption of a new provincial government in Massachusetts depends upon Patterson's analysis that conservatives and moderates in eastern Massachusetts used the authority of the Continental Congress to counter demands of western radicals for a completely popular government (p. 117). While Patterson's equation of politics and geography breaks down in certain specific instances (for example, with the Warren brothers), his account gives a lucid explanation of the complicated pattern of politics in the Bay State. On the 1774 movement to resume government under the old charter, see pp. 117–21. See also the older account by Harry A. Cushing, *History of the Transition from Provincial to Commonwealth Government in Massachusetts*, Studies in History, Economics and Public Law, vol. 7, no. 1 (New York, 1896), pp. 79–80.

10. "At a Meeting of the Committees of Correspondence from . . . the County of Worcester," Aug. 30–31, 1774, *Draper's Massachusetts Gazette*, Sept. 15, 1774.

11. Dr. Thomas Young to Samuel Adams, Sept. 4, 1774, S. Adams Papers, vol. 6; Joseph Warren to S. Adams, cited in Jensen, *Founding of a Nation*, p. 622.

12. *JCC* 1:62. See Chapter 3 for the action of the First Continental Congress on the committee's request to resume the old charter.

13. John Adams to James Burgh[?], Dec. 28, 1774, in Smith, ed., *LDC* 1:276. On moderate satisfaction, see, for example, John Andrews to William Barrell, Oct. 19, 1774, in Sargent, ed., *Andrews Letters*, p. 72. The determination of provincial moderates to go slowly was strengthened by warnings from moderates in other provinces regarding the dismay with which the unilateral assumption of government by Massachusetts would be viewed in those provinces. See John Dickinson to Thomas Cushing, Jan. 26, 1775: "I have lately been inform'd that a considerable part of your Province, are determined to resume the old Charter, and chuse a Governor &c. This Intelligence has given Me inexpressible Pain of Mind, . . . Why should a prudent People take a Step so full of the most dangerous Disunion? . . . I implore You, my dear Sir, in the Name of Almighty God to discourage by all the Means in Your Power, this, not only useless, but pernicious Scheme." Dickinson was assured by Cushing on February 13, 1775 that the idea had been turned down at the last Provincial Congress and that "you may depend upon it, no such thing will be moved at the present [Provincial] Congress." Smith, ed., *LDC* 1:301–2, 310–11. See also Thomas Cushing to Samuel Purviance, Sr., Feb. 13, 1775, ibid., p. 312.

14. Apr. 1, 1775, in Lincoln, ed., *Jour. Prov. Cong. of Mass.*, p. 116.

15. Ephraim Doolittle to John Hancock, Mar. 21, 1775, in Force, ed., *American Archives*, 4th ser., 2:177–78; James Warren to John Adams, May 7, 1775, in Ford, ed., *Warren-Adams Letters* 1:47; Joseph Warren to Samuel Adams, May 26, 1775, in S. Adams Papers, vol. 7.

16. May 4, 5, 1775, in Lincoln, ed., *Jour. Prov. Cong. of Mass.*, pp. 536, 197; James Warren to John Adams, May 7, 1775, in Ford, ed., *Warren-Adams Letters* 1:48. On May 4 and 5, the Provincial Congress rescinded its resolutions advising compliance with Gage's election writs; Lincoln, ed., *Jour. Prov. Cong. Mass.*, pp. 192–93.

17. David Cobb to Robert Treat Paine, May 12, 1775, R. T. Paine Papers Mass. Hist. Soc.; May 8, 9, 1775, in Lincoln, ed., *Jour. Prov. Cong. Mass.*, pp. 207–8.

18. May 12, 16, 1775, ibid., pp. 219, 230.

19. James Warren to Mercy Warren, May 18, 1775, in Ford, ed., *Warren-Adams Letters* 1:50; Elbridge Gerry to Massachusetts Delegates, June 4, 1775, in Austin, *Life of Gerry* 1:78–79; James Warren to John Adams, June 11, 1775, in Ford, ed., *Warren-Adams Letters* 1:56.

20. June 11, 1775, in Lincoln, ed., *Jour. Prov. Cong. Mass.*, p. 319. This letter was written by Joseph Hawley.

21. JCC 2:76–78.

22. Autobiography, June 2, 1775, in Butterfield, ed., *Adams Papers* 3:351–52. Adams's recollections of his prescience are, of course, open to question, and there is no contemporary confirmation that such a speech was made.

23. June 3, 7, 8, 9, 1775, in JCC 2:79, 81, 83–84. The committee consisted of John Rutledge, Thomas Johnson, John Jay, James Wilson, and Richard Henry Lee.

So important did the continental delegates consider it to be that the form of the charter of 1691 not be deviated from that they turned back a motion to allow the sitting Provincial Congress (rather than a newly elected House of Representatives) to choose the Provincial Council. The delegates agreed "that it was best to adhere as near to the Charter as possible & not to vary from it but in the Case of Absolute Necessity." Thomas Cushing to Joseph Hawley, June 10, 1775, in Smith, ed., *LDC* 1:470.

24. Quoted in Jensen, *Founding of a Nation*, p. 622. Joseph Warren to S. Adams, May 14, 1775, S. Adams Papers, vol. 7.

25. Joseph Warren to S. Adams, June 21, 1775, S. Adams Papers, vol. 7; Massachusetts Provincial Congress to Continental Congress, June 20, 1775, in Lincoln, ed., *Jour. Prov. Cong. Mass.*, p. 365. See also James Warren to John Adams, June 20, 1775: "I can't . . . say that I admire the form of Government prescribed. But we are all Submission." Ford, ed., *Warren-Adams Letters* 1:64.

26. Lincoln, ed., *Jour. Prov. Cong. Mass.*, pp. 358–60. Benjamin Church to S. Adams, Aug. 2, 1775, S. Adams Papers, vol. 7. See the official notices of the General Court through July and August 1775 in the *Boston Gazette* and the *Massachusetts Spy*. All the acts of the first session of the new Assembly are listed in *Boston Gazette*, Sept. 4, 1775. For the general understanding of the central role played by the Continental Congress in the assumption of the new provincial government, see "Democritus," *Massachusetts Spy*, July 5, 1775; and "Lycurgus," ibid., July 19, 1775.

27. Although the charter of 1691 was resumed, as the Continental Congress had directed, the process caused several political problems and much discontent. The most serious dispute arose in the fall of 1775 over the appointment of provincial militia officers. This power was vested in the governor by the charter of 1691, and the Council, which by the resolve of the Continental Congress was to exercise the powers of the "absent" governor, asserted that it, not the House, had the power of appointment. The dispute caused much bitterness and deepened discontent with the government prescribed by the Conti-

nental Congress. "I hate the name of Our Charter," wrote a frustrated James Warren to John Adams on November 14, "which fascinates and Shackles us." Taylor, ed. *Papers of Adams* 3:303. A full discussion of the militia dispute is in Elbridge Gerry to [John Adams], Nov. 11, 1775, ibid., pp. 287–91. See also James Warren to Samuel Adams, Nov. 22, 1775, S. Adams Papers, vol. 7.

28. The ability of the Congress to secure such obedience to its decisions allows us to say that as an institution it possessed "political authority," as defined, for example, by David Easton: "A policy is authoritative when the people to whom it is intended to apply or who are affected by it consider that they must or ought to obey it." *The Political System* (New York, 1953), p. 132.

29. The best account of the disintegration of royal authority in New Hampshire is Jere R. Daniell, *Experiment in Republicanism: New Hampshire Politics and the American Revolution, 1741–1794* (Cambridge, Mass., 1970), pp. 74–123, from which this account is largely drawn. See also an older but still useful narrative; Richard F. Upton, *Revolutionary New Hampshire* (Hanover, N.H., 1936), pp. 32–45, 63–68.

30. New Hampshire Provincial Congress to Continental Congress, May 23, 1775, in Force, ed., *American Archives*, 4th ser., 2:696; New Hampshire Provincial Congress to J. Sullivan and J. Langdon, May 23, 1775, in Otis G. Hammond, ed., "Letters and Papers of Major General John Sullivan, Continental Army," New Hampshire Historical Society, *Collections* 13 (1930): 63. New Hampshire's large defense requirements stemmed from the province's early attacks on British military authority. In late December 1774, a mob had seized the royal military supplies in Castle William and Mary in Portsmouth Harbor. Since that date the royal governor had been bombarding London with requests for reinforcements.

31. New Hampshire Committee of Safety to New Hampshire Delegates, July 8, 1775, in Nathaniel Bouton, ed., *Documents and Records Relating to the Province of New Hampshire* (Nashua, N.H., 1873–74), 7:560. Financial problems such as those experienced in New Hampshire represent an "important functional failure" on the part of governing authorities, notes Harry Eckstein, since "finance impinges on the ability of governments to perform all their functions." "On the Etiology of Internal Wars," *History and Theory* 4 (1965): 148.

32. New Hampshire Provincial Congress [Matthew Thornton] to J. Bartlett and J. Langdon, Sept. 1, 1775, *Letters by Josiah Bartlett, William Whipple and Others, Written Before and During the Revolution* (Philadelphia, 1889), p. 20. An excerpt from these instructions, undated, is printed in *JCC* 3:298 under the date of October 18, 1775. The parallel between New Hampshire and Massachusetts is also drawn by Douglass, *Rebels and Democrats*, p. 330.

33. Autobiography, June 2, 1775, in Butterfield, ed., *Adams Papers* 3:352; Oct. 18, 1775, in *JCC* 3:298. Thus, on October 2 the New Hampshire delegates urged the president of the New Hampshire Provincial Congress to use the occasion of their forthcoming meeting with the congressional committee visiting the army in Cambridge, "to mention the Convu[lse]d state of our Colony and the absolute Necessity of Govermt. and also to forward by them a Petition from our Convention, to take government." They had, they reported "Con-

sulted many of the members on the Matter" and were ready to "Motion for leave to take up the same government as Massachusetts Bay" as soon as Josiah Bartlett recovered from his smallpox inoculation. Oct. 2, 1775, Smith, ed., *LDC* 2:98–99.

34. New Hampshire Delegates to Matthew Thornton, in Smith, ed., *LDC* 3:293; Autobiography, Oct. 18, 1775, in Butterfield, ed., *Adams Papers* 3:355. The New Hampshire Committee consisted of John Rutledge, Richard Henry Lee, Samuel Ward, Roger Sherman, and Adams himself; Oct. 26, 1775, in *JCC* 3:307.

35. Nov. 2, 3, 1775, in *JCC* 3:317, 319. On the effect of the king's rejection of the petition and his Proclamation of Rebellion, see Chapter 2.

36. New Hampshire Delegates to Matthew Thornton, Nov. 3, 1775, in Smith, ed., *LDC* 2:293. The resolution was opposed by Dickinson and his allies, who believed it would make efforts to achieve a reconciliation much more difficult. It was in response to the New Hampshire resolution, and that regarding South Carolina passed on November 4, that he began this campaign to bind the Pennsylvania delegation with instructions that mandated that they "dissent from and utterly reject any propositions, should such be made, that may cause or lead to a Separation from our Mother Country, or a Change of the Form of this Government, or the Establishment of a Commonwealth." John Dickinson, Proposed Instructions [Nov. 9? 1775], in Smith, ed., *LDC* 2:320. See also Ryerson, *Revolution Is Now Begun*, pp. 140–41.

37. Proceedings of the New Hampshire Provincial Congress, Nov. 14, 16, 1775, in Force, ed., *American Archives*, 4th ser., 4:17; Upton, *Revolutionary New Hampshire*, p. 67; Daniell, *Experiment in Republicanism*, p. 109.

38. J. Sullivan to M. Weare, Dec. 11, 1775, in Thomas C. Amory, *The Military Services and Public Life of Major-General John Sullivan* (1868; reprint, Port Washington, N.Y., 1968), p. 17.

39. The New Hampshire delegates had recommended precisely this course when they had transmitted the November 3 resolution. "We would here beg leave to Suggest whether a government Somewhat Similar to the Massachusetts would not be best . . . and not to Proceed so far as [electing a] governor at Present." To Matthew Thornton, Nov. 3, 1775, in Smith, ed., *LDC* 2:293.

40. Jan. 5, 1776, in Bouton, ed., *Prov. Records of New Hampshire*, 7:642, 8:2; Daniell, *Experiment in Republicanism*, pp. 107–9. Even the assumption of this form of government engendered considerable resistance, and in fact provoked a subsequent petition to Congress from dissidents in the new House of Representatives. See Samuel Adams to John Adams, Jan. 15, 1776; Richard Smith Diary, March 1, 1776; Josiah Bartlett to Meshech Weare, Mar. 2, 1776; and Josiah Bartlett to John Langdon, Mar. 5, 1776; in Smith, ed., *LDC* 3:93, 318, 319–20 and n. 2, 333–34.

41. The most detailed authority on South Carolina during this period is still Edward McCrady, *The History of South Carolina in the Revolution, 1775–1780* (New York, 1901), especially pp. 1–32, 69–85. See also an excellent study that concentrates on the period after independence, Jerome Nadelhaft, *The Disorders of War: The Revolution in South Carolina* (Orono, Me., 1981), as well as Ed-

ward McCrady, *The History of South Carolina under the Royal Government, 1719–1776* (New York, 1899), 2:758–98; David D. Wallace, *The Life of Henry Laurens* (New York and London, 1915), pp. 204–12; Robert M. Weir, *"A Most Important Epocha": The Coming of the Revolution in South Carolina*, Tricentennial Booklet no. 5 (Columbia, S.C., 1970), p. 68; Robert H. Weir, *Colonial South Carolina* (Millwood, N.Y., 1983), pp. 321–40. McCrady and all subsequent historians of South Carolina during this period depend upon Drayton, *Memoirs of the Revolution,* for much of their information on the factional disputes within the South Carolina revolutionary bodies. On the chronic discontent in and underrepresentation of the backcountry, see Nadelhaft, *Disorders of War,* pp. 12–21.

42. Nadelhaft, *Disorders of War,* pp. 8–9, 21–23.

43. McCrady, *South Carolina in the Revolution,* pp. 53–68.

44. Ibid.; Nadelhaft, *Disorders of War,* pp. 8–9.

45. Weir, *Colonial South Carolina,* pp. 323–24. On Brown, see Gary D. Olson, "Loyalists and the American Revolution: Thomas Brown and the South Carolina Backcountry, 1775–1776," *South Carolina Historical Magazine* 68 (1967): 201–19; 69 (1968): 44–56.

46. Charles Drayton to William Henry Drayton, Sept. 16, 1775, in Clark, ed., *NDAR* 2:126. Their suspicions of Lord Campbell were justified. As far back as July 19, 1775, in the aftermath of Bunker Hill but during the period during which Campbell had reached an ostensible agreement with the patriot leadership, he reported to Lord Dartmouth that "The Committee and Council of Safety sit Night & Day; I am told they are debating about seizing the King's Officers and those few who have not yet signed the Association, and boldly changing the Government at once." Lord William Campbell to Lord Dartmouth, July 19, 1775, Haldimand Papers Additional MSS 21697, fol. 126.

47. Log of H.M.S. *Tamar,* Sept. 14, 15, 1775, ibid., pp. 102, 114.

48. Henry Laurens to John Laurens, Sept. 18, 1775, ibid., 144.

49. Diary of Captain Barnard Elliott, Sept. 14, 1775, ibid., p. 102.

50. Henry Laurens to William Henry Drayton, Sept. 16, 1775; Log of H.M.S. *Tamar,* Sept. 15, 1775; and Extract of a Letter from Charleston, Sept. 15, 1775, ibid., pp, 126, 114–15.

51. Extract of a Letter from Charleston, Sept. 15, 1775; and Arthur Middleton to William H. Drayton, Sept. 15, 1775, ibid., pp. 115, 117.

52. Henry Laurens to South Carolina Delegates in the Continental Congress, Sept. 18, 1775, ibid., pp. 140–44.

53. Nov. 23, 1775, in *JCC* 3:318, 319. The committee consisted of B. Harrison (Va.), A. Bulloch (Ga.), W. Hooper (N.C.), S. Chase (Md.), and S. Adams (Mass.). The names of John Rutledge and Thomas Lynch were interlineated. John Adams later recalled that John Rutledge had moved for the appointment of the committee. Autobiography, in Butterfield, ed., *Adams Papers* 3:357.

54. Nov. 4, 1775, in *JCC* 3:325–27.

55. See H. Laurens to South Carolina Delegates in the Continental Congress, Sept. 18, 1775, in Clark, ed., *NDAR* 2:140–44. Rutledge was one of the leading conservatives at the First Congress. See Chapter 3. On his conservatism within the context of South Carolina politics, see Richard H. Barry, *Mr. Rutledge of South Carolina* (New York, 1942), pp. 187–88.

56. The only other delegate who was also a member of both committees was Richard Henry Lee; *JCC* 2:81, 3:307.

57. On the divisions on the committee, see Nadelhaft, *Disorders of War*, pp. 28–29.

58. Drayton, *Memoirs of the Revolution* 2:172; McCrady, *South Carolina in the Revolution*, pp. 108–11. Adams's ideas are in his Autobiography; Butterfield, ed., *Adams Papers* 3:356–58.

59. McCrady, *South Carolina in the Revolution*, pp. 108–11, citing Drayton. These remarks call into question John Adams's recollection in his autobiography that Rutledge had heard his "new, strange and terrible doctrines" regarding the need to call conventions of the people in order to institute governments with "apparent pleasure," and that by the time Rutledge became a member of the New Hampshire Committee the following October he was "compleatly with Us, in our desire of revolutionizing all the Governments," and it was for this reason that as soon as the New Hampshire resolution was passed he "brought forward immediately, some representations from his own State" Autobiography, in Butterfield, ed., *Adams Papers* 3:357. But the *Journals* show clearly that Rutledge made his motion on November 2, the day before the adoption of the New Hampshire resolution; *JCC* 2:318, 319. In any event, it is certainly clear that the process by which the new government of South Carolina was instituted bore little resemblance to the plans put forward by Adams.

On the other hand, Rutledge's biographer, Barry, intimates that Rutledge secured the resolution solely to strengthen the position of his faction against the Gadsden-Drayton group. While this may be true, it is not necessarily inconsistent with the hypothesis presented here, that Rutledge's primary motivation was to secure the means to restore orderly government to the province, because, to a sincere conservative like Rutledge, the victory of his faction was tantamount to the achievement of peace, good order, and social harmony in the province. *Mr. Rutledge*, pp. 187–93.

60. Nadelhaft, *Disorder of War*, pp. 29–34. As he notes, "satisfied with old ways, the low country rulers had innovated little" (p. 34).

61. *South Carolina and American General Gazette*, Mar. 27–Apr. 3, 1776. For the reaction of the Charleston mechanics to the conservative 1776 constitution, see Walsh, *Charleston's Sons of Liberty*, p. 81. As the editors of the South Carolina Assembly journals emphasized, "the first constitution was . . . but a temporary substitution of government, undertaken with the slightest of changes in leadership in order to legitimize an accepted authority." William E. Hemphill, Wylma A. Water, and R. Nicholas Oldsberg, eds., *Journals of the General Assembly and House of Representatives, 1776–1780* (Columbia, S.C., 1970), pp. xi–xii. See also Nadelhaft, *Disorders of War*, p. 34.

62. Pendleton gave a synopsis of his political creed in a long letter he wrote to Joseph Chew on June 15, 1775:

The Crisis of our Fate in the present and unhappy Contest seems approaching nearer than may be imagined by us, and perhaps this Summer may determine whether we shall be slaves, or a Rotten, wicked Administration be sacrificed to Our Freedom, in such times there will be as great Variety of Sentiments as Constitutions, among those who have the same end in view. The Sanguine are for rash Measures without consideration, the Flegmatic to avoid that extreme are afraid to move at all, while a third Class take the middle way and endeavor all together to a Steddy, tho' Active Point of defense; but till this is done, it is natural to suppose the extremes will be blaming each other, and perhaps in terms not the most decent, and each at times will include the third class in that which is opposite to themselves, this I have frequently experienced; and must blame, since mutual Charity should lead Us, not to censure, but to endeavor to convince the Judgment of each other.

Smith, ed., *LDC* 1:488. He spoke for many of his colleagues among Virginia's leaders.

63. David J. Mays, *Edmund Pendleton, 1721–1803: A Biography* (Cambridge, Mass., 1952), 2:1–18; Richard Beeman, *Patrick Henry: A Biography* (New York, 1974), pp. 68–69; Hamilton J. Eckenrode, *The Revolution in Virginia* (Boston and New York, 1916), pp. 47–48, 50–53. For the domination of local committees by established moderate leaders, see Bowman, "Virginia County Committees," pp. 322–27.

64. On March 25, 1775, the Virginia Convention went so far as to pass a resolution approving the Indian expedition and thanking His Lordship for undertaking it; Force, ed., *American Archives*, 4th ser., 2:170. Richard Henry Lee was quite disturbed by what he regarded as inappropriate behavior on the part of Virginia's major institution of resistance. See R. H. Lee to John Dickinson, Apr. 7, 1775, in Smith, ed., *LDC* 1:328. When counseling his brother, Francis Lightfoot, on the course he wished to see pursued at the upcoming session of the Virginia Assembly, he wrote, "For heavens sake avoid compliments (except to the Soldiery) on the Indian expedition last summer. Nothing has given more concern and disgust to these northern Colonies than our unhappy vote of that sort in last Convention." He had been told, he reported, by "one of the first Men on the Continent for wisdom[,] sound judgment, good information, and integrity," that he was "much grieved and concerned for the honor and good sense of Virginia, when I saw that ill founded ill judged Compliment." May 21, 1775, ibid., p. 366.

65. Mays, *Pendleton* 2:30–31, Silas Deane to Mrs. Deane, May 24, 1775; and Samuel Ward Diary, May 24, 1775, in Smith, ed., *LDC* 1:402, 406.

66. Pendleton's pet name for the royal governor was "Wronghead." See Pendleton to William Woodford, July 4, 1775, ibid., p. 581. Not only was Dunmore's political judgment deplored but his private character was also questioned. See, for example, "To the Inhabitants of Virginia," Oct. 19, 1775, in Force, ed., *American Archives*, 4th ser., 3:1103–4.

67. Mays, *Pendleton* 2:31; Eckenrode, *Revolution in Virginia*, pp. 54–55. For a contemporary characterization of the governor's character and appearance, see Edmund Randolph, *History of Virginia*, edited by Arthur H. Shaffer (Charlottesville, Va., 1973), pp. 196–97. Pendleton's explanation of Dunmore's

flight is in E. Pendleton to Joseph Chew, June 15, 1775, in Smith, ed., *LDC* 1:490.

68. Dunmore's shipboard proclamation is cited in Francis Berkeley, *Dunmore's Proclamation of Emancipation* (Charlottesville, Va., 1941), unpaginated; Mays, *Pendleton* 2:50–52. Richard Henry Lee wrote of Dunmore's activities that "it seems indeed as if Lord Dunmore was taking true pains to incur the censure of the whole reasonable world." Lee to Robert Carter, July 1, 1775, in Smith, ed., *LDC* 1:569.

69. Mays, *Pendleton* 2:32–36; Benson, "Wealth and Power in Virginia," p. 295; George Mason to George Washington, Oct. 14, 1775, in Robert A. Rutland, ed., *The Papers of George Mason, 1725–1792* (Chapel Hill, N.C., 1970), 1:255.

70. Eckenrode, *Revolution in Virginia*, pp. 59–85. See the Oath of the Inhabitants of Princess Anne County, in Force, ed., *American Archives*, 4th ser., 3:1671.

71. Edmund Pendleton to Virginia Delegates, Oct. 28, 1775, in David J. Mays, ed., *Letters and Papers of Edmund Pendleton* (Charlottesville, Va., 1952), 1:125; Benson, "Wealth and Power in Virginia," pp. 284–94, 303. Benson indicates that under the new leadership, local committees began to charge their former leaders with toryism. Especially in counties directly threatened by Dunmore's forces, local action against suspected Tories partook again of the violence of 1774. Thus, for example, conservatives worried about a series of riots caused by the widespread shortage of salt (and thus potentially of winter food). See, for example, Robert Carter Nicholas to Thomas Jefferson, Nov. 10, 1775, in Boyd, ed., *Jefferson Papers* 1:255; E. Pendleton to Virginia delegates, Nov. 11, 1775, in Mays, ed., *Letters of Pendleton* 2:127; Prince William County Committee to Virginia Delegates, Nov. 14, 1775, Lee Family Papers, reel 2.

72. Eckenrode, *Revolution in Virginia*, pp. 69–71; Mays, *Pendleton* 2:53; Berkeley, *Dunmore's Proclamation*, n.p.

73. The text of the proclamation, dated Nov. 7, 1775, on board H.M.S. *William*, is in Berkeley, *Dunmore's Proclamation*, n.p., and in Force, ed., *American Archives*, 4th ser., 3:1385.

74. Nov. 11, 1775, Albion and Dodson, eds., *Fithian Journal*, p. 135; Benson, "Wealth and Power in Virginia," pp. 283, 286. Richard H. Lee to Catherine Macaulay, Nov. 29, 1775, in Smith, ed., *LDC* 2:406. On the impact of the proclamation, see also Benjamin Quarles, "Lord Dunmore as Liberator," *WMQ*, 3d ser., 15 (1958): 494–507.

75. Committee of Northampton County to Continental Congress, Nov. 2, 1775, in Force, ed., *American Archives*, 4th ser., 3:1669–71.

76. Dec. 2, 1775, in *JCC* 3:395–96.

77. The committee members were Samuel Adams, Thomas Lynch, Samuel Ward, James Wilson, and Thomas Johnson. On December 2, to emphasize the speed with which the Virginia Committee was expected to act, William Paca was appointed to sit in for the absent Johnson; *JCC* 3:344, 395.

78. Samuel Ward to Henry Ward, Dec. 3, 1775, in Smith, ed., *LDC* 2:432; E. Pendleton to R. H. Lee, Nov. 27, 1775, in Mays, ed., *Letters of Pendleton*

1:132–33; John Page to Thomas Jefferson, [Nov.] 24, 1775, in Boyd, ed., *Jefferson Papers* 1:265; John Page to Richard Henry Lee, Dec. 9, 1775, Lee Family Papers, reel 2.

79. Francis Lightfoot Lee to Robert W. Carter, [Dec. 2, 1775], in Smith, ed., *LDC* 2:425–26. Lee reiterated this conviction on December 12, after Congress had granted authorization to assume government. See Francis Lightfoot Lee to Landon Carter, Dec. 12, 1775, ibid., p. 480: "Is it not necessary that the Convention should establish some kind of Government as Ld. D. by his proclamation has utterly demolished the whole civil Government."

80. Dec. 4, 1775, *JCC* 3:403. The dire picture reported by the Virginia delegates is recounted in Samual Ward to Henry Ward, Dec. 3, 1775, ibid. 2:432–33. The close connection between Dunmore's declaration of martial law and the resolution authorizing government is also clear from Francis Lightfoot Lee to Landon Carter, Dec. 12, 1775; and Samuel Adams to James Warren, Dec. [5?], 1775, in Smith, ed., *LDC* 2:480, 439.

81. Mays, *Pendleton* 2:71–74; Eckenrode, *Revolution in Virginia*, pp. 80–85; Ordinances of the Virginia Convention, Dec. 20, 1775–Jan. 20, 1776, in Force, ed., *American Archives*, 4th ser., 4:141–42; Benson, "Wealth and Power in Virginia," pp. 311–16.

82. F. L. Lee to Landon Carter, Apr. 9, 1775, in Smith, ed., *LDC* 3:501; John A. Washington to R. H. Lee, Apr. 27, 1776, quoted in Benson, "Wealth and Power in Virginia," p. 352; R. H. Lee to Robert Carter Nicholas, Apr. 30, 1776, in Ballagh, ed., *Letters of Lee* 1:184. Benson systematically presents the view that the assumption of government in Virginia came as a direct result of the planters' fear that they were losing their traditional control of Virginia affairs. See "Wealth and Power in Virginia," pp. 335–53.

83. John Page to Thomas Jefferson, Apr. 26, 1776, in Boyd, ed., *Jefferson Papers* 1:288; E. Pendleton, "Address to the Virginia Convention of 1776," May 6, 1776, in May, ed., *Letters of Pendleton* 1:175.

84. The Virginia Constitution of 1776 has been hailed for so long as the foundation of American civil liberties that its description as a conservative document may need further explanation. Although the Declaration of Rights (and especially the provisions for religious freedom) were significant libertarian steps (if not democratic ones), the government established by the Constitution closely resembled the relatively conservative governments organized in the colonies discussed above. As Beeman notes, "There is little evidence in any of the actions of the members of the Virginia Convention, and considerable evidence to the contrary, that they were concerned about the advancement of democratic doctrine." There was certainly no great extension of the franchise, and there was a great continuity of leadership. Finally, the document was neither drawn up by a "constituent convention" nor ratified by the people—flaws that Jefferson, for one, considered fatal. See Beeman, *Patrick Henry*, p. 105, and, in general, pp. 99–109.

85. North Carolina was an exception. Perhaps conceiving itself to be included in the grant to South Carolina the previous November, the North Car-

olina Provincial Congress proceeded in early April 1776 to instruct its delegates to vote for independence, and it began the process of assuming a new
government for the province. As John Penn explained the move to John Adams, "We are endeavoring to form a Constitution as it is thought necessary to
exert all the powers of Government." April 17, 1776, in Taylor, ed., *Papers of
Adams* 4:128. On April 14 a committee was appointed to frame a temporary
constitution. By April 18 dissension within the committee was rampant, and
the leading conservative, Samuel Johnston, withdrew in disgust. After much
debate, on April 25 the committee was able to report a "temporary Civil Constitution" to the Provincial Congress. The debates in the full Provincial Congress were even more acrimonious than those in the committee had been, and
on April 30 the project was postponed until the next Provincial Congress
should meet the following summer. As Johnston wrote to James Iredell on
April 20, "We have not yet been able to agree on a Constitution. We . . . can
conclude nothing." On May 2 he reported to Iredell that "All ideas of forming
a permanent Constitution are, at this time, laid aside." McRee, *Iredell* 4:276,
279. On this process, see the Proceedings of the Provincial Congress of North
Carolina, in Saunders, *Colonial Records of North Carolina* 10:512, 545; Frank
Nash, *The North Carolina Constitution of 1776 and Its Makers*, James Sprunt Historical Publications, 11 (1912), pp. 11–13; R.D.W. Conner, *History of North Carolina: The Colonial and Revolutionary Periods* (Chicago and New York, 1919),
1:401–2; Thomas Jones to James Iredell, April 28, 1776, in McRee, *Iredell* 1:277–
78; Douglass, *Rebels and Democrats*, pp. 119–35. While the primary cause of the
failure is found in internal political struggles, it is nevertheless true that the
one attempt to form a temporary constitution without a direct authorization
from Congress was not successful.

86. May 10, 1776, in *JCC* 4:342.

87. May 15, 1776, in *JCC* 4:357–58.

88. Autobiography, in Butterfield, ed., *Adams Papers* 3:383. His recollections
are supported by a memorandum he drew up for himself in February 1776 of
"Measures to be Pursued in Congress." They included: "Government to be
assumed in every Colony" [February 9–23? 1776], in Smith, ed., *LDC* 3:218.

89. Autobiography, in Butterfield, ed., *Adams Papers* 3:335.

90. Adams later recalled more precisely that the preamble, not the resolution, had been the primary source of controversy; ibid., p. 383. See *JCC* 4:329,
330, 338, 340, 342.

91. John Adams to James Warren, May 12, 1776; William Floyd to John
McKesson, [May 9, 1776]; John Jay to Alexander McDougall, Apr. 11, 1776;
Caesar Rodney to John Haslet, May 14, 1776; and John Adams to John Win-
throp, May 12, [1776], in Smith, ed., *LDC* 3:661, 644, 506, 673, 663; Thomas
Jefferson to Thomas Nelson, May 16, 1776, in Boyd, ed., *Jefferson Papers* 1:292.

92. Compare, for example, Nov. 3, 1775, in *JCC* 3:319 (N.H.), with May 10,
1776, in *JCC* 4:342.

93. Carter Braxton to Landon Carter, May 17, 1776, in Smith, ed., *LDC* 4:19.
Dickinson is cited in Thomas Rodney to Caesar Rodney, May 19, 1776, in Ry-

den, ed., *Rodney Letters*, p. 82. According to Rodney (writing from Delaware), as he walked through town with Dickinson, Rodney mentioned the May 10 resolution.

> [Dickinson] answer'd it was made before he Left there; upon which I observed to him many advantages that would follow our assuming Government to which he agreed & observed many others "And that it would not prevent but perhaps promote a more speedy reconciliation, because the longer they let Government exist before they offer Terms the more firm that Government would be, & therefore the more difficult to effect a reconciliation." I should apprehend from the above sentiment that Mr. D—— has some glimmering hopes of reconciliation yet, or that he ment thereby, to flatter those who have such hopes, to acquiesce in the resolution of Congress.

Many conservatives drew a sharp distinction between the assumption of new governments and a declaration of independence. It was a common conservative assertion that the former would foster a reconciliation with Great Britain, because only authoritative governments could conduct serious negotiations with the British. See, for example, Rodney citation above; "Columbus," *New-York Journal*, June 12, 1776; and J. Iredell to Joseph Hewes, June 9, 1776, in McCree, *Iredell* 2:597–98. While this rationale rings somewhat false, or at least illogical, in modern ears, because the assumption of new state governments was such an obvious corollary of the movement to rid the colonies of royal authority, nevertheless, prior to the May 15 preamble no *explicit* connection was drawn between the assumption of new governments and the rejection of royal authority.

94. On the Pennsylvania instructions, see note 36.

95. See note 106.

96. The committee consisted of John Adams, Richard Henry Lee, and Edward Rutledge, May 10, 1776, in *JCC* 4:432. The preamble, written by Adams, is in *JCC* 4:351. James Duane to John Jay, May 11, 1776, in Smith, ed., *LDC* 3:652.

97. James Duane to John Jay, May 16, 1776, in Smith, ed., *LDC* 4:5.

98. Carter Braxton to Landon Carter, May 17, 1776; and John Adams, Notes of Debates [May 13–15], 1776, ibid., 4:19, 3:668–69.

99. Ibid. 3:669–70.

100. Thomas Stone to James Hollyday? May 20, 1776; and Carter Braxton to Landon Carter, May 17, 1776, in Smith, ed., *LDC* 4:47, 19. According to Braxton, the vote on the preamble was six colonies to four. This would have probably meant:

> For the preamble: Massachusetts, New Hampshire, Connecticut, Rhode Island, Virginia, and South Carolina
> Against: North Carolina, New York, New Jersey, and Delaware
> Abstaining: Pennsylvania and Maryland
> Absent: Georgia

This is the interpretation adopted by Hawke, *In the Midst of a Revolution*, p. 124 n. 53. However, according to the diary of James Allen, a Philadelphia lawyer who was not present at the vote, the final tally was seven to four. The editors of *LDC* hypothesize that if this is correct, then North Carolina probably joined the majority, while Pennsylvania voted against. Smith, ed., *LDC* 4:20 n. 3. However, Stone clearly reported that *two* colonies lacked a sufficient representation to vote, although the representatives were expected shortly. This seems to militate in favor of Braxton's count.

101. Ryerson has documented how closely the Philadelphia radicals worked with the Adams cousins in devising a strategy that would (1) bring down the Pennsylvania Assembly (the goal of provincial radicals) and (2) bring about a Pennsylvania vote for independence (the aim of the Adamses). Ryerson also notes that the Philadelphians considered a number of alternative strategies for bringing about the Assembly's downfall. The May 15 resolution was one method, but not the only one, that they could have—and would have—used to bring about their predetermined ends. See Ryerson, *The Revolution Is Now Begun*, pp. 207–28. On the close consultation between the congressional and provincial radicals, see also R. H. Lee to Thomas L. Lee, May 28, 1776, in Smith, ed., *LDC* 4:91, especially note 4 and sources cited therein.

102. "The ADDRESS and REMONSTRANCE of the INHABITANTS of the City and County of *Philadelphia*," in Votes of Assembly, May 29, 1776, in *Pennsylvania Archives*, 8th ser., 8:7526; Caesar Rodney to Thomas Rodney, May 29, 1776, in Ryden, ed., *Rodney Letters*, p. 85.

103. May 16, 20, 1776, Christopher Marshall Diary B, Hist. Soc. of Pa.; "The PROTEST of divers of the INHABITANTS of this Province . . ." [May 20, 1776] in Votes of Assembly, May 22, 1776, in *Pennsylvania Archives*, 8th ser., 8:7514–15; Ryerson, *Revolution Is Now Begun*, pp. 211–12; Hawke, *In the Midst of a Revolution*, pp. 130–36. See also John Adams to James Warren, May 20, 1776, in Ford, ed., *Warren-Adams Letters* 1:250–51.

104. "Votes of Assembly," May 20, 22, 1776, in *Pennsylvania Archives*, 8th ser., 8:7513–16. Reed describes the Assembly during this period as "perplexed and alarmed, threatened without, and distracted within." *Life of Reed* 1:186. The provincial radicals quickly responded to the conservatives' move by informing their allies in Congress. Benjamin Rush, for example, sent a hurried note to Richard Henry Lee, praying that he not "desert us in this trying exigency." Rush to R. H. Lee [May 22, 1776], in Smith, ed., *LDC* 4:91 n. 4. As Smith notes, Rush had "nothing to fear," because the Assembly was not sufficiently organized to lay such a petition before the Congress.

105. *Pennsylvania Archives*, 8th ser., 8:7542–43; June 12–18, Christopher Marshall Diary B, Hist. Soc. of Pa. An excellent recent account of the downfall of the Assembly is in Ryerson, *Revolution Is Now Begun*, pp. 219–28.

106. See Ryerson, *Revolution Is Now Begun*, pp. 211–12. It is, however, important to emphasize the different goals of the two groups. The provincial radicals sought to overthrow the Assembly in order to bring about a radical revolution within the province, the crowning achievement of which was the Pennsylvania Constitution of 1776. Their congressional allies, on the other

hand, worked solely to remove a substantial roadblock to independence. Compare, for example, the views of a proper state constitution expressed by John Adams in his letter to John Penn (Mar. 19–27? 1776), which became the basis of his *Thoughts on Government*, with the Pennsylvania Constitution of 1776. Smith, ed., *LDC* 3:399–406.

107. Maryland was the only colony that refused to implement the May 15 resolution. John Adams attributed the colony's singularity to eccentricity and fervently wished that Maryland "could exchange places with Halifax." John Adams to James Warren, May 20, 1776, in Ford, ed., *Warren-Adams Letters* 1:251. Yet Maryland's reaction to the resolution is fully comprehensible when one notes that the province's recent relations with the Congress had made it appear to conservative provincial leaders that the continental body was the promoter of disorder.

Through the months of April and May 1776, the conservatives who dominated the Maryland Convention and the the Council of Safety tried to secure the peaceful exit of the popular royal governor, Robert Eden. They were blocked by a radical coalition within the province, which was supported by several powerful Virginia radicals and by General Charles Lee, continental commander for the Southern Military District. For reasons largely concerning the military situation in Virginia, Lee and the Maryland radicals secured a continental resolution on April 17 calling for Eden's arrest. So miffed were the conservative members of Maryland's Council of Safety that they called for the full Convention to meet in early May to protest the continental resolution. This was the Convention that received the May 15 resolution. Not surprisingly, the Convention treated it as an unwarranted intrusion upon the internal affairs of the colony and replied to the continental delegates that Maryland had "a Jurisdiction competent to the Occasion" and contemplated no alteration in its government. Thus, in the only province that resisted the May 15 resolution, the Continental Congress appeared to be the opponent, rather than the supporter, of the forces of peace and good order, and its authority was consequently resisted. Daniel of St. Thomas Jenifer to J. Hancock, Apr. 18, 1776, in Papers of the Continental Congress, 1774–1789, National Archives Microfilm M-247, reel 84; *Maryland Gazette*, May 23, 1776. A full account of the Eden episode and its effect on relations between Maryland and the Continental Congress is presented in H. E. Klingelhofer, "The Cautious Revolution: Maryland and the Movement toward Independence, 1774–1776," *Maryland Historical Magazine* 60 (1965): 265–313; and, in general, David C. Skaggs, *Roots of Maryland Democracy, 1753–1776* (Westport, Conn., 1973), pp. 174–96.

108. John A. Munroe, "Revolution and Confederation," in H. Clay and Marion B. Reed, eds., *Delaware: A History of the First State* (New York, 1947), 1:108; J. Thomas Scharf, *History of Delaware, 1609–1888* (Philadelphia, 1888), 1:226–27, 229. The activities of the Tories are recounted in Harold B. Hancock, *The Delaware Loyalists* (Wilmington, Del., 1940); John Haslet to Caesar Rodney [May 1776], June 5 [1776], in Ryden, ed., *Rodney Letters*, pp. 87, 88–89. On the naval engagement between the *Roebuck* and the American forces, see Jackson, *The Pennsylvania Navy*, pp. 35–57.

109. Caesar Rodney to John Haslet, May 17, 1776, in Ryden, ed., *Rodney Letters*, pp. 79–80.

110. Ibid.

111. Ibid.

112. Ibid.

113. Caesar Rodney to Thomas Rodney, May 29, 1776, ibid., p. 85; Proceedings of the Delaware Assembly, June 14, July 27, 1776, in Force, ed., *American Archives*, 4th ser., 6:884; 5th ser., 1:618.

114. Jeanette Eckman, "Colony into State," in Reed and Reed, eds., *Delaware* 1:278. As John Munroe concluded, "Here in these Delaware counties the old order did not relinquish control. Gradually, not without occasional challenges from one side or the other, the colony was altered into a state. The colonial assembly, with some prodding, provided for a constitutional convention that the old moderate leadership dominated and where an old society was reorganized under a new name: the Delaware State." *History of Delaware* (Newark, Del., 1979), p. 63. Thus, although Delaware, like New York, called a constitutional convention to frame a new government, the conservative leadership both controlled the process by which the Convention was called and it dominated the Convention itself (see below).

115. Larry R. Gerlach, *Prologue to Independence: New Jersey in the Coming of the Revolution* (New Brunswick, N.J., 1976), pp. 327–45; Leonard Lundin, *Cockpit of the Revolution: The War for Independence in New Jersey* (Princeton, N.J., 1940), pp. 70–108; Richard P. McCormick, *New Jersey: From Colony to State* (Princeton, 1964), pp. 117–19. As Gerlach notes, "The prompt establishment of a functioning government was necessary to clear up the stagnation of the legal and judicial processes that had obtained since the termination of royal authority [i.e., Franklin's arrest], to prevent the chaos that would soon result from a prolonged absence of duly constituted political institutions, and to cope with the peril of the impending British invasion of New York." *Prologue to Independence*, p. 340.

116. Proceedings of the New Jersey Convention, June 21, 1776, in Force, ed., *American Archives*, 4th ser., 6:1628.

117. Gerlach, *Prologue to Revolution*, pp. 340–43.

118. Proceedings of the New Jersey Convention, June 24, 26, 29, 1776, in Force, ed., *American Archives*, 4th ser., 6:1629, 1631, 1635–36. See also Lucius Q. C. Elmer, "The Constitution and Government of the Province and State of New Jersey, . . ." New Jersey Historical Society, *Collections* 7 (1872): 27–31.

119. Becker, *Political Parties in New York*, exhaustively detailed the factional struggles in New York during this period. See also the work of Roger Champagne, "New York's Radicals and the Coming of Independence, 1776," *New York State Historical Association Quarterly* 46 (1962): 281–303; and Bernard Mason, *The Road to Independence: The Revolutionary Movement in New York, 1773–1777* (Lexington, Ky., 1966).

120. An excellent analysis of the weakness of the New York revolutionary authorities in the years prior to and immediately following independence is provided by Edward Countryman, "Consolidating Power in Revolutionary

America: The Case of New York: 1775–1783," *Journal of Interdisciplinary History* 6 (Spring 1976): 645–77. Through an interesting application of modern political theory, Countryman traces the gradual assumption of authority by the New York revolutionary authorities in the late 1770s and early 1780s. His thesis is presented in greater detail in his recent monograph, *A People in Revolution: The American Revolution and Political Society in New York, 1760–1790* (Baltimore, 1981), esp. pp. 131–60.

121. Egbert Benton to the Representative of Dutchess County, July 15, 1776, in Force, ed., *American Archives*, 5th ser., 1:357.

122. This account is taken from Countryman's perceptive analysis of the distinctions between the two provinces in *A People in Revolution*, pp. 163–66.

123. Robert R. Livingston to John Jay, May 17, 1776, in Henry P. Johnston, ed., *The Correspondence and Public Papers of John Jay* (New York and London, 1890–93), 1:59–60.

124. John Jay to James Duane, May 29, 1776; and John Jay to Robert Livingston, May 29, 1776, ibid., pp. 63–65.

125. The statements by "Columbus" are also in Force, ed., *American Archives*, 4th ser., 6:825–26.

126. Ibid.

127. For such opinion, see, for example, Morris, ed., *Letters of Gouverneur Morris* 1:6; and Charles Z. Lincoln, *The Constitutional History of New York* (New York, 1906), 1:483. On the actions taken by the Provincial Congress, see Alexander C. Flick, ed., *History of the State of New York* (New York, 1933), 4:155; May 24, 26, 31, 1775, New York (State) *Journals of the Provincial Congress, Provincial Convention, Committee of Safety, and Council of Safety of the State of New-York* (Albany, 1842), 2:460, 462, 466–67.

128. Countryman, *A People in Revolution*, p. 166. On the subsequent adoption of the New York Constitution of 1777, see ibid., pp. 166–69.

129. Caesar Rodney to John Haslet, May 17, 1776, in Ryden, ed., *Rodney Letters*, p. 79.

Chapter 10

1. See Labaree, *Royal Government in America, passim*.

2. Adams Autobiography, in Butterfield, ed., *Adams Papers* 3:352.

3. See Article 8, Silas Deane's Proposals to Congress [November 1? 1775], in Smith, ed., *LDC* 2:418–19; and Article 5, Benjamin Franklin's Draft Articles of Confederation, July 21, 1775, in *JCC* 2:196.

4. See, for example, remarks of John Witherspoon, in Thomas Jefferson, Notes of Proceedings in Congress [July 12–August 1, 1776], in Smith, ed., *LDC* 4:442.

5. *JCC* 2:80.

6. Ibid., p. 103.

7. Ibid., p. 221.

8. E. James Ferguson, *The Power of the Purse: A History of American Public Fi-

nance, 1776–1790 (Chapel Hill, N.C., 1961), p. 30. Ferguson notes that by the end of 1776 Congress had emitted $15,000,000, and by the end of 1779 it had emitted $226,000,000. Ibid. On Congress's early efforts to finance the war, see ibid., pp. 25–42. See also Jennings B. Sanders, *Evolution of the Executive Departments of the Continental Congress, 1774–1789* (Chapel Hill, N.C., 1945), pp. 50–51; Rakove, *Beginnings of National Politics*, pp. 210–11.

9. See, for example, resolve 7 of the Suffolk Resolves, in *JCC* 1:34. On colonial currency practices, see Ferguson, *Power of the Purse*, pp. 3–24.

10. On the political problems any such attempt would have engendered, see Rakove, *Beginnings of National Politics*, p. 205.

11. *JCC* 2:196. See Articles 10 and 12 of the Dickinson draft in Smith, ed., *LDC* 4:238; Articles ix and xi of the committee and August 20 drafts in *JCC* 5:677–78.

12. Dickinson draft in Smith, ed., *LDC* 4:233–34. See also Article 3, Franklin draft, in *JCC* 2:196; and Article iii, committee and August 20 drafts, in *JCC* 5:675.

13. Compare Article 4, Dickinson draft in Smith, ed., *LDC* 4:234–35, with committee draft in *JCC* 5:547.

14. Articles 7 and 8, Dickinson draft, in Smith, ed., *LDC* 4:236; Articles vi and vii, committee draft, and article vi, August 20 draft, in *JCC* 5:547, 676.

15. Article 5, Franklin draft, in *JCC* 2:196; Articles iv, xviii, committee draft; Articles iv, xiv, August 20 draft, in *JCC* 5:547, 550, 675, 681. On the commercial nature of treaties, see above, Chapter 7.

16. Article 9, Dickinson draft, in Smith, ed., *LDC* 4:237; Article viii, committee draft, and Article vi, August 20 draft, in *JCC* 5:544–48, 676. Thus, for example, although the United States had concluded a treaty granting most-favored-nation status to Holland, Virginia nevertheless gave preferential customs treatment to French brandy, a decision about which the Secretary for Foreign Affairs, John Jay, could do little except protest. See Sanders, *Executive Departments*, p. 124.

17. Articles 2, 15, and 16, Deane's Proposals to Congress [November ? 1775], in Smith, ed., *LDC* 2:418–19. Such a solution would not necessarily have been inconsistent with Congress's lack of power to lay "internal taxes," because, like the post office, such customs duties could be viewed as administrative, rather than revenue-producing, measures. This argument, of course, had long been urged by supporters of parliamentary regulation of colonial trade, and it was, in fact, the scheme pursued tirelessly, and almost successfully, by Robert Morris as Superintendent of the Treasury in the last years of the Confederation. See Sanders, *Executive Departments*, pp. 137–39; Ferguson, *Power of the Purse*, pp. 116–17, 146–76; and Rakove, *Development of National Politics*, pp. 297–329. See also E. Wayne Carp's perceptive explanation of the political ends Morris hoped to achieve with his financial plan in *To Starve the Army at Pleasure: Continental Army Administration and American Political Culture, 1775–1783* (Chapel Hill, N.C., 1984), pp. 207–14.

18. Articles xviii, xiv, in both the Committee draft, and the August 20 draft, *JCC* 5:681–83.

19. *JCC* 2:196. The discretionary legislative powers denied to the Confederation Congress became the foundation, in the guise of the commerce and "necessary and proper" clauses of the federal constitution, of the discretion the present Congress possesses to legislate on matters that intimately concern the "internal police" of the individual states. See, for example, *McCullough v. Maryland*, 17 U.S. 316 (4 Wheat.) (1819) (Marshall, C.J.): "But we think the sound construction of the constitution must allow to the national legislature that discretion, with respect to the means by which the powers it confers are to be carried into execution, which will enable that body to perform the high duties assigned to it. . . . Let the end be legitimate, let it be within the scope of the constitution, and all means which are appropriate, which are plainly adapted to that end, which are not prohibited, but consistant with the letter and spirit of the constitution, are constitutional." Also, *Heart of Atlanta Motel v. United States*, 379 U.S. 241 (1964): The determinative test of the exercise of power by the Congress under the Commerce Clause is simply whether the activity sought to be regulated is 'commerce which concerns more States than one' and has 'a real and substantial relation to the national interest.' "

20. Article 19, Dickinson draft, in Smith, ed., *LDC* 4:244; Article xviii, committee draft; Article xiv, August 20 draft, in *JCC* 5:683.

21. Deane proposed, "That where the Governor's are Now appointed by the Crown, they shall be appointed by the General Congress during good Behavior & the same with respect to Leiut. Governors. Councellors now appointed by the Crown as well as Judges & other Officers in the Royal Appointment in Royal Governments shall be elected by the Representatives of the People in their General Assembly, and so elected, to hold their Offices during good Behavior." Article 8, Silas Deane's Proposals to Congress [Nov.? 1775], in Smith, ed., *LDC* 2:418.

22. Autobiography, in Butterfield, ed., *Adams Papers* 3:352.

23. Price, *Additional Observations*, p. 8.

24. Connecticut Delegates to Governor Jonathan Trumbull, Oct. 10, 1774, in Smith, ed., *LDC* 1:169; John Adams to James Warren, July 11, 1775, in Ford, ed., *Warren-Adams Letters* 1:80.

25. John Adams to Mercy Warren, Nov. 25, 1775, in Smith, ed., *LDC* 2:387; John Adams to James Warren, July 24, 1775, in Ford, ed., *Warren-Adams Letters* 1:89; Silas Deane to Elizabeth Deane, June 3, 1775, in Smith, ed., *LDC* 1:436; Samuel Ward Diary [Nov. 2, 1775], ibid. 2:290.

26. John Adams to James Warren, July 23, 1775, ibid. 1:652.

27. For Adams's reminiscences of proceedings in committees of the whole, see his autobiography in Butterfield, ed., *Adams Papers* 3:381.

28. The standing committees were the Committees on Accounts, or Claims (created Sept. 25, 1775); Medicines (Sept. 14, 1775); Naval or Marine (Dec. 11, 1775); Prisoners (Nov. 17, 1775); Applications (Dec. 8, 1775); the Secret Committee (Sept. 19, 1775); and the Committee of Secret Correspondence (Nov. 29, 1775); see *JCC* 6:1065–67.

29. John Adams to Mercy Warren, Nov. 25, 1775; and Silas Deane to Elizabeth Deane, Sept. 22, 1775; in Smith, ed., *LDC* 2:387, 44; Caesar Rodney to

George Read, March 6, 1776, in Ryden, ed., *Rodney Letters*, p. 72; and Josiah Bartlett to John Langdon, Sept. 21, 1778, in Smith, ed., *LDC* 10:678.

30. Benjamin Harrison to George Washington, July 21, 1775, in Smith, ed., *LDC* 1:645. As Carp notes, "one result of Congress's decision to retain control of war administration and overload its members with work was a high turnover rate of congressmen. In addition, the army suffered from Congress's chronic delays in getting to pressing military matters. Both factors invariably disrupted the continuity of congressional policy making and interfered with the efficient administration of the army." *To Starve the Army at Pleasure*, p. 30.

31. Arthur St. Clair to James Wilson, May 14, 1776, Gratz Coll., case 4, box 14, Hist. Soc. of Pa.; Samuel Chase to Richard Henry Lee, May 17, 1776, in Smith, ed., *LDC* 4:22. See also Samuel Chase to John Sullivan, Dec. 24, 1776, ibid. 5:614 n. 2. For an imaginative study of the connection between the administrative inefficiency of Congress, the decline of congressional authority, and the development of a nationalist faction within and outside of the army, see Carp, *To Starve the Army at Pleasure*, passim, but especially pp. 191–222.

32. Richard Smith Diary, [March 19, 1776], in Smith, ed., *LDC* 3:412; Robert Morris to Silas Deane, Dec. 20, 1776; and to the Committee of Secret Correspondence, Dec. 16, 1776, ibid. 5:626, 609.

33. *JCC* 6:1041; James Wilson to Robert Morris, Jan. 14, 1777, in Smith, ed., *LDC* 6:103.

34. Sanders, *Executive Departments*, p. 5. On the reasons for the delay, see Rakove, *Development of National Politics*, pp. 198–205.

35. Sanders, *Executive Departments*, passim.

36. Eugene R. Sheridan and John M. Murrin, eds., *Congress at Princeton: Being the Letters of Charles Thomson to Hannah Thomson, June–October, 1783* (Princeton, 1985), p. xxxviii. The following analysis draws heavily upon that presented in the perceptive introductory essay to this collection.

37. For the development of the concept of the "sovereign people," and the embodiment of their power in constitutional conventions, see Robert R. Palmer, *The Age of the Democratic Revolution: A Political History of Europe and America, 1760–1800*, 2 vols. (Princeton, 1959–65); and Willi Paul Adams, *The First American Constitution: Republican Ideology and the Making of the State Constitutions in the Revolutionary Era* (Chapel Hill, N.C., 1980). This theme is developed in Sheridan and Murrin, eds., *Congress at Princeton*, pp. xxxiv–xxxv.

38. Remarks of James McHenry, May 29, 1787, in Farrand, ed., *Records of the Federal Convention* 1:26.

39. John Adams to Roger Sherman, July 17, 1789, in Charles F. Adams, *The Works of John Adams, with a Life of the Author, Notes and Illustrations* (Boston, 1850–56), 6:430.

Index

Library of Congress Cataloging-in-Publication Data

Marston, Jerrilyn Greene, 1945-
King and Congress.

Revision of the author's thesis (Ph.D.)—Boston University, 1975.
Bibliography: p.   Includes index.
1. United States—Politics and government—
Revolution, 1775-1783. 2. United States.
Continental Congress. 3. Executive power—
United States—History—18th century. I. Title.
E210.M36 1987   973.3'1   87-2439
ISBN 0-691-04745-6 (alk. paper)